Parenthood

ITS PSYCHOLOGY AND PSYCHOPATHOLOGY

LITTLE, BROWN AND COMPANY, BOSTON

Parenthood

Its Psychology and Psychopathology

By 29 Authors

EDITED BY

E. James Anthony, M.D., D.P.M.

Ittleson Professor of Child Psychiatry, Washington University
School of Medicine, St. Louis; Professorial Lecturer,
The University of Chicago School of Medicine; Training and
Teaching Analyst, Chicago Institute for Psychoanalysis, Chicago

AND

Therese Benedek, M.D.

Senior Staff Member, Chicago
Institute for Psychoanalysis, Chicago

Library of Congress catalog card No. 75–112005

ISBN 0–316–04370

First Edition

Seventh Printing

Printed in the United States of America

HAL

To my dear docents—Sasha, Stephanie, Sonia,
and Bruno—with love
                    E. J. A.

To my grandchildren
                    T. B.

Preface

The psychology and psychopathology of parenthood provide an inexhaustible array of subjects. A systematic presentation of these subjects would *natura rerum* fixate them in time and place to a particular civilization, thereby counteracting our main purpose, which is to discuss parenthood as a process in continual change. It seemed advantageous, therefore, to approach the problem in the form of a multi-authored book and to present the generally accepted facts and theories as they are applied by different investigators in pursuit of their own inquiries. This aim was not expressly formulated as such by the editors. As far as it formed the background of our thoughts, it was apparent only in the selection of contributors and in our request to them to write a chapter related to their particular area of interest in the field of family life but seen from the point of view of the parent as he or she functioned normally or abnormally. The assignment thus had broad dimensions, and it says much for the empathy of our contributors that they seemed to understand our purpose so immediately and completely. We envisaged our own task as editors in terms of adding continuity to the book as a whole by welding together the different chapters with clarifying editorial comments.

Naturally, we expected from Charles Kaufman, a psychoanalyst known for his research in the field of ethology, a contribution to the biology of parenthood; from Otto von Mering, a scholarly review of the anthropologic aspects of rearing children; from Gerald Handel, a segment of sociology to illustrate the function of the small social group of the family within the larger societal organizations. The psychobiology of parenthood, presented by one author, is based on her psychoanalytic investigations, and her experiences are presented here from a unified biopsychologic viewpoint.

Unexpected but gratifying to the editors were those parts of the book comprising Parts III, IV, and V. Written by psychoanalysts not in communication with one another and mainly interested in their own special field of investigation, they appear to fit together like pieces of a mosaic. In spite of the seeming diversity of these contributions, and although they do not offer a substitute for a systematic presentation of the psychology and psychopathology of parenthood, each chapter, in its own particular way and also as part of the whole, expresses the purpose and meaning of the book.

Since the overall purpose of this book is to present parenthood as a function of biology and, at the same time, as a tool of civilization, it necessarily aims at crossing the borders of specialties and enhancing interdisciplinary communications. With this in mind, we are hopeful that it will further the working knowledge of psychiatrists, psychologists, and social scientists of the related disciplines of anthropology, sociology, and education and the treatment skills of all those engaged in the various forms of therapeutics such as psychotherapy, casework, and counseling insofar as these deal with families, marital pairs, or parent-child units.

In handing over the work to our publisher, we think of those who by their contributions directly or by their encouragement indirectly helped us to complete our task. We owe special thanks for their unflagging loyalty to Mrs. Martha Kniepkamp and Mrs. Harold R. Gordon, who typed and retyped large sections of the material and responded to the heavy burdens of editorial work with patience and willing cooperation. Mrs. Kniepkamp, in St. Louis, had the additional task of preparing the final version for the publisher, and she did this with her habitual carefulness and attention to detail.

E. J. A.
T. B.

Contributing Authors

E. James Anthony, M.D., D.P.M.

Ittleson Professor of Child Psychiatry, Washington University School of Medicine, St. Louis; Professorial Lecturer, The University of Chicago School of Medicine; Training and Teaching Analyst, Chicago Institute for Psychoanalysis, Chicago

Marjorie L. Behrens, M.A.

Research Associate, The Family Institute, New York

Therese Benedek, M.D.

Senior Staff Member, Chicago Institute for Psychoanalysis, Chicago

Anni Bergman, M.S.

Senior Research Associate, Masters Children's Center, New York

Sylvia Brody, Ph.D.

Adjunct Professor of Psychology, Graduate Department of Psychology, and Director, Child Development Research Project, City University of New York, New York

James L. Foy, M.D.

Associate Professor of Psychiatry, Georgetown University School of Medicine, Washington

Contributing Authors

Anna Freud, Sc.D. (Hon.)
Director, Hampstead Child-Therapy Course and Clinic, London

Peter L. Giovacchini, M.D.
Clinical Professor of Psychiatry, University of Illinois College of Medicine, Chicago

William Goldfarb, M.D., Ph.D.
Clinical Professor of Psychiatry, Columbia University College of Physicians and Surgeons, New York; Director, Henry Ittleson Center for Child Research, Bronx

Gerald Handel, Ph.D.
Associate Professor of Sociology, City University of New York, New York

Hedwig Jahoda, Ph.D.
Late Psychologist, Henry Ittleson Center for Child Research, Bronx

Lucie Jessner, M.D.
Professor of Psychiatry, Georgetown University School of Medicine, Washington

I. Charles Kaufman, M.D.
Professor of Psychiatry, University of Colorado School of Medicine, Denver

Judith S. Kestenberg, M.D.
Clinical Associate Professor of Psychiatry, State University of New York Downstate Medical Center College of Medicine, Brooklyn; Visiting Consultant, Department of Pediatric Psychiatry, Long Island Jewish Hospital, New Hyde Park

Norman Kreitman, M.D., D.P.M.
Assistant Director, Medical Research Council Unit for Epidemiological Studies in Psychiatry, University of Edinburgh, Edinburgh

David M. Levy, M.D.
Lecturer in Psychiatry, Columbia University College of Physicians and Surgeons; Consultant Psychiatrist, Department of Public Health, New York

Margaret S. Mahler, M.D.

Clinical Professor of Psychiatry, Albert Einstein College of Medicine; Director of Research, Masters Children's Center, New York

Otto von Mering, Ph.D.

Professor of Anthropology, Departments of Anthropology and Psychiatry, University of Pittsburgh School of Medicine; Professor of Anthropology, Department of Psychiatry, Western Psychiatric Institute and Clinic, Pittsburgh

Mirta T. Mulhare, Ph.D.

Assistant Professor of Anthropology, Departments of Anthropology and Sociology, Carlow College; Maurice Falk Senior Research Assistant Fellow in Psychiatry, Western Psychiatric Institute and Clinic, Pittsburgh

Norman L. Paul, M.D.

Assistant Clinical Professor of Psychiatry, Tufts University School of Medicine, Boston

Fred Pine, Ph.D.

Associate Professor of Psychiatry (Psychology), Albert Einstein College of Medicine of Yeshiva University, Bronx

Leo Rangell, M.D.

Clinical Professor of Psychiatry, University of California at Los Angeles School of Medicine; Faculty Member and Training Analyst, Los Angeles Psychoanalytic Institute, Los Angeles; President, International Psychoanalytic Association; Past President, American Psychoanalytic Association

Marshall D. Schechter, M.D.

Professor of Child Psychiatry and Consultant Professor of Pediatrics, University of Oklahoma School of Medicine, Oklahoma City

Lillian Sibulkin, M.S.S.

Social Worker, Jewish Board of Guardians, New York

Melitta Sperling, M.D.

Clinical Professor of Psychiatry, Division of Psychoanalytic Education, State University of New York Downstate Medical Center College of Medicine, Brooklyn

Contributing Authors

René A. Spitz, M.D.

Visiting Professor and Lecturer in Psychiatry, University of Colorado School of Medicine, Denver

Brandt F. Steele, M.D.

Professor of Psychiatry, University of Colorado School of Medicine; Chief, Psychiatric Liaison Division, University of Colorado Medical Center, Denver

Edith Weigert, M.D.

Chairman of the Faculty, The Washington School of Psychiatry, Chevy Chase

Donald W. Winnicott, M.A., F.R.C.P. (Lond.)

Former Physician and Director, Department of Child Psychiatry, Paddington Green Children's Hospital, London

Contents

xiii

Contents

Contents

Part V. Some Clinical Correlations Between Parents and Children

Contents

Part VI.   Summing Up

Introduction

In this book we would like to extend the concept of dynamic process beyond its usual meaning in modern psychology to include the process of evolutionary biology as it repeats itself in each human being and directs human behavior, under the aegis of the genetic code, toward procreation and parenthood. Viewed in this context, parenthood is a manifestation of "natural man" and, as such, is governed by the laws of biologic processes that are universal. This factor of universality dominates both Freud's instinct theory and his basic thesis that human personality evolves under the influence of an innate organization of growth processes resulting from psychologic reactions to the environment.

Once the environment and its influence come under consideration, however, one moves from the universal to the specific, whether considering variations in parental behavior due to ethnic, cultural, or social factors or individual variations within a single group. Freud's formulation of the developmental processes that enable individuals of the same culture to transmit their cultural inheritance from one generation to the next was not intended to overshadow the universal validity of instincts that bring into being, through the organization of behavior, structures and functions essential to the survival of the species. At every step of the phasic development from infancy into adult life, conflicts between the biologic and the social must be solved. The behavior of the individual is determined by inescapable instincts,

and although man has gained for himself the privilege of choice, this is
limited not only by biologic laws but also by the intrinsic nature of
individual development that demands a resolution of the biosocial conflict at each and every stage. Moreover, the choices made may have
consequences that limit further choices, thus leading to behavior that
is not in the "nature of man" and, therefore, conducive to pathologic
states.

Parenthood in our age, as it evolves in individuals raised in our
culture under the pressure of our civilization, often appears to be far
removed from its biologic source, so much so that it is not infrequently
discussed in clinical terms as if some pathogenic conflict had replaced
the biologic processes of parenthood and assumed the function of universally motivating it. For this reason, it is important to keep in mind
the biologic roots whenever talking of psychologic mechanisms, so
that universals and particulars are not hopelessly confused. To add to
the difficulties, any delineation of human development tends to be
complicated by the fact that biologic growth is also responsive to environmental influences. It would seem, therefore, that development implies a long series of interactions between physiologic maturing and
environmental accommodation. For example, the adaptation of the
child to his parents rests on the continuous effort of educational measures to domesticate his instinctual urges. Only during the last two
decades has an interest in psychologic adaptation afforded us new insights into the complex reciprocal adjustments constantly made between parents and children, teachers and pupils, society at large and
the individual.

Two intriguing questions arise at this point: Why did psychoanalysts fail to perceive and to study the developmental situation
from the parents' point of view? And why did they get to know so
much more about children than about their parents? A third question
related to these two might also be asked: Why have psychoanalysts not
asked themselves these questions before?

The evolution of psychoanalytic theory, bound by the method
and material of its investigation, may answer these questions in depth.
In general, however, the solution of the riddle points to a universal
characteristic of adulthood that necessarily prevails in parents at any
time and in any civilization. Parents, unlike their children, form part
of the mainstream of life, and for this reason they cannot see them-

selves with the degree of separation necessary for objective description. To ourselves we seem to be what we are, real and self-evident, therefore beyond question and investigation. It is more possible to be definite and realistic about those who are different and at a distance from us. From this it is easy to understand why men at all times have been able to ask questions about the world around them, their *Umwelt*. They had to know about it since it lay outside the self, and for this reason it was important to ascertain whether it was good or bad, familiar or strange, safe or dangerous, in order to feel secure.

Evolutionary biology, in its role of "great organizer," has contrived for parents, the adults in their respective generation, to be part of the mainstream and responsible for offspring. Since children are expected to grow up and become like their parents, the parent generation can observe the children objectively and measure their health and happiness by their own selves, their own achievements and failures, by their anticipations, hopes, and disappointments. At the same time, parents disregard their role, or at best find it difficult to see themselves as parents, and are scarcely aware of their ingrained behavior and its influence upon the child. What follows from this, understandably, is that child development from birth to maturity is often carefully and completely described, whereas the psychology of parenthood has remained a grossly neglected topic of description and investigation. Writers and investigators, of course, are also part of the mainstream and therefore equally likely to take for granted the parental role with its apparently built-in love for the child and responsibility for his welfare. Furthermore, the growth of science inculcated the scientific attitude, setting a high value on objectivity and consequently making it less easy for the parent to look inward and to recognize the fact that limits his investigation—that he is both the subject and the object of the investigation.

Early psychoanalytic work tended to focus on the psychologic aspects of the parent-child relationship and to see it predominantly from the standpoint of the instinctual development of the child. The genetic theory defines the intrapsychic processes of the child isolated from the psychologic processes of the parent. This biologic concept of psychoanalysis has often been one-sidedly exaggerated because of the absence of a large concomitant factor from among those emphasized in each instance of psychopathology, namely, the parent's genetic influence upon and responsibility for neurotic symptom formations and other aberrations in the child. What was investigated in the parent's psychology was not his actual interaction with the child, and this served only to emphasize that the child's behavior was simply a derivative of his developmental experiences.

Although this still describes the general attitude, a modification is needed. It was 1914 when Freud first referred to the psychodynamics of parental love as a projection of the infantile self-love of the parent to his child [4]. This was only a single side-remark in an epoch-making paper that introduced an ego psychology based on the processes of introjection and identifications, and subsequently led to the structural theory of psychoanalysis in 1923 [5]. Structural theory and ego analysis dominated the field of psychoanalytic investigation and expanded our knowledge without conceptualizing the theory as essentially that of a nonverbal communication of infancy that modifies intrapsychic processes as well as the motivations and manifestations of behavior. It is true that the vicissitudes of introjected objects influence the outcome of subsequent developmental phases, but the theory of instincts by itself did not suffice to explain the phenomenon brought to light by ego psychology.

Heinz Hartmann then introduced another biologic concept into psychoanalysis when he integrated ego psychology with problems of adaptation [6] and opened up new avenues for psychoanalytic research, thus affording a broad perspective for investigations of growth and development as processes of adaptation to normally acceptable environmental conditions and pointing toward the variety of adaptive tasks necessitated by changes in the individual and his environment. It is interesting to note that the original publication remained almost unnoticed because of the disturbing world situation at the time and the rapid dissolution of psychoanalytic communities in Europe. It is even more surprising that following World War II the systematic investigations by Hartmann and his associates in the United States were directed chiefly at a clarification of significant aspects of already accepted psychoanalytic theories and not on the adaptive processes involved in the interpersonal relationships of the family, the first social environment of the child.[1]

[1] One might assume that the papers published from the 1940s to the middle of the 1950s were planned to support and uphold the basic theories of

Attention was directed to the problems of parenthood and the family, however, not only by the wartime upheaval that disrupted families and orphaned children but basically by the intrinsic course of psychoanalysis, which leads back, almost inevitably, to the earliest phases of individual existence [3]. Karl Abraham emphasized the significance of the oral phase as early as 1911, and in 1916 he published his seminal studies on the pregenital phases of development that culminate in the oedipus complex [1]. This core complex of personality development, representing an integration of the primary object relationships of the child with the phasic course of his instinctual development, was considered the cornerstone of maturation; it put such emphasis on the father's role in the family, however, that for a long time it adumbrated the psychologic significance of the mother's biologic function in the raising of her children.

Flugel was the first psychoanalyst to describe the interpersonal structure of the family on the basis of the psychoanalytic theory of development of his time [2]. Accordingly, in the center of his investigation was the oedipus complex as it functions unconsciously in the parents and sets the goal of development for each of the children. Just as the oedipus complex is a psychic representation of the patriarchal family, so was Flugel's study inescapably based on the conditions prevailing within Western patriarchal cultures at the time, which conceptualized parenthood as mature and relatively unchanging. In spite of these limitations, Flugel's contribution to the psychology of parenthood is significant. He anticipated aspects of later work when he emphasized that the development of the child requires corresponding readjustment in the parents' attitude and behavior at every stage, and that this is as necessary for the parent as for the child. He noted that the heterosexual development of parents is, to a considerable extent, related to the heterosexual development of the child, and that the hostile feelings of parents toward their children are often powerfully stimulated and reinforced by the unconscious process that identifies the child with the parents' own parents so that there tends to be some

Freud; they omitted any emphasis on Hartmann's own significant contribution, assuming that ego psychology, seen from the perspective of adaptive tasks, might easily lead (probably all too easily from the point of view of these investigators) to anthropology and sociology. Such attempts to conserve psychoanalysis in its purity may have been the cause of the slow diffusion and absorption of new ideas into the body of psychoanalysis, thus barring new perspectives from investigation.

similarity between the parent-child relationship of one generation and the parent-child relationship of the earlier generation. Parents, he observed, find themselves at times incompatible with their children, which eventually leads to strong resentments as the "hostage to Fortune" increasingly interferes with work and aspirations. To a large extent, however, Flugel's insights into the family as a functional social unit have been outdated by the consequences of the profound cultural changes that have affected contemporary living.

The period during which psychoanalysis shifted from a primarily patriarchal view of personality development to one in which the bio-psychologic role of the mother became understood coincides with the period during which the emancipation of women made powerful strides forward (from about 1914 to the recent decade), and both processes are still going on. Are they related to each other? Psychoanalytic insights were arrived at by the tedious investigations of single individuals in the privacy of the analytic chamber. Analysts did not react to the larger community directly, but the ongoing, enveloping social process rendered investigators within the field of psychoanalysis, as in neighboring fields, more perceptive and more responsive to the new problems that were arising.

The emancipation of women was prompted by the economic necessities created by two world wars and by the cultural factors that disseminated to women the personal need for higher individuation. These and many other factors helped to alter the interpersonal relationship between husband and wife and, with it, the parent-child relationship. Perhaps the most radical change came with the emancipation of women from the inevitable duties of childbearing. Improvement in contraceptive techniques brought with it striking alterations in family structure. One of these could be defined as the equalization of the sexes. As far as parenthood is concerned, this manifests itself by the father's greater interest and participation in the care of his infants and small children.

Thus, with changes in the status of women came changes in family structure, and concomitant with these and bearing vitally on them came changes in psychoanalysis itself. The focus of theoretical interest moved from the oedipal to the preoedipal stages, from the triadic concept, in which each participant was considered in a one-way communication with another, to the transactions between the participants; from the reconstruction of early infancy obtained from the analysis of adults to the direct observation of mother-infant trans- actions. Since the early preoccupation with instinctual vicissitudes shares our attention with concern for the ego and its autonomous functioning, instinctual derivatives have obtained new meaning as they appear in the group phenomena of the growing generation striv- ing for autonomy of a different kind.

From all that has been said in this introduction, it will be clear that both biologic and psychologic factors play a complex, correlated role in the development of parenthood. From these various points of view it becomes possible to systematize the human motivations for parenthood into various classes as follows:

1. The psychologic representation of the *basic biologic motiva- tion* is the instinct for survival, which activates the physiologic pro- cesses leading to conception, the maintenance of pregnancy, and the nursing of infants. It directs and coordinates the primary object relationship that ensures development, namely, the child's need for the mother and the mother's readiness to fulfill this need.

2. *Developmental motivations* originate in the psychosexual de- velopment of the personality. The interactions of physiologic processes with the environment influence and modify the primary biologic ten- dencies, which in adults are expressed in readiness for and adaptation to the progressive series of tasks culminating in parenthood. Today a great deal more is known about the positive and negative influences of the pregenital phases of development upon the parental tendencies of individuals of both sexes. Then there is the contribution from the oedipal phase during which object relationship with both parents is established, with internal representations reflecting the sex differences. The oedipal child, therefore, becomes able to have fantasies which project his experiences with his parents into his own future experience as a parent. Such derivatives, uncovered by the psychoanalytic pro- cess, are often taken as direct representations of the biologic urge for procreation. It should, however, be emphasized that the interpersonal experiences and their fantasied derivatives are motivations of the second order, as compared with the biologic motivations, and are modifiable by environmental and cultural factors. Consequently, the universal characteristic of the biologic motivation cannot be at- tributed to them.

3. The differentiation between primary biologic and secondary developmental motivations is the more important since their interaction activates motivations of a third order, namely, *cultural, anthropologic motivations.*

The complexity of motivations for parenthood in our society, the effects of cultural and societal pressures on parental behavior, and their influence upon molding the next generation indicate that in some direct and indirect ways all aspects of the humanities have relevance to parenthood and its problems. This assertion is such a commonplace that its repetition is justified only by stating that the intention of this publication is to disseminate the knowledge of psychodynamic processes beyond the fields of psychology and psychiatry to education, anthropology, and sociology, and to improve and enrich communication between parents and their children, that they may help themselves as they help their children. Such mutuality of give-and-take on all levels of interpersonal relationships is the premise of this endeavor.

Bibliography

1. Abraham, K.   The first pregenital stage of the libido. *Int. Z. Arztl. Psychoanal.* 4:71–97, 1916.
2. Flügel, J. C.   *The Psycho-Analytic Study of the Family.* London: Hogarth, 1921.
3. Freud, A., and Burlingham, D.   *Infants without Family.* New York: International Universities Press, 1944.
4. Freud, S.   On Narcissism: An Introduction (1914). In J. Strachey (Ed.), *The Standard Edition of the Complete Psychological Works of Sigmund Freud,* Vol. 14. London: Hogarth, 1957.
5. Freud, S.   The Ego and the Id (1923). In J. Strachey (Ed.), *The Standard Edition of the Complete Psychological Works of Sigmund Freud,* Vol. 19. London: Hogarth, 1961.
6. Hartmann, H.   *Ego Psychology and the Problem of Adaptation.* New York: International Universities Press, 1958.

Parenthood

ITS PSYCHOLOGY AND
PSYCHOPATHOLOGY

Part I

General Considerations

1

Biologic Considerations of Parenthood

I. Charles Kaufman

> What is the most humanly significant biological denominator common to all human beings and to all human groups? It occurred to me that this might be the concern of parents for their very young. This parental concern has a long biological heritage and is absolutely essential for survival of most species.
>
> F. FREMONT-SMITH [21]

In one sense parenthood is as old as life itself, since so far as we know all cells issue directly from other (parent) cells. Each organism is thus dependent upon others for at least part of its life history. This dependence is the ultimate basis of all evolved systems of parental behavior and indeed of all social existence. However, there is an obvious and enormous difference between the parental nature of a cell which gives rise by fission to daughter cells and that of a human mother or father. Yet, evolutionary theory provides a basis for examining the relationships among the various forms of life, both morphologically and behaviorally.

PHYLOGENETIC CONSIDERATIONS

Even after sexual reproduction had evolved in the seas, the relationship between parents in many species was limited to a single interaction in the breeding season, consisting of courtship behavior and spawning. In the stickleback, for example, males leave the school in the breeding season to take up territories. Females leave the school when ready to spawn; each goes through a complicated courtship with a male in the male's own territory, spawns, and then rejoins the school. The male fertilizes the eggs, takes over their care, and later cares for the fry. This system of external fertilization is wasteful since large numbers of gametes must be produced in order that relatively few zygotes may successfully become mature animals. Any arrangement that raises the chances that ova will be fertilized by sperm and that zygotes will grow to maturity is clearly advantageous to the species.

Internal fertilization by copulation had this advantage, and when it evolved, early reptiles became land animals, no longer dependent on water for external fertilization. Another evolutionary advance to favor the survival of a zygote that benefited the reptiles was the development of an amniote egg, with a shell and membranes to protect it and to enclose an aqueous environment on dry land. Zygotes growing inside shells must develop until they are large enough and fully formed enough to break out and fend for themselves; meanwhile they live on food supply, e.g., yolk, produced in the female reproductive tract just prior to the secretion of the shell. To insure a certain number of offspring, these reptiles still produced many eggs which were hidden and left to hatch alone. The young animals on their own were easy prey to carnivores. In many species of fish, reptiles, and certainly birds, however, parents protect eggs which are laid in special nests. As birds are warm-blooded, their eggs must be kept warm, which is accomplished by incubation, a task often shared by the parents. After hatching, many birds are naked and require brooding by the parents, as well as feeding. Also, in many species parents protect young birds against predators.

A major evolutionary advance was the development of the *placenta,* an elaboration of the uterus by means of which materials are exchanged between the blood of the mother and that of the developing embryo. Viviparity—keeping the fertilized egg and its nourishment within the mother until considerable growth has occurred—is a particular feature of the mammals, who thereby improved their reproductive economy, i.e., reduced the loss of eggs and young. The close association of mother and fetus in placental mammals provides great protection and a continuous supply of food and oxygen. The hemoglobin of mammalian embryos is even adjusted to this stage with an oxygen dissociation curve that differs from the mother's in such a way as to favor transfer of oxygen from mother to embryo across the membrane. In the higher primates, including man, a hemochorial placenta was evolved, in which only fetal tissue separates the fetal and maternal blood streams, with fetal vessels actually penetrating the endometrial vessels. This provides the optimum conditions for the embryo, an improved supply of oxygen and food, a better system for removing waste products, and improved transmission of antibodies.

Of at least equal significance, mammals also evolved a *behavioral* program of reproductive economy, namely, a higher order of *parental care* of the young after birth, without the consequence of which it is impossible to visualize the development of man. Care of the very young was already evolved in fish, reptiles, and especially birds, but what made possible the tremendous advance in mammals was the system of feeding the infant, through special glands, a substance, milk, which contains everything needed for growth and development. The improved feeding arrangement keeps the young physically close to the mother and thus safer from harm. The progressive reduction in mortality is reflected in a reduction in the number of eggs fertilized each year from millions in fishes to dozens in reptiles to one in the higher primates. Finally, and very importantly, the close physical relationship and the shared personal experience provided to the infant and mother by the feeding from her body constitute a degree of contact and intimacy which creates a new kind of bond, with durable characteristics, one major effect of which is to allow the infant a slower rate of growth.[1]

This bond, with its affective potential, loomed large in the further evolution of parental behavior and, in fact, of social behavior

---

[1] This character of slow development reaches its greatest extent and importance in human evolution, and will be discussed at considerable length later in this chapter.

generally. Darwin said: "The feeling of pleasure from society is probably an extension of the parental or filial affections, since the social instinct seems to be developed by the young remaining for a long time with their parents; and this extension may be attributed in part to habit, but chiefly to natural selection" [16]. The wisdom of this statement has been confirmed by various studies which show that, in organisms with advanced development of the central nervous system, repeated interactions (i.e., reciprocal stimulation) lead to the development of affective relationships [7, 110], that such affective relationships may be generalized or transferred [22], that the affective components reinforce the experiences they accompany and possess motivational status, and that affective relationships and societal living have been selected as biologic adaptations [31, 74].

Another significant step in the evolution of parental care occurred in the higher primates (anthropoidea), probably as an adaptation to an arboreal existence, namely, the birth of a *single offspring* [117]. A basic aspect of the evolutionary process is competition, which is usually more marked within a species than between species, because members of one species require the same habitat and food, whereas members of another species generally do not. Intraspecific competition is found in infants and embryos too, so that in animals that produce several young at one birth the intrauterine competition for a limited supply of nourishment and space is considerable. The production of a single fetus is thus of great advantage, eliminating the competition for survival and allowing for a slowing down of development. The longer the single offspring is preserved in the uterus the more unhurried its development may be, and the more likely that it will be preserved for the species. Even so the general slowing of development means that at birth the anthropoid infant is relatively helpless, which provides for a longer period of dependence upon the mother[2] and new kinds of social organization.

Social Structure and Biologic Adaptation

In the higher primates, social organization has reached much higher levels while clearly serving biologic adaptation [32, 114].

---

[2] The relation between slow development and dependence is not a simple causal one. See Washburn's comments ([111] and pp. 17–18) on the interrelation between cause and effect in natural selection.

6

Group living has functioned to provide mutual defense, a territory large enough to supply food for all its members, and an internal stability, largely derived from the dominance hierarchy, which serves to facilitate reproduction, as well as the education and socialization of the young in ways appropriate to their given environment. There is a pooled experience in a group which necessarily exceeds that of an individual mother or father. The social facilitation of learning was undoubtedly of major significance in the evolution of higher intelligence as well as culture.

Since the parent-young relationship is inextricably embedded in the social structure of the higher primates, we must examine this structure. It is highly variable. It used to be thought that there is no breeding season in monkeys and apes, and that the persistence throughout the year of social organization was due to continuous sexual attraction [120]. It is now clear that many species do in fact have a breeding season and a birth peak, a time of year at which births tend to be concentrated [65]. "This is highly adaptive for widely distributed species, for it allows the majority of births to occur at the optimum time for each locality while maintaining a widely variable basic pattern," according to Washburn et al. [116].

There is also considerable variation among species in frequency of copulation and in the number of sexual partners. Social patterning is variable as well. However, Hallowell has pointed out that the basis of most primate societies is a group consisting of X males, X females, X infants, and X juveniles [30]. This is generally true, although there are exceptions such as groups with only males or only mothers and offspring.

The most stable groups are those in which there are *dominance hierarchies* headed by males who lead the group and provide protection. Hierarchical structure is based on the emergence of three evolutionary developments: (1) intraspecific aggressiveness; (2) the capacity for individual recognition; and (3) patterns of submission which do not ordinarily involve flight, and in fact make flight unnecessary [76]. The submissive behavior has the function of controlling or preventing aggressiveness. There are also integrative behaviors in a hierarchy that tend to maintain affiliations. These allow the distance between neighbors to be reduced while actually decreasing the level of aggression. This process is aided by recognition, which implies also

7

the ability to distinguish strangers against whom aggression may be increased. Ordinarily, contact behaviors tend to reinforce affiliations (see fn. 6), and in many nonhuman primates mutual grooming is a major form of bond-servicing between individuals. (In human beings we frequently speak of keeping in touch when we do not mean physical contact, and small talk often seems to serve the same function that grooming does in other primates.)

By inhibiting aggression and fostering affiliations the dominance hierarchy provides order and stability. It also largely controls population growth. There are a variety of factors which control population density. Included among the key factors are fertility, disease and accidents, stress, migration, food supply, and war [35]. In most species dramatic fluctuations do not occur very often, and population control is generally maintained through the dominance hierarchy. In some instances fertility may be limited to the more dominant animals [12, 59, 113], but this is not the only mechanism at work. The dominant animals are the more advantaged in every way. They are usually bigger, stronger, and have the greatest freedom of action and the greatest access to food. Subordinate animals have a rather different existence. They are very often peripheral in a group and have less access to everything. If anything occurs to increase aggressive interactions within a group, e.g., an increase in density or a shortage of food, the aggression will be directed down the hierarchy. If the stress continues, it will often ultimately be relieved by the adaptation of dispersal. Invariably it is the subordinates who must disperse. If there are physical or social limitations on dispersal, it has been shown in a number of species that the stressed animals undergo a series of physiologic changes, primarily associated with an increase in size and activity of the adrenal glands, which in the short term are adaptive but in the long term have serious effects [10, 75, 85, 108]. Resistance is impaired to a wide range of stresses, including starvation, parasites, virus infections, and bacterial diseases. There may be suppression of growth and reproduction. Sexual maturity is delayed and at higher population densities totally inhibited. In mature females estrous cycles are prolonged, while ovulation and implantation decrease. Intrauterine mortality increases, and there are upsets in normal maternal behavior. These effects are themselves adaptive since they lower the reproductive performance of these particular animals and thus the

8

density of the group. In this way the culls are eliminated, while the selected reproduce. The advantage of dominance is clear.

In primates dominance depends at least in part upon the hierarchical status of the parents, acting through both genetic and ontogenetic factors. In addition to the selective factor the social status of the mother is in many species conferred upon the offspring [57, 58, 60, 96]. This comes about in several ways. First, in various species mothers and infants occupy a special location in the center of the group with the dominant males [41, 113]. As juveniles, most of the males are forced to the periphery where they become subordinate or subdominant. Exceptions are the male offspring of the dominant females, who remain in the center where they have privileged relations to the dominant males, with greater opportunity to learn from them, to identify with them, according to Imanishi, and then themselves to achieve top status [42]. Second, dominant mothers intercede on behalf of their offspring in encounters with other animals, so that the offspring have greater freedom of movement, and thus greater familiarity with the surround, and a greater repertoire of behaviors and coping techniques [52, 60]. Like the other aspects of primate society we have considered, the character of the dominance hierarchy also varies, in some species being very constant and rigid [2, 29, 47], and in others being very flexible or at times seemingly nonexistent [23, 98].

Maternal Behavior

There is one feature of primate social organization, however, that is constant—the enduring tie and economic responsibility of the mother for her offspring. Whatever the grouping may be in each species, young infants are invariably found with or near their mothers, who nurse them, raise them, and in various ways teach them that which their species needs to know in order to thrive in that environment [32]. The interest of other members of the group in infants is considerable but varies greatly among primate species, whereas the interest of the mother is constant. She generally cleans the neonate, usually eats the placenta, and often helps the infant cling during locomotion until it can hang on through its own strength. Ordinarily, primate mothers effectively nurse, groom, protect, and transport their young.

There are differences in maternal care, of course, both between

9

and within species [71]. Langur mothers, for example, allow other females to handle and carry their newborn [47]; bonnet macaque mothers immediately rejoin friendly huddles after parturition [54]; whereas pigtail and rhesus macaques [54, 102] tend to jealousy, holding their infants close and away from others. Within a species there are differences in efficiency. The experienced multipara tend to be the most efficient handlers of the young. They are more confident and expend less effort in keeping the newborn quiet [44]. Young inexperienced mothers are more cautious in handling their infants, and yet their motions are sometimes quick and startle them. According to Jay, "Females range from the very capable, through those which constantly readjust the infant's position, to a few extremely inept ones which hold the newborn infant too tightly, in awkward upside-down positions, or constantly away from their bodies" [45].

DeVore found that the baboon mother's status influences the infant very greatly. "There seemed to be a high correlation between the amount of frustration and 'insecurity' displayed by an infant and its mother's position in the female dominance hierarchy" [17]. He found infants to be very sensitive to the mother's emotional state so that when she was upset, as by a fight, the infant was very upset too and would run to her. Subordinate mothers who take a lot of punishment from dominant females he found to be short-tempered and less responsive to their infants. Jay found that the temperament and personality of langur mothers, most particularly their patience and calmness, affect their aptitude in handling their infants [45]. "A tense, nervous, and easily irritated female frequently startles the infant with quick or unpredictable motions; a calm, relaxed female makes few sudden movements."

Jay also found that langur mothers threaten, chase, or even slap males who accidentally frighten their infants [46]. Other adult females nearby may join in chasing the male away. Similar behavior has been reported for other species, including nonprimates.[3]

Mothers of various primate species have been known to tend to

---

[3] Altmann has reported that a moose cow in the beginning of the rutting season will not tolerate the courtship of a bull moose unless he is friendly toward her calf. She also reports that a moose cow has been known to beat up a bear which carried off her calf. "The maternal state obviously endows the moose cow with an aggressive spirit comparable to that of the broody hen defending her chicks" [1].

10

dead babies for days, to retrieve them, protect them, and carry them until only skin and skeleton remain [9]. After finally abandoning dead infants, chimpanzee mothers are reported to look intently at other infants for several days [24].

Recent studies of both monkeys and apes have shown clearly that the relationship between mother and offspring is a very intense one with considerable durability. Chimpanzees have been known to return periodically to their mothers until they are 12 years old and fully mature [23]. In several macaque species it has been demonstrated that all the offspring of a female, even when they are fully grown themselves, maintain a special relationship both to her and to their siblings, a clan relationship [55, 95]. It seems clear that the bond which develops between the mother and infant is the basis for much of subsequent social behavior. Grooming of the fur and skin is probably the most common social activity and serves not only to keep the skin clean and free of parasites but also to build up and maintain affectional bonds. Mothers groom young infants a great deal. At times it is clear, as the infant is growing older, that the grooming by the mother serves to keep the infant close to her at a time when he is on the verge of leaving [55]. Grooming is also seen to inhibit rising aggressiveness [95]. Members of a clan groom each other more than they do other animals in their troop. Maternal behavior and the mother-infant relationship are thus very literally the matrix of primate society. The bond between mother and infant generates the positive affect which ordinarily characterizes much of the behavior within primate groups.[4] Sexual relations between mother and son are said not to occur. In some instances this appears to be a consequence of inhibition by more dominant males, but in my laboratory it has also seemed clear that where there is a continuity of relationship[5] between mother and son that relationship retains certain special qualities, including dominance by the mother, which effectively inhibit sexual relationship between them.

Part of the socialization process in all species involves a pro-

---

[4] On the other hand, Carpenter described now under conditions of stress rhesus females may chase their infants away from food or even kill them over food, as when they were being brought from India to Puerto Rico by boat and were frustrated by confinement and a limited food supply [9].

[5] We have seen a 5-year-old pigtail copulate with his mother when placed with her after 3 years of separation.

11

gression from maximal dependence by the infant toward more independent functioning. Two factors have been cited as playing a significant role in this emancipation of the primate child from the mother. Some studies appear to show that the prime determinant of filial independence is maternal rejection, of which weaning is the most obvious aspect. Weaning appears very traumatic in some species such as the langur, with early mild rejection ultimately replaced by severely punitive behavior and total physical rejection, which sometimes leads to tantrums in the year-old infants [45]. If the mother has resumed estrus, the rejection during weaning is even more intense [17]. In response to the rejection the infant is thought to turn to peers and play, and thus develop greater independence [34, 48].

However, the various studies which indicate an enduring relationship to mother and clan in monkey and ape societies would tend to question this conclusion. Instead, the studies by J. H. Kaufmann of rhesus infants indicate: "Rejection of the infant seemed insignificant compared to the infant's interest in other monkeys, especially other infants" [56]. Also, in chimpanzees Goodall found little rejection by the mother, but a rather consistent initiative by the infant with respect to exploration and interactions with peers and older juveniles [23]. Studies in my laboratory tend also to favor the second thesis, namely, that the growing infant and juvenile primate has a very considerable exploratory tendency which is largely responsible for his growing independence. Rejection by the mother tends to increase dependent behavior by the infant rather than decrease it [53]. Also, as will be made clear in a comparison of bonnet and pigtail monkeys, the bonnet infants who were rejected less seemed to be both the more secure and the more independent. Finally, the drive toward independence of the young has been noted in the human [104] and stressed by Mahler in her studies of separation-individuation [68].

Paternal Behavior

The role of the father in primate society is variable. Paternal behavior by males shows little in the way of a distinct evolutionary course. Of course, in some fashion or another the male must fertilize the eggs externally or internally. This may or may not be preceded by courtship or followed by further close contact with the female or the young. Among mammals there are several species in which the males are strongly parental and normally participate in the care of the young. This is particularly true within the order Rodentia where the male may wash the young, rebuild the nest if destroyed, help the female move it if necessary, retrieve and clean young, or adopt foster young [4]. It has also been demonstrated that male (and virgin female) rats which have been repeatedly exposed to newborn young will care for infants of their own species.

Beach has pointed out that such behavior would likely be most highly developed in those species whose reproductive pattern includes formation of a pair bond and extended postparturitional association between the partners. Also, if the mother carries out her reproductive function within a well-structured group it is more likely that individuals other than the mother will be involved in care of the young. Beach states: "This feature characterizes the behavior of several species of primates, canids, and cetaceans" [4].

Primate males vary greatly in parental behavior. The South American monkey male usually carries the infant virtually all the time except when it is being nursed [72]. Barbary macaque dominant males have been reported to take active roles in infant care, although mothers provide the major care [64]. The dominant males handle the infants, groom them, and carry them around somewhat from the first day on. Usually the male first has to placate the mother, with lip-smacking or grooming, for example, before he can get the infant away from her.

In the Japanese macaque Itani has reported parental behavior by males of high rank that takes place at that time of year when females let their infants go so they may deliver new babies. Among 1-year-old infants protected by the males there are equal numbers of each sex, but among the 2-year-olds there are mostly females—by this time most of the males have formed into a juvenile group and been peripheralized, while the females stay in the central part of the troop. Itani makes it clear that there is no evidence of a blood relationship between the adult males and the infants they protect [43].

Male langurs apparently lack interest in young infants and associate only with older male infants [44]. A report by Sugiyama on Hanuman langurs describes how a previous bachelor male who was part of an all-male group, through a series of attacks by the group upon a troop with females and infants under a dominant male, became the new leader of the troop. He then proceeded to bite to death all the infants who were fairly quickly abandoned by their mothers. The mothers soon thereafter showed signs of estrus and then engaged in copulatory behavior with the new leader. This led to a distinct change in the troop, with replacement of the previous offspring by offspring of the new dominant male [106].

The relationship of adult male baboons to offspring tends to be close. In the chacma baboon, mothers with infants move to the center of the troop near the oldest, most dominant males, who protect them closely [113]. Juvenile and young adult males are not much interested in infants, but the older males are, and frequently come and touch the babies. They are very straightforward, and the mother cringes when a male fondles her infant. The males frequently accompany their approach with conciliatory lip-smacking. They may carry infants on their bellies, and they respond to distress cries immediately. DeVore says: "It is scarcely possible to overemphasize the significance of the newborn baboon for the other troop members. Of the many behavior patterns which bind the members of a baboon troop together, the presence of young infants is of foremost importance. Grooming is the most frequent and obvious expression of 'friendliness' and well-being, and the grooming clusters in a baboon troop are almost always formed around the mothers with the youngest infants. The protective presence of the adult males and the attraction of the infants combine to draw the other troop members toward the center of the troop" [17]. As infants grow older their own mothers and other females become less tolerant of them, but the adult males remain tolerant and play with them, which facilitates attachment of the older infants to the adult males. DeVore says: "The evidence from baboons and Japanese macaques suggests that social bonds between adult males and infants are very strong in these terrestrial species, in striking contrast to the weak bonds between infants and adult males in more arboreal species" [17]. This would go along with the increased sexual dimorphism of terrestrial species, notably the bigger bodies and larger canine teeth of the males. In monkeys it is clear that dimorphism is based primarily on the adaptation of the male for defense and fighting. Such differences do not appear as often in arboreal species, where escape is much easier and predators fewer. Campbell says, in accord with Darwin [16]: "Sexual dimorphism has evolved with

14

the male animal's role as defender of the primate troop as well as a result of sexual selection resulting from dominance" [8]. He says dimorphism has been reduced in man because man does not rely on physical strength and teeth, and the development of the family led to a reduction in intermale rivalry. McBride points out that dimorphism is related not so much to sex and reproduction, but rather to a division of labor in social functions [76]. Each caste makes a different contribution to the functioning of society and accordingly has specialized adaptations for different social functions that can be either behavioral or morphologic.

In my laboratory we have seen striking differences in two species of macaques in the behavior of the adult males with respect to the young. The adult male pigtail macaque is rather disinterested in the young and does not provide them with care, even if their mothers are removed [52]. In contrast, the male bonnet macaque will play with older infants, and if the mother is removed he may hold and carry the infant, as well as protect him [54].

It is difficult, then, to make a simple statement about paternal behavior in nonhuman primates. Adult males may be very attentive to infants or extremely indifferent, but they tend not to be overtly hostile; they may play with infants or juveniles. In species where protection of the group against predators is a major function of the males there is a greater likelihood of close interaction with infants, but even this is variable. At times, in certain species, under certain conditions, males will show maternal behaviors toward infants, perhaps when the mother is ill, occupied, or absent. More generally it seems that adult males play a role with older offspring, especially males, as they enter later stages of development in which gender identities become finalized. At such a point socialization by adult males becomes more critical.

In none of these instances is the parental behavior necessarily directed at the male's own offspring. In fact, in most primate groups there is no way even to know. Two exceptions are of interest. Among gibbons a single male and female pair and raise offspring. There is very little closeness, however, between the adult male and the offspring. He tolerates them until they are about 2½ years old but then he becomes increasingly antagonistic and protective of his own food supply; finally he appears to chase out the juveniles [19]. The other type of one-male group is exemplified by the hamadryas baboon of Ethiopia. Baboons generally sleep in tree tops, but in this barren region there are not very many trees; these baboons are found to sleep on rocky cliffs in groups of many hundreds. In the morning these very large groups break up into much smaller groups of perhaps fifty animals, which then further divide into family-sized one-male groups [62, 63]. The one-male groups, which contain one or several females and their young, remain stable over long periods of time. They maintain their identity as they gather at night with each other to form larger groups whose constituents are far more variable. The one-male groups come about by the male collecting juvenile females, one at a time, to form a small harem. He mates only with his own females and protects only his own and their offspring. This small grouping appears to be an adaptation to food scarcity; the savannah (or chacma) baboon at times of great food shortages has also been reported to break down into one-male units [27]. The same has been reported for the langur [106], the gelada [14], and the patas [28]. As we shall see later this may be homologous to a similar adaptation by man when he came down out of the trees.

Sexual Behavior

One aspect of monkey and ape parental behavior is disruptive to parental function. Female monkeys and apes have estrous cycles recurring monthly, at least throughout the breeding season. In many species the female has very evident external signs of estrus, particularly in the so-called sex skin which becomes engorged and very prominent. In other species it is not so evident visually, but there is very good evidence that the information is broadcast in odors [83]. In any case, the female in estrus shows a much greater interest in males, and they in turn show very great interest in her. During the time that estrus lasts, the female and associated males are very much preoccupied with sexual activity. Ordinarily there is, following birth and during lactation, a period of months in which estrus does not return. However, it does return long before the infants are fully grown or even juveniles. The sexual mania during estrus interrupts normal social behavior and interferes with the care of infants. Accordingly the loss of estrus in the human was a very significant change with respect to the development of family life. Behavior relating to estrus sheds some light on one role

16

of sexuality in sociality.[6] The female in estrus becomes of greater interest to the male, has greater privilege with him than at other times, and is less apt to receive aggressive behavior from him than at other times. In the monkey this privilege usually lasts only as long as estrus, but the mechanism may be of significance in the evolution of permanent relationships and the human family [20]. The sexual object is precious and privileged.

The loss of estrus in humans, i.e., the escape from endocrinologic domination of sexual behavior, made it possible for sexual behavior to be better controlled, for the female to have a longer period for rearing each child without the loss of sexual activity or reproductive capability, and for relatively permanent male-female relationships to develop in a less competitive sexual atmosphere. It thus seems to have played a great role in the formation of family life in the human.

The Emergence of Man

When the ape-man (Australopithecus) came down to the ground out of the trees, the evidence is that he was already largely bipedal and erect, capable of using primitive tools, but with a brain not much larger than the ape's and still largely a vegetarian. It seems likely that the scarcity of food in the open plains then led to the formation of one-male groups.[7]

Washburn has succinctly described the emergence of early man:

Some very limited bipedalism left the hands sufficiently free from locomotor function so that stones or sticks could be carried, played with and used. The advantage that these objects gave to their users led both to more

[6] Marler has recently noted that many behaviors which reduce distance or maintain proximity between primates are forms of contact which often involve the genitalia and/or mouth [69]. In addition he has noted the frequency with which embraces and other greeting gestures by males are accompanied by penile erections or involve mounting. The recurrence of sexual elements in situations that are obviously not copulatory suggests to him that they have an "alternate social role," i.e., to effect closeness. His proposal, based on studies of monkeys and apes, is remarkably like Freud's theoretical constructions on the broad social role of libido. Presumably, the tactile, olfactory, and visual stimuli from conspecifics may produce a pleasurable state, akin to sexual arousal, which serves to promote recognition and reinforce social interaction. I have proposed: "The basis of the continuity and ultimate unity of libidinal drive [in humans] must be sought . . . in some characteristic physiological mechanism underlying sexual excitation" [50].

[7] See earlier comments on the hamadryas baboon (p. 16).

bipedalism and to more efficient tool use. English lacks any neat expression for this sort of situation, forcing us to speak of cause and effects as if they were separated, whereas in natural selection cause and effect are interrelated. Selection is based on successful behavior, and in the man-apes the beginnings of the human way of life depended on both inherited locomotor capacity and on the learned skills of tool-using. The success of the new way of life based on the use of tools changed the selection pressures on many parts of the body, notably the teeth, hands and brain, as well as on the pelvis. . . . The emergence of man's large brain occasioned a profound change in the plan of human reproduction. The human mother-child relationship is unique among the primates. . . . In all the apes and monkeys the baby clings to the mother; to be able to do so, the baby must be born with its central nervous system in an advanced state of development. But the brain of the fetus must be small enough so that birth may take place. In man adaptation to bipedal locomotion decreased the size of the bony birth canal at the same time that the exigencies of tool use selected for larger brains. This obstetrical dilemma was solved by delivery of the fetus at a much earlier stage of development. But this was possible only because the mother, already bipedal and with hands free of locomotor necessities, could hold the helpless, immature infant. . . . Bipedalism, tool use and selection for large brains thus slowed human development and invoked far greater maternal responsibility. The slow-moving mother, carrying the baby, could not hunt, and the combination of the woman's obligation to care for slow-developing babies and the man's occupation of hunting imposed a fundamental pattern on the social organization of the human species [111].*

The great disadvantage in the helplessness of the newborn, including his poorly developed homeostatic mechanisms, was overcome by the evolution of diligent parental care.

With his bipedalism, increasing tool use, and brain capacity, man became a hunter. His ability to procure mammal meat through hunting opened up a whole new source of food supply and led to very great changes in social organization. In order to track and catch larger animals, men banded together in small groups. With the development of cooperative hunting in the Middle Pleistocene Age, females became finally and fully dependent on males for meat, and the one-male group became bonded together more closely, with a division of labor and economic dependence. The woman would gather food and rear the children, and in return she and the children would receive protection and meat.

With the need for cooperation among the males some form of marriage contract between each man and woman arose as part of the

* From Tools and human evolution, by Sherwood Washburn. Copyright © 1960 by Scientific American, Inc. All rights reserved.

political bond between descent groups. This was necessary for social stability, since man could survive only through the social hunt and other social institutions. Thus was the social group enlarged, not as a promiscuous troop but as a broad political structure which united descent groups through intermarriage. Exogamy, which requires the incest barrier, appears to have been the key to this type of social structure. Also the appearance of exogamy and the resultant increase in genetic mixture and variability may have played a great role in the further rapid evolution of the Hominidae, in contrast to the inbreeding monkeys who have not changed in millions of years.

The family became an integrated structure with a clear division of roles throughout; Campbell says these underlie the process of individualization. "The fact that particular males and females are interdependent means that one individual is ultimately important to another, if only at an economic level. With the appearance of one-male groups the interdependence became sexual and it expanded still further with the evolution of the family.[8] The wife and husband recognize each other as economic and social sexual partners. The frontal position in coitus enhances this recognition; role names, such as wife, husband, father, mother appeared and reflected the division of labor within the family" [8]. We can see the human family as having arisen as an adaptation to economic and political needs, as well as through permanent sexual relations. It is a unique group in that there are young of differing ages who have to remain with the parents for a very long time in order to reach maturity. This is possible not only because of the evolution of parents who care a great deal but also because various cultural institutions have evolved based on man's enormous biologic adaptability and capacity for learning.

The Adaptative Aspects of Slow
Growth and Development

A major factor accounting for man's vast cultural development was the evolution of a very slow rate of growth,[9] i.e., growth and development continue for a very long time. Every period of development is lengthened compared to other primates—gestation, the infan-

---

[8] The permanent bond between male and female brought the male into the mother-child relationship [8].

[9] It is of interest that among mammals the amount of protein in the milk is closely correlated with the early growth of the infant; the more protein in the milk the sooner is the birth weight doubled [101]. The human has the least.

19

tile period to the eruption of the first permanent teeth, the juvenile period to the eruption of the last permanent teeth, the adult period to the end of life, and the various stages of reproductive life. Also as mentioned before, man is born at an early stage[10] of development to overcome the limitation imposed by the size of the mother's pelvis. The brain at birth is only about one quarter of its final size. It grows rapidly for several years, reaches 90 percent of final weight by 6 years of age, but continues to grow until about age 20.

The human infant at birth is far more helpless than other primates, whose brains are at least half-grown at birth, and who have a much more developed motor apparatus and the ability to cling to the mother. The problem this creates, and the solution, are clear. Lidz [67] has pointed out that the prolonged helplessness of the human infant dictates that he be reared in a family whose members are attached to him and care about his needs.

The period of infant dependency, which is a matter of months in most mammals, a year in monkeys, and several years in apes, becomes 6 to 8 years in humans. Beyond this, of course, there is the long period of cultural dependency. The close relationship between generations which follows upon suckling and caring for the young makes it possible to transmit learned behavior in a variety of ways, instead of depending solely upon learning through direct experience, as happens in many lower species. The experience of generations can thus be assimilated during a long period of training and instruction. Prolonged dependency and the presence of experienced adults have clearly been major factors in the evolution of human society.

Our focus is on parental rather than infant behavior, but a few comments about the *learning* process during the long period of growth are in order. Lidz [67] has suggested a modification of Hartmann's statement that the infant is born adapted to survive in an average

[10] This is so in still another way, in that human evolution is believed to have been subject to neoteny, a process in which there is a retention of the fetal or juvenile plasticity of ancestral forms in the later postnatal stages of development [84]. Man retains many features that are fetal but not adult characteristics of apes, e..g., the cranial flexure and the absence of brow ridges and cranial crests. The idea is that an essential feature of human evolution has been the avoidance of the specializations of ancestral primates and the preservation into adulthood of the fetal and infantile characteristics of growth. The birth of only one offspring made possible the establishment of mutations favoring neoteny and slow development, there no longer being selective advantage in rapid development.

20

expectable environment. He proposes rather that within each society institutions arise that take into account the essential needs of the young. At the same time that parents provide physical care, they also communicate to the child the mores and instrumental techniques evolved by the society to deal with the environment. Parents provide the basic education in affective behavior and in techniques of communicating, relating, and living with others in social groups. In so doing, they and their ways become part of the child through identification.

Many similar processes are to be found in other species. Mead says:

There is one kind of transmitted experience in which—if we ignore for a moment the presence of language—there is no break between the kind of learning described for red deer or prairie dogs and that which occurs in human society, that is, learning which can occur only when the behaving, individual model is present, because the learning is unverbalized, inarticulate, recorded in no artifact, and represented in no symbolic form. Posture and gesture systems and the unsymbolized parts of a language—stress, cadence, and accent—all belong to this category. As the senior female red deer or the old ewes lead the herd or flock so older members of human groups guide the behavior of the younger members through the experience of a mass of patterned behaviors, specific to a given ecological setting and characteristic of a given society, with much of this never becoming conscious teaching or conscious learning [79].

Young monkeys and apes learn a great deal by observation and imitation, so that the behavior of the mother is very important to the education of the young. Futhermore, as Hall points out, "Early learning goes on in intimate relationship with positive emotional attitudes . . . in the affectional context provided by the mother and others" [26]. Many emotional reactions seem to be learned from observation or kinesthetically derived from the mother's reaction. Learning what is dangerous seems to be in this category. There is evidence that young monkeys showed no fear of snakes if they were raised in such a way as not to have the opportunity to see older monkeys react to snakes with fear [26].

Practice, as in play, is a major technique for primate learning. For example, male juvenile monkeys observe sexual behavior and then practice mounting with peers. Finally, estrous females help them learn to mount. Washburn says: "Play is the educational system for the nonhuman primate. The acts that will be important in adult life and learned in social situations are practiced in play" [112]. However, they rarely play with objects and are "tool dumb" [117].

This shows, say Washburn et al., that learning "is not a generalized ability; animals are able to learn some things with great ease and other things only with the greatest difficulty. Learning is part of the adaptive pattern of the species and can be understood only when it is seen as the process of acquiring skills and attitudes that are of evolutionary significance to a species when living in the environment to which it is adapted" [116].* Washburn and Hamburg state: "Learning can profitably be viewed in the adaptive context of evolutionary biology. The biology of a species expresses itself through behavior, and limits what can be learned. Evolution, through selection, has built the biological base so that many behaviors are easily, almost inevitably learned" [115].† Finally, Washburn says: "In the field studies we see the power of play, social learning, and identification creating adults whose biology and learning have both fitted them for their adult roles. The patas male is built to flee and he has learned when this behavior is appropriate. The baboon male is built to fight, and he has learned the behavior of his troop. Biology and experience make possible the appropriate behaviors of the species" [112].‡

The slow rate of growth as an opportunity for learning is seen in still other ways. Whereas in most primate species females enter upon *reproductive life* with the achievement of nubility, males usually experience a further lag. In chacma baboons, for example, young adult males are allowed to copulate, but usually only with females at the beginning of estrus, whereas older more dominant males take over later in estrus when ovulation takes place, so that it is the older dominant males who are fathering the young [113]. Thus the young male satisfies his sex drives but does not contribute much to the gene pool until he gets older. A similar situation is found in polygamous people even today, where the young men have to wait many years to take wives while the older men are taking their third and fourth [8]. The long apprenticeship provides maximum opportunity for weeding out

* From S. L. Washburn, P. C. Jay, and J. B. Lancaster. *Science* 150:1541–1547, 1965. Copyright 1965 by the American Association for the Advancement of Science.

† From I. DeVore (Ed.), *Primate Behavior*. New York: Holt, Rinehart and Winston, Inc., 1965.

‡ From S. L. Washburn [112]. Copyright © 1968 by The University of Chicago.

the unhealthy and less intelligent males while allowing the selected to gain further experience. In human society reproduction is thus delayed until the male is in a position to provide economically for his family.

Among females a delay in child-bearing after nubility occurs only in the human, and is clearly cultural. This delay is curiously at variance with a gradual change in the age of menarche in Western Europe over the last hundred years from 15 or 16 to around 13 years of age [107]. This is rather remarkable in that it is completely opposite from the overall direction of human evolution toward a slower growth rate. The earlier age of menarche is thought to be due to changed ecologic conditions, bringing about an increase in growth rate in the female. Yet reproduction remains delayed since culturally the assumption of parenthood at nubility seems inappropriate. This delay provides an opportunity for the young adult female to assimilate cultural traditions more fully before having to pass them on to her children. This seems to be a more recent development than the situation in males, where activity for the benefit of the society in many species has usually preceded a full reproductive role.

In connection with the above, it is of interest that among monkeys and apes, fairly early in development, a *behavioral dimorphism* becomes quite evident in most species. Juvenile and even infant males show in their play much more active and aggressive behaviors than do females; these behaviors then develop into the more adult types of aggressive behavior which characterize dominance encounters or group protective fighting [49, 90]. Young females, on the other hand, who do not show this kind of behavior, do show a great deal of interest in infants that is not shown by the young males. Female juveniles watch and then participate in the handling of young infants. There is also evidence, from several species, of maternal behavior by adult females without offspring, the so-called aunts [5, 93]. This practice would seem to serve the juveniles and aunts in good stead later when they become mothers. Supporting the importance of experience in the development of motherhood is the experimental work of Harlow et al. with rhesus females raised on dummy mothers in isolation [37]. They never received mothering, nor did they have an opportunity to observe or practice. They were totally inadequate mothers themselves when they had first infants. They were indifferent or abusive to them, and they did not feed them, so that the infants would have starved if they

23

had not been artifically fed. Yet even these females became more adequate mothers with second offspring.

In the nonhuman primates we can see how the early sexual differences interact with the social milieu to provide the experience relevant to the development of adult parental function. The same is true in the human to an even greater degree. The human family provides a much longer opportunity for observation, practice, and further acculturation even beyond nubility before reproduction takes place. In this learning of sexual behavior, gender role, and parental function we see neatly illustrated the relationship between biology and learning.[11]

Another aspect of the slow rate of growth is the *greater length of life* and the remarkable extent to which humans live beyond their reproductive years, especially women. This is an uncommon situation in other species. In trying to understand how this might have been selected in evolution we have to consider first the fact that, due to the slow growth of children, parents are needed for at least 15 to 20 years after birth, which in itself would take many mothers beyond the menopause. Secondly, the cultural contribution of the postreproductive individual appears to be great. The evolution of culture emphasized

[11] The roles of hormones and the central nervous system are critical in this regard. Studies in recent years have demonstrated fairly conclusively that sex hormones have a double-action effect on the brain [39]. During fetal and neonatal life they act on the undifferentiated brain as they do on the undifferentiated genital tract, in an inductive way to organize brain circuits in male or female patterns. In the adult they act on the nervous system in either an excitatory or an inhibitory way, affecting the neural regulation of sex hormone secretion and the expression of overt patterns of sexual behavior. In experiments pregnant monkeys have been given androgen injections, and as a consequence they have borne female pseudohermaphrodites who behave like male infants, especially in the increased amount of aggressive play, although they are clearly females [119]. In interpreting this, Hamburg and Lunde say: "Perhaps the influence of androgen during a critical period in brain development on the circuits destined later to mediate aggressive behavior would have central nervous system–differentiating effects that would facilitate the ease of learning aggressive patterns and increased readiness to learn such patterns. . . . [The] threshold of response to certain agonistic stimuli might be lowered, with the result that the stimuli might take on distinctly arousing properties. Or, certain patterns of action might become more rewarding as a result of the early hormone action on the central nervous system; e.g., the large muscle movements so critical in agonistic encounters might be experienced as highly gratifying and therefore be frequently repeated" [33]. This would suggest that the early action of sex hormones on the central nervous system produces a dimorphic predisposition— males to aggressive behavior and females to maternal behavior—which is then developed through social learning, and ultimately put to adaptively significant use. This is clearer in the monkeys and apes but may have some relevance to man as well.

24

the importance of learning and the value to the breeding population of the learned individual. Campbell says: "The wise old man will be greatly valued in a social group for his knowledge of hunting, tool-making, and other masculine activities, and in particular for his experience of rare and occasional events, such as flood, drought, locust infestation, and so on. Similarly, the old woman will be valued for her knowledge and experience in childbirth, child-rearing, food-gathering and preparation, and other household odds. The old make a unique contribution to the survival of the cultural animal, for they are the storehouse of knowledge and wisdom" [8].

BIOLOGIC ASPECTS OF BOND FORMATION

Earlier it was indicated that in order for the parent-infant bond and social structure to reach high levels of organization the mother had to be motivated to care for the offspring and the young to seek the care. Carpenter says: "A universal characteristic is that all social relations are, in varying degrees, reciprocal. The aroused motivation of one organism finds its satisfaction, or incentive, in an interacting organism or organisms. The nursing infant satisfies its hunger while at the same time it stimulates the nipple and breasts of the mother possitively and relieves the tension caused by accumulated milk. The infant is the incentive for a complex of the maternal drive" [9]. It used to be said that the mother has a maternal instinct to take care of the young. It is more satisfactory to delineate the processes which account for the behavior. It seems clear that natural selection has favored the emergence of processes which act to keep the young with one or both parents for an extended period of time so that mutual stimulation may occur and lead to the development of bonds, i.e., long-term interdependent behavior.

Tobach and Schneirla say: "The primary process involved in the formation of a social bond is the approach of one organism to another" [110].* Approach is based on the attractiveness of the stimulus object, and Schneirla has proposed a powerful theory in which attractiveness is ultimately derived from low-intensity (with withdrawal the response to high intensity) stimulation [99]. When the stimulus object is another organism the directed orientation reaction

---

* From *The Biologic Basis of Pediatric Practice,* edited by Robert E. Cooke. Copyright 1969 by McGraw-Hill. Used with permission of McGraw-Hill Book Company.

to it is called a biotaxis. A biotaxic aggregation arises when a number of organisms come together through a common response to a social stimulus, e.g., the collection of worker bees around the queen honeybee in response to the chemical secretion from her mandibular gland. Any form of sensory stimulation may elicit approach—the vibratory stridulation of the grasshopper, the visual appearance of the beak in many birds, the tactile stimuli of fur in many animals. Whatever the details, it is clear that aggregations based on biotaxic responses provide an opportunity for reciprocal stimulation of the animals. In lower forms the behavioral modifications resulting from reciprocal stimulation are limited by the neural equipment, according to Tobach and Schneirla, "so that patterns of action typically are determined rather directly by structural and physiologic factors . . . [which] limit the storage of the trace effects of experience and restrict the use of such trace effects in new situations. The type of group bond formed in such animals is of a situationally determined character, limited in scope, and is termed 'biosocial' " [110]. The social and migratory behaviors of the army ant exemplify the biosocial level of organization.

According to Tobach and Schneirla: "The levels of organization achieved in higher mammals are a function of the extent and speed with which the initial processes of biotaxis become elaborated and fused into higher processes as individual development proceeds, so that processes of *psychotaxis* occur. Psychotaxic processes arise through reactions to taxic and biotaxic stimuli which become modified through the integration of maturation and experience by virtue of such processes as conditioning, learning, and concept formation (among others) introducing a plasticity of behavior. 'Psychosocial' types of bond formation then arise, in which the meanings rather than the immediate physiological effects of stimuli are functional " [110].

In many species it has been demonstrated that early approach responses of a biotaxic nature facilitate the subsequent development of psychosocial behavior. For example, in the rat physiologic changes in the body of the female near the end of pregnancy serve to orient her attention toward the parts of her body that are most relevant to the impending parturition. Specifically, she licks her genital region a great deal, in part due to changes in salt metabolism and in part due to swelling and fluids. When the young are born with the birth fluids, she transfers the licking from her own body to them.

26

A number of factors influence this early biotaxic relationship. Hormones within the mother play a great role in the reproductive and maternal behavior of fish, birds, and mammals, but increasingly in the course of evolution the hormones came under neural regulation, thus providing for the increasing importance of external stimuli, learning, and experience [3]. The parental behavior of birds consists of nest-building, egg-laying, incubation, and brooding, and each of these is related to specific hormones [66]. Nest-building occurs under the influence of estrogen which has been secreted in response to pituitary stimulation. This secreting process follows hypothalamic stimulation that has occurred in response to visual stimulation by another bird (the male). Egg-laying occurs under the influence of progesterone, after stimulation by the nest and the male has activated the hypothalamus and pituitary. Incubation behavior is based on the increased vascularity of the incubation patch and the opportunity to dissipate heat to the cool egg; this is related to the effects of estrogen and prolactin. Brooding of the young appears to be related to prolactin activity.

However, it is clear that even among birds learning and experience importantly influence parental behavior. For example, multipara are generally better mothers than primipara. The recognition of individual young is based on learning (discrimination), whereas in lower forms recognition is based, for example, on a group scent. Lehrman has amply demonstrated the relation between *learning and hormones* in the ring dove [66]. Those with feeding experience will easily feed young after being given prolactin injections. The hormone causes their crop to become turgid; they peck at the head of the young to induce insertion of its head into their mouth to provoke regurgitation. Ring doves with incubating experience will incubate eggs after injections of progesterone. Naive birds do not respond to either of the injections in the same way. They do not easily feed or incubate, if at all. Yerkes and Tomlin stated: "Structurally determined patterns of activity are neither adequate nor dependable, but instead require facilitation, modification and supplementation through experience" [118].

Let us now examine various species as examples of early biotaxic responses providing opportunities for *reciprocal stimulation* and the development of psychosocial bonds. In many mammals the female becomes restless some time before giving birth and even aggressive, especially to previous offspring. Altmann has described how the elk

27

cow, for example, chases her calf away about 2 weeks before parturition, providing for greater closeness with the new offspring [1]. As mentioned earlier, the rat actively licks her genital area and then the neonate. The whole sequence is important to bond development; rats delivered by cesarean section later retrieve pups very inefficiently, since there is a poor bond.

The cat also, in delivering her young, responds to the attractive chemical stimuli in the amniotic fluid, and her licking brings her soon to the neonate which presents the most fluid in a concentrated area, as a consequence of which the licking soon becomes focused on the newborn; this one is licked most of all [100]. Regarding the neonate's behavior after birth the position of the female cat lying on her side with legs extended is a physical pattern that in effect guides the newborn to her, and her licking from this position also exerts a guiding effect. These initial biotaxic responses establish a situation of continuing reciprocal stimulation which leads to the formation of a social bond.

In goats and sheep the mother's physiologic state at parturition is important to acceptance of the newborn—she licks puddles of birth fluid and responds to distress cries of strange kids [11, 40]. Her own voice changes. The first response following birth is for the mother to turn at once and begin licking the membranes from the newborn; this is occasionally preceded by licking her own external genitalia, and it seems to be connected with the fresh birth odor. The thirst of the mother may be a factor, since she stops licking once the kid or lamb is dry. The bleating of the young induces the mother promptly to respond with vocalization and to go to the young. However, if it is not her own, she will not accept it. The mother goat defends her newborn against the approach of any other goat and thus prevents any disturbance of the interaction (reciprocal stimulation) which is needed to establish the firm bond. If the young lamb or kid is removed shortly after birth and kept away for several hours, the mother does not then accept it. She will not let it nurse and butts it away. Collias says, "Maternal rejection under these conditions demonstrates that the first few hours after parturition are critical to the development of the social bond between mother and young in sheep and goats" [11]. If she has had the young for an hour before removal she will accept it again. After birth there is a very rapid establishment of the social bond.

28

Odor, sound, tactile stimuli, and color cues are probably used by the females in learning their individual young.

Generalizing about various mammals, Tobach and Schneirla say:

The social bond which is basic and prior to later species-mate responses is initiated through the female's biotaxic responses intensified by excitatory effects from the gestation and parturitive processes themselves, in a complex sequence of reciprocal stimulative events. At first the stimulative effects are biotaxic, as the female is attracted either to the fluids or to the neonate on visual, tactile, or chemostimulative bases, and the neonates are attracted to the female through biotaxic effects such as temperature, visual, auditory and gentle tactual stimuli. These biotaxic stimuli operate reciprocally after parturition, so that within the first hours after delivery the formation of a psychosocial bond between parent and offspring is well begun. Tension-relief through nursing the young must intensify the female's perceptual reactivity to them, so that as she licks and nurses them they take on significance as objects and potential social "signs." For the young, tension-relief through feeding and bladder and bowel evacuation in the instance of relatively altricially born mammals, similarly organizes the percept of the parental animal [110].

In *nonhuman primates* chemical stimuli at birth still play a role, with vigorous licking of amniotic fluids and eating of the placenta by the mother [9, 109]. However, other factors seem to be strongly involved. Primate infants seem to be attractive to mothers and others through visual, auditory, tactile, and kinesthetic stimulation as well.

Jay believes that there are three elements about the infant langur which are important in releasing maternal behavior and inhibiting aggression—coat color, quality of movement, and vocalizations [45]. The natal coat in most monkeys is a different color from that of the adult, as is the skin. The duration of the color difference coincides with the period of maximum dependence. The changes in coat color usually coincide with increase in locomotor skill, so that the infant's increasing independence correlates with the general decrease in interest in him as his color changes to the adult type. The quality of movement of the newborn is another factor. Its movements are uncoordinated and awkward, and frequently the infant, in slipping, grasps its mother's fur. The infant's motions appear to stimulate necessary adjustments and to increase fondling by the mother. Finally, the cries of the newborn infant are distinct in quality, intensity, and volume, and can apparently communicate considerable information to the mother.

Similar factors have been described in other species [17, 88]. In connection with the continued interest of mothers in infants who have died, it is probably the lack of movement and vocalization that ultimately causes the mother to abandon the dead infant, but this usually takes place gradually over days.[12]

Tactile stimulation seems important in view of the clinging relationship which is so constant and critical to the infant in early life, as shown by Harlow's brilliant investigations [36]. The role of the clinging in stimulating the mother, however, is unclear. On the one hand, there is evidence that if the infant does not cling maternal behavior is deficient, e.g., with dead infants, and in an adoption experiment by Harlow et al. [38]. On the other hand, Rumbaugh tied a squirrel monkey infant's arms so that it could not cling, and the mother responded with active cradling [94].

There is evidence that the infant's appearance per se is attractive to the mother. Cross and Harlow showed that multiparous mothers which had been separated from their babies at birth chose to look at pictures of an infant rather than of a juvenile monkey. Nulliparous females showed no preference, and mothers tested before and after giving birth showed a very sudden and rapid rise in preference for infant-viewing after parturition [15].

The previous experience of the mother affects her behavior, as illustrated by the motherless rhesus mothers who were so inadequate with their first infants. Their ability to be more adequate mothers with their next infants illustrates the same point. The delivery experience also appears to be a factor. Meier reported that laboratory-reared, socially deprived mothers showed normal maternal behavior toward infants delivered by vagina but not toward infants delivered by cesarean section, whereas wild-born and -raised mothers displayed normal maternal behavior even toward infants delivered by cesarean section [81, 82]. Another factor that plays a role is the mother's postpartum condition. For example, a bonnet female in my laboratory suffered a prolapsed uterus with the delivery of her baby and soon stopped holding and carrying the baby. It had to be taken away from her to be artificially reared. She was debilitated by her experience and unable to provide maternal care.

[12] In some instances mothers have been known to switch gradually from grooming by mouth to taking little bites and actually eating the dead infant. We have seen it in the laboratory with pigtail mothers.

Harlow has described three stages in the development of the affectional system of the monkey mother—attachment,[13] ambivalence, and separation [38]. For the infant, Harlow [36] has stressed the importance of contact comfort and rocking while minimizing the role of nursing, but Tobach and Schneirla [110] have interpreted Harlow's own data to show the importance of early feeding in the socialization of the infant monkey. Later I shall present data from my laboratory that bear on the mother-infant relationship of monkeys.

Margaret Mead points out that among human beings much of early mother-infant behavior, even among primitive peoples, is culturally and not biologically determined. However, she also says: "It might be claimed that the biological mother establishes a shared tie with her newborn infant owing to the establishment during and after birth of a series of biologically given responses, to the infant's cry, to the smell of the mother's body, to the shape of the mother's nipple, to the nature of the infant's sucking reflex, that is of such an order that it will assure the kind of continuity of later care that the infant requires" [80].

Of the biologic factors in the early mother-infant relationship in humans we have most information about the *nursing* situation, which was recently reviewed by Newton and Newton [86]. Milk is delivered to the sucking infant via the milk ejection reflex, which is triggered by the sucking stimulus to the nipple; as a result oxytocin is discharged

[13] Cairns has reviewed the extensive studies of mammalian attachment behavior and has proposed a parsimonious theory with great explanatory power [7]. He says that an animal forms an attachment with respect to those objects with which it has been continuously maintained, and that the strength of the attachment depends on the length of association in a given context and on the relative cue weight of the object. Objects that appear recurrently in combination with other environmental or external events can become significant components in the stimulus patterns supporting an animal's behavior, including such basic maintenance response systems as drinking and eating. Animate objects by virtue of their salience and involvement in the animal's behavior are particularly apt to become conditioned. With respect to the early attachment of infant to mother, and vice versa, the typical insulation of the mother-young unit is an important factor, by focusing the attention of each on the other. In the more slowly maturing primates this isolation is assured by the incompetence of the neonate. Another important factor is the continuous involvement of each animal across a large number of the response system of the other. The prolonged and extensive interaction promotes a dyadic conditioning process in which the behaviors of each acquire significant cue function for the other. Rosenblatt and Lehrman's study, e.g., showed how the cues of the neonatal rat provide the stimuli for the maternal activities of licking and retrieving, and that licking in turn elicits and directs the neonate's elimination and sucking responses, and so on [89].

from the posterior pituitary and carried in the blood to the breast where it acts on the myoepithelial cells around the alveoli, causing them to contract and push out the milk into the larger ducts where it is more easily available. The reflex is very sensitive to small differences in oxytocin level, perhaps accounting for the fact that so many different factors may operate to affect it.

The sucking stimulus also causes the release from the anterior pituitary of prolactin (and probably somatotropin) which is responsible both for the milk production and the milk ejection. It is not surprising then that there is considerable evidence that restriction of sucking for any reason reduces lactation [18, 97]. The less the baby sucks or is allowed to suck, the less milk there is.

Since nursing is such an important aspect of maternal behavior it is worth considering other factors that influence it [86]. The physiologic responses in coitus and lactation are allied. Uterine contractions occur during suckling and during sexual excitement as does nipple erection. Milk ejection has been observed during sexual excitement. Breast stimulation may induce orgasm. Both involve skin changes, sexual excitement causing vascular changes and breast-feeding raising body temperature. The thermal skin response and the nipple erection reflex appear to be related to milk production. There is a strong positive correlation between milk supply and the rise in temperature of mammary skin due to nursing [13]. A study of nipple protractility found that those whose total nipple protractility was 2.5 cm. usually experience successful breast-feeding whereas those with as little as 0.25 to 0.50 cm. less protractility were notably less successful [25]. Nipple erection may cause an increase of 1 to 1.5 cm. in nipple length suggesting that the nipple erection reflex may lead to more efficient nursing [73].

A study comparing nursing and nonnursing postparturient women and mice showed in both species that the ones who nursed manifested a significantly heightened drive to be in close contact with the young [87].

There is good evidence that difficult labor is associated with a lower tendency to breast-feed, and that failure in breast-feeding leads to unwillingness in the future, whereas success leads to likely recurrence.

Since breast-feeding is a cooperative process, smooth function depends on the baby's behavior also, and the baby's behavior can be disturbed by inefficient sucking, dislike of the nursing situation, or lack of responsiveness. Ability to suckle effectively, for example, has been shown to be related to the amount of barbiturate medication given to the mother during labor [6]. The infants suck at significantly lower rates and pressures and consume less nutrient if the mother has been sedated, and the effect may last for 4 to 6 days [61]. No doubt this is related also to the disturbance in attention of neonates whose mothers are sedated [105].

One way in which the baby comes to reject breast-feeding is by being taught other techniques of sucking. This apparently leads to a loss of interest or effectiveness in the breast-feeding situation.

The pleasantness or unpleasantness of the feeding situation apparently influences the baby's behavior. Scheduling of a few large feedings causes the breast to be overfull, and when ejection occurs the milk may spurt out and choke the infant. Cutting off the air supply even temporarily may be a quick way to instill fear. Ejection reflex failures also may teach the baby to dislike the breast. It has been found that breast-feeding was significantly more successful when there was less fluctuation in the amount of milk obtained from one feeding to the next. Pleasure in breast-feeding is very obvious in older babies. "The total body shows signs of eagerness—rhythmic motions of hands, feet, fingers, and toes may occur along with the rhythm of sucking. Erection of the penis is common in male babies. After feeding, there is often a relaxation that is characteristic of the conclusion of satisfactory sexual response. The sensuous enjoyment of breast-feeding is likely to increase the baby's desire to suckle his mother frequently and fully, thus stimulating the secretion of milk," according to Newton and Newton [86].

Finally, it should be noted that since milk production and availability are so much under the influence of higher nervous mechanisms they are each very easily influenced by the mother's thoughts and feelings.

There have been many debates about the desirability of breast-feeding. One important consideration has been pointed out by Mead—biologically there may not be an adequate fit between mother and infant, either because the mother's nipple is not of the right length or protractility, or because the infant does not display certain sucking and breathing behavior essential to proper breast-feeding. Or, "It may be that the cues for maternal feeling which result in increased capacity for maternal performance, in lactation, tenderness, patience, and playfulness, depend on the types of congruity between the parent's hereditary equipment and the child's. The birth cry of some children may not be the cry for which some mothers are constitutionally prepared, and the quality of the mother-child tie may be determined by interaction between mutually reinforcing and releasing mechanisms, on the one hand, or by mechanisms which negate, mute, extinguish each other, on the other" [77]. Accordingly, she points out, it does not make sense to force a mother to breast-feed her child regardless of how well it is working, with the implication that otherwise she is a rejecting (bad) mother.

There is a little evidence about factors that might play a role in *weaning*. A study of dogs showed that hormonally based changes in the nursing bitch before the litter stops suckling typically result in her regurgitating partially digested solid food which the puppies feed upon [70]. A study of the cat showed that when the mutual approaches of female and young introductory to feeding increase in frequency the kittens direct more and more of their actions at each other and the female until it becomes a rather intense hyperactive approach "play" in which the other animal is clawed and pawed and licked and mouthed and climbed upon [100]. A lot of this behavior is directed at the female's mouth and face, as a consequence of which the kittens get a taste of adult food. In this way the kittens become accustomed to the mother's food, and when they encounter it in wandering about they begin to eat it independently. Meanwhile their rough behavior, together with their increasing strength and emerging teeth, all act to disturb the female and cause her to avoid them increasingly. Similar factors probably play a role in primates also, including humans.

Another factor to consider in parent-young bond formation is *territory*. Even in lower forms of life the environment is altered and reorganized in relation to young. Fish and reptiles show complicated behavior in which the delineation of an area seems important both to fertilization and parental activities. In ring doves it has been shown that behavior concerning territories and nests is crucially related to hormonal functions in the incubating parents [66]. Similar phenomena have been demonstrated in mammals. Physiologic changes in pregnant animals often lead to changes in the level of general activity and the need to regulate temperature; these limit the female's behavior to a place where she builds a nest. When deprived of the opportunity to create an adequate nest, parental responses to young may be weakened in rats and mice, leading to serious disruptions of behavior and an abnormally high neonatal mortality rate. Hamsters rebuild their nests several times during the litter period and stop only at the time nursing falls off due to hormonal changes. In the hamster the nest is so important to the bond that the female often will not nurse young that have been born outside the nest.

The nest site is important also to the young in various ways. Tobach and Schneirla say: "The environment naturally presented to neonates has physical properties and behavioral effects typical of the species, which not only favor the occurrence of the species-characteristic process of bond-formation but canalize the directions of their elaboration and development. The nest or 'home' site is frequently the focus of such properties and effects. The adaptive values of the nest clearly lie in its providing a center for feeding operations as well as an appreciable protection from disturbance and marauders and a place where the young may pass their early stages of development" [110]. In many species odor serves to attract the young to the home area.

Among nonhuman primates the home base or territory is portable. Every day as the troop moves out it changes its location, and for the infant home is where mother is. All its members have to move with the troop or be deserted, which is generally equivalent to death. Sick and wounded animals usually make enormous efforts to keep up with the troop. For the nonhuman primate a fatal illness or injury is one that separates it from the troop. In the human the situation has changed significantly, in that there is a home base. Washburn and DeVore state: "The whole evolutionary impact of disease and accident on the human species was changed when it became possible for an individual to stay in one place and not have to take part in the daily round of the troop. Certainly one of the reasons why it has been possible for man to migrate without building immunity to local disease is that his way of life allows him to be far sicker than a baboon and still recover" [114].

BIOLOGIC CONSIDERATIONS OF THE GOOD PARENT

Earlier, concerning the biologic fit in the nursing situation we considered the matter of the mother's adequacy. Let us now consider further what constitutes a good or adequate parent. From a purely biologic point of view the only criterion is reproductive success—a good parent is one whose offspring survive and reproduce. Everything else one could say about it would be descriptive, i.e., the techniques by which this is done. Obviously these would vary widely among different species, but the techniques of parenthood might be classified into such categories as nurturance, protection, teaching, and fostering independence. Things to be taught might include basic ecology (range, predators, food-getting, and its utilization); body care and maintenance; and social behavior (caste and gender role, hierarchical behaviors, emotional behaviors, bonding and bond-servicing, such as grooming, sexual, and parental behavior). Depending on the species, these techniques are more or less determined by biologic or cultural factors, which are subject to selective or cultural pressures. The goodness or adequacy of the parent is thus defined internally by the requirements of the species or culture. What is good for the goose may be good for the gander but probably not for the ram. What is appropriate for one species or culture is by no means necessarily appropriate for another.[14] Behavior, like morphology, is adaptive. When baboons came to the ground the males became big and strong to protect the troop, whereas the male patas monkey became a lean, fast runner who decoys a predator while mother and young freeze and hide. In this instance, the same problem led to different adaptations.

[14] In most species, and perhaps in early man, the infant who could not suckle or who was sickly was allowed to die. Contemporary human civilization appears to be committed to the preservation and survival of all offspring. Parents are told how to accomplish this and given considerable institutional assistance. Preservation of all life is a continuing goal, so that the infirm, the poorly acculturated, and the poor genotypes are all maintained. Nevertheless certain factors operate to limit the reproduction of these groups. Some homozygotes are lethal and not reproducible, e.g., sickle cell. Some major deviations, e.g., schizophrenia, have a lower rate of reproduction both because of cultural pressures and the nature of the deviation itself. Within a given society, pressures tend to be conservative, to favor reproduction of the stable pattern, not unlike the genetic situation. However, at the extremes of the normal curve are the parents who allow or foster cultural deviations. Most of these are not viable but the few that are provide for subsequent growth and change. There is a balance between stability and flexibility.

Living in the protection of the forest the langur mother may be found with her infant in any part of the troop, whereas the terrestrial baboon mother and her young are always found in the center of the troop where they may be guarded by the strong males. Jay says: "Maternal behavior is a complex of interactions between the adult female and the young infant. It is a well integrated system of patterns of behavior adapted to the efficient protection and nourishment of the dependent young monkey. . . . The meaning . . . can only be understood under the condition in which its adaptive value can be seen" [44]. A good langur mother would not be so good for a baboon baby.

Let us consider a comparison of two closely related species that have been studied in my laboratory. For 6½ years we have been studying numerous groups of two species of macaque, pigtails (*Macaca nemestrina*) and bonnets (*Macaca radiata*). Each group consists of a wild-born adult male, four or five wild-born adult females, and their laboratory-born offspring. There have been more than sixty infants born, of whom over 90 percent are still alive. Some mothers have had four or five offspring with whom they still live together in their original groups.

Although taxonomically close, and sharing many behaviors and social characteristics, there are some striking differences between these two species. Bonnet adults tend to remain physically close, often in huddles, whereas pigtail adults do not usually make physical contact with neighbors except to engage in a dynamic social interaction such as grooming, mating, or fighting. This difference is manifest also following parturition when bonnet females return to close contact (Fig. 1-1), whereas pigtail females with infants remain apart (Fig. 1-2) from other females. This difference in propinquity is consistent and statistically significant [92]. It appears to reflect a significant character of their social behavior, as it may be seen in the behavior of the mother-infant pair and the development of the young [53, 91].

To begin with, in both species there is a period of great closeness, with the infant on the mother's ventrum, nipple in mouth. After a few weeks the infant begins to initiate breaks in contact, but the mother restrains him. Then, as she allows the breaks, she follows along and guards him. Or, she watches very closely, and at a hint of danger rushes to retrieve him. In this stage the infant is striving for

37

Fig. 1-1. Characteristic huddle in a bonnet group. Five adult females are seen together, three with infants, two of whom are nursing.

Fig. 1-2. Characteristic spacing in a pigtail group. Reading from left to right, the group members on the upper bar are an adolescent male, mother with young, adult male, and an adolescent female. Three adult females are seen on the shelves. (From L. A. Rosenblum, I. C. Kaufman, and A. J. Stynes [92].)

separation while the mother resists. This is followed by more willingness on the mother's part as the infant goes further away from her, but they still spend considerable time together.

Then, in the third, and especially fourth, month, weaning efforts by the mother reach a peak, followed by a peak in punishing behaviors. Ventral contact and nipple contact progressively fall, although even at a year of age they still occupy 15 to 20 percent of the time while awake. Meanwhile there is in the second half-year of life a progressive increase in infant play behavior, first of an exercise (nonsocial) type and then involving peers.

Interesting and consistent differences appear between the two species. Bonnet mothers are more relaxed about their infants than are pigtail mothers: they allow them from the start more interaction with other adult females (mothers or not); in the early months they restrain, guard, and retrieve the infants less; later they wean less and punish less. Bonnet infants accordingly show differences from pigtails in their development. They appear to be more secure: they are less dependent on their mother in that they leave her more often to go farther away; they are freer to approach other members of the group, both adults and peers; and they spend more time in social play, whereas pigtails spend more time in exercise play, although the total play time is the same. We may see in the mother's behavior and the infants' development a mechanism of great consequence in the perpetuation of the species-characteristic difference in spatial patterning and temperament.

In considering the reaction of the infants to loss of the mother we may see the influence of the species-characteristic social behavior upon the infants' development in even more dramatic form. We removed mothers, one at a time, leaving infants with their usual group. Of four pigtails 4 to 6 months old, three became severely depressed [52] in a manner comparable to the anaclitic depression described by Spitz [103].

We reported:

The reaction during separation, in three infants, fell into three phases: agitation, depression, and recovery. The fourth infant showed only the first and third phases (Fig. 1-3). During the first phase pacing, searching head movements, frequent trips to the door and windows, sporadic and short-lived bursts of erratic play, and brief movements towards

FIG. 1-3.   Agitated pigtail infant fleeing from rebuff by adult female he had approached. Note fear grimace while screaming. (From I. C. Kaufman and L. A. Rosenblum [52].)

FIG. 1-4.   A depressed motherless pigtail infant showing the characteristic posture. He is completely disengaged from the mother (not his) and her infant sitting nearby in close ventral contact. (From I. C. Kaufman and L. A. Rosenblum, *Science* 155:1030–1031, 24 February, 1967. Copyright 1967 by the American Association for the Advancement of Science.)

other members of the group seemed constant. Cooing, the rather plaintive distress call of the young macaque, was frequent. There was an increased amount of self-directed behavior, such as sucking of digits, and mouthing and handling of other parts of the body, including the genitals. This reaction persisted throughout the first day, during which time the infant did not sleep.

After 24 to 36 hours the pattern in three infants changed strikingly. Each infant sat hunched over, almost rolled into a ball, with his head often down between his legs. Movement was rare except when the infant was actively displaced. The movement that did occur appeared to be in slow motion, except at feeding time or in response to aggression. The infant rarely responded to social invitation or made a social gesture, and play behavior virtually ceased. The infant apppeared disinterested in and disengaged from the environment (Fig. 1-4). Occasionally he would look up and coo (Fig. 1-5).

After persisting unchanged for 5 or 6 days the depression gradually began to lift. The recovery started with a resumption of a more upright posture and a resurgence of interest in the inanimate environment. Slow tentative exploration appeared with increasing frequency. Gradually, the motherless infant also began to interact with his social environment, primarily with his peers, and then he began to play once again. The depression continued, but in an abated form. Periods of depression alternated with periods of inanimate-object exploration and play. Movement increased in amount and tempo. Toward the end of the month the infant appeared alert and active a great deal of the time; yet he still did not behave like a typical infant of that age.

Fig. 1-5. Depressed pigtail infant showing characteristic posture and facies. (From I. C. Kaufman and L. A. Rosenblum [52].)

FIG. 1-6. Reunited pigtail mother and infant in ventral-ventral contact. Mother is grooming infant's ear. (From I. C. Kaufman and L. A. Rosenblum [52].)

The fourth infant, the offspring of the dominant female, did not show the phase of depression. During the agitation phase, unlike the other infants, she spent a great deal of her time with adult females in the group [51].*

In all four when the mother was returned after a month there was a marked and long-lasting intensification of the mother-infant relationship (Fig. 1-6).

We have also separated eight bonnet infants. In no instance has a bonnet infant shown a response resembling the severe depression

* From I. C. Kaufman and L. A. Rosenblum. *Science* 155:1030–1031, 1967. Copyright 1967 by the American Association for the Advancement of Science.

[54]. Some degree of agitation appeared with increased vocalization and self-directed orality, but there was not the same marked withdrawal of interest in the inanimate and especially the social environment. What characterized their reaction was an overwhelming increase in interaction with other adults, especially sustained ventral-ventral contact. Four of the infants achieved full adoptions by other females, including nursing. In one instance a female with an infant of her own cared for two separated infants (Fig. 1-7). The adult males were also solicitous toward the separated infants and even held or carried them, behavior we have never seen by pigtail males. In several instances the infant remained with the substitute mother for a time

Fig. 1-7. A bonnet mother with three infants in ventral contact with her. One is her own; the other two, who were separated from their mothers, she has adopted. One infant has her right nipple in his mouth. She nursed all three.

after the real mother's return, and in one case the infant never reestablished ventral contact with the real mother.

The gregarious quality of bonnet behavior, the influence of which we saw during development, became even more evident and fateful when the mother was lost. As with the one pigtail who did not react with depression, the readiness of all bonnet infants to move toward and be accepted by adults in their group was effective in preventing the otherwise debilitating effects of the mother's loss. It seems likely that the continuous interaction of the bonnet infant with adults[15] other than mother, beginning right after birth, provides a less precise boundary for the affectional bond than develops in the pigtail, whose attachment is so profoundly focused on his mother.

The birth of the next offspring always temporarily disturbs the relationship of the older infant and mother, especially among pigtails. The mother rebuffs all efforts to achieve ventral contact, and the infant shows a mild depression-like response (Fig. 1-8). He does not play as much and tends to stay near the mother, sitting quietly except for frequent digit-sucking (Fig. 1-9). Except for sleeping next to mother at night the older infant is not allowed physical contact with her until the younger one begins to leave her at 3 to 4 weeks of age. Then there is renewed ventral contact and even occasional nipple contact, together with a resumption of greater activity with playmates.

Recently we compared a bonnet and a pigtail group which had each lived undisturbed for 6 years in the laboratory while mothers had as many as four babies [55]. There were twelve offspring in each group. They were studied as to the frequency and duration of significant social activities such as grooming and physical contact with members of their clan (mother and her offspring) as compared to neighbors. Pigtails showed much more interaction with clanmates than did bonnets (Fig. 1-10). Furthermore, pigtails interacted primarily with clanmates, whereas bonnets did not. Among pigtails the attachment to mother continues into maturity and spreads to include siblings who are similarly attached, while all remain somewhat removed from neighbors, in contrast to the bonnets.

---

[15] With respect to the adult bonnet caretaking behavior, pilot work suggests that it too is based on previous interactional experience and is not simply solicitude for any separated infant or, more specifically, any separated bonnet infant. We placed a 4-month-old pigtail and a 4-month-old bonnet infant without their mothers into a strange bonnet group; they were each attacked and had to be removed.

FIG. 1-8. A pigtail mother with a young infant in ventral-ventral contact threatening away her older infant. (From I. C. Kaufman and L. A. Rosenblum, Effects of separation from mother on the emotional behavior of infant monkeys. *Ann. N.Y. Acad. Sci.* 159:681–695, 1969.)

FIG. 1-9. A pigtail mother nursing her young infant while her older infant sits in a corner sucking both thumbs. (From I. C. Kaufman and L. A. Rosenblum, Effects of separation from mother on the emotional behavior of infant monkeys. *Ann. N.Y. Acad. Sci.* 159:681–695, 1969.)

45

Fig.1-10. A pigtail clan showing three generations, mother with older infant on the right, older daughter with her young infant.

We must assume that the difference between the species arose as an adaptation, but as yet we do not have the field data to explain it. We might speculate that some aspect of basic ecology favored a limitation of the pigtail group to clan size, living either as a single group or as part of a colonial arrangement. Other speculations are equally likely, but the explanation awaits further study. Meanwhile it is clear that an important aspect of the difference between the species is the difference in maternal behavior. It is tempting, on first thought, to think that the bonnet is the better mother—her infant is more secure, less fearful, more independent, and less prone to debilitating depression. On second thought, however, it might appear that the pigtail is really the better mother—her infant forms closer attachments with greater affective significance. Then it becomes clear that both opinions are judgments based on human values that have no relevance to pigtails and bonnets and which evolved as they did in response to particular pressures.

What would happen to a pigtail infant raised by a bonnet mother in a bonnet group, or vice versa, is a subject for continuing

46

study which might clarify the relation between genetic and ontogenetic processes. However, the relevance to human beings could at best be only in terms of these processes. Such a study could never tell us how to bring up a child, since that depends on goals derived from consideration of peculiarly human values. For example, based on her studies of primitive peoples, Margaret Mead has argued against the tradition of exclusive upbringing by a close inseparable mother, since she believes that this practice fosters intense but few attachments [77]. She favors the Samoan way of rearing by many relatives without intense ties to parents. When the child is cared for by many warm, friendly people she thinks there is less liability to trauma. Samoans adapt very easily when they go abroad. She points out that we have not developed a method for our children that makes it easy for them to go away from a familiar environment so that they can tolerate "without fear strangers who look, speak, move, and smell very different. In a situation where the mother must take the child day by day to market, to the clinic, on the bus, on the underground, among strangers, the present tendency to advise very close ties between mother and child is doubtfully the best. Wider experience in the arms of many individuals known in different degrees of intimacy, if possible of different races, may be a much better preparation" [78]. Whether or not we agree with Mead as to what is desirable in our children, and whether or not we agree with her ontogenetic psychodynamic formulations about the relation between a rearing practice and its outcome, we recognize the appropriateness of her attempt to extrapolate from one human culture to another, even if we question whether a mothering system could be successfully transposed from a primitive culture to an urban one. When we study in monkeys parental behavior which arose in remote forests probably millions of years ago we hope to learn more about evolutionary processes of adaptation, but we do not expect to find literal models for human behavior.

ACKNOWLEDGMENT

In the preparation of this chapter I have drawn upon the work of many authors, all of whom have been cited. There are, however, several authors whose influence has been greater than may be indicated only by inclusion in the bibliography, and whom I wish to acknowledge separately. These are Bernard Campbell, David Hamburg, Phyllis Jay, Glenorchy McBride, Theodore Schneirla, Ethel Tobach, and Sherwood Washburn.

47

Bibliography

1. Altmann, M.   Naturalistic Studies of Maternal Care in Moose and Elk. In H. L. Rheingold (Ed.), *Maternal Behavior in Mammals.* New York: Wiley, 1963.
2. Altmann, S. A.   A field study of the sociobiology of rhesus monkeys, *Macaca mulatta. Ann. N.Y. Acad. Sci.* 102:338–435, 1962.
3. Beach, F. A.   Biological Bases for Reproductive Behavior. In W. Etkin (Ed.), *Social Behavior and Organization Among Vertebrates.* Chicago: University of Chicago Press, 1964.
4. Beach, F. A.   Maternal behavior in males of various species (Letter to the Editor). *Science* 157:1591, 1967.
5. Bowden, D., Winter, P., and Ploog, D.   Pregnancy and delivery behavior in the squirrel monkey (*Saimuri scuireus*) and other primates. *Folia Primat.* (Basel) 5:1–42, 1967.
6. Brazelton, T. B.   Psychophysiologic reactions in neonate: II. Effect of maternal medication on neonate and his behavior. *J. Pediat.* 58:513–518, 1961.
7. Cairns, R. B.   Attachment behavior of mammals. *Psychol. Rev.* 73:409–426, 1966.
8. Campbell, B.   *Human Evolution.* Chicago: Aldine, 1966.
9. Carpenter, C. R.   Societies of monkeys and apes. *Biol. Symp.* 8:177–204, 1942.
10. Christian, J. J., and Davis, D. E.   Endocrines, behavior and population. *Science* 146:1550–1560, 1964.
11. Collias, N. E.   The analysis of socialization in sheep and goats. *Ecology* 37:227–239, 1956.
12. Conaway, C. H., and Koford, C. B.   Estrous cycles and mating behavior in a free-ranging band of rhesus monkeys. *J. Mammal.* 45:577–588, 1964.
13. Cowie, A. T., and Folley, S. J.   The Mammary Gland and Lactation. In W. C. Young (Ed.), *Sex and Internal Secretions,* Vol. 1. Baltimore: Williams & Wilkins, 1961.
14. Crook, J. H.   Evolutionary change in primate societies. *Sci. J.* 3:66–72, 1967.
15. Cross, H. A., and Harlow, H. F.   Observations of infant monkeys by female monkeys. *Percept. Motor Skills* 16:11–15, 1963.
16. Darwin, C.   *The Descent of Man.* London: Murray, 1871.
17. DeVore, I.   Mother-Infant Relations in Free-Ranging Baboons. In H. L. Rheingold (Ed.), *Maternal Behavior in Mammals.* New York: Wiley, 1963.
18. Egli, G. E., Egli, N. S., and Newton, M.   Influence of number

of breast-feedings on milk production. *Pediatrics* 27:314–317, 1961.

19. Ellefson, J. O.   A natural history of gibbons (*Hylobates lar*) in the Malay Peninsula. Ph.D. thesis, University of California (Berkeley), 1967.

20. Etkin, W.   Social Behavior and the Evolution of Man's Mental Faculties. In M. F. A. Montagu (Ed.), *Culture and the Evolution of Man*. New York: Oxford University Press, 1962.

21. Fremont-Smith, F.   Comment in M. A. B. Brazier (Ed.), *The Central Nervous System and Behavior: Transactions of the Third Conference*. New York: Josiah Macy, Jr. Foundation, 1960.

22. Freud, S.   Group Psychology and the Analysis of the Ego (1921). In J. Strachey (Ed.), *The Standard Edition of the Complete Psychological Works of Sigmund Freud*. London: Hogarth, 1955. Vol. 18, pp. 67–143.

23. Goodall, J. Van Lawick-   Chimpanzees of the Gombe Stream Reserve. In I. DeVore (Ed.), *Primate Behavior*. New York: Holt, Rinehart & Winston, 1965.

24. Goodall, J. Van Lawick-   Mother-Offspring Relationships in Free-Ranging Chimpanzees. In D. Morris (Ed.), *Primate Ethology*. Chicago: Aldine, 1967.

25. Gunther, M.   Instinct and nursing couple. *Lancet* 1:575–578, 1955.

26. Hall, K. R. L.   Observational learning in monkeys and apes. *Brit. J. Psychol.* 54:201–226, 1963.

27. Hall, K. R. L.   Variations in the ecology of the chacma baboon, *Papio ursinus*. *Symp. Zool. Soc. Lond.* 10:1–28, 1963.

28. Hall, K. R. L.   Behaviour and ecology of wild patas monkeys, *Erythrocebus patas,* in Uganda. *J. Zool. Soc. Lond.* 148:15–87, 1965.

29. Hall, K. R. L., and DeVore, I.   Baboon Social Behavior. In I. DeVore (Ed.), *Primate Behavior*. New York: Holt, Rinehart & Winston, 1965.

30. Hallowell, A. I.   The Procultural Foundations of Human Adaptation. In S. L. Washburn (Ed.), *Social Life of Early Man*. Chicago: Aldine, 1961.

31. Hamburg, D. A.   Emotions in the Perspective of Human Evolution. In P. H. Knapp (Ed.), *Expression of the Emotions in Man*. New York: International Universities Press, 1963.

32. Hamburg, D. A.   Mother-Infant Interaction in Primate Field Studies. In B. Foss (Ed.), *Determinants of Infant Behaviour,* Vol. IV. London: Methuen, 1969.

33. Hamburg, D. A., and Lunde, D. T.   Sex Hormones in the Development of Sex Differences in Human Behavior. In E. E.

Maccoby (Ed.), *The Development of Sex Differences.* Stanford: Stanford University Press, 1966.

34. Hansen, E. W. The development of maternal and infant behavior in the rhesus monkey. *Behaviour* 27:107–149, 1966.
35. Harcourt, D. G., and Leroux, E. J. Population regulation in insects and man. *Amer. Sci.* 55:400–415, 1967.
36. Harlow, H. F. Love in infant monkeys. *Sci. Amer.* 200:68–74, 1959.
37. Harlow, H. F., Harlow, M. K., Dodsworth, R. D., and Arling, G. L. Maternal behavior of rhesus monkeys deprived of mothering and peer associations in infancy. *Proc. Amer. Phil. Soc.* 110:58–66, 1966.
38. Harlow, H. F., Harlow, M. K., and Hansen, E. W. The Maternal Affectional System of Rhesus Monkeys. In H. L. Rheingold (Ed.), *Maternal Behavior in Mammals.* New York: Wiley, 1963.
39. Harris, G. Sex hormones, brain development, and brain function. *Endocrinology* 175:627–648, 1964.
40. Hersher, L., Richmond, J. B., and Moore, A. U. Maternal Behavior in Sheep and Goats. In H. L. Rheingold (Ed.), *Maternal Behavior in Mammals.* New York: Wiley, 1963.
41. Imanishi, K. Social organization of subhuman primates in their natural habitat. *Curr. Anthrop.* 1:393–407, 1960.
42. Imanishi, K. Social Behavior in Japanese Monkeys, *Macaca fuscata.* In C. H. Southwick (Ed.), *Primate Social Behavior.* Princeton: Van Nostrand, 1963.
43. Itani, J. Parental Care in the Wild Japanese Monkey, *Macaca fuscata.* In C. H. Southwick (Ed.), *Primate Social Behavior.* Princeton: Van Nostrand, 1963.
44. Jay, P. C. Aspects of maternal behavior among langurs. *Ann. N. Y. Acad. Sci.* 102:468–476, 1962.
45. Jay, P. Mother-Infant Relations in Langurs. In H. L. Rheingold (Ed.), *Maternal Behavior in Mammals.* New York: Wiley, 1963.
46. Jay, P. The Indian Langur Monkey (*Presbytis entellus*). In C. H. Southwick (Ed.), *Primate Social Behavior.* Princeton: Van Nostrand, 1963.
47. Jay, P. The Common Langur of North India. In I. DeVore (Ed.), *Primate Behavior.* New York: Holt, Rinehart & Winston, 1965.
48. Jensen, G. D., and Bobbitt, R. A. Implications of Primate Research for Understanding Infant Development. In J. Helmuth (Ed.), *Exceptional Infant.* Vol. I, *The Normal Infant.* Seattle: Special Child Publications of the Seattle Seguin School, 1967.
49. Jensen, G. D., Bobbitt, R. A., and Gordon, B. N. Sex Differ-

ences in Mother-Infant Interaction. In J. Wortis (Ed.), *Recent Advances in Biological Psychiatry,* Vol. 8. New York: Plenum, 1967.

50. Kaufman, I. C. Some theoretical implications from animal behaviour studies for the psychoanalytic concepts of instinct, energy, and drive. *Int. J. Psychoanal.* 41:318–326, 1960.

51. Kaufman, I. C., and Rosenblum, L. A. Depression in infant monkeys separated from their mothers. *Science* 155:1030–1031, 1967.

52. Kaufman, I. C., and Rosenblum, L. A. The reaction to separation in infant monkeys: Anaclitic depression and conservation-withdrawal. *Psychosom. Med.* 29:648–675, 1967.

53. Kaufman, I. C., and Rosenblum, L. A. The Waning of the Mother-Infant Bond in Two Species of Macaque. In B. Foss (Ed.), *Determinants of Infant Behaviour,* Vol. IV. London: Methuen, 1969.

54. Kaufman, I. C., and Rosenblum, L. A. Effects of separation from mother on the emotional behavior of infant monkeys. *Ann. N.Y. Acad. Sci.* 159:681–695, 1969.

55. Kaufman, I. C., and Rosenblum, L. A. Unpublished data, 1963.

56. Kaufmann, J. H. Behavior of infant rhesus monkeys and their mothers in a free-ranging band. *Zoologica* 51:17–28, 1966.

57. Kawai, M. On the rank system in a natural group of Japanese monkeys: I. The basic and dependent rank. *Primates* 1:111–132, 1958.

58. Kawamura, S. The matriarchal social order in the Minoo-B group: A study on the rank system of Japanese macaque. *Primates* 1:149–153, 1958.

59. Koford, C. B. Group Relations in an Island Colony of Rhesus Monkeys. In C. H. Southwick (Ed.), *Primate Social Behavior.* Princeton: Van Nostrand, 1963.

60. Koford, C. B. Rank of mothers and sons in bands of rhesus monkeys. *Science* 141:356–357, 1963.

61. Kron, R. E., Stein, M., and Goddard, K. E. Newborn sucking behavior affected by obstetrical sedation. *Pediatrics* 37:1012–1016, 1966.

62. Kummer, H. *Social Organization of Hamadryas Baboons: A Field Study.* Chicago: University of Chicago Press, 1968.

63. Kummer, H., and Kurt, F. Social units of a free-living population of hamadryas baboons. *Folia Primat.* (Basel) 1:4–19, 1963.

64. Lahiri, R. K., and Southwick, C. H. Parental care in *Macaca sylvana. Folia Primat.* (Basel) 4:257–264, 1966.

65. Lancaster, J. B., and Lee, R. B. The Annual Reproductive

Cycle in Monkeys and Apes. In I. DeVore (Ed.), *Primate Behavior*. New York: Holt, Rinehart & Winston, 1965.

66. Lehrman, D. S.   Hormonal Regulation of Parental Behavior in Birds and Infrahuman Mammals. In W. C. Young (Ed.), *Sex and Internal Secretions* (3d ed.), Vol. II. Baltimore: Williams & Wilkins, 1961.
67. Lidz, T.   *The Family and Human Adaptation*. New York: International Universities Press, 1963.
68. Mahler, M. S., and McDevitt, J. B.   Observations on adaptation and defense in statu nascendi. *Psychoanal. Quart.* 37:1–21, 1968.
69. Marler, P.   Aggregation and Dispersal: Two Functions in Primate Communication. In P. Jay (Ed.), *Primates: Studies in Adaptation and Variability*. New York: Holt, Rinehart & Winston, 1968.
70. Martins, T.   Disgorging of food to the puppies by the lactating dog. *Physiol. Zool.* 22:169–172, 1949.
71. Mason, W. A.   The Social Development of Monkeys and Apes. In I. DeVore (Ed.), *Primate Behavior*. New York: Holt, Rinehart & Winston, 1965.
72. Mason, W. A.   Social organization of the South American monkey *Callicebus moloch:* A preliminary report. *Tulane Stud. Zool.* 13:23–28, 1966.
73. Masters, W. H.   Sexual response cycle of human female. *West. J. Surg. Obstet. Gynec.* 68:57–75, 1960.
74. McBride, G.   Society evolution. *Proc. Ecol. Soc. Aust.* 1:1–13, 1966.
75. McBride, G.   Behavioral Measurement of Social Stress. In E. S. E. Hafex (Ed.), *Adaptation of Domestic Animals*. Philadelphia: Lea & Febiger, 1968.
76. McBride, G.   Personal communication, 1969.
77. Mead, M.   Some theoretical considerations on the problem of mother-child separation. *Amer. J. Orthopsychiat.* 24:471–483, 1954.
78. Mead, M.   Changing patterns of parent-child relations in an urban culture. *Int. J. Psychoanal.* 38:1–10, 1957.
79. Mead, M.   Cultural Determinants of Behavior. In A. Roe and G. G. Simpson (Eds.) *Behavior and Evolution*. New Haven: Yale University Press, 1958.
80. Mead, M.   A cultural anthropologist's approach to maternal deprivation. *Public Health Papers* 14:45–62, 1962.
81. Meier, G. W.   Behavior of infant monkeys: Differences attributable to mode of birth. *Science* 143:968–970, 1964.
82. Meier, G. W.   Other data on the effects of social isolation during rearing upon adult reproductive behavior in the rhesus

monkey (*Macaca mulatta*). *Anim. Behav.* 13:228–231, 1965.
83. Michael, R. P. Unpublished data, 1968.
84. Montagu, M. F. A. Time, Morphology, and Neoteny in the Evolution of Man. In M. F. A. Montagu (Ed.), *Culture and the Evolution of Man*. New York: Oxford University Press, 1962.
85. Myers, K. The effects of density on sociality and health in mammals. *Proc. Ecol. Soc. Aust.* 1:40–64, 1966.
86. Newton, N., and Newton, M. Medical progress: Psychologic aspects of lactation. *New Eng. J. Med.* 277:1179–1188, 1967.
87. Newton, N., Peeler, D., and Rawlins, C. Unpublished data (as cited in [86]).
88. Poirier, F. E. The Nilgiri langur (*Presbytis johnii*) mother-infant dyad. *Primates* 9:45–68, 1968.
89. Rosenblatt, J. S., and Lehrman, D. S. Maternal Behavior of the Laboratory Rat. In H. L. Rheingold (Ed.), *Maternal Behavior in Mammals*. New York: Wiley, 1963.
90. Rosenblum, L. A. The Development of Social Behavior in the Rhesus Monkey. Ph.D. thesis, University of Wisconsin, 1961.
91. Rosenblum, L. A., and Kaufman, I. C. Laboratory Observations of early Mother-Infant Relations in Pigtail and Bonnet Macaques. In S. A. Altmann (Ed.), *Social Communication Among Primates*. Chicago: University of Chicago Press, 1967.
92. Rosenblum, L. A., Kaufman, I. C., and Stynes, A. J. Individual distance in two species of macaque. *Anim. Behav.* 12:338–342, 1964.
93. Rowell, T. E., Hinde, R. A., and Spencer-Booth, Y. "Aunt"-infant interaction in captive rhesus monkeys. *Anim. Behav.* 12:219–226, 1964.
94. Rumbaugh, D. M. Maternal care in relation to infant behavior in the squirrel monkey. *Psychol. Rep.* 16:171–176, 1965.
95. Sade, D. S. Some aspects of parent-offspring and sibling relations in a group of rhesus monkeys, with a discussion of grooming. *Amer. J. Phys. Anthrop.* 23:1–18, 1965.
96. Sade, D. S. Determinants of Dominance in a Group of Free-Ranging Rhesus Monkeys. In S. A. Altmann (Ed.), *Social Communication Among Primates*. Chicago: University of Chicago Press, 1967.
97. Salber, E. J. Effect of different feeding schedules on growth of Bantu babies in first week of life. *J. Trop. Pediat.* 2:97–102, 1956.
98. Schaller, G. B. Behavioral Comparisons of the Apes. In I. DeVore (Ed.), *Primate Behavior*. New York: Holt, Rinehart & Winston, 1965.
99. Schneirla, T. C. An Evolutionary and Developmental Theory

of Biphasic Processes Underlying Approach and Withdrawal. In M. R. Jones (Ed.), *Nebraska Symposium on Motivation.* Lincoln: University of Nebraska Press, 1959.

100. Schneirla, T. C., Rosenblatt, J. S., and Tobach, E. Maternal Behavior in the Cat. In H. L. Rheingold (Ed.), *Maternal Behavior in Mammals.* New York: Wiley, 1963.

101. Silversten, E. On the biology of the harp seal. *Hvalradets Skrifter* 26:1–166, 1941. Cited in B. Campbell, *Human Evolution.* Chicago: Aldine, 1966.

102. Southwick, C. H., Beg, M. A., and Siddiqi, M. R. Rhesus Monkeys in North India. In I. DeVore (Ed.), *Primate Behavior.* New York: Holt, Rinehart & Winston, 1965.

103. Spitz, R. A. Anaclitic depression. *Psychoanal. Stud. Child* 2:313, 1946.

104. Spock, B. The striving for autonomy and regressive object relationships. *Psychoanal. Stud. Child* 18:361–366, 1963.

105. Stechler, G. Newborn attention as affected by medication during labor. *Science* 144:315–317, 1964.

106. Sugiyama, Y. On the social change of Hanuman langurs (*Presbytis entellus*) in their natural condition. *Primates* 6:381–418, 1965.

107. Tanner, J. M. *Growth at Adolescence* (2d ed.). Oxford, Eng.: Blackwell, 1962.

108. Thiessen, D. D. Population density and behavior: A review of theoretical and physiological contributions. *Texas Rep. Biol. Med.* 22:266–313, 1964.

109. Tinkelpaugh, O. L., and Hartman, K. G. Behavior and maternal care of the newborn monkey (*Macaca mulatta*—"M. rhesus"). *J. Genet. Psychol.* 40:257–286, 1932.

110. Tobach, E., and Schneirla, T. C. The Biopsychology of Social Behavior in Animals. In R. E. Cooke (Ed.), The *Biologic Basis of Pediatric Practice.* New York: McGraw-Hill, 1969.

111. Washburn, S. L. Tools and human evolution. *Sci. Amer.* 203:63–75, 1960.

112. Washburn, S. L. Speculations on the Problem of Man Coming to the Ground. In B. Rothblatt (Ed.), *Changing Perspectives On Man.* Chicago: University of Chicago Press, 1968.

113. Washburn S. L., and DeVore, I. The social life of baboons. *Sci. Amer.* 204:62–71, 1961.

114. Washburn, S. L., and DeVore, I. Social Behavior of Baboons and Early Man. In S. L. Washburn (Ed.), *Social Life of Early Man.* Chicago: Aldine, 1961.

115. Washburn, S. L., and Hamburg, D. A. The Implications of Primate Research. In I. DeVore (Ed.), *Primate Behavior.* New

York: Holt, Rinehart & Winston, 1965.

116. Washburn, S. L., Jay, P. C., and Lancaster, J. B.   Field studies of old world monkeys and apes. *Science* 150:1541–1547, 1965.

117. Washburn, S. L., and Lancaster, J.   Human Evolution. In D. L. Sills (Ed.), *International Encyclopedia of the Social Sciences.* New York: Macmillan, 1968.

118. Yerkes, R. M., and Tomlin, M. I.   Mother-infant relations in chimpanzee. *J. Comp. Physiol. Psychol.* 20:321–359, 1935.

119. Young, W. C., Goy, R., and Phoenix, C.   Hormones and sexual behavior. *Science* 143:212–218, 1964.

120. Zuckerman, S.   *The Social Life of Monkeys and Apes.* London: Routledge and Kegan Paul, 1932.

2

Anthropological
Perspectives
on Socialization

Otto von Mering
Mirta T. Mulhare

T he study of parenthood and childhood is an inseparable part of the broad field of inquiry into the nature of how and why man becomes a social being as well as an individual member of the family of man. As such, this study is concerned with the formulation and testing of relevant statements about man's regulative thoughts and actions which make up the complex, life-long process of socialization and individuation. This process of becoming and remaining a variously contributing and supporting member of the human species, of a particular culture and of various component social groups, can only be understood as a patterned response to the universal categories of experiences of sex and reproduction, food and hunger, health and sickness.

Because man is subject to universal categories of experience and because he has evolved socially under many different "historically created explicit and implicit designs for living," the contemporary systematic study of socialization is a meeting place of all those disciplines and sciences which seek to explain what is common to man and also unique about his thoughts, feelings, works, and biological nature [96]. Scholarly interest in socialization and individuation is, of course, as old as the writings of the early philosophers. The roots of contemporary socialization theories, however, are traceable to the late nineteenth- and early twentieth-century social philosophies of F. P. Giddings, W. I. Thomas, Charles H. Cooley, John Dewey, and George H. Mead.

Traditionally, "anthropology has excavated and analyzed the remains of past civilization (archaeology); described and explained the evolution and present biological characteristics of our species (biological anthropology); traced the development and spread of customs and technologies over the face of the earth, showing how these forms, arts, faiths and tools satisfy the psychological needs of individuals and keep societies together (cultural and social anthropology); and defined the varieties of human speech and the relationship among the tongues of men (linguistics)" [96]. The theoretical and methodological impetus to the systematic study of socialization arose with the emergence of culture and personality studies in the 1920s, a subfield of inquiry within cultural and social anthropology. This subfield has been defined as constituting a body of theory and fact about the transmission of cultural norms and values in behavior (preferred, alternative, and idiosyncratic patterns of behaving), and about the formation of personal, social, and national character through socialization and unconscious processes in different cultures [158].

Anthropology is practiced as "a science *and* a humanistic discipline and is concerned with both the synchronic and diachronic approach" to the understanding of "man the physical beast and man the social animal" [95]. Hence, neither purely culturological nor strictly psychogenic formulas are regarded as having sufficient explanatory power by themselves to account for the *particular* processes of individuation and socialization in different cultural realities. This theme has been a consistent controversial undercurrent of the anthropological quest to understand the cultural component of personality development, a quest which has taken the anthropologist beyond the limits of complex Western society and its culture-bound psychological and social perspectives on normal and abnormal development.

The brief history of the theoretical and methodological vicissitudes of the studies in culture and personality is a record of anthropological efforts to account for the fact that "the worlds in which different societies [and individuals] live are distinct worlds, not merely the same world with different labels attached" [177]. These efforts also document the many difficulties the anthropologist faces when he attempts to "cut off a manageable field of reality of concern to him from the total flow of events" [54]. To a large extent, he has sought to over-

58

come these difficulties by borrowing selectively from the approaches and methods of neighboring sciences and disciplines. As a rule, anthropological formulations of how and why the individual goes about shaping himself within and apart from culture reflect a basic rule of research which may be stated as follows: In the study of cultural and individual phenomena and their interrelations, the anthropologist as field worker and observer generates and tests his own data, and is "guided not by what it would be practically helpful to learn, but by what it is possible to learn" [163].

It is suggested here that this investigative orientation is largely responsible for the fact that anthropology is currently being given credit for having contributed more to the rise of scientific interest in socialization in recent decades than any other single discipline [30]. In a sense, the developmental history of culture and personality studies began with a controversy over polar culturological and psychodynamic explanations of man's nature, behavior, and works. In 1920 A. L. Kroeber, in his review [98] of Freud's *Totem and Taboo* in the *American Anthropologist,* rejected Freud's reliance on analogies between cultural and biological evolution in advancing the thesis that "the beginnings of religion, ethics, society and art meet in the Oedipus Complex" [52]. Like many other anthropologists of the time, he saw no scientific basis to the argument that the long history of man's experiments with institution-building began, so to speak, with a case of parricide in the "primal horde."

Despite widespread initial rejection among anthropologists of the freudian view of evolution and social organization, psychoanalytic psychology has become the most important theoretical influence in the cultural study of personality and socialization. Indeed, it was Kroeber himself who nearly 20 years later, as the dean of American anthropologists, revised his evaluation of *Totem and Taboo* to the extent of according importance to the selective application and reformulation of psychoanalytic concepts to the study of culture in personality [99]. In taking note of the already growing body of such studies, both he and his colleagues recognized the need to direct greater investigative efforts to the life-cycle study of individuals within a culture as opposed to studies of whole cultures.

The reasons for the overriding influence of psychoanalysis on the field of anthropology [102] may be found in certain assumptions psychoanalysis shares with and which distinguish it from other

59

psychologies [103]. It "is the first psychology to take seriously the whole human body as a place to live in . . . to preoccupy itself with the purpose as opposed to the process of thinking . . . to pay significant attention to the symbolic content of thought," and to argue "that there are other kinds of sensual pleasure besides the sexual (genital)," even though the latter is dominant in an evolutionary or biological sense [103]. Among the several assumptions it shares with other psychologies is psychic determinism, which asserts that "everything that happens in the 'mind' is part of a lawfully determined universe" [103]. Another major shared premise rests on the psychoanalytic discovery "that all that goes on in the conscious mind does not exhaust the whole activity of the mind," and that the unconscious part of the psychic economy can be demonstrated through the technique of free association and the process of transference, for which "one must be present, either as analyst or analysand, in order to witness the data" [103]. These premises altogether explain why the anthropological, holistic view of man in nature, society and culture, coupled with the basic practice of obtaining first-hand data through prolonged, direct observation proved to be a most receptive soil for the psychoanalytic perspective of man as a thinking, feeling, and behaving biological organism.

During the period between Kroeber's first review of *Totem and Taboo* and his 1939 reassessment of the relevance of psychoanalytic thought to the study of culture, new approaches and methods integrating psychological and anthropological concepts appeared in the literature at an accelerated pace. This search for a more profound and balanced understanding of socialization and character formation in different cultures is still continuing. We shall present only some of the landmarks in its history.

As a pioneer anthropological investigator of the role of the unconscious among non-European peoples—a goal inspired by C. G. Seligman's 1924 address to the Royal Anthropological Institute—Bronislaw Malinowski sought to test the universality of the oedipus complex in his study of socialization processes among the Trobriand Islanders of the Western Pacific [122]. He concluded that the oedipus complex was only one of a number of possible nuclear complexes capable of patterning primary family affects in a way characteristic of the culture in which it occurred.

In support of his argument, Malinowski presented evidence that ambivalent feelings similar to those delineated by Freud with respect to father and son in a patriarchal nuclear family obtained between mother's brother and sister's son in the matrilineal kin groups of the Trobrianders. This manifest shift of the primary love-hate object from the father to the mother's brother, and related findings—such as the salience of the brother-sister incest taboo among the Trobrianders—reinforced Malinowski's view of the nonuniversality of the oedipus complex, and it kindled his famous debate with Ernest Jones on the subject. Several excellent recent reviews cover the basic issues involved, and also explore their continued relevance to evolving anthropological and psychoanalytic theory and research on the relation of culture to personality formation [51, 165, 201].

Both Margaret Mead and Edward Sapir occupy a singular place in the annals of anthropological studies of socialization and personality development. Mead, in her trilogy *Coming of Age in Samoa* [126], *Growing Up in New Guinea* [127], and *Sex and Temperament in Three Primitive Societies* [128], produced the first truly comparative, empirical studies on the cultural basis of childhood socialization, sexual development, adolescent behavior, and attitude formation. To Sapir goes the distinction of formally launching the study of culture and personality as a special conceptual and methodological sub-discipline within anthropology. In 1931, together with the psychologist John Dollard, he initiated a formal academic program on this subject at Yale University.

Mead, in stressing the significance of problem-oriented research to the field of anthropology, broke with the traditional approach which emphasized the detailed description of all aspects of culture regardless of their relevance to the systematic understanding of individual behavior or any other problem of being human. In organizing her investigations on the basis of both psychodynamic and cultural principles of human development, she did in fact, perform a crucial experiment in obtaining evidence to prove or disprove a general hypothesis [94]. The series of fundamental questions to which she addressed herself in the course of her field work in the South Pacific are as relevant to the scientific understanding of parenthood and socialization today as they were more than three decades ago.

Because they illustrate so well as yet unresolved issues in con-

61

temporary anthropopsychological research they are presented here in Mead's own words [129]. In 1925 she asked herself:

What is human nature? How flexible is human nature? How much can we learn about its limits and its potentialities from studies of societies so very different, so conveniently simpler than our own?

In 1930 she formulated her key questions in this way:

Human nature is flexible, but it is also elastic—it will tend to return to the form that was impressed upon it in earliest years.

In 1935 she raised the issue of:

. . . how we can frame our cultural expectations of human nature so as to make human nature either frustrating or fulfilling, [and that] human societies make assumptions about human nature which their educational systems are unable to carry out.

Margaret Mead's sense of problem in her empirical work has withstood the test of accumulated knowledge about processes of socialization and individuation [132, 134]. The same can be said about Edward Sapir's pioneer efforts at forging theoretical links between anthropological concepts and those derived from psychology and psychoanalysis in the study of the formative influence of culture in personality and abnormal conduct. In his words, a character structure "is carved out by the subtle interactions of those systems of ideas characteristic of a culture as a whole, as well as those systems of ideas which get established for the individual through more special types of participation with the physical and psychological needs of the individual organism" [177].

In discussing the interrelations between culture and individual emotional well-being, Sapir referred to the personal systems of need-related behavior as individual subcultures: "The personal meanings of the symbolisms of an individual's sub-culture are constantly being reaffirmed by society, or at least he likes to think they are. When they obviously cease to be, he loses his orientation—a system of sorts remains and causes his alienation from an impossible world" [177]. It is true that Sapir's cogent assessments of the role of culture in the unconscious patterning of personality did not consider the possible effects of material conditions under which a culture functions. Moreover, he discussed normative personality development in relation to particular cultures in a largely descriptive, nongeneralizing manner. Yet, his basic contributions to the understanding of psychological man within his cultural matrix have remained a milestone in the history of cross-disciplinary research.

The subsequent history of anthropopsychological researches on how and why man becomes and remains a social animal is a tapestry of many theoretical and methodological ventures. Only a discussion of those contributions having direct bearing on the topic of anthropological perspectives on parenthood, socialization, and abnormal behavior will be attempted here.

Ruth Benedict's impressionistic or "configurational approach" of relating whole cultures to polar Apollonian and Dionysian personality types [22] set the stage for many studies of national character, including her own on the Japanese [21]. Her psychological epitomizations of whole cultures have perhaps been more of inspirational than of scientific value to anthropological research [162]. On the other hand, her paper on Continuities and Discontinuities in Cultural Conditioning [20] runs counter to this approach. As a pioneer formulation of cultural forces and conflicts influencing individual development, it has become a classic anthropological statement on a fundamental problem of socialization.

The anthropopsychological studies of national character [55–59, 64, 65, 81, 101, 118, 123, 130, 136–139, 141, 146, 147, 150], such as the well-known "basic" and "modal" personality studies [40, 86–88], which appeared in the years just prior to and post–World War II, are historically significant because they established the pressing need for scientific precision in assessing the relationship between child-rearing patterns and character formation [23]. The national character studies, and the several attempts to relate causally adult personality traits to specific cultural modes of toilet training, weaning, and swaddling represent hypothesis-generating explorations rather than definitive works on the basic questions they raised [150]. Subsequent research has demonstrated the fallacy of conceptually holding constant the facts of individual diversity and intergenerational and culture change in the transformation of the child into a social adult through succeeding generations of elders.

The assumption of a common conflict structure and personality

underlying cultural institutions and individual behavior which dominated national character studies was also central to basic and modal
personality research. Neither approach, however, could provide sufficient proof to substantiate this theoretical formulation. The basic personality approach could not shed light on the problem of the frequency of occurrence of particular culturally conditioned behaviors,
and the modal-statistical personality studies could not elucidate the
problem of structure and pattern in human conduct [18, 194].

Nevertheless, this work became a powerful stimulus to the
extensive field testing of a wide range of specialized projective techniques [77], and to the examination of the function of dreams and
fantasies, folklore, and mythology in individual development [33, 43,
79]. These investigations demonstrated anew that it is essential to
raise not only the problem of the ways in which diversity of human
characteristics can be organized but also the question of divergent
patterns of reproducing behavioral uniformity from generation to generation.

Of equal significance is the fact that these studies build new and
lasting theoretical and investigative bridges between anthropologists
and other behavioral scientists seeking integrative interpretations of
individual development, society, culture, and geographic habitat.
Most notable of these efforts by nonanthropologists has been the work
of Erik Erikson, whose comparative explorations—among the Yurok,
the Sioux, and white and Negro Americans—of the critical importance of child-rearing experiences in the formation of adult personality have become modern classics in psychological anthropology [45–
47]. His developmental conceptualizations about the transformation
of culturally given goals into personally cathected motives through the
socialization process and its typical dilemmas or conflicts and "multiplicity of successive and tentative identifications" have left a lasting
imprint on all subsequent anthropological studies of "normal" human
development in different societies [48].

The retrospective life-history study of individuals and families
occupies a special place in the emergence and deepening of anthropological concern with man's ways of becoming both a distinctive person and a member of his culture. From the publication of the first
biographical study of an American Indian by Paul Radin in the year
that Kroeber first reviewed *Totem and Taboo* [169], to the well-
known recent anthropobiographies of whole families by Oscar Lewis

[110–114], the evolution of this approach [82, 92, 104] reflects the many theoretical cross-currents and emphases characteristic of anthropology as a whole.

Studies like Dyk's *Son of Old Man Hat* [41], Ford's *Smoke from Their Fires* [49], Simmons' *Sun Chief* [180], Leighton's *Gregorio, the Hand Trembler* [107], Marriott's *Maria, the Potter of San Ildefonso* [124], Aberle's *A Hopi Life History* [1], Winter's *Beyond the Mountains of the Moon: The Lives of Four Africans* [208], Lantis' *Eskimo Childhood* [105], and Pozas' *Juan, the Chamula* [166] have substantially advanced our knowledge of the range and limitations of this approach. In particular, the intensive retrospective study of the individual throughout his life-cycle, as well as of nuclear and extended whole families, has strengthened both the scientific and humanistic orientation of the anthropology of socialization and parenthood [115].

It is not the place here to review further the known conceptual shortcomings [190] and methodological problems [77] of human developmental studies drawn on the canvas of whole cultures. Nor will we compare the scientific difficulties encountered in these works with critiques of the statistical and interpretive cross-cultural surveys of variation in child-rearing practices [7, 32, 109, 125, 185]—surveys which arose since the establishment of the Human Relations Area Files (HRAF) at Yale University [4, 35, 184, 203, 204, 209].

Similarly, we shall not examine in detail the advantages and disadvantages [188] of the early and recent learning theory approaches to the cultural study of socialization [80, 83, 108, 121, 154, 172, 190, 195, 200]. Further, we will not dwell on the several important comparative approaches to social developmental processes within culturally defined family units which have been guided by modified psychoanalytical or psychological propositions [26, 39, 133, 135, 140, 151, 156, 165, 167, 173, 199, 201, 202, 206]. Nor will we assess the many and varied contemporary psychocultural studies of particular aspects of childhood training experiences and adolescent behavior [3, 6, 28, 34, 53, 89, 143–145, 152, 186–188]. All these studies exemplify the growing trend to theoretical and methodological pluralism in describing and analyzing the structural and dynamic aspects of socialization which shape the individual in the image of his culture as well as beyond its recognized profile.

It is true that the widely cherished conception of a direct and invariant relationship between culturally conditioned infancy and childhood experiences on the one hand, and adult character and behavior on the other has remained an unverified assumption [78, 164, 179]. Nevertheless, the work of anthropologists has fully documented the many-faceted unfolding experiences which transform a child into a culturally recognizable adult member of society, a person similar, though not identical, in behavior and role to his parents and grandparents before him [2].

Margaret Mead discussed the cumulative and sequential process of growing up in terms of the "simultaneity of impact" [142] of the total human environment. Thus, she took note of it not only as an inseparable aspect of "the behavior of each individual with whom the child comes in contact" but also as it is "mediated by ritual, drama, and the arts" [131]. She further elaborated this, stating that "the shape of a pot, the design on the temple door, the pattern of the courtyard, the form of the bed, the graveposts or the funeral urn, the dancer's headdress and the clown's mask, are again reinforcements and whole statements of the same pattern which the child is experiencing serially" [131].

Mead's conception of socialization grew out of her abiding interest in elucidating the cultural context, meaning, and form of communication or interaction between the child, his parents, and other significant parenting and peer figures. Largely because of her work, and subsequently through the researches of Gregory Bateson and Jules Henry, socialization studies have focused more and more on the communication system between parents and children in both "well" *and* "sick" families. These investigators shared her view that communication with culture begins long before the child acquires verbal skills, and that the formative influences of child-rearing need not be, indeed seldom are, the same for every child within a given family unit.

Attentiveness to the most minute detail of growing up enabled Mead to arrive at a comprehensive view of the many culturally engendered concordant and discordant impressions a child receives from the outside world, of how he decodes and internalizes his observations, and of how he expresses their formative influence on his behavior [138, 140, 141, 149, 151]. For the same reasons, Mead also cautioned against making cross-cultural generalizations on the basis

66

of abstracting a few common elements from observed behavior in different societies [140].

In his classic 1936 study of the Iatmul in the Sepik River region of New Guinea, Bateson examined the role and function of multiple ethoses in society—including those pertaining to the male-female, parent-child polarities of complementary behavior. He argued that a given ethos comes about through "a process of differentiation in the norms of individual behavior resulting from cumulative interaction between individuals" [12]. Since that time, the communication aspects of how and why each new generation—living through particular social learning experiences—is prepared to act in harmony *or* disharmony with the dominant cultural patterns of interpersonal relations have been the major focus of his work [8–11, 17].

Gregory Bateson's field experience in different cultures repeatedly raised certain fundamental questions: How does the child learn to perceive contradictory cultural and interpersonal themes about impulse control, and to manage appropriately the expression of fear and anger, frustration and rage in everyday living? How does it happen that in the course of learning about culturally sanctioned meanings of maleness and femaleness, some children learn to respond in a recognizable pathological rather than normal fashion? These and related questions led him to conduct his well-known studies of double-bind communications between parent and child as a part of ordinary patterns of family interaction, and to analyze the place and consequences of repeated "can't win" mother-child situations in schizophrenic households [13–16].

In a sense, Bateson's work reflects the abiding interest of his and later generations of anthropologists in coming to scientific terms with the problem of the relationship between culture and the development of different forms of mental and behavioral aberrations. Although both Sapir [175, 176] and Linton [116, 117] argued against using clinical pathological phenomena as the basis for explaining all human behavior or the workings of whole cultures, Benedict—as a cultural relativist—initially suggested that abnormals of one culture might well be normals in another [22].

The problem of making psychiatric nosologies and psychodynamic formulations of emotional malfunctioning cross-culturally relevant prompted many other definitional explorations by anthropologists [24, 27, 29, 44, 62, 90, 119, 160–162, 194, 196, 198]. In essence, these attempts sidestepped the issues of etiology and pathology and arrived at what could be referred to as cultural symptomatologies or social diagnoses of individual behavioral deviation.

A few anthropologists attempted to deal with the problem from a classic psychoanalytic position, especially George Devereux, who is noted for his exhaustive ethnopsychological and psychiatric study of the Mohave Indian since the early 1930s [38]. To date, his work has only had a limited influence on anthropological studies of socialization and parenthood. Nevertheless, his formulation of a healthy society as one which encourages the fullest factualization of Homo sapiens' potentialities for individuation and differentiation [36], and his perceptive psychodynamic interpretations of the individual within the sociocultural system [37] represent a significant effort to deal with the problem of psychopathology in everyday life.

The conceptual and methodological quandries about normal and abnormal development and behavior in different cultures stem from several sources. Few anthropologists have dealt with physical *and* emotional disorders or abnormality as a unitary problem of life under altered conditions; fewer still have viewed the problem of disease in man as an "ailing-healing unit" [188] of internal *and* external problem-solving. Although anthropologists would vigorously deny being influenced by the ancient mind-body dichotomy, they have nevertheless studied mental illness as if it were a distinct disease entity, and as if it represented a condition whose manifestations could be explained best in terms of the moral-magical order of tribal existence.

If the anthropological literature on mental phenomena in different cultures has been rich in descriptive detail, all too often the relevance of the many coexisting or underlying forms of disease other than the psychological have been left unexplored. Most of the important research questions which have been posed do not adequately reflect the fact that emotional aberration and bodily changes are *both* part of man's reactions to his total environment.

His many inquiries into the normal and abnormal of man's many "experiments in living" [120], however, have moved the anthropologist closer to the thesis that the culturally deviant individual openly practices what is concealed in the healthy person. Consequently, he has become more and more concerned with the question of "what changes the limits between the two forms of life" [25], and turned his trained senses on the character of everyday intimacy and familiarity with madness. Thus, more recent anthropological researches focused on the manifestations of madness within the family, kin, clan, neighbor, and society: The milieu which nurtures the growth of mental aberration gives it shelter and care and also serves as one of its expressions. In so doing, the anthropologist has been intent on exploring and defining its typical personifications; its unfolding and its spread; and its diagnosis, confinement, and treatment as they have emerged and exist in the context of particular cultures.

In order to leave the door open to the dialogue between cause and meaning, the anthropologist has as often pursued the study of the unusual or sick in man as the usual. The application of the life-under-altered-conditions principle of disease to mental illness has shown that for a few individuals in some cultures illness may be a legitimate way of life despite pain or suffering [106]. It has also been demonstrated that certain mental phenomena, such as hallucinations, are not necessarily experienced as personally disturbing and denotative of illness as such [193]. Instead, their content may be of great social interest and will be examined by the folk practitioner and the community for its significance within the framework of dominant cultural values. Under certain human circumstances, we can obtain singularly useful knowledge about the natural history of a disease, indeed about the particular condition of altered behavior itself, if we also scrutinize the value it may have in the way of life chosen by the individual.

If the anthropologist had only tried to explain the altered human condition known as disease in terms of specific causes such as physiological change, gene mutation, or trauma, he would not have addressed himself to the crucial question: Why and how do cultures expend collective energy and effort to suppress *or* expand individual sensitivity to and familiarity with so commonplace a phenomenon as mental illness? It has been suggested that unlike preliterate or non-Western societies, Western civilization of the past several centuries has tended to "conceal the interrelationship between exterior trauma and schizophrenic psychosis" [25]. The anthropologist's views about mental illness, unlike those of the psychiatrist, have not primarily developed on this basis. Rather, they stem from his extensive experience with tribal life, where he found that the utterances and behavior of

69

reason and unreason *together* are capable of revealing fundamental truths about mankind adapting.

In his work with primitive peoples, and lately with contemporary Western societies, the anthropologist has sought to encourage every informant to find his own voice instead of reporting facts alone. In listening often to the sound of deeds and thoughts dipped in the mold of private hopes, fears, and sloths, he has acquired a special sense of social history and individual development. This experience has equipped him to speak with some authority on the relationship between culture and personality.

For the same reason, however, it is not very hard to understand why some psychiatrists and analysts have tended to dismiss anthropological studies of so-called culture-bound syndromes like amok, *latah, windigo,* or *susto* as reports on nothing more than quaint variants of basic psychopathological states [91]. Whatever the merits of particular arguments about the significance of culture patterns and values in the determination of "pathoplastic features" of mental illness (e.g., delusions), few contemporary psychiatrists will deny the demonstrable relationship between cultural factors and "the incidence and character of psychic stresses [and conflicts] in different human societies quite additional to situational and organic factors" [61].

Just as in his work Freud, working within the peculiar "logic of the unconscious," achieved a "return to madness at the level of its language . . . ," that is, ". . . restored, in medical thought, the possibility of a dialogue with unreason" [1] [50], the anthropologist must also succeed in saying something relevant and meaningful about the general condition of man while studying the particular instance of his "fall from reason." His job neither begins nor ends with describing or "explaining" mental illness in terms of heredity, symptoms, and traumata, episodic flareups and chains of reaction, inner conflict and defense, or outer stress and strain.[2]

Like his colleague the practicing psychiatrist, the anthropologist

---

[1] In the psychoanalytic doctor-patient relationship, for example, reality may be "re-viewed" as if it were a myth, and myth may be relived as if it were reality. As such, the relationship is something outside ordinary human awareness and experience, and hence beyond normative social expectations and reciprocities.

[2] Despite many promising research leads, knowledge about the etiological significance of these and related factors in mental illness is still embarrassingly inconclusive [63, 85, 168, 174].

cannot deny reality to the desperate continuity and the pathetic binds of madness in man. Unlike some of his contemporaries, however, he need not become fettered by an extrinsic need to reduce objectively all that can be said about man and madness to "people who have mental disease" and need care. The anthropologist cannot allow himself to succumb to the unconscious as well as culturally sanctioned need to repress the irrational, deranged, or impulsive element in all forms of human existence.

A great many of us still underestimate the hidden dangers to sound research posed by the current fashions of transvaluing mental illness into a psychological or social problem, and then explaining and treating it exclusively on the basis of various related nosologies. Neither psychological nor social factors completely explain all forms of mental illness. It may be "easy to persuade oneself that neurotic patients do not suffer from a disease, but it is not so easy with schizophrenic patients" whose "spontaneous" symptoms approximate those provoked by many known pharmacological substances [5]. Although similar agents found in the schizophrenic patient cannot be taken as the cause of his condition, the burden of proof is on those who fail to see any relationship. It is evident that in his endeavor to illumine the particular problem of the development of abnormality in the context of culture, and especially in his own society, the anthropologist must exercise exceptional care not to let its values dim the chances of acquiring new and painful insights about disease and man.

In the anthropopsychological study of the unusual or abnormal in man's usual relationships with his fellow men, the work of Jules Henry occupies a special place of distinction. From the time he began his pioneer experimental and behavioral analysis of Pilaga Indian children [74] to his current work with whole families [68, 72, 73], he focused his trained senses on the utterances and behavior of reason and unreason in everyday life. In particular he sought to penetrate man's screen of ordinary intimacy and familiarity with these modes of communication in order to understand how they tend to function over time as a unitary formative experience, standardizing, so to speak, the emotional, cognitive, and social responses of the growing individual.

Jules Henry studied family life as he would a culture or other human grouping for three reasons. He argued that "direct observation encounters almost the full drama of family existence," that "unless direct [and continuous] observation is undertaken, important areas of etiology are concealed from us," and that "distortion through observer intrusion" can be minimized with experience [72]. This preference for the natural or "actual living experiment" over the "generated experiment," such as is produced through structured interviewing and testing, was backed by extensive field experience with the "directed observational," "structured activity," and projective test approaches to child development and human behavior in different institutions of culture [67, 70, 74, 76, 77, 153, 178].

It is granted that the cross-cultural anthropological literature on the psychosexual development of children, the expression of love and hate, in child-rearing patterns and sibling behavior, and the developmental analysis of ordinary speech habits and speech disturbances [66, 75] has been greatly enriched by the generated-experiment approaches [42, 66, 75, 84, 88, 155, 157, 170, 171, 182, 184]. Nonetheless, both Jules Henry and many fellow anthropologists remain convinced that the advantages of direct and continuous observation far outweigh its disadvantages.

A central theme of Jules Henry's many-faceted investigations has been the search for a culturally and clinically sound "formulation of the evidential bases of normality" [73]. This search for psychocultural invariants or social system constants which underlie intuitive judgments of normal and abnormal behavior began with his Pilaga Indian studies. It has come to fruition in his recent and current work on American culture and values [71], particularly his detailed analyses of parent-child interaction and the transmission of neurotic behavior from generation to generation in disturbed families [68, 72, 73].

Jules Henry's abiding motivation to formulate a systematic statement about these universal variants [69, 73] stems not only from the knowledge that "all cultures establish their own criteria of the normal"—of "good behavior." His empirical work also persuaded him of the fact that judgments of normality are intuitively based on certain structural, communication factors underlying *all* cultures. Restated, he refused to be satisfied with the idea that "normality is what the culture says it is," and explored the possibility of moving beyond a simple pragmatics of qualitative and quantitative criteria used by most other investigators.

He has stated his approach to the problem succinctly in relation to his work with clinically disturbed families:

In my daily clinical observations and research, I have become aware that I intuitively refer behavior to certain invariants. [It convinced me of the need] to elucidate some of these clinically derived "constants" with little regard for such existential problems as what is decent human behavior, whether an entire civilization can be sick for 4000 years, whether the so-called sick are often in better mental health than the so-called normal, and so on [73].

Moreover, he did not find it feasible to identify all the possible invariants and selected for special scrutiny a small number. He has called them "circumspection; circles of approval, affection, and communication; perception; communication and contradiction" [73].

In order to illustrate his approach, only the definitional elaboration of circumspection is presented here:

All cultures link people together systematically in relations of time, space, motion, and objects. Work is performed at certain times, at a certain pace, and with certain people who handle certain objects and not others. Another expression of the linkage of time, space, objects, and people is living together in one house or living far apart during certain times of the year or during certain periods of the life cycle. At certain ages children have to be close to their mothers, while at other ages they can be separated. At certain ages children can be high off the ground while at others they cannot. People must appear at certain times at certain places in order to perform certain tasks or obligations.

Martin Heidegger has called "circumspection" the inherent characteristic of the human mind that enables it to put things together. While circumspection is an inherent capacity of *homo sapiens,* it is expressed in different ways in different cultures. Every culture makes demands on circumspective capabilities, and failure to meet these demands is considered abnormal. When people lack circumspection, they are "pathogenic" in that particular culture [73].

Observational materials obtained from numerous live-in case studies of families of disturbed children not only demonstrate the nature and working of the universal variants but tend to support Jules Henry's argument that "their dynamic interrelationship constitutes the structural underpinning of culture" [73]. He concludes his argument with these cogent observations:

Wherever man has lived and is living, the total content of culture is "apportioned" by such variables so that no one group bears the entire cultural burden. These rules and criteria are the conventional bases for the judgment of normality.

73

All cultures have some measure of tolerance for deviation. These tolerances vary, depending upon which rules are transgressed, the number of rules transgressed, and the extent and frequency of violation. Gross abnormalities, called psychoses, are probably a combination of several transgressions and their mutually reinforcing "circular interlocks." Thus, massive environmental interventions which attack the underlying regularities of culture appear to be of paramount significance in producing individual psychotic behavior. When these are attacked in this way, there is no reason why the metabolization of adrenachrome should *not* be disturbed [73].

In this historical overview of anthropological perspectives on parenthood, personality, and the abnormal, we have named some knowns about man becoming a social person under usual and altered conditions of life in different cultural worlds. Such an overview would seem to present a strong argument for the principle of multiple determination in the assessment of man's unique and protracted ways of growing up different and yet the same. In exploring the relationship of meaning and cause between childhood experience and the socializing environment, we sampled many strategies of inquiry through the analysis of fact, and many ways of knowing through face-to-face experience and the interpretation of pattern.

Just as the field of anthropology will continue to ask many questions rather than a few, or only one at a time [197, 207], the scientific study of the child in man and of man growing up must continue to obey this rule: The simple yet all-inclusive question which prohibits a conditional answer—the experiment—is still the child and pupil of long, close observation.

Bibliography

1. Aberle, D. F. The psychosocial analysis of a Hopi life history. *Comp. Psychol. Monogr.* 21:1–33, 1951.
2. Aberle, D. F. Culture and Socialization. In F. L. K. Hsu (Ed.), *Psychological Anthropology: Approaches to Culture and Personality.* Homewood, Ill.: Dorsey, 1961.
3. Ammar, H. *Growing Up in an Egyptian Village.* New York: International Library, Grove Press, 1959.
4. Bacon, M. K., Child, I. L., and Barry, H. Relation of child training to subsistence economy. *Amer. Anthrop.* 61:51–63, 1959.
5. Bailey, P. Mental Illness Is a Biological Problem, Too. In

M. Rinkel (Ed.), *Biological Treatment of Mental Illness.* New York: Farrar, Straus and Giroux, 1966.

6. Balke, J. *Family Structure in Jamaica.* New York: Free Press of Glencoe, 1961.
7. Barkow, J. H. The causal interpretation of correlation in cross-cultural studies (Brief Communications). *Amer. Anthrop.* 69:506–519, 1967.
8. Bateson, G. Social Planning and the Concept of Deutero-Learning. In *Conference on Science, Philosophy and Religion, Second Symposium.* New York: Harper, 1942.
9. Bateson, G. Some systematic approaches to the study of culture and personality. *Charact. Personal.* 11:76–82, 1942–1943.
10. Bateson, G. Cultural Determinants of Personality. In J. M. Hunt (Ed.), *Personality and the Behavior Disorders.* New York: Ronald, 1944.
11. Bateson, G. Bali: The Value System as a Steady State. In M. Fortes (Ed.), *Social Structure Studies Presented to A. R. Radcliffe-Brown.* London: Oxford University Press, 1949. Pp. 35–53.
12. Bateson, G. *Naven* (2d ed.). (Orig. 1936.) Stanford: Stanford University Press, 1958.
13. Bateson, G. Cultural Problems Posed by a Study of Schizophrenic Process. In A. Auerback (Ed.), *Schizophrenia—An Integrated Approach.* New York: Ronald, 1959.
14. Bateson, G. Minimal requirements for a theory of schizophrenia. *Arch. Gen. Psychiat.* (Chicago) 2:477–491, 1960.
15. Bateson, G., Jackson, D. D., Haley, J., and Weakland, J. H. Toward a theory of schizophrenia. *Behav. Sci.* I:251–264, 1956.
16. Bateson, G., Jackson, D. D., Haley, J., and Weakland, J. A note on the double-bind—1962. *Family Proc.* 2:154–161, 1963.
17. Bateson, G., and Mead, M. *Balinese Character: A Photographic Analysis.* Special Publications of the New York Academy of Sciences, No. 2, 1942.
18. Beaglehole, E.,.and Ritchie, J. E. Basic Personality in a New Zealand Maori Community. In B. Kaplan (Ed.), *Studying Personality Cross-Culturally.* New York: Harper & Row, 1961.
19. Benedict, R. F. Anthropology and the abnormal. *J. Gen. Psychol.* 10:59–80, 1934.
20. Benedict, R. Continuities and discontinuities in cultural conditioning. *Psychiatry* 1:161–167, 1938.
21. Benedict, R. F. *The Chrysanthemum and the Sword.* Boston: Houghton Mifflin, 1946.
22. Benedict, R. *Patterns of Culture.* (Orig. Boston: Houghton Mifflin, 1934.) New York: Penguin, 1946.

23. Benedict, R. F. Child-rearing in certain European countries. *Amer. J. Orthopsychiat.* 19:342–350, 1949.
24. Benedict, P. K., and Jacks, I. Mental illness in primitive society. *Psychiatry* 17:377–389, 1954.
25. Bleuler, M. Conception of schizophrenia within the last fifty years and today. *Proc. Roy. Soc. Med.* 56:945–952, 1963.
26. Burton, R. V., and Whiting, J. W. M. The absent father and cross-sex identity. *Merrill-Palmer Quart.* 7:85–95, 1961.
27. Caudill, W. A. *Effects of Social and Cultural Systems in Reaction to Stress.* New York: Social Science Research Council, 1958.
28. Caudill, W. A., and DeVos, G. A. Achievement, culture and personality: The case of the Japanese Americans. *Amer. Anthrop.* 58:1102–1126, 1956.
29. Caudill, W. A., and Doi, L. T. Interrelations of Psychiatry, Culture and Emotion in Japan. In I. Galdston (Ed.), *Man's Image in Medicine and Anthropology.* New York: International Universities Press, 1963.
30. Clausen, J. A. A Historical and Comparative View of Socialization Theory and Research. In J. A. Clausen, O. G. Brim, A. Inkeles, R. Lippitt, E. E. Maccoby, and M. B. Smith (Eds.), *Socialization and Society.* Boston: Little, Brown, 1968. Pp. 18–72.
31. Codere, H. The amiable side of Kwakiutl life: The potlatch and the play potlatch. *Amer. Anthrop.* 58:334–351, 1956.
32. Cohen, Y. A. On alternative views of the individual in culture and personality studies. *Amer. Anthrop.* 68:355–361, 1966.
33. D'Andrade, R. G. Anthropological Studies of Dreams. In F. L. K. Hsu (Ed.), *Psychological Anthropology: Approaches to Culture and Personality.* Homewood, Ill.: Dorsey, 1961. Pp. 296–332.
34. DeLaguna, F. Childhood Among the Yakutat Tlingit. In M. B. Spiro (Ed.), *Context and Meaning in Cultural Anthropology; in Honor of A. Irving Hallowell.* New York: Macmillan, 1965.
35. Devereux, E. C., Jr., Bronfenbrenner, U., and Suci, G. J. Patterns of parent behavior in the United States of America and the Federal Republic of Germany: A cross-national comparison. *Int. Soc. Sci. J.* 14:488–506, 1962.
36. Devereux, G. Cultural factors in psychoanalytic therapy. *J. Amer. Psychoanal. Ass.* 1:629–655, 1953.
37. Devereux, G. Normal and Abnormal: The Key Problem of Psychiatric Anthropology. In *Some Uses of Anthropology: Theoretical and Applied.* Washington, D.C.: The Anthropological Society of Washington, 1956.
38. Devereux, G. *Mohave Ethnopsychiatry and Suicide: The Psy-*

chiatric Knowledge and the Psychic Disturbances of an Indian Tribe. Washington, D.C.: Smithsonian Institution, BAE Bulletin No. 175, 1961.

39. DeVos, G. The relation of guilt toward parents to achievement and arranged marriage among the Japanese. *Psychiatry* 23:287–301, 1960.

40. DuBois, C. *The People of Alor: A Social-Psychological Study of an East Indian Island.* (Orig. 1944.) Cambridge, Mass.: Harvard University Press, 1960.

41. Dyk, W. *Son of Old Man Hat: A Navaho Autobiography.* Recorded by Walter Dyk. Introduction by Edward Sapir. New York: Harcourt, Brace, 1938.

42. Earle, M. J. *Rakau Children from Six to Thirteen Years.* Wellington, N.Z.; Victoria University of Wellington Publications in Psychology, No. 11 (Monographs on Maori Social Life and Personality, No. 4), 1958.

43. Eggan, D. Dream Analysis. In B. Kaplan (Ed.), *Studying Personality Cross-Culturally.* Evanston, Ill.: Row, Peterson, 1961.

44. Engelmann, H. O. The non-literate, the psychotic, and the child: A reconsideration. *Anthrop. Quart.* 36:27–33, 1963.

45. Erikson, E. Childhood and tradition in two American Indian tribes (Yurok and Sioux). *Psychoanal. Stud. Child* 1:319–350, 1945.

46. Erikson, E. *Childhood and Society.* New York: Norton, 1950.

47. Erikson, E. H. On the Sense of Inner Identity. In R. P. Knight and C. R. Friedman (Eds.), *Psychoanalytic Psychiatry and Psychology.* New York: International Universities Press, 1954.

48. Erikson, E. H. The problem of ego identity. *J. Amer. Psychoanal. Ass.* 4:56–121, 1956.

49. Ford, C. S. *Smoke from Their Fires.* New Haven: Yale University Press, 1941.

50. Foucault, M. *Madness and Civilization.* New York: Pantheon, 1965.

51. Freeman, O. Totem and taboo: A reappraisal. *Psychoanal. Stud. Society* 4:9, 1967.

52. Freud, S. *Totem and Taboo.* (Translated by A. A. Brill.) New York: Moffat, Yard, 1918.

53. Geertz, C. *The Japanese Family: A Study of Kinship and Socialization.* New York: Free Press of Glencoe, 1961.

54. Gluckman, M. *Closed Systems and Open Minds: The Limits of Naivety in Social Anthropology.* Chicago: Aldine, 1964.

55. Gorer, G. Themes in Japanese culture. *Trans. N.Y. Acad. Sci.* 5:106–124, 1943.

56. Gorer, G. *The American People.* New York: Norton, 1948.

77

57. Gorer, G. The concept of national character. *Sci. News* 18: 105–123, 1950.
58. Gorer, G. Some notes on the British character. *Horizon* 20: 120–121, 369–379, 1950.
59. Gorer, G. Swaddling and the Russians. *New Leader* 34:19–20, 1951.
60. Gorer, G., and Rickman, J. *The People of Great Russia.* London: Cresset, 1949; New York: Chanticleer, 1950.
61. Hallowell, A. I. Psychic stresses and culture patterns. *Amer. J. Psychiat.* 92:1291–1310, 1936.
62. Hallowell, A. I. *Culture and Experience.* Philadelphia: University of Pennsylvania Press, 1955. Pp. 75–111.
63. Handel, G. *The Psychosocial Interior of the Family.* Chicago: Aldine, 1967. Chap. 23.
64. Haring, D. G. Aspects of personal character in Japan. *Far East. Quart.* 6:12–22, 1946.
65. Haring, D. G. Japanese national character: Cultural anthropology, psychoanalysis and history. *Yale Rev.* 42:373–392, 1953.
66. Henry, J. The linguistic expression of emotion. *Amer. Anthrop.* 38:250–256, 1936.
67. Henry, J. Rorschach technique in primitive culture. *Amer. J. Orthopsychiat.* 11:230–234, 1941.
68. Henry, J. Family structure and transmission of neurotic behavior. *Amer. J. Orthopsychiat.* 21:800–819, 1951.
69. Henry, J. Towards a system of socio-psychiatric invariants: A work paper. *J. Soc. Psychiat.* 37:133–161, 1953.
70. Henry, J. A cross-cultural outline of education. *Curr. Anthrop.* 1:267–305, 1960.
71. Henry, J. *Culture Against Man.* New York: Random House, 1963.
72. Henry, J. My Life with the Families of Psychotic Children. In G. Handel (Ed.), *The Psychosocial Interior of The Family.* Chicago: Aldine, 1967.
73. Henry, J. Normal and Abnormal. In O. von Mering and L. Kasdan (Eds.), *Anthropology and the Behavioral and Health Sciences.* Pittsburgh: University of Pittsburgh Press, 1970.
74. Henry, J., and Henry, Z. Doll Play of Pilaga Indian Children: An Experimental and Field Analysis of the Behavior of the Pilaga Indian Children. New York: American Orthopsychiatry Association, Research Monograph No. 4, 1944.
75. Henry, J., and Henry, Z. Speech disturbances in Pilaga children. *Amer. J. Orthopsychiat.* 10:362–369, 1950.
76. Henry, J., and Spiro, M. E. Psychological Techniques: Projective Tests in Field Work. In A. L. Kroeber (Ed.), *Anthro-*

pology Today. Chicago: University of Chicago Press, 1953.

77. Henry J., et. al. Symposium: Projective testing in ethnography. *Amer. Anthrop.* 57:245–270, 1955.

78. Hoffman, L. W., and Hoffman, M. L. (Eds.), *Review of Child Development Research.* New York: Russell Sage Foundation, 1966.

79. Honigmann, J. J. The Interpretation of Dreams in Anthropological Field Work: A Case Study. In B. Kaplan (Ed.), *Studying Personality Cross-Culturally.* Evanston, Ill.: Row, Peterson, 1961.

80. Honigmann, J. J. *Personality in Culture.* Harper & Row, 1967.

81. Hsu, F. L. K. American Core Values and National Character. In *Psychological Anthropology: Approaches to Culture and Personality.* Homewood, Ill.: Dorsey, 1961.

82. Hughes, C. C. The Life History in Cross-Cultural Psychiatric Research. In J. Murphy and A. Leighton (Eds.), *Approaches to Cross-Cultural Psychiatry.* Ithaca: Cornell University Press, 1965.

83. Hull, C. L. Mind, mechanism and adaptive behavior. *Psychol. Rev.* 44:1–32, 1937.

84. Hymes, D. Linguistic Aspects of Cross-Cultural Personality Study. In B. Kaplan (Ed.), *Studying Personality Cross-Culturally.* Evanston, Ill.: Row, Peterson, 1961. Pp. 313–359.

85. Jackson, D. D. *Etiology of Schizophrenia.* New York: Basic Books, 1960. Pp. 37–38.

86. Kardiner, A. *The Individual and His Society: The Psychodynamics of Primitive Social Organization.* With a Foreword and two ethnological reports by Ralph Linton. New York: Columbia University Press, 1939.

87. Kardiner, A. The Concept of Basic Personality Structure as an Operational Tool in the Social Sciences. In R. Linton (Ed.), *The Science of Man in the World Crisis.* New York: Columbia University Press, 1945.

88. Kardiner, A. *The Psychological Frontiers of Society.* New York: Columbia University Press, 1945.

89. Kaye, B. *Bringing Up Children in Ghana.* London: Allen & Unwin, 1962.

90. Kennedy, D. Key Issues in the Cross-Cultural Study of Mental Disorders. In B. Kaplan (Ed.), *Studying Personality Cross-Culturally.* Evanston, Ill.: Row, Peterson, 1961. Pp. 405–425.

91. Kiev, A. The study of folk psychiatry. *Int. J. Psychiat.* 1:524–552, 1965.

92. Kluckhohn, C. The Personal Document in Anthropological Science. In L. Gottschalk, C. Kluckhohn, and R. Angell (Eds.), *The Use of Personal Documents in History, Anthropology and*

Sociology. Social Science Research Council, Bull. No. 53, 1945.

93. Kluckhohn, C.   Southwestern studies of culture and personality. *Amer. Anthrop.* 56:685–695, 1954.

94. Kluckhohn, C.   The Influence of Psychiatry on Anthropology in America During the Past One Hundred Years. In D. Haring (Ed.), *Personal Character and Cultural Milieu* (3d ed.). (Orig. 1944.) Syracuse: Syracuse University Press, 1956.

95. Kluckhohn, C.   *Culture and Behavior: Collected Essays.* New York: Free Press of Glencoe, 1961.

96. Kluckhohn, C., and Kelly, W.   The Concept of Culture. In R. Linton (Ed.), *The Science of Man in the World of Crisis.* New York: Columbia University Press, 1945.

97. Kluckhohn, C., and Rosenzweig, J. C.   Two Navaho children over a five-year period. *Amer. J. Orthopsychiat.* 19:266–278, 1949.

98. Kroeber, A. L.   Totem and Taboo and Ethnologic Psychoanalysis. (Orig. 1920.) In *The Nature of Culture.* Chicago: University of Chicago Press, 1952.

99. Kroeber, A. L.   Totem and Taboo in Retrospect. (Originally published in *Amer. J. Soc.* 45:446–457, 1939.) Reprinted in *The Nature of Culture.* Chicago: University of Chicago Press, 1952.

100. Kroeber, A. L.   The Use of Autobiographical Evidence. (Originally published in A Yurok war reminiscence. *Southwest J. Anthrop.* 1:318–322, 1945.) Reprinted in *The Nature of Culture.* Chicago: University of Chicago Press, 1952. Pp. 320–322.

101. La Barre, W.   Some observations on character structure in the Orient: The Japanese. *Psychiatry* 8:319–342, 1945.

102. La Barre, W.   The influence of Freud on anthropology. *Amer. Image* 15:275–328, 1958.

103. La Barre, W.   Personality from a Psychoanalytic Viewpoint. In E. Norbeck (Ed.), *The Study of Personality.* New York: Holt, Rinehart and Winston, 1968. Pp. 65–87.

104. Langness, L. L.   *The Life History in Anthropological Science.* New York: Holt, Rinehart and Winston, 1965.

105. Lantis, M.   *Eskimo Childhood and Interpersonal Relationships: Nunivak Biographies and Genealogies.* Seattle: University of Washington Press, 1960.

106. Lebra, W. P.   The Okinawan Shaman. In A. H. Smith (Ed.), *Ryukyan Culture and Society.* Honolulu: University of Hawaii Press, 1964. Pp. 43–48.

107. Leighton, A. H.   *Gregorio, the Hand Trembler.* Cambridge, Mass.: Papers of the Peabody Museum of Archaeology and Ethnology, 1949.

108. LeVine, R. A.   The role of the family in authority systems:

A cross-cultural application of stimulus-generalization theory. *Behav. Sci.* 5:291–296, 1960.

109. Lewis, O.   Comparisons in Cultural Anthropology. In W. L. Thomas (Ed.), *Current Anthropology, a Supplement to Anthropology Today*. Chicago: University of Chicago Press, 1956. Pp. 259–292.

110. Lewis, O.   *Five Families*. New York: Basic Books, 1959.

111. Lewis, O.   *The Children of Sanchez*. New York: Random House, 1961.

112. Lewis, O.   *Pedro Martinez: A Mexican Peasant and His Family*. (Orig. 1914.) New York: Random House, 1964.

113. Lewis, O.   "La Vida": A Puerto Rican Family in the Culture of Poverty. New York: Random House, 1966.

114. Lewis, O.   An Anthropological Approach to Family Studies. In G. Handel (Ed.), *The Psychosocial Interior of the Family*. Chicago: Aldine, 1967.

115. Lewis, O.   The Children of Sanchez, Pedro Martinez, and La Vida (Book Review). *Curr. Anthrop.* 8:480, 1967.

116. Linton, R.   Culture, society and the individual. *J. Abnorm. Soc. Psychol.* 33:425–436, 1938.

117. Linton, R.   *The Cultural Background of Personality*. New York: Appleton-Century, 1945.

118. Linton, R.   The Concept of National Character. In A. H. Stanton and S. E. Perry (Eds.), *Personality and Political Crisis*. Glencoe, Ill.: Free Press, 1951.

119. Linton, R.   *Culture and Mental Disorders*. (Edited by G. Devereux.) Springfield, Ill.: Thomas, 1956.

120. MacBeath, A.   *Experiments in Living*. London: Macmillan, 1952.

121. Malinowski, B.   *The Dynamics of Culture Change: An Inquiry into Race Relations in Africa*. (Edited by P. M. Kaberry.) New Haven: Yale University Press; London: Oxford University Press, 1945.

122. Malinowski, B.   *Sex Repression in Savage Society*. (Orig. 1927.) New York: Meridian, 1955.

123. Mandelbaum, D. G.   On the study of national character. *Amer. Anthrop.* 55:174–187, 1953.

124. Marriott, A. L.   *Maria, the Potter of San Ildefonso*. Norman: University of Oklahoma Press, 1948.

125. McEwan, W. J.   Forms and problems of validation in social anthropology. *Curr. Anthrop.* 2:155–183, 1963.

126. Mead, M.   *Coming of Age in Samoa*. New York: Morrow, 1928.

127. Mead, M.   *Growing Up in New Guinea*. New York: Morrow, 1930.

128. Mead, M. *Sex and Temperament in Three Primitive Societies.*
New York: Morrow, 1935.
129. Mead, M. *From the South Seas, Studies of Adolescence and
Sex in Primitive Societies.* New York: Morrow, 1939.
130. Mead, M. *And Keep Your Powder Dry.* New York: Morrow,
1942.
131. Mead, M. The concept of culture and the psychosomatic approach. *Psychiatry* 10:57–76, 1947.
132. Mead, M. On the implications for anthropology of the Gesell-
Ilg approach to maturation. *Amer. Anthrop.* 49:69–77, 1947.
133. Mead, M. The contemporary American family as an anthropologist sees it. *Amer. J. Soc.* 53:453–459, 1948.
134. Mead, M. *Male and Female.* New York: Morrow, 1949.
135. Mead, M. Psychologic Weaning: Childhood and Adolescence.
In P. H. Hoch and J. Zubin (Eds.), *Psychosexual Development
in Health and Disease* (proceedings of the 38th annual meeting
of the American Psychopathological Association, 1948). New
York: Grune & Stratton, 1949.
136. Mead, M. The impact of personality development in the
United States today. *Understand. Child* 20:17–18, 1951.
137. Mead, M. The Study of National Character. In D. Lerner and
H. D. Lasswell (Eds.), *The Policy Sciences.* Stanford: Stanford
University Press, 1951.
138. Mead, M. National Character. In A. L. Kroeber (Ed.), *Anthropology Today.* Chicago: University of Chicago Press, 1953.
139. Mead, M. The swaddling hypothesis: Its reception. *Amer.
Anthrop.* 56:395–409, 1954.
140. Mead, M. Some theoretical considerations on the problem of
mother-child separation. *Amer. J. Orthopsychiat.* 24:471–483,
1954.
141. Mead, M. Effects of anthropological field work models on interdisciplinary communication in the study of national character. *J. Soc. Issues* 11:3–11, 1955.
142. Mead, M. The comparative study of child-rearing: Problems
of simultaneity and sequence. In *Human Development Bulletin*
(Seventh Annual Symposium, Committee on Human Development). Chicago: University of Chicago Press, 1956.
143. Mead, M. Cultural Differences in the Bathing of Babies. In
K. Soddy (Ed.), *Mental Health and Infant Development.* New
York: Basic Books, 1957.
144. Mead, M. Family and Child Development Patterns in Other
Cultures. In K. Soddy (Ed.), *Mental Health and Infant Development.* New York: Basic Books, 1957.
145. Mead, M. Cultural contexts of puberty and adolescence. *Bull.
Philadelphia Ass. Psychoanal.* 9:59–79, 1959.

146. Mead, M. National Character and the Science of Anthropology. In S. M. Lipset and L. Lowenthal (Eds.), *Culture and Social Character*. Glencoe, Ill.: Free Press, 1961.

147. Mead, M. The Idea of National Character. In R. L. Shinn (Ed.), *The Search for Identity: Essays on the American Character*. New York: Harper & Row, 1964.

148. Mead, M. *New Lives for Old*. (Orig. New York: Morrow, 1956.) Reprinted with new Preface. New York: Morrow, 1965.

149. Mead, M., and Macgregor, F. C. *Growth and Culture*. New York: Putnam, 1951.

150. Mead, M., and Metraux, R. (Eds.). *The Study of Culture at a Distance*. Chicago: University of Chicago Press, 1953.

151. Mead, M., and Wolfenstein, M. (Eds.). *Childhood in Contemporary Cultures*. Chicago: University of Chicago Press, 1955.

152. Mencher, J. Growing up in South Malabar. *Hum. Organiz.* 22:54–65, 1963.

153. Mensh, I. N., and Henry, J. Direct observation and psychological tests in anthropological field work. *Amer. Anthrop.* 55:469, 1953.

154. Miller, N. E., and Dollard, J. *Social Learning and Limitation*. New Haven: Yale University Press, 1941.

155. Miner, H. M., and DeVos, G. *Oasis and Casbah: Algerian Culture and Personality in Change*. Anthropological Papers, Museum of Anthropology, No. 15. Ann Arbor: University of Michigan Press, 1960.

156. Mischel, W. Father-absence and delay of gratification. *J. Abnorm. Soc. Psychol.* 63:116–124, 1961.

157. Mulligan, D. G. *Maori Adolescence in Rakau*. Wellington, N.Z.: Victoria University of Wellington Publications in Psychology, No. 9 (Monographs on Maori Social Life and Personality, No. 2), 1957.

158. Murdock, G. P. Sociology and Anthropology. In J. Gillin (Ed.), *Toward a Science of Social Man*. New York: Macmillan, 1954.

159. Newman, R. E. Personality development in a primitive adolescent group. *Z. Diagnost. Psychol.* 6:241–253, 1958.

160. Opler, M. K. *Culture, Psychiatry and Human Values*. Springfield, Ill.: Thomas, 1956.

161. Opler, M. K. *Culture and Mental Health*. New York: Macmillan, 1959. Pp. 273–289.

162. Opler, M. K. *Culture and Social Psychiatry*. New York: Atherton, 1967. P. 236.

163. Oppenheimer, J. R. *The Flying Trapeze: Three Crises for Physicists*. New York: Oxford University Press, 1964.

164. Orlansky, H.   Infant care and personality. *Psychol. Bull.* 46: 1–48, 1949.
165. Parsons, A.   Is the oedipus complex universal? (the Jones-Malinowski debate revisited and a South Italian nuclear complex). *Psychoanal. Stud. Society* 3:278, 1964.
166. Pozas, R.   *Juan, the Chamula.* Berkeley: University of California Press, 1962.
167. Prothro, E. T.   Patterns of permissiveness among preliterate peoples. *J. Abnorm. Soc. Psychol.* 61:151–154, 1960.
168. Rabkin, L. Y.   The patient's family: Research methods. *Family Proc.* 4:105–132, 1965.
169. Radin, P.   *Crashing Thunder: The Autobiography of an American Indian.* New York: Appleton, 1920.
170. Read, M.   *Children of Their Fathers: Growing Up Among the Ngoni of Nyasaland.* New Haven: Yale University Press, 1960.
171. Ritchie, J.   *Childhood in Rakau: The First Five Years of Life.* Wellington, N.Z.: Victoria University of Wellington Publications in Psychology, No. 10 (Monographs on Maori Social Life and Personality, No. 3), 1957.
172. Roberts, J. M., and Sutton-Smith, B.   Child training and game involvement. *Ethnology* 1:166–185, 1962.
173. Rosen, B. D., and D'Andrade, R.   The Psychosocial Origins of Achievement Motivation. In P. H. Mussen et al. (Eds.), *Readings in Child Development and Personality.* New York: Harper & Row, 1965.
174. Sanua, V. D.   Socio-cultural factors in families of schizophrenics. *Psychiatry* 24:246–265, 1961.
175. Sapir, E.   Cultural Anthropology and Psychiatry. (Orig. 1932.) In *Selected Writings in Language, Culture and Personality* (edited by D. G. Mandelbaum). Berkeley: University of California Press, 1949.
176. Sapir, E   The Emergence of the Concept of Personality in the Study of Cultures. (Orig. 1934.) In *Selected Writings in Language, Culture and Personality* (edited by D. G. Mandelbaum). Berkeley: University of California Press, 1949.
177. Sapir, E.   *Selected Writings in Language, Culture and Personality* (edited by D. G. Mandelbaum). Berkeley: University of California Press, 1949.
178. Schachtel, A. H., Henry, J., and Henry, Z.   Rorschach analysis of Pilaga Indian children. *Amer. J. Orthopsychiat.* 12:683, 1942.
179. Sewell, W. H.   Infant training and the personality of the child. *Amer. J. Soc.* 58:150–159, 1952.
180. Simmons, L.   *Sun Chief: The Autobiography of a Hopi Indian.* New Haven: Yale University Press, 1942.

181. Spiro, M. E.   Ghosts, Infaluck, and Teleological Functionalism. *Amer. Anthrop.* 54: No. 4, 1952.
182. Spiro, M. E.   *Kibbutz: Venture in Utopia.* New York: Schocken, 1963.
183. Spiro, M. E.   *Children of the Kibbutz.* New York: Schocken, 1965.
184. Stephens, W. N.   *The Oedipus Complex, Cross-Cultural Evidence.* Glencoe, Ill.: Free Press, 1962.
185. Strodtbeck, F. L.   Considerations of meta-method in cross-cultural studies. In A. K. Romney, and R. G. D'Andrade (Eds.), Transcultural studies in cognition. *Amer. Anthrop.* 66: No. 3, 1964.
186. von Mering, O.   Provisional parenthood, the foster child and neighborliness. *Penn. Psychiat. Quart.* 4:3–16, 1960.
187. von Mering, O.   Ways of Family Living Between Husband and Wife. In *Understanding Family Dynamics.* Pittsburgh: Family and Children Service and Buhl Foundation, 1960. Pp. 89–119.
188. von Mering, O.   Disease, healing and problem solving: A behavioral science approach. *Int. J. Soc. Psychiat.* 8:137–148, 1962.
189. von Mering, O.   The Latency Child in the Society of Little People. In *Proceedings, Seminar on Growth and Development.* West Virginia Department of Health, West Virginia, 1962. Pp. 42–49.
190. Wallace, A. F. C.   Individual differences and cultural uniformities. *Amer. Sociol. Rev.* 17:747–750, 1952.
191. Wallace, A. F. C.   The Modal Personality Structure of the Tuscarora Indians as Revealed by the Rorschach Test. *Bull. Amer. Ethnol.* No. 150, 1952.
192. Wallace, A. F. C.   Dreams and wishes of the soul: A type of psychoanalytic theory among the seventeenth century Iroquois. *Amer. Anthrop.* 60:234–248, 1958.
193. Wallace, A. F. C.   Cultural determinants of response to hallucinatory experience. *A.M.A. Arch. Gen. Psychiat.* (Chicago) 1:58–69, 1959.
194. Wallace, A. F. C.   The bio-cultural theory of schizophrenia. *Int. Rec. Med.* 173:700–714, 1960.
195. Wallace, A. F. C.   *Culture and Personality.* New York: Random House, 1961.
196. Wallace, A. F. C.   Mental Illness, Biology and Culture. In F. L. K. Hsu (Ed.), *Psychological Anthropology.* Homewood, Ill.: Dorsey, 1961. Pp. 255–295.
197. Wax, M.   The tree of social knowledge. *Psychiatry* 28:99–106, 1965.
198. Wegrocki, H. J.   A critique of cultural and statistical concepts

of abnormality. *J. Abnorm. Soc. Psychol.* 34:166–178, 1939.

199. Whiting, B. *Six Cultures: Studies of Child Rearing.* New York: Wiley, 1963.

200. Whiting, J. W. M. *Becoming a Kwoma: Teaching and Learning in a New Guinea Tribe.* Foreword by J. Dollard. New Haven: Yale University Press (Yale Institute of Human Relations Publication), 1941.

201. Whiting, J. W. M. Totem and Taboo—A Re-evaluation. In J. H. Masserman (Ed.), *Science and Psychoanalysis III.* New York: Grune & Stratton, 1960.

202. Whiting, J. W. M. Socialization Process and Personality. In F. L. K. Hsu (Ed.), *Psychological Anthropology; Approaches to Culture and Personality.* Homewood, Ill.: Dorsey, 1961.

203. Whiting, J., and Child, I. *Child Training and Personality: A Cross Cultural Study.* New Haven: Yale University Press, 1953.

204. Whiting, J. W. M., Kluckhohn, R., and Anthony, A. The Function of Male Initiation Ceremonies at Puberty. In E. E. Maccoby, T. M. Newcomb, and E. I. Hartley (Eds.), *Readings in Social Psychology* (3d ed.). New York: Holt, Rinehart & Winston, 1958.

205. Whiting, J. W. M., and Whiting, B. Contributions of Anthropology to the Methods of Studying Child Rearing. In P. H. Mussen (Ed.), *Handbook of Research Methods in Child Development.* New York: Wiley, 1960.

206. Whiting, J. W. M., et al. *Field Guide for the Study of Socialization.* New York: Wiley, 1966.

207. Winch, P. *The Idea of a Social Science.* London: Routledge & Kegan Paul, 1958.

208. Winter, E. H. *Beyond the Mountains of the Moon: The Lives of Four Africans.* Urbana: University of Illinois Press, 1959.

209. Young, F. W. The function of the male initiation ceremonies: A cross-cultural test of an alternative hypothesis. *Amer. J. Soc.* 67:379–396, 1962.

3

Sociological Aspects of Parenthood

Gerald Handel

Sociology,[1] like psychology and psychiatry, is concerned with understanding human behavior, thought, and feeling. Its distinctive task, however, is to understand how these phenomena are shaped by group life, a term whose scope encompasses a range from society in the large to two-person or dyadic relationships. Whereas psychology differentiates and elaborates upon the components of personality, studying behavior as the outcome of interrelationships among these components, sociology differentiates and elaborates upon the components of group life. To be sure, psychology attends to and investigates factors or environmental conditions that shape personality components, but it is not systematically concerned with the order that obtains among these extrapersonal conditions, treating them, rather, as discrete variables. In contrast, the guiding conception of sociology is that man lives in a socially ordered world, and that behavior is to be understood as a product of that order.

[1] Sociology shares an indistinct boundary with social psychology. I have tried to adhere to a strictly sociological presentation in order to highlight the effects of large-scale social forces on parenthood. For this reason and also because of space limitations, I do not discuss many topics which form part of the sociology of parenthood and which are of a more social psychological nature. For one approach on the other side of the boundary see G. Handel (Ed.), *The Psychosocial Interior of the Family* (Chicago: Aldine, 1967). Thanks are expressed to my wife, Ruth D. Handel, for editorial suggestions which have helped to sharpen the presentation.

87

Sociologically considered, parenthood is a position in a social structure. To say this is immediately to state that it is tied to other positions in a set of interconnected groups of institutions. To be a parent is to occupy a position that is connected in socially defined ways to such other social positions as parent of the opposite sex, child, neighbor, teacher, pediatrician. Each position is socially defined in terms of a set of expectations. The expectations that define a position in one group differ from those that define the same position in another group. Thus, for example, a teacher in a school serving a working-class neighborhood is expected by the parents to be more of a disciplinarian than is the case among parents in an upper-middle-class neighborhood. The latter, being generally more articulate and better educated, expect to have more influence in the curriculum content than would working-class parents. More generally, upper-middle-class parents expect to exert more direct influence on their children's schooling than do working-class parents.[2]

From this illustration it can be seen that parenthood is definable not only in reference to such institutionalized positions as teacher but also in terms of more embracing, though noninstitutionalized, aspects of social order such as social class. The way in which the position of parent is enacted is shaped, then, not only by the expectations deriving from other institutionally based positions but, more importantly, by more pervasive aspects of the social order. The structure of the society as a whole is one such pervasive shaping factor. Thus, in an industrial society, a father does not typically teach his son an occupation. In an agricultural society, a father who is a farmer will teach his son to earn his living by farming. In the two types of society, the position of father is defined by different expectations concerning preparation of the child for an occupation.

While the structure of society as a whole sets certain general expectations, no society of any size is homogeneous. It is, rather, differentiated into a variety of different kinds of segments, of which the most significant are social class and (in our society) ethnic group.

[2] The author has studied one school system in which upper-middle-class parents succeeded in pressing the Board of Education to provide foreign language instruction in elementary schools in upper-middle-class neighborhoods, over the opposition of the Board's own professional staff of educational administrators. The administrators spoke more approvingly of parents in lower-middle-class and working-class neighborhoods who "support" the schools but don't "interfere."

Other segmentations which have some importance are religion, occupation, and type of community (e.g., suburban vs. urban). These social segmentations cut across each other in multifarious ways, and one task of sociology is to identify what kind of importance each type of segmentation has upon the way in which parenthood is performed. This task has not yet been carried out so comprehensively and systematically that we can, say, differentiate the parental performance of the upper-middle-class, Irish Catholic, suburban mother married to a professional man from an upper-middle-class, Irish Catholic, suburban mother married to a businessman, or from an upper-middle-class Negro or Jewish mother married to either a professional or businessman and living in either a suburb or in a city. In other words, each of these segmentations (social class, ethnicity, religion, community type) has been shown to have some effect on how parenthood is performed, but not enough work has yet been done to provide a comprehensive and composite picture of how they all interact. In addition, it must be noted that the significance of each type of segment changes through time so that the relative importance of different kinds of segmentation changes. Thus, for families of a given social class level, but diverse in ethnic origin, who have moved to the suburbs, the fact of being suburban probably has a greater effect on how parenthood is enacted than the fact of being Irish or Swedish in ethnic origin. A conclusion of this kind, is, however, somewhat inferential, based on the general knowledge that ethnic origin among whites is somewhat less important in the suburbs than it was in the areas of earlier settlement in the city.

So far as the study of parenthood and child-rearing is concerned, more concentrated attention has probably been given to the importance of social class than to other types of social segmentation. This is due, in part, to the fact that attention was emphatically drawn to the existence of social classes in America by a series of researches during the 1930s, particularly those conducted by W. Lloyd Warner and his associates. Although Warner's particular approach to social class became the subject of some dispute, sociologists thereafter generally had no difficulty recognizing the importance of this type of segmentation in America. Even so, the emphatic enunciation of the existence of social classes in the United States challenged the vague but prevalent ideas of universal equality of opportunity. If social classes

89

exist, children start out in life with systematically different preparation. Indeed, the notion that children were starting out in life with equal opportunity to participate in a wide-open race in which they were all running had to be modified in two major respects. Investigation began to suggest not only that they did not start out with equal opportunity but that they were not even being prepared for the same race. It became evident, rather, that parents in each social class were primarily preparing their children to become adult members of the same social class into which they were born, rather than to compete in a kind of free-for-all in which the members of each succeeding generation would sort themselves out independent of their origins.

Prior to Warner's work, students of child development had discovered that children's mental development was affected by their socioeconomic status. But these earlier studies did not examine parental behavior, attitudes, and values. Two of Warner's principal co-workers, Allison Davis and Robert J. Havighurst, applied his concepts of social class to the study of parental behavior [6]. This study stimulated various efforts first to replicate it, then to improve upon it, and thus played an important part in setting the problem for a whole series of later studies.

Over time, the most sustained attention, then, has been given to social class as a factor influencing parental performance. This dimension has emerged as the most enduringly significant large-scale social influence on parenthood in the United States. The importance of rural-urban differences has shrunk, in view of the increasing urbanization of the American people. With the decrease in immigration, ethnic differences became less important, the principal exception to this being the Negro-white difference, which is partly a social class difference. Religion as a segmenting factor retains some importance, as will be suggested, but its significance is attenuated. In any case, it has not attracted the same concentration of interest that social class has. For these reasons, the reader will find more frequent references to social class than to other large-scale social factors in the balance of this chapter. However, it should also be noted that as knowledge has grown, some efforts have been made to draw distinctions within social class and also to locate smaller-scale social groupings that mediate the effects of social class.

THE SOCIOLOGY OF REPRODUCTION

No society commits suicide. Every society seeks in various ways to maintain itself, to preserve its continuity. It does this by such means as fashioning legends of its past which it then cherishes and transmits to its young. It seeks to preserve its territorial boundaries against encroachment from other societies. Not the least important, it recruits new members through reproduction. Parents are, then, society's agents for replenishing its population. Society reveals its interest in this process through various official means which encourage or discourage the rate of reproduction: programs to limit family size when overpopulation threatens, programs to stimulate reproduction when the net reproduction rate is insufficient to maintain the population at its existing size or to sustain a desired growth rate. Most fundamentally, society declares its interest in reproduction by establishing norms for the legitimacy of unions and their offspring. Certain unions and their offspring are defined as illegitimate; these are, at the very least, denied the honor that society accords to legitimate unions and births. Often, illegitimacy is subject to additional penalty beyond dishonor. Various legal and social disabilities still attach to illegitimacy; efforts to moderate or abolish these continue in the United States at the present time. The social significance of illegitimacy is highlighted in these observations by Vincent:

Because of their greater visibility, and consequently their greater threat to the value judgments sustaining marriage, illicit births are given far greater attention than is given to the more generic problem of *unwanted pregnancy*—licit and illicit. Not all illicit births are unwanted and pose a social problem; and not all licit births are desired and problem-free. This becomes evident when we consider whose value judgments determine which births are unwanted by whom. *Illicit pregnancies* may be unwanted by the mothers and society, as in cases of rape and incest; they may be wanted by the mothers but not by society, as in some cases of very low-income unwed mothers receiving public assistance; and they may be unwanted by the mothers but highly desired by other couples, as in cases of unwed mothers who release their children for adoption and enable childless couples to establish families. Similarly, *licit pregnancies* may be unwanted by the mothers and society, as in cases involving severe genetic abnormalities or economic deprivation; they may be unwanted by the mothers but desired by childless couples, as in the case of the estimated 15% of adoptions that involve children relinquished by married couples; and *licit pregnancies* may be wanted by the mothers but not by society, as in some cases of extreme economic deprivation, or unwanted by the mothers but wanted by society as in some cases of affluent and brilliant parents. . . .

The far greater public concern about illegitimacy than about the more generic problem of unwanted pregnancy is consistent with the value judgments and social mores involved in the following: (1) The amount of public (and research) interest in a social problem is closely related to the visibility and public expense of the problem; unwed parenthood not only is the most visible of the various alternatives in coping with unwanted pregnancy, but in cases of very young and poor females it imposes the greatest cost upon the public. (2) The "principle of legitimacy" is maintained by censuring the unwed mother. . . . Censuring her is believed to serve as an object lesson to prevent these mores from "dying out in the conscience" of society. (3) The greater concern with illegitimacy is also consistent with the mores which prescribe that the sexual relationship be a private, covert experience [18].

Vincent's analysis of the statistical data on rates of illegitimacy reveals that, contrary to widespread belief, the rate of increase in illegitimacy between 1938 and 1963 was far greater in age groups over 20 than among teen-agers.

The biological route to parenthood is the same for all parents, but the social route is not. Whether or not an act of sexual intercourse that has a high probability of resulting in a pregnancy will occur is influenced by various social factors which operate at various junctures in the time sequence between mental concept and biological conception. The most comprehensive study of this problem is that by Rainwater; in what follows we draw upon his study except where otherwise indicated [13]. The study is of interest also because it reveals the complex interplay of social factors in parenthood.

The general problem to which Rainwater addresses himself is that of family size—how families come to have the particular number of children that they do. As Rainwater phrases it: "Each couple is confronted with the twin goals (and necessities) of having 'enough' children and not having 'too many.'" Most generally, the number of children that a couple has is a function of (1) the number of children that they desire, and (2) the effectiveness with which they practice contraception. The first, second, third, or nth child may be the result of a planned effort to conceive in order to realize some ideal concerning family size or it may be the result of failure in the use of contraception and thus a defeat in the effort to realize a goal. The inquiry follows out these two proximate determinants of family size to *their* determinants; that is, the study investigates the factors influencing number of children desired and the factors influencing effectiveness of contraceptive practice. From a summary of some of the main findings of the study, it will be evident that conception has social as well as biological and psychological determinants.

The research is based on interviews with 409 persons—152 couples plus 50 men and 55 women not married to each other. The sample includes members of four social classes—upper-middle class, lower-middle class, working class, and lower class; it also includes Catholics and Protestants, and whites and Negroes, since it was anticipated that family size would reflect these three aspects of social segmentation. Since the investigator was interested not simply in showing the existence of a relationship between these large social groupings and family size but also in indicating how membership in such groupings was related to marriage, the data gathered included information on conjugal role relationships[3] and on sexual relations. These five major factors—social class, religion, race, type of conjugal role relationship, and social psychological aspects of sexual relations—significantly affect the number of children a family will have, because they affect both the number of children desired and the effectiveness with which contraception is practiced.

The Rainwater study yields a great number of specific findings which are not readily summarizable in brief compass. A short statement of certain highlights will, however, indicate the complex interplay of social determinants of parenthood: Protestants tend to want fewer children than do Catholics at all social class levels except the lower class, where there is no difference between the two religious groups. (In a study of the effects of religion on family life, Lenski found that Protestant mothers are somewhat more likely than Catholic mothers to feel that children are burdensome [11].) Family size preferences tend to shift during the course of marriage, with middle-

---

[3] This concept was introduced by Elizabeth Bott in *Family and Social Network* (London: Tavistock Publications, 1957). As adopted by Rainwater, it refers to "those aspects of the relationship between husband and wife that consist of reciprocal role expectations and the activities of each spouse in relation to the other." Three types of role relationship are distinguished: (1) *Joint:* the pattern is one in which most husband-wife activities are either shared or interchangeable; (2) *Segregated:* husband's and wife's activities are separated and different, sometimes carried out with minimum day-to-day articulation, sometimes fitted together to achieve coordination; (3) *Intermediate:* sharing and interchangeability of task performance are valued, but more formal division of household tasks is maintained than in the joint conjugal role organization.

class couples often wanting fewer children than when they were first married and lower-class couples wanting more (as a passive adaptation to the larger number actually born to them because of ineffective contraception). But within the middle class, couples who have a joint conjugal role organization, with much husband-wife sharing and interchanging of activities and responsibilities, are more likely to want a small family than couples with a lower level of husband-wife involvement. But irrespective of social class or religion, large families tend to be more often desired by those couples in which both members consider sexual relations very important than by those couples in which one or both partners say sexual relations are not very important.

Effective use of contraception (regular and consistent use of a method that has a high degree of effectiveness when used appropriately) varies according to the same general factors as does desired size of family. To begin, middle-class Protestants are more optimistic than other groups studied that the size of family they want can be achieved. Middle-class Catholics and working-class whites and Negroes are hopeful but less confident. Lower-class whites and Negroes are passive and fatalistic; they do nothing because they do not think anything will help, or they go through the motions of using a method in which they have little confidence and thus do not use it consistently. As would be anticipated from such basic attitudes, among the middle-class Protestants alone, of the groups studied, is there much serious discussion of family planning between husband and wife early in the marriage. Not surprisingly, middle-class Protestants are most likely to use effective contraceptive practices before the birth of the last child they want. After the birth of the last wanted child, this contraceptive superiority is maintained by the middle-class Protestants, although an increased number of couples in all groups learn to use the methods more effectively (98 percent of middle- and working-class Protestants; 73 percent of middle- and working-class Catholics; 50 percent of working-class Negroes; 33 percent of lower-class Protestants, and 13 percent of lower-class Negroes and Catholics use contraception effectively after the birth of the last wanted child). Within the lower class, after the birth of the last wanted child, effective contraceptive practice is more likely in couples maintaining joint or intermediate conjugal role relationships than segregated, and in couples in

94

which the wife finds sexual relations gratifying and important marriage.

It can be seen from the summary of Rainwater's study t likelihood of a couple's becoming the parents of yet another not a chance event but is influenced by the particular position ᴏꜰ ᴛʜᴇ parents in the social structure. Conception of a child has societal determinants as well as biological and psychodynamic ones.

INFANT CARE AND CHILD REARING

From a sociological point of view, the principal task of parents is to prepare their children to become adult members of society. This involves various kinds of care, the inculcation of values and norms, training in certain specific kinds of behavior, provision of models of adult roles upon which the child can draw in forming his concept of himself and his place in society, and the fostering of appropriate self-regard—all of which are summed up in the concept of socialization.

Although socialization begins with the birth of the child, the earliest days of life have been little, if at all, studied by sociologists; the field has essentially been left to psychologists and psychiatrists, so that we do not as yet have a sociology of the neonate. Sociological attention has been directed to that point in the infant's development at which the explicit imposition of "discipline" begins. The control of feeding has been regarded as the first major socializing experience, followed by toilet training. Recognition of the importance of these activities had been stimulated by psychoanalysis, and efforts were then made to place their significance in a larger social context.

The Davis-Havighurst study mentioned above aroused particular interest. The studies which followed in its wake resulted in various findings which seemed incompatible. Bronfenbrenner has endeavored to integrate results obtained from fifteen studies done over a 25-year span from 1932 to 1957 [3]. Over time, he finds that whereas the middle-class mothers were previously more strict than working- and lower-class mothers, they have become more permissive. Middle-class mothers, in contrast to their earlier practice and in contrast to working- and lower-class mothers, now more often allow self-demand feeding and wean later from the bottle, although breast-feeding is apparently becoming less common in all social classes. As part of the same

95

overall trend toward increased permissiveness, middle-class mothers at the end of the period reviewed were instituting bowel and bladder training later than were working- and lower-class mothers, reversing the situation that existed at the beginning of the period.

The basic trend that Bronfenbrenner identifies is an increase in middle-class permissiveness, although he finds also a less marked trend in the same direction for the working and lower classes. An interesting aspect of his analysis is his relating of his survey to Wolfenstein's survey of successive editions of the U.S. Children's Bureau bulletin on infant care [19]. Her study showed that over substantially the same time period the advice issued by this publication changed from an emphasis on dominating and "taming" the child to an emphasis on meeting his needs. Research has indicated that middle-class mothers have been more likely to read not only this bulletin but other child-care literature such as Spock's *Baby and Child Care*. Bronfenbrenner concludes: "Taken as a whole, the correspondence between Wolfenstein's data and our own suggests a general hypothesis extending beyond the confines of social class as such: *child rearing practices are likely to change most quickly in those segments of society which have closest access and are most receptive to the agencies or agents of change (e.g., public media, clinics, physicians, and counselors)*. From this point of view, one additional trend suggested by the available data is worthy of note: rural families appear to lag behind the times somewhat in their practices of infant care" [3].

Bronfenbrenner finds similar trends in the training of children beyond the age of 2. In the 1930s and 1940s, the middle-class mother was more restrictive of freedom of movement; since then, less so. Also, since World War II, the middle-class mother has become more permissive toward the child's expressed needs and wishes in such diverse areas as oral behavior, toilet accidents, dependency, sex, aggressiveness, and freedom of movement outside the home. At the same time, however, the middle-class mother has higher expectations for the child with respect to independence and achievement.

Methods of discipline were found to differ. Working- and lower-class mothers are more likely to use physical punishment, while the middle-class mothers use more symbolic and manipulative techniques such as reasoning, isolation, and appeals to guilt. But over the 25-year period surveyed, the overall parent-child relationship in the middle

96

class was reported as being more acceptant and egalitarian than in the working class, which is more oriented toward maintaining order and obedience.

The differences in the parent-child relationship between the middle class and the working and lower classes arise from systematically different life experiences which, in turn, lead to differences in basic outlook and life style. Rainwater, Coleman, and Handel found these important characteristics of the working-class mother: Central to her outlook is her underlying conviction that most significant action originates from the world external to herself rather than from within herself [15]. Further, she sees the world beyond her doorstep and neighborhood as fairly chaotic and potentially catastrophic. She feels she has little ability to influence events, and her outlook is shaded by a fairly pervasive anxiety over possible fundamental deprivations. Similarly, she feels it is difficult to influence the behavior of her children. The study found that "the middle-class woman is more likely to perceive her child's behavior as complex, requiring understanding. The working-class mother is more likely to see her child's behavior as mysterious, beyond understanding. The latter, consequently, looks for rules or authoritative guidance which she hopes will work and take hold on the child." Middle-class mothers want to give their children "worthwhile experiences" to make them well-rounded; working-class mothers want their children to grow up to be moral, upright, and religious-minded.

How can we explain the apparent contradiction resulting from our finding that working-class mothers want specific rules or authoritative guidance in dealing with their children and Bronfenbrenner's finding that middle-class women are more attentive to child-care experts and literature? Kohn argues—substantially correctly, we believe —that middle-class parents' attentiveness to experts and other sources of relevant information represents not a search for new values but for better techniques of realizing the values they already have [9]. He believes that middle-class values have remained substantially the same over the period surveyed by Bronfenbrenner, but that the attentiveness of middle-class parents to expertise stems from greater readiness to accept innovation in the service of their unchanging basic goals and from the fact that these parents regard child-rearing as more problematic than do those of the working and lower classes. His interpretation that the middle class is not only more receptive to—but also more in search of—innovation than the working classes and lower classes is borne out by much research. However, the conclusion that basic middle-class values have not changed over 25 years is somewhat more open to question. It does not seem sufficient to say that earlier middle-class rigidity and more recent middle-class permissiveness are simply two different techniques in the service of the value of self-direction. Various social analysts have noted, for example, a change from production-oriented to consumption-oriented values. Insofar as such a shift in value emphasis has occurred, the increased permissiveness in child-rearing documented by Bronfenbrenner may derive from a more general acceptance of impulsivity in the middle class.

Kohn believes that sociological emphasis on child-rearing techniques is somewhat misplaced, and he seeks to redirect attention from specific techniques to the larger question of how the social structure influences behavior. His analysis takes the following general form: Values (conceptions of the desirable which influence choices) are products of life conditions. Middle-class and working-class parents live under different conditions; they therefore have different values, although they also have some values in common. The value differences result in differential parental behavior in the different social classes. To understand parental behavior one must know what their values are, particularly those concerned with child-rearing.

Filling in the specifics of his analytic model, Kohn notes that the significant value difference is that working-class and lower-class parents want conformity to external proscriptions while middle-class parents want their children to become self-directing. The life conditions which most directly determine these values are occupational, educational, and economic. Middle-class occupations deal more with manipulation of symbols, ideas, and interpersonal relations; working-class occupations, with manipulation of things. Middle-class occupations are more subject to self-direction, and getting ahead in them depends more on the individual, whereas working-class occupations are more subject to standardization and direct supervision, and getting ahead in them depends more on the collective action of labor unions.

The greater income and higher educational preparation of middle-class parents enables them to be more attentive to motives and feelings, including their children's. Thus, in disciplining them, middle-class mothers are more concerned with the child's intent; working-class mothers are more concerned with the overt consequences of the child's act. A more general consequence of the value difference is that middle-class mothers tend to feel a greater obligation to be supportive of their children, whereas working-class and lower-class mothers are more attentive to the parental obligation to impose constraints. In keeping with this, middle-class mothers want their husbands to be supportive of the children, especially the sons, but do not expect them to impose constraints to any great extent. In the working class, the reverse holds: the wives expect their husbands to be more directive and look less to them to give emotional support to the children. However, Kohn finds that while middle-class fathers' own role expectations for themselves accord with what their wives expect, this is not as frequently true in the working class, since the working-class father believes that the most important thing is that the child be taught proper limits, and it doesn't much matter who does the teaching. He would rather not be bothered, and expects his wife to take major responsibility for child care.

A few years ago, after some 10 or 15 years of postwar growth in affluence, there was a growing belief that "now everyone is middle class." This notion proved to have a rather short life, since it was followed by the "rediscovery of poverty." During the interim of popular illusion, however, some research was directed to this question, particularly since it was unmistakable that some working-class families were moving to suburbs and an increasing number of their children were going to college. The fact that suburbanization became a mass phenomenon during the 1950s lent credence to the illusion. Berger, however, studied a new tract suburb settled largely by working-class families and found that the increased level of material comfort had not resulted in any significant shift in outlook or life style as compared with their life before the move to the new suburb [2]. Berger's basic conclusion is that the fact of being of the working class was more influential than the fact of having moved to a suburb. Berger's results are understandable in terms of Kohn's analysis, since the men remained in working-class occupations. At the same time, it should also

99

be said that Berger's study was done only two and one-half years after the settling of the new community, perhaps too soon for any suburbanizing effects to become evident. Even so, residence basically follows from occupational level, rather than the other way around, so that the "working classness" of a working-class suburb is likely to remain more consequential than its "suburbanness."

Handel and Rainwater also studied the question of change in the working class and found it useful to distinguish between a traditional and a modern working class. Nonetheless, the basic difference in values between middle class and working class endures, although some changes in outlook occur. For example, the growing working-class interest in a college education for their children is largely focused on their sons, for whom it is seen as a means to a better-paying job rather than as a means of personal inner growth. College education for girls is discouraged unless the girl has a definite vocational objective such as becoming a nurse or a teacher; a year or two of college that does not lead to a definite vocation is seen as wasted [8].

FATHER ABSENCE AND UNEMPLOYMENT

Until now, the parental differences we have sketched assume intact families. They assume further that the father is engaged in some kind of gainful work. The presence or absence of the father in the home has significant consequences. The kind of work he does—or his lack of work—is scarcely less consequential. It is therefore useful to indicate here some facts concerning father absence and unemployment, particularly their uneven incidence. Clausen observes that the 1960 U. S. Census reports that 11 percent of all American households with children under 18 had only one parent present; the absent parent was usually the father [5]. Moynihan, in his summary of statistical data pertaining to Negro families, states that 36 percent of Negro children are living in broken homes at any given time [12]. In addition, he reports an estimate that only a minority of Negro children reach the age of 18 having lived all their lives with both parents. More than 20 percent of Negro households are headed by a female, as compared to 9 percent of white households.[4] Moynihan shows that over

[4] A social psychological analysis of the lower-class female-headed Negro family is presented by L. Rainwater in his "Crucible of Identity" [14].

100

a period of years from 1951 to 1963 the number of broken Ne families rises and falls with Negro male unemployment. Althou both series of statistics show a long-run rising trend, there are num ous fluctuations during the period; an increase in unemployment tends to be followed a year later by an increase in separations, and a decrease in unemployment by a decrease in separations. In 1960, Negro unemployment was double that of whites; even so, as Moynihan points out, the usual way of reporting unemployment understates the problem. The average monthly Negro unemployment rate for males in 1964 was 9 percent, but during 1964 some 29 percent of Negro males were unemployed at one time or other.

The father's occupation is obviously of enormous significance for parenthood. When the father has no sustained gainful occupation, the consequences for the family can be devastating. The discrimination in education and employment directed to the Negro male plays a significant part in undermining the Negro (particularly lower-class) family. The destructive effects of unemployment on the family, now most clearly evident among Negroes in American society,[5] but also apparent wherever unemployment is pervasive and long-enduring, were epidemic during the Great Depression [1, 10]. The amount of evidence accumulated to date is substantial: Long-continued unemployment among males, especially fathers (though also among young unmarried men), is one of the most important causes of pathological conditions within the family, with far-reaching consequences for both parents and children, as well as for the entire society.

STRUCTURED STRAIN IN BECOMING A PARENT

The traditional interest in the study of parenthood, in sociology as in psychiatry and psychology, has been to ascertain the consequences of different kinds of parental performance on the child. In concluding this chapter, it is appropriate to take note of a relatively new line of sociological inquiry, the socially structured strains in becoming a parent, particularly in the middle class and particularly for women. This problem has been addressed most directly by Alice Rossi, who argues that the transition to parenthood is more difficult in

[5] For a comparable picture among Appalachian whites, see Caudill's *Night Comes to the Cumberlands* [4]. The way in which family relationships are affected by larger social forces has seldom been more effectively traced than in this beautifully written book.

American society than either marital or occupational adjustment [6] [16]. She notes Therese Benedek's point that the child's need for mothering is absolute, while the need of an adult woman to mother is relative. Mrs. Rossi then observes: "Yet our family system of isolated households, increasingly distant from kinswomen to assist in mothering, requires that new mothers shoulder total responsibility for the infant precisely for that stage of the child's life when his need for mothering is far in excess of the mother's need for the child." Thus, she continues, what is often interpreted as an individual mother's failure to be adequately maternal "may in fact be a failure of the society to provide institutionalized substitutes for the extended kin to assist in the care of infants and young children." Rossi notes these additional strains in the transition to parenthood: (1) There is great cultural pressure on growing girls and young women to consider maternity necessary for individual fulfillment and adult status. (2) Pregnancy is not always a voluntary decision, but society does not allow the termination of unwanted pregnancies. (3) First pregnancy is now the major transition point in a woman's life, because of the spread of effective contraception. This is a change from the past, when marriage was the major transition and first pregnancy followed closely upon marriage. (4) Parenthood is irrevocable, since society allows one to be rid of wives and jobs but not children, and one consequence of this social fact for women with unwanted children is that "the personal outcome of experience in the parent role is not a higher level of maturation but the negative outcome of a depressed sense of self-worth. . . . The possibility must be faced, and at some point researched, that women lose ground in personal development and self-esteem during the early and middle years of adulthood, whereas men gain ground in these respects during the same years." (5) American society does not provide adequate preparation and training for the role of mother. (6) The period of pregnancy does not allow adequate training, unlike the period of anticipatory socialization for marriage (i.e., engagement). (7) Finally, the transition from pregnancy to motherhood is abrupt; it does not allow for a gradual taking on of responsibility, as is true in a professional work role.

Thus, Rossi seems to be describing two main kinds of strain:

[6] I wish to express my thanks to my colleague Dr. Betty Yorburg for bringing this article to my attention.

(1) American culture presses many women into maternity who are not very maternal and perhaps should not become mothers and (2) motherhood in America is difficult because the role demands exceed woman's capacity to meet them adequately and, further, because the social structure provides no built-in surrogates to help the mother, particularly right after delivery but also throughout the rearing of the young.

Rossi's analysis of the strains in the transition to motherhood locates them in the basic structure of American society rather than in any particular segment of it. Some questions arise. Her argument turns to some extent on characterizing our family system as consisting of isolated households which thus deprive the new mother of kinswomen to help in mothering. However, some sociologists have conducted studies which show that the nuclear family is not nearly so isolated as had been commonly supposed. Sussmann is most closely identified with this line of inquiry [17]. But while this work shows that there is much more help among kin (including that of parents to their married children and to their minor grandchildren) than had been supposed, the findings are not specific enough to confirm or disconfirm Rossi's specific claim that basic mothering is a solitary task rather than one shared with others, as formerly. Another source of doubt: perhaps Rossi's analysis holds for the middle class but not for the working class. Numerous studies have shown that working-class married women in several societies retain close ties with their own mothers and other kin. A brief overview will be found in Gans's study of working-class Italians [7]. The evidence would seem to suggest that Rossi's analysis may be less tenable for the working class, though again the evidence is not in a form that permits a confident confirmation or disconfirmation of her analysis.

What about the abruptness of full-scale mothering responsibilities in the middle class? Rossi's strongest case would seem to be located here, but numerous questions will have to be laid to rest before it can be accepted. For example, many young newly delivered mothers hire a practical nurse to live in for at least a week after returning home from hospital confinement; others have their own mothers visit and help out. We do not know how widespread such practices are in the middle class. Perhaps this is true in only a small "deviant" group of middle-class mothers. Or perhaps Rossi's mothers constitute the

103

small deviant group rather than the basic pattern to which the middle class is tending. Another informal observation: rooming-in arrangements in maternity hospitals seem to be growing in popularity. If this is a demonstrable fact, how does it fit with Rossi's analysis?

Rossi offers her paper to raise questions and to stimulate re-thinking of important issues rather than to provide answers. The largest question she raises is that of the goodness of fit between psychological propensities and the social arrangements which channel wishes, motives, and behavior. This is one of sociology's enduring questions, one that follows close on the heels of the master question: How does society structure wish, motive, and behavior?

Bibliography

1. Angell, R. C. *The Family Encounters the Depression.* New York: Scribners, 1936.
2. Berger, B. M. *Working-Class Suburb: A Study of Auto Workers in Suburbia.* Berkeley: University of California Press, 1960.
3. Bronfenbrenner, U. Socialization and Social Class Through Time and Space. In E. E. Maccoby, T. M. Newcomb, and E. L. Hartley (Eds.), *Readings in Social Psychology* (3d ed.). New York: Holt, Rinehart and Winston, 1958.
4. Caudill, H. *Night Comes to the Cumberlands.* Boston: Little, Brown, 1963.
5. Clausen, J. Family Structure, Socialization and Personality. In M. Hoffman (Ed.), *Review of Child Development Research,* Vol. II. New York: Russell Sage, 1967.
6. Davis, A., and Havighurst, R. J. Social class and color differences in child rearing. *Amer. Sociol. Rev.* 11:698–710, 1946.
7. Gans, H. J. *The Urban Villagers: Group and Class in the Life of Italian-Americans.* New York: Free Press, 1962. Pp. 238 ff.
8. Handel, G., and Rainwater, L. Persistence and change in working class life style. *Sociol. Soc. Res.* 48:280–288, 1964. Reprinted in A. Shostak and W. Gomberg (Eds.), *Blue-Collar World.* Englewood Cliffs, N.J.: Prentice-Hall, 1964.
9. Kohn, M. L. Social class and parent-child relationships: An interpretation. *Amer. J. Sociol.* 68:471–480, 1963. Reprinted in B. Farber (Ed.), *Kinship and Family Organization.* New York: Wiley, 1966.
10. Komarovsky, M. *The Unemployed Man and His Family.* New York: Dryden, 1940.

104

11. Lenski, G.   *The Religious Factor: A Sociological Study of Religion's Impact on Politics, Economics and Family Life* (rev. ed.). Garden City, N.Y.: Anchor, 1963. P. 221.
12. Moynihan, D. P.   *The Negro Family: The Case for National Action*. Washington: Office of Policy Planning and Research, U.S. Department of Labor, March, 1965. Pp. 6, 9. Reprinted in L. Rainwater and W. L. Yancey, *The Moynihan Report and the Politics of Controversy*. Cambridge, Mass.: Massachusetts Institute of Technology Press, 1967.
13. Rainwater, L.   *Family Design: Marital Sexuality, Family Size and Contraception*. Chicago: Aldine, 1965.
14. Rainwater, L.   Crucible of identity: The Negro lower class family. *Daedalus* 95: No. 1 (Winter), 1966. Reprinted in G. Handel (Ed.), *The Psychosocial Interior of the Family*. Chicago: Aldine, 1967.
15. Rainwater, L., Coleman, R., and Handel, G.   *Workingman's Wife: Her Personality, World and Life Style*. New York: Oceana, 1959; paperback ed., Macfadden, 1962.
16. Rossi, A. S.   Transition to parenthood. *J. Marriage Family* 30:26–39, 1968.
17. Sussman, M. B.   The Isolated Nuclear Family: Fact or Fiction? *and* The Help Pattern in the Middle-Class Family. In M. B. Sussman (Ed.), *Sourcebook in Marriage and the Family*. Boston: Houghton Mifflin, 1963.
18. Vincent, C. E.   Teen-age unwed mothers in American society. *J. Soc. Issues* 22:22–23, 1966.
19. Wolfenstein, M.   Trends in infant care. *Amer. J. Orthopsychiat.* 23:120–130, 1953.

Part II
The Psychobiologic Approach to Parenthood

4

The Family as a Psychologic Field

Therese Benedek

Tempora mutantur et nos mutamur in illis. (The times change and we change with them.) This Latin proverb [11], the origins of which it would be worthwhile to trace, came to my mind with stunning persuasiveness when, in preparation for this publication, I read over an earlier paper of mine, The Emotional Structure of the Family [3]. What has changed? What is permanent? Psychoanalytic investigations have led to the understanding of psychodynamic processes which bring about psychosexual maturation of the individual and also the interpersonal relationships as they unfold in our culture, not only within the family, but also from generation to generation. Freud disclosed the process through which the individual becomes the carrier of cultural inheritance and relives "the traces which the biological and historical fate of mankind left behind in the id" [7]. This has not changed, but a rapidly progressing technologic civilization compounded by fears of wars brings about cultural changes at a pace which threatens the stability of the family and weakens its effectiveness. The "crisis about being" alerts us to the need to know more about the family, to investigate even more thoroughly the processes by which parents convey the cultural inheritance to their children. The current fear and simultaneous acceptance of the alienation between generations indicate a hitch in the processes by which parents fulfill their biologically given function of raising their children.

Psychoanalysis, i.e., the biologic approach to psychology, "affords the framework within which biology, psychology and sociology as continuum can be explained" [10]. This contribution written in that framework intends to expand the psychoanalytic theory of development by considering the transactional processes between parents and between parents and their children, thus viewing the family as a psychologic field.

The core of this field is the marital couple—husband and wife —who bring to their marriage their particular personalities as they have developed from infancy through adolescence in transactions with their own parents and with other significant persons and events of their environment. In the language of communication theory, the core of the family—the marital couple—represents one "system," while the personality of each represents a "subsystem." Normally the subsystems become welded together by the reciprocal adaptations evolving through the marriage and, even more, biologically through parenthood.

At this point, it seems necessary to discuss briefly the psychodynamic processes of love and marriage, since the cultural changes which influence the core of the family necessarily affect the crucial experience of husband and wife, their parenthood. Through this it will influence the content of the culture which they convey to their children, while the psychodynamic processes maintaining the continuum remain unchanged.

THE DYNAMICS OF LOVE IN MARRIAGE

There has been little written in psychoanalytic literature about the psychodynamics of "being in love." In his paper, On Narcissism: An Introduction [6], Freud truly introduced ego psychology, especially what today we call the object relationship aspect of ego psychology, and he illustrated this with the dynamics of "being in love." [1]

Freud differentiated two kinds of object love between adults; one he called "anaclitic," the other "narcissistic love." The model of

---

[1] The German word *Verliebtheit* expresses the sense of "being lost" in the state of acute love, but it does not have such depreciating connotation as the word *infatuation*.

anaclitic love is the child's need for the mother. Adults who love in this way seek in their love object the mother who feeds, or the father who provides and protects. The other, the narcissistic love, seeks in the object the idealized self, the ego ideal. Heterosexual attraction sets in motion a process of idealization of the love object. Freud theorized that the lover's ego libido (narcissistic libido) overflows and cathects (charges) the object of one's desire, causing impoverishment of the self. (The word *yearning* expresses an intensity of longing which in that emotional state implies emotional dependence.) If the lover feels his love fulfilled, the libido floods back, enhanced by the gratification, and cathects the ego of the lover. Just as the infant with each feeding introjects the object (feeding mother), so the lover introjects with the gratification of his need the object who has gratified his need. Through the repetition of such processes, lovers become mutually a part of the self-system of the other. Thus it is inherent in the dynamics of inter-personal relationship that the dividing line between anaclitic and narcissistic love disappears during the course of a successful marriage.

As long as society concentrated its ethics and customs on securing stability for marriage, there was little need to investigate the dynamics of love itself. Indeed, in stable patriarchal family structures, marriages were arranged without consideration of individual choice and love. It was assumed in the West, just as in the Orient, that love, by which was meant an enduring relationship, would develop during the marriage, mainly through parenthood. The acute phase of love again seems to be in discredit. Considered as a state of narcissistic imbalance such as the adolescent struggle for maturity, sociologists, psychiatrists, and even psychoanalysts do not consider romantic love to be a dependable basis for a lasting marriage [13]. Whatever the professional opinions and advice may be, individuals who are in love project the need for each other into the future and strongly believe that they will live happily ever after. Heterosexual love, however, is not a simple need for an object who gratifies one's sexual desire. It is a complex attainment, a result of individual development. Its permanence in marriage depends on the total personality; it requires an ego organization that does not become discouraged by the changing aspects of love as an experience, since it invests the marriage as an institution with narcissistic libido, i.e., with the ego aspirations of the personality. If such ego investment exists, the feedback from being married and being a parent supports the interpersonal relationship between the marital partners through the vicissitudes of marriage. According to evidence, probably the great majority of marriages even in our individualistic culture, would support this point, although our culture tends to make love the sole basis of marriage. Marriage, however, offers not only social status and economic security; more significantly, it offers the security of being loved, being attached, not being alone. This aspect of love might be overshadowed by the light of flaming love, but it comes again to full significance when it is experienced that love is not static, it is a process; its dynamic implies change.

I am almost embarrassed as I attempt to abstract from love—that eternal theme of poets, the inexhaustible source of creativity—in brief formulations its interpersonal dynamics during marriage: (1) Passionate love is an attempt of the personality to fulfill the self through the love of the sexual object. (2) When the tension of ungratified love is relieved by sexual gratification, the sense of suspense disappears. In the intimacy of marriage the uncertainty about being loved diminishes. (3) The fulfillment of love in marriage changes the psychodynamic interaction between the marital partners. Before fulfillment, before marriage, there was an exchange of ego ideals; in marriage this becomes a relationship between two individuals who share the same reality. Common ambitions, desires, children, achievements of goals and/or their frustrations all may strengthen the identification between marital partners, be they positive or negative in their outcome. The depth of the identification is a consequence of the original intensity of the need which brought husband and wife together, and it gives the relationship its exclusive significance, even after sexual passion has declined and the marriage appears to be a matter of convenience. (4) The desexualization of the introjected ego-ideal (the marital partner) proceeds, and as it becomes a part of the self-system it also becomes part of the superego. The marital partners, besides everything else, become a critical measure of each other. It depends on the earlier development of the two personalities and also on the course of their love whether the introjected image of the husband will create a fear against which the wife has to defend herself, or bring about a gratifying awareness that as a wife she has satisfied the wishes and needs of her husband. The husband in turn attains sincere gratification if his personality and achievements satisfy the woman he has loved with passion, even if the object of his love now psychodynamically has become more a mother than the girl with whom he fell in love.

Thus the love of husband and wife for each other is not lost when it becomes desexualized; it survives in the manifold identifications of the marital partners who accept each other, being more or less aware of their mutual responsibility for the personality changes of the partner. Individuals having normal capacities for development through mature love accept the responsibilities that grow out of love. Only infantile personalities become deeply resentful and unable to adjust to the consequences of the dynamic processes which change the surface of the marriage.

The traditional marriage of the patriarchal family emphasized the actual aims of the marriage. By blocking divorce, it forced compromises until adjustment, sometimes dearly paid for with individual unhappiness and neurotic disturbances, was achieved. The domineering role of the patriarchal husband and the apparently dependent situation of the wife formed the core of the traditional family. In the modern marriage the balance between husband and wife has shifted. Each of the marital partners represents the double aspiration of our culture. The role of the husband is not free from the responsibilities and illusions of the patriarchal husband-father. Although he is expected to perform his functions to satisfy that ideology, he also is expected to recognize the equality and, very often, the independence or even superiority of his wife. The wife, though she is not free from the psychosexual desire for a strong man as a husband, in other areas of her personality requires of him the acceptance of her drive for independence. Thus the modern marriage, in each of its partners, manifests the conflict between the passing patriarchal and the present individualistic society. Yet in writing this, I feel that this transition already belongs to the past. The oncoming generation, ready for marriage, is farther away from the patriarchal tradition than their parents. Having been raised by liberal principles of enlightened parents, they have not incorporated domineering parental images and therefore they may lack the convictions necessary to convey well-integrated value systems to their children.

The aim of this seeming deviation from my theme is to indicate

113

that it is not the passion of love or its blindness that is at fault in the bankruptcy of many marriages, but the immaturity of the ego organization of one or both partners who did not develop to the level in which gratifications could be postponed and aims and responsibilities could be shared. This must be emphasized especially now when our cultural modes encourage relationships between the sexes before the personalities of the partners have matured enough to experience the deep gratifications and serious responsibilities of marriage. Marriage between immature people, more often than not, is a weak, unstable core to support the multiple functions of the family. Fortunately, there are exceptions. There are many young people who, having married too young, become parents prematurely and yet have the capacity for further development through the transactional processes of marriage and parenthood. The dialectic of marriage and its goal is this: Each of the partners, stimulated by the ongoing psychodynamic interactions with each other, achieves another level of integration of his or her personality. The process of maturation gains another dimension through parenthood.

Our age of planned parenthood affords opportunities to investigate the psychodynamic components of man's propagative instinct. Investigation of the sexual cycle in women has revealed the psychobiologic tendencies which in monthly periodicity express a genuine quality of female sexuality, the instinctual motivation of motherhood. The psychobiologic processes of parenthood in both sexes will be discussed in subsequent chapters of this book; this reference is included here to introduce the biologic-psychologic continuum of the family from which the superstructure of society and the variety of its culture have evolved.

THE TRANSACTIONAL PROCESSES DURING
THE SYMBIOTIC PHASE

To elaborate the parent-child relationship in its transactional significance, it is useful to consider the family as a psychologic field. This idea might raise questions in many readers' minds, and even cause some eyebrows to lift. Is it necessary to introduce the terminology of another discipline to explain what is obvious? Don't psychoanalysts know well enough the significance even of the earliest object relationship for the organization of the personality? Yes, they do. The term might be alien but the phenomena of transactional processes are not new to psychoanalysis. I have referred in this chapter to Freud's discussion of the psychodynamics of object-relationships in adults, to cite a classic example of transactional process. Two lovers whose emotional state changes from suspense and frustration, accompanied by a decline of self-esteem (regression), to recovery through increasing self-esteem if love is returned, introject the memories of their drive experiences which affect their personalities. The desexualization of passionate love, as described above, leads to identifications between marital partners, not only in the actualities of their life situations, in their children, in their goals, but also in the deeper strata of their personalities which affect their characters.

The function of the family as a psychologic field is even more convincingly illustrated by the psychoanalytic theory of personality development. The primary process of object relationship is as old as the concept of libido as psychic energy. Freud assumed that libido reaches out, like pseudopodia of amoebas, from its reservoir to the object from which it can be withdrawn to its source again [5]. From this beginning Freud developed the metapsychology of object-relationship—introjection and identification—and its influence upon the personality organization. On the basis of processes which he studied in Mourning and Melancholia (1916) Freud stated: "The character of the ego is a precipitate of abandoned object cathexes and it contains a record of past object choices" [7]. Since that time an abundance of clinical and theoretic studies have discussed the object-relationship aspect of personality development in all age levels leading to normal or to pathologic manifestations. (Such psychoanalytic investigations, following the model developed by Freud, have considered development as a process occurring in the closed system of the child's psychic apparatus from infancy to maturity. Even as recently as in René Spitz's beautiful discourse Life and the Dialogue, the developmental process is viewed only from the point of view of the child [16]. The poetic symbol *dialogue* refers to the nonverbal communications between mother and infant, from which the infant derives stimulation for his mental-emotional development, but the responses of the mother's psychic system, its gains or losses, are not considered.)

Alice Balint, however, questioned the concept of a one-way

115

receptive relationship between mother and child. In her paper based upon anthropologic and psychoanalytic material she used the term *symbiosis* not as a metaphor but to designate a mutual instinctual need for communication between mother and child [1]. My own elaboration of the concept of symbiosis was based on a study of the psychosomatic processes of the female sexual cycle, of pregnancy, and of the postpartum period [4].

Introjections and identifications are primary processes by which mental structures develop. Thus they constitute "theoretical bridges between biology and personality, and between personalities and social groups" [9]. In this sense, introjection and identification are terms which refer to processes by which memory traces of drive-motivated, interpersonal relationships are stored during the course of life, as illustrated by Freud, in the course of heterosexual love.

Closer to their biologic sources, however, are the drive experiences of the newborn and his mother. In the neonate the drive experience relates mainly to alimentation. The primary model is simple: need = hunger→mother = food→satiation. All other requirements and their gratifications—all kinds of olfactory, tactile, auditory, and visual sensations—seem to be submerged in the experience of alimentation. The repetition of these experiences adds up to the introject of "pleasant, feeding mother," which is equated with the experience of pleasantly fed = satiated self. The same mother in dissimilar feeding situations or even during different phases of the same feeding may also be associated with unpleasant memory traces. With the memory traces of discomfort and pain, just as with the sensation of unrelieved hunger, is introjected the experience of painful, angry self = painful, bad mother. On the other side is the mother. If she is unable to satisfy the need of her child, the manifestations of the child's frustration—his anger, his crying fits—affect the mother. She introjects the memory trace: frustrated child = inefficient, frustrating, bad mother = bad self. Thus the introjected drive experience merges with the self and thereby object-representations and self-representations become established in inseparable connection with each other. There develops a spiral of interpersonal processes which substitute for the biologic symbiosis of pregnancy an emotional symbiosis. "This term refers to reciprocal interactions between mother and infant which, through processes of introjection and identification, create structural changes in both of the participants" [4].

116

In time, the infant, adapting to the external realities and the multiple sensory gratifications offered by the mother's care, develops the expectation that hunger will be relieved by satiation. As he learns to know mother as the need-gratifying "object" outside the self, he develops "confidence" which enables him to project expectations of gratification into the future. Confidence is a primary mental construct[2] in which are integrated the object-representations of "good mother" and the self-representations of "good self." (Observations show that the 3- to-5-month-old infant may reveal a confident attitude at the time of feeding even in a state of moderate hunger. Protected from the sense of frustration by a psychic structure of libidinal origin, the infant has learned, commensurate with his maturational level, to wait.) Yet confidence means more than the expression of a positive object-relationship. It is the infant's own psychic equipment which acts as an organizer of all later object-relationships. In that early age it represents a step toward differentiation between *I* and *you* and at the same time it maintains the mother-child unity on an intrapsychic level.

Parallel with the experiences which lead to *confidence* in the infant, the mother, by introjecting her own gratifying experiences of mothering and their object, her thriving child, establishes *self-confidence* in her motherliness. Her confidence in her motherliness is not just a reflection of the child's gratification. From the time of conception, she has experienced the stimulation of the drive organization that motivates the psychobiology of motherhood and the activities of mothering. Now, observing her child whose smile is her reward, whose crying is her punishment, her self-concept expands through the gratifying introject: good, thriving infant = good mother, good self. As the consequence of the positive balance of the symbiotic processes establishes in the child the primary mental attitude of confidence which will influence his object-relationships in the future, the mother through her successful mothering unconsciously relives the primary experiences of her infancy; her self-confidence in her motherliness leads step by step to amelioration or resolution of her infantile conflicts with her mother and through this to conquering her fear of motherhood, her fear of her child.

---

[2] Erik Erikson termed the same primary mental construct *trust* and attributed to it the same origin and the same intrapsychic function as I do to *confidence*. Alice Balint [6] refers to the same as *primary love*.

117

The significance of the symbiotic relationship between mother and infant is more obvious in those instances in which the developmental conflicts of the mother motivate her sense of inadequacy in her motherliness. Then any crying fit of the infant may mobilize the anxiety which increases her inability to summon the "right response" to the child's need from the instinctual reservoir of motherliness. Since the "wrong response" intensifies the crying fit, it enhances in the child the memory traces of frustrating, bad mother = frustrated, angry self; parallel with this, in the mother it intensifies the feeling: crying, angry infant = inadequate, bad mother, bad self. Through memory traces charged by aggressive energy, the infant establishes in his psychic structure the ambivalent core of his personality. In the mother the parallel experiences activate a regressive spiral which, by intensifying her sense of inadequacy, increases her fear of and hostility toward her child.[3]

Confidence and the ambivalent core are primary mental constructs. Each of these primary structures interacts with the other in the further development of the child's personality and concurrently modifies in a specific way the further "emotional symbiosis," i.e., the reciprocal relationship between mother and child. Thus conceptualization of the processes resulting in confidence and in the ambivalent core also serves as a model of the transactional processes between parent and child in their later developmental phases. Here, instead of illustrating this proposition with references to well-known clinical examples, we prefer to emphasize the feedback cycles of interpersonal communications which result, in our own terminology, in reciprocal identifications. In the model of emotional symbiosis mother and infant can be considered the two foci within a dynamic field. The communication of the foci is accomplished not by direct energy exchange but by "emotional communication" within a field which is maintained by libidinal energy. In the transactional processes between mother and infant the source of energy is close to its physiologic source which energizes the processes of motherhood and the activities of mothering. The other example is the husband-wife unit which, representing two foci in the dynamic field, maintains the axis of the family by their

[3] Pathologic manifestations of the mother's reactions may lead to the "disruption of the maternal affectional system" often with tragic consequences, as illustrated in Chapter 22, Parental Abuse of Infants and Small Children, in this volume.

mutual libidinal needs for each other, leading to their parenthood. Both of these examples illustrate the reciprocal processes that induce intrapsychic changes in each of the participants according to their level of maturity (i.e., their drive-motivated need) and their function in the particular interaction.

EMPATHY: ITS ROLE IN PARENTAL FUNCTIONING

Now the question arises whether there is a psychic manifestation of energy which basically maintains the communication within the family and directs it toward its goal by providing for and protecting the growth and development of the children. The answer to this question comes more directly if we observe communications between animals.

Begetting and bearing the offspring is a biologically designed function of each species; caring for the offspring is under hormonal control, and its performance is considered "instinctual behavior." Taking the precision of instinctual behavior for granted, it was rarely if ever questioned whether animal mothers recognize their offspring after the procreative cycle has run its course and the hormonal stimulation which coordinated their feeding behavior has abated. At least, this is what we assume unless ethologists prove it otherwise.[4] It is only Homo sapiens which has the distinction and the responsibility for raising its children beyond that procreative cycle which produced the particular child to full maturity and adulthood. Because of this, in the psychologic functioning of the family, we can observe the manifestations of a psychic energy which, originating in the libidinal processes of the procreative function, reaches beyond them and maintains communications beyond the parent-child unity to encompass the family as a whole.

Thus empathy* is a specific human quality, a result of evolution that has created a psychic apparatus which enables man to sublimate, and so to continue on a purely psychic level, processes which originate in biology. *Empathy* in psychoanalytic terms is an unconscious function of the psychic apparatus, a manifestation of Freud's broadest definition of libido, according to which "libido is integrating

---

[4] Recent investigations of primate behavior [4a] and of that of some other mammals indicate that mother-offspring interactions in various subhuman species extend beyond the period of lactation.

* See also Chapter 16 in this volume.

psychic energy." Empathy in itself is just an energy charge which directs the ego's attention and facilitates perceptions and further integrations within the psychic apparatus.

In general, empathy enlarges the psychic field of any individual and enables him to encompass in his empathic responsiveness everyone and everything to which he might relate.

It was 60 years ago when a German philosopher defined empathy as "activation of oneself toward another" [19]. Whether it is the infant who activates the mother or the attentive gaze of the mother that awakens the sleeping infant, or when similar exchange occurs between lovers, whether a landscape or a piece of art mobilizes emotions, empathy expands the ego and enables the individual to perceive several aspects of external and intrapsychic events almost simultaneously. Indeed, empathy can be recognized as a direct effect of libido which opens up one person to another, bringing them closer to each other,[5] or farther apart, since the empathic response is a result of sundry interacting situations. While empathy itself remains unconscious, the empathic response appears usually as an intuitive or spontaneous reaction which often mobilizes affects and motivates behavior. Although empathic responsiveness is a genuine quality of human psyche, there are great individual differences regarding the facility and directness of empathic responses. Many individuals, especially in highly cultivated social groups, are so well defended, overly guarded against their emotions, that they suppress their primary responses and by this also their empathy even in sexual interaction and in transactions with their children.

Closest to its biologic source is the mother's empathy for her infant that gives impulses to the variety and subtlety of parental responses and adds up to successful mothering. As the child develops and becomes more and more a person in his own right, even parental empathy has to undergo intrapsychic processes in order to become empathic understanding since this is often necessary for the guidance of the evolving individuality of the child. Empathic response is a direct instinctual or intuitive reaction to the child's need. Empathic understanding, in contrast, is arrived at by a preconscious process of self-

---

[5] The German word for empathy is *Einfühlung,* which implies feeling oneself into another; it is not feeling with a person. Feeling into a person— empathy—is the primary phase of the process of identification.

reflection that leads the parent to an understanding of the motivations of his own reactions to the child's behavior. This implies also the parent's spontaneous or well-thought-out insight into motivations of the child's behavior. Only the empathic understanding of the ongoing process (between himself and the child) can guide the parent's interaction with the child toward a successful end.

This may appear abstract, as if it would not affect parents and children or other individuals within a family interacting with each other continually. This is not so, however. Only very young children do not reflect on their behavior. However, young children often reveal a surprising capacity to think of their parents pragmatically and not only anticipate but also evaluate their parents' behavior on the basis of their reciprocal emotional reactions. Indeed, emotional learning occurs promptly; its results hold fast and long in the grooves of the mind. Parents, being adults, could often help themselves and their children if they would attempt to understand the motivation of their own responses to their children's needs and behavior.

THE PSYCHODYNAMIC SIGNIFICANCE OF COMMUNICATION

Empathy, as a psychic representation of integrating energy, is the vehicle of communication within the psychologic field of the family. Through the evolving complexity of communications the biologically prearranged mutuality of needs and responses become modified by experiences and memories; the past and current emotional experiences give content and, with time, a pattern to the evolving interpersonal relationship that is a subsystem of the family.

The family, even the core family—mother, father, child—represents a hierarchy of subsystems. We have outlined the course of the psychodynamic processes which bind husband and wife. Through parenthood their bond is strengthened, since each of them become part of a subsystem: mother ↔ child, and father ↔ child. These subsystems are in continual interaction with each other and through them father and mother are in constant communication through and for the sake of the child. Thus none of the subsystems in a family represents a dyad only, since even during pregnancy and the postpartum period, when the psychodynamic processes between mother and infant are closest to

121

their biologic origin, the husband-father is an active participant in the family triad. He responds to the receptive-dependent needs of his wife which are increased by her pregnancy, by her anxieties about parturition and the care of the child. By supporting his wife's emotional needs, the husband participates in her pregnancy and prepares himself for the object-relationship to the child. As the infant begins to look, smile, and coo at him, he reactivates his "motherliness," the memory traces introjected during his own infancy. The father, soothing, comforting, and playing with the child, receives pleasure from the child. Besides this primary libidinal gratification he also experiences narcissistic ego gratification. Reassured by the feeling of being a good father, he achieves one of the aspirations of his ego-ideal.

The evolution of motherliness and fatherliness will be discussed in Chapters 6 and 7. Here it serves to illustrate that these complex feelings, rooted in the personality development of each of the parents and nurtured by the dynamism of their interpersonal relationship, unfold toward their child, creating with him an intrinsic psychodynamic unit which is the *triangle*—father-mother-child. In this triangle the child, even before he is born, plays a dynamic part, as the German poet, Anton Wildgans, succinctly said: "Weil, wo wir zwei sind, du wir beide bist." (Because, where we are two, you are both of us.) [18].

Psychoanalytic investigations confirm the poet's intuition. In the child, with each child in a different way, the mother and also the father unconsciously relive certain parts of their developmental problems. Under fortunate circumstances—i.e., if the child does not stir up deep-rooted conflicts in either of his parents—by gratifying their most significant aspirations, he enlarges the scope of their personalities, enhances their sense of identity, and deepens the meaning of their marriage. In the transactional processes of parenthood the family triangle represents a psychologic field which supports the individual development of each of the participants.

The first such triangle in the family—the relationship between the parents and the first child—may exist undisturbed, based on the intrinsic relationship of the three of them as long as the child is an only child. The balance is disturbed and changed from the point of view of all the participants by each additional child, or even by any other emotional experience of either of the parents which is significant

122

enough to break through the exclusiveness of the parents' relationship with each other and therefore with the child. Although each child forms a distinct triangle with the parents, each triangle unit is in dynamic interaction with and is influenced by the other units within the family.

However complex a description of these interacting forces and their effects on the cohesion of the family may be, the configuration of its several triangles is so deeply ingrained in all of us that it needs but a little training to evoke very definite associations in relation to any mention of an individual's place within his family. Every case history begins by stating that the patient is the nth among x number of children, for only a few details are then necessary to tell a great deal about the emotional constellation of that person within his family. But in addition to the primary and permanent triads, there are transient triads, or even larger interacting groups, forming between the children and with one or the other parent or with both parents. Such transitory groupings of interacting forces arising from current problems in the family, might have differing significance for the harmonious collaboration of the whole and, by this, for the development of any of its members.

Considering the family as a dynamic system, one can describe the relationships in terms of the hierarchical order of its subsystems. Since the whole system moves with time, the hierarchic order of its subsystems changes in their relationship with each other depending on age, developmental processes, and attainments of the interacting individuals (Chap. 8). The family is a closely knit organism thriving on a delicate balance of its emotional currents. It is a keenly sensitive balance which must continually be reestablished in adjustment to everyday events. There are always happenings, pleasant and unpleasant; there are always tensions which may come and go, or which may come to represent critical periods in the life of the family and, by this, in the development of each of the children. The continuity of the relationships is disrupted if one member of the family dies; similarly traumatic might be separation necessitated by military service during wartime. Such separation also disturbs the existing balance and exposes conflicts which have already receded into the background through the usual adjustments of living [2].

123

PARENTHOOD AS A DEVELOPMENTAL PROCESS

The psychodynamic processes within the family are usually discussed in psychoanalytic literature only as factors motivating the child's development from infancy to maturity. This study of the family as a field of transactional processes, however, is based on the proposition that the parents' drive-motivated, emotional investment in the child brings about reciprocal intrapsychic processes in the parents which normally account for developmental changes in their personalities.

The tendency to internalize outer reality is hereditary, as is the central organization which, in man, permits manifold working-over of the interacting psychic patterns from their incipient drive-object—self-representations—to their integration within the ego organization and the personality. Conceptualizing these phenomena from the point of view of the parent, it should be emphasized that the parent is not a *total object* for the infant. The parents, however, meet the child's needs as adults. They take in the newborn as the *total object* of their parental needs. They observe the infant, his motility, his sucking behavior, his crying, his looks, and they respond to him with their fondest hopes and expectations; as these motivate their emotional attitudes, they influence the intrapsychic processes of the child to which, in turn, the parent responds. Indeed, it is the narcissistic investment of the loving parent in the child which represents a demand on the child for support of the parent's self-system by not frustrating his projected self-expectations.[6] They are happy children and fortunate parents.

It is not possible to describe here the parental reactions to the evolving self-action patterns of the infant.[7] Long before the rewarding smiling response of the 8-week-old has become spontaneous, there are signs watched for and responded to with pleasure. Whoever has observed parents responding to the infant's eyes following an upheld,

[6] The right to punish in educational systems and of parents (even with capital punishment as provided by Greek and Roman law) is based on this self-righteousness of the parent.

[7] Margaret Mahler has studied these processes in detail and describes them as "individuation," as "hatching from the symbiotic state" [14]. The term *self-action pattern,* as used by Margaret Fries [8] and others, emphasizes the evolving innate characteristics of the infant such as sucking behavior, motility, appetite, rate of maturation, etc.

124

moving finger, or turning his head in response to the cooing sound of the mother, knows the pleasure which has many meanings. The gratification of nonverbal communication is a confirmation of one's ability to be one with the child and is a promise for the future when one's identity as a parent will be confirmed by the child. In the countless communications with the child, the parents introject the lasting gratifications and the fleeting frustrations of being a parent and by this the "indentification" with the child becomes step-by-step organized in their self-systems.

The parents, however, live with the real child at the same time that they are fostering the intrapsychic child as a hope of their self-realization. Their maturity is put to the test when the child's self-action pattern evolves from its neuromuscular anlage to the semantic expression of No as the opposite of the gestures saying Yes [15]. From the viewpoint of the parent, the Yes of the infant represents a manifestation of a satisfactory projection of the self-image; it keeps the child included in the parent's self-system, enhancing love and hope and the expectations for the future of the child and, through this, for the parent himself. The response is different to the child's consistent No or intensively negativistic behavior. Then the response depends upon the genuineness of the parental feelings, and also upon the role of the original object whom the child has come to represent for the parent. But beyond this, and even more important, the parents' responses are motivated by their awareness of their function as educators of the child. "Since the negativistic behavior of the child separates him from the self-system of the parents, it forces the parent to see what he or she does not like within himself (or in significant objects of his present or past). If this activates a regressive pattern, the opposed parent feels compelled to oppose the child. Under the impact of frustration by the child, the parent's ego boundaries weaken so that the angry parent identifies with the angry child. The healthy, adaptive response to negativistic behavior of the child strengthens the ego boundaries of the parent, making him conscious of his role as educator. The culturally assigned role of the parent derives its motivations, however, not only from its conscious goal but also from repressed or remembered significant events of his developmental experiences. These— both the current situation with his child and his past experiences with his parents—will motivate the parent's reaction to the child" [4].

125

Based upon the model of reciprocal interactions between parent and child during the oral phase, we may generalize that the spiral of transactions in each phase of development can be interpreted on two levels of motivations in terms of each participant. The parent's behavior is unconsciously determined by his developmental past, and consciously by a current reaction to the child's behavior or to his need. The child's behavior, depending upon his maturational level, is motivated primarily by his actual need or impulse. With time, however, as the child has "incorporated"—"learned"—the parents' responses, he acquires a "past" which enables him to anticipate his parents' responses to his behavior. This introduces a third aspect into the motivational pattern, namely, the anticipation of the emotional course of future experiences.

The significance of the child's anticipation of the parent's reactions to his behavior is well known. The child's confident expectation of gratification, his fear of frustration and punishment, modify his sense of security with his parents. Through many minute happenings the child learns to trust his anticipation. This more than massive anxiety accounts for the autoplastic and alloplastic adaptive patterns in the ego of the child. It is expected that it would be different with the parents. It is, or used to be, generally assumed that the parent's ego organization is such that he is not subject to changes through his object-relationship with his growing or grown child. Indeed, the self assurance of the parent in his motivations toward his child seems to justify his authority. His authority functions, however, not only to protect the child but also the insure himself against being affected by the child's behavior. It helps the parent to repress and deny his fears and anticipations, his unconscious feelings toward the child. Today it is difficult to imagine the emotional security of the Victorian parent toward his child, so aware are we of the modern parent's anxieties. Anticipating negativistic attitudes in their children, parents feel insecure, afraid, and often angry even before the child gives them cause. This then mobilizes their punitive behavior toward the child which, even though it may be appropriate for educational purposes, in modern parents often mobilizes a sense of guilt, and by this may increase the insecurity toward their children. The regressive, i.e., the more or less pathogenic and/or pathologic reactions of parents toward their children can be relatively easily observed and investigated.

Is there, however, any psychoanalytic evidence which would support the thesis that the child, being the object of the parents' drive, has, psychologically speaking, a similar function in the psychic structure of the parent? Does the child, evoking and maintaining reciprocal intrapsychic processes in the parent, become instrumental in the further developmental integration of the parent? In an attempt to find the answer to this question we shall cite here some well-investigated aspects of parent-child interaction, such as *imitation*.[8]

Imitation is a means of communication and as such enters into the spiral of emotional transactions and influences the parent-child relationship. The imitating child holds up a mirror image to the parent. Thus the parent responding to the mirror image may recognize and even say to the child: "This is your father; this is me in you" [18]. If the child's imitative behavior shows the positive aspect of their relationship, the parent will like what he sees and consequently feel that both child and parent are lovable. Imitation then reinforces the positive balance of identifications. It can also happen that the child shocks the parent by exposing the representation of hostile experiences in the past and in the present. In this event the parent feels the child's rejection and withdraws from the child (even if just for a moment), since the unloved self equals the unloved child. Imitation, externalizing what has been internalized from early infancy on, brings the child sometimes closer to the parent; at other times it pushes the child away. If this is a transient phenomenon soon relieved by reassurance, it creates an adaptive task and might stimulate growth and development in the child, and in the parents an attempt to change their behavior toward the child.

We know so much more about the child than about the parent's intrapyschic reactions to the child that in order to explain the parent, we have to take the child as a model.

The self-action patterns of the child lean on the parent and use imitation as a vehicle; the playful imitation of the parents' activities means learning coordination and function. As the 2- or 3-year-old boy and girl alike imitate the mother sweeping or drying dishes, as the little boy learns to use a toy hammer or lawnmower, as the little girl with great attention gives the

[8] Imitation is usually investigated only as it concerns the intrapsychic processes of the child. Jacobson states: ". . . imitation of parental emotional expression influences the child's own discharge patterns . . . to induce identical affective phenomena" [12].

bottle to the baby-doll, the parents delight in the skillfulness of the child and are gratified by such impersonation. For the child, imitation functions in the same way as fantasy; it forecasts what he will be able to do, to be, sometime in the future. In imitating the parent, the child charges his actions with the wonderment and admiration which he feels for adults. This increases the child's self-assurance. Perceiving the parents' pleasure in his achievement, the child's confidence in his parents increases and gains new nourishment. The positive communication between parent and child suggests the elaboration of confidence on the developmental level of the pre-oedipal child. During the oral phase of development the confidence that needs will be satisfied provides intrapsychic protection against the fear of frustration. Paralleling the growing independence of the child, a more complex introject, identification with the omnipotent parents, is needed to maintain the parent-child unity on the psychologic level, while it is being severed step-by-step in reality. While the secondary narcissistic elaboration of confidence is the source of omnipotent fantasies of the child, it is also the antecedent of the child's idealization of the parent [4].

What is the corresponding psychic process in the parent? Since the omnipotent fantasies of the child and the corresponding idealization of the parent comprise the positive arc of the transactional pattern, it facilitates the parent's positive identification with the child. The child's fantasies, unknown by the parent yet perceived through his play actions, reactivate in the parent the omnipotent fantasies of his own childhood; in addition, the parent, identifying with the fantasies of the child, accepts the role of omnipotence attributed to him. The normal parent, in spite of his insight into his realistic limitations, embraces the gratifying role of omnipotence. It induces him to identify with his own parent as he had anticipated being able to do in his childhood fantasies. Whatever the real course of events was between himself and his parents, as long as the fantasies of the child do not become hostile against him, the parent derives from the process of preoedipal identifications the reassurance that he is a good parent and, even more, the hope that he is or can be better than his parents were. The reciprocal interaction of positive fantasies, if not disrupted too often and by too intense ambivalent interplay, makes the task of the parent-educator easy. This is the process by which the value system of the parent becomes integrated into the precursors of the superego of the child. As the child's acculturation proceeds, the parent's self-assurance in his own parental capacity grows with rewarding pleasure and hope.

With the increasing expansion of the self-actions of the child,

128

his self-differentiation develops to express itself in the manifestations of the gender-pattern of the oedipal phase.

Normally, the child's idealization of the parent feeds the parent with gratification. There is no need to dwell upon the father's response to the admiration of his son or to the flirtation of his 4-year-old daughter. Just as obvious is the mother's pleasure in her daughter's wish to become like her and/or her son's promise to marry her because she is the best or most beautiful mother. The manifestation of the child's love for the parent intensifies the parent's libidinal feelings for the child. Indeed, one could compare the libidinal feelings of the oedipal child—who is not in possession of mature sexual drive and its physiologic equipment—with the tender, libidinous feelings of the parent toward the child which, according to the requirements of our culture, prevail in spite of, or probably because of, complete repression and sublimation of sexual drive toward the child. Yet it happens more often than our case histories or conceptualizations account for that the psychoanalyses of individuals of high superego standards reveal various forms of neurosis resulting from a disturbance of the interactions between parent and child, beginning, for example, when a father becomes aware of a genital response to his daughter, or when a mother is shocked by her fascination with her son's penis. The incestuous impulse revives in the parent his childhood struggle against oedipal tendencies. The intensity of the castration fear when he was a child resulted in the strictness of his superego which is now severely censoring his own impulses and also the sexual impulses of his children. Similarly, the intensity of the mother's sexual fear and guilt when she was a girl motivates her acute anxiety regarding her own impulses and also toward the manifestations of sexual impulses in her children, be they daughters or sons.

Since the child is the object of the parent's libido, he activates in the parent a new process of repression and neutralization of energies participating in the conflict. The intrapsychic struggle is, in the parent as in the child, between the id impulse and the repressing forces. In the child the precursor of his superego and fear of punishment press toward repression. In the parent the integrated superego maintains the barrier reinforced by the dynamic processes of parenthood. Thus a new phase in the parent's superego evolves. This encompasses the object-representations of the child and self-representations

129

originating in the experiences with the child. The conflicts which were incorporated in the superego when the parent was a child were worked over through the experiences of parenthood; this accounts for a new phase of maturation in the parent. "Through the successful relationship of the parent with his child or children, his superego loses some of its strictness and, as it allows for a broader, deeper capacity of experience, it indicates a new step toward the dissolution of its infantile origin. The opposite may also be true. Unsuccessful experience of the parent with unsuccessful children undermines the parent's self-esteem and enhances the strictness of his superego, thus rendering it pathogenic for the parent and consequently for the child. Incorporated into the psychic system of the parent, the child may mitigate or intensify the strictness of the parent's superego" [4].

Here I recall again Wildgans' poem. Musing about his newborn son the poet said, "Our judge you may become—you are he already" [18]. In a few words he expresses what modern parents, deprived of the security of parents of less individualistic, more authoritarian cultures, so often feel with more or less anxiety. The child at birth is an enigma. He represents hope and promise for self-realization and at the same time he forewarns that he may expose not one's virtues but one's faults. This threat to the parent's self-esteem implies his anxious anticipation of the child's failure. Such interacting motivations activate the parent's hesitation in directing the child according to the educational aims. The hesitation might lead to exaggerated watchfulness and intensified strictness in order to avert errors, or to laxity which leaves the child to his own devices. In either case the anticipation of the child's failure brings about, as projections often do, what one was afraid of—developmental conflict and failure in the area where the parents anxiously anticipated it.

Psychoanalytic investigations have revealed that parents anticipate the child's failure in the area of their own developmental conflicts. Unaware, as parents mostly are, of the repressed conflicts of their childhood, the transactional processes evolve relatively smoothly until the child reaches the developmental level at which the parent, because of his own developmental conflict, unconsciously anticipates the child's conflict and therefore become insecure in his responses to the child's behavior. It is the task of the "psychopathology of parenthood" to study the manifestations and the intrapsychic and interpersonal dynamics of the regressive spirals that evolve in such critical phases of parenthood which leave transient or permanent scars in the parent and in the child.

In this chapter, however, the emphasis is on parenthood as a normal developmental process. Although the parent's development occurs through the repetition of childhood conflicts, this does not lead necessarily to a pathologic condition. We assume that the opposite happens more often. We have hinted at processes which indicate that the reworking of the childhood conflicts leads to resolving them, i.e., to intrapsychic changes in the parents. It would be difficult to generalize in a meaningful way about the multitudinal psychic resources which support the parents' egos in their functioning. One is rooted in past experiences, in the fact that adults can counteract their fears by reliance on their achievements, in their conviction that they were able to overcome their conflicts. The other is the love for the child which maintains the hope that the child will become a better man than his father was. Each parent has to deal in his own way with the positive as well as the negative revelations of himself in the child. It is the individually varying degree of confidence in oneself and in the child which enables the parent not to overemphasize the positive and not be overwhelmed by the negative aspects of the self as it is exposed through the child. The varying manifestations of the parent's self-image in the child alternates, fortunately, with such swiftness that it rarely leaves time to respond to all the minute changes, but maintains the balance between contrasting experiences. With the help of the positive manifestations of the child's development, the parents' confidence in their children grows and with it grows the heartwarming and self-assuring conviction that they are achieving the goal of their existence. This is not just a phrase. In terms of dynamic psychology it means that while the parent consciously tries to help the child achieve his developmental goal, he cannot help but deal with his own conflicts unconsciously and by this, normally, achieve a new level of maturation.

THE CULTURAL FUNCTION OF THE FAMILY

In discussing the transactional processes within the family, our aim was to elaborate the psychodynamic processes by which the family achieves its cultural function. The intrapsychic instrument of this function is the *superego,* which evolves in each individual from the struggle between the instinctual needs of the child and his loving, protecting, but restricting environment. The model of that environment was the patriarchal family, in which not only the roles of the father and the mother were set and relatively static, but also their personalities were assumed to be stable and not influenced by their experience with the children. The idea of growing up with the children was not yet conceived, since the parent by his function as parent was assumed to be adult = mature. Indeed, this constellation of the family, just as the weltanschauung and the concepts of the physical world of that period, supported that concept of personality development.[9] The task of the family was then to transmit well-established patterns of a homogeneous and almost repetitious developmental goal.

Today we are aware that expectations for such slowly shifting but predictable repetitions of parental models of their children often meet with disappointment. Unaware of the psychologic factors that bring about conflicts between generations, we usually investigate them from the points of view of the individuals who are involved. Yet the cultural process that leads to changes in parental attitudes in one generation, by affecting the superego development of their children, influences also the yet unborn generation of their grandchildren. The transactional processes between parents and children explain the double aspect of the cultural function of the family; like Janus it has two faces. It is conservative and conserving, since it secures the attainment of the past; it is progressive since it transmits new cultural gains; by this it furthers differences between the generations of parents and their children. Clashes between fathers and sons have always occurred and provided not only subject matter for great literary achievements but also leaders of the progress of civilization [17]. In our era, however, it seems to constitute a built-in source of failure in the modern family.

What is it in our culture that, instead of securing the function of the family, complicates it, threatening the parents with failure? No

---

[9] The closed systems of the physical world agreed with the concept of *closed psychic systems,* although the physiologic dependence and the psychologic interaction were unquestioned and studied in detail.

doubt many books have been and will be written in an attempt to answer this question. Knowing that each and every aspect of cultural and socioeconomic changes exerts influence upon the family and also that all these events converge toward the ideal of our culture, namely, the higher individuation of all participants in the social process, we arrive at the question—how does the aim of high individuation affect the function of the family?

The pleasures and pains, the gratifications and sorrows of parenthood, are essential components of human existence. Experienced through untold generations, parental emotions are evident, unmistakably open to the empathy of human beings. Probably this is the reason why the metapsychology of parenthood, i.e., the intrapsychic changes occurring in parents due to responses to their children, has not been adequately investigated. In this presentation also these processes can only be intimated in order to indicate that as the parents are instrumental in the development of the superego and ego ideal of their children, so are children agents of intrapsychic changes in the parents. Whatever the psychologic and cultural lag is between the generations of parents and their children, the psychic structure of the parent cannot remain unaffected by the psychologic processes of child-rearing itself.

Choosing parenthood for unconscious motivations but with "free will" increases the modern parents' sense of responsibility toward the child. Not only the ambivalent or hostile parent's but also the loving parent's motherliness is weighted down by concerns kept alive by an ever-watchful superego. Parents in stable patriarchal societies offered themselves in good conscience as examples to their children. Modern parents in the best of circumstances offer themselves as guides and teachers, respecting the individuality of the child, even in opposition to the child's needs for guidance and control. Thus the foundation of the child's individuality becomes precarious.

Infant care in the modern family facilitates the fusion of primary introjects of the mother image with that of the father image. Whatever the effects of such fusion on the ego development of the child may be, from the further developmental transactions in the family triangle we can assume that when the child passes the oedipal phase and integrates the images of his parents, those images are inevitably more complex than they were in the past. All sorts of terms which we use to define psychologic characteristics in general, such as *active-passive, masculine-feminine, prohibitive-permissive,* etc., may be attributed to either of the parents. Whatever this might mean for the sense of identity of the individual generally, we can conclude that the declining authoritative behavior of parents, especially of the father, diminishes the intensity of the oedipal conflict and thus the impetus for the organization of the superego. Consequently, such a superego does not convey the cultural requirements from generation to generation in simple, categorical terms.

It is at the time of adolescence when such results become manifest in behavior and bring about a sense of alienation. Yet after adolescents have lived down their period of rebellion and become parents in their own turn, it becomes evident in their attitude toward their children and in their emotional problems with them that they have incorporated from their parents, along with the aims of high individuation, their doubts and insecurities in the parental role. The next generation will then be raised by less secure parents toward less stable goals in an insecure world.

The awareness of such a menacing, downward spiral between generations prompts wide and keen interest in the psychology of the family. Only a more precise knowledge of the psychology of parenthood can provide methods which will enable parents to find a golden, middle path that will lead safely to the multiple goals of parenthood. The goals of parenthood are inseparable from the maturation of the parent. The physical and emotional well-being of the child cannot be safeguarded if the parents do not feel secure in their educational role. Yet this role can no longer be fulfilled by the simple formula of authoritarian parenthood. To raise children in a democratic society by individualistic parents in order to achieve their own individuality and by this become assets to society is a complex and urgent task of parenthood. It cannot be left, as in earlier times, to the indirect and circuitous influences of socioeconomic and cultural events. Educators in the various fields of endeavor—sociologists, teachers, psychiatrists—must combine their efforts in order to develop in parents a conscious awareness of the complexity of their task, to face it as a challenge, and to live up to it.

SUMMARY

In this chapter I have tried to demonstrate the dynamic processes which, originating in the instinct for survival, maintain the family as a psychologic field, an open system in continual transaction with its environment. I have illustrated the psychologic field by the processes of introjection and identification by which husband and wife, as two foci of the core of the family, are welded into a functional unit through their parenthood. We have illustrated the mother and child as two foci of the other node of the field which, through introjection with the need-satisfying and need-frustrating mother, establishes reciprocal developmental processes in both mother and infant.

The basic assumption of our deliberation is that parenthood as a biopsychologic experience activates and maintains a developmental process in the parent. Each parent is a link in the chain of generations. Psychoanalytic investigations of members of three generations in the same family often reveal the interfamilial processes that influence the shifts in the structure of the superego. From such experiences one might generalize that raising the aim of individuation of the parents renders them insecure in their parental functioning. This, in turn, brings into focus the never-ending cycle of transactional processes that, via parenthood, maintains the biologic, psychologic, and cultural continuum.

Bibliography

1. Balint, A.   Love for the mother and mother-love. *Int. J. Psychoanal.* 30:251–259, 1949.
2. Benedek, T.   *Insight and Personality Adjustment.* New York: Ronald, 1946.
3. Benedek, T.   The Emotional Structure of the Family. In R. N. Anshen (Ed.), *The Family: Its Function and Destiny.* Science of Culture Series, Vol. V. New York: Harper, 1949. Pp. 202–225.
4. Benedek, T.   Parenthood as a developmental phase. *J. Amer. Psychoanal. Ass.* 7:389–417, 1959.
4a. DeVore, I.   *Primate Behavior.* New York: Holt, Rinehart and Winston, 1965.

135

5. Freud, S. *Three Contributions to the Theory of Sex.* New York: Nervous and Mental Disease Monographs, 1948.
6. Freud, S. On Narcissism: An Introduction. In J. Strachey (Ed.), *The Standard Edition of the Complete Psychological Works of Sigmund Freud.* London: Hogarth, 1957. Vol. 14, pp. 67–102.
7. Freud, S. The Ego and the Id. In J. Strachey (Ed.), *The Standard Edition of the Complete Psychological Works of Sigmund Freud.* London: Hogarth, 1961. Vol. 19, pp. 19–27.
8. Fries, M. E., and Woolf, P. J. Some hypotheses on the role of the congenital activity type in personality development. *Psychoanal. Stud. Child* 8:48–62, 1953.
9. Grinker, R. R. On identification. *Int. J. Psychoanal.* 38:379–390, 1957.
10. Hartmann, H., Kris, E., and Lowenstein, R. M. Some Psychoanalytic Comments on "Culture and Personality." In G. B. Wilbur and W. Muensterberger (Eds.), *Psychoanalysis and Culture.* New York: International Universities Press, 1951. Pp. 3–31.
11. Holinshed, R. In *The Chronicles of England,* 1577. (Earlier sources not traced.)
12. Jacobson, E. The self and the object world. *Psychoanal. Stud. Child* 9:75–127, 1954.
13. Kubie, L. Psychoanalysis and Marriage. In V. W. Eisenstein (Ed.), *Neurotic Interaction in Marriage.* New York: Basic Books, 1956.
14. Mahler, M. S. Thoughts about development and individuation. *Psychoanal. Stud. Child.* 18:307–324, 1963.
15. Spitz, R. *No and Yes; On the Genesis of Human Communication.* New York: International Universities Press, 1957.
16. Spitz, R. Life and the Dialogue. In H. Gaskill (Ed.), *Counterpoint.* New York: International Universities Press, 1963.
17. Turgenev, I. *Fathers and Sons.* (Edited by R. Matlaw.) New York: Norton, 1966.
18. Wildgans, A. Im Anschauen meines Kinder. In *Dichtungen,* 1913.
19. Worringer, W. *Abstraction and Empathy* (1908). New York: International Universities Press, 1967.

5

The Psychobiology
of Pregnancy

Therese Benedek

Pregnancy is a "critical phase" in the life of a woman. Using the term as ethologists use it, it implies that pregnancy, like puberty, is a biologically motivated step in the maturation of the individual which requires physiologic adjustments and psychologic adaptations to lead to a new level of integration that, normally, represents development. For a long time the significance of the psychobiologic processes of pregnancy was neglected by psychoanalysts. Freud, impressed by the emotional calmness of pregnant women, considered pregnancy as a period during which the woman lives in the bliss of her basic wish being gratified; therefore, he assumed that pregnant women are not in need of or accessible to psychoanalytic therapy. Since then psychoanalytic investigations have revealed the two opposing poles which account for pregnancy as a critical phase. One is rooted in the drive organization of the female procreative function, the other in the emotional disequilibrium caused by the stresses of pregnancy and the danger of parturition.

Recently, Rheingold collected into a large volume references regarding women's "fear of being a woman," with emphasis on the fear of death connected with childbearing [12]. This concept is so deeply ingrained in the human mind that even Freud failed to recognize the emotional manifestations of the instinctual tendency to bear children in the drive organization of women. Helene Deutsch, in her major work, attributes "the devoted patience which women of uncounted generations have shown in the service of the species" to the

137

necessity of woman's socioeconomic dependence on man [9]. An ever-growing literature abounds in the discussion of this concept, drawing its arguments from folklore, religion, mythology, and from the history of civilizations [8]. Against such telling evidence it may seem foolhardy to propose the results arrived at by psychoanalytic investigations. Yet it seems safe to do so since investigations have revealed the psychobiologic process of the female reproductive function without which mankind would not exist.

An investigation begun thirty years ago with the aim of discovering whether psychologic correlates of ovulation could be detected by psychoanalytic method fortunately directed my attention to the emotional accompaniments of the hormonal processes during the menstrual cycle [3]. Neither a description of that investigation nor the precise correlations of the emotional cycle with the cyclic changes of the gonadal hormones—the sexual cycle—are relevant here. However, a brief discussion of the psychologic processes corresponding to ovulation and the postovulative phase of the sexual cycle is unavoidable, since they, by elucidating the psychodynamic processes of the reproductive drive, facilitate our understanding of the well-being and also of the psychopathology of pregnant women. In the perspective of the psychobiologic processes of pregnancy, one can evaluate the clinical significance of the developmental conflicts and their constellation in the personality organization of women; these conflicts, revived during pregnancy, influence women's feelings about motherhood and their attitude toward their child and/or children. Psychoanalyses of pregnant women or women in the postpartum period thus provide clues to the interactions of three generations in the psychology of parenthood.

Growth, neurophysiologic maturation, and psychosexual development are intrinsically interwoven processes. The master gland, the anterior lobe of the pituitary, secretes the hormones which regulate metabolism, growth, and the propagative functions, including lactation and maternal behavior. In accordance with the two phases of the female reproductive function, copulation and childbearing, the ovaries produce two groups of gonadal hormones: estrogen, the follicle-ripening hormone, and lutein, the hormone of progestation; the latter is also termed progesterone, since it prepares the uterus for implantation of the fertilized ovum and helps to maintain pregnancy. Corre-

138

sponding to the follicle-ripening phase, the prevalent emotions are motivated by an active, i.e., object-directed, heterosexual tendency, the biologic aim of which is to bring about copulation. With ovulation, the direction of the dominant sexual tendency changes and libido becomes directed toward the self.

The impact of ovulation is accompanied by systemic reactions. Among these the best known is the heightened basal body temperature by which ovulation is often diagnosed. On the psychologic side, a sense of relaxation and well-being seems to flood the woman with libido. As if the psychic apparatus has registered the somatic preparation for pregnancy, the emotional concern shifts to the body and its welfare. The manifestly narcissisic emotional response to ovulation corresponds with the peak of the hormonal cycle and expresses the psychobiologic readiness for conception.

On the basis of psychoanalytic observations Helene Deutsch generalized that a deep-rooted passivity and a specific tendency toward introversion are characteristic qualities of the female psyche [9]. Investigation of the sexual cycle has revealed that these propensities reappear in intensified form correlated with the specifically female gonadal hormone, lutein, during the postovulative phase of the cycle. Such observations justify the assumption that the emotional manifestations of the specific receptive tendency and the self-centered retentive tendency are the psychodynamic correlates of a biologic need for motherhood. Thus motherhood is not secondary, not a substitute for the missing penis, nor is it forced by men upon women "in the service of the species," but the manifestation of the all-pervading instinct for survival in the child that is the primary organizer of the woman's sexual drive, and by this also her personality. Thus the specific attributes of femininity originate in that indwelling quality of woman's psyche which is the manifestation and result of the central organization of receptive and retentive tendencies of the reproductive drive that becomes the source of motherliness.

The 4 to 6 days following ovulation—the lutein phase of the sexual cycle—represent a plateau of high hormone production, since both hormones, estrogen and progesterone, are produced. Yet in the psychoanalytic material, in dreams and fantasies—rarely, however, in behavior—the heterosexual tendency appears masked by psychologic expressions of the preparation for motherhood. Parallel with the preparation of the uterine mucosa for nidation, the emotional manifestations of intensified receptive-retentive tendencies represent the psychologic preparation for pregnancy. Correspondingly, the overt behavior as well as dreams and fantasies reveal the wish to receive and retain, or the defenses against that wish, if the woman is for any reason unconsciously or consciously afraid of pregnancy.

The comparative study of lutein phases in several women, through a number of cycles, affords evidence of the significance of lutein stimulation in the development toward motherhood. Introduced by an introversion of psychic energies at the time of ovulation, the receptive and retentive tendencies, characteristic of infancy, become intensified and recharge the memory traces introjected during infancy. These unconscious memories, interacting with the emotional reality of the individual, induce a great variety of phenomena. Most accessible to psychoanalytic observations are the repetitions of developmental identifications and conflicts with the mother. The psychoanalytic material reveals attempts at resolution of these conflicts as well as failures of such attempts. The latter eventuality is usually in the center of our attention since failures frequently motivate symptoms of "oral" origin. Psychoanalytic investigation of several consecutive cycles, or several cycles at greater intervals, reveals the factors upon which success or failure of attempts to resolve the developmental conflicts depend. From puberty to menopause, in monthly repetition, as her physiology prepares the woman for childbearing, her personality organization evolves that sublimation of psychic energies which we call motherliness (for further discussion of motherliness, see Chap. 6).

It is a physiologic characteristic of woman that her reproductive function requires an increase of metabolic processes. Each phase directly connected with childbearing—the lutein phase of the cycle, pregnancy, and lactation—goes hand in hand with an increase of receptive and retentive tendencies; these phases are the psychic representations of the need for fuel to supply energy for growth. At the time of ovulation and during the lutein phase, the actual increase in metabolic need must be minimal, yet the psychic responses are recognizable. This signifies that in the presence of signal stimulation the psychic apparatus sets in motion an innate pattern of responses which, if actually not needed, affords learning by repetition.[1]

[1] The unconscious repetition of memory traces of early infancy under the

140

When conception occurs, the cyclic function of the ovaries is interrupted and is not reestablished with regularity until after lactation is finished. Because of the uninterrupted and enhanced function of the corpus luteum, the psychobiology of pregnancy can be best understood as an immense intensification of the lutein phase of the cycle. While this seems to be an oversimplification of the complexity of the physiologic and psychologic processes of pregnancy, it refers to its foundation, namely, to the increased hormonal and metabolic processes and their psychologic manifestations motivated by intensified receptive and retentive tendencies.

Pregnancy is a biologically normal but exceptional period in the life of women. At conception a "biologic symbiosis" begins that steers the woman between the happy fulfillment of her biologic destiny and its menacing failures. The heightened hormonal and metabolic processes which are necessary to maintain the normal growth of the fetus augment the vital energies of the mother. It is the interlocking physiologic processes between mother and fetus that make the pregnant woman's body abound in libidinous feelings. As metabolic and emotional processes replenish the libido reservoir of the pregnant woman, this supply of primary narcissism becomes a wellspring of her motherliness. Self-centered as it may appear, it increases her pleasure in bearing her child, stimulates her hopeful fantasies, diminishes her anxieties. One can, however, observe differences in women's reactions to this psychobiologic state. A woman whose personality organization makes her a natural mother enjoys the narcissistic state with vegetative calmness, while a less fortunate woman defends herself, often consciously, against that experience. As women succeed in adjusting to the hormonal influences of pregnancy, the initial fatigue, sleepiness, some of the physical reactions such as vertigo or morning sickness, diminish. Thus women are able to respond to their physical and emotional well-being by expanding and enjoying their activities. While the pregnant woman feels her growing capacity to love and to care for her

stimulation of the hormones of the corpus luteum is a good example of "psychosomatic learning." These memory traces interacting with later levels of mother identifications influence the psychic representations of motherhood and modify the anticipations connected with it. Thus the monthly repetition of the intrapsychic processes of the sexual cycle illustrates that psychosomatic learning occurs not only in infancy but throughout life as a result of integration of maturational and developmental processes.

child, she experiences a general improvement in her emotional state. Many neurotic women who suffer from severe anxiety states are free from them during pregnancy; others, in spite of morning sickness or in spite of realistic worries caused by the pregnancy, feel stable and have their best time while they are pregnant. Healthy women demonstrate during pregnancy just as during the high hormone phases of the cycle an increased integrative capacity of the ego.

Yet the drive organization which accounts for the gratifications of pregnancy harbors its inherent dangers. It tests the physiologic and psychologic reserves of women. Realistic fears, insecurities motivated by conception out of wedlock, economic worries, unhappy marriages make the test more arduous. Yet even such pregnancies usually have a normal course. We might assume that such pregnancies, in our age of relatively free use of contraceptives, are often deliberately or unconsciously chosen for their drive gratification and therefore have a curative effect. To this assumption one might object, since we all know that the hope for a change for the better in an interpersonal relationship or in an external situation may enhance the gratification of pregnancy. To this, however, I would answer that the increased libidinal state of pregnancy enhances hope and by this might favorably influence not only the pregnancy but also the realities of the environmental situation. Whether the hope will be fulfilled or disappointed, the fact is that hope arising from the libidinal state of pregnancy is often the motivation of motherhood. The point to be emphasized is: *only if the psychosexual organization of the woman is loaded with conflicts toward motherhood do actual conditions stir up deeper conflicts and disturb the psychophysiologic balance of pregnancy.*

PSYCHOPATHOLOGY OF PREGNANCY

Since the complex steps toward maturity, motherhood, and motherliness begin with infancy, the psychodynamic processes of normal and pathologic pregnancy can be discussed in terms of the oral dependent phase of the mother's development. Receptive-dependent needs having been revived, pregnant women thrive on the solicitude of their environment and suffer, sometimes unduly, if such needs are frustrated. It seems that the exceptional condition brings about exceptional needs, which by requiring attention provide for emotional gratification. Well-known symptoms such as the perverse appetite of preg-

142

nant women, even nausea and morning sickness, might be so motivated, since such symptoms seem to diminish under the changing attitudes toward pregnancy. Yet the question remains—which changes in attitude affect the emotional health of pregnant women? Grete Bibring, in her preliminary publication of a large-scale investigation of the psychologic processes in pregnancy, assumes that much of the psychopathology of pregnancy in our current culture might be activated by our "scientific" approach to pregnancy, which does not pay enough attention to the emotional needs of pregnant women [7]. This scientific attitude communicates to women a scientific requirement, namely, to take a natural, i.e., an objective, attitude toward themselves, toward their condition during pregnancy. However, self-imposed frustration of needs and repression of fears might also be a factor in activating pathologic reactions.

The inner-directed psychologic state of pregnancy has a regressive pull which brings about mood swings from the calm elation of the narcissistic state to the anxious depressive mood of deep-seated insecurity. The intensification of receptive and retentive tendencies activated by the physiology of pregnancy brings about id regression in the service of the species, to paraphrase the felicitous formulation of Kris, which under certain circumstances might bring about a regression of the ego, hence the vulnerable ego state of pregnant women [11].

Whether the woman fully enjoys her pregnancy or is ambivalent toward her motherhood, in any case the integrative task of pregnancy and motherhood—biologically, psychologically, and realistically—is much greater than a woman has ever faced before. In some cases the adaptive task appears greater with the first child, when the woman experiences something completely new. The physiologic and emotional maturation of the first pregnancy usually makes motherhood easier with the second and third child. Yet it also happens that women, fatigued by the never-ceasing labor of motherhood, afraid of the burden of another child, experience pathogenic regression during later pregnancies. Yet the security of marriage, the considerate affection of a good husband, the pleasure in her children, and the support of her parental family supply the feedback which helps to keep in balance the emotional household of a pregnant woman. Actual deprivations, by increasing the integrative task, intensify the regression and stir up the basic instinctual conflict at the root of the procreative function of woman. Concern about her future increases her need, and by

143

this the intensity of her frustration. Unrelieved frustration and the accompanying helpless, hopeless anger interrupt the well-being of the physiologic symbiosis. Then the pregnant woman, like an angry, frustrated infant, cannot find gratification in her pregnancy. Ungratified, the frustrated woman feels unable to love and satisfy her unborn child; this, in turn, activates her anxiety. The rejection of the pregnancy goes hand in hand with the hostility toward the self, with the rejection of the self.

It is known that extreme rage may lead to spontaneous abortion, especially during the first trimester of pregnancy. In the less acute cases, anorexia, vomiting, and consequent severe metabolic disturbances may result from the woman's destructive tendencies toward herself and toward her unborn child. It is pertinent here to note that such symptoms appear even under the most satisfactory emotional and socioeconomic circumstances, and they occur often in women who as infants had severe anorexia and/or other psychosomatic illnesses of the gastrointestinal tract. This again demonstrates that as the psychodynamic processes inherent in pregnancy revive the infantile ambivalence toward mother and motherhood, they reactivate the anxieties, frustrations, and pains referable to the pregnant woman's infancy, her oral phase of development.

In 1911 Karl Abraham conceptualized the pathogenesis of depression [1]. Since then it has been a well-established concept of psychoanalysis that regression to the oral phase of development is the psychodynamic condition of depression. "Since such regression is inherent in the physiology of pregnancy and lactation—even in the lutein phase of the sexual cycle—depressions of varying severity and psychosomatic conditions of oral structure are the basic manifestations of the psychopathology of the female propagative function" [5].

The further elaboration and symptomatic manifestation of that regression depend on all the factors, constitutional and experiential (environmental), which account for the personality organization of the individual. Among the experiential factors, as emphasized earlier (Chap. 4), are the vicissitudes of the female child's identifications with her mother. If this is not charged with intense hostility, the woman accepts her heterosexual desires without anxiety and motherhood as a desired goal. At the other end of the innumerable solutions to the same infantile conflicts is the extreme fear of pregnancy and

144

motherhood which, under certain conditions, might lead to infertility.

Infertility, if not caused by organic pathology, can be considered a defense against the dangers inherent in the procreative function [4]. The conflicts leading to infertility are usually so deeply repressed that such women, some time in their lives, becoming aware of their inability to bear children, clamor with an anxious desire for a cure. Then psychoanalysis discovers the conflicts and ego defenses which, by enabling them to avoid pregnancy, protect them from the anxiety [6], which could shatter their personality organization. Other women, having similar primary conflicts but a constitution which enables them to conceive easily, still might be protected from their anxiety through spontaneous abortions or by psychosomatic symptoms which, by the severity of the illness, direct the anxiety away from its source, the pregnancy, and away from its object, the fetus. In illness the anxiety can be concentrated upon the self, upon one's own survival. Even without illness the anxiety stirred up by the threat to the ego might remain concentrated on the pregnancy itself; then the woman might become hypochondriacal, afraid of dying during or as a result of delivery. In other cases the hostility toward the fetus is closer to consciousness as the cause of death; in these instances, women fantasy about harboring a cancerous growth, a gnawing animal, or even a monster. Such fantasies, alien to the ego and often in traumatic contrast to the woman's wish for pregnancy and motherhood, activate grave anxiety frequently experienced as losing her mind. Whoever has observed a pregnant woman's ego struggling to master her panic knows that the biologically motivated introversion magnifies the psychologic and consequently also the realistic task of motherhood. Many women have enough ego resources to overcome the panic, but even if the panic lasts only a few minutes, the victory is paid for dearly. Having become painfully aware of her fear of and hostility toward her unborn child, the anxiety might lead to severe phobic defenses against the sense of inadequacy in her motherliness. This, in turn, might create a vicious circle in the transactional processes between mother and her infant. Thus the disturbance of the biologic symbiosis, although we generally assume that it is experienced by the mother only, might disturb the postpartum symbiosis and the ensuing developmental interactions between a mother and her child.

145

DERIVATIVES OF THE OEDIPUS COMPLEX
AND OTHER FANTASIES

Until now we have concentrated on those representations of the primary object relationships which have a deleterious effect upon the emotional course of pregnancy, but they are the exceptions representing variations of pathologic states. While we are impressed by and concerned with pathology, we should not forget that infants grow up with the ability for normal motherhood. What is evident in the population statistics is confirmed by psychoanalytic investigation of many women of childbearing age, i.e., the positive balance of introjects during infancy, in spite of its oscillations, increases the wish for motherhood and the gratifications of pregnancy.

However, not all the fantasies about childbearing originate in the oral phase of development. Since the psychic representations of the primary object relationships are in continual interaction with all later object relationships during the development of an individual, the later course of her development also bears upon the woman's attitude toward pregnancy and motherhood. Many fantasies originating in later developmental phases revived during pregnancy by well-tolerated physiologic regression add to the enjoyment of pregnancy and color the woman's anticipations of her motherhood. Many of these can be grouped under the heading, fantasies about the content of the womb. They have different but significant meanings in the psychic economy of pregnancy. Among these the most important regarding the psychology of pregnancy is Freud's assumption that the fantasied content of the womb is the incorporated penis of the father.

It is well established that the outcome of the girl's oedipal development, although dependent upon the vicissitudes of the preoedipal phases, influences the woman's attitude toward the other sex, her acceptance of her sexual role in coitus. As the father influences the girl's heterosexual maturation, he alleviates her fear of being a woman and of bearing children. The investigation of the sexual cycle confirmed these assumptions; it demonstrated that during the follicle-ripening, estrogen phase, the developmental wish to become equal to mother and to have a similar sexual role with father is repeated. Oedipal wishes reactivated during pregnancy might motivate the fantasy that the content of the womb is the representation of the received and retained penis of the father. Although this fantasy is not as ubiquitous as it is interpreted, it demonstrates the integration of the two phases of the female reproductive drive, the heterosexual drive and the tendency to receive and retain, i.e., conceive. Although this fantasy cannot carry the weight of the psychobiologic concept of woman's propagative function, psychoanalysis in many instances has demonstrated its motivational power in women's attitudes during pregnancy.

EFFECTS OF OTHER (COMMON) FANTASIES

There are many common infantile fantasies. One or the other of them might have greater significance in the girl's development toward motherhood. Rekindled by the regressive processes, such a fantasy might influence the emotional course of the pregnancy and by this the mother's attitude toward her child. Such influence might be beneficial or anxiety-provoking. The main and most natural source of her fantasies is the pregnant woman's body, abundant with libido. Since the fetus is a part of the woman's body, it is cathected with narcissistic libido. But there are many aspects of the self-image charged with ambivalence. Is the fetus identified with the loving and loved self? If so, this is fortunate for both mother and infant. Or does the fetus represent the "bad, aggressive = devouring self," engendering fear of carrying a monster, creating panic or depression, and by this devaluating mother and child. The fetus might also represent the once-admired beauty or the envied pregnancy of the pregnant woman's mother. Such fantasies express hope for fulfillment in the child, or they may revive the hostility once felt toward the envied mother or sibling. Or does the fetus represent the missing and wished-for penis, as Freud assumed? Even this would not always represent an object charged exclusively with positive feelings. More often and closer to consciousness are fantasies which identify the fetus with its begetter. In such fantasies the oneness of the pregnant woman with her mate encompasses their yet unborn child, creating the psychodynamic foundation of the triad: father-mother-child.

The fetus does not always represent a genital symbol, even in the happy pregnant woman's fantasies. Some women identify the content of the womb, the fetus, with the content of the bowels, with feces;

147

by this they relive the mysteries of the infantile fantasy, the anal child. Such fantasies charged with the once strictly forbidden pleasure of anal eroticism allow parents to indulge each other in their shared regression and in this way anticipate their future communication with their child in the language of infancy.

It is noteworthy to add here that husbands can and often do share the libidinous, happy fantasies of their wives if the latter are not embarrassed to talk about them. Women, understandably, do not talk about their aggressive, hostile fantasies unless they cannot help it; because of their mounting anxiety, they have to ask for help, for reassurance, for love. If love is available and is enough to relieve their anxiety, pregnancy will continue without a renewed flare-up of unconscious conflicts. Such confirmation of their love—his power and her reception of it—deepens the bond between husband and wife; it gives another perspective to her pregnancy which then encompasses both of them and their unborn child. It is different if the hostility and anxiety cannot be alleviated. Whether it spills over to the husband or not, it alienates the marital partners. Since the husband does not experience a regression motivated by the state of pregnancy, he often cannot have deep-rooted empathy with the incomprehensible reaction of his wife to a normally healthy, happy condition. However considerate the husband tries to be regarding the suffering of his wife, sooner or later he begins to resent her pathologic state, since it deprives him of the gratification of his virility in having impregnated his wife. This plants dissension between them. The child born out of that pregnancy often remains the center of the disunity of the parents. Thus the primary ambivalence, the root of the mother's pathologic state, might bring to the fore the ambivalent attitude in the father toward the child. The disunity between the parents endangers the emotional development of the child, since the transactional processes in such triads are reciprocally affected by the ambivalence of each of its members.

Citing the most frequent (typical) fantasies of pregnant women has proved to be rewarding, since it illustrates different levels of ego operations in response to (or motivated by) the biologic regression inherent in the physiology of pregnancy. A microscopic analysis of any one of the examples is beyond the scope of this presentation, but altogether they illustrate the psychobiologic continuum.

148

One participant of this continuum seems to have been left out —the fetus itself. Does the psychobiologic disequilibrium influence the intrauterine environment and by this the fetus itself? Folklore takes it for granted that acute anxiety, sorrow, or worry disturbs the fetus and causes physical harm.[2] There are obvious reasons why investigations of this far-reaching problem are relatively recent and far from conclusive. Yet a rapidly growing interest and promisingly developing methodology of investigations of the fetal environment and the response by its inhabitor—the fetus—might expand our knowledge of the psychobiologic continuum to include fetal-maternal and neonatal-maternal processes into the ontogenesis of individuals. That which has long been a part of mythology and folklore has been brought into the focus of scientific inquiry during the second quarter of this century. Beginning with investigations that proved an infectious disease of the mother, rubella, causes malformations and mental retardation in the child, Sontag expanded his research to include more subtle effects of differences in the fetal environment and its effect on fetal behavior and physiology [13, 14]. An even more courageous move in the same direction was presented by Green [10], whose investigation led him to the premise that some kinds of objects are perceived very early by the developing human organism, that objects perceived via somatic rather than psychologic processes afford the organism a degree of variation in tension which maintains communication between mother–fetal environment–fetus.

Psychoanalytic investigation of pregnancy as a psychobiologic process reveals its significance for the individual and for the three generations which pregnancy links in sequence. The psychosexual maturity of the individual woman is the result of the girl's introjected developmental experiences. These form the self-image of being a woman and her characteristic attitudes, her acceptance of, or her rebellion against, her sexual role in intercourse and in motherhood. As these psychic precursors of motherhood come to be influenced by the

---

[2] For example, it is a widespread belief that the fetus will be born with a birthmark (nevus flammeus) on the face if the pregnant woman in sudden anxiety covers her face with her hands.

physiologic processes of pregnancy, they mature and expand to encompass the yet unborn child with anticipation of fulfillment. Normal mother-and-child relationships are a relatively unobtrusive evolution of the culturally accepted manifestations of motherly love and care. Deviation from the normal demands attention. Clinical observations of the postpartum and later interactions between mother and infant reveal that the mother's ambivalence toward her procreative function influences her motherliness; it inhibits and blocks the natural flow of her mothering behavior. Since the father's attitude toward the child might be influenced by the communicated experience of his wife, the emotional course of the pregnancy is largely responsible for the psychologic environment of the child; since it might confirm or undermine the meaning of the marriage, it may stabilize or disrupt the primary social unit, the family.

Bibliography

1. Abraham, K.   Notes on the Psycho-Analytical Investigation and Treatment of Manic-Depressive Insanity and Allied Conditions. In K. Abraham (Ed.), *Selected Papers*. London: Hogarth, 1927. Pp. 137–156.
2. Alexander, F.   *Psychosomatic Medicine*. New York: Norton, 1950.
3. Benedek, T., and Rubenstein, B. B.   *The Sexual Cycle in Women*. Washington, D.C.: National Research Council, 1942.
4. Benedek, T.   Infertility as a psychosomatic defense. *Fertil. Steril.* 3:527–537, 1952.
5. Benedek, T.   *Psychosexual Functions in Women*. New York: Ronald, 1952.
6. Benedek, T., Ham, G. C., Robbins, F. P., and Rubenstein, B. B. Some emotional factors in infertility. *Psychosom. Med.* 15:485–498, 1953
7. Bibring, G. L.   Some considerations of the psychological processes of pregnancy. *Psychoanal. Stud. Child* 14:113–121, 1959.
8. de Beauvoir, S.   *The Second Sex*. (Translated by H. M. Parshley.) New York: Knopf, 1953.
9. Deutsch, H.   *The Psychology of Women*. New York: Grune & Stratton, Vol. I, 1944; Vol. II, 1945.
10. Green, W. A.   Early object relations, somatic, affective and personal. *J. Nerv. Ment. Dis.*, 126:225–253, 1958.

11. Kris, E. *Psychoanalytic Explorations in Art.* New York: International Universities Press, 1952. Pp. 173–188.
12. Rheingold, J. C. *The Fear of Being a Woman.* New York: Grune & Stratton, 1964.
13. Sontag, L. W. The significance of fetal environmental differences. *Amer. J. Obstet. Gynec.* 42:996–1003, 1941.
14. Sontag, L. W. Differences in modifiability of fetal behavior and physiology. *Psychosom. Med.* 6:151–154, 1944.

6

Motherhood
and Nurturing

Therese Benedek

All creatures are endowed with innate patterns of coordinated physiologic processes which, when set in motion by the act of conception, unfold to protect the growth and maturation of the embryo and to regulate parturition and the care of the young until they are able to fend for themselves. Thus "mothering" is a biologic and hormonally regulated function, as is motherhood itself. This, however, does not hold true without qualification for Homo sapiens. Having reached the highest rung of the ladder in selective evolution, the slow ontogenic maturation of human offspring necessitated the evolution of social structures which, in turn, allow for and require a broad range of modifications in mothering behavior. It is only the species of Homo sapiens that has the distinction, the privilege, and the responsibility of raising its children beyond that procreative cycle that produced the particular child to full maturity and adulthood. It is only the human female whose mothering behavior has two resources: One is, as in any other creature, rooted in her physiology; the other evolves as an expression of her personality which has developed under environmental influences that can modify her "motherliness." In the individual mother's experience, the derivatives of these two origins are tightly interwoven and cannot be isolated from the child who is part of the weave. Because of its independence from the strict limitations of physiologic, preformed patterns, the motherliness of the human mother is tested with each of her children during the phasic development of the child; one probably could say it is tested day by day. It is

153

tried by environmental expectations as well as by the mother's ego ideal and superego; its final judge is, however, the child itself; only his satisfactory development brings about in the mother's psyche harmony between external and internal demands which the work of mothering exacts. This might sound like an exaggeration speaking of a drive-motivated function, and certainly if compared with the exquisitely accurate mothering behavior of birds or with the seemingly patient tenderness of mothering of mammalian females; it appears exaggerated even if compared with the blissfully unconcerned nursing behavior of primitive mothers, be they in Samoa or Mexico. But studying the mothering behavior of women in Western civilization we are impressed and concerned by its differences and oscillations. These sensitive women, imbued by awareness of their "motherly" functioning, often conscious of their motherly tenderness, frequently become impatient. They may be gloriously proud of their competence or anxiously troubled by the possible shortcomings of their mothering behavior.

INSTINCTUAL ORIGINS OF MOTHERLINESS

The action of the pituitary hormone upon the integration of mothering behavior has been well studied in animals. In the human female, however, only lactation proper is under direct hormonal stimulation. Mothering is a complex, more or less culturally determined, learned behavior; the many practical attitudes necessary to take care of the infant and guide his primary learning are facilitated by a characteristic quality of woman's personality, i.e., motherliness. Motherliness in woman is not a simple response to hormonal stimulation brought about by pregnancy and the ensuing necessity to care for the young. Nevertheless, the study of the sexual cycle permits the assumption that hormonal stimulation exerts influence upon the integration of motherliness from puberty on (Chap. 5). The integration of motherliness is a complex and as yet uninvestigated process. One aspect of its psychodynamics could be defined as a process by which the infant's passive tendency "to be fed," "to be given," changes to the active tendency "to feed, to give, to succor." While the girl is growing up and her ego is learning the techniques and attitudes of giving, her ego ideal incorporates the aspiration to feed, to be a mother, a good mother.

154

Motherliness is a function of the human mental apparatus that through evolution has developed to become able to modify drive patterns mainly through integration of memory traces into personality organizations and ego functions. This accounts for the differences in motherliness of women belonging to the same civilization, social group, even to the same family.

The hormonal and metabolic changes that induce parturition, the labor pains, and the excitement of delivery interrupt the continuity of the mother-fetus symbiosis. After delivery, an emotional symbiosis is brought about by the mother's care for the infant, facilitated particularly by lactation. The hormonal function which stimulates milk secretion usually suppresses the gonad function and induces an emotional state motivated by intensified receptive and retentive tendencies. These tendencies become dominant motivating factors of mothering. The mother's desire to nurse the baby, to be close to him bodily, represents a continuation of the physiologic symbiosis. While the infant incorporates the breast, the mother feels united with him. The identification with the infant permits the mother to regress and repeat in her mothering behavior memory traces of her infantile experiences. As the reciprocal (transactional) emotional experiences of lactation mediate identifications between mother and infant, they facilitate the integration of motherliness. Not only lactation, but bottle-feeding or any other frequent and intimate contact with a thriving infant has a stimulating and integrating effect on motherliness.

Motherliness as a normal characteristic of femininity, of women's psychosexual maturity, and as part and parcel of motherhood, belongs to those enigmatic features of woman's psychology that have eluded investigation. Because its manifestations even in little children appear sublime and sublimated, it did not seem to fit in the frame of libido theory. Kestenberg has made strenuous efforts to fill this gap by proposing, on the basis of psychoanalytic study of children, that the vagina is an erotogenic zone [6]. Others before her also have reported observations which demonstrate that the vagina is not a hidden organ but has cathexis which directs the young child's attention (the preoedipal child's attention) to libidinous feelings derived from that part of the body.[1] Kestenberg, however, goes further in her proposi-

[1] This has to be put vaguely since libidinal sensations arising from the vaginal area could also be clitoral, perineal, or anal.

tion. She assumes that vaginal libido is the source of motherly feelings as expressed by primary motherliness, for example, in the doll play of little girls; her further conclusions lead to the assumption that through the vicissitudes of female development the vaginal libido, desexualized, becomes integrated as motherliness in mature women [7]. Her studies represent a significant link in the search for the origins of motherliness; they confirm and support the hypothesis that when the gonadal hormones set in motion the reproductive physiology, they coordinate already prepared organ sensibilities with prepared drive patterns.

But even such dovetailing of hypotheses does not assure the role of vaginal libido in the development of motherliness. The doll play of little boys, their not infrequent wish for a baby, and even more the keenly sensitive motherliness of many mature men turn our attention from libidinal zones to the central nervous organization of all processes pertaining to the reproductive functions. The psychophysiologic system of motherliness is part of that organization, the maturation of which begins immediately after birth.

Recent investigation of ethologists reveal that the diffuse, overall body contact between the animal mother and her litter is prerequisite for the maturation of mating, motherhood, and mothering behavior in animals [5]. These findings have direct bearing on the psychoanalytic concepts of identification, especially on hypotheses which, derived from direct observations or arrived at by psychoanalytic investigations, assume that woman's emotional attitude toward motherhood, her mothering behavior, and her motherliness are derivatives of her developmental identification with her mother.

The term *identification* is often used to represent the incorporated image of the total mother, either as the ideal, good mother or the opposite. In Chapters 4 and 5 the term refers to transactional processes of drive-motivated experiences during infancy. I assume that a woman's acceptance of her feminine role and her motherliness is dependent upon and is influenced to a high degree by the vector of an infinite number of minute experiences. Since readers and even scientists are inclined to accept an often-repeated hypothesis for fact, I want to underline the qualification implied in the foregoing statement, *dependent upon and influenced by,* but not *caused by.*

If there is a genetic anlage to motherliness—and I believe there must be—we might assume that it reveals itself in primary motherliness mostly during the preoedipal phase of development. This could also indicate that primary motherliness is the result of positive identification with the mother. But many observations could testify that a 3-year-old girl holds her doll more securely, arranges the equipment of the baby carriage with more natural skill, than her mother had ever taught her or her siblings. What are the developmental hazards of that exquisite motherliness observed in little girls? We have enough opportunity to observe that the same girl who was such a talented little mother cannot or does not behave with similar tender competence with her own children. We can observe also that some women show more intuitive motherliness to children of others than to their own. Indeed, we cannot avoid realizing that motherliness, as it became a human attribute, had to be burdened by conflicts. One source of the conflicts lies in the psychosexual development of the personality, the other in the actual tasks of motherhood. For the human mother, the task surpasses the care of the infant.

MOTHERLINESS IN ACTION

"Nurturing" does not only mean giving nourishment, tenderly nursing or suckling the infant; the word according to the dictionary implies breeding, rearing, tutelage, training, moral training, even discipline. The whole range of the sociocultural role of motherhood is expressed in the word, the primary meaning of which is the psychobiologic function of motherhood. All the minute details of this far-reaching activity require choices and decisions. In making their decisions mothers are led by their motherliness and by their ego which, having developed from its congenital anlage and having been trained by environmental influences, is expected to direct the mothers' intuition toward "right" decisions. The ego in this function, however, might also be under the influence of affects and emotions which distort the meaning of motherliness, for the function of this unconsciously functioning faculty lies in the facilitation of a sedulous and adept responsiveness to the child's physical and emotional needs. In this context the term *need* refers not only to drive-motivated, immediate necessities but also to the requirements of the child's personality development. Mothers, however, may be victims of emotions which

157

motivate behavioral responses that do not serve that purpose and fail, particularly in the distant goals of mothering.

This brings us to the problems of motherliness in action, and there are many. Motherliness in action receives its direction from the mother's empathic reaction to the child's needs. But just as "love is not enough" [2], empathy by itself is not enough either. It can be too much or too little; it can also give false advice originating in the mother's neurotic needs and distorted ideas about child-rearing. Therefore the mother's empathy has to be confronted, most often by her own intuitive primary process thinking, but sometimes by careful evaluation, not only with the immediate need and situation but also with the developmental tasks and goals of that growing child. Thus the choices that mothers make begin early and probably never end. They have to change with age, maturation, and life situations but they do not end so long as the mother is in active interaction with her child. Therefore I chose to speak here not about mothering behavior, which is the primary manifestation of motherliness, but of motherliness in action. The former is to a high degree determined by the physiologic processes of lactation—or nursing by bottle-feeding—and has been discussed in previous chapters. Early mothering behavior to a high degree is influenced by culture and by modes and leaves the mother's personality fewer choices than the later processes of nurturing. While a serious pathologic condition of the mother in relation to motherhood becomes obvious in the postpartum period and infancy, the neurotic patterns of motherliness become more manifest later. Since these choices depend on many conditions of the individual mother—her growing child, the socioeconomic situation, cultural influences, and personal aims—they hardly can be generalized. Therefore, I take the primary task of mothering, i.e., nursing the infant, to illustrate some problems which influence motherliness in action.

The modes of infant feeding have undergone almost revolutionary changes in Western civilization. This began around the turn of the century when an Austrian pediatrician [3] described the harmfulness of unrestricted breast-feeding. Until then the natural nursing technique was—and under primitive conditions still is—to nurse the baby any time it seemed hungry. Babies lying in bed at the mother's side could take one or more swallows from the breast without waking and awakening their usually tired mothers. No doubt, this procedure, while it caused eczema and constipation and also might have caused rickets (rachitis) by one-sided overfeeding, helped to maintain the biologic symbiosis almost until the infant was ready to walk away from it. The strict recommendation that babies be fed only every 4 hours and not more than five times in 24 hours overcame the Western world. In the United States, Watson [10] added fuel to the fire by frightening mothers with the dangers of "spoiling the child." Aldrich [1], a pediatrician, and Ribble [9], a psychoanalyst, recognized the psychologic dangers of such child-rearing practices, and they fought for the "right of the infant." The infant's frustrations were sometimes remedied either by the doctors' recommendations and/or many more times by the instinctual (intuitive) behavior of the mother, who fed the baby rather than let the hungry child cry, who picked up the crying infant and even rocked him (horribile dictu) rather than let him lie for hours without attention. But what had been done naturally was now followed by remorse, by the mother's fear that she might have harmed her child.

Pediatricians tried to find a compromise and the stiff Czerny regime became "demand feeding," a recommendation to feed the normal infant when he was hungry, thus relaxing the rigidity of the hospital schedule. There are many mothers who can easily get their demand-fed baby on a regular schedule. Most infants have an inborn ability to regulate their feeding-sleeping schedule. But the natural rhythm of the infant may be easily upset if the mother, in her anxious eagerness, responds to any sign of the infant's discomfort with an attempt to feed him lest he go hungry. Thus anxious mothers have restless babies, and restless babies increase their mothers' insecurity. Consequently, the feeding difficulty may spiral and upset the normal course of the emotional symbiosis.

The insecurity of the mother interferes with the effective functioning of her motherliness, since this requires that she trust her empathy; this, in turn, is an effect of her self-confidence. Empathy and confidence in the judgment based on empathic understanding are prerequisite for educators, be they mothers or teachers, on any level. This needs further qualification, especially for mothers. Self-confidence has to be accessible to intuitive awareness of its effect on the child in order to achieve the desirable result, which sometimes requires modification in the mother's attitude and/or behavior. The difficulties of

159

young mothers are often caused by oscillations between insecurity and overcompensatory self-confidence. Here we can hardly avoid thinking of the overly self-confident mother. Such self-confidence, if it has served as a defense against insecurity, against the fear of being wrong, distorts the mother's empathy for the child. Such an attitude also may be in undisturbed balance with a thriving infant and therefore gain in intensity with the gratifications of mothering, yet it tends to isolate the mother from the child later when his individuation expresses his growing tendency for independence, for separation from his mother.

The negative influence of mothers upon the development of their children has been investigated in its various manifestations as effects of the mother's ambivalence and aggression that submerges motherly love. Here I want to view it as a derivative of the mother's separation anxiety. The mastery of this anxiety, its neutralization to the level of signal anxiety [4], is the result of the total personality development that expresses itself in the mother's ability to "separate" from the child on a psychobiologic level but to maintain motherliness as a positive attribute in the service of the child's development.

Psychiatrists and, even more often, social workers have to deal with women for whom the physiologic gratification of pregnancy and mothering remains an everlasting temptation, who enjoy pregnancy, lactation, and caring for the infant as long as he is completely dependent. They neglect each child as they become pregnant with the next. As if the procreative function of such women were completely under physiologic control, they are unable (seemingly unwilling) to maintain object relationship beyond infancy, and often abandon their children since they cannot cope with responsibilities to growing individuals. Their personality organization is immature; their ego is weak. Yet they seem not to have separation anxiety; actually, they do not have object relationship, in the human sense, with their children. These seriously pathologic individuals, whatever diagnostic label might be attached to them, can be considered to have been arrested in their development before they could integrate the image of good-normal-mother–"good-motherly-self" in their personalities.

But not all women who do not cathect their infants with the intensity of emotions that we consider normal in our culture abandon their children. Some who are considered apathetic mothers have ego strength enough to protect themselves against the shame and guilt of

160

such action by using the emotional distance as partial separation, separation not only from the children but from their own destructive impulses [8]. Although careless mothers and sloppy housekeepers, they often train the oldest child to take care of the younger siblings, especially if she is a daughter and even if she is only 5 or 6 years old. Thus they avoid making decisions and choices in behalf of their children after they have outgrown infancy.

It would be a mistake, however, to forget the anthropologic, socioeconomic facts, the different family structures which, keeping women at home with their children, afford mothers time (not necessarily leisure) to live in symbiotic relationship with their children until the normal, developmental separation of the child. The behavior of such mothers is efficient, calm, and goal-directed, tender but rarely demonstratively affectionate. They are adequately responsive to any event in the child's life, be it threatening to his health and security or to the progress in his life. In the same way they further and participate in his success and happiness. This is common-sense knowledge that I wanted to explain by discussing the psychology of motherliness, indicating also that motherliness may also lead to pathology if the ego's weakness impedes the mother's ability to overcome the symbiotic phase of her motherliness.

CONFLICTS OF MOTHERLINESS

The development of the ego, so intensely influenced by the cultural milieu of the individual, harbors the conflicts of motherliness. In simple societies the biologic and ego aspirations of women are easily integrated into their ego ideals. In our culture women in the course of their psychophysiologic development toward motherhood incorporate also an active, extraverted, "masculine" ego ideal. This may conflict with the passive tendencies inherent in the propagative function. Consequently, many women cannot permit themselves the regression that lactation and the bodily care of an infant imply. The often anxious distance from the infant depletes their source of motherliness. Such women often respond with guilt and with a sense of frustration because of their inability to live up to their biologic function of mothering with natural, intuitive ease.

The conflict between the biologic and cultural ego aspirations

161

would probably suffice to explain the mother's reactive ego operations. Psychoanalysis reveals that as mothers relive with their children memory traces of their own childhood, they act upon the motivations of those drive components that have become integrated in their personalities as character trends. In this sense we describe and might categorize mothers as *overindulgent, oversolicitous, overprotective,* and/or *perfectionistic.* Analyzing the mother's behavior as a symptom, we find that the counterphobic behavior serves to avoid separation from the child, to prolong the emotional symbiosis beyond what his development would require. Whether we analyze the behavior of overindulgent, oversolicitous, overprotective, even of perfectionistic mothers, each of these variations serves the same goal, i.e., to undo the harm, to alleviate the guilt which the sensation of alienation from the infant has activated. The feeling of alienation might be fleeting and forgotten by the fortunate woman whose love for the child wells up when she hears the first cry of the newborn, when she first has the baby in her arms, investigates his face and feels relieved from fears and happy.

From the time of conception the fetus has stimulated the receptive tendencies of the mother; after parturition, the infant by the very fact of his existence represents the most significant fulfillment of the mother's receptive needs. With her baby the mother feels whole, complete, but not without him. Many young mothers, especially in the first half-year after delivery, feel an emptiness when they leave the child even for a short while; often they become anxious about the infant and feel compelled to overeat. This indicates an increased tension of their receptive needs. The affect hunger of the mother, her need for love and affection, her wish to reunite with her baby, to overprotect and overpossess him are all exaggerated manifestations of the very emotions which originate in the psychobiologic processes of motherhood. The intensity of these emotions indicates the meaning of the separation trauma of parturition for the mother. As if the separation could be undone, mothering and each loving sensation for the infant are fused with a need "to incorporate the child," "to eat him up," to hold on to him. As the mother clings to her child, he becomes, at least partially, the needed, loved, and hated object of her own past, and with it also the representation of the loved and hated self.

Normally, the intensity of these manifest emotions diminishes. As it energizes the activities of mothering, it becomes absorbed (sublimated) in the reservoir of motherliness. As the postpartum emotional symbiosis evolves, parallel with the integration of her motherliness, the mother goes through a process of "individuation." Becoming secure in her ability to care for and love her child, the mother regains a sense of herself free from the reproductive cycle just experienced. Because of such biologically prepared distancing from the child, her motherliness can function normally, i.e., in the direction of making the right choice for the sake of the child, even as the infant through his own individuation requires decisions which with time become more and more remote from the biologic sources of motherliness.

It is different with those mothers whose personality organization harbors intensely charged separation anxiety. Reactivated by motherhood, the psychic energy necessary to repress the anxiety mobilizes emotions, attitudes, and behavior that create the illusion that separation can be delayed or even avoided. Psychoanalysis might then reveal and distinguish factors which determine whether they will fall into the group of oversolicitous or overprotective mothers who, with zealous vigilance, watch over the child's welfare and, with (almost) hypochondriacal anxiety, try to protect him against any possible harm. The dominant motivation of such mothers might originate in the compelling need (wish) to supply the child with more of what they did not have enough of; or it might be that the mothers, by too much attention, by love and care given to them in a way that crippled their independence, now cannot be different from their own mothers. Whatever their case history may be, oversolicitous and overprotective mothers struggle with their power of giving against the fear of their child's separating from them, hating them as they unconsciously hated their mothers. The evolving interaction between mother and child is pathogenic. The child, affected by the incorporative need of the mother which does not allow his self-differentiation, responds to his own impulses toward independence, as his mother does, as if it meant separation, deprivation of love and protection. The manifestations of the ambivalently charged symbiosis, while they inhibit the normal development of the child, become pathogenic for the mother also, since, as time passes, she experiences her own failure in the child with remorse and anxiety. There are situations in which such a dark prognosis proves to be wrong. Rare as they are, they are encouraging. There are fathers who are able to counteract the influence of these overanxious mothers. There are situations in which the husband's love for the

163

wife and for the child is enough and is expressed in such a way that the father does not alienate the child from the mother but helps them both. Mothers are often helped by the reassuring development of their children. There are also children who are endowed with such ability to love, and with such strength in pursuing their individuation, that they "cure" their mothers, at least as long as everything is going well.

The overindulgent and perfectionistic mothers can be easily separated from the former group. Oversolicitous and overprotective mothers usually are anxious, often feel helpless, feel that they don't do enough; they hold themselves in low esteem. The overindulgent and perfectionistic mothers are narcissistic personalities, although the metapsychology of their narcissism and also its behavioral manifestations toward their children differ. Mothers might be overindulgent because their narcissistic identification with the child does not allow them to see any fault in the child; they cannot apply control because they do not permit themselves to see where and when discipline is necessary, or they do not apply it even if they are aware of its necessity. The child reigns supreme, often at the cost of the masochistic mother. The perfectionistic mothers' narcissism requires the opposite behavior. Convinced of their own perfection or the perfection of the ideal in whose image they want to model the child, they concentrate on raising the child to perfection. For the sake of achieving this aim, these mothers are vigorously controlling and consistently, often compulsively, punitive.

It is obvious that such powerful emotions embedded in the neurotic personality of the mother affect her empathic responsiveness to the child's needs. Since mothers rationalize their behavior from the point of view of their neurotic need, they rarely can have insight into its meaning and influence upon the child before the child is more or less seriously affected by it.

The psychopathology which evolves in the child has been described in innumerable case histories, although not systematized. Such systematization probably cannot be approached, since there are many factors—innate and environmental influences—which may be responsible for the pathologic effect or for its amelioration and cure (see Chap. 19). It would be unfair to mothers in general, and would detract from the significance of the function of motherliness in the organization of the psychosexual personality of women, if this discussion did not refer again and summarize what has been previously discussed (Chap. 4 and above). Motherliness is a quality resulting from the psychobiologic organization of the individual. When actual motherhood or motherly tasks activate its functioning, it becomes instrumental in the development of the child and of the mother. As motherliness facilitates the normal symbiotic processes between mother and child, it supplies the matrix for the healthy development of the child; at the same time, as it enables the mother to encompass the growing child in her own personality, it also prepares her for the individuation of her child and for his separation from her. Even the normal maturation of the child represents, in every phase, a new adaptive task to parents. The character trends and personalities of the parents, of both father and mother, are in continual transaction with their growing and maturing children. The elaboration of these problems will be found in Chapter 8.

Bibliography

1. Aldrich, C. A. *Babies Are Human Beings.* New York: Macmillan, 1944.
2. Bettelheim, B. *Love Is Not Enough.* Chicago: University of Chicago Press, 1950.
3. Czerny, A. *Der Arzt als Erzieher des Kindes* (5th ed.). Leipzig and Vienna: Deuticke, 1919.
4. Freud, S. Inhibitions, Symptoms and Anxiety. In J. Strachey (Ed.), *The Standard Edition of the Complete Psychological Works of Sigmund Freud,* Vol. 20. London: Hogarth, 1959.
5. Harlow, H. R. Primary affectional patterns in primates. *Amer. J. Orthopsychiat.* 30:676–684, 1960.
6. Kestenberg, J. S. On the development of maternal feelings in early childhood. *Psychoanal. Stud. Child* 11:257–291, 1956.
7. Kestenberg, J. S. Vicissitudes of female sexuality. *J. Amer. Psychoanal. Ass.* 4:453–476, 1956.
8. Rheingold, J. C. *The Fear of Being a Woman.* New York: Grune & Stratton, 1964.
9. Ribble, M. *The Right of Infants.* New York: Columbia University Press, 1943.
10. Watson, J. B. *The Psychological Care of Infant and Child.* London: Allen & Unwin, 1928.

7

Fatherhood
and Providing

Therese Benedek

T he child is father to the man" [8]. The psychoanalytic theory
of personality development illuminates this poetic statement (now a
proverb) by conceptualizing the processes by which the child develops, reaches the level of "genital primacy," and becomes able to beget
his child. But what does it say about the man as father of the child?
The psychobiology of fatherhood seems to have evaded investigation
as if it were hidden by the physiology of male sexuality and by the
socioeconomic functions of fathers as providers. While biology defines
the role which the male invariably plays in the propagation of the
species, the role of fathers as providers changes with cultural and so-
cioecologic conditions. Nevertheless, the latter seems to be taken almost as much for granted as the former. Surprising as this might appear, it becomes understandable, since the socioeconomic function of
providing as well as the characterologic quality of fatherliness are derivatives of the instinct for survival. Indeed, the functions which
represent fatherhood, fatherliness, and providing are parallel to motherhood, motherliness, and nurturing. Fatherhood and motherhood are
complementary processes which evolve within the culturally established family structure to safeguard the physical and emotional development of the child. The role of the father within his family and his
relationship with his children appear to be further removed from instinctual roots than those of the mother. It is the burden of this chapter to offer observations in support of the hypothesis that fatherhood,
i.e., the human male's role in procreation, has instinctual roots be-

yond the drive organization of mating behavior to include his function as provider and to develop the ties of fatherliness that make his relationship with his children a mutual developmental experience.

Observations of patients who grew up in the patriarchal, pseudopuritanical family organization of the late nineteenth-century Vienna and the unique experience of his self-analysis supplied the data which Freud conceptualized in his "first instinct theory" (1905) [4]. In this he differentiated the "sexual instincts" that are in the service of propagation of the species from the "instinct of self-preservation" (ego instinct) and concluded that the psychic derivatives of these instincts, as well as their behavioral manifestations, are of necessity in conflict with each other. The adaptive processes, compelled from within by instinctual conflicts and from without by the environment, cause modifications of instincts as well as developmental changes in the "psychic apparatus" thus bringing about the human personality with its individual variations.

In his paper Instincts and Their Vicissitudes (1915) [5], Freud dealt with the modifications of instincts. In elaborating instincts Freud laid the foundation of a psychodynamic theory of drives. What appears as a semantic confusion was caused by the fact that the German language has one word for both concepts; the word *Trieb* might refer to instincts and also to drives, yet the two concepts refer to different kinds of biologic phenomena. In terms of evolutionary biology, instincts can be defined as primary organizers in the service of natural selection leading to evolution of structures and functions that secure the survival of the species. Drives, in contrast, are energy structures which, by responding to needs, activate physiologic processes in the appropriate organ systems to eliminate the need and thus secure survival. Needs are signs of disequilibrium in the homeostatic and hormostatic systems caused by interacting internal and environmental conditions perceived by the mental apparatus. The qualitative and quantitative aspects of needs and the corresponding intensity of drives can be subjectively experienced. Thus drives, their manifestations as needs, their gratification and frustrations, as well as the ensuing psychologic responses, are subject matters of psychoanalytic investigation; instincts, however, as philogenetic organizers are not accessible to experience; their purposive function is deducible from the drive-motivated behavior.

168

Ethologists in recent decades investigating behavior in a great variety of animal species have differentiated a hierarchy of instincts which, directed by immediate needs, organize behavior toward the "solution of the problem" in the service of survival. Recently Konrad Lorenz [6] investigated aggression as a manifestation of the instinct of survival. Robert Ardrey [1] has formulated the concept of "territorial instinct," under which he subsumes all other instinctual behavior necessary for the survival of the species. The territory is the base of security; it supplies food and water, safety for forming pair-bonds, mating and care for the offspring. It offers protection from animals of other species including the most dangerous—man. Animals from the most primitive organisms to man have developed instinctually organized systems of defenses, often referred to with the slogan "fight or flight."

The psychoanalytic study of the drive organization of parenthood [2] reveals the similarities and differences according to the role of the sexes in procreation. In contrast to the phasic organizer of the female propagative function, which is under the control of the cyclical changes of two ovarian hormones, the propagative function of the male is under the control of one group of gonadal hormones—androgens—and is discharged in a single act of cohabitation. Since paternity depends on one act, the motivation for which is experienced as a compelling desire for orgasmic discharge of sexual tension, one might ask the questions: Is there a genuine instinctual drive for fatherhood? Is fatherhood primarily a social accomplishment that takes advantage of the sexual need to induce man to shoulder the responsibilities for his offspring?

Such questions may have been justifiable some decades ago when one assumed that living in families, different as their structure might have been, is a specifically human privilege and burden. The extensive study of animal behavior in its natural habitat and/or under experimental conditions has offered a quantity of evidence for the existence of rudimentary and temporary "pair-bonds" cooperating in the care of the offspring. There are species, especially among fish, in which the male takes over completely the care even of the fertilized ova. Among birds and mammals the male participates according to an instinctually preformed pattern in the care of the offspring, providing food and security of the territory which is their home. These observations prove that providing food and security is not a culturally imposed burden on the male of the species but "nature's order." No doubt, this order is greatly disturbed by the ability of our species to control and, to a degree, even surpass nature's order.

The physiologic process of the heterosexual act has been described by Masters and Johnson [7] with exactitude without reference to its biologic aim of procreation. Since sexual physiology conceals the biologic tendency in men more than in women,[1] we have to search for signs and manifestations of psychodynamic tendencies which would reveal that in men, as in women, one can differentiate two goals of the reproductive drive: One becomes manifest in the wish to become a father, and the other in the ability to be one, being the provider in the human sense.

THE INSTINCTUAL DRIVE OF FATHERHOOD

Under conditions which impede the propagative function, such as the sterility of either of the marital partners or enforced separation, man's instinct for survival in his offspring becomes urgent and therefore accessible to psychoanalysis. World War II, which threatened the survival of millions of men, like a great experiment exposed the psychodynamic motivations of the wish to become a father. In our age of planned parenthood we had reason to be surprised by the increased birth rate during the war, since the external circumstances of war in our society would seem to interfere with the natural urge for parenthood. The father-to-be knew that he would not be able to help his wife during the pregnancy; he would not share her worries or her elation; he would not be able to see his baby, perhaps for months or years, if ever. Yet he was deeply happy in being able to go away with

---

[1] Since man's sexual apparatus (which includes the central and spinal nervous system) is extremely susceptible to external and internal stimulation, the sexual response in man appears to be more under the influence of psychologic mechanisms than under gonadal control, as if semen, continuously produced and collected in its receptacles, is but waiting for stimulation to be released. There is an obvious variation of frequency and intensity depending on virility and potency; there is great variation in preparatory actions and their fantasy-stimulated effectiveness. These, however, are determined in men, as in women, by individual development. In humans the pattern of preparatory actions is determined by the individual's psychosexual development and, unlike preparatory actions in subhuman species, undergoes changes in the same individual.

170

the feeling that his life would be continued, that he had created a tie which gave him a sense of obligation and, by this, an aspiration to life. Many men were aware of using the fact of survival in their child as a means of increasing the chances of surviving the war. Letters written by many soldiers have revealed repeatedly that fantasizing about their child or children helped them to overcome hardships and deprivations, and increased their resourcefulness in actual danger.

Psychoanalyses of several individuals have revealed that the threat of impending separation increased the individual's dependency upon all his significant relationships, especially upon his wife and his mother. The dependency needs are usually in conflict with the ego aspirations of young men; they would lose self-esteem were they to recognize their dependency, their regressive tendencies. Such conflicts increase a man's narcissistic defenses and make him vulnerable to individuals and situations which remind him of his conflicts. In his conscious desire for procreation, however, he overcomes his regressive trends through his virility. While he achieves gratification in heterosexual love, he reassures himself of his masculinity and elevates himself above his fears. When he pledges to his wife his willingness to take on responsibility, he creates in his child the representation of his maturity. When man fears that his survival is threatened, his desire for reproduction becomes a process of reparation, a means of overcoming anxiety.

The biologic root of fatherhood is in the instinctual drive for survival. Man's desire to survive in the child of his own sex is documented by rites, religions, customs, and socioeconomic organizations. Even in our civilization, so advanced in the equalization of the sexes, there are signs of an almost universal preference for a male child, rationalized by different motivations. Among these, society's higher evaluation of the male sex is kept in the foreground by men and women alike; yet this is actually secondary to the narcissistic motivation of parenthood in the male. Biologically, of course, it does not make any difference; men have to beget children of both sexes just as women have to bear and give birth to boys and girls alike. Yet as if parenthood were intended for the continuation of the self, fathers and mothers seem to have more direct gratification from a child of their own sex. This is more obvious in the attitudes of men. It is to no avail to try to deny the father's overflowing gratification in his newborn, especially if the first-born child is a son, or to minimize the emotional adjustment which is necessary if it is a daughter. Since his identification with his son is immediate, he can project into him the aspirations of his ego ideal, anticipating unconsciously his future self-realization in the son. The professed preference for a male child is only secondary in women. It might be, as is generally assumed by psychoanalysts, a fulfillment of the woman's unconscious desire for masculinity now accomplished through her child; it might be motivated by her desire to produce what is most valued by society and, therefore, represents success for her now and in the future; it is also in keeping with her love for her husband to wish to reproduce him, to give him what he values the most. Psychoanalysis of women reveals that no matter how intense the conscious desire for a son may be, in the deeper layers of the unconscious, there is the biologic tendency to reproduce herself in her daughter.

Of course, in men and women alike, the identification with the child of one's own sex is not, of necessity, free from conflict. It would lead us astray from the psychobiologic aspects of parenthood if we began to discuss the sources and motivations of conflicts which make fathers and mothers struggle within themselves against a deep-rooted ambivalence toward themselves. The projection of that hostility toward the child anticipated with anxiety may produce interference with parental love. Not infrequently the desire for children of the opposite sex is motivated by an intuitive awareness of the wish to avoid reexperiencing with the child the conflicts that were incorporated through the developmental interactions with the parent of the same sex.

Fatherhood is, however, not only a biologic fulfillment. It is also the means for further evolution of the parent's personality. One aspect of this process was indicated earlier in relevance to man's urge to conquer his regressive-dependent tendencies manifest under the threat of impending separation; the other can be subsumed as the male child's wish to become like his father. Competition with his father is recognized as an attribute of the male child from the time of his oedipal phase. This competition is the manifestation of the biologic tendency to develop masculine maturity. During the process of growth it passes through vicissitudes that leave their mark on the character. Sometimes it has to be repressed because of fear; at other times it can be exhibited with pride, with confidence in the father's pleasure in his son. With the act of reproduction the son not only asserts his biologic function, he also achieves the goal of the competition with his father; he has become a father. When he gives a child to his wife, he not only conquers his fears, but when he himself has become a link in the chain of generations between his father and his child, he has reached a further stage of development in his psychosexual maturity.

It is interesting to emphasize here the difference in the psychodynamic processes correlated with the reproductive function. In order to become a mother, women experience a biologic regression with each phase of their reproductive physiology. Men, in contrast, have to overcome their regressive tendencies to assert their virility in the heterosexual act and they have to integrate active, extraverted psychic potentials to fulfill the role of the father as protector and provider.

ORIGINS AND CONFLICTS OF FATHERLINESS

The emotional relationship of the father with his child or children has two sources of motivation: One is the father's identification with his child and the other the father's identification with his own father. In the frame of these identifications the emotional needs and gratifications of fatherhood can be easily understood. These two levels of identification normally complement each other and are integrated into the father's behavior toward the child. While one facilitates the father's empathy for the child, the other gives form to the culturally established norms for fathers raising their children. All this comes naturally to fathers and their children in slow-moving civilizations, in stable family structures. Fathers who were raised to tend the soil as their fathers did, who then raised their sons to follow in their footsteps, were probably not as often afraid of their sons' competitiveness, not even as downcast if they felt outgrown by them. Sons, on the other hand, who were content to live their lives as their forefathers did, did not need to struggle for their identity as they now do.

This nostalgic reference to past civilizations aims to emphasize the significance of the father's role in raising his children; his strength and dependability create the "father-image" which becomes a permanent axis of the child's development. But beneath the established role of a stable father, in spite of his maturity in the love for his wife and empathic hope for his children, there is a flow of repressed memories and emotions of the father's developmental experiences which may become mobilized in response to the child's development. There are preverbal memories integrated in the personality which are manifest in the father's parental attitude; there are memories proudly remembered and easy to talk about as encouraging examples for the children in keeping with the father's self-image which he wants to transplant in his sons. There are memories of conflicts and disappointments which are recalled with shame or guilt such as masturbation or enuresis. Just as it is normal for parents to enjoy the manifestations of the constructive aspects of their personalities in their children, it is also normal, in the sense of the psychodynamics of parent-child interaction, that fathers watch with anxious anticipation for signs which indicate that the child might have conflicts and develop problems similar to those they had to struggle against. In either case, the constructive as well as the pathognomic results of the parents' identifications with the child are more direct and effective with the child of their own sex.

Parental narcissism plays a primary role also in conveying delinquency from one generation to the other. Fathers who take pride in outwitting the police, defying the social order by criminal action, implant by normal psychodynamic processes the criminal tendency in their children. One might say that the child's normal ego is then criminal.

In spite of our emphasis on the repetition of the developmental processes through parenthood, we must point out the normal striving of young parents for differentiation from their own parents, not only in their goals for their children but also in their behavior toward them, no matter how often with questionable results. Fathers respond with shame and guilt when they find themselves acting toward their sons in anger exactly as their fathers acted toward them some decades before. One who realizes that his father might have felt the same remorseful devotion toward him as he feels now toward his child might take a step forward in resolving his conflict with his father; those who feel self-righteous in their anger toward the child are so because they cannot help retaining their bitter conflicts with their parents.

Since it is impossible to enumerate here the phase-determined variations of the father's influence upon the development of his child or the father's unconsciously motivated responses to his child's behavior, it should be emphasized that the tasks, the burdens and problems of fatherhood, become alleviated for the father as well as for his children by his *genuine fatherliness*.

What is genuine fatherliness? How does it come about? Fatherliness is an instinctually rooted character trend which enables the father to act toward his child or all children with immediate empathic responsiveness. Fatherliness is not rooted as directly as fatherhood itself in the instinct for survival in the child, yet it is derivative of the reproductive drive organization. Its sources can be traced to the biologic bisexuality and to the biologic dependency on the mother. Bisexuality enables individuals of both sexes to have empathy for each other and enables them to have empathy for their children of either sex. Individually, empathy develops through the experience of the primary dependency on the mother. Men too are borne and nursed by their mothers; each man's earliest security as well as his earliest orientation to his world were conveyed to him by his mother and were learned by him through identification with her. In the normal course of the development of the male child, the early emotional dependence upon and identification with the mother have to be overcome by developmental identifications with the father directed by the innate maleness of the boy. One area of developmental identifications with the father directs the processes of sexual maturation, the other the learning of the role of the father as protector and provider. These secondary manifestations of maleness are in continual transaction with those primary psychic representations which were established as a result of the oral dependent relationship with the mother. Therefore, the boy's development is often wrought with conflicts and anxieties, not only because of the fear of the father but also because our civilization expects men to repress and/or deny every manifestation of their emotional dependency which is considered contradictory to virility.

The boy's development toward sexual maturity, toward male identity, implies not only heterosexual maturity but also the acceptance of its consequence by becoming a father = protector-provider and the ability to fulfill these functions with the empathic quality of fatherliness. Fatherliness is the result not only of memory traces originating in the infant boy's oral, alimentary experiences with the mother, but these become integrated with memory traces of the boy's developmental experiences with his father. A tender, loving father reenforces the male child's acceptance of his own tender feelings; a rigidly strict and punitive father, activating in the boy these defensive qualities, compels him to repress his tenderness and thus inhibits the development of his fatherliness.

Fatherliness has many manifestations. It might begin with the

175

father's first smile at his infant. It expresses itself in the father's ability to hold an infant, to cradle it securely, or by practicing his fatherhood in giving the infant his bottle or diapering him, as is usual in our modern families. In the traditional patriarchal family the father became acquainted with his child only later. After the first smile at the newborn, the father's interest appeared superficial; fathers had little or no participation in the physical care of the infant; their participation began when the baby was old enough to require their attention actively. Then genuine fatherliness expressed itself in readiness to respond to the child, in patience and inventiveness in playing and holding the child's interest. In this way, fatherly fathers became active in promoting the normal ego development of the child. The fathers' inventiveness in playing with the child, mainly by finding a task that the child was able to solve, gave them the opportunity to become the teachers of the little child. They could sustain their relationship with the child by promoting his development by encouragement, by examples, by smiles of approval, by omitting an expected punishment, by sitting at the bedside when the child was too sick to play. The countless variations in the manifestations of fatherliness conveyed then, as today, to the child that sense of protectedness and security which remains the source of an enduring, warm, positive relationship between that child and his father. As the father-teacher becomes a model for the child, his fatherly attitudes become incorporated in the child's mind as a pattern to become a source and support for his fatherliness when he becomes a father himself.

The family is the relay station of the processes by which the effects of the shifts and changes in social structures are transmitted to the intrapsychic processes of individuals. Therefore, it is pertinent to recall here the influence that the father's changing position within his family exerts upon the personality development of his children, especially upon his sons. The repercussions of these changes upon the parents will be considered in Chapter 8.

THE CHANGING ROLE OF THE FATHER IN THE FAMILY

Most middle-aged or somewhat older Americans, and many of the younger ones as well, were raised in the puritan tradition of the patriarchal family. The emotional structure of such a family appeared to be unchangeably set. Its main representant, the father-husband, was assumed to be strong, active, providing for his wife and children not only a livelihood but also the means of emotional security. In return, his authority was not questioned; his own goals and aims were the goals and aims of his children. His wife, linked to her husband in a lasting marriage, derived her emotional security not only from her husband but, even more, from and through her children. Bearing them without questioning the laws of nature, she raised them in the security of their love, appreciation, and gratefulness to her. The children, in turn, accepted parental authority with devotion and with a sense of obligation (or, at least, they were expected to do so). Having incorporated firm ideals (one might say, rigid ideals) of parenthood, the same children when fully grown acted according to those ideals, i.e., they accepted their function of parenthood with the same hopes and expectations, with the same responsibilities and ideals as their own parents once did. The fatherliness of those fathers was not questioned and was not even required; as far as the contact with their children was concerned, they were disciplinarians, building strong superegos based, as Freud discovered, on the fear of the father and the ensuing castration complex.

With the change of the authoritarian family to an individualistic structure, education turned from a prohibitive to a permissive attitude toward sexuality from early childhood on. Since fatherliness now includes discerning tolerance toward the sexual strivings of children, it diminishes that emotional distance which formed the psychologic basis of the father's authority, especially in regard to the sons. No doubt this deeply influences the psychosexual development of the children of both sexes, but its effects are more directly intelligible in the sons. There are no psychoanalytic investigations which compare and comprehensively evaluate the factors which account for the differences in the personality organization from one generation to the other.[2] One of these factors is the effect of the diminishing castration fear which, although it is one of the causes of the diminishing authority of the father, in itself promises a more direct, mutually free communication between fathers and sons. Consequently, fathers can play a more fruitful, healthier role in the individuation of their sons than

[2] For example, there are innumerable references to the current frequency of "identity crisis" as a clinical diagnosis that hardly existed two decades ago. How the identity crisis of the adolescent might effect the parental generation is discussed in Chapter 14.

177

before when that relationship, muffled by the burden of castration fear, often brought about the variety of pathologic manifestations of superego development. Yet the positive effects of the more relaxed relationship between fathers and sons comes only rarely to full fruition since the socioeconomic situation of most families in our industrial civilization tends to alienate fathers from their families and modifies their roles as ego-builders.

Today the good father often takes over the role of his wife with his small children; as they grow, he tries to or actually does play with them, but his children rarely have an opportunity to work with him. Sons rarely can introject the image of the working father; they know about his work only in the abstract or in its consequence, since he brings home the money. How much more real, psychologically effective, is the son's identification with the working father in situations in which the father of necessity wants the son to be his helper [3], whether in mending a fence or delivering packages to his customers, especially when he can show the child that his help is needed and appreciated. Work is an ego-builder. It has a different meaning for the child when his father lets him help in washing the car or when the father helps the child to put together his electric train. Important as such communications are, they convey to the child more often the feeling that father is bending down, descending to his childish level and by this he stimulates his dependency rather than his growing up. But such common experiences also give a firmer foundation for the father-son relationship than an occasional common experience of watching a baseball game together, since father has neither time, interest, nor patience to do more with his growing son. The father's role as provider, which is his public function, and the intimate, private experience of his fatherliness are intricately interwoven. The socioeconomic conditions, by modifying the father's role as provider, change the manifestations of his fatherliness; they alter the experience of his fatherliness for himself and also for his children.

PSYCHOLOGIC CONSEQUENCES OF THE
FUNCTION OF PROVIDING

In all living organisms in which the survival of the species depends upon the interrelated instinctual functions of two sexes, it is the male's role to protect the territory, the nest, thus to provide some degree of security to the female during the time of her labor, and to supply her with food while she is tied to the nest by her litter. Even in predatory mammals such division of labor is recognizable. In animals such behavior impresses us as fatherly providing, just as the female's mothering behavior appears to be tender, unfailing motherliness. While in females, mothering behavior is regulated by a pituitary hormone, in males no hormonal regulation of the providing is recognizable. Yet this behavior in the male disappears when the particular reproductive cycle of the female is terminated—in human idiom one could say, when the father can expect the offspring to fend for themselves. Thus the correlations between male and female parental function are evidently biologic "givens."

The human father's role as a provider is a more distant derivative of the instinct of survival. It extends beyond the periods of particular reproductive cycles of his wife and, as far as his children are concerned, is expected to last until the children become able to earn their living. Through the permanence of the human family and its consequences in socioeconomic organizations, all significant cultures have developed on the basis that the husband-father is the chief protector and provider of the family. Repeated through uncounted generations, transferred from fathers to sons, man's role as provider has become relatively independent of its biologic roots. In our acquisitive civilization his ego aspirations are invested in his capacity to produce beyond the necessity of providing for his family. (This, of course, brings about material wealth not only for his family but also for his immediate or larger community.)

Man's self-esteem primarily derives from his sense of virility, but virility in the mature adult includes not only his sexual potency but also his productive and creative capacity. His ego-libido thus invested in his role as provider, his self-esteem, can be maintained by his ego aspirations alone. Often their goals are pursued with great intensity just for the sake of man's ego aggrandizement. As they become narcissistic goals, successful as they might be, they conflict with the psychobiologic aims of fatherliness; channeling his physical and emotional energies away from the primary emotional experiences with his family, his ambitions might alienate the father from his children and lead to an emotional impoverishment of the family.

179

Discussing the psychodynamic sources of distortion of mother-liness, we emphasized the mother's fear of separation from the child, i.e., a regressive tendency of clinging to the child, not because there would not be other pathologic states or because the need to cling could not be a reaction formation to the wish to be free of the child, but because the wish to be one with the child is the deeply rooted source of the wish to be a good mother. In contrast, what interferes with fatherliness, in general, is the extraverted activity, especially if pursued with an exaggerated ambition. This too is rooted in the primary requisite of a good, efficient father-husband and thus is a derivative of biologic sources. Yet if it is not balanced by emotional feedback from the wife and children, it leads to rigidity of the man's personality. On the other hand, the ambitious, one-sided preoccupation of the husband-father with his own work might make him unreceptive to emotional approaches from his wife and children. Disappointed in their frustrated efforts, they withdraw from him, offering him justification for his relentless pursuit of his ambition. The ensuing emotional and physical consequences endanger not only the coherence of the family but also his health.

Fatherliness, just as motherliness, has pathogenic manifestations motivated by different characteristics of the father. One of the manifestations of virility is a diffuse, not easily describable but clearly recognizable attribute of maleness termed *dominance*. In animals it is expressed in the total behavior and is effective in choosing and gaining females to mate and also in leadership, since dominance is acknowledged and respected by the other males and females of the herd. (How this reflects on the ego of the dominant male we do not know and we should not anthropomorphize.) In human males, while its frequency seems to be decreasing, its significance for the male ego is increasing. Since its manifestation is self-assurance, it supplies the male ego with an almost steady flow of libido, enhancing his narcissism from within and from without through his successful experiences with women and by achievements in his work. No doubt, those husband-fathers are admired by their wives and by their children.

How does this affect their fatherliness? One could assume that such men should have the happiest families and the happiest children. No doubt this happens, but not as often as one would wish or imagine. That such a father's ambitions might interfere with his fatherliness has already been mentioned. The other motivation of the modification of his fatherliness lies in his narcissism. Unbridled, this might be projected to the child—to the son for one reason and to the daughter for another; the child is expected to be born perfect and to grow up as a perfect specimen. The narcissistic father is perfectionistic and is extremely disappointed if his son does not have his qualities, even more and better. Whatever attributes his son has, if they are not what he appreciates the most, he depreciates them. As if it were not hard enough for the son who is aware that he cannot become like his admired father, he suffers also from the depreciation and neglect by his father. This effect on the son can be even more pathogenic if the father does not have the rich self-gratification of the successful, dominant male, so that he projects to the son not only his gratifications but also the anticipation of his frustrations. Even if the son fulfills the expectation, trouble between fathers and sons might arise from the father's competition with the son; he might withdraw in depression or in obvious anger from the successful son, by whom he feels defeated.

Narcissistic fathers, if they are somewhat less actively driving, might fall in the category of the overindulgent parent since they, like overindulgent mothers, love the child as an extension and future realization of their perfect self-image. Their disappointment might come later when the overindulged child reveals himself as the spoiled one who, since he has not internalized controls, cannot apply self-discipline. One knows also about overprotective and oversolicitous fathers in terms of their narcissistic identifications with their children. Their personality organization is, however, not as one-sidedly dominated by their drive for achievement. Not that these fathers would not be achievers and providers, but their fatherliness, motivated by the integrated positive experience of their infancy, can express itself freely, undisturbed by internal awareness or by social disapproval of femininity.

The innate bisexual anlage, however, exerts a pull on masculine personality organization that often causes serious pathologic states and may interfere with an ego organization that can support the multiple responsibilities of fatherhood. It is not within the scope of this chapter to discuss the great variety of exceptions from the normal biosociologic pattern. We know men often avoid marriage and parenthood, afraid of the responsibilities involved. There are fathers who

181

abandon wife and child; often such men become "bums" (vaga-bonds) only after they have failed completely as fathers. Their guilt and shame about their failure in the primary function of masculinity make them avoid civilization and life normally adjusted to it. There are fathers who, instead of being providers, become dependent and a burden on their wives and children because of the pathologic nature of their personalities. Among these, alcoholism is most frequent; it shows also most clearly the underlying regression to the oral phase of development and the depression which usually accompanies it. These vignettes of character structures which motivate the father's function as provider are, of course, superficial generalizations. They serve the purpose of indicating the wide span in which the personality functions to fulfill the emotional and socioeconomic tasks of paternity.

Just as there are crucial phases in motherhood, when the trans-actional processes between mother and child become charged with conflicting tensions, there are also crucial phases of fatherhood. Yet complete failures in fatherliness are, fortunately, relatively rare, al-though alienation between fathers and their children seems to be on the increase. But very often the crucial phases, just because they reach deep into the instinctual reservoir of the parent and the child, may bring up constructive factors in the interacting individuals and lead to reconciliation where previously there has been a rift. Illness or death in the family, or threatening divorce, often lead to reconciliation be-tween marital partners or between parents and children.

To conclude this discussion of the psychobiology of parenthood during the procreative phase, the basic difference between the sexes should be pointed out as revealed by the stresses of fatherhood in contrast with those of motherhood. The basic conflict of motherhood is inherent in the psychobiologic regression of pregnancy, and in the pains and dangers of parturition. The conflict itself does not involve society, the world around, directly. The basic conflict of fatherhood is not within the procreative function itself but in its derivative, in the father's function as provider. This has always required work of one kind or another. In modern, urban civilization, work includes ever greater segments of society and ever-increasing complexity of interde-pendence of extrafamilial contingencies. It depends on the many in-teracting factors in any man's personality that enable him to adapt to the stresses of the realities of his work, without decreasing the emotional interest which maintains his age-adequate, fatherly participation in the ever-changing emotional life of his family. Frustrations and disappointments, however, might originate not only in the work situation but also, and even more painfully, in the family. As the two main areas of man's world are continually interacting, they participate in enriching or impoverishing, maintaining or jeopardizing, his mental health. Because of this, the mental health of the adult male, and by this his fruitful fatherliness, are best guaranteed by a smoothly functioning interchange between primary libidinal gratification provided by his family, community, and friends, and by his secondary ego gratifications provided by his work achievements.

Bibliography

1. Ardrey, R.   *The Territorial Imperative.* New York: Atheneum, 1966.
2. Benedek, T.   The organization of the reproductive drive. *Int. J. Psychoanal.* 41:1–15, 1960.
3. Engel, M.   Children who work. Conference on normal behavior. *Arch. Gen. Psychiat.* (Chicago) 17:291–297, 1967.
4. Freud, S.   Three Essays on the Theory of Sexuality. In J. Strachey (Ed.), *The Standard Edition of the Complete Psychological Works of Sigmund Freud,* Vol. 7. London: Hogarth, 1953.
5. Freud, S.   Instincts and Their Vicissitudes. In J. Strachey (Ed.), *The Standard Edition of the Complete Psychological Works of Sigmund Freud,* Vol. 14. London: Hogarth, 1957.
6. Lorenz, K.   *On Aggression.* New York: Harcourt, Brace, 1966.
7. Masters, W. H., and Johnson, V. E.   *Human Sexual Response.* Boston: Little, Brown, 1966.
8. Wordsworth, W.   *The Poetical Works of Wordsworth.* (Edited by T. Hutchinson.) London: Oxford University Press, 1959.

8

Parenthood
During the
Life Cycle

Therese Benedek

Parenthood as a psychobiologic process ends only with the death of the parent. This statement, evocative as it is, might call for a second thought in the minds of many readers who in the foregoing chapters accepted parenthood as a developmental process and expect its reciprocal psychobiologic involvements to end with the maturation of the children. Such an assumption is a fallacy, however, probably based on the experience that children appear to outgrow their parents when they become parents themselves. The fact is that their parents just then begin to relive the memories of their early parenthood as these memories become revived by the parental behavior of their children and in the developmental responsiveness of their grandchildren. Even after that period, in their old age, parents cling to the status that parenthood gave them, since it helps them to maintain their self-esteem.

Thus parenthood, supplied by memories of past experiences, is timeless. Yet it is (like any living process) under the inescapable domination of time. Time means change and change requires adaptation. Concerning parenthood this implies continuous adaptation to physiologic and psychologic changes within the self of the parent, parallel to, and in transaction with, changes in the child and to his expanding world. To describe parenthood as a psychologic process throughout the life cycle appears to be an overwhelming task. To re-

185

duce it to dimensions manageable in this chapter, its crucial problems will be pointed out as they arise in critical periods of parenthood.

What are critical periods of parenthood? How and why should one differentiate *critical period* from *critical phase?* Critical phase, as it was defined to characterize the interactions of physiologic and psychologic processes during pregnancy, is a biologically motivated process of maturation which requires psychologic adaptation to achieve a new level of development. This definition can be applied to the postpartum period also. With some modification it can be attributed to all those transactional processes between parent and child which, motivated by the phasic libidinal development of the child, reactivate in the parent conflicts originating in that developmental phase of the parent. Transactional processes between parents and their children, however, in time become more and more distant from the primary physiologic and emotional processes of parenthood. Since significant emotional transactions between parents and children frequently occur at typical age levels and in psychologically characteristic situations throughout life, we refer to the combination of these factors as critical periods. They offer focal points for the orderly presentation of the material of this chapter.

On the basis of psychoanalytic theory and observation, those transactional processes can be conceptualized with relative ease in reference to infancy, when communication between parent and child is motivated by primary biologic needs. Paradoxically, communication becomes more complicated as it becomes verbal, when consciousness of its aims covers up its deeper, unconscious meaning. At first, when the child is just beginning to speak, it is pure pleasure for the parents to participate in his baby-talk, to observe the evolution of his language and enjoy how much more he knows than they expected. During the early years of verbal communication, parents respond to the spontaneous expressions of the child with a sense of gratification, since they experience him as a lucky extension of themselves. It is later, when the child's individuality emerges, forecasting its definite contours, that communication becomes less understandable by empathy. Then the child, harboring the images of both parents but motivated mainly by his non-yet-tamed drives, begins to reveal himself as an individual groping for and grasping at opportunities to exert himself as such.

186

Several chapters of this volume deal with the early phases of parenthood. They describe from different viewpoints motivations of parental attitudes from the birth of the child through his oedipal phase; they describe the parents' participation in the symbiotic needs of the infant, the parental response to the dependency of the child, and also the often-conflicting reactions to the child's individuation. But, except for the actually seductive pathogenic behavior of parents, very little has been written about the parents' participation in the development of the normal oedipal phase. This can be explained by the normal parents' reserved, even restrained, physical contact with the child at this age, by the tendency to hide, to forget, and actually repress libidinal impulses toward the child, even during the preoedipal phases of his development. Yet we know about the conflicts of many mothers who compulsively avoid looking at the penis of their little sons, who mistrust their own behavior, even just bathing their children; there are fathers who are so afraid of the slightest physical contact with their daughters that the little girl becomes afraid of the stranger, father. On the other side are those parents who under cultural influences assume that any control, especially sexual control, would be inhibiting the child's psychosexual development. This mistaken rationalization allows them to expose their children to undue sexual stimulation.[1] The personality development of their children is often described in case histories. The parents themselves, so free and unconcerned with their young children, often have to struggle with their own conflicts, with the psychologic consequences of their laxity during the later phases of their parenthood.

During the oedipal phase, with its normally diminishing physical intimacy, the parents' libidinal impulses toward the child decrease;

---

[1] In defending their behavior as advantageous to the development of their children, these parents often cite anthropologists who describe parental behavior in now-passing primitive societies, where children are not screened from the sexual life of their parents or from other adults. This is true, or has been true, in cultures where all families have or used to have, before wars and Western civilization reached them, the same customs, rites, and standards. In our culture, however, children raised by such sexual concepts still are exceptions, who, being raised differently in one respect, are expected to live up to the other standards of our culture in other aspects. Thus what the children of Samoa do not need to overcome but our children have to struggle with is a multiplicity of double standards, which creates conflicts and leads to serious distortions of the personality. (See Margaret Mead, *Growing Up in New Guinea* [7].)

they are also more strictly controlled. That which the parent prohibits to himself becomes incorporated in the child's psychic structure and forms the core of his superego. Thus we know more about the parent's role in the repression and resolution of the oedipus complex than we know about how parents are affected by this phase of the child's development [4]. Since, normally, the culturally sanctioned, prohibitive behavior of the parents reassures them about the correctness of their behavior, it helps them to repress their conflicts in this area. Yet the parents' strictly prohibitive behavior toward this phase of the child's development reflects not only the developmental past of the parents; it indicates also that they were unable to resolve that conflict through their adolescence and even through their apparently healthy sex life. Since the derivatives of the repressed oedipus complex demand more and more repressing energy, they forecast the possibility that those defenses might break down later in reaction to the sexual maturation and especially in connection with the marriages of their children. Thus the pathologic consequences caused by the transactional processes of the oedipal phase (aiming at sexual repression) become manifest often in the middle or old age of parents (see Chap. 15). One of the most complex tasks of sexual education is to achieve that maturity in parents which enables them to guide their children through the repression of their oedipal phase, a prerequisite of superego development, without embedding into their personality the neurotic derivatives of that complex.

EARLY PHASE OF PARENTHOOD

In discussing the manifestations of recurring psychologic conflicts during the life cycle of parents, it is helpful to consider parenthood as a process which has an early, a middle, and a late phase. It would seem less clumsy to speak of young, middle-aged, and old parents, yet this would not be quite correct, since young parents can be and often are persons who are middle-aged. Parenthood as an experience is more in focus during the period of *total parenthood*. This term of Kestenberg (see Chap. 13) refers to the parents' involvement with and responsibility for the child from his birth to school age. During this time parents have their children most completely as their own.[2]

[2] There are many exceptions to total parenthood even during infancy.

Interestingly, the beginning of school in Western civilization coincides with the age and maturational level to which Freud attributed the end of the oedipal phase. Before that age the child's developmental needs for expansion were under parental surveillance. After this period, the routine of school hours, the expanding environment of the classroom, diminish the parents' almost exclusive influence and control over the child up to that time. School, a socially required and regulated partial separation of parents and children, facilitates the repression of the oedipus complex; the steadily expanding ego of the child that encompasses gradually increasing sections of his environment slowly liberates him from the bonds of his dependence on his parents. Kestenberg states: "Latency stands out as a time of 'part-time parenthood' preparing parents for the state of 'childless parenthood' at the end of the child's adolescence." (See Chap. 13.)

Although Kestenberg means by this only the diminishing activities involved in child-rearing, it is fortunate that even such separation evolves slowly, since most families have more than one child and frequently at the time the first child leaves for college or for military service, there remains at home a child probably just entering grade school. Otherwise, such a childless parenthood might activate an even more serious reaction in parents to separation from their children than we usually observe.[3] I believe that describing parenthood according to its early, middle, and late phases will afford a better opportunity to organize the most frequent problems of parenthood as they change in time, keeping in focus the transactional processes between the generations.

The beginning of the early phase is easy to define, whether one puts it at the conception of the first child or at his birth. The end of

---

One just has to think of cultures in which mothers have many helpers within the kinship; of social and economic strata where maids, nurses, governesses have taken over the mother's duties; and nowadays when women, even young mothers, are working, leaving even their babies to the care of others.

[3] It would be worth investigating whether the current trend toward large families in our urban population practicing birth control is motivated by the fear of the empty nursery. Not having a baby or, at least, a preschool child at home means for many mothers being left empty-handed, or having to face the necessity of reorienting their lives toward activities outside the family. No matter how stimulatingly this author or others write about this aspect of middle-aged women's lives, it is difficult for many women, especially for those who preferred an early marriage to special training, to enter new activities and face competition [2, 5].

this phase, however, overlaps with the middle phase, especially in the parents of several children. The parents are total parents with each of their children, and live through the early phase of parenthood with each of them until and through various stretches of their adolescence. Keeping in mind the overlap between the early and middle phases of parenthood, one could say that the early phase of parenthood lasts until the youngest child reaches adolescence. This, of course, does not exclude the fact that parents are in their middle phase regarding their older children, who at that time have already married and have become parents themselves. Thus, being a young grandparent can coincide and interact in various ways with the early phase of parenthood with their younger children.

Yet parents always hold on to the incorporated psychic images of their children as separate individuals. They may compare their children directly in their presence or among each other; they may admit, mostly however to themselves only, that they love one child more, that they find another more gratifying, but—unless a serious pathologic state causes changes in the parents—they do not confuse, do not blend the mental images of their children. They remain distinct entities although continually changing with time, but unless the parents' mental health fails, the process that integrates past and present never ceases; the child is never alien, never a stranger. Just the opposite, parents love to add new experiences of their children to the past to embellish the present and bring closer to reality that early image of the hopeful ideal that was projected to the child during his early infancy. Pathologic conditions arise, either in the parent or in the child or in both, when parents hold on to the early images and expectations with a tenacity that does not allow change, that does not recognize the broad range of normal variations occurring with maturation and refuses adjustments which become necessary if the child does not turn out as the parents hoped.

It is the *latency period* when school intrudes upon the intrafamilial triangle of father–mother–child and tests the parent's capacity to share their influence and, by this, help the child to adapt to the requirements of extrafamilial environments. Normally, parents welcome the school age of the child; they participate in his pleasure and try to alleviate his anxiety connected with his new experiences. The marked separation anxiety of some mothers, their overconcern about their children while they are in school, is justifiably considered a manifestation of conflicts that are often responsible for the school phobias of children. Also the parents' fear of and consequent resistance against the authority of the school are symptoms that originate in the personality problems of the parents and may bring about the children's rebellion and maladaptation to school. Parents with such problems have not achieved that intrapsychic separation from the child which is necessary for the child's maturation to function well in his age-graded role. Parents remaining so involved with their child maintain on the level of latency and adolescence the transactional processes by which they achieve what they are afraid of, since the child who is troublesome in school often gives cause for worry and embarrassment to the parents later on.

The question arises, what are the psychologic factors that characterize parenthood in correlation with the period of latency and adolescence of their children? Attempting to answer this question we realize that it is easier to conceptualize the interpersonal dynamics between parent and child during the early developmental phases of the child than later on. Yet the answer is probably simple, at least, in general terms. During the preoedipal and oedipal phases, the evolution of the dominant libidinal conflicts and the corresponding ego growth are brought about by the physiologic processes of maturation. Although they activate unconsciously motivated characteristic responses in the parent, they pass quickly, giving way to other reactions to the newly arising developmental trends in the child. Parents, secure in their love for the child, rarely feel involved in or responsible for his passing problems, since all that happens seems to be open to the empathic understanding of the parent and therefore responded to with the feeling that it is natural and the child will outgrow it.

With school age this security becomes troubled by apprehensions. School means to the parent that their child's behavior, his performance at work and in play, will be exposed to a comparative scrutiny and by this the parents themselves feel exposed. (See Chap. 13.) Although they are less total parents in one sense, they feel more identified with the child in another sense. In order to diminish the disconcerting feeling of responsibility, parents, especially in our urban communities, eagerly watch the various sources of extrafamilial influences to which their children are exposed and their vigilance is often biased by prejudices and preconceived ideas. Playmates and neighbors attain a significance they did not have before; television programs, on the other hand, are considered welcome entertainment since, while it keeps the child busy at home, its influence upon the child—good or bad—usually cannot be assessed by the parents. Yet parents watch with concern that their children are growing up faster, that they know more than we did at that age. It seems that parents in the early phase of their parenthood very often would like to slow down the tempo of that externalization that characterizes the growth of the latency period. In this respect, again, parents can only rarely avoid their ambivalence. On one hand, they would like to hang on to the past, when they felt they knew everything about the child; on the other, they cannot help but participate in the comparative scrutiny of their children. In this respect they may exert a harmful influence, since their scrutiny is often contaminated by their underlying ambition, i.e., that their children should be the best or, at least, should perform on every level with adequate competence. Yet the pursuit of even such normal parental endeavor by the modern parent is undermined by apprehensions. Consciously striving to raise independent, self-secure, and efficient individuals, they refrain from applying controls lest their child become inhibited, from punishment lest their children grow up to hate them.

These are commonplace examples of problems of parenthood during latency. They are cited to illustrate that in this period of development and in subsequent periods, the parents' empathic, affective, and goal-directed responses are not evoked by the manifestations of relatively well-defined libidinal phases, but by the evolving complex personality organization of the maturing individual. Correspondingly, the parents' response to this pressure, whether it is intuitive, dictated by common sense, or is an expression of elaborate educational principles, is the result of a many-faceted, intrapsychic experience. The parents' response is a derivative of their developmental past integrated with experiences of interactions with a given child. Whereas regarding young children the parents' developmental past refers prevalently to unconscious processes, in response to latency children and adolescents, parents remember their own behavior and its consequences. Thus conscientious parents' emotional responses to the problems of their children of that age are motivated by reaction-formations to the actual or psychologic consequences of their own experiences. This

192

conceptualization of parental decision-making can be illustrated by many kinds of situations. Regarding the topic of this chapter, however, mainly the parents' unconscious and manifest reactions to the sexual development and behavior of their children are pertinent. This is the thread which, beginning with parenthood, winds its way through the middle phase of parenthood, links the generations in grandparenthood, and leads to the desexualized, childless parenthood of old age.

This prompts us to return once more to the oedipus complex ". . . that has apical importance not only as much as the nucleus of neuroses, but as the nucleus of normal character structure" [6]. Just as its vicissitudes formed the personality of the parents and motivated their life experiences, when they are confronted with the sexual behavior of their maturing children, their responses to them are motivated by the derivatives of the oedipus complex and by the memories of actual experience. These form the basis of their identifications with and differentiations from the child and his particular problem. Such intrapsychic processes then motivate parents to promote, even indulge, the wishes of their adolescent children in instances of identification with them, or to dissuade them from pursuing their desires, not abstaining from threats and punishments.

PARENTAL REACTIONS TO THE SEXUALITY OF THEIR CHILDREN

It seems that parents nowadays are not too disturbed by noticing that a young child is playing with his genitals. The father who threatens a 3-year-old that he will "cut it off," although not extinct, is becoming rare. During the boy's latency, fathers usually are more concerned with the manifestations of his athletic abilities, of his general manliness than with his sexual behavior. Toward their daughters they are normally defensive; i.e., they suppress their libidinal interest and consequently assume that girls are blissfully innocent, not troubled by sex. Mothers are different. Being more aware of their defensiveness against their sexual impulses, they often become suspicious when children, even of the same sex, play together behind closed doors and are too quiet. They are intent on protecting their children, their daughters more than their sons, against the dangers of sexuality, yet they often feel helpless. This mood takes hold more often of those mothers who are aware of their conflicting tendencies regarding the experiences of their children. Their worries begin at the time when the period of dating comes along and rarely cease until the child, whether daughter or son, lands safely in marriage.

In order to generalize about these problems of motherhood, it is practical to group our observations in reference to women who feel positively about their femininity and enjoy sexuality, and to those who basically deny the gratifications of woman's life and are resistant against sexuality. Women belonging in the first group, especially as long as they are in the fullness of their sexual life, usually trust their children, since they trust themselves and their own experiences. In their intuitive confidence in the power of their own personalities, they feel that they have conveyed to their children their own value systems and what is within that is anticipated without anxiety. Nowadays even such mothers are sometimes shocked by disappointment. Self-confident parents have such an intrinsic need to trust their children, to assume that, "what should not happen cannot happen," that nothing seems easier than to pull the wool over the eyes of trusting parents. Children in puberty hide their sexual impulses and behavior because of the fear and guilt generated by it; for this reason, they do not trust their parents. Adolescents who have come to terms with their sexuality, because of their intense drive for independence, see in "trusting" the parent a submission, a manifestation of their own weakness. They confide in them only in extreme need. Therefore, even trusting parents often are left in the dark about the most important experiences of their children. On the other hand, parents who, because of neurotic reasons, cannot bear their children's secretiveness do not gain their trust either.

Mothers whose behavior toward their children is characterized by intrusive vigilance belong usually in our second group. Women having little or no confidence in their femininity usually succeed in conveying their insecurity to their children. When the period of dating comes along, they are frightened by the results of their competitive scrutiny. They realize that their daughters are not popular, their sons do not date. Correspondingly, they relive their own adolescence with pangs of waiting, of being left out, alone. They project their own urgency for their children's happiness, for their success, at least for having a good time, to them, and by disguising the fact that they suffer

194

from the inferiority feelings of their children, these mothers begin to push their adolescent children; they advise and scheme in order to help them out from what parents feel to be an impasse, a failure. It is not surprising that the emotional tension of mothers, their concentration upon the children's chances for marriage, increase as the mothers approach menopause. Painfully aware of the well-meant but unbearable influence, daughters try to escape it; sometimes working away from home or going to college brings relief to both and often leads to the emancipation of the daughter by allowing her new experiences away from the watchful eyes at home.

Fathers' neuroses express themselves very differently. They are usually tolerant of the lack of popularity of their daughters. The more usual complaint of daughters about their fathers is that they scrutinize the boys too closely, too frankly, and/or often make fun of them in their presence, not to mention those fathers who become offensive toward the young men and often try, all too successfully, to scare them away.

Different as their responses may be, when it comes to going out, father and mother together watch the clock for their daughter's return, hoping that in some not far-distant part of the city the young man's parents are just as intensively concerned. His mother might be, but his father is probably sleeping, totally unconcerned. While fathers watch with Argus eyes over the virginity of their daughters, they instinctively have a double standard. Unconsciously identifying with their son's experience, they readily smile at the young girl with whom the son is in love as long as everything is proper. For fathers, traditionally, propriety ends when the son comes home downhearted to announce that the girl is pregnant.

THE MIDDLE PHASE OF PARENTHOOD

Not only adolescents but also their parents pass a crossroad in their development when the sexual maturation of the child introduces the middle phase of their parenthood. The variations of individual experiences of the middle phase of parenthood may be innumerable, but the main characteristic is the parent's involvement in and preoccupation with their children's sexual life. Whether this be the traditional courtship under the watchful eyes of the parents or the now more frequent series of boyfriends and love affairs leading to consecutive promiscuity before marriage, all are intended to culminate in marriage. Whether the parents' marriage is happy, just tolerable, or a cauldron of explosive emotions, no matter how deeply these intramarital struggles influence their children and cast a shadow over their future marriages, the past is forgotten and the future appears rosy in the light of a new marriage. Except when differences in race, religion, and social status threaten the traditions of the families, both sets of parents unite their children in the hope that they will live happily ever after.

With a child's marriage, the immediate responsibility of parenthood for that child is discontinued. The parents cease to be closest of kin by law, since the new husband and wife, even if they have known each other for only a few weeks or months, have become the next of kin. Their own parents, having lived with them through the early and the middle phases of their parenthood, enter a new, last phase of parenthood. They are not, however, old people yet; they might still be living in the unity of early parenthood with their younger children.

In cultures where the young wife customarily has to live in the home of the husband, usually in his parental home, the marriage of a daughter represents an almost complete separation between mother and daughter. In such cases, the young wife's mother has neither the right nor the opportunity to remain involved with her daughter by helping her to adjust to her new way of life. In our civilization, formerly, it was not uncommon that both sets of parents of a young married couple lived close to each other—were neighbors or friends by trade or profession—and that the young people had probably known each other from childhood on. Marriage under such conditions did not entail such a sharp separation from the old, did not require a difficult adjustment to a new situation. It is different in our current mode of living when neither social nor geographic boundaries are as confining as they used to be. Thus the marriage of a daughter or of a son now might imply a more actual separation of parents from their children than it did formerly, thus bringing about a critical period in the parents' lives.

The parents have a new developmental task to accomplish; they have to encompass the husband of their daughter or the wife of their son, not only in their own family but also in their own psychic systems as an object of their love. The process by which this is accomplished is the identification with their own child. But the object relationship to the in-law remains shaky for some time. The underlying ambivalence flares up any time there is reason (or even if there is none) to be concerned about the happiness of their own child. In this respect, now, just as at the time the child first went to school, parental narcissism is at work and the fault is seen in the other rather than in one's own child, with whom one usually identifies.

Intrafamilial conflicts can be easily conceptualized in terms of the parents' ability to separate from their married child, objectify their parental relationship, and thus become able to be more objective and less ambivalent toward the in-law. This is not achieved as easily as it can be prescribed. The beginning relationship can be well compared to an armed truce watched by both parties. The young husband and wife, although they quickly learn to call their in-laws "Mom and Dad," see in them strangers toward whom they feel somewhat guilty and therefore whose love they would like to win. Yet their communications are cautious and lack spontaneity. If their attempts do not succeed, they withdraw in anger and feel justified in not making any further attempts. The parents, either in response to the behavior of the children or following their natural inclinations, prefer to keep their distance. This is more true for fathers than for mothers. Fathers, of course, might also be caught in the web of their oedipus complex which, being revived toward the daughter, causes them to be jealous of the son-in-law, sometimes to a degree of paranoid reaction. This, however, is a manifestation of pathology and its frequency is hardly comparable to the interferences of mothers in the lives of their young married daughters and/or sons.

Mothers very often cannot live up to the adaptive tasks that the marriages of their children set for them. Instead of consciously attempting to relax their influence upon their daughters, they unconsciously identify with them and want to be involved in every detail of their new life. Frequent visits to the daughter's household, meant to be helpful, often become like an inspection that enrages the daughter and irritates her husband. It can go even farther, becoming a kind of inquisition regarding her life with her husband, his work, his income, etc., which enrages the son-in-law and in turn makes the mother-in-law an unwelcome visitor. Only the steps in the process are different if

197

it is the husband's mother who discloses her ambivalence toward her daughter-in-law. Daughters-in-law often make excuses for their husbands' mothers by telling themselves or their friends that they have taken away her only son, her favorite son, her first son, or her youngest. But if the mother-in-law does not relent, the enmity of the daughter-in-law can be lifelong and often costs that mother the love of her son.

For many generations jokes were made about the unwelcome and often ludicrous mother-in-law. It seems that in the last 20 years or so these jokes have almost disappeared from magazines. Irrelevant as this observation may seem, it is an indicator of social-psychologic changes that have resulted in a gradual emancipation of daughters from the influence of their mothers. This has significance beyond its direct relevance to parenthood. As long as daughters grew up in families in which the dependent mother's love and care could be rewarded only by abject dependency and even after marriage had to be accepted by unquestioning deference to her opinions, husbands had reason to be afraid of their mothers-in-law. Since their wives could rarely muster the independence to side with their husbands, such visits often stirred up conflicts, leaving both in emotional disarray. Now mothers can no longer be sure that their daughters will side with them. On the contrary, they can be certain that if there is no compelling reason to justify their attitude, they will not be welcome guests again in the households of their daughters. Moreover, the mother who cannot accept the necessary separation from her daughter and attempts to maintain her influence as a manifestation of the bond between them might bring about the breaking of the bond and alienation.

But even this elaboration would not make the shifts in interfamilial relationships pertinent to our discussion of parenthood if it did not illustrate a prevalent psychologic problem during the late phase of parenthood. One of the characteristics of the late phase of parenthood is the emotional consequence of the married childrens' alienation from their parents. Whether the parents are chronologically young, middle-aged, or older, their "child" who is now a parent is not as dependent as she or he was before: the psychic structure has changed. The married person has an ally. This deepening object relationship with the spouse is instrumental in changing the psychic structure of the young parent. As young parents encompass the experiences of their own parenthood, they become emotionally distant from their parents. Thus the "middle age of parenthood" is a critical period which requires adaptation of parents to the alienation of their children, adaptation to not being needed, which usually reduces self-esteem.

Often the overinvolvement of mothers in their married children's lives is a defense against and overcompensation for such depressing feelings. Since this often coincides with the climacteric, the psychophysiologic reactions of women to "the change of life" intensify the emotional reactions of the mother to such a degree that it might bring about a rift in the family which, in turn, aggravates the mother's "climacteric depression." It is not surprising that fathers usually do not get into the same trouble of alienation at a relatively early age, since they usually have more distance from the interpersonal affairs of the family. As long as their ability to work is not diminished, aging has a mellowing effect on fathers' attitudes toward their children. In the threatening experience of alienation of their married children, fathers frequently function as negotiators, trying to make peace and avoid a rift. But if they do not succeed, they usually feel compelled to protect their wives. Thus the late phase of parenthood arrives later for fathers than for mothers for many reasons.

GRANDPARENTHOOD

Before the last phase of parenthood, however, there come the gratifying experiences of *grandparenthood*. Very little has been written about the psychology of grandparenthood. In earlier psychoanalytic literature a few vague references indicate similarities in the grandchildren's gestures and attitudes to that of their grandparents. In previous chapters we have discussed the psychodynamic processes which account for similarities which might be regarded as identifications even if the grandchild has never seen his grandparents. But this does not explain the emotional significance of grandparenthood. It is often referred to as a "new lease on life" by grandparents themselves and also by the new parents who are proud of their ability to bestow this status on their parents.

The psychoanalyses of individuals, men and women, whose married children are childless, whether voluntarily or because of infertility, reveal the disappointment and frustration caused by this condition. Are such individuals just waiting for their children to supply them with a living toy to brighten their lives, already somehow impoverished in libidinal pleasure? I have had the opportunity to analyze the dreams of several such persons and found indications of the sources of their frustration and anxiety. Sometimes these individuals expressed guilty feelings for wishing for something beyond their ken and cautioned themselves to moderation lest they put an emotional burden on the unfortunate children. I analyzed a would-be grandmother who developed a reactive depression after repeated miscarriages of her daughter, since her daughter's condition deprived her of having grandchildren. The somatic correlations of that depression revealed the wish to survive in the grandchildren and also the depth of the identification with her daughter, since she appeared to live somatically and emotionally through her daughter's experiences. When the daughter finally gave birth to a living infant, the grandmother's elation probably surpassed the calmer expressions of the gratification of her daughter. Much careful research, however, is necessary to confirm or disprove the notions based on analytic study of a variety of cases and situations.

There is, of course, a noticeable difference in the attitudes of the prospective grandparents toward the pregnancy of the daughter. Both father and mother want the grandchild and the health of both the pregnant woman and the child. But the father does not identify with the experience of pregnancy as the mother does. The prospective grandmother remembers what her mother told her about her pregnancy, the pleasurable and/or the frightening experiences of the delivery and lactation. Now while she is preparing her own daughter, she may recall these childhood memories affectively, i.e., she may abreact the anxiety that she encapsulated as a child. But more deeply and unconsciously she relives her own pregnancies in identification with her daughter's. It is not unusual that the "expectant" grandmother, in her wish to protect her daughter, conveys her anxiety to the pregnant woman and by this nullifies the good that the empathic protectiveness of an experienced mother could provide. In such anxious overidentification of the prospective grandmother, one can see again the aging woman's wish to live her daughter's life. Such an attitude, however, often interferes with the actual bliss of grandparenthood.

Grandparenthood is a new lease on life because grandparents—

grandmothers more intensely than grandfathers—relive the memories of the early phase of their own parenthood in observing the growth and development of their grandchildren. Grandparenthood is, however, parenthood one step removed. Relieved from the immediate stresses of motherhood and the responsibilities of fatherhood, grandparents appear to enjoy their grandchildren more than they enjoyed their own children. Their instinctual wish to survive being gratified, they project the hope of the fulfillment of their narcissistic self-image to their grandchildren. Since they do not have the responsibility for raising the child toward that unconscious goal, their love is not as burdened by doubts and anxieties as it was when their own children were young.

The indulgence of grandparents toward their grandchildren has its deep-rooted instinctual origin, hence its psychodynamic motivation. How does it work out in the transactional processes of the family? Assuming that the relationship between the grandparents and the parents of the child is not hostile and that the grandparents can feel free to love the grandchildren, children will take the normal advantages that genuine love offers them. This does not mean candy and toys or time spent in playing. The love of grandparents gives the child a sense of security in being loved without always deserving it. Thus the undemanding love of the grandparents preserves for the child a piece of the self-indulgent sense of omnipotence experienced unconsciously during infancy. What does the grandparent receive in return? A loving glance from a happy child, a trusting hand, an actual appeal for help, a warm, feverish body clinging—whatever it is, for better or for worse, it is a message conveyed to the grandparent that he or she is needed, wanted, and loved, so they really feel like good parents, accepted gratefully by the child. This is the token of the new lease on life cherished by all.

We have dealt here with grandparenthood as if it were the same for everyone. It is obvious that there are differences depending on the personalities of all the interacting individuals belonging to three generations in family structures. Thus the emotional content of grandparents toward their children and grandchildren, and also what is expected of them as grandparents, depend upon the cultural and socioeconomic changes in family structures. Thus the emotional content of grandparenthood cannot remain the same for all time and for all persons.

Of the many factors which exert influence upon the emotional

201

significance of grandparenthood, only one should be mentioned here, the age of the grandparents. The experience of grandparenthood has a different emotional coloring if the grandparents are young, still in possession of their reproductive capacities. It is unusual but not an unheard of situation when a grandmother can nurse her grandchild, when family relationships become difficult to clarify since the uncle is younger than his nephew. It is obvious that in such families the wish for survival in the grandchild does not approach consciousness; the involvement of the grandparents with their own, still young children overshadows their emotional need for grandchildren. It is different if the grandparents are well over their own procreative period and if they have had to wait a long time for grandchildren.

Grandchildren, however, grow up and grow away from doting grandparents. As they reach adolescence, their attitude toward their grandparents appears to reach that postambivalent phase of object relationship which Karl Abraham described as characteristic of maturity [1]. The ambivalence of adolescence, the rebellion of youth, is directed toward the parents who are the objects of their conflicting instinctual drives. Since the relationship with the grandparents was never so highly charged with the energy of conflicting drives, the grandparents become the recipients of considerate and indulging behavior of the maturing individuals who, in the fullness of their strength, see the weakness in the doting grandparents, even earlier than would be justified. The grandparents respond to the manifestations of the protective, even if somehow condescending, love of their grandchildren as balm for whatever wounds old age inflicts upon them.

Old age, if not hastened by illness, arrives slowly and brings with it the adaptive tasks to aging itself. For aging is a normal process but its physiology has somatic and psychic attributes and consequences which at times lead to more or less serious pathologic conditions and finally to death. From the multitude of adaptive tasks, only those will be mentioned which influence intrafamilial relationships and with it the old parents' status and function in the family. In order to put this in the psychodynamic frame of reference which is basic to these chapters, the overall psychodynamic character of each major phase of the life cycle should be pointed out: (1) From infancy through adolescence the vector of metabolic and psychologic processes is self-directed, i.e., receptive. (2) During the reproductive period the vector is expressed in the object-directed, expansive, giving attitude of parenthood. (3) As the supply of vital energies declines with aging, the positive, extraverted tendencies slowly become outweighed by the energy-conserving, restricting, self-centered tendencies of old age. These are the unconscious factors that bring about the psychologic (often psychiatric) manifestations of old age. Thus the gradual involution of old age makes understandable the psychologic processes which bring about the age-determined changes between parents and their children [3].

Sociologists agree that chronologic age is not the significant variable by which to order most social and psychologic data of aging. Social psychologists offer statistical evidence for what seems natural to psychoanalysts, namely, that the style of aging depends more upon the personality pattern than on chronologic age. Thus one might be generally satisfied with the notion that character changes in later life are merely variations of the existing character traits. Since aging reduces the libidinal expansiveness of the individual, in old age the negative hostile components of the character become more pronounced and even dominant. This explains the domineering know-it-all behavior of many aging mothers and grandmothers who become embittered if the younger generation does not follow suit.

The object-relationship changes between a parent and each of his children, motivated by the gratifications and frustrations that the parent experienced in his emotional relationship with that individual. When the pattern and the course of the psychodynamic processes of the parent are known, it is not difficult to establish the distortions caused by the involutional processes of the parent and understand with sympathy the influence that old age exerts upon the interpersonal relationships within the family.

Middle-aged fathers are not infrequently jealous of the virility of their adult sons. This may be playful and may be handled for some time with mutual understanding and humor, but in many instances the jealousy sooner or later ossifies into pathologic behavior.[4] Sexual competition brings about the manifestation of the reversed oedipus complex (see Chap. 15) with its manifold pathologic manifestations. When analyzing individuals in that stage of life, one can uncover the

[4] Mother's climacteric reactions to daughters have been discussed earlier.

complexity of intrapsychic processes by which the individual is defending himself against the experience of being old.

The competition between the aging father and his son becomes manifest also in the area of work achievement. Disappointing as the unsuccessful son may be, the success of the son does not always (and necessarily) lead to harmony between the generations. It happens very often, especially in the business world, that the father takes all the credit for success and consequently depreciates the productive achievements of his son. It may be also that the son does not give the father what he needs—the acknowledgment of the father's merit in the son's accomplishment. It is difficult for a son to empathize with the emotions of his once powerful father who, in his declining ego-strength, is dependent upon the expression of the son's love, respect, and even admiration. Just as once the son developed through the father's love, in his old age the father needs the son's generous, loving attitude to maintain his self-esteem. Thus the father becomes dependent upon the son. Here economic dependency must be differentiated from emotional dependency. If the father is dependent upon his son for financial support, his already hurt self-esteem increases his need for respect and his sensitivity to realistic or imagined offenses. Even without such realistic dependency, old parents, whether mothers or fathers, become dependent upon their adult children for emotional support, since the emotional reactions to aging depend on the current emotional balance of the individual and of his anticipation of his future. The insecurity and fear which this engenders is one of the most significant factors in the psychopathologic processes of aging. If respect and love can be expected, aging will be less painful, less anxiety-ridden.

There is no doubt about the specific blend of narcissism in the aged which, since it cannot draw upon fresh resources of libido, enlarges the remaining resources by identification with the young and by rekindling the memories of past gratifications. Current frustrations increase the preoccupation with memories of youthful experiences. Being engrossed in what one has been often becomes irritating even to the grandchildren, let alone to their parents. But frustrations increase the need and thus the senescent parent exhibits more and more inconsiderate demands. With the aging process an elderly person's ability for empathy with the younger generation diminishes; the defenses of the self-centered personality become more tenacious so that the younger generation complains about the egotism of the old, and with justification. It is frustrating to the younger generation that the solace which is offered does not gratify the demands of the old parent. These demands are often irrational. Just as a child expects that his parents can relieve his pain, undo all harm, so does the senescent parent unconsciously expect his children to remove the burdens of his age. While he is dissatisfied with himself, the senescent person demands from his children the impossible, namely, that they make him unaware of his weakness.

One could go on with the elaboration of the manifestations of the state of "nonparenthood" with "nonchildren." Why include it at all? For two reasons—one is that it demonstrates the complete turn of the cycle. As once the parent was the need-fulfilling object of the child, now the "adult child" is the need-fulfilling object of the aged parent. The other is that it demonstrates the significance of parenthood in the identity of the parent. Originating in the instinct for survival in the offspring, parenthood establishes a sense of identity that integrates the biologic and social functions of the personality.

Being a parent is in the center of a normal parent's self concept. In old age, removed from his reproductive period by two generations, he clings to his adult children and seeks in them the psychic images of what they had once been and therefore will always remain, his children. Thus in the sense of intrapsychic processes, parenthood ends when memory is lost and intrapsychic images fade out. Only great poets can grasp and convey the emotional power of memories which, even if faded, live on and can be revived in crucial moments of living such as might occur in dying.[5]

Bibliography

1. Abraham, K.   A Short Study of the Development of the Libido, Viewed in the Light of Mental Disorders: II. Origins and Growth of Object-Love. In K. Abraham (Ed.), *Selected Papers*. London: Hogarth, 1927.

[5] I am thinking of Thomas Wolfe's description of old Mr. Gant dying in *Of Time and the River*.

2. Benedek, T.   Climacterium: A developmental phase. *Psychoanal. Quart.* 19:1–27, 1950.
3. Benedek, T.   Personality Development. In F. Alexander and H. Ross (Eds.), *Dynamic Psychiatry.* Chicago: University of Chicago Press, 1952.
4. Freud, S.   The passing of the oedipus complex. *Int. J. Psychoanal.* 5:419–424, 1924.
5. Friedan, B.   *The Feminine Mystique.* New York: Norton, 1963.
6. Gitelson, M.   Re-evaluation of the role of the oedipus complex. *Int. J. Psychoanal.* 33:351–354, 1952.
7. Mead, M.   *Growing Up in New Guinea; a Comparative Study of Primitive Education.* New York: Morrow, 1930.
8. Mead, M.   *Coming of Age in Samoa; a Psychological Study of Primitive Youth for Western Civilization.* New York: Blue Ribbon Books, 1936.

Part III

Developmental Aspects of Parenthood

9

The Development
of Parental Attitudes
During Pregnancy

Lucie Jessner
Edith Weigert
James L. Foy

Editors' Introduction

The many-faceted observations presented in the following chapter can be viewed as an elaboration of the psychobiology (or, more aptly, biopsychology) of pregnancy as revealed by a group of contemporary women of the same cultural background and interpreted within the broad psychoanalytic framework of the authors. The study of the development of parental attitudes during pregnancy illustrates in a broad scope the complexity of motivations of the third order referred to in the introductory chapter as the cultural motivations. From observations of women who "chose" to become pregnant, the study revealed the complexity of problems created by conflicts between the "culturally given" free choice of the individual and the limitations of the personality determined by the physiologic and psychologic development.

The attention given to fathers is both timely and appropriate in any consideration of pregnancy. As the authors point out, there is as yet only a slight literature on expectant fatherhood, and they make an excellent attempt here to remedy this. They draw not only from their own clinical and research experience but also, as Freud did in his work, on the insights provided by the great intuitive writers. Quite rightly they point out that fatherhood is largely a secondary phenomenon and cannot be described in terms of its biological immediacy. It is not essential to the survival of offspring but, with the help of powerful developmental and cultural motivations, it has gained for itself a significant place in the cycle of human life.

E. J. A.
T. B.

Pregnancy is a human situation which announces a teeming realm of possibilities not only for the unborn at the threshold of existence but also for his parents who now enter a new configuration of relatedness to one another and to their not yet visible but present offspring. Preparation for parenthood is a long and complex development, even antecedent to the period of gestation. However, pregnancy unfolds a significant anticipatory parenthood in both expectant mother and father. The disposition for parenthood trails back into an individual's past; nevertheless, latent dispositions become manifest during the course of pregnancy. In former decades the psychologic exploration of pregnancy proceeded with some reservation and avoidance of intrusion into this period of constant psychophysiologic change and upheaval. During the past decade the psychologic investigation of pregnancy has become commonplace, and there has emerged a growing recognition of a need for counseling, consultation, or psychotherapy both in preparation for pregnancy and during the period. Such a need is not only determined in the case of women with problems of adaptation but also in the case of some prospective fathers. The attention of psychologists and psychiatrists has focused on specific and typical conflicts and anxieties of the period of pregnancy; understanding them is important for the healthy future development of both generations of parents and children.

The authors wish to acknowledge the sources of their clinical observations and impressions. They have been based on materials from the practice of psychiatry and psychoanalysis and upon findings from two recent research investigations of expectant parenthood and pregnancy. One of the authors was principal investigator of a multidisciplinary team of researchers studying first pregnancy in a group of wives of university students.[1] Another of the authors was coinvestigator on a research team of psychoanalysts and psychologists studying the emotional aspects of pregnancy among a group of 52 women, primiparas and multiparas, who were followed through the last two

---

[1] This project was conducted at the University of North Carolina by a team of psychiatrists, Marianne Breslin, Virginia Clower, Harold G. Harris, Lucie Jessner, Cornelius Lansing, and Milton L. Miller; an obstetrician, Charles E. Flowers; a psychologist, Marilyn T. Erickson; and two sociologists, R. J. McCorkel and Jean Thrasher. Publications related to the project have already appeared; see Erickson, Flowers, Jessner, and Thrasher [12, 16, 23, 36].

trimesters of pregnancy and for three months postpartum.[2] The subjects in both studies were middle-class white women, most of them with some education beyond the high school level. Additional source material derives from a current investigation of unmarried pregnancy being conducted by one of the authors.[3]

MOTIVATIONS FOR PREGNANCY

The complexities of human motivations concerning the commitment to parenthood are thrown into relief when we compare human procreation with the merely instinct-directed behavior of animals that determines their cohabitation and care for the offspring. In all higher primates, except human females, the hormonal cycle separates breeding episodes from periods of exclusive care for the dependent offspring, and estrus returns only when the offspring can shift for himself. The much longer dependency of the human child and the vanishing of seasonal division between periods of heightened sexual desire and periods of maternal preoccupation create conflicts of motivations which represent a challenge to the potentialities of human integration.

The extended knowledge of birth control in recent decades has, on the conscious level of deliberations, separated procreation from the abandonment to sexual passion. While the impulse for sexual union spontaneously arises in all seasons, the act of procreation can be timed by rational decisions. But the foresight of planned parenthood has not abolished the conflicts of motivations: We have become increasingly aware of the complexities of conscious and unconscious motives. Our studies could only deal with conscious motivations but they permitted inferences concerning unconscious motivations. An unplanned pregnancy revealed itself frequently as welcome in the course of pregnancy. A carefully planned pregnancy sometimes met with unexpected resistances at a later date.

The commitment to parenthood, more than the nuptial vows,

[2] This project, under the auspices of the Washington School of Psychiatry, was supported by a National Institute of Mental Health Research Grant, No. R11-MH-1193. The investigators were: Mabel B. Cohen, John M. Fearing, Robert G. Kvarnes, Edward M. Ohaneson, Sarah Saltzman, Edith V. Weigert, and Naomi K. Wenner. Publications related to the project have appeared in the literature; see Cohen, Wenner, and Wenner and Ohaneson [5, 39, 40].

[3] Maternal Attitudes During Unmarried Pregnancy Approached Through Expressive Drawings and Painting, principal investigator, James L. Foy, conducted at the Florence Crittenton Home, Washington, D.C.

implies a decision for lifetime, at least for the long life span until the children become independent, since many parents hesitate to burden their dependent children with the hardships of a broken family. When one or both partners are unable to renew their commitment freely, parenthood can become a trap, and both partners are bound to level accusations at each other about the loss of mutually granted freedom and respect.

It is difficult to unravel the motivations that militate against the commitment to parenthood, since public opinion expects the adult man, and particularly the adult woman, to be gratified by procreation and child-bearing. Thus married couples often feel ashamed of voluntary or involuntary infertility. This traditional pressure, bolstered by sentimentalities of motherhood cults and religious exhortations to fulfill the divine command of fertility, certainly influences the planning of parenthood, since the need for conformity to social roles frequently takes precedence over the authenticity of individual decisions. The fear of overpopulation is used as rationalization of individual decisions against procreation. The striving for prestige of parenthood frequently conceals a deeper insecurity about a person's identity and personal aims in life.

Parenthood as a stage in the life cycle, described by Erikson as well as by Benedek, represents an important step in human development beyond the level of genital maturity [2, 13]. It implies a struggle between identification and differentiation in relation to the parents, or the image of the parent, embedded in the ego ideals of the younger generation, but the surface appearances conceal deeper conflicts.

A daughter wants to fulfill her parents' wish for grandchildren, but this conventional motivation conceals the guilt-laden oedipal wish of childhood to be impregnated by the father. He sometimes is her secret accomplice. He really does not want to yield his authority to the son-in-law; he does not want to step into the background. A famous German architect said jokingly at his daughter's wedding: "I tell you one thing, my grandchildren I make myself."

At the verge of parenthood both men and women feel either vaguely, or more intensely than at any previous step in adulthood, that they can no longer find the way back—"the beautiful way into the land of childhood" (line of a German song). However, unfulfilled

212

infantile dependency needs are inescapable. They may find their expression in oceanic feelings, in religious yearnings, or in political strivings for an ideal society of human fellowship. But there is also an uncanny emotion involved in this nostalgia, a vague recognition that a perfect fulfillment of this yearning would mean individual death. Freud has interpreted this nostalgia as a familiar, yet uncanny, longing for a return to mother's womb, a reunion with Mother Earth [20].

The decision for parenthood touches off, particularly in the woman, a nostalgia for her mother to relive in the union with her future child a reversal of the original mother-child symbiosis. Exhilaration at the prospect of motherhood covers unconscious anxieties. An intensification of nostalgia for mother may lead to the illusion of a parthenogenetic pregnancy which tends to ignore the role of the husband in parenthood. Strong ambivalent attitudes of a woman toward her mother may supply negative motivations for pregnancy.

A young woman in psychoanalysis because of phobias, depressive tendencies, and rages against her daughter had had a postpartum psychosis and several miscarriages. During her analysis, she became pregnant again and was fearful of delivery and another postpartum disturbance. While consciously wanting another child, she became aware of opposing unconscious tendencies; she kept on losing things and had frightening dreams. In one she went to visit a cathedral with grotesque gargoyles that leaped about and bit. She associated the dream to the concern over being injured in pregnancy like her mother, who had much trouble while carrying the patient. In another dream a lot of baby black widow spiders came out of the mother spider and the patient thought: "They can kill you." She finally worked through her symbiotic tie to her mother and her guilt feelings toward her.

Fear of success and castration anxieties enter into the male's motivations for parenthood. The adolescent wants to show to the world his potency by procreation. But some young men are afraid to become domesticated by parenthood; they consider their parental potentialities as a sign of weakness, of effeminacy. The fear of parenthood in a male often stems from repressed rage and anger in relation to unloving, rejecting parents. These repressed resentments make him insecure about his capacity to love. As far as parenthood represents a success, the type of male that Freud described as "wrecked by suc-

213

cess" is afraid of being a successor to his father, exposed to all the angry accusations that he had repressed in relation to his predecessor [18].

Rebellion against fatherhood is often caused by holding on to adolescent ideals. In the discussion of parenthood a young scientist brought up his ardent wish for a racing car, which he did not need and could not afford. He brought it up each time his wife pleaded for a pregnancy. He gradually agreed that he would like to have a son, but that he would antagonize his Greek Orthodox parents by not baptizing the son and by naming him Darwin. Such a rebellious break with tradition does not yet indicate the freedom of individuation; it can be an inevitable sign of transition, but it burdens the conflict of motivations with the ambivalent struggle between infantile dependency and mature dependency in the sense of Fairbairn [15].

For the most part men are more ashamed of their dependency needs than women. They express them more obliquely. They hope that parenthood represents security and emotional stability in the family home, but many men protest that security and dependability are more desirable for women than for men, since the women carry the greater burden. This inequality elicits the male suspicion that the woman may use a pregnancy as a means to hold on to a seemingly or truly wayward husband. Her conscious or unconscious intention frequently fails, since he senses her anxieties and increased dependency needs. He may be contaminated by her anxieties and instead of giving support, his own dependency needs may be reinforced. They dampen his erotic enthusiasm, and she loses her spontaneous charm. The young husband often holds on to the adolescent ideal image of slender feminine beauty, and the woman fears to be rejected in pregnancy. Puritanical prejudices that dissociate sexuality from dignified parenthood may threaten both partners or one of them with a loss of sexual gratification. The husband may even fear to see in his pregnant wife the castrating woman, the threatening, voracious mother of his childhood who turned away from him when she became heavy with another pregnancy.

An estrangement between marital partners may arouse the wish for parenthood to make up for the lack of meaningful partnership. There is a feeling of inner emptiness, unfilled inner spaces, loneliness and boredom, particularly on the part of women who feel inferior to overactive, extroverted husbands. A woman seen in private consultation had five children. The marriage was deeply disturbed by the husband's outbreaks of violent rage to which the woman reacted with submissive docility. She had no training for any activities outside the home. She was lonely and bored, boring to the husband and her older children. The husband felt threatened when she engaged in anything but cooking, cleaning, and caring for him. The wife was happy only when she was with child and in the nursing period. When the child reached the toddler age, showed signs of independence and negativism, she lost her enthusiasm. Dreams, fantasies, and slips in daily care indicated unconscious murderous impulses against this child. She reacted with guilt feelings, became depressed, and demanded another pregnancy. The husband gave in, mainly motivated by the need to show his masculine prowess without being able to admit his resentful jealousy of his children in an estranged marital relation. One could call this a case of addiction to pregnancy on the part of a dissatisfied woman.

The decision for multiple pregnancies is difficult even in more harmonious marriages. There is the rational motivation that it is not good for a single child to grow up in isolation without learning to endure the frictions of sibling rivalry. Disappointment in the first child or children and hope for a more perfect offspring play a role in the parental motivation; on the other hand the second, third, and further pregnancies elicit less enthusiasm than the first one. The commitment to multiple pregnancies is loaded with additional anxieties. The doubt whether the parents can provide sufficient care, can be better parents than they have been heretofore, takes its toll, as does the fear of the children's competitive envy and hostilities. These anxieties were illustrated by a subject's dream, a woman in the beginning of her third pregnancy: This woman swam in a pool with three children. One was drowning; she hastened to save him. Meanwhile, the others were drowning. When she hurried to them, the first one was drowning. The dream continued: One child was attacked by a bull. While saving him, the bull attacked the other ones. When she came to their rescue, the first was attacked again. The drowning symbolized a dangerous mother, the bull a threatening father.

In spite of the various conscious and unconscious anxieties that are mobilized by the prospect of parenthood, the positive motivations prevail in many human beings who decide to become parents. Many prospective parents take up the responsibilities of parenthood soberly, not necessarily with exhilaration. Ecstatic emotions frequently compensate for concealed anxieties and imply denial of the tragic aspects of life. The man not only wants to silence his doubts about his procreative abilities and prove his manliness, but he trusts that fatherhood will expand his horizon and develop his human potentialities. A woman wants to experience her full feminine potentialities in motherhood, leave behind infantile dependency and the adolescent ideal of irresistible seductiveness. Motherliness, as Deutsch has pointed out, is an inherent quality of the feminine character, also in women who have never borne a child [8]. Motherhood provides an opportunity to develop this feminine quality, even in women who previously have escaped into a pretense of masculinity out of fear of being more vulnerable as a woman. It is true, women who take up the burden of motherhood are more vulnerable, less self-sufficient, and more dependent on their male partner. They are raising children who will gradually leave them, continuously growing away from the symbiotic intimacy. But it is not merely neurotic masochism that makes women accept the pains, anxieties, drudgeries, and possible tragic losses of motherhood, it is the courage of endurance, the capacity to forego momentary pleasures and comforts for the sake of future gratifications, even beyond her own life span. The husband, too, is not exempt from sacrifices and curtailment of freedom. He accepts his burdens and responsibilities with a courage that transcends the juvenile ideals of manliness. If unmanageable, escalating anxieties do not alienate the parents from each other, they find in parenthood a deeper meaning to mutuality that fortifies the trust in life.

EXPECTANT MOTHERHOOD

During pregnancy a woman experiences a sequence of transformations, and this is especially so during the first pregnancy. These changes are experienced in different ways during the trimesters of pregnancy.[4]

During the first trimester the subtle changes within the body are usually the focus of attention: swelling of the breasts, nausea, morning sickness; an aversion against or craving for certain foods, which

[4] Some material in this section has been published previously [23].

216

may be related to infantile fantasies about oral conception; and also a general weakness, fatigue, indolence, inexplicable mood swings, irritability, and easily hurt feelings make most women think of themselves as not the same person anymore. "It seems like an illness without being sick."

A feeling of loneliness and distance from others, even the husband, and a separateness and uniqueness coincide with a changing self. At the same time there is the strong wish to be protected, to be taken care of, which cannot be fulfilled by even the most solicitous husband. "Nobody really understands the predicament that I am thrown into," said Mrs. B.

The world seems at times to recede and then again to encompass her in a new way. Abigail Lewis[5] at the seaside found herself (in the third month of her pregnancy) struck by the sight of a whale swimming among innumerable little fish: "Lower animals may astonish by sheer number, but mammals astonish by their aloneness and individuality. And I, newly conscious of being a mammal, can begin to understand what it means." *

The embryo at this time is there by intimation, not as a separate entity. To the feeling of widened space—being a part of the whole animate universe—comes the feeling of an extension in time, a transcendence of herself. She is struck by the idea of a chain of generations and herself as a link between past and future.

Some women experience pregnancy as a proof of being really a woman, a reassurance against the fear of being unable to conceive. It becomes obvious that the wish to be pregnant is not always the wish for a child. Mrs. M. dreaded having a child but proceeded in a methodical way to become pregnant by forcing her husband to have intercourse at the precise time of ovulation. During the second month of her hard-won pregnancy, she attended her brother's wedding in a maternity dress. During the third month, however, she vomited every afternoon and became aware that she wanted to get rid of the baby. She took antihistamines and tranquilizers against medical advice, with guilt feelings for possibly doing harm to the baby. She dreamed that

[5] This author wrote a perceptive diary of her first pregnancy published under the title *An Interesting Condition* [25].

* From *An Interesting Condition* by Abigail Lewis. Copyright 1950 by Doubleday & Company, Inc. Copyright 1950 by McCall Corporation. Reprinted by permission of Doubleday & Company, Inc.

she gave birth to the child but had no place to put it. She was determined against breast-feeding, because she did not want to be devoured
by a jackal—her image of the baby.

In one case the coming child was consciously, even intensely,
desired, but the pregnancy seemed almost unbearable due to hyper-
emesis. The mother lost 18 pounds in the first trimester, and a therapeutic interruption of the pregnancy had to be considered. This 21-
year-old woman had a very hostile relation to her mother, who had
"beat the good-for-nothing father out of her." After a divorce from
the first husband and remarriage, the mother had exploited this
daughter as nursemaid to rear her step-siblings; the girl could not
manage the stepbrothers; she was undernourished and overworked,
but she had a motherly attachment to her youngest stepsister, for
whom she was planning to name her own daughter. Her husband,
who was twenty-five years older than she, was able with his warm
parental solicitude to carry her through the most painful first months
of pregnancy, which seemed to revive the intense ambivalence about
the care of an infant and the anxieties and bitter resentments of her
childhood.

In the second trimester a sudden shift occurs with quickening;
feeling the movements of the fetus makes him real. The perceptions
of fetal movements, according to our women subjects, at first have a
delicate, exquisite quality, "like holding a butterfly in your hand, and
it was fluttering," or "gentle strokings from a soft glove." The otherness within is a crucial experience of the second trimester. Sometimes
the fetus seems a stranger not belonging to her.

For most women this is a time of fulfillment and delight. They
experience what Erikson calls the "relevance of the productive interior . . . a sense of vital inner potential" [14]. They seem to confirm this author's suggestion that "in female experience an 'inner
space' is at the center of despair even as it is the very center of potential fulfillment."

Some women experience the fetus with ambivalence, fluctuating
between bliss and resentment of the intruder. "Oh God, the black rage
that comes over me sometimes, especially at night. The nerve of this
creature, the impudence, placidly leeching food from my body without even an invitation!" [25].

Most women feel that they now eat for two. Food poses conflict. They become very hungry, but warned by their obstetrician

against gaining weight, eating becomes an issue and loses much of its spontaneous pleasure. So does sex. Many complain about losing enthusiasm and the capacity to become involved. Intercourse becomes a matter of concern, something that might harm the baby. This fear seems astonishing, because all the women in the study were assured by the obstetrician that they could safely have intercourse until the time of delivery. But childhood concepts of sex as sinful or impure, irreconcilable with the idea of a mother, would not let them accept the medical dictum with ease. A few women experienced heightened sexual needs induced by anxiety.

The body now visibly and tangibly loses its familiar shape. The woman gives up her usual clothes—which were part of her body image—and wears maternity dresses. This change makes her proud, but also at times distressed because of the loss of beauty and of youth. She is concerned that she will not be attractive to men anymore and that she will lose her husband's love.

Mrs. O. was plagued by a dream: She was in an auditorium and a girl in a sexy black dress was there too. Mrs. O.'s husband got up to sit with the girl. The dream reminded Mrs. O. that she is self-conscious about her figure and afraid of losing what had been most precious in her life—to be a woman loved and in love. Her own feelings had become less passionate, and intercourse had become a duty for her. She found some comfort in her husband's objection to breast-feeding. He had said her breasts belonged to him. She agreed with him, although she had heard that nursing a baby was a most exquisite sensation. But keeping a part of herself and her beauty reserved for her husband gave her some confidence; she might be a mother and an attractive woman as well.

A redefining of femininity is common. Abigail Lewis writes about herself: "The defiant tomboy that was me will be finally and irrevocably lost, but someone else will be born, though not so apparently as the baby is born." Some of our subjects too struggled against giving up masculine aspects of themselves.

It might be helpful to convey to such women that this is not an absolute either/or proposition. Freud said there is a great deal of the masculine aspect in females, and it is important for a woman to know where to apply her masculinity appropriately [19]. Pregnancy, labor, and delivery indeed call for activity as well as passivity.

Others who had accepted their female destiny experienced the shift from being a girl to being a woman, some with nostalgia, others with apprehension of not being ready for this new self. Other aspects of the personality are challenged too: Women for whom a career or some form of self-actualization means a great deal regard motherhood as a dilemma.

Mrs. N. W. came to the emergency ward in her fifth month because she suddenly could not breathe, and she thought she was dying. An acute anxiety attack was diagnosed. This episode passed. However, she remained apprehensive, depressed, and lost her appetite. A few weeks later she had a second attack of "suffocation." Following this the patient was seen in a number of interviews. She was a professional musician, and it was found that she thought having children would be the end of her music. She loved babies and had previously felt "a little unfulfilled." She despised women who sacrifice their children for a career but at the same time she was critical of women who sacrifice themselves for their children. Expressed in these terms, she found her conflict irreconcilable. The working through allowed her to alter this either/or position and to see that being a musician and a mother were not necessarily incompatible.

There is a major problem with this type of conflict. Deutsch, describing adolescent girls who plan for both profession and family, feels that they are unaware of a deep and powerful conflict of emotional energy that cannot serve one goal without being drawn away from the other [9]. She has given up her former optimistic view that this conflict can be resolved. We still maintain this optimism. Surrounded by psychiatric residents who are mothers, we have been impressed with the difficulty of divided devotion, but this also has persuaded us that the compromise allows these young mothers the experience of themselves as whole persons and allows a genuine enjoyment of their children without burdening their offspring with resentment or expecting them to compensate for the sacrifice. What matters is being emotionally available and responsive to the child. It is difficult for the mother to give up an essential part of herself; by becoming a mother an equilibrium may not be reached during pregnancy, but an awareness of the conflict and partial resolution are important for a comfortable mother-infant relationship.

To be dedicated to a vocation of one's choice is a middle-class prerogative. But also, we found that even women in jobs they considered rather boring regretted giving up a life of activity and companionship for the solitude of the home. The structured, busy day alleviated fears and tensions—it also served to attenuate the full impact of pregnancy, the drama inside.

But even when the internal drama is covered with a layer of busy distractions, one sees the tendency of the woman to turn inward, alternating with the tendency to turn more than before to others. Our observations confirm Deutsch's statement: "A typical and unique phenomenon of pregnancy is the interweaving of intensified introversion with the simultaneously intensified turn towards reality" [8].

The turning inward also affects the relationship with her husband. There is less romantic longing, less desire for union in embrace —the unity with the baby within seems to have replaced it. On the other hand there is a marked orientation toward rather unspecified outsiders, to the community for instance, to which she seems to belong more than before. Sometimes waves of tenderness radiate into the world. Mrs. O., for example, felt like mothering everyone. Bibring has observed that the pregnant woman nowadays lacks the support given to previous generations by the extended family, and she also lacks the carefully worked-out traditional customs which guided them [3]. The women in the University of North Carolina study managed to get such support and guidelines mainly from each other and from their obstetrician.

Inwardly the most relevant person to the pregnant woman is now her mother, who in most cases that we observed lived at geographical distance, often kept away on purpose. While outwardly the prospective mother takes her model from contemporaries, she is flooded with memories of her mother. Some idealize their mother as the prototype they would like to embody. Some struggle against an identification with her, e.g., Mrs. L. was horrified at the thought that she might become a mother like her own, who engulfs everyone and knows no boundaries between herself and other people, especially her children. She was afraid her child would push her away as she had done with her parents. She was determined to avoid what her mother did, namely, keep the child too close to her. One time, when she woke from a cheerful dream in which she was able to soothe a crying baby, she suddenly had the frightening thought that her child would be the child of a stranger, her husband—whereas the infant should be her father's or her brother's child. She realized how much her parents were a part of herself and that she carried her mother within her, no

221

matter how much she wanted to eradicate her. Mrs. L. also worried that her child might do to her what she did to her parents—play one off against the other, destroying the harmony between them. She—like several others—perceived the future child as an intruder in her marriage.

The difficulty of loosening the ties to incorporated objects of the past brings up one potential interference with motherliness: the displacement of feelings on to the future child, e.g., Mrs. D., who took care of a younger brother born when she was not quite 8 years old, relived her jealousy and anger against him. She recalled with pleasure having spanked him with a hair brush, bruising his bottom. She had enjoyed recently seeing her little niece taking the pillow from underneath her infant brother's head and putting it over his face. She resented her husband's interest in the future child. We predicted that Mrs. D. would be able to control the tendency for displacement. Indeed, she was able to overcome feelings of rivalry and jealousy because, as she said, "I'm not competing for my mother's attention then." She accepted her ambivalence, "I am sure I feel like putting that baby under the bed sometimes." She was sure enough of her tender feelings for him not to get upset. On postpartum follow-up visits she seemed happy and at ease with her little boy.

The feeling of being at the mercy of the unborn, of having no control over the growing creature within, alternates in most women with the concern that whatever they do, eat, think, or wish will have an influence on the future child—which indeed it may to some degree [33].

All the women were haunted at times by the fear of producing a monster or a dead infant. These concerns, however, were not very realistic; they reflect the experience of the uncanny and of magic powers. Enjoyable images of the child alternate with these apprehensions, which usually have their origin in guilt feelings.

Most women begin to prepare actively for the baby's arrival. Some postpone this task. The omission of preparing for the baby's arrival is generally regarded as an expression of unconscious rejection of the child [3]. While this is the case in some, in others it has seemed to stem from the belief that they could not truly produce a child.

In the third trimester the body becomes more and more a burdensome weight, an embarrassing discomfiture, and a distorted shape.

"I look like a stranded whale," said one woman. The disfigurement doesn't mean as much at this time as before. To quote Abigail Lewis again, "In the early months I was very self-conscious about myself. There are about three stages of this self-consciousness. The first is when you wonder if you are noticeable or not and don't know if it is better to have people realize you are pregnant or just let them think you are getting fat. The second covers all the middle months when you are quite obviously pregnant; then it is a queer naked feeling to walk along the street and feel no longer anonymous, realizing that there is one secret of your life that everyone who looks can know— that at least one private incident of your past has become almost incredibly public and that you can bear, as it were, the stigma of past passion wherever you go. The third stage, which I have mercifully entered now, is when you don't care very much; the event is so close that you are living more in the future than in the present."

Straus, describing the world of the obsessive, writes: "Normally we can surround ourselves with attractive things and expel the others to a sequestered spot" [35]. This division is not possible in the last stage of pregnancy: Frequency and urgency of urination, laxatives for constipation, and hemorrhoids are some of the disagreeable aspects which intrude. Some women can take these symptoms as negligible nuisances but most feel degraded and humiliated, reminded of childhood accidents with excretion. Medical invasion of privacy through checkups and as preparation for delivery insult their dignity. Mrs. L., for example, could accept the vagina as an organ for lovemaking, but not for the purpose of medical inspection and manipulation.

The fetus by now seems like a giant or like twins. His movements are welcome as a reassurance that he is alive, but they are not gentle anymore and are sometimes painful, suggesting injury. The conversations with the fetus lose the tenderness of the previous months and become more like one of our patients' admonitions: "Wait 'till you are out and I'll show you!" Most women experience the fetus now as an enemy, who is injuring the kidneys or the womb. He arouses their rage as he moves vigorously just when they lie down to rest or sleep. While they usually know that this is due to the change in their position, it seems as if he does this just to torture them. Sensations of bursting occur. One of the students' wives saw in one of the Rorschach cards, "a ship losing cargo on four sides."

There is often a new and strong attachment to the husband and a conviction of a new bond, something they will have in common, that adds to their marriage another dimension. But there is also a sudden awareness of the disparity between the sexes: that a man, in spite of his empathy (shown by some of our husbands through a variety of physical symptoms and manifestations reminiscent of couvade*) cannot have the experience she is thrown into. Some women wish mother would come and take care, others fight this wish vehemently.

Time now has a focus: the date of delivery, which is usually waited for with impatience to get it over with, finally to see and have that baby which makes its presence so unmistakably felt day and night. But most women also anticipate a feeling of losing a unique union. There comes the saddening awareness that the child will—and should—move further away from her. Delivery thus is anticipated with a polarity of feelings. The inner conflicts stirred up in the second trimester and the vehement struggle for a new identity are submerged in an atmosphere of anxiety. Mrs. L. envisaged that the child would not be like a visitor; he would not leave and she could never again be alone with her husband. She also dreaded being empty inside after the delivery. The expression: "moon on the wane" came to her mind at night—it seemed to refer to her figure after delivery, but also to her death. She got up and wrote down a list of friends who should get announcements of the baby's birth, including their addresses, so that somebody else could send them in case she should die. She felt that one generation pushes the former one away, killing it. Delivery initiates in the mother fantasies of death and rebirth.[6]

Editors' note: The term *couvade* is derived from the French verb *couver* meaning to brood or hatch. In its nonclinical or ritual form, it has been practiced in many different races in many different parts of the world and for many centuries upon the occasion of the birth of a child. It was first reported as 60 B.C. by Diodorus Siculus.

According to Sir James Frazer there are two main groups: First the prenatal or pseudomaternal couvade, which aims primarily and ostensibly at a magical transference of the mother's labor pains onto the person of the father, the father pretending to undergo what the mother experiences in reality; and second, the postnatal or dietetic couvade, in which the father pretends to be weak or ailing for a certain time after the birth of his child, during which time he keeps to his bed and refrains from eating certain foods. This seems to be directed not at the mother but at the child and stems apparently from the idea that an intimate relationship already exists between the father and child so that the child can be affected by the father's activities.

[6] Experiences of anxiety in many forms and morbid preoccupations in women during the last weeks of pregnancy were observed in all pregnant subjects studied. What was not observed in these women was any organized state

In summary, in the first trimester the embryo was considered a part of the mother's own body; the focus of concern was on changes within herself, a slight estrangement from herself and others but also a merging with nature, with mankind. With quickening the fetus became a being by himself, and the second trimester also brought on a new attitude toward herself as becoming a mother. Fluctuations between regressive and maturational tendencies occurred. Conflicts arose between the wish for a child and hostility against it as the enemy within, or the intruder in the marriage or the interfering agent against self-actualization. The relationship to her own mother with accepting or rejecting identification entered into the woman's image of herself as a future mother. In the third trimester fear of death of herself or the baby, of deformities of the baby, or damage to her own body prevailed.

We have reports on the behavior of the research subjects during delivery which, in spite of their cultural similarity, demonstrated many individual varieties. We gained the impression that most neurotic women were not the greatest complainers; some had surprisingly easy deliveries. It seemed that their neurotic guilt feelings were attenuated by the painful process of delivery. A number of women asked urgently for anesthesia at the beginning of the delivery. They wanted to lose consciousness and not participate in a process that mobilized such intense anxieties and pains. But there were also many women who had prepared themselves for natural childbirth in a training course following some modification of Dr. Read's recommendations. When such training had not been available, a number of women insisted on maintaining consciousness as long as possible. Where spinal anesthesia was applied, allowing the women to observe in the mirror sometimes strengthened the active participation, particularly in the terminal process of delivery. (Compare H. Deutsch, p. 229 [8].) In the majority of deliveries the trusting relation to the obstetrician visibly lessened the mothers' anxieties, while a belated appearance of the familiar obstetrician, or his substitution by a less familiar colleague, sometimes triggered off panic reactions. Some women com-

---

of withdrawal or dissociation comparable to that described by Winnicott as a "primary maternal preoccupation" of the last trimester [42]. In our observations this phenomenon can occasionally appear in the first two trimesters of pregnancy or more frequently after delivery, when the mother is confronted with the responsibility of infant care.

225

plained about the officious coldness of their nurses. Anxieties were mitigated by more personal, encouraging nursing care.

A certain number of women requested that the husband accompany them into the delivery room and stay with them. But the obstetricians wisely rejected this request when they were not convinced of the stability and endurance of the husband. Some women seemed to have vindictive motivations for wanting the husband to witness the delivery. Others wanted to spare the husband's disgust or guilt feelings and were proud of enduring the delivery without his attending support.

The wife of a law student delivered on the day her husband had to pass his final public examination. She sat in the audience through the long hours of this examination with mounting labor pains. When he finished, she calmly asked him to drive her to the hospital. After their arrival he offered to stay with her, but she sent him home for a good night's sleep after his strenuous day, and she joyfully presented the newborn infant to him in the morning.

Another woman arranged for her delivery all by herself. She had lost her mother due to suicide when she was ten. She could not share her grief with anybody, since her father, a seafaring captain, was unapproachable. Her marriage with a former homosexual did not permit any closeness; nevertheless, she insisted on impregnation before his departure to foreign countries with the intention of divorce. She was ecstatically happy during her pregnancy and prepared for the delivery most efficiently. Her elated mood carried her through the delivery and the breast-feeding period, and left her with a mild depression after weaning in spite of, or because of, the return of the husband to the family.

In another subject, who was deeply frustrated by her alcoholic husband's bankruptcy at the time of her delivery, a delay in the birth process made a cesarean section necessary. She was ashamed of this "defeat" in the natural delivery and blamed this failure on the irresponsible husband and her childishly careless mother. In a dream she crushed her mother's head and hung her in the cellar.

After a satisfactory delivery some women complained that they could not immediately feel love for the infant, who looked like a stranger to them. Exhaustion and resentment against the creature who has caused so much anxiety and pain make this estrangement under-

226

standable. This emotional lag was mostly overcome in a couple of days, however, greatly helped by the initiation of breast-feeding.

What follows is a case history covering one woman's experiences through the three trimesters of pregnancy. She had difficulty in disengaging herself from the past and orienting herself toward the future. This account underscores a number of neurotic conflicts reactivated at different stages during a first pregnancy. Mrs. E. was 25 years old and married for 6 years when—as she put it—she finally could have what she wanted, what she had been agitating for all those years. She had been obliged to postpone her pregnancy in order to support her husband.

Her mother, a college graduate and a teacher, was her model. She spoke of her father as "the most wonderful, kind man I have ever known." Mrs. E. was the middle of three children, a position she deplored. She therefore wanted to have either two or four children.

Her older brother, whom she adored, was a physician. Her younger sister had been graduated from college and had two sons. This was what their mother expected from all her children: that they finish their education and have a family. Mrs. E. had not lived up to this model. She had left college after two years to marry, with the faint hope of returning to college later. Although she called her marriage happy, she felt deprived and angry with her husband. Having a child was a big step forward to becoming what she felt she should be. She also expected pregnancy and childbirth to improve her looks, described by interviewer and observers as "rather unattractive." Her father had always told her she was overweight, and she was determined to lose weight in pregnancy. Pregnancy also held the promise of satisfying some of her dependency needs. She expected her mother to stay with her after delivery to take care of her, her husband, who "can't boil an egg," and the baby, whom she would not know how to handle. Her brother and the obstetrician would watch over her health.

She wanted the baby to be a girl. This wish was overdetermined, e.g., (1) her husband did not want a boy and early in her pregnancy allegedly said he would throw him out of the window; however, he later changed his mind and was willing to accept whatever might come. (2) She was afraid a boy would be like her husband and their respective bad tempers would clash. In the sentence completion test, she said that boys "are mighty cute as babies but can be real stinkers later," while girls "can be such help to mother and such joy to father." (3) Her brother and sister-in-law couldn't have children of their own and had adopted a little boy—just before Mrs. E. had tried to become pregnant—and "they would like to have our child grow with their child." It was inferred that Mrs. E. unconsciously wanted a daughter as an extension of herself, to grow up with her brother's son, repeating her own childhood experience with him but unhampered by the taboo of incest. She seemed to produce a child for her brother.

Our early predictions were that Mrs. E. needed a child mainly to fulfill her own needs, but that due to her strict superego she would be a responsible mother, although not able to love the child as an independent being.

During the second trimester she defended herself against anxiety that something might happen to her. She had never been afraid of pregnancy and delivery because her mother described it as a wonderful experience. She proudly denied any physical discomfort, irritability, or fatigue. She was especially pleased that she didn't gain much weight.

She expressed some concern about the baby. "I am anxious to know the baby is all right. I hope it will be alive. I always felt like childbearing is one of the main things I was put here for and I am awfully anxious to fulfill it." She felt somewhat guilty for not making preparations for the baby and not having read the government booklet on prenatal care. In a book about expectant motherhood she read only to the point of going to the hospital but not about delivery. Her association to this was that she never liked to read murder mysteries —which seemed to indicate her fear of being killed or killing. She read instead *Look Homeward, Angel*.

Her defenses against these anxieties held up, even when in the eighth month she fell ill with a pyelonephritis. She was in an oxygen tent for 2 hours, and her physician told her she was not taking in enough oxygen to take care of her and the baby both. In spite of this hint she seemed not concerned about the baby but about her record being spoiled. "It disgusted me more than anything else because here I am eight months pregnant, and I haven't had the slightest bit of trouble, and then all of a sudden, kaboom. It was just miserable; I wasn't paying much attention to the baby. I wish I could go ahead and get it over with." She defended herself against guilt feelings for her

228

illness, which she believed was caused by her eating pizza while she was on a salt-free diet. Her brother should have put his foot down when she was eating pizza in his house. "There was nothing that I had done wrong." She was pleased to have lost 4 pounds during her illness. Meanwhile, her husband had become solicitous, helping her with housework, setting up a crib for the baby. Her relationship to him began to change, and she seemed to be able to transfer positive feelings and confidence from her brother to her husband. In the ninth month she became increasingly impatient "to get it over with." During delivery she was given an anesthetic and did not mind missing the experience of birth. The baby was a boy and looked exactly like her husband, for whom he was named.

When seen together with her baby 3 weeks after delivery, Mrs. E. seemed proud and happy. "I guess I'm taking care of him real well; he seems to be thriving." She and her husband were feeding him his bottle alternately. "We [sic] started out nursing him, and it wasn't very satisfactory. He just doesn't work hard enough to get anything" —a reproach reminiscent of her former objections to her husband. However, she suffered much from the pain of drying up, which she found worse than having the baby. "The whole thing got so messy, I just wanted to get it all over with." Now she can share a much cleaner procedure with her husband, who "thinks this boy is one of the wonderful things in the world. It is really amazing." She was ready to go through it again. "Evidently I was just made for it." She weighed 14 pounds less than before her pregnancy, and that pleased her husband and her father. After she had gotten home she became depressed for a few days. She wondered if she would be able to take care of the baby. She hoped people would come to look at him, but they didn't. She was satisfied that he was a good boy and did not cry without reason. He had something in common with her, "he doesn't like to have wet pants on."

Look Homeward, Angel seemed the right title for Mrs. E.'s case, illustrating her overattachment to her past and (since the title refers to a cemetery statue) to her deep fear of death. Mrs. E. appeared strongly attached to her family and distant and hostile toward her husband. We suspected that she wanted in her husband a mother as well as a strong, important brother. Obsessive-compulsive characteristics were marked, and projection and denial outstanding defenses.

229

Her wish for pregnancy grew out of narcissistic needs. She conceived of herself as a failure that could be remedied by having children. The wish for pregnancy was highly enhanced by her rivalry with her sister and unconscious incestuous longings for her brother.

Pregnancy and the possession of a child gave her the assurance that she lived up to the image of herself as a woman and a mother. It also gratified her deep wish for dependency on mother, brother, obstetrician and last, not least—her husband. It was in her new relationship to her husband that we felt Mrs. E. became more mature during pregnancy and that the warmth and confidence in the marital relationship would benefit the child.

Mr. E. apparently did grow up during his wife's pregnancy. This in turn made it possible for her to loosen her ties to the past and to face the future. She seemed interested in the child but still regarded him mainly as a narcissistic supply. Narcissistic satisfaction, of course, is a legitimate premium of childbearing. But in Mrs. E.'s case it seemed excessive in the sense that emphasis was on her having performed well, and the shift to the infant as love object did not occur.

EXPECTANT FATHERHOOD

Compared to the abundance of clinical and theoretic knowledge about expectant motherhood, the literature on expectant fatherhood is slight. Jarvis published a clinical article in which he discussed effects of pregnancy and childbirth upon husbands who were in psychoanalysis [22]. Wainwright has written of fatherhood as a significant precipitant of mental illness, while reporting briefly on ten relevant cases [38]. Liebenberg recently presented a paper on the anxieties and symptoms of a group of sixty-four first-time expectant fathers [26]. Theoretic articles published by Brunswick, Benedek, and Jacobson relate to the adaptational situation of fatherhood [2, 4, 21]. In Erikson's papers there is explicit emphasis on generativity and generosity within the adult stages of ego development [13].

Becoming a father, however, is to a great extent still covered with the dust of stereotypes and convention. The stereotype is mainly built up by the role assigned to the father by others: his wife, parents, in-laws, and peers. This role evolves during the pregnancy, delivery, and the postpartum period. The stereotype underscores two principal features: the maturational transition of first fatherhood, youth into adult, and the phallic achievement of the boastful, beaming father. The convention of the gift of a cigar upon the birth of a child fits with both of these cliché images of fatherhood. In spite of a narcissistic enhancement bestowed by these so frequently offered images, the stereotype also presents the father as a slightly comical figure, that is, someone who has done his job and deserves praise but who, during most of pregnancy and childbirth, must content himself with a supporting role while the real drama is enacted by wife and obstetrician.

The image of the *pater familias* evokes associations of middle-aged stuffiness and distance, but this image is decidedly undergoing a change with the convergence of several important cultural factors. Some of these trends leading to modification and perhaps a new concept of the role of the father are (1) acceptance of previous psychoanalytic findings and recognition of the emotional importance of fatherhood; (2) changing family structure in the new urban environment; (3) shifts in the cultural definition of masculinity.

Therese Benedek has written: "The emotional attitude of the father in the family triad is significant from conception on. He responds to the receptive-dependent needs of his wife which are increased by her pregnancy, by her anxieties about parturition and the care of the child. . . . Independent of hormonal stimulation (in contrast to the pregnant wife), the father's relationship to the child is directed more by hope than by drive" [2]. The father's involvement is gaining special recognition, and husbands are included in prenatal courses and instructions prior to delivery [11]. Increasingly, husbands are encouraged to be with their wives in labor and delivery rooms. Many obstetricians seek and maintain contact with the husbands of their patients [32].

The evolving social structure of middle-class America redefines and emphasizes the participant role of the expectant father and the new father. Sociologists have described the prevailing pattern of family urban life as a residential isolation of the nuclear family from collateral and generational relatives. A most important, if still ill-defined, change is the shift in the concept of masculinity and a narrowing of the differences in culturally approved behavior of males and females [29, 31].

In regard to this change in role assigned to him, a man might respond with enthusiasm, with resistance, or with ambivalence. These cultural changes, which give a husband his meaningful place by the side of his wife, may signal the danger of a new convention, one which coaxes a couple into an artificial togetherness, while discounting individual style and unconscious processes. The possibility of a new stereotype, narrowly and rigidly defined, raises the specter of rapidly assimilated and culture-sanctioned attitudes.[7] Fatherliness is humanized by a new emphasis on participation, but if it is seen as identical with motherliness instead of complementary to it, there is distortion of the authentic paternal role.

In the multidisciplinary study of first pregnancy in wives of university students, mentioned earlier in this chapter, McCorkel, a sociologist, conducted interviews with twenty-nine husbands [28]. He explored three facets of expectant fatherhood: (1) changes in the husband's self-concept while anticipating his father role; (2) changes in his relation to his wife; (3) changes in his social world outside of the home. His major research question became, "What is the nature of the crisis in becoming a father and what are the adaptive responses to it?" He found that for each particular husband, the definition of his situation changed throughout the pregnancy. Despite differences among these normal subjects there were natural groupings of the husbands based upon similar reactions to the event of pregnancy. Three groups, according to their dominant orientation toward marriage and pregnancy, were delineated: (1) those with a romantic orientation; (2) those with a family orientation; (3) those with a career orientation.

The husbands with a romantic orientation had a casual approach to parenthood. Pregnancy brought about a general feeling of awe in these students at the prospect of having to support a wife and a child, where previously they were supported by parents or wives. They felt responsibility in new ways at different times as the pregnancy progressed. The career-oriented husbands regarded prospective fatherhood as a burden that interfered with professional responsibilities. One of them planned a trip to New York City, explaining, "This is our last chance to be human beings. After this we're going to be parents." Two of these men said that state nurseries were great. They all had in common a pattern of ritualistic reaffirmation of the habits and expec-

---

[7] Cf. Coleman, Kris, and Provence [6] in respect to the introduction of psychoanalytic viewpoints into child-rearing practices.

tations which were in force before the pregnancy and of wishing to postpone or avoid acceptance of new responsibilities as parents.

The family-oriented husbands on the other hand accepted the new responsibilities easily and experienced fulfillment in the prospect of being a father and a "family man." The pregnancy was considered a gift, and the relationship to their wives became closer. While previous studies made the assumption that fatherhood begins at the time the child is born, McCorkel observed anticipatory fatherhood occurring during pregnancy. The husbands extended themselves toward the unborn and a transformation of identity began. At the first stage, when his wife missed her period or immediately after medical confirmation of pregnancy, the image of the child was vague. A second stage came with quickening and fetal movements felt by the husbands— "the whole thing becomes more real." A third stage coincided with the perceivable changes in his wife's shape. Several husbands remarked how they noticed and watched children more than before. "Fatherhood is something that grows on you."

Among the three groups the career-oriented husbands actively denied an identity transformation. Their old self was held to be adequate for the change in life situation. For the family-oriented husbands, their transformation into fathers had begun before pregnancy but was intensified and detailed during the months of anticipation.

For the romantically oriented husbands, becoming a father was largely a maturational experience. First pregnancy was a sharp reminder that they were adults and no longer carefree adolescents. The transition was frequently accompanied by marital crisis and conflict with relatives. One of them remarked how he did a lot of thinking above having children, who grow up to have children, whose children have children, and so on to infinity.

During psychoanalysis and psychotherapy with expectant fathers, their conscious and preconscious involvement in the pregnancy comes into focus. In the therapeutic situation a range of unconscious forces, overdetermined fantasies, and distortions of adaptive structures can be investigated. Somatic symptoms in the prospective father, varying from vague gastrointestinal sensations to couvade, and psychologic experiences, reflecting or complementing the emotions of his wife, often accompany the progress of pregnancy. Confronted with the changes in her physical appearance during the second and

233

third trimesters, the man's psychosexual responses to his wife undergo change. Some husbands experience a greater need for sexual intercourse, which may reflect a wish for more closeness to counteract the impending threat of an intruder into the marital union. Some express jealousy, the fear of losing their wife's love, when sexual advances are discouraged or unenthusiastically tolerated. Feelings of inadequacy can be aggravated by a shift in the balance of interdependence.

For other men the sight of the protuberant pregnant abdomen is a deterrent to sexual feelings. Mr. B. had been in psychotherapy for long-standing neurotic difficulties and had eagerly desired and planned to have a child. In the course of his wife's first pregnancy he became acutely disturbed, was disgusted by the roundness and fullness of his wife's body, and felt irresistibly attracted to slim young girls. In the therapeutic situation he relived the rage and contempt he had felt at age 10 when his mother was pregnant. After working through residual oedipal conflicts, his rejection of his wife subsided. A resolution of remnants from the oedipal conflict are relevant for the development of a fatherly attitude.

Another case illustrates a tragic failure and denial of fatherliness attendant upon a reentry into oedipal strivings and conflicts. Mr. W., a 26-year-old clerk, entered psychotherapy with a complaint of inhibited speech when answering a telephone or meeting strangers. He was unable to speak his own name in introducing himself. He claimed his mother had a similar problem. He denied any marital discord; however, 3 months after starting treatment his young wife left him, taking their 2-year-old daughter with her. From a distant town she informed him that she was pregnant and that he was the father, which he conceded. As the pregnancy progressed, he strictly avoided confrontation with his wife and all moves toward reconciliation. Strong ambivalent feelings emerged toward his wife, the unborn child (always referred to as his son), and his daughter. He planned a visit to his wife at the time of her delivery but canceled it at the last minute. Throughout the pregnancy he moved closer to his parents and counseled with them.

Another aspect of the adaptation to early fatherhood is thrown into relief because of the increasing demands, mentioned above, to involve the new father in the actual care of the infant. For some men this participation is a threat to their masculine ego ideal. Freud wrote:

". . . in human beings pure masculinity or femininity is not to be found either in a psychological or biological sense. Every individual on the contrary displays a mixture of character traits belonging to his own and to the opposite sex" [19]. The appeal to their feminine traits arouses defenses in some men, while others feel enriched by developing these potentials.

The emergence of gentle, tender feelings, formerly suppressed for the sake of masculine toughness in a rigid, conventional character had been described by Tolstoy in his novel *Anna Karenina*. Karenin had returned to his wife, Anna, who had given birth to the child of her lover. She was desperately ill and expected to die.

> By his sick wife's bedside he had given way for the first time in his life to that feeling of sympathetic compassion which the suffering of others produced in him, and which he had hitherto been ashamed of, as of a pernicious weakness . . . For the new-born girl he felt a quite peculiar sentiment, not of pity only but of tenderness. At first sheer pity had drawn his attention to the delicate little creature, who was not his child, and who had been cast on one side during her mother's illness, and would certainly have died if he had not troubled about her; and he did not realize how fond he became of her. Several times a day he would go to the nursery, and remain there. . . . At such moments especially Karenin felt quite calm and at peace with himself, and saw nothing abnormal in his position . . . [37].

By way of contrast Tolstoy describes another man's difficulty in experiencing tender, fatherly feelings. Levin, the counterpart to the mundane, ambitious, and romantic characters in the novel, who searches for faith in God and a way to serve humanity, is at a loss when he is confronted with the reality of his wife's pregnancy and later the sight of his newborn son.

> Just as Levin had disliked all the trivial wedding preparations for detracting from the majesty of the event, so now he felt even more of an affront the preparations for the coming birth, the date of which they seemed to be reckoning on their fingers . . . The birth of a son (he was certain it would be a son) which they promised him, but which he still could not believe in, appeared to him on the one hand such an immense and therefore incredible happiness; on the other, an event so mysterious that this assumption of knowledge of what would be, and consequent preparation for it as for something ordinary, something brought about by human beings, shocked and humiliated him. . . . Gazing at this pitiful little bit of humanity, Levin searched his soul in vain for some trace of paternal feeling. He could feel nothing but aversion. . . . His feelings

for this little creature were not at all what he had expected. There was not an atom of pride or joy in them; on the contrary, he was oppressed by a new sense of apprehension—the consciousness of another vulnerable region [37].

This example highlights another vicissitude in the development of fatherliness in idealistic or overintellectualized men, who love their offspring in the abstract but have varying degress of incapacity in establishing object love when they are faced by their infants in the flesh. Such a man might also be highly invested in anticipatory fatherhood during his wife's pregnancy, with intense expectations about the sex of the unborn but disappointment or perhaps disillusion in the infant when confronted with the result.

In some husbands the appeal to their own feminine traits leads to a further identification with their pregnant wives, manifested by an array of somatic symptoms or, more drastically, by couvade. Some men, in the course of psychotherapy or psychoanalysis, acknowledge a deep envy of the capacity to bear and to deliver a child. This archaic wish is fulfilled in Greek mythology with Zeus carrying Dionysus sewed up in his thigh until ripe for birth and also in Athena's birth from the head of Zeus. The procreative wish reaches sublimated actualization in the creative activity of male artists, writers, and scientists.

In an essay entitled The Creative Vow as Essence of Fatherhood, the French existentialist Gabriel Marcel writes: "The gesture of procreation can be accomplished under such conditions that the man only has an indistinct recollection of it and is able to wash his hands of all its consequences since they will take place outside him, in another world as it were, a world with which he has no direct communication. . . . The experience of fatherhood, whatever it may be, or rather become, whatever its special characteristics and its almost innumerable varieties, develops from what must certainly be called a nothingness [néant] of experience. It is exactly the contrary of what is true in motherhood" [27]. This "nothingness," however, is not a void; it is prepared in imagination.

In childhood experiences of boys, both clinical observation and psychoanalytic findings reveal parental fantasies and actions which precede the stages of puberty and genital primacy. There are two aspects to childhood experiences: the boy's wish to have a baby and fantasies attendant to it, and a parental attitude displayed toward younger siblings or playmates. Freud recorded pregnancy fantasies in his paper on little Hans [17]. Winnicott in an early paper on appetite and emotional disorders reported a pregnancy fantasy in a boy with belly pain [41]. Jacobson published an important paper on the wish for a child in boys [21]. Jessner and her co-workers, while conducting a clinical investigation of emotional implications of tonsillectomy, observed several boys who expected to leave the hospital with a baby, as their mothers had done before them [24]. In recent articles Bell has emphasized the organizing role that scrotal sac and testes play in feminine identifications of prepubertal boys and documentation of the wish for a baby in 4-year-olds [1].

In her paper (already mentioned) Jacobson wrote: ". . . narcissistic components in a man's longing for children are apt to revive again his infantile frustrated reproductive wishes. Especially, when he has had experiences of his mother's pregnancy in childhood, they will lend themselves to his present fantasies. As his wife gets pregnant, oedipal and preoedipal experiences will be easily mobilized and give his attitudes a special coloring. Many men show a particular enthusiasm for their work during their wife's pregnancy; others develop neurotic behavior or symptoms which show identification with the pregnant woman. . . . Man approaches the birth of his children with all varieties of mature or infantile object-libidinous, and also highly narcissistic, fantasies and conflicts" [21].

Since Plato, thinkers have been struck by the parallel between procreation and creation, between bodily gestation and the spiritual gestation of a work of the imagination. The creative endeavor of the artist can perhaps be interpreted as a sublimation of his infantile wish to bear a child. The behavior of a creative and gifted man during the time of his wife's pregnancy provides a most interesting area for the study of conflicts and rivalries as they impinge on the emergence of paternal attitudes. A remarkable illustration, with considerable neurotic conflict before arrival at fatherliness, can be found in the biography of Fyodor Dostoevsky and his experience during the first two pregnancies of his young wife.

In 1867 the novelist married his stenographer, 25 years younger than himself. He had been a widower 3 years and his previous marriage had been childless, although Dostoevsky was devoted to a stepson. During the spring he and his bride left Russia to be free

237

from creditors and debtors' prison. During the first 6 months of his wife's pregnancy he avoided work on his projected novel, *The Idiot,* and undertook disastrous gambling excursions. Of all his novels, *The Idiot* came hardest for the writer. "The idea I have is so good and so pregnant with meaning that I worship it. And yet what will come of it? I know beforehand. I'll work on it for eight or nine months, and I'll make a mess of it. Two or three years are necessary for something of this kind" [10].

A daughter, Sonia, was born and Dostoevsky later wrote to a friend: "For the past month I have become aware of quite new sensations, from the first moment I caught sight of my Sonia for the first time, to the moment when, awhile ago, we bathed her. . . . Your god-daughter is a very pretty little thing, in spite of being impossibly, even comically like me . . . I would not have believed it if I had not seen it. The baby is only a month old, and has exactly my expression, even, and exactly the same face, even to the wrinkles on the forehead; —she lies there for all the world as if she were composing a novel!" [7].

The infant died very suddenly, and in another letter Dostoevsky wrote: "That little, three-month-old creature, so pitiful, so tiny,—was already an individual and a person for me. She was beginning to know me and love me, and smiled when I went near. When I sang to her in my ridiculous voice, she liked to listen. She did not cry or frown when I kissed her; she stopped crying when I went to her. And now people say to comfort me that I shall have other children. But where is Sonia? Where is that little person for whom, I am bold to say, I would accept crucifixion if it meant she would live? But enough of this, my wife is crying" [7].

When he finished *The Idiot* there was also the happy news of a second pregnancy. During this pregnancy gambling, guilt, poverty again prevailed but accompanied by intense work on his next novel, *The Possessed*. A daughter, Lyubov, was born and she survived.

The formation of paternal feelings is grounded upon a man's wish to produce a child, his envy of female childbearing, his productive capacities, and his identification with his own father. There remains the all-important conclusive element of his identification with his offspring and a transformation of this emotional bond into an object-related, altruistic love. The risks of fatherhood are as obvious as

238

its opportunities. In becoming a father a man may also become the child he was, reinstalling himself into the oedipal constellation, or a man may deny his fatherhood with all the imaginable deleterious consequences for the couple [30].

Expectant fatherhood is not governed by those impelling psychophysiologic events: gestation, quickening, fetal growth, parturition, and lactation, which provide the sequence in which mother and child discover their separateness. During pregnancy and its aftermath the father experiences these stages at second hand. The perception of fetal movements of his unborn child through sight and touch lack the continuous, visceral knowing felt by his wife. After childbirth a woman will frequently have an enlightening, "So it was you!" experience which is not accessible to her husband. The inevitable distance between the father and the unborn child shrinks at the time of delivery and the visibility of the newborn inaugurates the reality of his otherness. Relationship proceeds from this point, and the possibilities of a father-child tenderness emerge.

It would seem that during pregnancy expectant fatherhood cannot be described in terms of its biologic immediacy. Instead description must fall back upon experiential components such as hope, appropriation, and responsibility. The meaning of fatherhood is grafted upon the procreative act. There is a sense in which fatherliness crystallizes in a decision and a responsibility recognized and accepted. Marcel writes of this aspect of fatherhood as a vital creative vow [27].

In Marcel's perspective of fatherhood as decision, responsibility, and participation it becomes possible to understand the authentic foundations of adoptive parenthood. Adoptive parenthood is by no means a pale and bloodless copy of the real thing, since it partakes of the same essential human elements which are intrinsic to all parent-child relationships.

EXPECTANT PARENTHOOD

The optimal condition for parenthood is a marriage based on a compatible partnership, which can reduce the frustration, anxiety, and anger of everyday life to a tolerable minimum and which at the same time can provide a creative reciprocity and spontaneous solidarity.

The clinical vignettes introduced in this chapter indicate the large number of intrapsychic, interpersonal, and cultural variables that converge in the enterprise of becoming a parent. Voluntary parenthood is an ideal that is endangered but not necessarily violated when obscure and immature motivations enter into the decision for pregnancy. Even accidental or unwanted pregnancy may under some circumstances initiate the response of mature and responsible parenthood.

Insecurity of one partner may be compensated for by the strength of the other; however, this kind of inequality shifts the balance of interdependence to a precariously one-sided dependency. Such a dependency, which is more commonly seen in the expectant mother, becomes exaggerated when the husband is unable to respond adequately to her outspoken or unspoken demands, or when she is intimidated by conflict between her individual aspirations and the duties of motherhood. Conflict is sharpened when a woman cannot encounter or emulate the good mother of her childhood. She sees in motherhood an unreachable perfection and consequently fears she may become the bad mother, or she anticipates motherhood as the beginning of a long martyrdom. These fears are reinforced by the psychiatric preoccupation with schizophrenogenic or neurotogenic mothers and the general tendency to blame all psychopathology in the offspring on the malfunctions of mothering care.

Increased dependency in the expectant father is likely to introduce more serious imbalance and discord. Some pregnant wives, however, practice their mothering skills on their husbands, and in the absence of such a solution an anxious and overdependent man may seek support in male companionship or from another woman. Just as women anticipate conflict between individual ambition and parental duty, so do men. For a man whose masculinity is grounded upon excessive competitive strivings in his work or extramarital erotic conquests, conflict during pregnancy can be intense, uncovering a deep inadequacy in the father-to-be. The readiness to sacrifice a part of himself, his ambition, his freedom in order to become a good father requires a strong fatherly model from a man's own past. It is surprising, however, that often juvenile notions of masculinity in young men are revised and upgraded during pregnancy, or once they face their infant offspring.

Expectant parenthood provides a field for the study of what

Georg Simmel described as the transformation of a dyadic group into a triadic group [34]. For the couple without children their marriage does not signify a superpersonal existence, nor does it appear as a special structure over and above themselves. Their group ceases to exist socially if one partner dies or departs, which is not the case in a family with one or more children. The couple does exhibit unity and synthesis, a coexistence in which coresponsibility is clearly visible, but the couple also embodies internal antithesis and opposition. With the knowledge that the twosome will become a threesome, married persons are keenly aware of the changing nature of their family group. The entrance of a third person will cause considerable realignment. Expectation of the arrival of a first child institutes an authentic super-individual family unity, and it also changes the direct and immediate reciprocity between husband and wife. To have a child is to know a new commitment to marriage and family and to recognize the newcomer as triangling the relationship between the couple.

The entrance of the third person is anticipated as meaning transition, conciliation, and renunciation both of the immediate reciprocity and the direct opposition. Three new structures can evolve in family dynamics upon the arrival of the first child: (1) a third party mediation for disputes between a pair; (2) a nonpartisan self-promotion at the expense of a pair; (3) a third-party power play by means of *divide et impera*. During pregnancy couples gain a growing awareness of these dawning possibilities, and some of these triadic configurations are realized even before the birth of the child. The fetus may become a mediator preventing disruption of unity or unmanageable opposition. Anticipation of the possibilities for taking sides, for splitting, for being excluded, or for being tyrannized may all disturb the expectant parent.

Pregnancy is an opening-out experience and a commencement which powerfully stimulates the potentialites for mutual concern, intimacy, and tenderness. Many expectant parents revise their memories of childhood and discover a new order of reconciliation with their parents within their own experience of becoming parents. It is true that the gap between the generations is wider than it was in the past, but there is more readiness for mutual cooperative aid between contemporaries and an acceptance of psychotherapeutic support by the generation of young parents. Male and female ideals are no longer so

241

dissimilar. Mutuality and empathic understanding can prevent sado-masochistic deterioration of the marital partnership. The expectation of parenthood may or may not counteract the tendency toward narcissistic withdrawal; it does introduce the possibility of responsible, organized activity in a woman and patient tenderness in a man. Although this rapprochement between man and woman is not always successful, common concern for the helplessly dependent infant promotes an integrating union of the prospective parents; and this solidarity strengthens the endurance of anxieties and frustrations as much as it fosters dedication to the child and his future.

Bibliography

1. Bell, A. Significance of scrotal sac and testicles for the pre-puberty male. *Psychoanal. Quart.* 34:182–206, 1965.
2. Benedek, T. Parenthood as a developmental phase: A contribution to the libido theory. *J. Amer. Psychoanal. Ass.* 7:389–417, 1959.
3. Bibring, G. L., Dwyer, T. F., Huntington, D. S., and Valenstein, A. F. A study of the psychological processes in pregnancy and of the earliest mother-child relationship: I. Some propositions and comments. *Psychoanal. Stud. Child* 16:9–24, 1961.
4. Brunswick, R. M. The preoedipal phase of the libido development. *Psychoanal. Quart.* 9:293–319, 1940.
5. Cohen, M. B. Personal identity and sexual identity. *Psychiatry* 29:1–14, 1966.
6. Coleman, R. W., Kris, E., and Provence, S. The study of variations of early parental attitudes. *Psychoanal. Stud. Child* 8:20–47, 1953.
7. Coulson, J. *Dostoevsky: A Self-Portrait.* London: Oxford University Press, 1962. Pp. 176–177.
8. Deutsch, H. *The Psychology of Women.* Vol. II, *Motherhood.* New York: Grune & Stratton, 1945.
9. Deutsch, H. *Selected Problems of Adolescence.* New York: International Universities Press, 1967.
10. Dostoevsky, F. M. Letter quoted in E. Wasiolek (Ed.), *The Notebooks for "The Idiot."* Chicago: University of Chicago Press, 1967. P. 1.
11. English, O. S., and Foster, C. J. *Fathers Are Parents, Too.* New York: Putnam, 1951.
12. Erickson, M. T. Method for frequent assessment of symptomology during pregnancy. *Psychol. Rep.* 20:447–450, 1967.

13. Erikson, E. H.   Identity and the life cycle: Selected papers. *Psychol. Issues* 1:1–171, 1959.
14. Erikson, E. H.   Inner and outer space: Reflections on womanhood. *Daedalus* 93:582–608, 1964.
15. Fairbairn, W.   *The Psychoanalytic Studies of Personality.* London: Tavistock, 1952. P. 145.
16. Flowers, C. E.   The Obstetrician's Responsibility in Reducing Stress Due to Pregnancy. In E. M. Nash, L. Jessner, and D. W. Abse (Eds.), *Marriage Counseling in Medical Practice.* Chapel Hill: University of North Carolina Press, 1964.
17. Freud, S.   Analysis of a Phobia in a Five-Year-Old Boy (1909). In J. Strachey (Ed.), *The Standard Edition of the Complete Psychological Works of Sigmund Freud.* London: Hogarth, 1955. Vol. 10, pp. 1–149.
18. Freud, S.   Some Character-Types Met with in Psycho-Analytic Work (1916). In J. Strachey (Ed.), *The Standard Edition of the Complete Psychological Works of Sigmund Freud.* London: Hogarth, 1957. Vol. 14, pp. 309–333.
19. Freud, S.   Three Essays on the Theory of Sexuality (1905). In J. Strachey (Ed.), *The Standard Edition of the Complete Psychological Works of Sigmund Freud.* London: Hogarth, 1953. Vol. 7, p. 220.
20. Freud, S.   The "Uncanny" (1919). In J. Strachey (Ed.), *The Standard Edition of the Complete Psychological Works of Sigmund Freud.* London: Hogarth, 1955. Vol. 17, pp. 217–256.
21. Jacobson, E.   Development of the wish for a child in boys. *Psychoanal. Stud. Child* 5:139–152, 1950.
22. Jarvis, W.   Some effects of pregnancy and childbirth in men. *J. Amer. Psychoanal. Ass.* 10:689–699, 1962.
23. Jessner, L.   On Becoming a Mother. In R. Griffith (Ed.), *Conditio Humana.* Berlin: Springer, 1966.
24. Jessner, L., Blom, G. E., and Waldfogel, S.   Emotional implications of tonsillectomy and adenoidectomy on children. *Psychoanal. Stud. Child* 7:126–169, 1952.
25. Lewis, A.   *An Interesting Condition.* New York: Doubleday, 1950.
26. Liebenberg, B.   Expectant fathers (digest). *Amer. J. Orthopsychiat.* 37:358–359, 1967.
27. Marcel, G.   *Homo Viator.* New York: Harper & Row, 1962. Pp. 102–103.
28. McCorkel, R. J., Jr.   Husbands and Pregnancy: An Exploratory Study. University of North Carolina M.A. thesis, 1964.
29. Mead, M.   *Male and Female.* New York: New American Library, 1955.
30. Merleau-Ponty, M.   Preface to A. Hesnard, *L'Oeuvre de Freud.* Paris: Payot, 1960.

243

31. Odenwald, R. P. *Disappearing Sexes.* New York: Random House, 1966.
32. Schaefer, G. The expectant father: His care and management. *Postgrad. Med.* 38:658–663, 1965.
33. Sontag, L. W. Differences in modifiability of fetal behavior and physiology. *Psychosom. Med.* 6:151–154, 1944.
34. Spykman, N. J. *The Social Theory of Georg Simmel.* New York: Atherton, 1966.
35. Straus, E. W. *On Obsession.* New York: Nervous and Mental Disease Monographs, 1948.
36. Thrasher, J. H. *The Subculture of Pregnancy in a College Community.* Chapel Hill: University of North Carolina Press, 1963.
37. Tolstoy, L. *Anna Karenina.* (Translated by R. E. Edmonds.) Baltimore: Penguin, 1954.
38. Wainwright, W. H. Fatherhood as a precipitant of mental illness. *Amer. J. Psychiat.* 123:40–44, 1966.
39. Wenner, N. K. Dependency Patterns in Pregnancy. In J. H. Masserman (Ed.), *Science and Psychoanalysis,* Vol. X. New York: Grune & Stratton, 1966.
40. Wenner, N. K., and Ohaneson, E. M. Motivations for pregnancy (digest). *Amer. J. Orthopsychiat.* 37:357–358, 1967.
41. Winnicott, D. W. Appetite and Emotional Disorder. In *Collected Papers: Through Paediatrics to Psycho-Analysis.* New York: Basic Books, 1958.
42. Winnicott, D. W. Primary Maternal Preoccupation. In *Collected Papers: Through Paediatrics to Psycho-Analysis.* New York: Basic Books, 1958.

10

The Mother-Infant
Experience of
Mutuality

Donald W. Winnicott

EDITORS' INTRODUCTION

The physiologic exchange between the pregnant mother and her fetus—the physiologic symbiosis—is continued postpartum in the body language and other preverbal communications between the mother and her infant. The conceptualization of the effects of these interactions evolved relatively late, when psychoanalysts learned to recognize, in the transference, manifestations of the patient's pathogenic potentials of that early phase of development.

The following chapter is a moving illustration of the depth and intensity of a psychoanalyst's experience. By studying the behavior of infants the author arrived at the conviction that the nonverbal experiences between an infant and his mother establish a mutuality which unconsciously sets the emotional tone of interpersonal experiences and their intrapsychic coloring throughout life. The intense experiencing of the discovery seems to overshadow the knowledge that this discovery has been made by several other psychoanalysts and its derivations studied in various contexts since 1938. Since the meaning of the mutuality of the infant's nonverbal experiences becomes woven into the texture of the psychic apparatus, its significance for a particular individual comes sharply into focus in the regression of the psychoanalytic process, especially—as the author emphasizes—if the therapist can permit it. The author, instead of providing a theoretic explanation of what is going on, describes the patient's regressive experience in transference and the analyst's controlled regression in response as an illustration of how this primitive mutuality can (when indicated) serve a therapeutic purpose in the psychoanalytic process.

E. J. A.
T. B.

Whereas it is generally known that there is almost infinite subtlety in a mother's management of her baby, it took a long time for psychoanalytic theory to reach to this area of living experience. It is not difficult to see some of the reasons for the delay. Psychoanalysis, in its beginnings, had to emphasize the powerfulness of feelings and of conflicting feelings and had to explore the defenses against them. In terms of childhood, psychoanalysis occupied itself for several decades with the oedipus complex and all the complications that arise out of the feelings of boys and girls who have become whole persons related to whole persons.

Psychoanalysis gradually began to encroach on the experiences of younger children and explored the conflicts within the psyche and developed the concepts covered by words and moods and the persecutions from within and without. The psychoanalyst was always fighting the battle for the individual against those who ascribed troubles to environmental influence.

Gradually the inevitable happened and psychoanalysts, carrying with them their unique belief in the significance of details, had to start to look at dependence, that is to say, the early stages of the development of the human child when dependence is so great that the behavior of those representing the environment could no longer be ignored.

We are now right in the study of these very early mutual influences. We must expect resistance to the work we do, this time not because of the operation of repression and of anxiety in those who meet our work, but resistance that belongs to the feeling that a sacred area is being encroached upon. It is as if a work of art were being subjected to an analytic process. Can one be sure that the capacity to appreciate the work of art fully will not be destroyed by the searchlight that is played upon the picture? It could indeed be well argued that these very early phenomena ought to be left alone, and I who have found myself making a study of them could not but insist that what we think we know about these intimacies is not useful reading material for artists or for young mothers. The sort of thing that can be discussed when we look at these early phenomena cannot be taught. It is remarkable, however, that certain people, even fathers and mothers, do like to read about these things after they have been through the experiences.

For our part as psychiatrists we have another reason why we must go ahead in our work with the examination of the subtleties of the parent-infant relationship. We have to take into consideration that this is an area of research which can throw light on the etiology of the group of disorders that are labeled psychotic or schizoid, that is to say that are not the affective disorders or those that are called psychoneurotic. In fact, if in our psychoanalytic work or in any other kind of psychotherapy we find ourselves temporarily involved with schizoid processes in our patients, we know that we shall be dealing in our consulting rooms with the same phenomena that characterize the experiences of mothers and infants. We shall be caught up in the immense needs of the dependent infant and in the countertransference with the massive responsive processes which show us to some extent what is happening to parents when they have a child. As psychiatrists, therefore, we are left with no alternative but to go ahead and try to describe something of what we find, taking care not to put our views forward in the form of advice to mothers and fathers and childminders, but to keep what we say in reserve for the use of colleagues who must find themselves involved from time to time with patients who develop dependence that is near absolute.

It is a relief that psychoanalysis has nearly come through the phase, which lasted a half century, in which, when analysts referred to babies, they could only speak in terms of the baby's erotic and aggressive drives. It was all a matter of pregenital instinct, of oral and anal eroticism and reactions to frustration, with some rather wild additions in terms of natural aggressive behavior and destructive ideas, *agressivité*. Work of this kind had its value and continues to have value; but it is necessary now for analysts who refer to the nature of the baby to see what else is there to be seen. There are some shocks in store for the orthodox analyst if he looks further.

THE SUBJECTIVE OBJECT

In order to study the way in which the human infant achieves the capacity to objectify, it is necessary to accept that at first there is no such capacity. To allow for this the theorist needs to be able to

247

give up some tenets of which he has rightly been proud in all the years since Freud gave us the concept of the oedipus complex, the idea of infantile sexuality, and the psychoanalytic technique for investigation that is the same as the psychoanalytic technique for therapy.

In this new area, the idea of the individual rather than of the environment (a major psychoanalytic contribution) needs to be modified or even dropped. When it is said that a baby is dependent, and at the beginning absolutely dependent, and this is really meant, then it follows that what the environment is like has significance because it is a part of the baby.

A baby is not what one may postulate by assessing that baby's potential. A baby is a complex phenomenon that includes the baby's potential *plus* the environment. To understand this idea we may look at a child of 2. We may say: This child has not been the same since the new baby was born. In many cases we may diagnose illness patterns, and these illness patterns (shown as rigidity of defense organizations) call for treatment. The existence of illness patterns must not be allowed to obscure the reality that the child in question is a child *with a younger brother or sister.* With the same potential, this child would be different if he or she were the youngest child or the only child, or if a baby had been born but had died. No one would object to this idea in terms of a 2-year-old, which of course does not alter the fact that it is possible to give effective psychotherapy in respect of the child's psychopathology. Psychopathology, however, is a different thing from health and from the effect on the child of the innumerable environmental features that belong to the child who is not far from absolute dependence and is but a short way along the path toward independence.

To carry the argument back to the very early stages, the significance of the environment for the baby when there is near-absolute dependence is such that *we cannot describe the baby without describing the environment.*

The stage of absolute dependence or near-absolute dependence belongs to the state of the baby at the beginning who has not yet separated a *not-me* from what is *me,* of the baby who is not yet equipped to perform this task. In other words, the object is a subjective object, not objectively perceived. Even if it is repudiated, put over there, the object is still an aspect of the baby.

How does the next stage come about? Its development and establishment are not due to the operation of the child's inherited tendencies (toward integration, object-seeking, psychosomatic collusion,
etc.). In any one case it may never happen in spite of perfectly good
inherited tendencies in the baby. This development takes place *because of the baby's experiences of the mother's* (or mother substitute's) *adaptive behavior*. The mother's adaptive behavior makes it
possible for the baby to find outside the self that which is needed and
expected. By means of the *experience* of good enough mothering the
baby goes over into objective perception, having inherited the tendency to do this *and* having been given the perceptual equipment and
opportunity.

In order to understand the part played by the mother it is necessary to have a concept such as the one that I have described in Primary Maternal Preoccupation [6]. I have tried to show that we may
expect good enough mothering from the mothers of the world, and of
the past ages, because of something that happens to women during
pregnancy, something that lasts for some weeks after the baby's birth
unless a psychiatric disturbance in the mother prevents this temporary
change in her nature from occurring.

In addition, it is necessary to be able to think of a baby as
beginning to have some capacity for objectivity, and yet being generally unable to objectify, with a forward and backward movement in
this area of development.

COMMUNICATION

In order to clarify our concepts we can usefully bring ourselves
to think in terms of communication. To explain how this can help I
wish to give an example.

From birth a baby can be seen to take food. Let us say that the
baby finds the breast and sucks and ingests a quantity sufficient for
satisfaction of instinct and for growth. This can be the same whether
the baby has a brain that will one day develop as a good one or
whether the baby's brain is in fact defective or damaged. What we
need to know about is the communication that goes or does not go
with the feeding process. It is difficult to be sure of such matters by
the instrument of infant-observation, though it does seem that some

babies watch the mother's face in a meaningful way even in the first weeks. At 12 weeks, however, babies can give us information from which we can do more than guess that communication is a fact.

ILLUSTRATION 1.   Although normal babies vary considerably in their rate of development (especially as measured by observable phenomena), it can be said that at 12 weeks they are capable of play such as this: Settled in for a (breast) feed, the baby looks at the mother's face and his or her hand reaches up so that in play the baby is feeding the mother by means of a finger in her mouth.

It may be that the mother has played a part in the establishment of this play detail, but even though this is true it does not invalidate the conclusion that I draw from the fact that this kind of playing can happen [5].

I draw the conclusion from this that, whereas all babies take in food, there does not exist a communication between the baby and the mother except insofar as there develops a mutual feeding situation. The baby feeds and the baby's experience includes the idea that the mother knows what it is like to be fed.

If this happens for all to see at 12 weeks, then in some way or other it can (but need not) be true in some obscure way at an earlier date.

In this way we actually witness a *mutuality* which is the beginning of a communication between two people; this (in the baby) is a developmental achievement, one that is dependent on the baby's inherited processes leading toward emotional growth and likewise dependent on the mother and her attitude and her capacity to make real what the baby is ready to reach out for, to discover, to create.[1]

Babies feed, and this may mean much to the mother, and the ingestion of food may give the baby gratification in terms of drive satisfactions. Another thing, however, is the communication between the baby and the mother, something that is a matter of experience and that depends on the mutuality that results from cross-identifications.

Melanie Klein has done full justice to the subject of projective and introjective identifications, and it is on the basis of her develop-

[1] This has a direct relationship to Sechehaye's term *symbolic realization,* which means enabling a real thing to become a meaningful symbol of mutuality in a specialized setting [4].

ment of Freud's ideas of this kind that we are able to build this part of theory in which communication has significance greater than that which is usually called "object-relating" [3].

In giving this illustration, I have remained close to the familiar framework of psychoanalytic statements concerning object-relating because I wish to keep open the bridges that lead from older theory to newer theory. Nevertheless, I am obviously near to Fairbairn's statement made in 1944 that psychoanalytic theory was emphasizing drive-satisfaction at the expense of what Fairbairn called "object-seeking." And Fairbairn was working, as I am here, on the ways in which psychoanalytic theory needed to be developed or modified if the analyst could hope to become able to cope with schizoid phenomena in the treatment of patients.[2]

At this point it is necessary to interpolate a reference to the obvious fact that the mother and the baby come to the point of mutuality in different ways. The mother has been a cared-for baby; also she has played at babies and at mothers; she has perhaps experienced the arrival of siblings, cared for younger babies in her own family or in other families; and she has perhaps learned or read about baby care and she may have strong views of her own on what is right and wrong in baby management.

The baby, on the other hand, is being a baby for the first time, has never been a mother, and has certainly received no instruction. The only passport the baby brings to the customs' barrier is the sum of the inherited features and inborn tendencies toward growth and development.

Consequently, whereas the mother can identify with the baby, even with a baby unborn or in process of being born, and in a highly sophisticated way, the baby brings to the situation only a developing capacity to achieve cross-identifications in the *experience of mutuality* that is made a fact. This mutuality belongs to the mother's capacity to adapt to the baby's needs.[3]

---

[2] See Fairbairn, page 88: ". . . since it is only ego structures that can *seek* [my italics] relationships with objects" [1].

[3] The word *need* has significance here just as *drive* has significance in the area of satisfaction of instinct. The word wish is out of place as it belongs to sophistication that is not to be assumed at this stage of immaturity that is under consideration.

MUTUALITY UNRELATED TO DRIVES

It is possible now to enter the deep waters of mutuality that does not directly relate to drives or to instinct tension. Traveling toward this, another example may be given.

Like so much of what we know of these very early babyhood experiences, this example derives from the work that has to be done in the analysis of older children or of adults when the patient is in a phase, long or short, in which regression to dependence is the main characteristic of the transference. Work of this kind always has two aspects, the first being the positive discovery in the transference of early types of experience that were missed out or distorted in the patient's own historical past, in the very early relationship to the mother; and the second being the patient's use of the therapist's failures in technique. These failures produce anger, and this has value because the anger brings the past into the present. At the time of the initial failure (or relative failure) the baby's ego organization was not organized sufficiently for so complex a matter as anger about a specific matter.

Analysts with a rigid analytic morality that does not allow touch miss a great deal of that which is now being described. One thing they never know, for instance, is that the analyst makes a little twitch whenever he or she goes to sleep for a moment or even wanders over in the mind (as may well happen) to some fantasy of his or her own. This twitch is the equivalent of a failure to hold in terms of mother and baby. The mind has dropped the patient. (These cases put a strain on us. There are long periods of quiescence, sometimes at a room temperature that is higher than the analyst would choose to work in.)

ILLUSTRATION 2. A boy of 6 years was able to give me accurate information in a one-session therapeutic consultation about the way his mother went to sleep while holding him when he was 14 months old [7].

This was the nearest he could get to giving me the information that his mother had a depressive illness at that date which started with her developing a tendency to go to sleep.

In the language of this paper, the boy experienced a series of failures of communication at the points at which the mother became withdrawn.

My understanding of the child's communication in this one session enabled the boy to go forward in his development. A year later when I saw him, he was a normal boyish boy who brought his younger brother to see me. This was his own idea. He remembered the work that we had done together [7].

ILLUSTRATION 3.   This example is taken from the analysis of a woman of 40 years (married, two children) who had failed to make full recovery in a 6-year analysis with a woman colleague. I agreed with my colleague to see what analysis with a man might produce, and so started a second treatment.

The detail I have chosen for description has to do with the absolute need this patient had, from time to time, to be in contact with me. (She had feared to make this step with a woman analyst because of the homosexual implications.)

A variety of intimacies were tried out, chiefly those that belong to infant feeding and management. There were violent episodes. Eventually it came about that she and I were together with her head in my hands.

Without deliberate action on the part of either of us there developed a rocking rhythm. The rhythm was rather a rapid one, about 70 per minute (c.f. heartbeat), and I had to do some work to adapt to this rate. Nevertheless, there we were with *mutuality* expressed in terms of a slight but persistent rocking movement. We were *communicating* with each other without words. This was taking place at a level of development that did not require the patient to have maturity in advance of that which she found herself possessing in the regression to dependence of the phase of her analysis.

This experience, often repeated, was crucial to the therapy, and the violence that had led up to it was only now seen to be a preparation and a complex test of the analyst's capacity to meet the various communicating techniques of early infancy.

This shared rocking experience illustrates what I wish to refer to in the early stages of baby care. The baby's instinctual drives are not specifically involved. The main thing is a communication between the baby and the mother in terms of the anatomy and physiology of live bodies. The subject can easily be elaborated, and the significant phenomena will be the crude evidences of life, such as the heartbeat, breathing movements, breath warmth, movements that indicate a need for change of position, etc.

BASIC CARE

These primitive techniques that have intercommunication as a by-product lead naturally to still more primitive or fundamental interactions that are of the nature of silent communications; that is to say, the communication only becomes noisy when it fails.

Here I am in the area covered, I think, by Hartmann's phrase, "the average expectable environment," though I cannot be sure that Hartmann intended to refer to these very early silent communications.

What I have to say here is covered by the term *holding*. A wide extension of *holding* allows this one term to describe all that a mother does in the physical care of her baby, even including putting the baby down when a moment has come for the impersonal experience of being held by suitable nonhuman materials.

In giving consideration to these matters, it is necessary to postulate a state of the mother who is (temporarily) identified with her baby so that she knows without thinking about it more or less what the baby needs. She does this, in health, without losing her own identity.[4]

I have tried elsewhere to develop the theme of the developmental processes in the baby that need, for their becoming actual, the mother's holding [8]. The "silent" communication is one of reliability which, in fact, protects the baby from *automatic reactions* to impingement from external reality, these reactions breaking the baby's line of life and constituting traumata. A trauma is that against which an individual has no organized defense so that a confusional state supervenes, followed perhaps by a reorganization of defenses, defenses of a more primitive kind than those which were good enough before the occurrence of the trauma.[5]

Examination of the baby being held shows that communication is either silent (reliability taken for granted) or else traumatic (producing the experience of unthinkable or archaic anxiety).

This divides the world of babies into two categories:

1. Babies who have not been significantly "let down" in infancy, and whose belief in reliability leads toward the acquisition of a personal reliability which is an important ingredient of the state which may be termed "toward independence." These babies have a line of life and retain a capacity to move forward and backward (developmentally) and become able to take all the risks because of being well-insured.

[4] In psychopathology she may be so much identified with the baby that she loses her maternal capacity and, if she retains some sanity, she hands the baby over to the care of a nurse. In this way she vicariously gets well held, and one can see in this a natural seeking for that which the patient may get in the analytic transference in phases of regression to dependence.
[5] Khan has developed this aspect of trauma [2].

2. Babies who have been significantly "let down" once or in a pattern of environmental failures (related to the psychopathologic state of the mother or mother-substitute). These babies carry with them the experience of unthinkable or archaic anxiety. They know what it is to be in a state of acute confusion or the agony of disintegration. They know what it is like to be dropped, to fall forever, or to become split into psychosomatic disunion.

In other words, they have experienced trauma, and their personalities have to be built round the reorganization of defenses following traumata, defenses that must needs retain primitive features such as personality splitting.[6]

Of course, the world of human beings is not made up of examples of these two extremes. Those who are started off well, as most babies surely are, may be let down at later stages and suffer traumata of a kind; and *per contra* babies who have been badly let down in early stages may be almost "cured" of their disastrous beginnings by therapeutic care at later stages.

Nevertheless, it is valuable for the student of human nature to keep in mind the two extremes. Especially is it valuable for the psychiatrist and the psychotherapist to know of these matters, since a study of the etiology and psychopathology of the schizoid states and of the special features of the schizoid or psychotic transference leads right back to the reorganization of defenses of primitive quality following the experienced acute confusional states of early infancy; these follow traumas in the area in which the baby (for healthy development) must be able to take reliability for granted, the area that is almost covered by an extended use of the term *holding*. But reliable holding of a baby is something that needs to be communicated, and this is a matter of the baby's experiences. Just here psychology involves communication in physical terms, the language of which is mutuality in experience.

Bibliography

1. Fairbairn, W. R. D. *Psychoanalytic Studies of the Personality.* London: Tavistock, 1952.

[6] Phobic states are loose organizations in defense against defense failures.

2. Khan, M. M. R.   Ego distortion, cumulative trauma, and the role of reconstruction in the analytic situation. *Int. J. Psychoanal.* 45:272–279, 1964.
3. Klein, M.   *The Psycho-Analysis of Children.* London: Hogarth, 1954.
4. Sechehaye, M. A.   *Symbolic Realization.* New York: International Universities Press, 1951.
5. Winnicott, D. W.   Getting to Know Your Baby. In J. Hardenberg (Ed.), *The Child and the Family: First Relationships.* London: Tavistock, 1957.
6. Winnicott, D. W.   Primary Maternal Preoccupation. In *Collected Papers: Through Paediatrics to Psycho-Analysis.* London: Tavistock, 1958; New York: Basic Books, 1958.
7. Winnicott, D. W.   A clinical study of the effect of a failure of the average expectable environment on a child's mental functioning. *Int. J. Psychoanal.* 46:81–87, 1965.
8. Winnicott, D. W.   *The Maturational Processes and the Facilitating Environment: Studies in the Theory of Emotional Development.* London: Hogarth, 1965.

11

The Mother's Reaction
to Her Toddler's Drive
for Individuation

Margaret S. Mahler
Fred Pine
Anni Bergman

EDITORS' INTRODUCTION

This chapter represents a significant development in the history of the psychoanalytic theory of personality development. At an earlier stage of the history, Karl Abraham described the toddler period in terms of "the late oral phase" and "early and late anal phases." In the current era of psychoanalytic ego psychology, the term formulated by Mahler is more comprehensive, the processes of separation-individuation encompassing both the libidinal phases and the object-relationship aspects of the oral and anal stages of development.

An assessment of the influence of mothers upon the libidinal development of their children required only indirect and relatively crude methods of observation, the data deriving from reports furnished by the mothers or deduced from the psychoanalysis of mothers and children. Mothers were not studied in direct interaction with their children. It is a circuitous road that has led psychoanalytic theory, winding between the biology and pathology of mental processes, to the current conceptualization that personality development is a function of the reciprocal interchanges between mother and child. So now, in order to obtain answers to problems set by the mutuality of communication and contact between parents and children, direct methods of observation have become necessary.

This expansion of psychoanalytic research methodology does not diminish the significance of psychoanalysis itself as an incomparable tool of investigation because of its unique propensity for generating hypotheses and conceptualizing observations. There is now, in addition, a continual transaction between direct observational methods of investigation and theory-building. Observations check, support, confirm, or contradict hypotheses; hypotheses, on the other hand, pose new problems for investigation, thus enlarging the scope of observation and demanding refinement of its tools.

In this chapter the authors present one aspect of their extensive investigations, and in so doing offer a splendid illustration of the fruitful interaction of psychoanalytic hypothesis and direct observation.

E. J. A.
T. B.

V arious inferences may be drawn about intrapsychic events that seem to occur in the mother when confronted with the double-edged problem of separation-individuation, i.e., the impending (symbiotic) object-loss on the one hand, and on the other, the promise of and actual gain in object relationship to an individuating love object —the growing child.

There is a diversity in reactions on the part of different mothers to specific indicative maturational events in the child's life. These "events" all manifest the transition from totally dependent lap baby into and through the separation-individuation phase [5, 6]. Decreased molding and increased visual and visual-motor exploration, the specific smiling response, weaning, stranger reactions, separation anxiety, locomotor advances and walking, and finally, verbalization, accompanied by vivid affectomotor gestures, express the child's aims and feelings. In each case, the change is from a more symbiotic dependence upon the mother (matched in varying degrees by the mother's own symbiotic needs) to more developed object relationship. Most striking, of course, are the reactions of mothers who make a sharp turnabout in the overall quality of their maternal care in response to these maturational events. Often, however, the mother's reaction stops short of a gross impact upon overt behavior. In these cases the actual response may be discernible through insight into the reconstruction of her fantasies.

In order to indicate the range and the significance of these reactions, available data of widely differing origins and degrees of abstraction are drawn upon: (1) psychoanalytic data from mothers whose analyses have enabled us to understand these reactions; (2) fantasy material from interviews with mothers who were observed regularly during the course of their child's separation-individuation as well as from spontaneous conversations between the mothers; and (3) observations of the same mothers in interaction with their children during this phase, and as these maturational events were taking place, during the 8 years of our observational study.

During the course of our study of the symbiotic and separation-individuation phases of normal development, we have observed mothers who perform their mothering function better with their child as lap baby than as toddler; with other mothers the situation was reversed. Still others were able gradually to grow in their maternal role to a higher level and to achieve greater distance from the child, compatible with the changes in their individuating child [6, 10]. Although not all mothers show either marked worsening or significant improvement in their maternal functioning, among those who do, the "fit" of their behavior with what appear to be maturational givens in the first two years is suggestive enough to warrant comment [2].

Schematically, these maternal reactions are organized around two aspects of the child's maturation: (1) his increasing awareness of separateness from mother and (2) his increasing mastery of the ego apparatuses, most notably his increasing control over motility and the increased specificity of his psychologic communications (as opposed to mere cueing). Once again schematically, the mother may respond to either or both of these as though they meant a loss of the child's symbiotic dependence upon her, or as a step forward in clarity of communication with an autonomous and separate being—a gain in object relationship.

In reality, of course, the situation is far more complex. The infant's stage of total dependence upon mother—a stage marked by inexplicit cues from the young infant with regard to the specific sources of his periodic discomfort—can obviously be quite distressing to some mothers. Further, the child's progress through the separation-individuation phase includes not only his separation from mother, but also an increased appeal to and claim upon the mother. The mother's reaction may therefore reflect not only loss of symbiosis but the sense of relief from it, and not only gain in object relationship but also apprehension about the new claims that this may make upon her.

Though the focus is on the mothers, we should not fail to note that the impact is circular—the mother's reaction to her individuating child reverberates upon her child and then back again. If an inner sense of autonomy is to develop in the child, it is necessary for the individuation process to be gradual and progressive [7]. A mother who self-protectively withdraws from or actively opposes her child's drive for individuation will, in either case, bring this autonomy closer into the sphere of conflict.

The changes in the child that mark the opening of and passage through the separation-individuation subphases unfortunately cannot be elaborated here. One of the authors has described four subphases through which normal children characteristically pass during the separation-individuation process from 6 to 36 months of age, and we must refer to these descriptions [5, 6, 9]. Given the unending variety and range of maternal reactions to the process of separation-individuation, in this short chapter we can only illustrate a few of these around certain systematic issues.

What begins for the child as an increasing awareness of separateness from his mother, with attendant anxieties, and culminates optimally in his ability to sustain intrapsychic and physical separateness can be, for the mother, a progressive sense of loss of the child. Thus, if pregnancy and birth potentially signify for the mother the attainment of diverse wishes (for breast, penis, mother, father, for example), birth itself signals the onset of the process of loss. The work of Helene Deutsch is relevant here [3], as is the widely occurring phenomenon of postpartum depression. Following the long period of gestation, the infant ceases to be a part of the mother's body. Similarly, during the initial months of the infant's life, the inevitable repeated distress which he experiences, and the mother's frequent helplessness in dealing with it, can puncture her narcissistically invested image of the ideal child as well as her image of herself as a competent mother. From about the fifth month on, the normal infant resists being enveloped in exclusive symbiosis [12]. Gradually, the maturational "flux" is stepped up, and autonomy carries him out of the mother's lap. At first he merely resists molding to her; later, his behavior reveals that he has his own aims. The mother thereby loses her symbiotic union with the child in spite of any wishes or fantasies she may have of retaining it.[1]

Another major maturational current having important consequences for the mother-child relationship is the child's progressive internal differentiation and his mastery of cognitive and motor apparatuses. Just as the process leading to cessation of the symbiotic union may be experienced by the mother as a sense of loss, individuation may be experienced as one of gain.

When we speak of "individuation" we are referring to those

---

[1] The process of loss does not, of course, end at this point; it continues in the child's growing relationships with persons "other than mother" and in the gradual shift of his attention outward onto an ever-widening environment.

intrapsychic advances that mark the child's development of skills, styles, and individual characteristics. The child begins to have more specific preferences; he can make them known more clearly; and later, he can, on his own, find routes to their satisfaction. The horizons of his world widen as his increasing perceptual acuity, intellectual grasp, and motor skills enable him to record, in memory, experiences of a wide variety of persons and things.

The mother who is so disposed may find pleasure in the child's autonomous achievements, since the increasing complexity and richness of his aims and capacities for communication are leading to opportunities for new forms of parent-child contact. "He's finally a person," parents say, or "he's good company now." The mother can now have contact with her child through play, baby games, walking together, and through his eagerness to share with and learn from both mother and father. Concerning the last, Phyllis Greenacre has pointed out the importance of companionship with the father in the child's second year; the romping games [4] are especially important (cf. also Mahler's discussion of Greenacre's paper, October, 1966, unpublished).

Thus, the child's maturation provides the beginnings not only of the mother's experience of losing the symbiotic object, but also of her finding an object relationship with her child, as well as a basis for identification with him. Her actual response to these new opportunities will of necessity be shaped by her own intrapsychic processes.

These two maturational trends are, of course, two aspects of one complex growth process. The child's ability to separate himself from mother depends upon his maturational achievements in regard to the motor apparatus; similarly, his capacity to sustain separation depends upon those particular achievements in memory, anticipation, and affect control which we refer to collectively as the attainment of libidinal object-constancy. And while the mother may experience alternations of loss and increased closeness to her child, the total experience is a unified intrapsychically determined one, and not a balance of opposing trends.

Although it is during the second year of the child's life that perhaps the major steps in both of these maturational sequences take place, we should note, however, two contrasting reactions on the part of mothers to the *first* months of the child's life. For some, confrontation with the infant's helplessness and total dependence upon her, coupled with his often unclear signals, proves to be a frightening experience, attended by anxiety lest the fragile infant somehow be damaged. For other mothers, the very *lack* of clear-cut cues from the infant provides the opportunity to live out a fantasy of symbiotic union with him.

Benedek and Winnicott have described in detail the symbiotic or holding behavior of the average mother toward her young infant during the first half of the first year [1, 13]. We would add that, in our study of average mothers with their infants, we have been impressed by the enormous variation in these mothers' ability to read and react to the normal baby's cues [8, 9]. Certainly not all mothers fall into the aforementioned categories—either anxiously misreading cues or ignoring the child's more individual needs so as to satisfy their own. Some of the most striking *changes* that occur in mothering can best be understood against one or the other of these backgrounds.

Proceeding then into the period of the child's separation-individuation, we can see that this new era in both the child's and the mother's life can produce reactions which are diverse not only among mothers, but within each individual mother as well. For example, she may suffer feelings of loss of the previous symbiotic oneness and completeness, as well as feelings of relief from the demands of the previous symbiotic-parasitic relationship. She may find pleasure in the new object relationship and in the child's "choice" of relationship to *his* mother, while finding that his concentration upon her and unwillingness to accept substitute mothering objects are new and possibly threatening kinds of demands.

From the standpoint of the child's increased mastery of communication and other ego functions (this is simply the other side of the coin), the mother may experience each step the child makes as a signal of his progressive independence, and as a consequent loss, just as, in contrast, she may respond to the now-increased clarity of his demands with pleasure. She may feel confident that she "finally knows, for the first time" what it is that the child wants. Whereas this "first time" reaction is probably more common or at least more dramatic among fathers, we have seen it in some mothers as well. (In fathers it undoubtedly reflects not only a response to the increasing clarity of the child's communications and social responses, but also to the child's turning outward to a world that includes father.)

To say that the child's maturation may confront a mother with

263

the experience of loss (or of gain)—even if we then speak more precisely of loss of symbiotic union (or gain of object relationship)—is to make only the most universal of statements. *What* is lost (in the mother's fantasy) or *what* the mother hopes to find in the object relationship to the child must be spelled out differently for each individual. The extent to which the lost part of the self symbolizes the phallus, for example, or the extent to which the object-relationship with the child has the quality of a relationship to a parent, a sibling, or a child varies from mother to mother. The only universal element is the fact of *some* impact upon the mother of the child's maturational advances toward separateness and individuation. The extent of the impact, as well as the content of the mother's experience of it, is individual, and equally specific is the kind and degree of intrapsychic conflict in the mother. A mother may be torn between her wishes for the infantile symbiotic child and for the fantasied autonomous and powerfully complementing object. She may struggle between her desire to retain the symbiosis by infantilization and her shame and/or guilt over so doing, or she may be in conflict between her wish for the child as the sadomasochistically cathected sibling and guilt over that wish.

What we shall attempt to do below, rather than giving one or two case reports, is to give a number of brief clinical sketches, along with comments about specific maturational steps, in order to provide a better indication of the wide range of variations. In each of these, some from analyses and some from our observational study, we shall attempt to show aspects of the mother's sense of loss and/or gain in response to the child's maturation, as well as to give some indication of the fantasies underlying this and the specific thoughts and behavior through which it was expressed.

Some Clinical Vignettes from Psychoanalyses of Mothers

Particularly among mothers who breast-feed their infants, a major intrapsychic conflict, which is traceable in their analysis, may occur around the problem of weaning—that landmark of the infant's beginning differentiation which has a multitude of aspects and implications. In the psychoanalytic treatment of such mothers, one can observe the waverings back and forth between the impulse to wean and the impulse to retain this so meaningful symbol of symbiotic unity. Some mothers experience as rejection the normal infant's expanding interest in looking and stretching beyond the orbit of the symbiotic dual unity; others unconsciously anticipate it as an impending loss to be quasi-passively endured, and thus impulsively wean the infant. It seems to us that whereas a great deal has been written about the infant's trauma in weaning, the mother's side of the experience has been given much less attention. Most mothers, and particularly those who breast-feed, react strongly and often irrationally to the loss of this uniquely close bodily tie with their infant. In the following patient we explored in analysis the specific meaning of this loss:

CASE 1. Mrs. A., a tall, stately, and stunningly beautiful 23-year-old woman, came for analysis during the second month of her first pregnancy, mainly, she alleged, in order to adjust better to a difficult husband. Her very first dreams, however, suggested that one of her core problems was the fear that the child might be born defective. Mrs. A.'s competition with her husband was largely unconscious, as was her equation of body-phallus which, with her pregnancy, had shifted to a conflicting phallus-baby wish. In her analysis, prior to the baby's birth, she was made aware of the baby's role in her fantasy. Some of her conflict about these fantasies could be interpreted. This led to a lessening of her accumulated resentment toward her husband, whom she had felt was her superior only by virtue of his anatomy, and to a reduction of guilt feelings about her wish for a phallus-baby. Her fear of bearing a defective child was thus partially worked through prior to her confinement.

At term Mrs. A. gave birth to a son. She was very insistent about wishing to breast-feed, and during the breast-feeding period her former intense rivalry with her husband disappeared. She felt fully satisfied and compensated by the excellent symbiotic relationship she had with her suckling infant. During the third month of breast-feeding, a crisis occurred. Severe mastitis caused both her physician and husband to try to persuade her that the baby should be weaned. She became almost panicky, refused absolutely that course of action, changed physicians, pumped her breast, and subsequently breast-fed her baby for 5 additional months.

By that time, the baby was able to crawl rapidly about—he was wholly in the practicing subphase of the individuation process; that is, he was at or near the peak of the second subphase of individuation, a period marked by a massive shift of libido from its former exclusive investment in the mother-infant symbiotic dual unity onto the child's own functions and onto the expanding segment of his external reality. This maturational change in the baby precipitated an intrapsychic conflict in the mother which manifested itself in the following ways:

She began to skip many of her analytic appointments. During the few sessions that she did come, she described her exasperation with the inconsistency and unreadability of her 8- to 9-month-old infant's signals and communications, which was her way of experiencing the increasing break in the symbiotic union. Her ambivalence about this break appeared in her alternating wish that the baby give up the breast for the "independence" of the bottle and her disappointment when he finally did so. Dreams and associations at this time began to reveal that she was withdrawing some of her libidinal investment from the baby and shifting cathexis back to her individual self and her husband. Mrs. A. rationalized her resistance to further analysis by the baby's recurring colds and her difficulties with babysitters, and thus, for the time being, it became impossible to continue analytic work. It did not surprise the analyst to hear that a few weeks after termination of treatment, she had promptly become pregnant again. It appeared that she was seeking a replacement for her individuating first phallus-child. She became pregnant approximately 10 weeks after the termination of breast-feeding and 6 weeks after the termination of treatment.

In summary, not only did Mrs. A. regard her small son's drive for individuation as a rejection and loss, but by means of it she suffered a blow to her marked body-narcissism. The multifaceted equation of phallus-baby played a very important role in her fantasies about her body and in her competition with her husband and with her own mother. Apparently, her maternal feelings were secondary to these intrapsychic issues. She would not risk sharing with the "mother-analyst" her wish to replace the lost phallus-baby by way of a new pregnancy or delaying the fulfillment of this wish.

In way of comparison, let us sketch the case of another mother, whose relationship to her children improved as the symbiosis lessened and a more developed object relationship grew.

CASE 2. Mrs. L.'s analysis clearly indicated a less than optimal empathy first with her son and later with her daughter in their early months. When each of her newborn babies was first put on her shoulder (she did not breast-feed), she thought: "This red little creature is my child, and he is entirely dependent for life or death on me; he is so frail, alien, and ugly." She then decided intellectually to be a good—a fair and dutiful—mother. Mrs. L. was critical of herself throughout her child-raising. She believed that she must never tie her children, and especially her son, emotionally to herself. By nature somewhat undemonstrative, Mrs. L. tried deliberately from the first months on not to "spoil" her children—that is, from her point of view, not to damage her infants by close bodily contact. Underlying these ideas were fantasies of the destructiveness of symbiotic closeness.

As soon as each child reached toddler age, Mrs. L. felt more at ease, and once they were able to express themselves verbally, she particularly enjoyed the companionship of her children. When the son, however, had reached the rapprochement period soon after the second subphase of individuation, he was encouraged by the mother to seek his father's companionship rather than her own [6]. The mother developed a close, even optimal, relationship with the daughter, following her full individuation. It was clear in the analysis that the daughter as a love object fulfilled the mother's unconscious longing for a female sibling, in reparation for her earlier "inferiority" as a female among many male siblings and a powerful father. (In a later follow-up, Mrs. L. was still found to have an optimal relationship with her adolescent daughter, although the latter showed some scars that seemed related to deficiencies in mothering during her early months in life.)

This mother, then, in contrast to the first mother, could hardly wait to discharge her symbiotic duties and achieve verbal rapport with her toddlers. As she continued with analysis, it was possible in her case to follow the shift in her relation to her children as they moved through the specific fantasies determining her reaction to both the symbiotic and to the more individuated, object-related, phases.

Let us refer briefly to a third mother.

CASE 3. After her analysis, Mrs. T. bore four children, the youngest of whom is 7 years old at this writing. She insists that all that has remained in her memory are two periods in her children's life with her. One is the intense sensual pleasure that the breast-feeding of all four afforded her, and the other is the continual satisfaction that she has been experiencing in the companionship of all four growing children. The steps of separation-individuation, the minutiae of its back-and-forth movements, seem to be absent from her memory.

Although this reaction may seem unusual, it appears to be a particularly common one. This mother was one who enjoyed the early bodily tie as well as the later companionship, but who was nonetheless unable to remember any of the Sturm und Drang of the movement from one subphase of separation-individuation to the other. Even though many mothers during our study have specifically told us how helpful and clarifying it was to learn of the changing moods and demands of their children in the course of the separation-individuation process, and although often struck by their own concordant observations of this, it seems that they soon forget it all. We are prone to speculate that in the *parent,* as well as in the child, a partial repression of these events takes place. This appears to result from the conflictual experiences of loss in this period, and from the conflictual fantasies that gain heightened investment in response first to the child's helplessness, and, later, to his individuation.

267

An important additional factor for the forgetting of the sub-phase of the child's separation-individuation seems to be due to the great fluidity of the shift of cathexis of the individuating toddler. Mothers and fathers cannot possibly commensurately invest in those rapid and massive shifts and turns in the developmental process; so, it is probable that these events every so often register rather superficially or unclearly to begin with in the minds of the parents whose ability as adults to synchronize experientially with these rapidly changing states of the individuating child is naturally limited.

Thus far we have given illustrative material drawn from three analyses. Especially in the first two cases, we have tried to give some hint of the manner in which specific maternal fantasies can affect maternal mood, attitudes, and behavior.

If psychoanalysis is the method par excellence for understanding such fantasies, the direct observation of mothers and their children is, we feel, the ideal method of recognizing specific behavioral mechanisms by which such fantasies are expressed and affect the child.

In our observational study of the mother-child relationship, our material is drawn from twenty mothers, whom we studied intensively, in continual attendance with their children, from the child's fifth month (or earlier) to the end of the third year.[2] Although the project was concerned with many aspects of maternal behavior, we shall limit ourselves here to a description of reactions related to the main theme of this paper: the mother's holding on to or fear of the symbiotic tie to the infant, and her avoidance of or longing for an object relationship to the individuating child.

We shall describe two cases at opposite poles of the spectrum: (1) a mother who both consciously and unconsciously infantilizes her children excessively while resisting and creating obstacles to every step of their separation-individuation and (2) a mother who is extremely uncomfortable and inept with her totally dependent, "vulnerable" lap baby, and who can barely wait for the infant to become a toddler.

In addition, of course, there exists a wide spectrum of maternal attitudes and an as yet undetermined number of mothers who, as did

---

[2] Sixteen additional mother-child pairs, whom we began to see only after their infants' earliest symbiotic and differentiation phases, i.e., at 11 to 12 months of age, are not included here.

the third of the analyzed mothers, enjoy breast-feeding, follow their toddlers' steps in the individuation process with minimal interest and subsequent scant memory of the period of separation-individuation, and who have a good relationship and enjoy the companionship with the older child when he "makes sense" to them.

The first mother we shall describe, comparable to the first analytic case discussed earlier, is one who thoroughly, in fact excessively, enjoyed the breast-feeding and actively opposed the child's individuation:

CASE 4. We had the opportunity to study Mrs. K. with two of her babies (one from the fifth month and the second almost from birth). Mrs. K. was maximally attuned to her breast-fed babies. She breast-fed the first well into the second year, and the second past the age of 2, the unmistakable active aversive behaviors on the part of the individuating toddler notwithstanding. Each baby fought valiantly from quite early on for his own autonomy, while the mother fought every step of the baby's separation-individuation.

When she came to join our research study with her first-born son, Mrs. K. was in her thirties. While in the study, after a visit to her parents' home, she described herself as having reacted again as she had as a child: Her mother criticized everything she did, and Mrs. K. found herself doing nothing while her mother, all the while complaining, took over for her. Mrs. K. was married to a man who was extremely critical of her every shortcoming even though he himself was extremely helpless and demanding, and required his wife's constant attention and mothering. Thus, Mrs. K. retained her own mother's criticism in her relation to her husband, but she identified with her mother's all-pervasive mothering (though somehow without the martyred complaining) with both her husband and her children.

Mrs. K. saw herself as a "supermother," and described herself as placid, easy-going, good-natured, and long-suffering. This self-image corresponded only partially to the facts, as she was far from placid, but actually quite energetic, high-powered, efficient, and bossy. Long-suffering she was, however, not only with her demanding husband and both of her little sons, but even with her two cats, for which she cooked special food and which walked on the furniture and jumped into the baby's bed. She was ready to take care of not only the needs of her own family but those of other families as well, by way of unsolicited advice, on any subject, to the other mothers. Even though she extended herself for other people, there was a most intrusive and obtuse quality about her offerings: she did not easily fit into our group of typically more reserved mothers.

With both of her infant sons, Mrs. K. found motherhood inspiring and exciting, and she never complained about being tired or bored. She saw the first one, especially, as the perfect baby, and "loved" to breast-feed him. Observers were at first enchanted with this perfect mother-baby pair, but it was the baby who seemed to know better. He started to pull away from his mother, pushed against her body as early as 4 months of age, and soon thereafter began to prefer the laps of the "other-than-mother."

The mode of maternal impact upon this child first became apparent in the area of locomotion. At 5 months of age, Sam had not yet turned over. Mrs. K. thought it was because she was always there to make his position more comfortable. Two weeks later, she admitted that she did not give him much opportunity to move, as he spent most of his time in the small baby carriage close to his parents' bed, in which he even slept. Mrs. K. thoroughly enjoyed the dependency of her lap baby, and she did her utmost to keep him physically in that state. She was satisfied only if she could direct his every move, and did nothing to encourage his independent functioning.

With the inevitable maturational advance of the child's locomotor capacity, the mother evolved a number of ways to undo its significance. Thus, when Sam was 7 months of age and made movements suggesting his readiness to crawl, the mother minimized the importance of this by saying he had been doing it for months. At 9 months, when most infants are well into their practicing period, Mrs. K. continued to watch her baby like a hawk; it seemed as if everything in which Sam was interested had to be related to her and had to be done in unison with her; the mother-child symbiosis was thus greatly prolonged. When this first baby was over a year old, the mother's interviewer could not help but talk to her about a growing baby's need for independence. Mrs. K. agreed wholeheartedly, then promptly picked him up to engage him in a head-bumping game. When he did not respond she stimulated and tickled him until she forced an hysterical laugh from him. Finally, when, at the age of 17 months, he at last walked on his own, Mrs. K. reported how pleased *he* was with himself—quickly adding that he had *always* been pleased with himself—in this way devaluating her toddler's tremendous feeling of accomplishment and joy in upright locomotion, with its attendant sense of autonomy.

From then on a definite change took place in Mrs. K.'s relationship to her child. Here was a mother who could not be compensated for the loss of symbiosis by a gain in object relationship, and once the baby was no longer part of her, her interest in him greatly diminished. She would pay little attention to him other than to ask for signs of affection. She began to talk about planning a new pregnancy at this time, and also decided to take up sculpting, something she had never done before. The feeling of the clay pleased her, she said, and she called it an agreeable and absorbing occupation. This particular hobby, at that particular time, seemed to suggest not only her need for active, tactile stimulation, but also the need to control and form.

In summary, Mrs. K.'s particular wish to be a supermother required that she have a complementary symbiotic object on which her mothering could be applied, and who had no autonomous wishes. The child's progressive individuation continually shattered this state until finally the mother in large part withdrew her libidinal attachment and sought substitution in another pregnancy.

The Mother's Reaction to Her Toddler's Drive for Individuation

CASE 5. Mrs. M., another mother from our observational study, illustrates the reverse pattern, with a relationship to the individuating child which was far superior to the earlier symbiotic union. We met Mrs. M. when she joined our project with her first child, a daughter then 1 year old. A young woman in her early twenties, Mrs. M. was the oldest of four sisters, and she described her childhood as having been a happy one. It was clear that her father had played the most important role in her life, and she described the close companionship between them during her childhood which, however, was marred in later years by his serious illness. During her last year in college, when her parents had moved to the West Coast, Mrs. M., who had always done well in school, suddenly felt that with her father so far away there was no one for whom it would be worthwhile to be a good student. She lost interest in her work. Her husband, whom she had met that year, was an only son, much doted on by his own mother, and it seemed as though there was not too much stimulation or satisfaction in the marriage for Mrs. M. and that for that reason she seemed to put most of her energies into motherhood.

Mrs. M. participated faithfully (with all three of her children) during the entire duration of our study, and has been a sensitive and intelligent observer and informer (definitely fatherlike in this respect). Unlike Mrs. K., she often felt bored and lonely as the mother of young children, and she welcomed the intellectual stimulation afforded her by the sharing of observations of her children with the members of the research team.

When we first met Mrs. M. with her daughter, a most charming and precocious little girl of 11 months, whom she brought to our study at its inception, all observers found them enchanting and fascinating. Mrs. M. was well attuned to the child's needs, yet always encouraged her independent functioning. At 1 year of age the child impressed everyone as a small person in her own right, rather than as a baby. Not only did she walk well by then, but she had an outstanding language development (she used whole sentences by 13 months), all of which was greatly enjoyed and encouraged by her mother.

Two years later, when Cathy was 3 years old, Mrs. M. gave birth, probably at term, to her second child, a tiny baby boy. To our great surprise she was not at all attuned to this baby's needs. (She did not breastfeed any of her children as she "did not feel like it.") When holding Philip she never looked happy or comfortable. She did not cradle him, but instead jiggled him up and down in a rather nervous and awkward way. She seemed unable to help him relax, she could not read his cues, and when feeding him, which was her exclusive way of comforting him, she held him on her lap, but facing *away* from her. The baby fretted almost constantly.

Mrs. M. complained a lot at this time, saying that she really did not like babies. Some of her fantasies were probably expressed by the anxiety she felt about her son—she woke him frequently from fear that he might have stopped breathing. This anxiety was usually concealed by an overly casual attitude which only stopped near the point of neglect. On occasion, despite the baby's severe diaper rash, she would not change his diaper all morning. We had been used to her pleasure in talking about the girl at a year and older; she now resented even being questioned about Philip. Both she and the child appeared pale and unkempt.

271

All of this changed radically as soon as her son began to emerge from the symbiotic relationship. Once he was able to move about and show active interest in the environment beyond the mother-infant orbit, and especially when he could more clearly communicate his needs to her, the mother started to emerge from her depression. Suddenly, she became well attuned to Philip's needs, took pleasure in watching his achievements, and consistently and adequately (according to the requirements of the subphase) supported him in his growing independence. With this child and with a third one that we observed into toddlerhood, Mrs. M. demonstrated her ability to respond to each of her children as individuals. She could take in stride the developmental difficulties of a child growing through the later subphases of the separation-individuation process, and had no need to deny them. She also took great pleasure in her growing children's companionship without pushing them into premature functioning.

CASE 6. The last mother, Mrs. P., experienced stress every step of the way of her child's separation-individuation. It is our impression that, as in the third analytic case (Mrs. T.), these difficulties lapsed into repression once an object relationship to the individuated child had been established.

Mrs. P. came to us when her firstborn, Bobby, was 1 year old. She was a slim, attractive woman in her thirties, vivacious and interested, although somewhat ill at ease. Unlike the two other mothers described, Mrs. P.'s memories of her childhood were none too happy. When she was 16 years old her mother had died, and she ascribed this early death to her mother's having borne too many children. Mrs. P. talked more than the other mothers about her husband, who was many years her senior. She enjoyed their married life, and was obviously more interested in homemaking for him than in mothering her children.

In our study Mrs. P. welcomed the opportunity to talk about herself and her children with observers and with the other mothers. Although she wanted to be a good mother and worked hard at it, the "art of mothering" did not come easily. She resented her loss of personal freedom and was aware of the anger that she thus felt toward the baby. Nevertheless, she did not have too much difficulty in the beginning. She breast-fed her son for 5 months, and while not obtaining great enjoyment in the experience, with the help and support of her husband she nonetheless slowly became used to being a mother.

In general, what Mrs. P. found most difficult to accept and cope with were Bobby's autonomous feelings. At 6 to 7 months he developed intense stranger and separation anxieties, and from that time on Mrs. P. found him extremely difficult to care for. She began to sneak out on him, so as not to have to face his tears at separation [11]. The occasion which most drastically exemplified the difficulty was Mrs. P.'s second pregnancy (at the time Bobby was a little over 2 years old). In a multitude of ways the child indicated to his mother that he knew there would be a new baby, but Mrs. P. could not bring herself to tell him about it. She went to the hospital to give birth without having prepared him in any way.

In general, Mrs. P. could not face turbulent feelings, and she tended to forget them quickly once they were over. By the age of 3 years, Bobby had turned into a well-functioning little boy, a little too serious perhaps, but a separate individual. Now Mrs. P. could join him in many activities, could teach him to do things, take him on trips, and enjoy his company. He did very well in nursery school, another aspect of his life in which his mother could take pleasure and pride. Mrs. P. soon forgot that she had ever found Bobby a difficult child in the Sturm und Drang period of separation-individuation, as she became more involved in their activities together.

SUMMARY

The child's progress through the separation-individuation process presents contrasting opportunities to the mother—to experience loss of the symbiotic object and/or gain in object relationship with her individuating child; that the mother must confront this issue again and again, in the form of concrete maturational events—diminished bodily molding, weaning, independent locomotion, verbalization—all of which signal the child's increasing separation and individuation; and that a mother's unique response to these events depends upon her specific wishes, fantasies, and anxieties.

The particular intrapsychic stability that an individual achieves at a given point in time is always a temporary state, constantly upset by the stimulations and frustrations that everyday life entails. In the course of development, this stability is also upset in a major way by intrinsic maturational events such as the movement from one to another stage of the infantile sexual organization, puberty, and menarche. But for the mother, it is more the rapid maturational steps taken by her child than her own more slowly paced maturational changes that regularly upset her intrapsychic equilibrium and require that new adjustments be made.

ACKNOWLEDGMENTS

The material in this chapter is partly based on research supported by the National Institute of Mental Health, United States Public Health Service Grant MH–08238 and previously by the Field Foundation, the Taconic Foundation, and the Psychoanalytic Research and Development Fund, Inc., and carried out at the Masters Children's Center. (Also, Dr. Pine was supported by a research Career Development Award [#K3–MH–

18 375] from the National Institute of Mental Health, U.S. Public Health Service, during much of the period of the work, while he was at the Department of Psychiatry, State University of New York Downstate Medical Center.

Bibliography

1. Benedek, T.   The psychosomatic implications of the primary unit—mother-child. *Amer. J. Orthopsychiat.* 19:642–654, 1949.
2. Coleman, R. W., Kris, E., and Provence, S.   The study of variations of early parental attitudes: A preliminary report. *Psychoanal. Stud. Child* 8:20–47, 1953.
3. Deutsch, H.   *The Psychology of Women.* New York: Grune & Stratton, 1944.
4. Greenacre, P.   Problems of overidealization of the analyst and of analysis. *Psychoanal. Stud. Child* 21:193–212, 1966.
5. Mahler, M. S.   Thoughts about development and individuation. *Psychoanal. Stud. Child* 18:307–324, 1963.
6. Mahler, M. S.   On the Significance of the Normal Separation-Individuation Phase. In M. Schur (Ed.), *Drives, Affects, and Behavior.* New York: International Universities Press, 1965. Vol. II, pp. 161–169.
7. Mahler, M. S.   On human symbiosis and the vicissitudes of individuation. *J. Amer. Psychoanal. Ass.* 15:740–763, 1967.
8. Mahler, M. S., and Furer, M.   Certain aspects of the separation-individuation phase. *Psychoanal. Quart.* 32:1–14, 1963.
9. Mahler, M. S., and LaPerriere. K.   Mother-child interaction during separation-individuation. *Psychoanal. Quart.* 34:483–498, 1965.
10. Mahler, M. S., and McDevitt, J.   Observations on adaptation and defense in statu nascendi. *Psychoanal. Quart.* 37:1–21, 1968.
11. McDevitt, J.   The Preoedipal Determinants of an Infantile Neurosis. Paper presented to the New York Psychoanalytic Society, 1968.
12. Spock, B.   The striving for autonomy and regressive object relationships. *Psychoanal. Stud. Child* 18:361–364, 1963.
13. Winnicott, D. W.   The theory of the parent-infant relationship. *Int. J. Psychoanal.* 41:585–595, 1960.

12

The Reactions
of Parents to
the Oedipal Child

E. James Anthony

EDITORS' INTRODUCTION

Parents who have read with interest the psychiatric or psycho-analytic literature or have been in psychiatric or psychoanalytic treatment themselves may come to feel that this special knowledge or experience is conducive to beneficial repercussions on the psychologic development of their child. There is little doubt that the child gains from the therapy of his parents, especially if it has taught them to trust their own parental instincts and if it has allowed them to form a more direct and less neurotic form of empathy for the child. On the other hand, the child stands rather to lose if the parents begin to rely too completely on authoritative texts or attempt to transform the parental into a therapeutic relationship. Should the parent be tempted into the therapist's role, his "countertransference" may prove to be a factor in fixating the child at this level of development.

In this presentation the author has tried to bring some of the psychodynamic transactions that occur between parents and children during the time of the oedipal period into sharper focus, and he raises as yet unanswered questions such as what constitutes a normal oedipus complex or a normal resolution of the nuclear conflict, or under what conditions the oedipus complex settles down to become the core structure of normal personality development.

In Chapter 15 Leo Rangell demonstrates the persistence of an unresolved oedipal conflict into adult life and its reactivation under the stimulus provided by children.

E. J. A.
T. B.

T he seductiveness of the oedipal child is not without effect upon the parents, although the unsophisticated among them may be hard put to say what it is specifically in the child's behavior that disquiets them. They may talk of the child's "cuteness," his ability to twist them round his finger, his cajoling and wheedling ways, and his inordinate wish to remain constantly and irritatingly at the center of the stage, but they will not be able to disguise, in many cases, the vicarious gratification that the behavior affords them. The perceptive parents confess to being charmed, manipulated, and possessed. They may be aware of the intense jealousy directed by the oedipal child at every other member of the family transacting in any way with the beloved parent.

With stronger reactions, they may be forced into recognizing the insistent demands and pleas of a passionate young lover who may insist on rights and prerogatives like any adult counterpart. Under the enduring qualities of this mannequin, however, the sexual undercurrents may become sufficiently obtrusive and disturbing to provoke ambivalent responses. The result is that the child is often treated with an inconsistent mixture of teasing acceptance and angry repudiation, at times admired and at times laughed at. This may take the form of an oedipal game which alternates between pretense and seriousness in a way not too dissimilar from the early courtship behavior of immature adults.

If the relationship is allowed to progress further, the importunity of the child may eventually lead to a strict and punitive compensatory reaction in the parent and to the pronouncement of threats, especially with regard to the masturbatory outlets of the child. This may precipitate in turn an oedipal crisis with an overt outpouring of feelings and fantasies that may frighten the parents with their intensity. Another development may take the form of an infantile neurosis, such as a phobia or dissociated state.

In certain instances a chronic state of oedipal discontent ensues in which the frustrations of the child become perpetuated in a persistent attitude of carping dissatisfaction which inevitably casts a blight on family life and relationships, often to the detriment of the marital union. The parents quarrel constantly over the handling of the child,

276

the one making accusations of "spoiling" and demanding suppressive measures and the other insinuating a lack of understanding and feeling and pressing for better consideration of the child's needs.

It should be emphasized, however, that in the great majority of cases the oedipal period represents a silent revolution in which highly significant intrapsychic shifts occur without the participants becoming consciously aware of their involvement. At the end of this development, it may be reported that the child has "grown up suddenly," "become more mature," "settled down," or "now seems much easier to manage."

At times, the seductiveness of the child may strain the incest barrier to breaking point, so that the parents may find ways and means of increasing their contact with the child either through very tender interchanges, pregenital ministrations during toileting and bathing, or by punitive maneuvers such as beatings on the bare bottom.

The partially impotent or frigid parent may react to the child's genital overtures with strong repugnance and may reproach him for his wickedness. The preoedipal parent, on the other hand, may take umbrage at the child's burgeoning sexuality and scold him for his dirtiness. Both sets of parents may react to the child's masturbation as if they were reacting to his masturbatory fantasies and may threaten castration.

The reactivation of oedipal wishes in the parent is stimulated by the oedipal behavior of the child, so that there may be disguised or open erotic desires and daydreams that arouse a great deal of guilt.

Occasionally, an oedipal crisis in a child may bring about an oedipal crisis in the parent which may be acted out in some dramatic fashion. At other times, the parental response may be of such a quality or vehemence as to swing the child from a positive to a negative oedipal development or vice versa.

These various reactions will now be illustrated from case histories.

THE CLASSIC REACTION

The parents of Freud's patient, little Hans, were close followers of psychoanalysis and both had been analyzed [3]. The mother, described by Freud as an excellent and devoted one, had had neurotic difficulties as an adolescent. There were obviously marital problems, because a few years later she divorced Hans's father. The little boy's animal phobia or "nonsense" (as he called it) developed during a summer vacation taken by the family.

The relationship of the mother to her oedipal son was described in the following sequence of events starting from the time when Hans was 3½ years old.

CASE 1.   At 3.6 years, Hans was found by his mother with his hand on his penis. She threatened to send for the doctor to cut off his "widdler." At 3.9 years, he was looking on one day while his mother undressed. She became suddenly conscious of him and asked why he was staring at her like that. He replied that he was only looking to see if she had a "widdler." Her immediate response was: "Of course I have. Didn't you know that?" At 4.3 years, as she was giving him his daily bath and powdering him, his mother was careful not to touch his penis and he asked her why she did not. "Because that would be piggish," she replied, to which his comment was, "What's that? Piggish? Why?" Her defensive answer then was: "Because it's not proper." Hans laughed. "But it's great fun!" At 4.9 years, Hans learned that his mother could be persuaded, when he was in a certain sad mood, to take him into her bed and "coax" with him (Hans's expression for caressing). Likewise, when he came into the parents' room in the morning, his mother could not resist taking him into bed with her. The father warned her not to do so, but she answered, somewhat irritably, that it was all nonsense and that a few minutes in bed with her couldn't make all that difference. At about 5.0 years, his mother asked him whether he still touched his "widdler" and he admitted that he did every evening when in bed. She warned him not to do so, and when he woke up in the morning, she questioned him again and found that the warning had been of no avail. At about 5.3 years, Hans reported that his mother took off her black drawers in the morning when she went out and then put them back again when she returned. To her husband, she denied that she had changed her drawers on this occasion, but not that she habitually changed her drawers in front of the boy. A little later, the husband questioned his wife whether Hans often went with her into the toilet. Her answer was: "Yes, often. He goes on pestering me until I let him. Children are like that!" Hans also admitted that he had been very often to the toilet with his mother and liked to watch her "widdle" very much.

Hans's father found it easy to recognize the covert angry feelings that his son felt toward him as well as the desire that the boy had to replace him in the mother's affections. It was, however, less easy for him to acknowledge the positive feelings that came his way when Hans swung into a negative oedipal phase and it was extremely difficult for him to admit to his own counteraggressive feelings toward his son. For example, when the pair visited Freud for a consultation, the father had completely forgotten that he had smacked the boy "reflexly" after he had been butted by him in the stomach that morning. Also, for all his analytic understanding, he was adamant that Hans should not even allow himself to think his angry thoughts about his sister. On several occasions, he seemed almost to force Hans into confessing to extreme feelings toward his parents, such as that he wanted to whip his mother, which Hans admitted at first but subsequently retracted.

There was no doubt that Hans was an attractive child. Freud describes him as "a cheerful, amiable, active-minded young fellow who might give pleasure to more people than his own father." There was also no doubt that he was, as with most gifted children, both sexually and intellectually precocious and that the environment in which he was brought up was both stimulating and tolerant and allowed him a sense of security in the expression of unconventional thoughts and feelings. Certainly, at the end of the period of treatment, the boy managed to get on rather familiar terms with his father, who reported this with some amusement.

The father seemed curiously sure that if Hans stopped masturbating and getting into his mother's bed, he would get rid of his phobia. He was even more convinced that the mother's excessive display of affection toward her son was largely responsible for the outbreak of the child's neurosis, although, as Freud pointed out, she could as easily be blamed for having precipitated the disturbance by her energetic rejection of Hans's seductive advances ("That would be piggish!"). However, she did undress in front of him, did coax with him in bed, and did take him to the toilet with her, at the same time making light of her behavior. The father, for his part, did seem to let his therapeutic role go to his head, carrying on, in spite of Freud's supervision, a little bit of a "wild" analysis. His persistent cross-examination of Hans clearly gave him a lot of vicarious satisfaction, and we find the boy fabricating stories in self-defense or pleading with his father to please leave him alone. A typically defensive response of Hans to his father's interrogation was: "You know everything; I don't know anything."

Both parents, therefore, in their several ways were responding to the boy's oedipal provocations and pressures in expectable ways that have been replicated in subsequent studies. Nevertheless, it is rare in any of these for the analyst's attention to be focused on the parental reaction. Freud's consistent view was that the oedipal development unfolded in the nature of things, and he does not regard parental participation as collusive in the genesis of the infantile neurosis.

THE NEOCLASSIC ILLUSTRATION

The treatment of nightmares in a 7-year-old boy, making use of the father again as therapist, was conducted by correspondence by Rangell [6]. There were striking parallels and similarities in occurrences and background events between this case and Freud's, suggesting that childhood neuroses, in contrast to adult ones, according to

279

Rangell, "are rooted more in universal experiences than in specific individual determinants." Like Hans, Paul had an animal phobia and, as in the case of Hans, a summer vacation played an important part in the development of the disturbance, since it involved intimate contact with the mother, with the father as an irregular visitor. Again, like Hans, Paul is of superior intelligence, precocious, sensitive, and imaginative, and the birth of a little sister not only brought about a similar threat to the relationship with the parents but at the same time revived the memory traces of the child's earliest pleasure experiences.

In Rangell's case, the mother is also described as having anxiety symptoms, but little more is said about the reactions of the parents except the comment, when mother had neglected to mention that Paul was once again sleeping in the parental bedroom, that "We must by now wonder whether the ease with which Paul keeps bobbing up in his parents' bedroom may not be an indication of a proclivity on the parents' part to bring this about, perhaps for unconscious reasons of their own." Except for this, the analysis of the oedipal complex is confined to the boy. The parents are described as affectionate, permissive, and enlightened in their approach to children, understandably anxious about the child's symptoms and perhaps a little given to "over-affection and kissing and bending over backwards in [their] concern." The same is true for Kubie's report [5], and those of Grotjahn [4] and Barrett [1, 2]. The therapeutic role of the parents is seen to dominate the case description as if this were the only reaction open to them.

PARENTAL REACTION TO AN OEDIPAL CRISIS

The oedipal disturbance of the child may take any of a series of forms ranging from quiet to tempestuous. In its most unobtrusive variety, there is little apparent conflict, and the triangular relationship with the parents is not parceled into polarities of love and hate. In such cases, the child has often dealt competently with his pregenital ambivalence and dependency needs so that very little of this overflows into the oedipal situation as contaminant. In the next form of an oedipal crisis, the conflict remains phase-specific, but for various reasons the oedipal strivings become suddenly urgent and manifest. As a result, there is an oedipal outpouring lasting for a short period of weeks and the matter then subsides as quickly as it arose. Where there is collusion in the environment with much counterseductiveness and aggressiveness, a clinical infantile neurosis may emerge in the form of phobias and nightmares, and the period of disturbance is extended over a much longer time. In certain cases, where there has been a marked preoedipal disturbance, the oedipal disturbance not only becomes protracted and intense, but is obfuscated by pregenital components and is more difficult to resolve. There is a chronic quality about it that can best be summed up by the term "oedipal discontentment."

The oedipal crisis may be precipitated by the birth of a sibling, by hospitalization or surgery, or even by some small act of favoritism manifested to another child. The parents are often bewildered by the sudden revelation of the deeper feelings and fantasies and may display anxiety, anger, curiosity, and even disgust. In the case about to be described, the precipitating factor seemed to be a reversal in the contact with the parents, the mother going out to work as a nurse and the father staying at home with the children because he was able to conduct his business from the house.

CASE 2. Mark was a 5-year-old boy, the second of four children, all boys. He was described as affectionate, appealing, open, and "wholesome" with some counterphobic concerns with needles, doctors, and hospitals. The parents were religious with fundamentalistic beliefs, but showed considerable warmth in their relationship with the children. The father was an architect and the mother a nurse and, at the time of the crisis, the latter was going out to work while the former carried on his occupation at home.

The mother described herself as being a disciplinarian at work but extremely tolerant and laissez-faire at home. She was easygoing and inconsistent in the handling of the children, and breast-fed her babies openly in front of the other children. As an adolescent she had suffered from emotional problems with associated menstrual disorders. She had married her first date because he seemed to represent a combination of her father (passive and preoccupied) and her mother (religious), but she had always retained fantasies of marrying a "real" man.

The father was shy, quiet, and diffident and always ready to help out with the children. When the mother began to work, he assumed a much more maternal role in the household, although he was not in any way an effeminate man.

Both the father and Mark suffered from allergies for which mother gave them "shots." Mark preferred to get the injection from the mother "even though it hurt just as much." He was a highly intelligent child with an "adult flow" to his speech. His mother felt that like herself he had grown up too quickly. She also regarded him as somewhat special since he had been the smallest of her babies.

Soon after the change in their work schedule, the parents found two little letters written by Mark, the one addressed to his mother and the other to his father. The first read as follows: "Mother, I love you. I hope you have a good time at work. Love, Mark." In the second, he had written: "Daddy, I hope you have a good time at home when Mother is working. Love, Mark."

The father phoned in a very excited state and said that his son had "really opened up" with him the night before and he did not know what to do about it. This was the first time Mark had really indicated to his father much about what went on inside him, and it was rather startling. The mother was working the evening shift as a nurse and so he put the children to bed. A little later Mark came downstairs, saying that he could not sleep because something bothered him. He referred repeatedly, during the subsequent conversation with his father, to certain "clues" that he had and said that he wanted to get more clues. In the course of the night, he came down several times to talk. The father eventually let him lie in bed with him so as to encourage, he said, his son's confidence and reduce his fear. Mark's conversation was apparently rambling—"all in bits and pieces," said the father—and he seemed to be relating things just as they came to his mind.

He spoke of bad dreams which he had not told anybody and of having "another daddy who when you got a shot in the arm would give you something that would stop it from hurting." This daddy was a robot and appeared constantly in his dreams. He also dreamed frequently of his little brother, Jimmy, but the father found it difficult to follow Mark's description regarding his dreams of Jimmy as his associations at this point became very disjointed. However, there were recurrent dreams of pushing Jimmy off all sorts of bridges. He spoke of feeling "real sad" that he had attacked Jimmy for making a hole in one of his balls with a pin.

The father attempted to cope with Mark's anxiety by reassuring him that God and his angels were there with him to protect him, but Mark's response to this was: "Suppose you hurt somebody, how would you know they were there." He then made his father promise solemnly not to tell anybody about the things that he was revealing.

He then went on to say that in his dreams he often thought of women and girls, about "their wee-wees," and was adamant that his mommy would never find out about this part of his dreams. He said that he felt very guilty about the "bad things" he had done and thought about his mother as she was "so nice to him." He insisted on getting a quarter from his bank to give to her, but accepted a temporary loan from his father so that he could hand it to her in the morning. The father now learned that his wife concealed very little from the children, so that the boys could go in and out of the bathroom while she was taking a bath. It also appeared that they had seen and speculated on blood on the toilet during the time the mother was menstruating. Mark referred to his mother's genitalia as "her wee-wee," the same term used for the penis in the family.

The father had also noted that lately Mark seemed roused and blushed intensely when he saw any romantic scenes, such as kissing, on the television. He was also aware that his son spoke romantically about the little girls in the neighborhood and would often end up kissing them. When the father mentioned this to him, Mark had some associations about the Holy Family saying that he imagined himself as Joseph and the girls as Mary. He added that when he thought about kissing the girls, this gave him another clue which involved things that were bad that he thought about girls. He then proceeded to talk about thoughts in connection with his mother in the bathroom without clothes on and also about seeing other women. Seemingly, about a month previously, Mark had mentioned to his mother that he had bad dreams but said nothing more until now, when he told his father that he "felt so bad inside and scared to death" and apparently guilty about "a lot of things."

While Mark was talking, he would occasionally interject "God dammit!" At the time, the father said nothing. He recollected that one such expression had been made in connection with Mark relating how his mother had owed him a dollar and that though he had expressed only pleasure at the time, he now said to his father: "She'd better give it back to me or else . . . !" Mark also remembered a time when he and his father drove some women home after church and one of them had wanted to give the boy a quarter. His father had allowed him to keep it and, in calling the incident to mind, the boy said that he guessed that from then on he could trust his father. He thought that he would probably get other clues in the future and he suggested an arrangement whereby he would signal to his father when he had them so that they could both go up to the bathroom where he would reveal them to his father. At this point, he became a little anxious at the thought that his brother might be listening at the door and might overhear them.

Nine days later, the father phoned again to say that Mark was continuing to talk at high pressure and seemed to be very disturbed. The boy likened the situation in his mind to "a fight between good things and bad things and the bad things had won out." He had gone on to say that there was nothing he could do about it but "cut my brain out." He said that it was all hopeless and that something on the television he had seen lately was just the same. This was a documentary in which the religious beliefs of the Chinese communists were described. Mark said it was just as hopeless behind the Iron Curtain because there were not enough Christians to tell the people about God. Nothing could therefore be done about it! He had also been thinking of the countless poor and starving children in the world, wanting to be able to give them food and money, but, again, felt completely powerless to do anything about them.

This flow of florid fantasy continued for another week during which time Mark frequently sought to be close to his father in bed at bedtime so that an exclusive relationship was established between the two. More and more, the father was forced into a therapeutic role listening, attempting to understand, and reassuring, although at times genuinely alarmed by the nature of the things that he heard. As in Rangell's case, an oedipal realignment took place, the strong, erotic feelings for the mother gradually giving place to an intense interest in the father who was showing so much concern for him. There was no doubt that this negative oedipal development was a new source of gratification for the father and he began to look forward to the evening sessions with curiosity and pleasure. He began to probe the boy about his clues and, as he became more "therapeutic," his wife grew more and more upset and instead of characteristically sympathizing with him, she began either to condemn the boy or to inform him calmly that he could not possibly mean the things he said. Mark also began to react to his new and special position in the family. He was very much the center of his parents' attention and the more dreams and fantasies he produced, the more intrigued they seemed to become. The difference in the parental reaction became more marked in time. Whereas the mother began to complain of being tired and fed up and unable to take it any longer, the father became markedly less diffident and appeared to thrive on the situation. Mark himself began to grow more cheerful and active, questioned his father about childbirth, and sang songs like "Here comes the girl in the mini mini-skirt." The acute episode subsided and the next 6 months witnessed a marked change in Mark's development. He developed a close identification with his father and imitated him closely in many of his activities. Whereas, before, he had "shadowed" his mother and manifested anxiety in her absence, he was now happy to do things with his father. He demanded a great deal less attention from his mother physically and turned increasingly to peer group activities. He began to develop friendships and to retain them. He entered his first grade in good shape. The marital relationship steadily improved under the aegis of the mother's new respect for the father. She even began to speak of curtailing her nursing and becoming an "everyday mother" again.

PARENTAL REACTION TO OEDIPAL DISCONTENTMENT

When the parents are suffering from a well-defined neurosis, especially with a great deal of associated anxiety, the oedipal development may be affected. A circular transaction is set up between parents and child, and the feedback mechanism is conducive to increasing chronicity to the oedipal disturbance. In the case of a boy, the mother may suffer from an anxiety neurosis with neurasthenic symptoms which she may tend to displace onto the child at all stages of his development, leading to overprotection and oversolicitude. From an early period on, the child may be disposed to psychosomatic symptoms, headaches, tummy pains, and sniffles which would gain prominence at certain strategic moments. In other cases, an obsessive-compulsive neurosis would dominate the clinical picture in the mother. There would still be a tendency to overprotection, but associated with more obvious ambivalence.

CASE 3. Joey, aged 7, had become a real problem for his family. He made life miserable for each and every member, seemed to take no pleasure in anything whatsoever, and complained constantly about the way things were being done to him or for him. This was especially notice-able when his mother was around, since he not only craved her sole atten-tion but used her as a sounding board for his many complaints. As his father put it, he seemed to have a constant "chip on his shoulder." Within the past 2 years he had shown a strong antagonism toward his father which was both resented and reciprocated. He would do anything to avoid being left alone with his father, and considered it a great imposition to have to be taken anywhere by him. Surprisingly enough, when he did certain things with his dad, he had a much better time than he had ex-pected, but he was the last to admit this.

He was a bed wetter for 6 years and a constant "pain in the neck" for his sisters, both of whom were older than he. He also suffered from time to time with headaches, abdominal pain, and chronic constipation. Whereas he was regarded by the family as impossible to live with, he did extremely well at school and was reported as being a bright, reliable, and engaging personality. "He seems to change completely as he walks in through the front door," said his mother.

She felt that she must stand up for him since the others misunder-stood him and reacted to him with so much hostility. Her relationship with her husband had deteriorated sadly over the past year. She accused him of being unavailable to Joey and absorbed in his own work. She complained that she saw nothing of him and that when she did, he had very little to say to her. She became very depressed at times and suffered from recurrent tension headaches. She stated that if her husband was of the opinion that she did too much for the boy, he should try to spend a little more time with her. She turned to Joey because he needed her and because she needed him. Both of them were to some extent rejected by the father. On the other hand, her husband insisted that he got on famously with Joey in the mother's absence and that as soon as she appeared the boy's behavior deteriorated and he became obnoxious. He felt that she spoiled him and that the only hope was for her to make him understand that he was not the most important member of the family. At this point, the father had begun to have disturbing dreams in which Joey met with severe accidents leading to a loss of limb. Joey, in his turn, dreamed that he was sitting in the driveway at home talking with his mother when his father swung his car in and tried to run over him.

Recently, the father presented his wife with an ultimatum that she would have to choose between him and *her* son and that if she did not reform her ways, he was going to move out of the house. The two girls vowed that they would leave with him because sitting at the table with their brother was a constant martyrdom. The father continued to insist that the boy was emotionally sick whereas the mother believed he was just deeply misunderstood.

PARENTAL REACTIONS TO THE OEDIPAL GIRL

The typical oedipal girl may cry at night and when her mother goes in to her, shrink from her and say, with all the directness of a 5-

year-old: "I don't want you, I want my daddy." The mother explains patiently that daddy is very busy doing his work and cannot come, but the child is adamant. She does not want her mother. The mother gets up with tears in her eyes, feeling sad and helpless. She feels rejected and cannot understand why her little girl has no further use for her. She realizes that love has gone, and she cries half the night and gets no sleep.

The oedipal girl is often very conscious of her power over a susceptible father. She will often take exclusive possession of him, sometimes with the tolerant understanding of the other siblings in the family, who may have an unconscious appreciation of her greater need during this particular phase. Her perceptions are often mixed. She may see her father as a father-mother admixture and, on the one hand, she may demand that he love her in maternal fashion because she is his baby and must be carried and rocked by him. On the other hand, she is ready to become his "little housewife" and cater to his needs maturely. At other times she can play the role of girl because he wants a woman around, or become a tomboy because he wants to be active and wrestle or throw a ball. In her attempt to be all things to her father, she may oscillate uncertainly between regression and progression, masculinity and femininity. Every now and then, the incest barrier looms ahead and she may escape from him in panic.

In some cases, the father may be so overwhelmed by the tenderness of this relationship that his involvement with his little daughter may occasion rank jealousy on the part of the mother. Some borderline and psychotic women may make insinuations about erotic interchanges, and since the physical contact may be very close, there may be a certain amount of truth in this in most cases. The proof of erotic involvement may be derived from frankly sexual dreams that may be disturbing in their openness as compared with maternal dreams of the oedipal boy.

CASE 4. Sandra was an attractive 5-year-old child with a happy outgoing personality. She fell in love with her father in a rather dramatic way. She had been somewhat naughty on a particular day and had been scolded several times by her father, who eventually lost his patience with her and gave her a spanking. She seemed so upset by this that he began to feel very guilty and went out and bought her a chocolate Santa Claus. She appeared overwhelmed by the gift and stammered her thanks several times. She could not bring herself to eat it but set it by her pillow at night and took it with her wherever she went. Later she took to carrying her Santa inside her underpants, which had elastic bands around her thighs. In this position, the chocolate softened with the heat and the figure was soon distorted into an unpleasant-looking lump.

When the father heard about these exploits with his chocolate Santa, he became curiously excited and insisted that they had what he termed "a love feast," in which they would solemnly divest Father Christmas of his silver paper covering and eat him up together. On the following night the father had a dream in which he was pregnant and was about to give birth to a monster. It was a very disturbing dream for him and caused him to change his behavior radically with Sandra. He treated her with sternness, aloofness, and some contempt. He would pick on her faults and magnify them, to her great distress. When she approached him to sit on his lap, he would mock her for being a baby. He seemed almost compelled to tease her and reduce her to tears. The mother would often side with her daughter against these attacks and would attempt to get her husband to stop behaving sadistically toward the child. On such occasions, Sandra would explode with rage against her mother and scream at her to leave them alone. This would leave the mother sad and hurt.

There is no doubt that the oedipal phase in the child can reactivate the repressed oedipal struggles of the parents so that the parents transfer onto the child the sexual and aggressive wishes and feelings of the earlier time. The child catalyzes this response and then incorporates some of the ensuing struggle with the parent into his own nuclear neurosis. The degree to which the oedipal conflict is still unresolved in the parent will influence the oedipus complex in the child in the direction of nonresolution. In the immature parent, the stimulus of the child's oedipal phase may be responded to with a preoedipal defense reaction against the "piggishness" of the child.

When the child's oedipal development meets with some insuperable obstacle, it may be thrown back into an earlier phase of pregenital organization. The suppression of masturbation can sometimes act in this way. The child's sexual life then may take on an anal sadistic character so that he becomes irritable, tormenting, and cruel. The sadism may be turned around in fantasy and converted into masochism, so that beating fantasies arise. Occasionally the child will behave in an unmanageable way in order to provoke punishment, hoping for a beating as a simultaneous means of setting his sense of guilt at rest and of satisfying his masochistic sexual trend. The parents of the regressed oedipal child may respond to this provocation, the child's desire for a beating, and may then be caught up guiltily in a recurrent sadomasochistic transaction.

287

Bibliography

1. Barrett, W. A childhood anxiety. *Psychoanal. Quart.* 6:530–535, 1937.
2. Barrett, W. Penis envy and urinary control; pregnancy fantasies and constipation; episodes in the life of a little girl. *Psychoanal. Quart.* 8:211–218, 1939.
3. Freud, S. Analysis of a Phobia in a Five-Year-Old Boy. In J. Strachey (Ed.), *The Standard Edition of the Complete Psychological Works of Sigmund Freud.* London: Hogarth, 1955. Vol. 10, pp. 1–149.
4. Grotjahn, M. The relation of child analysis to education in milieu of psychoanalytically directed school. *Bull. Menninger Clin.* 1:184–191, 1937.
5. Kubie, L. S. Resolution of a traffic phobia in conversations between a father and son. *Psychoanal. Quart.* 6:223–226, 1937.
6. Rangell, L. A treatment of nightmares in a seven-year-old boy. *Psychoanal. Stud. Child* 5:358–390, 1950.

13

The Effect on Parents of the Child's Transition into and out of Latency

Judith S. Kestenberg

EDITORS' INTRODUCTION

Parenthood is a process of progressive adaptation. As the child becomes a person who learns to communicate in play and work with persons outside the family, the tasks of parenthood include adaptation to the changing world of the child. Parents, more aware now than parents in previous generations that the world around us is changing, respond with more or less anxiety to their own emotional problems stirred up by their attempts to grow up with their children. In the following chapter the author presents her keen observation of the emotional problems of parents specific to the particular developmental levels of the child. The background of her clinical observations is, of course, the genetic theory of psychoanalytic development, integrated with the hypotheses gained from her investigations regarding the libidinal sensations inside the body during early childhood.

E. J. A.
T. B.

Each transition from one phase to the next presents a challenge to both parents and children to give up outdated forms of interaction and to adopt a new system of coexistence. The ability of a parent to meet his side of this challenge depends on his inner preparedness to accept the new image the child forms of him and to erect a new image of his child. Only with flexibility in shifting roles and assigning the child a new identity, based on the actuality of his maturational advances, does parenthood become a developmental phase [1, 10]. Through successive subphases of parenthood the parent's own identity undergoes a continuous transformation until parenthood assumes a subordinate position in the individuality of a new life of "parents without children."

Latency has been defined as a phase in which childhood sexuality is dormant. It is more useful to look upon latency as a phase dominated by desexualized, drive-derivative behavioral patterns. Instinctual breakthroughs and sexualization of adaptive behavior do occur but are subordinated to the overall dominance of desexualized psychic structures. The developmental task of latency is the progressive consolidation of the newly acquired psychic agencies which is assured by the maintenance of desexualized, relatively autonomous ego and superego functions. The latency child's independence from id strivings and drive objects is reinforced by his partial separation from his parents. Ability to separate from the child and to surrender him to teachers, who act as guardians of desexualization, enforcers of independence from parents, and organizers of systematic skills, is an indicator of the parents' acceptance of the child's latency.

In transition to latency, parents must take the lead in the institutionalization of desexualized functioning. This constitutes an important step in their own separation-individuation process [19]. To highlight the crucial transition into "part-time parenthood" in latency, let us survey problems of transition in general and glance at the succession of past transformations that paved the way for the current one.

PARENTS IN TRANSITION

An intermingling of progression and regression characterizes transitional periods. To cope with the confusion created by conflicting clues in the child's behavior, parents use four sets of reference as aids in the adjustment to the changing identity of the child. They rely on tangible signs of maturation such as visible physical changes or acquisitions of skills. They follow ritualized customs of child-rearing, such as those prescribed for specific ages for weaning, training, school entry, etc. They act on the basis of positive and negative identifications with their own parents and adapt these practices to current views of influential authorities such as physicians or teachers. The younger the child, the greater the parents' reliance on intuitive understanding, an understanding based on memory traces of similar childhood states, now revived through closeness to the child and identification with him. In this manner parents can regress and progress with their children [9]. But their regression is held in check by their ability to maintain their identity as parents and to use clues other than those transmitted by the child's change of state. Their empathic understanding is tempered by their knowledge, foresight, and a stability born from adult constancy of object relationships.

In transition from one phase to the next, the child threatens the continuity of the parent's working ego. In transforming himself and demanding that parents also change to suit the needs of his next developmental phase, the child seems to reject the parents. As a result parents feel hurt and inadequate. They too become estranged from the child and, so to say, reject him. Before they can erect a new, ego-syntonic identity as parents, they must give up the Johnny they know to become acquainted with the new Johnny. But once the strange child loses his strangeness and becomes "familiar" again, the discontinuity of the relationship is bridged over and the period of alienation has passed.

A transition is in progress when a parent makes a remark such as the one Gesell and Ilg attribute to mothers of 6-year-old children [11]: "He is a changed child and I do not know what has gotten into him." We sense that a transition has been accomplished when we hear parents say: "We don't have a baby anymore. Glenda goes to school. She is a big girl and does not need us the way she used to." The child has changed, she is not the same any more, and neither parent can remain the same [9]. There is regret, but pride in the child's advancement is there too.

Every transition from one phase to the next generates aggres-

291

sion. Parents and children blame each other for each step in their progressive separation, but each new phase brings on a reconciliation, a rapprochement on a new level of coexistence [19]. A successful transition dissolves not only the barrier between parent and child but also the isolation of the parental ego from the rest of the adult ego [10]. Before a new isolation sets in, the parent has developed not only as a parent but also as an individual. Intrinsic to this progress is the task of every transition: to give up not only the real child—as he was and is not any more—but also to revise and re-form the revived imaginary baby of one's own childhood.

THE CHANGING IMAGE OF THE CHILD

The image of the child changes throughout development in accordance with the shifting dominance of drive components and their organization. In this image we find the most concise and brief representation of the totality of psychic functioning in a given phase. To clarify the following synopsis of child images, characteristic for successive developmental phases, the author's classification of phases, which differs somewhat from common psychoanalytic usage, must preface this section of the chapter (For a more comprehensive presentation of this classification see [18]):

1. *Pregenital* phases (oral, anal, urethral).
2. *Inner-genital* phase during which inner-genital tensions predominate over others. At this time the child becomes capable of giving ideational content to oral, anal, urethral, and inner-genital representations of the inside structure of his body, in accordance with their specific products. Externalization of inner-genital impulses helps the child to integrate pregenital and genital component drives before he can cathect his external genitalia, and thus subordinate other bodily pleasures to theu rgency of phallic needs, dominant in the next phase.
3. *Phallic* phase during which the whole body serves phallic modes of expression, and impulses from the inside genitalia are externalized and condensed in the child's body-phallus representation of himself. The growth and differentiation of this phase become the organizational base of psychic structure formation.

292

4. *Latency* is a phase of dominance of drive-derivative functioning and is characterized by a consolidation of newly acquired psychic structures.

5. *Prepuberty* revives the organization of the prephallic, inner-genital phase. Its developmental task is the reintegration of pregenital, inner-genital, and outer-genital drive components into patterns of organization suitable for genital dominance.

6. *Puberty* repeats the growth and differentiation patterns of the phallic phase on a genital level, and results in a reformation of psychic structure that becomes the basis for adult autonomous functioning.

7. *Preadult* phase of consolidation repeats on a higher level the organization of latency, thus establishing the dominance of drive-derivative functioning over expressions of untamed sexuality and aggression.

8. *Adulthood* phases subordinate drive expression to a variety of demands so that instinctual needs can be fulfilled with a normal degree of independence from drive tension and from fixation on primary objects.

A long and circuitous road leads from early concepts of babies to the reality of being a parent of a real infant, soon a toddler, and now a school child. Can one define what a child *is,* how his image remains constant and yet keeps changing through the developmental phases, from one's own childless infancy through the vicissitudes of real parenthood to the childless state of senescence? A scientific definition may not do justice to the feeling that pervades the creativity of parenthood through all ages.

A child is part of me and part of you, a link between us . . . a bond of constancy that holds us together when we are apart. Something of you and something of me. . . . it belongs . . . it's ours. Created with our insides and our outsides, in our own image . . . in the image of our parents . . . and yet different . . . strange, new, forever changing . . . a possession . . . a new life and now a separate being with a life of his own.

Giving vent to our own feelings brought us closer to the infant's feelings about his first possession—a transitional object—he created out of his bodily needs, his closeness to his mother, and his emerging

293

self-realization [23]. The transitional object is in a more real sense the infant's first baby than are the toddler's symbolic equations of the baby with food, feces, and urine that leave their imprint on the "inner-genital" image of the baby of the 2- to 3- or 4-year-old [16]. Equated with the mother's and the child's own inner genital, and externalized onto the toddler's cherished, desexualized possessions—his toys—the inner-genital baby belongs to mother and child. In contrast, the phallic baby is a gift received from the father or given to the mother, the fruit of a forbidden union, a shared sin. With the resolution of the oedipus complex emerges the image of the acceptable, desexualized child, a school child to be shared with a teacher. The latency child transfers much of his allegiance to school [7, 8], and, even in his play at home, he often assumes the role of the teacher rather than that of the parent.

In adolescence parenthood is anticipated with a mixture of reality and fantasy, with love, repudiation, and fear. In prepuberty, increased inner-genital tensions, vying with regressive pregenital and phallic urges, resexualize and distort the baby image at the same time that the child's image of his parents and his own self becomes distorted. Even though a more realistic child image emerges out of this chaos [16, 18], it undergoes repression with the revival of oedipal wishes in puberty. When fertility becomes a reality in adolescence, the realization of the wish for a child is postponed and the image of the child is once more desexualized in the final phase of adolescence which is similar in organization to latency [18]. The new wish for a child grows out of a need for a permanent love relationship with a nonincestuous object in a new home and a new family.

The removal from primary objects [14] is sealed, so to say, when the young adult can become a parent not only by virtue of his biologic readiness but also with the full approval of society.

The real "approved" child draws his acceptable qualities from the desexualized child image, created in a preadult phase of adolescence and its precursor in latency [18]. But these qualities are never free from traces of earlier baby images that emerge from repression and resexualize the parent-child relationship. These unconscious roots of parenthood exert a regressive pull from which empathy to the real child arises. They form the id core of ego regression in the service of adaptation to the child's needs. In normal parenthood, the ego's adap-

294

tive regression to the phase of the child's maturity is confined within the limits of this specifically parental form of adaptation that is isolated from the remainder of the parents' ego and superego [10].

The nursing mother feels relieved when the child is satiated and uncomfortable when he is hungry. She may even feel like "eating up the baby, he is so cute." But she does not radically change her own eating habits. She does not become a baby herself. As her child grows older, she allows her parenthood to encroach less and less into her life as nonparent. In this she finds support from her husband who can split off his fatherhood from the rest of his life much better than she can split off her motherhood.

With the passing of pregenital phases, the parents give up their control over the child's bodily functions and relinquish him as a possession. At the time the preoedipal toddler invents his own baby and identifies with the "lost" mother of his babyhood, parents too feel a need for a new baby as they give up the image of the toddler as a baby [6a, 17]. Sharing a real or toy baby with his mother, the 3-year-old child involves her and the father in the process of integration of pregenital and early genital drives he must accomplish before entering the phallic-oedipal phase. By a shift of cathexis from the inside of the body to the outside, parents and children re-form the "inner-genital baby image" and build the image of a child as a phallus. The resolution of the child's oedipus complex gives parents a chance to revise their own. A sensible desexualized "brain-child" becomes the heir to the phallic child, conceived with a parent. The desexualization of the parent-child relationship creates a distance between them in more ways than one.

TRANSITION INTO LATENCY

With the onset of their child's latency parents not only give up the forbidden phallic-oedipal child, but they become "partially childless" in reality as they release the child—his body and mind—to teachers who represent their own parents [4, 5, 7]. With this crucial separation, children and parents also go their own ways in divergent organizations of their lives. Consolidation of the newly formed psychic structure is the developmental task of latency [18]. Parents assist in this process but, in contrast to preceding phases, their own pattern of organization is different. The liberation of large quantities of narcissistic cathexis invested in the child as a possession, the confrontation with extrafamilial authorities and with expressions of the child's new autonomy, all call for a reintegration of old and new attitudes and a working-through of the revision of the parent's own oedipus complex.

The 5½-year-old child acts like an older edition of the 2½-year-old child [12, 13]. For parents, both of these periods represent successive steps in relinquishing the child as a possession. But latency initiates a much more crucial phase of parenthood that will later serve as a model for the reorientation to the "state of childlessness" when parents separate from their grown sons and daughters.

Some societies regard the 3-year-old child as the adult's helper, but all societies entrust the 6-year-old with responsibilities [13]. The 3-year-old child's autonomy was based on his new ability to verbalize and channel his thoughts into secondary process thinking [15]. But the 6-year-old child has real "sense" [12]. He should not only give lip service to what is right and wrong, he should know it. Although his thinking is syncretistic and concrete, he can reason and communicate in an adultlike manner [13, 20]. But parents are disappointed because he is losing the ability to remember and integrate the past with the present he had acquired as a toddler [21], and the scintillating, creative mind he exhibited at 5 years gives way to the prosaic concreteness and reticence of latency [22]. Repression reduces his passionate interests and his daydreams lack vitality. In addition, his new achievements are easily undone by regressive processes. Adults doubt his reliability when they discover his "lies" or small thefts, find evidence of "accidents" in his underwear, and discover his enchantment with "duty (bathroom) talk." They doubt his advances even more when they realize that he behaves "as though he were living by the rules of the secondary process" (i.e., conforming to reality) only to please them [2].

In relinquishing the phallic-oedipal child, parents shift much of their narcissistic investment in the child as their phallus upward to the child as their "brain"; from the child as proof of their guilty incestuous sexuality to the child as representative of their morality. They hope to exhibit a precociously bright, well-brought-up extension of themselves to the admiring eyes of the teacher. But at the very point when the 6-year-old child becomes ready to be exhibited and subject for evaluation, he lets his parents down. Their shame and guilt become tinged with regressive wishes to hide the evidence of "sins" they had committed against the child. Analysis of their fear of exposure to the teacher reveals parents' guilt about masturbatory practices, which the child's deficiency will disclose. The physician, who examined the child's body, was the parents' trusted ally who repaired the damage they might have caused. The teacher is a stranger who tests the child, judges his performance, and grades him publicly.

Parents and Teachers

The image of the teacher varies [3, 4]. She is sometimes thought of as a good fairy who rescues children and transforms them into angels who purify their parents. On the other hand, she is sometimes thought of as a cruel, witchlike stepmother who kills bad parents and castrates their children.

CASE 1.   A mother, observing in the classroom of her not yet 6-year-old first-grader, noted that her son was restless and not as well behaved as the other children. She felt publicly exposed when the teacher singled out Paul for reprimand and demanded that he stop scratching his leg. All eyes focused on little Paul but he kept on scratching. In a dulcet voice the teacher suggested that the offending leg might have to be cut off so that Paul could stop scratching and the classwork could be resumed. Paul stopped instantly. The teacher regained her leadership, and the children learned what might happen if they "move in a forbidden way."

Paul's mother regarded the teacher's threat as an attack upon herself. She had hoped to find her own beloved grammar school teacher, an idealized mother image. Instead, she found one resembling her punitive older sister who had enjoyed exposing her and undermining her relationship to their mother. She looked to her husband for help. Paul's father reminisced about his early failure in grammar school. He had not become a star pupil until his father had tutored him in second grade. He advised his wife to stay out of the situation. She too responded by a feeling long familiar. There was nothing else to do but placate the teacher as she had in the past placated her "castrating" sister. She advised Paul to behave himself in school. But Paul's battle with the teacher continued.

While the teacher was out of the classroom, Paul told the children that they were all "full of duty." The children "snitched" on him and heard the teacher tell him: "No gentleman talks that way." Thus Paul was publicly branded as already "castrated" as a result of his sinful persistence in masturbation substitutes and regressive rebelliousness. However, Paul did not give up. After a while he pulled down his pants and thus proved to his audience that he was indeed still a "gentleman." The stunnned teacher consulted the principal who agreed with her that the boy's outrageous behavior was the result of a misguided, progressive education at home. Paul's parents were advised to have the child "tested."

Needless to say, the conflict between school and home varies with the individuality of child and parent. Paul's mother wanted to share a good teacher with him. Another mother was competitive with the teacher. When she offered to give a guitar recital to the first-graders, the teacher agreed reluctantly and reported the problem to the principal. He summoned the "delinquent mother" and told her that, even though a performing artist and a teacher herself, she was not a teacher in *his* school but *merely* a mother. Reduced to tears, the mother not only resolved to retreat from the school as enemy territory but spread the word around and thus helped the principal to squash the parent-rebellion.

The foregoing examples illustrate how "bad teachers" can enforce parent-child separation and the surrendering of the child to them by castration threats and aggressive setting of boundaries, which delineate the role of the child and mother in relation to school authorities. The next vignette of parent-child-teacher interaction will serve to illustrate how "good teachers" can hinder parent-child separation by fostering use of the child's school status to prolong the parents' narcissistic investment in the child, and how a "bad teacher" can help establish a proper balance between family and school.

CASE 2. Glenda's parents prepared themselves for their separation from their baby girl by having a new baby. They not only accepted but accelerated their daughter's growing up. She had to give up her transitional object to qualify for admission to kindergarten. As an older sister and a schoolchild, Glenda vied for the teacher's attention in lieu of recapturing her position as a favorite child at home. She became the teacher's pet. Her mother shared in her glory when the teacher gave Glenda "the biggest and the most beautiful ribbon." In first grade, Glenda was restless but her cute appearance and the compliments she paid the teacher assured her continuation of her role as teacher's pet. Despite her gratification, Glenda's mother betrayed her anger at her daughter's liaison with the teacher by occasionally neglecting to be home when Glenda returned from school. The dormant battle between home and school was climaxed in second grade, when a "bad, old teacher" summoned the parents to complain about their child's poor performance. Both parents became greatly upset and the father cried in sympathy with his daughter. But the "bad" teacher brought Glenda and her parents closer. They began to rely less on the teacher as source of narcissistic supply. They ceased to regard Glenda as an object of display, they accepted her femininity, and were able to ease her transition from latency into puberty.

298

It is tempting to explore further the role of the teacher in the development of parents. Suffice it to say that to many parents she represents a voice of the superego, superordinated over their own. As keeper of desexualization in the form of learning and acceptable behavior, the teacher contributes to the redistribution of parents' instinctual and neutralized cathexis and to the reorganization of parental superego.

CASE 3. Nancy's parents, living in dire circumstances, neglected their home and children. As a baby, Nancy was never brought to the hospital for a change in formula or routine injections. In the first grade, when the teacher gave her a prize for attendance and neatness, both parents felt commended not only as parents but also as people. When she failed in school, Nancy's father took it upon himself to drill her until she could pass. The total readjustment of the family during their youngest child's latency brought an unprecedented order into their home.[1] Mother went to work and the whole family began to attend church. When normal standards fell short of the desired appearance, a code of concealment was invoked. When Nancy was reluctant to reveal to the interviewer that she shared her bed with her brother, her father praised her for her reticence. Despite these superego lacunae, the reorganization of parental ego and superego attitudes brought a new dignity to the whole family. Never before did Nancy feel ashamed, and never before did the father feel as calm facing an intruding strange visitor (the author) who represented the hostile society that had victimized him.

This example illustrated the beneficial influence of school on parental attitudes toward the child which, otherwise uncensored and unsupervised, might hinder desexualization and retard development. The next section will exemplify how the child himself contributes to the reorganization of parental ego—and superego—attitudes by invoking extrafamilial authority.

God and the Parents

The child's early superego is fraught with archaic features derived from his own id strivings. These combine with old and new teachings in a form that may be alien to the parent.

---

[1] Even though the examples used concern children from families of more than one child, the comments in this chapter are geared to the first and only child. It is not possible here to discuss the complexities of parents' developmental phases when several children present them with problems from different developmental phases. Neither is it possible to consider the variations stemming from relationships to first, second, youngest, or only children. Only passing references could be made to the differences between fathers and mothers, as each of them relate in a sex-specific way to different children and different age groups.

"Nancy is bad," her mother told the interviewer. "Recently her conscience bothered her. She asked me: 'When a child does something bad to her mother and father, does God fix that?' " Nancy's mother reacted to the question with a mixture of amusement and surprise but seemed pleased with the unexpected help given by God to parents of "bad" children.

Charlie, at the age of 6, punished his mother for interfering with the repression of his curiosity by introducing rituals into homework that deadlocked both mother's and teacher's endeavors to help him. One morning he surprised his mother by saying: "Oh, mother, the sun came out. It is beautiful. Come to the window. Let's pray." Thanking God for the beauty of the sun, Charlie ingratiated himself with his father and invited his mother to join in bowing to the father's superior phallic force. Charlie was teaching his mother to give him up as a phallic object and to accept him as subordinate to father figures. His mother "got a charge out of it" but also felt a new respect for the unteachable child who was becoming her teacher.

The 6-year-old child who invokes God in his dealings with parents seems endowed with special powers that make him appear wise beyond his years. The awed parent may feel that out of the babe's mouth speaks the voice of the omnipotent parent of his own childhood.

The invocation of extrafamilial authority challenges the parents to revive their everyday working conscience to conform to the child's high ideals. As the child's superego becomes reinforced by principles of fair play, impartiality, justice, and consistency of standards, learned in school, he gradually relies less and less on archaic superego demands. But he still imparts to the parent what he learned and becomes the parent's guide at home. At no point in the parents' development are they more forcefully confronted with their double standard of morality. To protect the young from too harsh a reality, to maintain the myth of parents' omnipotence, and, foremost, to deny evidences of adult sexuality, parents tend to deceive their young children. Latency morality challenges them to become honest for the sake of their children.

Parents and the Regressed Child

The 6- or 7-year-old moralist who has made honest people out of his parents is neither consistently honest himself nor able to conform to other ideals he holds the parents to. He regresses as he progresses.

To combat his masturbatory impulses he resorts to pregenital modes of behavior. In the process of transforming them into desexualized patterns of work he seesaws precariously between pleasing and displeasing adults. Adult desexualization of pregenital components of good work habits is far beyond his meager beginnings. Neither parents nor teachers accept what is self-evident to 6- and 7-year-olds: the connection between work and "do your duty," between effort and straining, between ambitious aspirations and "aim your sissy in the toilet." A long time has elapsed since parents themselves introduced these links. They demand an isolation between these original and derivative functions that the young latency child cannot consistently uphold. To him the teacher takes on the quality of the training mother, especially since the strange adult things he must learn (incorporate), memorize (retain), and produce on command (eliminate) seem as important to the adult world as his toilet training once was. "Duty" talk and anal jokes offend adult sensibilities more, the more they feel degraded and caricatured by the child.[2]

The average parent understands and even welcomes the child's regression when he comes home from school. But the pleasure in the return of the "lost child" [6a] may be overshadowed by the intrusion into the house of school in the form of homework for which parents are made responsible [17]. Even the many illnesses of early latency are not entirely free from the shadow of school life [11]. In providing reports to school, the physician loses his status as the parents' trusted ally and sharer of the child's body [6]. But he can still alleviate parents' guilt by mediating between them and teachers and taking responsibility for the child's temporary removal from school.

As illnesses renew bodily closeness between the child and the parents, the parents become more tolerant of his regression. Their unsupervised intimacy gives parents a new chance to identify with the child's way of thinking. They may, for instance, help the child to transform pregenital interests into jokes. Latency witticism, as strange as it is to adults, teaches parents to be more tolerant and less concerned with the child's regressive reactions to his learning experience. As they revise the image of their child, they also revise the image of

[2] In this category also belong moron jokes and riddles of later latency in which the child caricatures the wisdom of teachers who belittle children = morons. These also make fun of the literal approach to learning the children have just overcome.

301

their own parents and feel freer to pursue interests renounced in the past.

Parents' Readjustment During Their Child's Latency

As parents reintegrate their ego ideals and superego demands, they can assist the child in strengthening, amplifying, and making concrete his self-image as a schoolchild and his self-esteem as an achiever. To keep up with their children, in identification with them or with their teachers, parents reorganize their own learning patterns and integrate new knowledge with the core of learning automatized in childhood. Many become students themselves to make up for past deficiencies in their education. Fathers revive old interests in hobbies and sports they share with their children. Mothers have time now to paint or write, to resume old friendships, to join clubs, or go back to work. The children's own widening social contact and outlets for sublimation also guide their parents' socialization. Scouting and parent-teacher organizations are among the many fields of activity in which parents of latency children meet people from several social groups and assume new identities as members of the community. Whatever these new interests, they do give parents wider perspective which promotes reintegration of old and new cultural influences.

After the initial reorganization of parental attitudes and activities, life becomes peaceful and settled. The child in late latency has made great strides in the development from bodily needs to physical and intellectual skills, from play to work, from dependence to self-reliance, and from proneness to regression to a consistency in progression [5]. Parents have learned to rely on his stability. They treat infractions and disturbances of peace, such as sibling fights or school setbacks, as temporary phenomena that can be settled by proper handling and reasoning. To continue the peaceful coexistence with their children, parents try to prolong latency and tend to ignore signs of impending adolescent changes.

TRANSITION INTO PREPUBERTY

In late latency the body begins to change in structure and function. Physical complaints become more frequent and habits begin to deteriorate. Parents tend to ignore or deny the significance of these

302

changes. Even prodromal syndromes of disorders do not disquiet them until they become fulminant in prepuberty.

CASE 4.   Belinda, an only child of loving parents, began to lose weight at the age of 10. Her parents attributed her loss of appetite, her decrease in sociability, and the decline in her school work to their having just moved from another state. By the time Belinda was 11 she had become so haggard that the pediatrician suspected Simmond's disease. When this was ruled out, the parents were relieved and accepted the child's thinness. They helped her with schoolwork and encouraged her to call friends. But they did not notice Belinda's depression.

Belinda was obedient. She did all that was expected of her, but reduced it to "daily minimum requirements." Only with the onset of prepuberty did she become negativistic to a degree that alarmed her parents. They seemed unprepared for what they now accepted as their child's illness. They had forgotten how sensitive she had been as an infant and how easily hurt and frightened as a toddler. They reiterated what an outstanding student she had been when they lived in Florida; how industrious and adult she had been at home, in school, and in church. They were so impressed with her high religious and ethical standards that they considered becoming more observant Catholics to please her. The whole family had become involved in the child's illness as long as she perpetuated and exaggerated a latency pattern [18].

When parents cling to the peace of latency, even normal children may contain their inner turmoil. They give the appearance of stability and solidity by maintaining empty latency forms to disguise their nagging unrest. Politeness without consideration, conversation without content, and mechanical performance without personal involvement can mask the early signs of prepuberty diffusion and feign the persistence of latency.

Once parents become engaged in the process of transition out of latency, they resexualize the image of the child. Approaching adolescence emphasizes the dichotomy between sexes not only in children but in parents as well. Physical development and preoccupation with the body meet a responsive feeling tone in the girl's mother. She lets the father participate in her observations without involving him directly. A boy's fears about his changing body, especially concerning his inner-genital maturation, are often scoffed at by both parents, who consider such concerns feminine [18]. Mothers are embarrassed to talk about them and fathers, more often than not, are too threatened by homosexual temptations that may beset father and son in intimate talks about the body. But fathers, less involved with children's bodies than mothers and more inclined to maintain distance from their older children, regress less at this time than mothers do. Consequently they act out less and reject their children less in transition into adolescence. Father's longer persistence in "parental latency" and his better composure help mother to endure prepuberty sexuality. Maternal poise in turn assists the father when he regresses in response to aggressive or asocial acts or unreasonable outbursts of "independence" that foreshadow adolescence.

The changing image of the child creates problems for which parents are not prepared. What children feel inside their bodies calls for an outward expression that is not available. Girls want brassieres before they need them. Boys tell their mothers with disgust: "Gee, mom, you don't know nothing about what guys wear." Parents are discarded for friends, who serve as mirror images for self-observation [18].

Through a successful reintegration of her body-image and identity, Glenda's mother was able to guide her out of latency with a smoothness born out of her native gift for harmonizing with the child. But she did discourage friendships and held on to the closeness with her daughter. In accepting the child's femininity, she tended to exaggerate it. Glenda began to pout and complained, "She makes me wear dresses." In retaliation she attacked her mother's physical appearance: "You could not wear clothes like me, even when you were my age." She missed a mirror image of herself. She yearned for a close girl friend.

Most parents become annoyed by exaggerated expressions of friendship in late latency. But the loss of the child to a friend has its compensations. Bouts of diffuse, undirected excitement that grow out of incipient inner-genital sensations are contagious to parents and evoke archaic fears. A transient dissolution on body boundaries, a beginning diffusion of thought, and a greater need to externalize all add up to mutual dissatisfaction between children and parents. Regressing with the child, parents often blame each other for the waves of unrest created by the child. After a rainy afternoon at home, parents are only too glad to surrender the intimacy with their child to his bosom friend. Listening to preteen conversations from a safe distance, they become acquainted with the new customs of the "almost adolescent," which differ from those in their own childhood. A temporary estrangement from the child allows parents to regain their equilibrium and accept the waning of latency. The more deeply rooted the reintegration of psychic structure in the parents during their child's latency, the better prepared they are to participate constructively in their children's adolescent struggle.

SUMMARY

Latency stands out as a period of *"part-time parenthood"* during which parents learn to share their child with the community and in which distance from the child facilitates the *desexualization* of his image as well as a phase of redistribution of cathexis and *reorganization* of ego and superego attitudes that *prepares* the ground for the paradoxical ultimate goal of child-rearing, the state of "childless parenthood" at the end of the child's adolescence.

Bibliography

1. Benedek, T. Parenthood as a developmental phase. *J. Amer. Psychoanal. Ass.* 7:389–417, 1959.
2. Bornstein, B. On latency. *Psychoanal. Stud. Child* 6:279–285, 1951.
3. Ekstein, R. The child, the teacher and learning. *Young Children* (National Association for the Education of Young Children) 22:195–209, 1967.
4. Freud, A. The role of the teacher. *Harvard Educ. Rev.* 22:229–232, 1952.
5. Freud, A. *Normality and Pathology in Childhood: Assessment of Development.* New York: International Universities Press, 1965.
6. Freud, A. Discussion at the Panel: The Role of Physical Illness in the Emotional Development of Children. Congress of the International Psychoanalytic Association, Copenhagen, 1967.
6a. Freud, A. About losing and being lost. *Psychoanal. Stud. Child* 22:9–19, 1967.
7. Freud, S. Some Reflections on School-Boy Psychology (1914). In J. Strachey (Ed.), *The Standard Edition of the Complete Psychological Works of Sigmund Freud.* London: Hogarth, 1955. Vol. 13, pp. 241–244.
8. Freud, S. The Ego and the Id (1923). In J. Strachey (Ed.), *The Standard Edition of the Complete Psychological Works of Sigmund Freud.* London: Hogarth, 1961. Vol. 19, pp. 1–66.

305

9. Fries, M. Psychosomatic relationships between mother and infant. *Psychosom. Med.* 6:159–162, 1944.
10. Furman, E. Theoretical and Clinical Considerations in the Assessment of Parents. In E. Furman and A. Katan (Eds.), *Therapeutic Nursery School.* New York: International Universities Press, 1969.
11. Gesell, A., and Ilg, F. *The Child from Five to Ten.* New York: Harper, 1946.
12. Guthrie, G. M., and Jacobs, P. J. *Child Rearing and Personality Development in the Philippines.* University Park: Pennsylvania State University Press, 1966.
13. Inhelder, B., and Piaget, J. *The Growth of Logical Thinking from Childhood to Adolescence.* New York: Basic Books, 1958.
14. Katan, A. The role of "displacement" in agoraphobia. *Int. J. Psychoanal.* 32:41–50, 1951.
15. Katan, A. Some thoughts about the role of verbalization in early childhood. *Psychoanal. Stud. Child* 16:184–188, 1961.
16. Kestenberg, J. On the development of maternal feelings in early childhood. *Psychoanal. Stud. Child* 11:257–291, 1956.
17. Kestenberg, J. Acting Out in the Analysis of Children and Adults. Presented at the meeting of the American Association for Child Analysis, 1967. Unpublished data. (Condensed version in *Int. J. Psychoanal.* 49:341, 1968.)
18. Kestenberg, J. Phases of adolescence: With suggestions for a correlation of psychic and hormonal organizations. *J. Amer. Acad. Child Psych.* (Part I) 6:426–463, 1967; (Part II) 6:577–614, 1967; (Part III) 7:108–151, 1968.
19. Mahler, M., and La Perriere, K. Mother-child interaction during separation-individuation. *Psychoanal. Quart.* 34:483–498, 1965.
20. Piaget, J. *The Psychology of Intelligence.* New York: Harcourt, Brace, 1950.
21. Schur, H. An observation and comments on the development of memory. *Psychoanal. Stud. Child* 21:468–479, 1966.
22. Williams, M. Discussion of J. Kestenberg [17]. Unpublished data.
23. Winnicott, D. W. Transitional objects and transitional phenomena. *Int. J. Psychoanal.* 34:89–97, 1953.

14

The Reactions of Parents
to Adolescents and to
Their Behavior

E. James Anthony

EDITORS' INTRODUCTION

The period of adolescence is being gradually extended, especially in the Western world, as the social and cultural environment grows in complexity. What was once regarded as a fairly short transitional phase leading from childhood into adult life, and of only transitional significance, has emerged in the past few decades as a major developmental stage requiring its own specialized services in medicine and psychiatry. The reason for this evolution seems to lie in the fact that the characteristic developmental conflicts between regressive and progressive forces occurring within the individual at this time have become intensified by the contemporary malaise affecting the cultural milieu.

The anthropologic and sociologic data offered in this chapter serve to illustrate the marked differences that have arisen between civilized living today and the human condition within simple societies of less recent times. To the adult onlooker, and to the adolescent himself, youth culture would appear to be undergoing a rapid change resembling that of a state of constant flux whether in rebellion, regression, or retreat, as compared with the more "expectable" environment of the adult or the more stable setting of his adolescence. The child today, in many ways, is growing up in a different sort of world from the one peopled by his parents during their development. The discrepancy in life styles may be as large as that between immigrant parents and their children.

The average parent tries to anticipate, accept, and adjust to the behavioral changes that take place in his offspring in the course of development. This adaptation comes harder to some parents than to others who are more flexible, but all parents experience some degree of anxious tension, since they have not traveled the same developmental pathway or incorporated the newer elements that come into the family with the contemporary adolescent. Even the more enlightened parents are surprised by the size of the generation gap when they go out of their way to agree and understand, only to be confronted by the mystifying comment, "You don't understand at all." The gap has currently reached such proportions that parents, out of empathy if not sympathy with adolescence, have almost abrogated their parental rights to decide anything more for their children.

E. J. A.
T. B.

In recent years," remarks Adelson, "the adolescent has come to weigh oppressively on the American consciousness," and to occupy "a peculiarly intense place in American thought and feeling" [1]. This is in contrast to the attitude in earlier times, when the adolescent was generally regarded with tolerant condescension as a simple-minded character living "outside the world of adult happenings" and inhabiting "an Eden of preresponsibility." In our time he has "invaded the adult world" in two antithetical stereotyped forms. In one he is the *victimizer,* "leather-jacketed, cruel, sinister, and amoral," the carrier of society's sadistic and sexual projections, replacing the gangster and Negro in this role. In the other, he is pictured as the *victim,* passive and powerless in the face of adult corruption that seeks to exploit his gullibility.

A QUESTION OF STEREOTYPES

These adolescent stereotypes are not the only ones available to the adult population, but they present an element of ruthlessness and sadism that resonate disturbingly in the minds of the older group and are seized upon as shibboleths in the ongoing "conflict of the generations." So powerful have been these oversimplified preconceptions and so resistant to rebuttal by opposing facts that they have made their influence felt even within the family circle, causing parents to respond to their adolescent children as if they were embodiments of negative ideas rather than real people.

To compound the mischief even further, the stereotypes have also functioned as mirrors held up to the adolescent by society reflecting an image of himself that the adolescent gradually comes to regard as authentic and according to which he shapes his behavior. In this way, he completes the circle of expectation. The adult is convinced of the validity of his stereotypes since the predicted behavior does in fact

Reprinted from Excerpta Medica International Congress Series No. 108, *Proceedings of the Sixth International Congress of the International Association for Child Psychiatry and Allied Professions,* Edinburgh, July 24–29, 1966; and reprinted in modified form from Chapter 5 of *Adolescence: A Psychosocial Perspective,* edited by Gerald Caplan and Serge Lebovici, © 1969 by Basic Books, Inc., Publishers, New York.

occur; the adolescent is convinced that he is simply doing what everyone is expecting him to do; and society at large is convinced that it has a problem on its hands by the daily news of incidents chronicled luridly by its reporters.

The response of any parent to the adolescent child may therefore be dictated by a collusion of three factors: a collective reaction as represented by the stereotype, an idiosyncratic reaction based on the personalities and experiences involved, and the "transference" reaction in which preexisting factors from an earlier phase of life exert an influence unbeknown to the participants on their attitudes, affects, and actions, often to the detriment of the relationship. There is probably no human transaction in which any of these occurs uncontaminated by the presence of the other two, and the situation to a large extent determines which one predominates. As a general rule, the more negative the relationship, the less operative is the person-to-person response and the more conspicuous the stereotypic and irrational, unconscious modes of transacting.

In the next section follow various contemporary polarities of stereotypic thinking in their nascent form unmodified by personal considerations. The adolescent will be seen as victimizer and victim; as dangerous and endangered; as sexually rampant, requiring restraint, and as sexually inadequate, needing encouragement; as emotionally maladjusted, crying out for treatment, and as emotionally free, emitting a breath of fresh therapeutic air onto stale adult conflicts; as an enviable object to be cut down and as a repository of the adult's unfulfilled ambitions to be built up; as a redundant family member to be extruded with as much haste as decency will permit and as a lost object to be mourned in passing. Both adult and adolescent oscillate between these extreme images, and when the pair are not in phase, the resulting interaction may occasion a high degee of perplexity with the bewilderment evident in the inconsistent and confused communications that then flow between the participants.

The inherently dichotomous nature of the stereotype is reflected in the good or bad images created. The behavior of the adolescent is more of a continuum with the reactions distributed along a Gaussian curve, the extreme manifestations occurring with lesser frequency. However, because they tend to gain greater publicity, the impression is created that they are the statistically expectable modes of teen-age behavior. The "headline intelligence" characteristic of the public mind has come to consider adolescence and delinquency as synonymous, interchangeable labels. The clinician does little to correct this misconception, since he himself is constantly confronted with extreme reactions and may eventually be led to regard them as typical rather than atypical and infrequent. The "good" adolescent, although representing perhaps three-quarters of the adolescent population, is so effectively camouflaged by his conformity to the standards of a given culture that he is scarcely credited with existence. Instead of victim or victimizer, his role with respect to the adult has a special and satisfying quality to it that was not present in his dependent status as a child and will not be present in his ultimate status as an adult. In large measure, it can be viewed as a learning experience in which the adolescent is constantly practicing the adult role under the experienced tutelage of a friendly and encouraging adult. The relationship is regarded as basically helpful and trustworthy, even if a little avuncular and out of date. Since this chapter is directed mainly toward clinicians, it must be understood that the clinical viewpoint, with its more pathologic emphasis, will be salient. Since the stereotypic reaction and the vicious misunderstanding it engenders are felt to make major contributions to a pathologic condition, the two factors, the clinical and the stereotypic, will be interwoven in the account that follows.

THE STEREOTYPIC REACTIONS TO THE ADOLESCENT AS A DANGEROUS AND ENDANGERED OBJECT

The image of the "victimizer," slowly, relentlessly and ruthlessly stalking the terrified adult, calls attention to a surprising metamorphosis in the life of the individual through which the weak and helpless child is transformed into a potent and menacing figure that can now threaten the adult on whom he once depended for his security and sustenance. Every period of human history has accorded recognition to the potential dangerousness of this transitional period, and complex procedures have been instituted to control the situation. In the darwinian and later freudian speculation on the "primal horde," the threat to the father with the supervention of adolescence ended with the killing and eating of the father. It was never clear in the theory to what extent such a termination was inevitable and "natu-

311

ral," but one would expect that when the primal hordes banded together in the form of communities, the fathers would begin to legislate in favor of their own survival, perhaps resorting to the extrusion of the adolescent male as a first resort and then eventually subduing him by means of institutional techniques. In this context, it is interesting to note that adolescent male monkeys, when caged with a typical monkey family—father, three or four wives, and one or two adolescent females helping to care for a few infants—are often slain by the father at the onset of puberty.

The later institutional methods of dealing with the same problem initiation rites, secret adult societies, and prolonged apprenticeships —were generally effective in subduing any revolutionary trends present in the adolescent and in suppressing any inordinate wishes he might entertain for possession of the women, the works and the food of the adults.

There is another side to the adult's reaction other than this preoccupation with the dangerousness of the adolescent. It takes the form of marked concern for the safety of the younger person and may express itself in practical measures to safeguard him against premature exposure to the physical and emotional stresses of the adult world. The minor is protected legally against exploitation by the unscrupulous adult and may react to the protection as overprotection, regarding the prohibitions imposed as ways of thwarting his normal and necessary drives. He is quick to detect the hostility behind the solicitude, and he is often inclined to react to the former rather than to the latter component of the adult's ambivalence.

The same mixture of intention is present in the reactions of primitives. In many parts of the world, girls are suspended between earth and sky inside a dark, airless, and filthy contraption at the time of their first menstruation, not only because there is a fear that they will blight the crops, blunt the weapons, sour the milk, and cause cattle to miscarry, but also because they themselves, if exposed to light, may suffer from sores, grow blind, or shrivel up into skeletons. The precautions taken, therefore, to isolate and insulate them are activated as much by concern for their safety as for the safety of the adults [6].

As far as institutional measures go, the more advanced societies appear to ignore adolescence almost as completely as the primitive recognize it, but the sense of danger still remains. In the words of one anthropologist: "We prescribe no ritual; the girl continues on a round of school or work, but she is constantly confronted by a mysterious apprehensiveness in her parents and guardians. . . . The society in which she lives has all the tensity of a room full of people who expect the latest arrival to throw a bomb" [11].

Psychotherapists, confronted by the adolescent, have put forward as many reasons and rationalizations as parents and adults in general for treating the adolescent with special care and caution or not treating him at all. They have argued cogently in favor of treatment but by other therapists and in other institutions. Many have concluded, on the basis of sound reason, that it is better to leave adolescents psychotherapeutically alone during adolescence because of their well-known proclivity to act out and drop out. The vivid metaphors they have coined possess a strong deterrent quality. "One cannot analyze an adolescent in the middle phase," says one prominent author; "It is like running next to an express train" [7]. Another likens adolescence to "an active volcanic process with continuous eruptions taking place, preventing the crust from solidifying" [8]. Once the psychotherapist gets it into his head that he has to deal with a bomb that might explode or a volcano that might erupt or an express train that will outpace him, he will approach the treatment situation with very mixed feelings. If one adds to this array of stereotypes the reputation that even the mildest adolescents have for resorting to slight delinquencies at the least provocation, then the psychotherapist's reason for bypassing adolescence is easier to understand if not to condone. The teen-age patients that do come to therapy and remain in therapy are generally severe passive character disorders that are developmentally preadolescent in their makeup. They behave with the cooperativeness of the average adult and child patient, but they remain largely untouched by the therapeutic process.

Within the last decade these various considerations plus a growing sense of responsibility toward a neglected group have led clinicians to conclude that adolescents are best dealt with by psychiatrists who, whatever their major affiliations are, wish to deal with adolescents. There are child psychiatrists as well as adult psychiatrists who have a "built-in" flair for resonating sympathetically and empathizing deeply with the "in-between" situation. This gives them a sufficiency of comfort and confidence in coping with even tempestuous teen-agers and dampens down the fluctuations between the cautious and the carefree. Adolescents are especially sensitive to the "phony" attitudes and mannerisms of adults who are not too sure whether to talk "down" or "up" or "on the level" with them and are liable to exploit this uncertainty to the full by taking up provocative counterpositions.

THE STEREOTYPIC RESPONSE TO THE ADOLESCENT AS A SEXUAL OBJECT

Even in these pseudosophisticated days, when information on infantile sexuality can be purchased in every drug store and vivid accounts of prepubertal heterosexual activities have been reported in the press, the emergence of biologic sexual maturity in children invariably seems to take the family off guard as if it were completely unprepared for this natural and long-expected event. It would appear that early manifestations of the sexual impulse are in some way disregarded or depreciated as "child's play" and therefore not to be taken too seriously. With the development of the secondary sexual characteristics and the occurrence of seminal emissions and menstrual flow, the family becomes uneasily aware of the new sexual object in its midst. Its response varies from family to family. In some, the succession of pubertal events may be shared by the family members as in the manner of other achievements, whereas in others, it is hushed up and confined to the privacy of the bedroom and bathroom.

Parental reactions to puberty are closely correlated with the extent to which sexuality has found a comfortable acceptance in the household as gauged by the affectionate demonstrations between the members and the level of accurate biologic knowledge possessed by the children. There are parents who regard it as the consummation of their own psychosexual development, rounding off the cycle of the generations. There are others who are pruriently intrigued by the shy and groping sexuality of the novitiate and obtain vicarious enjoyment in stimulating its appearance and mocking its ineptness. A third group of parents, with a high degree of sexual repression, may react with dismay and displeasure at the slightest display of erotic feeling. The frigid woman, psychosexually infantile, not only insists on maintaining an asexual status for herself but also for her children [14]. She is blind to the pubertal indexes and repulsed by any form of adult hetero-sexuality. On the other hand, she is not greatly perturbed when the adolescent displays homosexual tendencies, symptoms indicating oral and anal fixations, or incestuous concerns. The hostile reactions to maturity contrast with the overflow of pathologic tenderness occasioned by immaturity, so that the children are caught up in a vortex of changing attitudes and behavior that bewilder them even more than the biologic events taking place in them. Unable to accept her own femininity, the frigid woman is inevitably led to sabotage the sexual development of her adolescent daughter. As long as the little girl is "neuter," the mother remains on good terms with her, but with puberty, a dynamic conflict comes into focus and a fierce hostility takes hold of the mother. She cannot and will not allow her daughter to become a woman, and the resulting conflict around the sexual identity in the daughter reactivates her own identity problem. It is difficult for any child to develop beyond the neurotic inhibitions of its parents, but nowhere is this truer than in the development of sexual identity.

The transition from "asexual" child to sexual adolescent may not only put the parent's psychosexual maturity to the test, but also tax his relationship with the child. "The very individual towards whom the parent was able to show overt signs of love during childhood has now become a sexually stimulating and taboo object. As a result the parent must mobilize defenses to handle the anxiety provoked by his own incestuous fantasy" [3].

Another effect of adolescence on adults is the reactivation of their own adolescent struggles with overt autoerotic, homosexual, and oedipal conflicts with the development of what amounts to an adolescent decompensation in retrospect. Not infrequently, this upsurge of suppressed adolescent feeling may drive the parent into psychotherapy. A given family may therefore have two crises occurring concomitantly—the crisis of adolescence in the child and a reactivated adolescent crisis in his parent.

These roused sexual impulses may confine themselves to the realm of psychopathology, but a breakthrough into everyday life is not so uncommon, especially in homes where there is a general degradation of living conditions as a result of economic privations, alcoholism, and mental illness. A weak incest barrier may give way under these circumstances, and a spate of miscarriages and pregnancies may

315

result. In one survey at an obstetrical hospital, it was calculated that at least one-third of the illegitimate pregnancies were the products of incestuous union, mainly with the father. It is surprising that the figure is not even greater when one takes into account the prevalence of Lolita fantasies in middle-aged men with adolescent daughters, as revealed in psychotherapy. It is also characteristic of fathers who have near-incestuous relationships with their daughters to react to any adult heterosexual interests on the part of the girls with prudish indignation.

The ambivalence noted in the parent's response to the adolescent as a dangerous object is equally true of the present consideration. An analysis of transactions between parents and adolescents around a covertly sexual conflict can illustrate how both sides play out their conscious and unconscious roles in response to wishes and fears that are implied but seldom verbalized. At one level, the parent may react with justifiable anxiety in keeping with his cultural standards and the adolescent, in turn, may behave in a way appropriate to the codes prevalent in the peer group. Underlying this reaction, there may be another less conscious one in which the parent may be provoking the adolescent to act out some of his own urgent repressed fantasies, at the same time punishing him for attempting to do so. The child may be dimly aware of this unconscious manipulation and may respond to the conflicting communications of the two levels with a double-bind communication of his own. For example, he may deny that he has done anything bad, be indignant at the suspicion, and, at the same time, "blow up" the experience, making a sexual mountain out of an ignominious mole hill. On still another level, the parent may be reacting to a deep dissatisfaction with his own sexual lot in life and envious that his child is getting something while he is being deprived. The adolescent, in his turn, may react with anger because he is being accused of engaging in activities which the father has often desired but cannot bring to pass because of his own inhibitions or the inhibitions of his partner. Under these circumstances, both parents and child may feel that his biologic drives are setting up an insuperable barrier between them [13].

The sexual rivalry appearing in the family at this time can have disruptive effects on marriage. An attractive daughter may become a serious rival to a mother who has been thwarting her husband for many years. The father begins to take notice of his daughter and finds reasons for taking her out in place of her mother. He may also begin to respond to other "dates" in a jealously hostile manner, either sulkily ignoring their existence or else referring to them in terms of scathing criticism. (One young girl amusingly referred to her father as suffering from an attack of "oedipops.")

The mother-daughter rivalry has its most extreme expression within the setting of the "menopausal-menarche" syndrome, when the mother's waning reproductive life is confronted with the flowering sexuality of the girl. The interaction stirs up considerable anxiety and depression in both, and the nagging relationship of prepuberty is transformed into an open warfare in which the Geneva conventions are abandoned.

The reactions of adults to the sexual pressures produced by their adolescent children may run the gamut of sexual psychopathology from the autoerotic to heterosexual acting out, so that unfaithfulness may enter the marriage for the first time. There is no doubt that the sexuality of the adolescent is a stimulus for the sexuality of the parent. This is well demonstrated again in the primitive situation when the adolescent is initiated into sexual life and the adult seizes upon the occasion to be openly sexual. "The use of obscene language, expressions of desire for prohibited sexual relationships, public mention of the sexual act and its mechanics, immodest exposure and hip movements—all these ordinarily shocking acts are expected and performed by women leading the novices back from the initiation ceremony" [10].

The Stereotypic Response to the Adolescent as an Object of Envy

It is clear that psychologically speaking the adolescent is on his way up when the caretaking adults are on their way down. This basic anabolic-catabolic distinction understandably provokes in the adult envy for the adolescent's youthful vigor with all its freedom, freshness, and joyful foolishness. The envy may show itself in a contrast derision at the simplicity and awkwardness of the younger person and at his lack of experience in worldly matters. At its worst, it can take the form of highly sadistic measures disguised in the form of initiation rites and rituals.

A frequent cause of disturbances in the family is the narcissistic parent in competition with the adolescent of the same sex. He has long been better at doing most things than his son and he can hardly conceive that the latter is now overtaking him. At this point, the better-adjusted parent will retire gracefully from the scene, acknowledging the new state of affairs, while his immature counterpart will attempt strenuously to outdo his rival in every activity even to the point of a coronary attack, as occurred in one case recently when a father undertook to beat his teen-age son in ten different athletic events and was rushed to hospital at the end of the eighth.

The envious response to the biologic events of puberty may take a variety of forms. A woman analyst [4] has discussed the sadistic manifestations of the mother in her treatment of the girl at her first menstrual period: ". . . many mothers do their best to keep young and to deny, even to themselves, the fact that they are growing older and find an adolescent daughter an uncomfortable reminder of what they are striving to forget or to hide from others. It often happens that the first menstruation may coincide with the mother's menopause, and this will greatly magnify her reactions."

In primitive communities, the attack on the pubertal child is institutionalized and, therefore, more open. An anthropologist offers this description of the reaction of the mothers to the removal of the clitoris at a ceremony for female initiation: "As soon as the piece of flesh has dropped to the ground, the crowd of women begin trilling loudly, gaily screaming and shouting, and in some cases dancing individually" [10].

The conflict of the generations is therefore directed in some part at keeping upcoming youth—with all his enthusiasm, his drive, his developing skills and knowledge, his relatively open mind, and his colossal capacity for assimilating new ways and new ideas—from overthrowing the establishment and upsetting the adult roles. Initiation rites help to keep him in his place, and so do qualifying examinations [15]. The examiner may regard the examination as a means of "getting his own back on his father" or of getting his own children to "toe the line" and do exactly what they are told. The hostility of some examiners on these occasions has passed into the student folklore, but it does lead to a great deal of impotent counterhostility on the part of the students. It is interesting to recall that following examinations during the Middle Ages, the candidate was required to take an oath that he would not "take vengeance on the examiner."

The mechanisms of envy in the adult frequently feed on the differences between the child's experience of life and what the parent himself had to go through as a child. "I never had a car at your age, and I do not see why you should. You get more allowance in a week than I got in a year. I had to work my way through high school, but you go to a private one." The feelings are exacerbated by grandparents, once so hard on the parents and now so intent apparently on "spoiling" the adolescent grandchild.

One way the parents have developed in dealing with these scarifying feelings of envy is by identifying with the newcomer and making his future narcissistically their own. He can then carry the parents' unrealized ambitions and aspirations and the energies are thus harnessed to pushing the adolescent up rather than keeping him down, although the process may generate as much conflict and resentment in the younger person.

The Stereotypic Reaction to Adolescents as Lost Objects

Many writers have commented on the depression that invades the earlier part of adolescence when the children are decathecting their childhood objects. The children lose their parents, but parents also begin to lose their children, and it is this depression that may evolve into a serious clinical melancholia. The parents experience a sense of emptiness about the home and an absence of goals that had motivated them so strongly and consistently throughout the childhood of their children.

The attempt to recapture the vanishing object can be strenuous. With every artifice at their command, certain parents will attempt to close the doors and raise the drawbridges and dig deep moats to keep their burgeoning offspring in, for they cannot bring themselves to realize that the loss entailed is almost as inevitable as death and almost as irreversible. They may offer themselves as apparently new objects, disguised as adolescent playmates, but the adolescent readily detects the old object in the new and struggles to escape even more strenuously. They may attempt to keep pace with the young and wear themselves out in so doing, or, at least for a while, they may successfully deny entrance to any new object.

It may take some time to discover that gaining new objects and

319

losing old ones go hand in hand in the course of normal adolescent development and that their only chance of preventing the escape of the adolescent is to set about systematically enslaving the child from his earliest years, so that by the time he reaches adolescence, the incestuous enthrallment is complete. This is the type of child who never seems to enter adolescence. Childhood is prolonged indefinitely and the parent certainly has possession of the child. The ambivalence involved in the fixation is so severe, and the pathologic developments of the child so extreme, that the conservation is associated with little real happiness for the parent.

A surer way of retaining some part at least of the lost child is by helping the process of separation and individuation to its completion and culmination in the adult child. A new relationship then becomes possible in which two adults, linked by mutual happy memories, find to their surprise (not knowing the strength of the identification processes) that they have many interests in common and discover a new mature pleasure in each other as people. This pleasure is no longer derived from the old anaclitic model but depends on the rediscovery of the child as an adult object, the parent having gracefully relinquished the child at the start of adolescence.

THE STEREOTYPIC RESPONSE TO THE ADOLESCENT AS A MALADJUSTED INDIVIDUAL

In one of the many current portraits of the adolescent, the author refers to "a fluent, loose-jointed restlessness alternating with catatonic repose" [5]. A puzzled teacher likened the experience of his contact with adolescents to a ride on the big dipper, "sometimes you are up and sometimes you are down, but you never know for certain when the next swing is coming." The adult in our Western culture has apparently learned to expect a state of acute disequilibrium and anticipates the "storm and stress" in his adolescent child as he once anticipated the negativism of his 2-year-old. The expectation has seemingly been incorporated into the literature of psychologic development and it may take methodic research and many years of endeavor to remove it from the textbooks. There is, however, growing anthropologic and sociologic support for the concept that society gets the type of adolescent it expects and deserves, and this is true of even those members who come into daily contact with the ordinary teen-ager. In a recent poll of teachers, for example, more than 80 percent of them subscribed to the opinion that adolescence was a phase of "great emotional disturbance," and more than half believed that the child at this time underwent a complete personality change [5].

It is not surprising, from what we said earlier, that adolescents themselves begin to share this opinion and to assume that their mood swings and waywardness are signs of incipient insanity. The referral to the psychiatrist may help to confirm this inner apprehension and it is at this age that the fear of the psychiatrist is at its greatest. It is at this age that the altered body image, the alienation of parts of the psychic structure, and the intense masturbatory conflicts all give rise to the same terrible speculation with the panic-stricken reaction: "I am not nuts. I do not need a nut doctor."

The immature, unstable parent, like the sexually inhibited one, helps to aggravate these feelings of inner looseness and uncoordination. In fact, the unstable parent may respond to the increased pressures introduced by adolescence by regressing into helplessness himself and may invite and obtain a protective, solicitous, almost therapeutic response from the adolescent. This "reversal of generations," which can be looked upon as a natural development of life when the parent figures shift into the helplessness of old age, is sometimes prematurely in evidence at this early stage. In his "therapeutic" role the adolescent may be burdened with many of the adjustment problems of the parent. "At last I have got someone to talk to. I have never been able to say this to anyone else. I have never been able to tell anyone what a sexual brute your father really was. Now that you know all about sex, you can realize what I have been through with him," etc.

Adolescent feelings persisting in the parents do not always work negatively for the adolescent child. They can and do often lead to greater sympathy, empathy, and understanding. The parent with a better recollection of his own adolescent difficulties can use this constructively in dealing with his child and, in so doing, may be able to help himself. The capacity to identify with the adolescent will permit the parent to handle the usual type of adolescent problem with a lighter touch. They may react, as one author puts it, with "a felt nostalgia for the youthful exuberance, fresh love impulses, and a sneaking adoption of the rebellion" [12]. This "ectopic youthfulness" enhances the sensitivity of the individual in relationship to younger individuals.

The fluctuations characteristic of adolescence demand flexibility on the part of the parent, the changing mood and manners calling constantly for changing attitudes and behavior toward them. It is not easy for even the average parent to shift comfortably in rhythm with these emotional swings since he is so often left completely in the dark as to what has occasioned them. A transient depression, for example, may reflect an intercurrent scholastic or vocational difficulty, a setback in a love affair, a nostalgia for the lost world of childhood and its love objects, or an upsurge of guilt from a reactivation of unconscious sexual and aggressive urges leading to a hostile retreat from the world. On the other hand, it may be no more than a phase of introspection as the adolescent stops to take stock of himself. The same variety of causes may underlie states of happiness, and it is therefore not surprising that the psychologically untutored parents, however devoted, may find themselves exasperated by the unpredictable nature of the affect [9].

A great many therapists find it highly uncomfortable to treat children during the earlier phase of adolescence when they neither play nor talk nor look to a friendly adult for help, but seem merely bent on escape. The patient is bored and restless, may yawn openly in response to a well-thought-out interpretation, and, when the therapist attempts to focus on the relationship, they will counter with a description of their passionate involvements at school and elsewhere. The therapist finds himself put on the shelf with a hundred other objects currently competing for the adolescent's attention. He will be irritated, and parents will readily recognize and sympathize with the essence of his irritation. "Most of the young adolescents I have seen consider all adults their natural enemies. If they say anything at all, they will barely state a complaint, and then defiantly wait for you to do something magically about it. I have never found any way to handle this, and the only children of this age I have treated are those who started with me at an early age or were quite immature . . . a great deal of environmental manipulation is usually required, and as soon as external pressures are relieved, the patient tends to drop out of treatment" [2].

322

The high dropout rate in psychotherapy has given the adolescent a bad name in therapeutic circles, and therapists are wary of taking them on for any form of intensive treatment. The main complaint is that they do not seem to form a stable working relationship, but this is like saying that the seasons vary throughout the year and that you cannot depend on having warm days and blue skies for picnics in the middle of March. It is in "the nature of things." Once the therapist has accepted the fluctuating responses and the irregular attendance as a natural part of the general variability of the period, he can then settle down to incorporating them into his technical approach, even to the extent of regularizing anticipated breaks from treatment.

THE "GOOD" REACTION TO ADOLESCENCE

Normality in psychology and psychiatry is a concept difficult to define in operational terms. One can point to the observation that the majority of adolescents seem to come through adolescence and develop into average adults with average reactions as an indication that things cannot be as bad as they look under a closer clinical scrutiny. Although we might be dissatisfied with the finished products and aware that many of them will eventually find their way into mental hospitals, divorce courts, coroner's courts, prisons, and homes for alcoholics and addicts, the larger group who achieve statistically average lives must have been subjected to "good enough" reactions.

The good or good enough reaction is one in which the stereotypic response is minimal or absent, the adult responding on a person-to-person basis. It is a reaction which is relatively free from the irrational influence of "transference," so that once again, the adult responds not in terms of the there-and-then but of the here-and-now. The third ingredient in a good reaction is the element of empathy and sympathy originating in a satisfactory adolescent experience; not satisfactory in the sense of being free from conflict, but satisfactory in the sense of having gone some distance toward making these conflicts conscious and resolving them. The acceptance of the once adolescent provides a sounding board to test out all future reactions for adolescent consumption.

323

Bibliography

1. Adelson, J.   The mystique of adolescence. *Psychiatry* 27:1–5, 1964.
2. Beiser, H.   Personal communication, 1962.
3. Bell, A.   The Role of Parents in Adolescence. In A. S. Lorand and H. I. Schneer (Eds.), *Adolescents: Psychoanalytic Approach to Problems and Therapy*. New York: Hoeber, 1961.
4. Chadwick, M.   The psychological effects of menstruation. *Nerv. Ment. Dis. Monogr.* 56:1, 1932.
5. Denny, T., Feldhusen, J., and Condon, C.   Anxiety, divergent thinking, and achievement. *J. Educ. Psychol.* 56:40–45, 1965.
6. Frazer, J.   *The Golden Bough* (abridged ed.). London: Macmillan, 1949.
7. Freud, A.   Adolescence. *Psychoanal. Stud. Child* 13:255–278, 1958.
8. Geleerd, E. R.   Some aspects of psychoanalytic technique in adolescents. *Psychoanal. Stud. Child* 12:263–283, 1957.
9. Jacobson, E.   Adolescent moods and the remodeling of psychic structures in adolescence. *Psychoanal. Stud. Child* 16:164–183, 1961.
10. LeVine, R. A., and Levine, B. B.   Nyansongo: A Gussi Community in Kenya. In B. B. Whiting (Ed.), *Six Cultures*. New York: Wiley, 1963. P. 15.
11. Mead, M.   Adolescence in Primitive and Modern Society. In V. F. Calverton and S. Schmalhausen (Eds.), *The New Generation*. New York: Macaulay, 1930. P. 169.
12. Miller, E.   Individual and social approach to the study of adolescence. *Brit. J. Med. Psychol.* 35:211–224, 1962.
13. Spiegel, J. P.   Interpersonal Influences Within the Family. In B. Schaffner (Ed.), *Group Processes*. Transactions of the Third Conference. New York: Josiah Macy, Jr. Foundation. 1957. P. 23.
14. Stekel, W.   Frigidity in Mothers. In V. F. Calverton and S. Schmalhausen (Eds.), *The New Generation*. New York: Macaulay, 1930. P. 24.
15. Sutherland, J. D.   Three cases of anxiety and failure in examinations. *Brit. J. Med. Psychol.* 19:73–81, 1941.

15

The Return of the
Repressed "Oedipus"

Leo Rangell

EDITORS' INTRODUCTION

Since Freud's publication of The Passing of the Oedipus Complex [2] it has become part of psychoanalytic theory that the drive-cathexes of the repressed oedipus complex become the core of the psychic structure of internalized controls, termed the *superego*. It is also implicit in psychoanalytic theory that the vicissitudes of the oedipus complex are a determining factor in the organization of the personality, affecting normal character development as well as psychopathology. The culturally traditioned variations of parental behavior disguise the role of the parents in the evolution of the oedipal phase of the child who is supposed to "outgrow" his oedipal phase. However, "resolution of an instinctual conflict," i.e., its absorption by the intrapsychic processes of the developmental organization, often remains incomplete. Even if the deficiencies of the developmental processes are not great enough to cause serious deviations from the normal in the young parent's behavior toward his young child, a shift in the intrapsychic balance of the parent might occur in any of the "critical phases" of parenthood. It might be the parent's reaction to the maturation of his child, or it might be his awareness of signs of his own aging; it is the diminishing repressive strength of the ego which brings about the psychopathologic state in the reversed manifestations of the oedipus complex.

E. J. A.
T. B.

The oedipus complex in psychodynamics and in clinical psychiatry is usually viewed from the standpoint of the child's part in the affair. It is worthwhile pointing out that clinical material is also seen which stems from and has as its basis the adult or parental role in this relationship. This short communication will accordingly be devoted to a consideration of some of the dynamisms and relevant clinical instances as seen from the parent's point of view.

For example, certain anxiety symptoms in a 47-year-old man were found in analysis to be due to a repressed erotic attachment to his attractive 21-year-old daughter. This man displayed during this period in his life an irritability and an antagonism toward his wife and an irrationally critical attitude and strong hatred for his daughter's boyfriend. The patient recognized that his feelings toward his daughter's boyfriend were exaggerated and unreasonable but attempted to rationalize these feelings in many ways. In his work he showed an especial tenderness toward young secretaries, pioneered certain causes in their favor, and without consciously setting out to do so, became extremely popular and desired by all of them. This finally culminated in one of the young girls "breaking down" and telling him that she loved him. The patient then assumed a benevolent and patronizing manner, although he became upset and had an exacerbation of anxiety and conversion symptoms.

Occurrences such as this are not uncommon in psychiatric or analytic practice. The starting point of a train of neurotic symptoms in an older adult is not infrequently discovered to be the actual or impending marriage of an offspring. The family drama takes place and produces effects not only with regard to the impulses streaming from child to parent, but also, simultaneously in connection with feelings in the opposite direction, from the parent to the child. Looking at the oedipus complex through the eyes of the parent, one can observe the same variations in its clinical manifestations and forms as when one is oriented from the vantage point of the child. These phenomena in the parents, though they probably exist earlier, become clinically most visible and significant when their children begin to emerge from adolescence and to become more obvious and overt sexual objects.

Thus, paralleling the case of the child's impulses, the classic situation at this time is, as in the case described above, for the parent to be (unconsciously) drawn to the child of the opposite sex, with unconscious hostile rivalry with the love objects chosen by the latter. This rivalry is, of course, camouflaged and rationalized in sundry well-known ways. Classically a mother is reluctant to give up her son and begins to resent any potential daughter-in-law, while the father feels protective and possessive toward the daughter with antagonism developing toward her boyfriends and then husband. "The Father of the Bride" is in a well-known traumatic and rejected state.

In contrast to this, there undoubtedly is less of an object loss when a mother sees her daughter married or a father his son. Each parent, in fact, then acquires a new potential love object in the mate of the child of the same sex. Thus the mother often cannot wait for her daughter to marry and then begins to make up to her son-in-law. The father is proud to "give away" his son and begins to dress smartly and act mischievously toward his new daughter-in-law.

The clinical variations deriving from this repressed unconscious nucleus are manifold. One possible outcome, resulting from a relatively undistorted acting out of the impulse, is seen in the recent wave of handsome middle-aged men in public life marrying fresh, younger girls and also in the glamorization of this theme in some hit musical comedies. The appeal with which this sweeps over the public is testimony to the prevalence of the unconscious emotional impulse being described and the extent of identification with it. It is, of course, bilateral, with the younger person as well as the older one acting out repressed oedipal wishes, the younger toward the parent, and the older toward the child.

Another set of clinical data stems from the rivalry side of the oedipal triangle. Just as in the case of the child the attraction to the opposite parent is accompanied by hostile rivalry with the parent of the same sex, so the same competitive jealousy may emanate from the parent toward the child of the same sex. A woman patient complained frequently of her mother's unveiled hostility toward her (a complaint which seemed realistic), while at the same time the mother was extremely flirtatious and flattering to the patient's husband. During this patient's previous adolescence and courtship days, the mother had resented the patient's going out, while demanding to know and eagerly listening to the details of each evening. This prototype is well known.

327

A mother waits up nervously and angrily for her young daughter to return home in the early hours. It is not difficult to see beneath the surface her jealousy of her daughter's activities. In another variation, a father-in-law had the habit of hugging and effusively greeting his son's attractive wife, to the accompaniment of a pat on her buttocks, which, although it embarrassed the girl considerably, she could do nothing but ignore. At the same time he was surly and hostile toward his son, depreciating his ability and activities and "taking the wind from his sails" in every venture which the son attempted.

A woman patient recalls many instances of how, during her early life, she used to be jealous of her mother, whereas in recent years since the patient is married, she has the feeling that it is now her mother who is jealous of her. The mother's hostile jealousy comes out in subtle criticisms, for example, of her daughter's hair or figure, and during one recent exchange, the mother remarked critically, "Well, you know you have more pubic hair than I ever had." The turn of events in such instances seems to depend on the state of impulse satisfaction. The victorious one in this competitive rivalry is the one who, at least in the mind of the other, is at the age of most satisfaction of instincts, roughly corresponding to the third and fourth decades. Thus, during this patient's childhood and adolescence, the parent is in the enviable position while during the parent's declining years it is the child who is at the peak of satisfaction and therefore envied. The oedipus complex in this way reverses itself.

The proverbial mother-in-law is another variant and derivative of this situation. Her hostility, when directed toward a daughter-in-law, is usually traceable to a relatively undistorted rivalry for the possession of the son. An example of this is the following. A woman patient developed a strongly paranoid attitude, although not yet a delusional one, toward her son's newly acquired wife. On the way home from the wedding ceremony, the patient managed to get into the back seat of the car, with the son sitting between wife and mother. Her symptoms and attitude began because the son held his wife's hand and not hers during this ride. The patient kept coming back repeatedly to this, regarding it as the beginning evidence of her son's ungratefulness, his preference for his wife, and his neglect of her, the mother. She also refused to leave town with her husband immediately after the wedding for a combined business-vacation trip because she felt that her son and daughter-in-law, who were staying in the city for their honeymoon, "might need" her. When this same attitude is manifested toward a son-in-law, there is an added layer of distortion, it being now the hostility of the rejected suitor toward the desired and frustrating object. This sensitive latter relationship, between mother-in-law and son-in-law, and its roots in these underlying conflicting ambivalent feelings, was described and commented upon by Freud in *Totem and Taboo,* in which he also traces the powerful taboos resulting therefrom among primitive races, where mother-in-law and son-in-law avoid each other's presence [2].

Another determinant for this parental oedipal participation, pointed out by Hanna Fenichel, is also worthy of note, namely the role played by old primal scene conflicts and the remobilization of the parents' repressed scoptophilic impulses [1]. The situation being described is thus perhaps more likely to ensue when this particular repression has been tenuous or labile. The parents are now in a position to look on and see what their children are doing, this being a revival and reversal of their old primal scene experiences and conflicts. A vivid example of this dynamism in action can be seen in the following clinical extract.

A man of 58 had exacerbations of a severe anxiety neurosis when each of his three sons married. This man subsequently became close to and a confidant of all three of his daughters-in-law, two of whom soon went into analysis. He was "so close to his sons" that they too discussed with him freely their intimate problems, and the reasons for their respective wives' going into therapy. In the case of one it was because of frigidity. Our patient kept close tabs on the progress of this symptom and expressed great interest in its course and its gradual resolution.

In the previous history of this man, there had emerged during the course of treatment, to the accompaniment of intense emotional catharsis, a history of an incestuous sexual relationship with an older sister which had lasted 8 years during his latency and early adolescence. In addition to this, in the slum area in which he had been brought up, with its crowded conditions, he had been repeatedly exposed to readily accessible primal scene experiences. Two of the five children, including the patient, had shared one bed with the mother, while the other three had slept with the father. On infrequent but definite occasions the father would come into this maternal bed during the night for his marital claims, within the immediate sight and hearing of the two children.

The patient's present intimacies with his sons and their wives, rationalized on the grounds of his being a devoted and intelligent and "liberated" parent, stemmed in reality from these old primal scenes and were linked directly to his own overstimulated and never-solved incestuous wishes, for his sister and for both his parents, as well as to the heightened and intense accompanying scoptophilic impulses. He was now continuing and finishing with his married children what had been interrupted with his parents. And it was precisely the anticipated and feared eruption of this very process from behind the wall of repression, foreshadowed by each child's marriage, that had brought on the successive anxiety attacks.

Not infrequently this parental oedipal involvement will become manifest at an earlier period than that described, particularly if current frustration hastens its onset. Thus a young attractive mother, who had a shallow and unsatisfying relationship with her husband, practically seduced her son of 6 years into bed with her and then expressed coy curiosity and sham anxiety about his having erections in her presence. She was, among other things, repeating with her son what she unconsciously had longed to have her father do with her.

In another similar instance, this same situation became manifest even earlier, in the following manner. A young mother hesitatingly related to the analyst her feelings and actions toward her new firstborn infant son of but a few months. She observed that her constant and almost uncontrollable kissing of the child had reached such proportions as to almost pass beyond the maternal into the more overtly sensual sphere. "I sort of kiss him on the neck and behind the ears and get such a feeling out of it," she confessed. Her husband made similar observations and even remarked that her sexual activities with him, the husband, seemed now to consist mainly of what she could not or did not dare finish with her child. Leaving aside for our purposes the implications of this with regard to the husband, the patient for her part confessed that such an interpretation indeed bore some validity.

This rather exaggerated and patent behavior toward her child was related to and had its origins in certain specific historical background events: From her earliest childhood up until the present day, this patient has had an intense and almost obsessive relationship with dolls. For years she had collected and clung to and loved dolls, especially some early favorite ones, with loyal and undying devotion. In her earliest life, her dolls took the place of friends, family, and all people, and she lived both her actual and fantasy lives intensely with them. She collected miniature clothes and furniture for them, all of which she has saved intact and cared for up to the present day. Through this medium she enacted the family drama, with herself in complete control and with wish fulfillment exerting an undistorted role. The proudest member of this fantasy world was her big teddy bear, much larger than she, who sat in a seat of great importance and whom she hugged and kissed and loved and married. He was the father. When she explained one day how she used to sit on Teddy Bear's lap, she made a slip and said "on Teddy's bare lap." This teddy, as all the others, was endowed with an animate existence. He still today occupies a place in her bedroom, and on cold nights she covers him with a blanket.

Only now, with the advent of her real live baby, has Teddy's position suddenly undergone a change. Her great love has shifted from her Teddy to her baby, and she has noted, not without some regret and remorse, that "Teddy is now just a teddy." Her baby has thus not only replaced the artificially animated, make-believe figure, but serves to reactivate and revive once again the family romance. He is both herself, one of the little dolls, now loved by the real parent, and the father Teddy, whom she can control and from whom she can extract love at will. This early make-believe world of course had its counterpart and origin in her relation to her real father, which came to light only during the analysis. It has now become meaningful and understandable to her why her father, when he objected strongly to her proposed marriage, chased her across the country and, in an effort to emphasize to her how little she needed her worthless fiancé, kept repeating to her desperately, "If I were a young man, I'd marry you in a minute." This was a revelation of his real feelings for her, which had been amply returned, unconsciously, from her to him. Now she was directing hers again downward, to her own new son.

It was thus the intensity and lack of resolution of her own oedipal problem which served as the background soil upon which this patient promptly renewed the family drama with her newly arrived infant son.

The oedipus complex has a continuous and dynamic line of development, from its earliest origin through various phases in the life of man, and the described phenomena are but stages in this continual moving stream. By no means is it an event which plays a tumultuous but short-lived role limited to the phallic scene of the play of life, but it is rather a constantly reappearing character which comes across the stage in new and changing roles progressing with the ages of man. The primeval, original complex of the oedipal phallic period of development goes through its well-known history and possible vicissitudes and is then "solved" in one way or another for the time being. Though dormant, however, it remains a powerful dynamic force in the unconscious, propelling itself from within and susceptible to attraction from without. It has from this point on a cyclic history, characterized by rejuvenations during certain crucial periods in life, at which time distorted derivatives of it may appear, with relatively quiescent and dormant intervals in between.

Periods in which revival of the oedipal struggle is stimulated are, for example, at the time of the endocrine upsurge of puberty, with its intensification of instinctual pressures, or at the onset of the marriageable age. In each instance the specific manifestations seen depend on the particular history and earlier type of resolution. The phenomena referred to and described in this communication must represent another recrudescence of the same complex in another form at another crucial period in life. This occurs usually in the fifth decade when the period of marriageability of the first-born child begins to arrive and to threaten again the old oedipal longings which, by this time, one would think are at rest forever. The subject now is looking backward instead of forward, and the derivatives which one sees are those which have been described.

Even this is not yet the last temptation, for further distorted derivatives appear even in geriatric patients. "Silly old grandfathers" show it in their proclivity to and "fooling around with" young girls, sometimes when these older men are still mentally clear, although more often when senility or arteriosclerosis has intervened and weakened the defenses. Or a grandmother may have a final opportunity to act out her lingering conflicts with her own daughter or son by adopting or using their children—her grandchildren—against them. Or, and as likely, she may use the latter for more direct and positive impulse gratification, reliving again the pleasures she derived from her own young children years ago.

The following can thus be said to be a schematic characterization of the course and fate of the oedipus complex. Early in life it is born and relatively quickly "solved," in the service of the recently acquired reality principle and the newly developed superego, almost like a flight into health in order that life may proceed. From then, up until young adulthood, the situation in the unconscious from which derivatives are produced is with the subject at the infantile point of the triangle, looking forward and upward (to higher age levels) for perhaps eventual gratification. In the third, fourth, and fifth decades, when the opportunity for impulse satisfaction is at its height and maximum attainment is possible, at least as far as external realistic barriers are concerned, the striving for satisfaction is less distorted and is directed toward one's contemporaries. Gratification is now within reach, with a minimum amount of compromise; one must of course still make his own extrafamilial life. The neuroses at this period, due to the continuation of inner prohibitions and defenses and unfulfilled desires, attest to the frequency of failure to achieve this goal.

In later life, frustration and revived longings may occur as described, stimulated both by the sense of declining power and, in contrast, by the lusty coming of age of our children, with an exacerbation of the unconscious pressure, but this time with a reversal of the process. The individual now looks not forward, but backward. The object now is not one's own powerful parent, but one's child, grown to his zenith. It is still one's own, a narcissistic extension of the self.

The philosophic attitude of old age may connote a final resignation to frustration, a repetition of the original oedipal "solution," and a final bowing to the dictates of reality. "I can never have my own, but only a stranger." Just as years before the child finally had to sever the tie to his parents and proceed outward, so now later in life he must see and allow the same process to take place with his children. Moreover, just as in the original oedipal problem the solution was largely effected by identification with the rival parent, or with certain aspects of both parents, so in the reverse process healthy derivatives again ensue by means of the process of identification. Thus satisfactions are again

333

intensified by identifying with the fruitful current lives and fortunes of one's children. Later still, there is even another chance, when, as a grandparent, one can again repeat the process of identification and vicariously relive the youthful hopes and deeds of still the next generation.

The foregoing by no means claims exclusivity as an explanation of unconscious neurotic attitudes of parent toward child. Rather it describes and elaborates upon one particular source of emotional conflict and interference, the residuals and derivatives of the parent's own unresolved oedipal problems. This still leaves room, of course, for other possible neurotic motivations, as the unwillingness of a parent to let go of a child on the basis of an anal possessiveness in general, or an oral needful clinging to the child with a feeling of loss and deprivation when the latter moves on, or the host of other possible vicissitudes and influences which can color and affect the bond between parent and child.

Bibliography

1. Fenichel, H.   Personal communication, 1952.
2. Freud, S.   Totem and Taboo. In J. Strachey (Ed.), *The Standard Edition of the Complete Psychological Works of Sigmund Freud,* Vol. XIII. London: Hogarth, 1955.

Part IV

Clinical Attitudes and Behavior of Parents

16

Parental Empathy

Norman L. Paul

> So often, below the words
> spoken is a thing known and
> unspoken.
>
> HAROLD PINTER [2]

EDITORS' INTRODUCTION

This presentation illustrates with subtlety and feeling the mysterious process of empathy as it operates in family life. Dr. Paul has commented elsewhere on the dearth of reference to this basic phenomenon in the literature and concludes that there may be an actual aversion on the part of the scientific worker to an essentially nonintellectual experience which appears to have no physical basis [1]. He quotes Sullivan in this context: "Although empathy may sound mysterious, remember that there is much that sounds mysterious in the universe, only you have got used to it; and perhaps you will get used to empathy" [3]. Not only is there a barrier of mystery but there is also a resistance because of fear, and here he recalls Pinter, the playwright, when he says: "To enter into someone else's life is too frightening," since tuning in on the other's experience demands the acceptance of comparable feelings in one's self [2]. William James once remarked that the major problem in life was the fact that one cannot feel another's toothache. Empathy affords us the nearest thing to the actual experience and it is, therefore, not surprising to find Dr. Paul postulating the existence of a "basic empathic hunger" in every human being related to "a wish for an intimacy which can nullify, if only for a moment, our sense of emptiness and aloneness" which can become, in his opinion, "the cornerstone of the healing process." The classic psychoanalytic situation tends to obscure the empathy of the analyst although it is an essential tool of the analytic process. This hiding of empathy is probably a source of countertransference feelings.

E. J. A.
T. B.

337

Bibliography

1. Paul, N. L.   The Use of Empathy in the Resolution of Grief. Strecker Monograph Series 3, 1966.
2. Pinter, H.   Writing for the theater. *Evergreen Rev.* 8:80–82, 1964.
3. Sullivan, H. S.   *The Interpersonal Theory of Psychiatry.* New York: Norton, 1953.

Dearest Father, You asked me recently why I maintain that I am afraid of you." With these words, Franz Kafka, then in his thirty-sixth year, began a letter to his father [2].* "I was a timid child. For all that, I am sure I was also obstinate, as children are. I am sure that Mother spoilt me too, but I cannot believe I was particularly difficult to manage; I cannot believe that a kindly word, a quiet taking by the hand, a friendly look, could not have got me to do anything that was wanted of me. Now you are, after all, at bottom a kindly and soft-hearted person . . . but not every child has the endurance and fear-lessness to go on searching until it comes to the kindliness that lies beneath the surface." With example upon example, Kafka went on to describe the frightening gulf between father and son and the strains in their relationship that Kafka blamed for his own lack of confidence and for his inability to marry. The lack of empathy between father and son was interrupted occasionally and accidentally when Kafka was able to catch glimpses of his father expressing feelings of sorrow and tenderness.

"Fortunately, there were exceptions to all this, mostly when you suffered in silence, and affection and kindliness by their own strength overcame all obstacles, and moved me immediately. Rare as this was, it was wonderful. For instance, in earlier years, in hot summers, when you were tired after lunch, I saw you having a nap at the office, your elbow on the desk; or you joined us in the country, in the summer holidays, on Sundays, worn out from work; or the time Mother was gravely ill and you stood holding on to the bookcase, shaking with sobs; or when, during my last illness, you came tiptoeing to Ottla's room to see me, stopping in the doorway, craning your neck to see me, and out of consideration only waved to me with your hand. At such times one would lie back and weep for happiness, and one weeps again now, writing it down."

Kafka apparently hoped that his long letter might improve their relationship, that "it might reassure us both a little and make our living and our dying easier." He gave it to his mother, possibly with the thought that she would pass it along; ironically, she did not.

* Reprinted by permission of Schocken Books Inc. from *Letter to His Father* by Franz Kafka, translated by Ernst Kaiser and Eithne Wilkins, copyright © 1954, 1966 by Schocken Books Inc., and by permission of Martin Secker & Warburg Ltd., London.

THE NATURE OF EMPATHY

Kafka's detailed plaint about failures of parental empathy is unusual in being given such forceful literary expression, but the situation itself resembles that in many families. All of us hunger for empathy so as to feel that we are not alone in our progress through life. Too often we experience it only vicariously in the theater or in response to a painting or a poem. Since the need for empathy is universal, it is useful to focus attention upon it, to discover what it is, how it works, and how the empathic potential in all of us can be released and increased. Although there is a kind of empathy that is called "intellectual," in which persons identify with each other in terms of their verbalized thoughts, here empathy means "affective empathy," which seeks to meet emotional rather than intellectual needs and involves all feelings, not only those that are verbalized.

As so often is the case, the very act of describing, of putting a complicated feeling into words, is baffling and simplistic. Samuel Butler cautions that definitions of vital processes are undesirable because such vivisection is likely to suspend if not destroy them [1]. Since we must fall back on words, however, Olden's definition of empathy is a useful approach—"the capacity of the subject instinctively and intuitively to feel as the object does. It [empathy] is a process of the ego, more specifically, an emotional ego expression . . . the subject temporarily gives up his own ego for that of the object" [3]. An empathizer, or subject, accepts, for a brief period, the object's total emotional individuality, not only his simple emotions but his whole state of being—the history of his desires, feelings, and thoughts as well as other forces and experiences that are expressed in his behavior. The object senses the empathizer's response and realizes that for a brief point in time they two have fused. If he then takes the initiative of communicating more of his experience and feelings, he provides a basic stimulus for what can become a mutual empathic process.

Empathy is different from sympathy; the two processes are, in fact, mutually exclusive. In sympathy, the subject is principally absorbed in his own feelings as they are projected into the object and has little concern for the reality and validity of the object's special experience. Sympathy bypasses real understanding of the other person, and that other is denied his own sense of being. Empathy, on the other

340

hand, presupposes the existence of the object as a separate individual, entitled to his own feelings, ideas, and emotional history. The empathizer makes no judgments about what the other *should* feel, but solicits the expression of whatever he *does* feel and, for brief periods, experiences these feelings as his own. The empathizer oscillates between such subjective involvement and a detached recognition of the shared feelings. The periods of his objective detachment do not seem to the other to be spells of indifference, as they would in sympathy; they are, instead, evidence that the subject respects himself and the object as separate people. Secure in his sense of self and his own emotional boundaries, the empathizer attempts to nurture a similar security in the other.

Empathy in the Family Setting

One relationship in which empathy is a critical component but is often stifled is that between parent and child. Even the "normal" family is often painfully impoverished in such empathic processes. In our time, many families are wound up in social, professional, and educational fabrics that inhibit the empathic potential. Although this inhibition is serious under any circumstances, it is most conspicuous and most damaging at moments when members of a family make critical choices or face new experiences.

What typically happens in these situations? Let us imagine a family that is apparently functioning well as it progresses through some of these critical incidents. A 6-year-old son is to begin school. The parents recognize that this implies a dramatic change for their child. Instead of relatively unstructured play, he will be subjected to a routine. Instead of his familiar house and immediate neighborhood and the supervision of an interested mother, he will shift to an impersonal milieu where he will be surrounded by strangers. How do the parents prepare him for this leap? Too frequently, by giving him a pencil case and stimulating his interest with remarks like: "You're a big boy now. Won't it be exciting to go to school! Now you'll be with all the other children your age." Perhaps the parents have forgotten their own fears and misgivings about the first day of school, their own sense of loss and bewilderment when enclosed in a classroom for the first time. Those who remember often suppose that it would be better to shield their child from such anxieties in the hope that he will not repeat their own experience. The child finds school terrifying or restrictive or both, and concludes that he must be somehow inadequate. Didn't his parents imply that it would be exciting and pleasant? Is there something wrong with him because he dreads the ringing of the school bell, finds the teacher a threatening, large person, and distrusts all the children who sit around him? Although he is experiencing the very feelings that many others have experienced, he is left with an impression of aloneness in his trouble. Ashamed of his inadequacy, he pretends at home that all is well. The parents are relieved that he has already adjusted to school. And the whole painful process of getting used to the new life is submerged in silence or euphemisms.

The years pass and the boy perhaps forgets his own intense emotional reaction to those early days in the first grade. He is accustomed to school now, has made friends, and can cope with most of the teachers that come his way. One day, he and some other boys cut school and go instead to a ball game. When the truancy is discovered, the family is confronted with another critical issue, another moment at which an empathic response would prove valuable for all three of them. How do they handle the situation? Faced with the anxiety that the child might become a discipline problem and with their embarrassment before the school authorities, the parents probably express disapproval toward their son. Does the father remember the lure of the ball park during his own school days? If he does, he is apt not to mention it. Do the parents try to discover why their son absented himself from school without permission, why, on that particular occasion, he made a choice which he knew would be unapproved and might bring serious consequences? Probably they are focused on the offense to the exclusion of searching for its cause. The boy is punished and made to feel guilty, somehow exceptional in his delinquency, a family member who has embarked on a strange and aberrant course.

Again time passes and the boy reaches early adolescence. Suddenly his hitherto permanent environment is shattered by the death of a favorite uncle, his mother's brother. The family is saddened by this loss. How do they behave among themselves? The mother, deeply moved by her brother's death, feels that she must bear up bravely for the sake of her husband and son. She has responsibilities to them and to their home. The father tries to comfort his wife by keeping the household on an even keel. He wants to show his family that life will go on as before, that they can still enjoy happiness together. Perhaps he can make up for the present grief by being especially kind and solicitous. The boy is crushed by having lost his favorite relative outside the nuclear family, but feels that he must not weep childishly or bemoan his loss; instead, he should emulate his father, the male model for his behavior. At the dinner table, the three talk about other things to "keep their minds off" the unhappy topic. At the funeral services they are quiet and solemn, but make no expansive display of grief. Afterward, they resume their routine in order to "forget." Each member of the family has been deeply touched by the death of a loved person, yet each shuts himself off in emotional solitude from the others, shielding them from his own anguish, protecting himself from a vulnerable exposure of feelings.

These are three incidents in the family's history that show a child alone with his fear, his guilt, his grief. And these three are undoubtedly interspersed with dozens of other occasions on which there is no sharing of feelings among people who live together in relative harmony and who love each other. The opportunities and the need for empathy are present, but there is no empathy. Why?

The Lack of Empathy and Its Causes

One answer seems to lie in the insufficient attention parents give to their own emotional histories, the accumulations of experiences and feelings that have brought them to their present modes of adapting to events. Surely both parents have lived through situations comparable to those through which their son is charting his hesitant course; surely the events, at the time they were fresh, generated important emotional responses. Yet the memories of these feelings have been relegated to the silent past as though they were no longer pertinent. They are either forgotten or at least not recalled in words. The parents' silences, their failures to revivify past moments of doubt, guilt, or grief and to share fully these recollected feelings may be repetitions of similar silences on the part of their own parents. They are behaving toward their son as their parents behaved toward them. A habit of restraint, a stifling of empathic potential, can run through a family from generation to generation as each new set of parents accords its young the treatment that it received earlier. And so each child is left to traverse life's problems alone, as though his responses were so unique and uncharacteristic that they must be kept private.

One matrix where parental empathy could be nurtured is the

empathy between marital partners themselves. If parents are able to share even the most uncomfortable feelings with each other, they are more likely to initiate empathic relationships with their children. Often, however, the vicious circle operates here as well. A child growing up in a family may be keenly aware of the visible interactions between his parents, their expressions of affection and anger. He is likely, however, to be totally unaware of the antecedent feelings that culminate in these overt expressions. He moves on to his own marriage, then, with little understanding of how feelings can be shared; he has neither observed such sharing between his parents nor experienced their sharing with him. His whole history of feelings, therefore, a history that would be vitally pertinent to his adjustment in marriage, is not brought out for review but held silently, sometimes with the resolution to "cancel out" the past in favor of a new beginning. If his marriage partner is similarly unprepared for an empathic relationship, the illusion of oneness in courtship may soon give way to an acute sense of separate loneliness and feelings of disappointment in the marriage. Their children, in turn, will be denied the opportunity to share feelings freely, and the cycle will begin again. As generation after generation emulates the models observed in early years and values these at the expense of expressing feelings, the possibilities for empathic sharing diminish; there is no precedent.

One of the impediments to an increase of empathy within the parent-child relationship is the position of power in which parents stand vis-à-vis their children. Up until adolescence the child sees his parents not only as larger than himself, but different in kind. Adults set his standards, monitor his behavior, seem always to know what is to be done and how to do it. Their wishes, insofar as the child can observe, can often be translated directly into reality, whereas his own often remain just wishes. Their evaluations of him, sometimes given hastily, in frustration, or to produce some effect in behavior, are accepted by the child as accurate. He expects strangers to assess him at the same value.

Parental behavior toward the child often reinforces this sense of power. The parent is likely to feel that his own day-to-day experiences in childhood have little relevance to his behavior as a parent; he forgets or shunts aside the fears and anxieties that haunted his early life. They belong to an early history of experience that is over, replaced by

344

a new adult history. This failure to review fully his own sum of past experiences thwarts a parent's ability to feel within himself the child's similar fears and anxieties. Instead, he imposes his own mature evaluations on the child's feelings. "You shouldn't be afraid of the dark. It's unreasonable." "Boys who steal candy when they are small are likely to rob banks when they are men." "We are only insisting that you learn to swim for your own good." Pronouncements like these bypass the child's own feelings. The child is viewed not as a separate individual, entitled to his own emotional development, but as an extension of the parents' wisdom accumulated through the years, clay to be shaped into pattern.

In respect to their current doubts and sorrows, parents are likely to be similarly restrained, though for different reasons. Unlike childhood feelings, these are conspicuously at the forefront of the parents' concerns. But many parents suppose that they will contaminate their child's happy environment if they express their feelings. Children are not made a party to their parents' disappointments; they may sense that something has gone wrong but be unable to explain it. In such an arrangement, the gulf between children and parents widens. The child may come to regard adults as people who always know what they are doing, who usually succeed in meeting their goals, but who do not cry when they fail.

The very culture in which we live contains elements that inhibit the empathic potential between parent and child. Preliterate cultures link the generations tightly, since the young depend on their elders for what can be passed on orally. Though words always oversimplify the things, including feelings, that they represent, the written word, unaccompanied by gesture and expressive nuance, oversimplifies more than the spoken word. In a preliterate society, the old must remember their histories and transfer them to the young in story, song, and dance. The society built around books, however, diminishes the parent's personal history in favor of expert generalizations available in print. The spread of literacy has, of course, liberated readers from some old chains of fear and ignorance; but it has imposed others. More and more crises to which a child is likely to have intense emotional reactions are moved from home to the more neutral atmosphere of the school, from a talking to a reading situation in which there is less opportunity for the exchange of feelings [4]. The mother whose child is harassed by nightmares is less likely to think back to her own childhood fears and to share her child's terror than to consult a book on child development that shows her how to cope with an "unusual" circumstance. The father whose son is undisciplined at school is less likely to review his own school behavior than to arrange a conference with the guidance counselor. And so the very situations in which parental empathy could function with mutual benefits are transferred to another context where they can be examined impersonally and dispassionately.

The schizophrenic family, that is, the family with at least one schizophrenic member, demonstrates the extreme effects of the blocking of parental empathy. Such families are usually characterized by a degree of equilibrium that is abnormal. As a defense against recognizing the passage of time and the losses incurred through deaths and separations, the family resists further changes resolutely. This often involves keeping a child in a perpetually dependent position as evidence that changes have not occurred. The child so treated within his family is, of course, denied his own separateness, the right to his own emotional development. He becomes, instead, a pivot upon which the family can function in its static equilibrium. In the schizophrenic family, members are tied to each other in ways that prevent their living lives where they can achieve a sense of independent mastery of the situations they encounter. The family is bound by its defenses, and these defenses preclude the sharing of feelings. In fact, expressions of anger or hostility by the dependent member are typically interpreted as the bizarre evidence of his inability to be independent.

Enhancing the Empathic Process During Development

How can we develop a climate in which empathy between parent and child will flourish? Major changes in customs and the social structure are obviously long-range processes, and in these a potential increase in empathy will have to be measured against other gains and losses. But there is opportunity to increase the empathic potential within individual families.

The underlying importance of marital empathy as a precondition for parental empathy is so marked that it merits thorough consideration. How can marital partners establish empathic relationships between themselves? The courtship period prior to marriage seems a logical place to begin. Ideally, courtship should include a shared review by both partners of their emotional histories, the disappointments they have suffered, the fears they have experienced, and the events they have met successfully. Such a review would both establish their separate emotional identities and provide stimuli for further empathic responses between them. With this accomplished in courtship, the surfacing of various feelings after marriage should prove less surprising and disruptive. This requires that couples take a new point of view toward courtship. It is not a "fresh start" for which earlier experiences can be erased so that two separate people can become permanently one. It is, rather, a stage of the individual's continuing journey, through which he carries the accumulation of all his past experience; the accumulation will continue to grow in marriage, so it is well to have a full inventory of the freight in advance.

The courtship review of experience brings into the open each partner's recollection of his own childhood, his relationship with his parents, his confusions and frustrations in a world dominated by adults. If he can empathize with himself as he once was, that is, feel again the way he felt then, he will be more likely to empathize with his future children when they pass through similar experiences. The review shared between partners establishes their separate emotional histories, thus enabling each to respect the other's individuality. This will also have later benefits in helping them to acknowledge the separateness of their own child. The child's feelings, then, can be accepted without evaluation. The parent will be able to oscillate between experiencing the child's feelings as his own and drawing back into an objective view of the feelings; this is the oscillation characteristic of empathy.

Pregnancy and birth, especially of the couple's first child, is another phase during which the empathic process between marital partners should be purposefully encouraged. Before conception and in the early stages of a pregnancy, the couple's attitude is often one of optimism and undiluted happiness. As pregnancy progresses, there are physical discomforts and an increase in uncertainties for both prospective parents. Fears about a decrease in lovemaking, worries over whether the child will be normal, anxieties about parental roles and their demands are typical feelings. A sharing of such feelings will reinforce the empathic process established in courtship and build a foundation for the exchange of feelings during later difficulties.

Exhilaration over the birth of a normal child is soon clouded by ambivalent feelings, particularly in the new mother. The responsibility for a baby carries with it a weight of uncertainty about what the child will be like. The new mother is likely to recollect her relationship with her own mother, and the recollection may make her uncertain of her willingness to assume a similar role. Although the mother has considerable power over the infant she cares for, he has great influence over her life because of his requirements for survival. In this situation, the mother needs to have her own repeatedly depleted emotional resources replenished, and this can best be achieved through empathic sharing of feelings with her husband. Such replenishment may very well forestall her harboring a covert resentment toward the baby, a feeling that, though the mother may not be aware of it, can be conveyed to the child by her facial expression and her way of handling him.

As the child grows, the empathic parent will feel and show his respect for the child as a separate person with his own emotional being. This involves permitting the child openly to prefer one parent to another for a particular situation. It also increasingly involves an acknowledgment of the child's need for strangers, since his small family circle needs to be replaced by ever-widening contacts. It is interesting, in this connection, to contrast children in schizophrenic families with those children raised in the *kibbutzim* in Israel [5]; their problems of adjustment are almost diametrically opposite. The schizophrenic family's child, frozen into a pathologic static relationship with his family, finds it difficult, if not impossible, to establish relationships with strangers; the family will not let the circle widen. The *kibbutz* child, on the other hand, is raised in an environment that provides easy, natural cooperation among unrelated people of the same age, but few close relationships within the nuclear family. Such a child often has difficulties in adjusting to marriage, to forming a close relationship with a nonstranger. Both of these situations, though ostensibly in contrast, illustrate difficulties of adjustment that arise from the absence of parental empathy.

348

THE TREATMENT OF EMPATHY DEFICIENCY

Some families which cannot achieve empathic understanding among themselves may be helped toward this process through therapy. Family therapy, where members of the nuclear family meet as a group with the therapist and where their group is sometimes augmented by other relatives, is a setting particularly favorable to the unblocking of the empathic flow. The therapist asks family members about incidents in their history that may not have been adequately expressed within the family—a death, a family secret, a guilt-ridden feeling of hostility to someone close. There is, of course, often some initial resistance to these questions. Once the evasions trickle out and real feelings begin to be exposed by a family member, the therapist's own empathic stance toward that person in his sorrow can serve as a model for other family members. If the session progresses well, they may begin to empathize with that member who is reviewing his suffering. The sharing of grief, the admission of anger, the exposure of guilt among loved persons who can experience the feelings as their own have a cathartic effect upon the whole family and free them for further empathic understanding. For some children, the family therapy session provides their first opportunity to see their parents in a state of suffering and sorrow, a situation that reassures them by demonstrating that powerful parental figures also experience intense feelings of helplessness.

The induction of empathy in a therapeutic setting can best be illustrated by a specific case history from my own practice.

CASE REPORT.   My patient, Mrs. X, was 28 years old, and her presenting problems were the prospect of her divorce, grief over the death of a child, and a low level of self-esteem. In individual therapeutic sessions the history behind these problems emerged. She had been adopted as an infant of 9 months. She described her adopting parents as kind, generous, and supportive, but mentioned that her adoptive mother has attempted to manage her life too closely. She had grown up and married and had two daughters, then aged 6 and 5. A third child, a son, had died suddenly in an accident at 2 months of age. After this dreadful episode her husband's parents took their whole family on a holiday to Mexico to help everyone forget the recent loss. At the vacation resort where they stayed, Mrs. X and her father-in-law were discovered nude by her husband and his younger sister. The chain reaction following this discovery led to Mr. X's initiating divorce proceedings. Mrs. X was resigned to the divorce, but eager to obtain custody of the girls and to be a responsible mother to them.

349

Subsequent sessions with Mrs. X brought to light further pertinent historical detail. Her marriage, she revealed, had progressed smoothly until her first pregnancy. At that time, she began to wonder who her real parents were, thinking, at times, that her mother may have been a prostitute and a vulgar person, her father a sailor or gangster. She felt resentful toward the mother who had given her away for adoption. At times she wondered whether she would prove to be like her adoptive mother, that is, unable to bear children. At other times she feared a resemblance to her real mother and worried about whether she would give her child away. When her daughter was born, she experienced feelings of jealousy toward the child who had a real mother with her. She felt ashamed of these feelings. And at this time her relationship with her husband began to deteriorate as she became increasingly repelled by sexual contact with him.

She began to drink shortly afterward, a habit of which her husband disapproved. His father, however, seemed to understand her drinking and frequently joined her. Eventually, the two had initiated an affair that had been going on for the past 3 years. Mrs. X maintained that she loved her father-in-law and wanted to marry him when her divorce was accomplished. She claimed that her affection for her husband had died long ago; nevertheless she described him as a charming person and an excellent father.

I solicited the presence of Mr. X, the husband, on the basis that it was important for both parents to develop a consistent explanation of their divorce for their two daughters. Mr. X attended three therapeutic sessions so as to have some counseling about the divorce. These three meetings succeeded in beginning the empathic process among family members.

In the first meeting, the husband expressed his pronounced resentment of his wife's affair with his father and revealed that he had suspected it for some years. Mrs. X had been fortified in individual therapy sessions by discussions about her husband's strong reaction. She was, therefore, able to accept his distress about her unfaithfulness and to understand the intensity of his feelings.

The second meeting provided an opportunity for reverse understanding. In this session, Mrs. X revealed in detail the anxiety she had experienced all through her childhood over being adopted and her feelings of being different from other children. She reviewed the fantasies that evolved during her pregnancy when this early distress resurfaced. This was the first time that Mr. X had realized that her adoption and its relationship to her own role as a mother was an important concern for his wife. He was visibly moved by her review of these feelings, feelings hitherto unexpressed.

The third meeting included the two little girls. Mr. X had maintained firmly that his daughters were not afraid of the impending divorce and were accepting it calmly. In the course of the therapeutic session, however, it became obvious that both girls were terrified by the collapse of their environment. For a brief moment, Mr. X was able to empathize with his daughters' fears.

These meetings had a profound effect on the X family. Two weeks later, Mrs. X phoned me to say that her husband wanted her back and asked my advice. I arranged a series of joint meetings for the couple, and Mr. X soon dropped the divorce proceedings. Subsequently, Mr. and Mrs. X were able to achieve a degree of marital empathy and harmony that had never existed in their courtship or in their early marriage. Once they were reunited, they were able to review with each other and with their daughters the loss of their son so that all family members could express and share their feelings of grief over this event.

The specific turning point in this case seems to have been Mr. X's parental empathy for his children's fears and anxieties. He was able to imagine himself as a child faced with the divorce of his own parents, and so to experience intensely his children's feelings. This breakthrough led to an altered relationship with his wife and accruing gains in all of the family's interrelationships.

It is easy after the fact to look at the X family and suggest stages in their history where an empathic process might have forestalled the events that brought them to therapy. Mrs. X's feelings about being adopted seem not to have been shared with her adoptive parents. A lack of information about her natural parents gave rise to fantasies about them and about herself. Her fears of being different were kept private in her family of origin, and the same silence was maintained through her courtship, marriage, and pregnancy. Consequently, Mr. X had no sense of the importance of his wife's feelings or of her emotional history. Her drinking and adultery were not viewed by him as being connected in any way with the past, but seemed instead an immediate rejection of himself. The family had not shared their feelings over the loss of a son or assessed this event at its real level of importance. They went on vacation "to forget," and another opportunity for empathy was neglected. Finally, neither partner, but especially Mr. X, had solicited expressions of feelings from the daughters about the impending divorce. The X family's history illustrates the vicious circle in which empathic potential can be strangled—lack of parental empathy in the family of origin, resulting in failure to develop marital empathy, resulting in lack of parental empathy in the family of procreation.

CONCLUSION

Therapy can cut into this circle in only a minority of cases. We have only a limited number of therapists, and they usually encounter

351

only those individuals and families where failures of empathy have had conspicuous effects. What can be done for the many, many more families where restricted empathy is ignored because it has as yet had no repercussions that are dramatically disruptive? It seems pertinent to ask what techniques and programs can be devised to further empathic processes in "normal" families so as to diminish their members' sense of aloneness, so as to make "their living and their dying easier."

Man's need for empathic relationships is recognized, especially in parent-child contacts where what is learned will affect the far future, perhaps for several generations. We are only at the beginning of groping for ways of meeting this need, of helping families to maintain their unity while simultaneously allowing each member his separate individuality. We seek, to put it simply, to help the family form that kind of coalition that is strong enough to endure sincere diversity among its members and weak enough to dissolve itself gracefully with the passage of time, the deaths of older members, and the marriage of the children. Our very need is our mandate for further searching.

Bibliography

1. Butler, S. Thought and Language. Reprinted in M. Black (Ed.), *The Importance of Language.* Englewood Cliffs, N.J.: Prentice-Hall, 1962.
2. Kafka, F. *Letter to His Father.* (Translated by E. Kaiser and E. Wilkins.) New York: Schocken, 1966.
3. Olden, C. On adult empathy with children. *Psychoanal. Stud. Child* 8:111–126, 1953.
4. Riesman, D. The Oral and Written Traditions. Reprinted in E. Carpenter and M. McLuhan (Eds.), *Explorations in Communication.* Boston: Beacon, 1967.
5. Spiro, M. E. *Children of the Kibbutz.* New York: Schocken, 1965.

17

About Adoptive Parents

Marshall D. Schechter

EDITORS' INTRODUCTION

Adoptive parents are parents who, by whatever motivation, assume the sociologic and ethical responsibility of biologic parents. Their parental attitudes and behavior, just as those of biologic parents, are determined by their personality development which defines their empathy for and adaptive capacity to the child.

Since in our society the prevalent reason for adoption is infertility of one or both of the marital partners, the following chapter deals mainly with the influence of this condition upon the adoptive processes of parenthood. Although in our civilization infertility is not a valid reason for divorce, it remains a problem that is usually solved, at least on the surface, before the prospective parents begin the steps which lead to "getting a child." The emotional state of expectant parenthood, although not as biologically motivated as begetting a child and pregnancy, mobilizes the repressed levels of those developmental processes which have been described as "secondary," i.e., psychodynamic motivations of parental behavior.[1] The fantasies so motivated might stir up potential pathologic responses and even deter some couples from adopting. In most instances—and only those are promising—the waiting period serves to "expand the motherliness and fatherliness" of the future parents; their desire for a child and children deepens if the period does not last longer than their tolerance. The future of the adoption, however, depends upon the adoptive parents' ability to encompass the child into their self-systems as their own.

This emphasizes the significance of receiving the child early, if possible, directly from the hospital. This gives the adoptive mother, deprived of the experience of pregnancy, a chance to engage in the processes of emotional symbiosis with the child; sharing these with her husband, together they achieve the triadic unity in parenthood.

[1] Chapters 5, 6, and 7.

353

The problems which may be activated in the parents corresponding to developmental accomplishments and/or deficiencies in the child might be as manifold in adoptive as in biologic parents, but in analyzing these factors one recognizes some differences between adoptive and biologic parents.

Generally, one is inclined to assume that parenthood is easier, more satisfactory, and more successful for biologic than for adoptive parents. This is not necessarily the case, however. One psychodynamic factor which often serves better as a "protective device" for adoptive parents than for biologic parents is an "emotional distance" which permits the child individuation without depriving him of warmth and support. No doubt, there are adoptive parents who overcompensate for the lack of "blood relationship" by neurotically exaggerated closeness that interferes with the child's normal development. It is, however, more frequent and biologically understandable that adoptive parents retain unconsciously an "emotional distance"; this then functions as a defense against "overidentification" with the child if this would gratify the narcissistic need of the parent or would protect him from deep narcissistic injury if the child causes disappointment. Thus adoptive parents might often be better defended than natural parents against the pathologic spiral of transactional processes.

E. J. A.
T. B.

Our society, as all cultures before, has a number of naturally occurring experimental situations. Among them there have always been parentless, homeless, neglected, and even abused children who deserve and need special attention. A vast majority of societies have had and still have severe taboos against out-of-wedlock pregnancies, and the culture in the United States is still influenced by the same puritanical attitudes described in 1850 by Hawthorne in *The Scarlet Letter* [5]. Today, women who have become pregnant out of wedlock are often rejected by their own families as well as by the putative father. These mothers-to-be often have no opportunity to go to a protective home and thus be temporarily isolated from society. Our civilization needs to segregate these women not only because of compassionate considerations but also to protect itself from a sort of contagion, as these women are frequently considered hypersexual, promiscuous, and impulse-ridden.

There are many couples who want children to complete their family but who unfortunately are not able to have children themselves. It is natural for a childless couple to care for parentless children who need care and for infants whose biologic mothers sign releases for them. Problems, which frequently are minor, do occur. If problems are persistent and major, the personalities of each of the individuals involved (adoptive parents as well as the adoptee) and the effect of these interacting vector forces on the total family situation should be considered.

There is evidence that parental infertility and the circumstances surrounding raising someone else's child create stresses in the adoptive situation that are different from those occurring in the biologically derived family [2, 10]. Specific adaptive devices are brought into play even in the healthiest and most relaxed of adoptive parents and adopted children. Assumptions about growth and development, and the transactional relationships or intrapsychic or environmental pressures embodied in Hartmann's concept of an "average expectable environment" cannot be presumed in the adoptive placement [4]. Most of the psychopathologic states that arise can yield to psychoanalytic or psychotherapeutic intervention [11]. Too many times, however, problem areas are concealed or denied in attempts to make the adop-

355

tive situation the same as the biologic. In order not to disguise or becloud the dilemmas of adopters and adoptees, it is important to analyze the particular and unusual strains and stresses to which this nonbiologically derived relationship can be subjected.

STRESS FACTORS IN THE PSYCHOLOGY OF ADOPTERS

Just as one can ask almost any verbal child about his vocational future, so can his hoped-for marital status and the number of children he would like to have be elicited from practically any child. The game of playing house that is so ubiquitous is obviously in preparation for parenthood. Themes of pregnancy, birth (as in the doctor game), and child care are all part of this essential learning process in children. The concept of being a mother or father does not undergo the shifts that vocational choice does. A child's choice of vocation, however, is more dependent upon the stages of psychosexual development and major conflicts. Within the past 15 years I have asked certain children how many children they would like to have. Usually children in the latency years or older will match the number in their own family circle. When I have then asked how many children they would have if they had to adopt, they most often selected a lesser number. The implication is that most children and young adults take their fertility for granted. When confronted by an inability to bear children, however, an adult must make a major revision in his body-image and self-concept. This is in contrast to the ease with which vocational alternatives can be changed, indicating a marked difference in the depth of the struggle, as childbearing involves processes of identification and object choice.

The woman who conceives and carries her child to term develops an intimate relationship between the fetus and herself. Pregnancy is indeed a developmental phase during which fantasies are actively stimulated and parental attitudes develop, shift, and modify. But most important, especially with the first child, is the internal change—the parents' matriculation from the childhood conception to the adult actualization and realization of themselves as parents. This development (initiated by pregnancy itself, which helps place the final stamp on female and male identifications) is not in the living experience of the nonfecund couple. Few adoptive individuals have ever had much contact with adopters or with adoptees and their families as they grew up, so that role models for their future positions are not available to reflect upon. Much support for the pregnant woman comes from all segments of the community, adding to the whole pregnancy and coming parenthood. The nonfecund couple misses this vital support.

And what does the adopting couple hear from the community? When sympathy is expressed, many sense it false since others have no precedent by which to judge how the nonfecund feel. The adopting couple are told how lucky they are not to have any children, because children are troublesome. Even though they recognize these statements are made to comfort them, the childless increasingly find themselves resenting such comments, since they would readily trade their emptiness for all the sleepless nights and worries just to become parents. A number of childless couples, when asked if they had any children, reacted with stony silence, as though they did not have children because they did not like them. Special kinds of remarks are directed at adopters and adoptees. Parents of an almost albino child, who themselves were swarthy, were constantly asked, "How could you ever have taken such a child?" Whereas the child was asked jokingly by family friends and by complete strangers, "Whose child are you? You really don't belong to them, do you?" In a father-son gathering, I recently heard one man say to the adoptive father of an award-winning son, "You sure picked a good one!" At another time, this same father was told, "I wonder if your son knows how lucky he was to get you as parents. Can you imagine how he would have turned out if someone else had gotten him?" Many adoptive mothers have been told, "You don't know how lucky you are not to have had to go through the unpleasantness of a pregnancy. My figure never came back and all those stretch marks! You really are lucky. I think the next time, I'll try to adopt too." "You seem to love her as much as if she were really yours. How can you do it?" "Don't you ever wonder about his background?" "What do your parents feel about your adopting a child?" "How and when do you plan on telling her she's adopted?" Questions and statements such as these reflect social attitudes that can only drive wedges between adopter and adoptee, as they emphasize the differences between the biologic family and the adoptive family. Since many adoptive families attempt to deny any differences, including the basic problem (infertility), which resulted

357

in their need to acquire a family in this manner, these remarks are reminders that society will not allow them or their children to forget.

The feelings of being different and missing a most essential part of life are continuous usually after a year of being unable to conceive. It is by no means unusual both prospectively (before placement) or retrospectively (many years after placement) for the following feelings to be revealed. These I have gleaned from a series of interviews with persons who came for psychiatric help themselves or for their children, and from interviews with a nonpsychiatric population (taken randomly from agency files) who volunteered to be interviewed. Women seemed much more sorely affected. Some of the attitudes were: "I felt different—out of the mainstream of what other women and couples were experiencing." "I was resentful, bitter—as if God had forgotten me." "I was disappointed and depressed." "Each time I'd be examined before early miscarriages, I'd become hopeful. But after the fifth examination and treatment and still no results, I was so depressed that I felt maybe the doctors were right that I had deep psychological problems that prevented me from carrying the baby to term." (This woman suffered from what is called an incompetent cervical os for which a simple surgical procedure has been devised subsequent to her adopting three children.) Although there is no question that psychologic mechanisms might cause infertility, there also are certain physical dysfunctions of unknown etiology that may be the cause of infertility. "My daydream as a child was to be a mother and a teacher of small children. I became a teacher, but with each year of not becoming pregnant, I began to resent all the inadequate parents whose children I'd be teaching and resent fate or God for having played a dirty trick on me." "I just didn't feel like a whole woman. It was reemphasized each time we'd go to a party. All the women would split off and talk about babies and children and all the good and troublesome things that go on with them. They would ask me why didn't I become pregnant. It was awfully uncomfortable and I always felt something must be drastically wrong inside of me." "It was as if I carried a heavy sad load around with me all the time. It became almost unbearably powerful when I'd see a baby—even in a movie. I was furious with the adoption agency when, after trying for 5 years to have a child of our own, they told me we'd have to wait and try more as we weren't married long enough to know if we could have a child." "I felt freakish."

In spite of the anguish, however, the women frequently assumed that the fault was theirs even if investigation revealed the sterility of the male. They intuitively felt that such a deficiency would be seen by their husbands as severely affecting their masculine ego and so in public (including the sheltering intimacy of the physician's consultation room) they were willing to assume the defect. The acute sensitivity of these women to potential narcissistic hurts in their husbands often led to delays in requests for adoption of a child. So many women seen in all aspects of an active psychoanalytic, psychiatric, and consultative practice feel definitely that they have a number of children plus one (their husband) to care for—and their reality-testing frequently is extremely accurate. Despite the injury to their own narcissism, represented in their lack of fecundity, women generally have found it much easier to admit to their defect than men, who were the cause of the couple's infertility.

It is my impression this same type of immaturity expressed by the male's acute sensitivity to his masculine identity is partly inherent in the remarks of males, exemplified by the following: "Sure I was disappointed, but I really didn't think having a baby was so important. We really enjoyed partying, the symphony, the theater, lectures, etc." "My major concern was for my wife. She longed so for a child. I was afraid it would become an obsession." "I am vitally involved in my job. My company transfers me every so often and I know how much finding and furnishing a new house, making new friends, and reestablishing a routine (even like where's the coffee section in the market) means to my wife. Frankly, I wondered what kind of father I'd make with all my activities. I even thought I'd resent having to stay home nights or gear my vacations to what would be good for the children." "I felt inadequate and depressed for some time. Then I became active in the community and felt good."

The physician that is first consulted when a couple is unable to conceive is the obstetrician because, I think, the concern is mainly that of the woman. Without being aware of it, many physicians add to the problems by the remarks or even the sounds ("hmmm!") they make in the examining room; these tend, however, to underline their own uncertainties more often than not. The woman, and often her husband too, is tense and therefore has a greater tendency to misinterpret what is said. Much of the present medical understanding of problems of infertility is still unclear. Each procedure—tubal insufflation, varying hormones, uterine suspension, artificial insemination, etc.—carries with it the hopes and desires that this procedure will be *the* one that allows for conception. With each failure, the feelings of frustration and depression increase. This all helps set the stage for feelings of hopelessness that can only be compounded when the physician says, "Since I can find no reason, i.e., organic [sic!], for your infertility, it must be psychologic. It must be you *really* don't want to have children."

Since the relationship of the obstetrician is with the wife, it is at times more difficult to get the husband to submit to tests. The resistance of the male is rooted in his unconscious fears of infertility, which would mean castration. From the remarks of men, we can see their interests in their business or other activities besides children. There are many suggestions, however, that men look upon wives as mother figures and upon children with a good deal of sibling rivalry.

When problems or unacceptable traits arise in one's biologic children, there is often the tendency to look into family backgrounds, and usually to find the undesirable characteristic in the family tree of one's spouse. In the case of adopters the child's genetic pool is most often unknown, or at best there is a most superficial knowledge of it. This allows for an increase in fantasies about the child's biologic parents which are skewed in directions determined by the adopters' own personality and conflict states.

CASE 1. Despite Ted's severe learning problems, stemming from moderate mental retardation, his adoptive mother continued to insist on his taking piano lessons. She recognized the apparent contradiction but, she explained, the adoption agency told her both biologic parents were music majors in college.

THE PAINS OF INFERTILITY

To be infertile represents an enormous narcissistic blow to male and female alike. The repeated failures in carrying pregnancies to term, the repeated physical examinations, the intense scrutiny of adoption agencies, and the constant searching questions of family and friends are reminders of the need to modify self-concepts. The non-fecund might have to readjust their self-image in a manner similar to that of the amputee. Along with these major cathectic shifts vis-à-vis their own body image are the repeated frustrations in attempts to conceive. Sexual feelings that for many were spontaneous, warm, exciting, and pleasurable become restricted and inhibited as coitus is attempted mainly on prescription. Occurring as this does at the time of ovulation, extraordinary tensions develop, depending on the preconscious awareness of the husband's or wife's responsibility for the infertility.

Women find their place in the continuum of the chain of generations in their ability to bear children. The male has no such reassurance that his seed has a niche in the annals of human society. In many cases, adoptive and nonadoptive, the male perpetuates himself by having a male child who will bear his name into the future. It is true that some of the adoptive parents interviewed had a need for a male child. Yet many more adoptive parents request female children than male children, which would suggest that adoptive parents are not strongly motivated by the need to perpetuate the family name [6].

There are probably many other determinants in deciding to adopt a girl rather than a boy. Two such, built into folklore, have entered (at least in part) into some adoptions. The first is that girls are usually closer to the mothers and the second is that when a girl marries she brings her husband into her own family. There are, besides, stronger unconscious incest taboos between mother and son than between father and daughter. (In the adoptive situation, however, there is a greater latitude for incestuous fantasy, which is possible because of the lack of the "blood-tie taboo," but it is still stronger for the mother-son relationship.)

In the case of extrafamilial adoptions (which constitute about one-half of all adoptions), the law permits a wedge of uncertainty between the child and parent by its delay in giving full parenthood status immediately and allowing a "return of damaged goods." In a sense, the institutionalization of this legal loophole may serve to protect families from a few defective children. It seems to be an anachronistic carry-over from the times when adoptions were mainly to meet the needs of the adopters, rather than to protect the adoptee [1]. Despite extraordinary, competent casework practices in many agencies, adoptive placement is more often the reflection of the personality of the specific worker assigned to this most difficult area. The following illustration of poor casework occurred in a reputable agency and, of course, affected the lives of the people involved.

CASE 2. During the probationary period, the caseworker not only had appointments with the parents in her office and on scheduled times at their home but arrived unannounced at 11:00 P.M. to check on "the way they really lived."

CASE 3. Not only did the worker obtain the income tax report and a financial statement from the bank, but she insisted on going with the couple to their safe deposit box to count their stocks and bonds.

CASE 4. The biologic mother had already signed the relinquishment papers. Her social worker continued counseling, emphasizing the need of the child to have contact with its biologic family. The woman reversed her stand and sued the adoptive parents for the return of her child 5 months after placement. This was the fourth case in which the worker exerted this type of influence. The director of the agency on reviewing all the cases felt that the worker was biased toward out-of-wedlock mothers and toward having them keep their children.

CASE 5. Because the child seemed less well-endowed intellectually than the adoptive parents (a questionable fact "established" by testing at age 5 months), the caseworker insisted on taking the child back since it was not "matched" properly. This was in spite of the parents' recognition of the relative slowness of the child (completely incorrect as 20 years of living have proved) and a positive decision to keep the child no matter what was wrong.

MALADAPTIVE RESPONSES IN ADOPTION

The knowledge (or assumption) of the out-of-wedlock origins of the child elicits specific responses from the adoptive parents which cannot be checked in reality. Just as society often visits the sins of the parents on their children, so too in the adoptive situation; the child carries the stigma of his out-of-wedlock birth. Aggressiveness and sexuality can be viewed as constitutional drives derived from promiscuous, impulse-ridden biologic parents.

CASE 6. The complaint from school was that Mike, age 9, was destructive, annoying the other children, and most recently chasing the younger girls and pulling down their underpants. At first Mike's parents refused the referral to a psychiatric clinic for an evaluation. As the behavior continued unabated, the school authorities made the referral a requirement for retaining Mike in school. During the intake interview Mike's parents told of his adoption, and when they spoke of Mike's behavior in school they indicated that it was all understandable. "You know the kind of girl his mother must have been," they said!

Rescue fantasies are often stimulated during the adoption process. These are especially evident in adoptions of older, multiracial, and handicapped children. Whenever these savior fantasies are frustrated—for example, when problems arise with the child—considerable aggression can be unleashed against him. To counter the expression of irrational angers, parents, just as irrationally, become inconsistent in their discipline. This may lead to the clinical picture of a child with an impulse disorder which further develops in the adoptive parents a vicious cycle of anger and guilt.

CASE 7. A judge of the Juvenile Court requested an evaluation of Bill, who was in custody for attempted rape. His parents also were interviewed. The father told of the severe beatings he administered for any infraction of rules. But when he talked of the current charges against Bill, he said, "Well, boys will be boys."

The need to adopt is usually based on factors that cause infertility which then lead to an extrafamilial adoption. Some couples respond to this dilemma with intense feelings of deprivation and anger, which occasionally are reflected in their child-rearing attitudes. Some adoptive parents recoil from telling the child that he is adopted, lest this activate *in them* the feeling of being defective. Conversely in a number of known cases the child was told about adoption early, frequently, and persistently, almost as a counterphobic mechanism to deny the parents' feelings of being different [7]. With other adoptive parents the problem lay in their inability to allow normal separation and individuation, since any disengagement from themselves heralded an attachment to others and placed them in the state of being childless once again. This problem of the parent can lead to the development of school phobias and even more severe pathologic states in the child.

One of the central concerns of the adoptive parent may be the adopted child's tendency to recover his biologic parents. Oedipus provides an example of the classic search for the mother.

CASE 8. Sue, an only child, had been placed at 5 days of age, with legal adoption completed one year later. The adoptive parents felt that there were no problems until her sixteenth year, when she began increasingly to run away and look for her biologic parents. They were most troubled because Sue's searching reminded them, the adoptive parents, that they were about to lose their only "place in the history of mankind."

363

The inability to have children, for women as well as for men too, is a narcissistic blow to the adult's infantile fantasies of omnipotence. During the course of development, as the child passes through his own stage of omnipotence, there is a revival of similar feelings within the parents. The reality of their infertility and the reality of their adopted adolescent seeking his biologic parents often destroy the security of the regression to the stage of omnipotence. The resultant frustration, their inability to enjoy the satisfaction of this period, can turn into anger directed at the frustrating object—the child. All the ambivalent aggression related to the late oral and early anal phases potentially can be mobilized with consequent symptomatic transactions with the child or the development of psychophysiologic disorders in themselves.

As every child goes through each psychosexual phase of development, all parents—natural and adoptive—go through a reactivation of their own analogous earlier periods. Implicit in this concept is that the parents can pass from stage to stage (as does the child) to final adult psychic organization. Since the infertile do not go through the maturational phase during pregnancy, some of them are fixated at an earlier stage of psychosexual development. The possibility of stress creating regression is therefore greater. If the adoptive parents interact at pregenital levels of psychic evolution, the child's oedipal struggles will more likely evoke anxieties about sexuality and aggression. This anxiety and the fantasies about the child's heritage (e.g., "born of sin," impulsive, reckless, and sexually abandoned parents, birth the result of rape or incest, etc.) create tremendous uncertainties within the parents causing, at times, wide swings in discipline—from excessively harsh and suppressive to unrestrained, provocative, and even seductive behavior toward their children.

As has been mentioned before, adolescence is a particularly stressful time for parents and child. Insofar as an adopted female is concerned, there is quite often the fear that she will be like her biologic mother.

CASE 9. In spite of adequate chaperoning and long, satisfactory, comfortable relationships with the boys in their daughter's church group, Mary's parents refused to allow her to go to any of the church parties. They felt that to begin even this supervised dating situation would ultimately lead Mary into the wrong crowd and finally to a seduction. This restrictive attitude spread to every moment away from home—at school, at clubs, and at the homes of girl friends. In their attempts to prevent a repetition of history (that Mary would do what her biologic mother did), they questioned her unmercifully. Finally, Mary's response after a single sexual experience was, "If I've got the name, I'll play the game."

There is often a more subtle apprehension. The adoptive mother's response to the sexual maturation of her daughter is characterized by a revival of an envy of women capable of bearing children. Conflict can also arise as a result of sexual rivalry, since the usual taboo is not so effective in the adopted family. The adolescent female becomes even more of a direct competitor for the adoptive father's affections. The same conflicting interactions pertain between adoptive fathers and adolescent sons. It would seem that both parents have a tendency to deemphasize the adoptee's maturation, attempting rather to infantilize their children, as if trying to prevent adolescence.

It has been my impression that psychologic maturity does not come at the end of adolescence for any adults—whether they become biologic or adoptive parents. Nor do I feel it occurs just with parenthood. These are indeed nodal points of development. But the point in time where psychic maturity is most likely to occur is when a parent has allowed his adolescent child full separation. Nonfecund couples who have adopted a child to complete their family or to solve problems between themselves find separation from their adolescent particularly difficult. The suggestion that the child will leave the home reproduces the childless (i.e., infertile) state once again. This feeling is particularly keen in families whose adolescent or young adult begins to look for his biologic parents ("reunion urgency") [3]. In these cases, the anxiety is that the child will never return to them but, rather, he will discard them in favor of his blood relatives. This fear can unconsciously force the adoptive family to prove their "unity" by denying information to their child, indicating in this way their desire for the child to remain with them.

When an infant of a month or younger is adopted, the adopting parents are essentially the only parents this child has, since the intrapsychic images established within the child are of the adoptive parents. When the child is adopted later in its life (e.g., 2 years and older), however, he carries with him the intrapsychic images of possibly one or more previous parents (or parent surrogates). Many pathologic states arise in children adopted beyond the infancy stage because they always feel like a stranger in the house. This attitude on the part of the child elicits animosity from the adoptive parents who then grossly or subtly attempt to break the will of the child. Indeed, the resistances the parents encounter are in no way derived from the child's stubborn refusal to acknowledge them. Rather the child is reacting to the prior internalized parents (or surrogates) as the familiar persons, while the new parent is the stranger to him. Thus the adoptive parent blames the child for acting like a stranger, but the accusation (if one must be made) should be applied to the "strange" previous caretakers, as it is these revenants from the past with whom the adopters are in competition.

CASE 10. Sally, adopted at age 3, had been in a series of foster homes prior to final placement. The adoptive parents had decided that if they had a female child of their own they would name her Pam. Thus they decided to call Sally, their newly adopted child, Pam. In later years, Sally demanded by word and action that her parents call her by her right name. Her favorite quotation was from Shakespeare's *Othello,* where Iago says: "Good name in man and woman, dear my lord, Is the immediate jewel of their souls: Who steals my purse steals trash; 'tis something, nothing; 'Twas mine, 'tis his, and has been slave to thousands; But he that filches from me my good name, Robs me of that which not enriches him, And makes me poor indeed." (Act III, Sc. III, ll. 154–161)

CASE 11. The two children, Kent, age 17, and Jan, age 13, were adopted at different ages. Jan was a few days old when she was placed, whereas Kent was 10 years old at placement. Both parents felt a warmth and affection from Jan, but always felt that Kent acted like a boarder in their home. Jan increasingly complained of being left alone with Kent when the parents went out for the evening. The parents questioned Jan closely when they became aware of her considerable tension. She related that Kent approached her sexually on many occasions. Kent's explanations were casual and candid. Jan was not his sister, and they were not his parents. But if they wanted him to desist, he would. When the parents partially talked through some of their concerns about the current situation, they were able to focus on their own interaction with Kent from the time of placement on. Both parents recognized that they had immediately expected from Kent the same degree of affection that they had received from Jan, and when it was not forthcoming they (retrospectively) noted that their own antagonism had interfered with their acceptance of him. The parents were able to see how essentially they contributed to Kent's remaining "a stranger in the home."

To a degree, similar problems can occur in intrafamilial adoptions. The major and most outstanding variable from the extrafamilial adoptees is that these children still have a consistent object that is available to sustain the vitality of their established internal images. What problems do occur in the intrafamilial adoptee are complicated by the process of mourning for the lost object that accompanies divorce or death and the division of loyalties accompanying divorce and separation.

"TELLING"

Of all the material contained in my original paper on adoption, the very small, tangential, and tentative remarks made about telling the adoptee about his background received the greatest response [9]. These responses were both positive and highly emotional. Although that paper was published a number of years ago, heated discussions with charges and countercharges continue not only unabated but perhaps even with increasing frequency. It seems clear that telling the adoptee about his background elicits extremely intense feelings, some of which might relate to any of the pathologic states noted earlier in this chapter. Yet this issue, as so many other socially derived mores and customs, developed from the experiences of individuals and their internal psychic elaborations. Historically it has only been in recent years that adoption laws have been directed specifically toward the protection and the needs of the children involved. Prior to this point, adoption was concerned mainly with the protection of the adopters.

Because of this, concerns about what and how and when to tell children about their biologic parents were not considered. These concerns came to the forefront around the turn of the twentieth century, when a series of incidents of delinquent acting out occurred in teenagers. The incidents occurred at the time they learned of their adoptive status. The longer social scientists looked at this situation, the more advisable it seemed to tell the child early and repeatedly that he was adopted.

Interestingly, the advice given for telling is based on the assumption that the earlier the word "adoption" is used, the less traumatic it will be when heard later by the child, especially from someone other than his parents. Advice was given (and still is customarily) by placement agencies to start talking about adoption as soon as the child is able to understand. (One couple was told to put their infant child to sleep saying, "Go to sleep, my darling adopted baby.")

If such advice is followed, one can assume that below age 4 (and sometimes much older) the child is not aware of the meaning of the word "adoption" and therefore is usually nonreactive to it. This, however, does not forecast the reaction the child may experience if and when he becomes fully aware of the meaning of the word.

It is true that in a number of circumstances, the telling about adoption is not particularly an option the adoptive parents have. I refer to cases where the child is placed between 3 to 5 years of age or even older. I also refer to cases in which there are many adopted children in a family and the older ones are already aware of their being adopted. In instances in which alternatives are possible, however, it would seem best to adjust the time and way of telling about adoption to the character structure and the personality type of the given child [8, 12]. Since the concept of another set of parents existing somewhere in the world might be traumatic for some children, it would be most worthwhile to consider telling in the same way that we think of elective surgery.

If the surgery can wait for a time when it can best be handled intrapsychically, the advice would be to wait until the major stages in psychosexual development have occurred. It should be emphasized again that the telling about adoption should be given to the child in doses, according to his ability to incorporate this information, and he should be given sufficient time to ask questions. Although the telling may in general be best during latency, the major determinant must be the individual child and his own special needs.

It has often been said that whenever or whatever is told to the child, it is the parental reaction that tends to determine the meaning of the communication. There seems no doubt about this idea as it relates to any piece of potentially unsettling information. As Kirk has suggested, there is considerable understanding within the parents regarding their defects (infertility specifically) that can allow them to empathize with the adopted child, who also has a defect (his being given up by his biologic parents) [7]. This can be the most vital force in the process of identification, permitting a vital unification of both the bad and the good parent images intrapsychically.

Giving information to the child about his adoption can be compared with the giving of sexual information. When a child is 3½ years old, he is unable to grasp all the facts about conception and most of the time is not really interested in the father's role specifically. Later, questions are asked as to how the baby gets out of the mother and these, too, can be answered simply and without elaboration. The full story of conception (even if told earlier) needs repeating on many occasions, but it is during the latency phase that the information seems to be assimilated.

Children adopted at birth want to know the same answers to the same questions as do nonadopted children. If they are told as above, the information concerning the details of their birth can and should be added during the latency phase. One way of doing so could be after the 6-year-old asks again as to where do babies come from, get out, and get in by adding: "And in your case, you were carried in another woman's uterus until you were born. Then, because she could not take care of you (she didn't have a daddy around, and you know how children need daddies as well as mommies), she let an agency help find a special and proper home for you with a Daddy and Mommy to love and take care of you. We could not have a child of our own and so when we went to the agency, you seemed to pick us out by smiling your own special smile. We knew right away that you were the very one for us."

Stories of this sort do not encompass all the facts, nor should they in the beginning. Parents who can accept the out-of-wedlock conception and can allow the adolescent adoptee even to look for his biologic family are in a far more strategic position because their entire relationship is based on honesty. In the same way, adoptive parents need to face the possibility of their children saying in anger, "You can't tell me what to do. You aren't my real parents anyway!" This concept should be met with a determined, "Oh yes, I am in every way. Maybe I didn't carry you in my uterus, but from then on we've done everything any other parent has done—and then some. You might be angry and that's your prerogative. But you'll do things the way we do them here."

CASE 12. Discussions about his adoption were always open and candid between Bill, age 16, and his parents. The relationship among all three was always excellent. Bill's father, a physician, was away at a medical convention when Bill asked his mother if he could drive a stock car at a drag strip. His mother said he could not. Uncharacteristically, Bill became furious, saying his mother never let him do anything. He said that each time he made movements toward independence and maturity, she

369

stood in his way. He stated he would not take this kind of treatment, especially since the other guys were depending on him. Besides, he finally exploded, she couldn't tell him what to do or not to do as she wasn't his real mother anyway.

Repetitious telling children of their origins is not only of no value but gives rise to suspicions in the child's thinking. "If I was chosen, why was I given up in the first place?" Persistent questions from children always indicate that the answers given are insufficient, inadequate, or unclear. The adoptive parent can ask the child what more he wants to know or what seems obscure. Telling an adopted child that his parents are dead (unless it is actually true) may backfire with sad consequences. Full and complete honesty between parent and child, dealt out according to the child's ability to understand and assimilate, is by far the best and most rewarding policy.

SUMMARY

Nonbiologic parenthood has been a fact in all recorded human history. There are evident problems distinguishing adoptive from biologic parents. Most of these problems are understandable and represent normal psychologic responses of parents and their adopted children, and the families, like natural families, derive a great deal of support from the social institutions around them. Psychopathologic reactions can more easily occur in adoptive parents because adoption offers an extremely fertile field for the development of maladaptive fantasies that may lead to untoward and misguided actions. Psychoanalytic intervention is of significant value in a crisis as well as in chronic pathologic interactions.

Bibliography

1. Bradley, T. *An Exploration of Caseworkers' Perceptions of Adoptive Applicants*. Child Welfare League of America, Inc., 1967. Reprint Q.
2. Deutsch, H. *The Psychology of Women*. New York: Grune & Stratton, 1945. Vol. II, Chap. 11, pp. 393–433.
3. Gonzalez, A. Quoted by Remus-Araico in Some Aspects in Early Orphan Adults' Analysis. Read at New York Psycho-

analytic Society, September 15, 1964, and Washington Psychoanalytic Society, September 18, 1964.

4. Hartmann, H. *Essays on Ego Psychology*. (Translated by D. Rapoport.) New York: International Universities Press, 1964. P. 16.

5. Hawthorne, N. *The Scarlet Letter*. Washington Square Press, 1948.

6. Kirk, H. D. Differential sex preference in family formation; a serendipitous datum followed up. *Canad. Rev. Soc. Anthrop.* 1:31–48, 1964.

7. Kirk, H. D. *Shared Fate*. New York: Free Press of Glencoe, 1964.

8. Murphy, L. B. *Personality in Young Children,* Vols. I & II. New York: Basic Books, 1956.

9. Schechter, M. D. Observations on adopted children. *Arch. Gen. Psychiat.* (Chicago) 3:21–32, 1960.

10. Schechter, M. D. Psychoanalytic theory as it relates to adoption. *J. Amer. Psychoanal. Ass.* 15:695–708, 1967.

11. Schechter, M. D., Carlson, P., Simmons, J., and Work, H. Emotional problems of the adoptee. *Arch. Gen. Psychiat.* (Chicago) 10:37–46, 1964.

12. Thomas, A., Birch, H., Chess, S., Hertzig, M., and Korn, S. *Behavioral Individuality in Early Childhood*. New York: New York University Press, 1963.

Maternal Rejection, Overprotection, and Perplexity

Editors' Introduction to Chapters 18–20

Parental attitudes and behavior are so varied, dependent on so many individual, familial, and societal factors, that they appear to defy classification. Psychoanalysis, however, offers a classification based on the motivational pattern of the prevailing attitude of the parent toward the child. Concise as such categorizations are, they include all shadings of behavioral manifestations under a single diagnostic label that indicates the typical behavior. Investigators of parental behavior, therefore, must always be aware that although the characteristic mode of action says a great deal about the parents' attitudes toward the child, it does not forecast its future development with any degree of certainty; the steadily changing vector of the interacting processes between parent and child often brings about unexpected results, since it is not possible to take all the factors of the past into account or to predict latent unconscious influences that change the adaptive potentials of the parent and, even more so, those of the child.

The following three chapters deal with concepts often applied in the diagnostic evaluation of parental behavior.

Anna Freud has focused her presentation upon the hazards of misusing the concept of the "rejecting mother" either by forgetting that only a thin line separates the normal and necessary from the pathogenic or by failing to consider that what is pathogenic at one time might be made better by interactions during other periods of development; or, in reverse, that the positive attitude of the mother or father might turn negative under conditions which change the parent's sentiments toward the child or which lastingly influence the parent's personality.[1]

[1] The effects of "willful neglect" and severe rejection of infants referred to in this chapter are discussed in more detail in Chap. 24.

This is, of course, equally valid for those parental attitudes sub-sumed under the concept of "maternal overprotection." There is, however, a significant difference: Maternal rejection is most destructive toward the newborn, whereas maternal overprotectiveness for the newborn can hardly be exaggerated. If it appears so, the suppressed hostility of the mother is revealed in overprotective behavior, since this can serve as a defense against guilty feelings aroused by rejection. Genuinely responsive protectiveness is a manifestation of normal motherliness. It is a developmental process in the mother that enables her to "outgrow" the symbiotic phase of motherhood and thus to overcome her resistances against the child's individuation. The latter is often disguised by overprotection.

The terms *maternal rejection* and *maternal overprotection* cover the range of parental attitudes from normal—biologically and psychologically useful—to pathogenic, that is, in different degrees harmful to the child. In themselves neither of the terms signifies an actual pathologic condition in the mother but only the inclination to respond to the child according to the tendencies represented in these terms.

In contrast, *parental perplexity,* as presented here, is a well-defined symptom of the parent generating a definable symptom in the child. It is an interesting presentation of the spiral of interaction between parents and children. Yet the perplexity of parents as a clinical phenomenon often characterizes the emotional reactions of young parents, fortunately, in a less extreme form. The great experience of being a mother coupled with the responsibility for the child brings about a sense of helplessness, especially in young mothers facing this novel situation for the first time. With fathers it is different. Amazed and insecure when confronted with the miracle of their own infant, they are better defended against perplexity than mothers, since it is not their biologic function to take care of the infant. This does not mean that they are less eager to do so, but their anxiety about being unable to function adequately is rooted in the more superficial layers of their personality. Normally, the mother takes over and grows into the function of her motherhood through the unconscious processes of her biologic learning. Surprises are always lurking; they are welcome as long as her infant is like all other infants or the surprise indicates his growth and development in an expected direction. Whenever the unexpected behavior is responded to by the parent with disappointment, it can be understood as signifying a threat to the self-system of the parent. If the sense of being sufficient which a thriving infant provides for the parent is not forthcoming, the latter may become aware of its increasing need for help. Inadequate to allay the rising tension in the baby, the pressure upon her increases as she feels both her own and the child's frustrated need. This frustration brings about a regression (even if temporary) of the parent's ego and causes her to feel helpless. The helpless parent, however, is not a child. She feels her responsibility for the child's well-being; if she fails, she feels guilty. The guilt is a burden from within while the frustrated child's crying is a burden from without. As she experiences the alienation of the child from her self-system, her guilt intensifies the sense of conflict and helplessness. At the same time, and in response to the parent's help-lessness, the frustration of the child becomes focused on its source, the parent. The child feels rejected, abandoned, and the source of frustration becomes the hated object, the hated parent. If the relation-ship between child and parents survives the repetitions of such trans-actions, the child develops and learns to see the parent as a complex source of frustrations and gratifications as well as a weak and inade-quate object outside himself. Since the infant, or even an older child, remains dependent on the parents, he often learns that he can receive attention and gratification only by a manifestation of his own help-lessness, and he uses this to manipulate them.

The following chapter illustrates these transactional processes. While the child's developing pathologic state can be viewed as caused by the perplexity of the parent, we know little about the minute details of the intrapsychic processes of the parent. Nevertheless, there is al-ways hope that the adult person's psychic resources will be replen-ished, step by step, either by good turns in the child's development or by other resources that help to balance the emotional homeostasis.

E. J. A.
T. B.

18

The Concept of the Rejecting Mother

Anna Freud

The facts of infantile sexuality, the oedipus and castration complexes, the problems of ego and superego development, and the role of aggression having been established, psychoanalytic study then turned to the child's first year of life, i.e., to the beginning of mental functioning and the first emotional contact of the infant with his environment. This brought into special focus how all-important the person of the mother and her attitude are to her child. It was demonstrated that all advantages of a later family life may be wasted on a child who has lacked a warm and satisfying mother relationship in the first instance. The conditions necessary for establishing this first contact to the best advantage have been described by many authors.[1] In this earliest partnership in an individual's life, that of infant and mother, the demands are all on one side (the infant's), while the obligations are all on the other side (the mother's). It is the mother's task to be attentive to the child's needs (for food, sleep, warmth, movement, comfort, company), not to misunderstand them or to confuse them with each other, and to fulfill them not according to her own speed

This paper is also included in *The Writings of Anna Freud,* Volume IV: *Indications for Child Analysis and Other Papers,* New York: International Universities Press, 1968. It also appears in *Casework Papers, 1954,* New York: Family Service Association of America, 1955; and in *Child Welfare,* New York: Child Welfare League of America, Inc., March, 1955.

[1] By none better than by D. W. Winnicott in his popular pamphlet The Ordinary Devoted Mother and Her Baby [11].

and rhythm but by adapting her actions to the child's. The infant is dependent on the mother for his satisfactions. If she proves a gratifying and accommodating provider for his pressing needs, he begins to love, not only his experiences of wish fulfillment, but her person. Thereby the infant's original state of self-centeredness is changed into an attitude of emotional interest in his environment and he becomes capable of loving, first the mother and—after her—the father and other important figures in his external world.

It is maintained by many analytic authors that it lies wholly with the mother of an infant whether this beneficial development occurs. When the mother welcomes the child's first outflow of feeling toward her and responds to it, she favors his progress from self-centeredness to object love. When she fails in her task at some point and thereby rejects his advances, she may destroy an all-important potentiality in her infant, with disastrous consequences for his future healthy development.

This development of analytic theory did not fail to direct the attention of workers in all professions caring for the welfare of little children toward the earliest ages and thus, perhaps, to the beginning of all troubles. They started to take serious notice of the vital bond which exists between mother and infant, to protect it against forcible interruptions, to foster its existence where they found it, and to urge mothers to be more forthcoming with their feelings where they seemed reluctant.

These were the legitimate applications of a new insight. But, whether owing to the fault of the analysts who were too emphatic in their statements, or owing to the fault of psychiatrists and caseworkers who were too bent on exchanging a multitude of causes of mental trouble for one single, simple, causal factor—the idea of being rejected by the mother suddenly began to overrun the fields of clinical work and casework. On the clinical side, more and more of the gravest disturbances (such as autism, atypical and psychotic development, mental backwardness, retardation of speech, etc.) were attributed to the presence of rejection. On the caseworker's side, more and more mothers were pronounced to be cold, not outgoing, unresponsive, unloving, hating, in short, rejecting their children. This caused much heart-searching and also much self-accusation, especially among the mothers of abnormal children.

Inquiry into the Concept
of the Rejecting Mother

There is, of course, no lack of evidence for the occurrence of rejection of infants. Many infants, instead of being kept as near to the mother as possible, spend many hours of the day in isolation; many are subjected to traumatic separations from their mothers; many, at the end of infancy, have good reason to feel deserted when another child is born; many are, indeed, unwanted. Nevertheless, there is behind these happenings a variety of determinants which decides their outcome. There is not one type of rejecting mother, there are many. There are those who are responsible for their rejecting attitude, who can be exhorted, advised, and helped toward a better adjustment to their child; there are also those for whom rejecting is beyond their control.

Children are deprived of the company and care of their mothers for external, physical reasons, and for internal, mental ones; or both factors are inextricably intermixed in other cases. Also, no child is wholly loved. The idea of rejection in its present form is imprecise, vague, and through overuse has become almost meaningless. Nothing short of definition and classification of the degrees and types of withdrawal of mother love from the infant can restore the term to its initial usefulness; hence the present inquiry into the concept of the rejecting mother.

Rejection by Unwillingness of the Mother

No one who has ever worked in a child guidance clinic, a well baby clinic, or a welfare agency will deny that there are bad mothers, in the same sense in which there are bad partners in every type of human relationship, whether they are mothers or fathers, wives or husbands. As described above, the relationship of a mother to her infant is an exacting one. It is too much to expect that she will fulfill her task if she has not taken on the role of motherhood voluntarily, if it has been forced upon her. That leaves on one side, classed as unwilling, all mothers who never meant to have a baby, or did not mean to have one at the particular time when pregnancy occurred.

The reasons for their unwillingness may be external ones:

financial difficulties, lack of their own home or of space, the burden of too many earlier children, or illegitimacy of the relations with the child's father. There are emotional reasons such as lack of affection for the husband, which is extended to his child. Or the reasons, rationalized merely on the surface by external conditions, may lie much deeper in the mother's nature. There are many women who are incapacitated for motherhood by virtue of their masculinity. They may wish for children for reasons of pride and possessiveness, but their humiliation at finding themselves female, their longing for a career, their competition with the husband preclude any real enjoyment of or with the infant.

There are, further, the mothers who waver between rejection and acceptance of the mother role. During her pregnancy a woman may be wholly unwilling and then be seduced and tempted by the infant himself until she enters into an affectionate relationship; in such cases the living presence of the child arouses in her what one used to call the mother instinct.

Or there may be conflict between internal and external pressure. This is well known from casework with unmarried mothers who reject their infants for social considerations, while they accept them emotionally.

It is also interesting to note that wholly external influences are capable of interfering with the mother's tie to the child. When mother and infant are separated for long periods and the mother is relieved of all responsibility for the child—as happened in wartime England for safety's sake or as happens in hospitals when either mother or child has to be isolated—under such conditions mothers have been seen to lose their attachment to the child and to become unwilling to resume it. Such experiences make one feel that the mother's attachment is bound up with the appeal made by an infant's helplessness and urgent need for care rather than being a mere instinct. This might explain too why mothers who entrust the care of their infants to paid nurses are so often described as rejecting.

On the whole, it is not the truly unwilling mother who exerts the most disastrous influence on her child's future. When she refuses altogether to play her part, the door is left wide open for an accepting mother substitute, as found in adoption and in foster families. It is the mother who wavers between rejection and possessiveness who does

379

the more irreparable harm by forcing her child into an unproductive partnership in which he fails to develop his capacities for object love.

REJECTION THROUGH ABNORMALITY OF THE MOTHER

Unwillingness, for conscious or unconscious reasons, to assume the special task of motherhood should not be confused with the general failure to establish normal human relationships, as it exists in women whose personalities are distorted by psychotic elements or who suffer from a circumscribed psychosis. The effect of a psychotic mother on the development of her child has been discussed frequently and by many authors in recent years. There is no doubt that infants may react to the lack of outgoing warmth in such a mother as if she rejected them. On the other hand, harmful consequences of an opposite nature can also be observed. The psychotic mother may include a child in her own world of self-centered (narcissistic) feelings and reactions, regarding him as a part of her own self. The normal symbiosis of a mother and infant may then become prolonged in an abnormal manner, and mother and child together become an isolated couple in an apparently hostile external world [8]. Such a state of affairs delays, or prevents, the growing child's normal adaptation to the social environment [1].

REJECTION BY SEPARATION

In contrast to these first two groups, there are the mother-child relationships in which a good beginning is made in every respect. The mother may be devoted, happy with her baby, accepting, and responsive. The child may respond to her care and make the first steps toward emotional attachment. Then there follows rejection brought about by sudden separation of the couple. Such separations may be the mother's fault (when she leaves the child in the care of strangers for trivial reasons such as trips, visits), but they need not be. The mother may be ill, have to go to the hospital, undergo an operation, need convalescence. The illness of an older child or the needs of the father may remove her from the infant. External conditions may interfere, as they did in wartime. The mother may die and leave her child an orphan.

Such separations act on the child irrespective of their causes. Since the infant cannot grasp the reason for the mother's disappearance, every separation equals for him desertion on her part. Before his sense of time develops, the pressure of his needs makes every period of waiting seem agonizingly long; therefore he does not distinguish between separations of short and long duration. Everybody's sympathy and understanding are automatically extended to the infant whose mother dies; if the mother is absent merely for a few weeks, we are less concerned. Wrongly so; *we* know that the mother will return; the *child* does not. Separations between mother and infant are *rejections,* whether they are brought about for good or bad reasons, whether they are long or short. The infant who is torn from the partnership with his mother is emotionally orphaned, even though he may be an artificial orphan with a living mother [3]. It is revealing, for example, that analyses show that adults who, when infants, lost their mothers through death unconsciously have never ceased to blame their mothers for desertion.

Dorothy Burlingham's and my wartime study *Infants Without Families* [4], John Bowlby's work on separation anxiety [2], James Robertson's film *A Two-Year-Old Goes to Hospital* [9], René Spitz's film studies [10], etc., have revealed some of the consequences of "rejection by separation." Here I can only summarize results. The shock of separation is often expressed by disturbance of the body functions such as upsets of sleep, feeding, of the digestive apparatus; there is also at such times an increased susceptibility to infection. Further, many infants make backward moves in their development: those who have just learned to talk give up speech; those who have just begun to move independently give up walking; those who have already undergone toilet training wet and soil again. It is almost invariably the most recent achievement in development which is lost first.

On the emotional side, all variations have been described, from incessant crying to silent despair. It seems to be as painful for the infant to withdraw his feelings from the loved person as it is for an adult in mourning. The main difference between the two emotional states seems to be that the adult is capable of withdrawing his feelings into himself and attaching them to an inner image of the lost object. The infant needs a living person in the external world who is capable of fulfilling his material needs besides serving as a love object: he

381

cannot live without a mother substitute. Therefore, the interval between withdrawal of affection from the mother and search for another object is a short one. But this ability, or rather need, of the young child to form new ties should not deceive us as to the seriousness of what has happened. The first attempt at object love has been destroyed; the next one will not be of quite the same quality, will be more demanding, more intent on immediate wish fulfillments, i.e., further removed from the more mature forms of "love." Repeated rejection by separation intensifies this process of deterioration and produces individuals who are dissatisfied, shallow, and, worst of all, promiscuous in their relationships.

REJECTION BY INCONSTANCY OF FEELING

There are many young children who show the effects of rejection, although they have never been subjected to a physical separation from their mothers. The fact is that infants demand more than the bodily presence of the mother, they demand too that the mother's regard for them should not undergo any fluctuations in degree. The younger the infant, the greater is his sensitivity for any lessening in the mother's love, even if this is a very temporary phenomenon. Even when the mother is oblivious of such a change in intensity of feeling, the child is not.

In a more specialized paper on the subject, About Losing and Being Lost, I was able to show how young children react if they feel less loved [6]. The mother's loving interest in the child ties him to her and he feels securely held in an atmosphere which is charged with her affection. When the charge (the libido cathexis, to use the technical term) diminishes, insecurity sets in, and the child feels "lost." When the infant is old enough to be capable of independent movement, he may even get lost physically; i.e., he may venture away from the mother into what is normally for him "out of bounds" and not find his way back to her. There is an interesting analogy here between our own hold on our material possessions and a mother's hold on her young child. We are apt to lose possessions if we withdraw interest from them, if "our mind is elsewhere." Mothers, under the same conditions, may lose their emotional hold on their young children; this, in its turn, may induce the child to stray, to lose himself, to run away.

Seen from the mother's side, it is an unreasonable demand that there should be no fluctuations in the intensity of her feelings for the child. There are many other claims on her emotions. The most devoted mother of an infant may have older children who have older claims; there are the husband's claims to satisfy, and needs vary. Mothers may suffer the loss of another child or of their own parents. If this happens, their feelings become withdrawn from the infant and are engaged in mourning. Infants react to such happenings as they do to rejections and desertions, with illness, with standstills or regressions in development, or with increased naughtiness and aggression toward the mother. The same happens if the mother falls into a morbid depression of some kind, or if there is an upheaval in her love life, or if there are troubles in the marital relations which absorb her interest.

Rejection by desertion also seems to be the most potent factor in the young child's emotional upheaval when a next child is born. So far as the mother is concerned, nothing is more natural, healthy, and even biologically necessary than that she should turn her attention to the newborn. But all the psychologic advice to mothers on how to handle the older child at that juncture, all the devices of giving him a doll to bathe, of letting him help with the new baby, of telling him what a big child he already is—all this will not for a moment blind him to the all-important fact that his mother has withdrawn libido from him. The child's own explanation of such rejection is invariably that he is no good, or that the mother is no good, both versions leading to anxiety, feelings of guilt, and regressions in behavior.

When the withdrawal of love is occasioned by the birth of a new baby or by some happening in the mother's love life, the child will react with normal jealousy. When mourning or depressions are the cause, children usually react with withdrawal and (immediate or later) pathologic depressions of their own.

ALTERNATION OF REJECTION AND ACCEPTANCE

It is only natural that a mother's relationship to her child fluctuates with his phases of development. Some mothers during their pregnancy feel a pride, possessiveness, and love for the unborn—attitudes which they can never recapture later on. Others are wholly de-

383

voted to the helpless baby and withdraw devotion when the child begins to move and help himself. To most mothers, the appeal of the hungry child is very different from the appeal (or lack of it) of the dirty or obstreperous one. Some mothers find it difficult to tolerate the awakening masculinity of the 3-year-old, and withdraw from him at a period when others turn toward the child with increased and proud affection. A mother may be rejecting toward her baby in his first stages and become accepting at the stage when the child is teachable, etc. [5].

Such alternations of rejection and acceptance (not of the child as a whole but of his changing aspects) are anchored in the depth of the mother's mind. She cannot help reacting to (i.e., rejecting) the child if his behavior arouses old conflicts of her own. His oral demands on her arouse once more her own struggles with her own mother in her own babyhood. His dirtiness and the need for her to be concerned with his body products arouse fantasies and battles of the anal phase. Her reaction to the child's phallic development will be determined by her castration complex and her penis envy. In short, the relationship to the developing infant shakes her personality to its foundations. Her behavior toward the child is understood best when viewed in terms of her own conflicts. She acts rejecting when she defends her own repressions, and accepting when the child's behavior meets with secret wishes and fantasies of her own which she can tolerate.

It is a frequent occurrence that a mother is so fixed to a certain libidinal phase of her own development that her obvious predilection for it acts on the child as a seduction. Thus, mother and child as a couple may meet on the basis of an exaggerated sadomasochistic relationship, provoking each other to endless quarrels. Or their relationship may remain predominantly within the sphere of oral fantasies; in the latter event, their partnership becomes the breeding ground for pathologic reactions, such as battles over food, eating and stomach troubles, and attitudes of craving and addiction.

REJECTION IN SPITE OF DEVOTION

Although, as said before, no human being is wholly loved, there are some women who come very near to fulfilling this achievement for their child. They are, emotionally, mothers rather than wives, with few other ties and interests, to whom the possession of a child means the fulfillment of their deepest wishes. They give themselves unreservedly to the infant; they do not separate from him and they do not allow other claims to diminish their attention. Their infant frequently remains their only child. But, surprisingly enough, they too do not escape the blame of being rejecting in the eyes of their children. New light is thrown on the factor of rejection when we realize that no degree of devotion on the part of the mother can successfully cope with the boundless demands made on her by the child.

There is another, more intricate, factor which should not be underrated. Every good mother of an infant shares his experience. Not only does she provide satisfactions, she also is at hand when the infant is uncomfortable, in pain, and suffering. It is not reasonable to expect that the child will connect her person only with his pleasures. As the first representative of the external world, in which the infant has to learn to orient himself, she becomes the symbol of both frustration and satisfaction, pain and pleasure.[2] The nearer she is to the child, the more convincingly will both roles be thrust on her. Paradoxically enough, the most devoted mother may in this way become the most rejecting one for the child.

Actually, we should have been prepared for this result through earlier observations concerning the role given to the father in the oedipus complex of the boy. There, too, the gentlest and most well-meaning fathers find themselves distorted in the boys' conscious and unconscious fantasies, until they take on the aspect of monsters and ogres; i.e., frightening, terrifying, castrating figures. Analysis has shown that the father assumes this aspect for the child as the representative of the culture in which incest with the mother is forbidden. He is no more, and no less, than a symbol of the moral code. I believe we can say that any infant's mother, for all her reality aspects, is a symbol too. In appraising the circumstances we, the observers, must not share the infants' delusion. We must guard against the error of confusing the inevitably frustrating aspects of extrauterine life with the rejecting actions or attitudes of the individual mothers.

This inquiry into the concept of the rejecting mother was under-

---

[2] See in this connection Melanie Klein's concept of the good and bad mother [7].

taken to demonstrate the necessity for discrimination of the factors that motivate the mother's attitude and behavior toward the child. Only careful evaluation of the reality and fantasy life can explain willful neglect and inescapable fateful situations and enable us to differentiate them from the many puzzling, delicate, and difficult situations that become remembered by the child as rejection by the mother.

Bibliography

1. Bonnard, A. Conscious and unconscious fidelity. *Psyche* (Stuttgart) 9:603–609, 1956.
2. Bowlby, J. *Maternal Care and Mental Health*. Geneva: World Health Organization, 1951.
3. Burlingham, D., and Freud, A. *Young Children in Wartime: A Year's Working Residential War Nursery*. London: Allen & Unwin, 1942.
4. Burlingham, D., and Freud, A. *Infants Without Families: The Case for and against Residential Nurseries*. New York: International Universities Press, 1944.
5. Coleman, R. W., Kris, E., and Provence, S. The study of variations of early parental attitudes. *Psychoanal. Stud. Child* 13:20–47, 1953.
6. Freud, A. About losing and being lost. *Psychoanal. Stud. Child* 22:9–19, 1967.
7. Klein, M. *The Psycho-Analysis of Children*. London: Hogarth, 1932.
8. Mahler, M. On child psychosis and schizophrenia: Autistic and symbiotic infantile psychoses. *Psychoanal. Stud. Child* 7:286–305, 1952.
9. Robertson, J. A Two-Year-Old Goes to Hospital (Film), 1952. (Available from New York University Film Library.)
10. Spitz, R. A. Grief, a Peril in Infancy (Film), 1947. (Available from New York University Film Library.)
11. Winnicott, D. W. The Ordinary Devoted Mother and Her Baby (1949). Nine Broadcast Talks. Republished in J. Hardenberg (Ed.), *The Child and the Family: First Relationships*. London: Tavistock, 1957.

19

The Concept of Maternal Overprotection

David M. Levy

It is generally accepted that the most potent of all influences on social behavior is derived from the primary social experience with the mother. If a mother maintains toward the child a consistent attitude of, let us say, indifference and hostility, the assumption is made that the child's personality is greatly affected thereby. His outlook on life, his attitude toward people, his entire psychic well-being, and his destiny are presumed to be altered by the maternal attitude. Life under a regime of maternal indifference develops a psychic pattern of a very different mold than it does under a regime of maternal overprotection. Psychiatrists regard the difference as great as though the children concerned lived in entirely different worlds. Indeed, two children of the same parents manifest profound differences in personality when the mother exhibits a different attitude toward each, and these personality differences are manifested on that basis alone. If human behavior is influenced so markedly by maternal attitudes, then surely the most important study of man as a social being is a study of his mother's influence on his early life.[1] The play of social response between mothers and children would then represent the foundation of social life,

Reprinted in modified form from D. M. Levy, *Maternal Overprotection*. New York: Columbia University Press, 1943.

[1] What follows is based on a series of studies in maternal overprotection conducted by the author at the former Institute for Child Guidance in New York. More than 2000 case records were examined in the search for "pure" cases, and follow-up evaluations were carried out 3, 7, and 10 years later.

and its investigation the pivotal attack on the problem of social behavior. The conviction that the destiny of the individual rests in the hands of his mother (or mother-substitute) is based on the thesis that the social forces operating on the infant affect his entire life.

THE MOTHER-CHILD MONOPOLY

The concept of maternal overprotection tries to delineate the dimensions of one such decisive type of relationship between the attitudes and behavior of the mother and the development of the child, the conditions of a mother-child monopoly. As an example take the case of a mother who, soon after the birth of her child, manifests a strong overprotective attitude. She "lives only for her child." Her life is devoted to him. She is uncomfortable whenever she is away from him, if only for a few minutes. She allows the husband to have little or no share in her baby's training. It is her baby, not his. She threatens to leave the house if her husband "dare lay a finger on the child." The husband's role as father is negligible and remains so throughout the life of the child. The mother's career becomes more and more exclusively maternal. Her sexual and social difficulties with the husband increase. They no longer go out together. The baby, later the child, becomes the everlasting excuse for the gradual elimination of the wifely role. Social life, previously active, becomes more and more restricted. When the child goes to school the mother accompanies him there, long past the time when the neighbors' children are on their way alone. She helps him with all his studies, allows him no friends for fear they will contaminate him, and is uncritical in her attitude toward him.

The clinical picture shows how, once an overprotective attitude is well developed, a mother-child monopoly gradually comes to fulfillment. When the mother finds in her child the solution for all her emotional needs, she gets caught by a social bond that automatically loosens all the others.

TYPES OF OVERPROTECTION

A clinical classification of overprotection would include the following types: (1) nonmaternal, (2) transient, (3) mild, (4) mixed, (5) guilt-provoked, and (6) pure.

Nonmaternal overprotection by fathers, siblings, grandparents, or other relatives can also occur, and in a number of cases of maternal overprotection there is often a reinforcement of the maternal attitude by others. Relatively few cases of marked paternal overprotection are found, although cases of paternal favoritism, shown usually to a daughter, are very common. There are several possible reasons for this infrequency. It is very rare that fathers are in as frequent social contact with children as mothers are. Cases in which the parental roles are reversed so that the father stays home and does the housework while the mother goes out to work are oddities. The opportunities for a constant overdose of paternal contact are therefore limited, especially in the important infantile years. Where a relatively strong father-daughter overprotection occurs, the problems arising may not affect the child so that she will be referred for treatment. (There are, in fact, a large variety of difficulties that do not become overt or available for treatment until adult life, if ever. Children are more likely to be referred for acts of aggression—quarreling, disobedience, temper tantrums, rebellious behavior—than for excessive obedience and submission. When overprotection results in an apparently successful parent-child relationship, especially in the form of a model child, the problems are more likely to become manifest when adaptation to adult life without parental support becomes necessary. A number of children, nevertheless, are found in the maternal overprotection group who are obedient and well behaved, and are referred to the clinic for help from sources outside the home.)

Overprotection by a grandparent, especially a grandmother—maternal or paternal—living in the patient's home, is a frequent finding. Such cases are complicated, especially when the mother is still striving unsuccessfully to free herself from the daughter relationship and her marital adjustment finds the presence of the grandmother a constant stumbling block. When the grandmother successfully absorbs all parental authority, the child has a means of escaping parental modifications, yet displays a pattern of behavior that differs from pure maternal overprotective forms.

A fair number of persons may be found in whom maternal overprotection, though no longer present, existed in marked degree during infancy or until the advent of a second child. A striking example is afforded by an immature parental pair who were constantly at the beck and call of their first child, a daughter. They brought her

389

about for all the neighbors to admire, and then discarded her like a forgotten doll when the second child arrived. A typical intense jealousy and open hostility against the newcomer was the reason for referral. Sibling rivalry appears to be generally proportionate to the degree of maternal overprotection and the degree of threat at the time of the birth of the rival.

There are a number of mild and mixed forms of overprotection that require description. Early overprotection followed by rejection is an example. Theoretically, a frank rejection of a child may be followed by pure overprotection, though we have no cases to illustrate that sequence. A mother absorbed in a first child and indifferent to the second may, after a dangerous illness of the second child has necessitated much nursing care on her part, shift about in her reactions. Such responses are a form of guilt-overprotection. There are children, also, who experience temporary periods of overprotection, or alternating periods of overprotection and rejection, or mixtures of overprotection and severity. In this connection, those children also should be included who are seen by their mothers for brief periods of time during the day, yet, in the time available, receive strongly overprotective care. They are often children of professional women. The latter act as though they must make up for their hours of absence from the child through the intensity of their devotion in every minute of contact.

Mild maternal overprotection is presumably an attenuated form and very common. A quantitative distribution of overprotective manifestations would show, no doubt, a graduated progressive series. In the mild forms, however, many extraneous problems complicate evaluation and selection. Since we are dealing with mothers of various cultural backgrounds and of different economic and social groups, patterns of maternal behavior with children, correctly estimated as overprotective in one group, may in another group be typical phenomena. Breast-feeding over a period of 2 years, for example, may be a symptom of overprotection. On the other hand, it may be typical behavior in certain cultural groups.

The most frequent clinical type of maternal overprotection is found in the group in which the overprotection masks a strong rejection or is compensatory to it.

Intensification of maternal care initiated by conditions in the child of severe illness, accident, or deformity is a very common occurrence in family life. That mothers tend to favor the weaker, sicklier, and generally more dependent child is an honored lay observation. Some mothers describe the response to the child during a severe illness in terms of a distinct change of attitude as in the remark: "Until he had that sickness I did not realize what being a mother meant."

An example of maternal overprotection that varied with external factors is shown by Mrs. R. When her first child was 4 years old, her second died of pneumonia following a cold. After that event she became overprotective toward the surviving child, especially during his frequent colds. After the birth of a third child, her overprotection of the first diminished considerably.

Overprotection during infancy followed by rejection is well-illustrated in the case of a 6-year-old girl referred because of fighting, quarreling, and constant show-off behavior. Born of doting parents, constantly caressed and petted, kept at the breast 18 months, she was shown in triumph and spoiled by relatives and neighbors. During several illnesses the father and mother took turns walking the floor with her all night. The weaning process was a difficult one, starting with peppering the nipples and achieved finally by forced feeding.

At the age of 4 the patient's world collapsed, the central position usurped by a baby sister. Until the birth of the second child, the patient was cheerful and happy, though troublesome because of excessive demands for attention. After the arrival of the new baby, according to the mother she became "mean and nasty," and was rejected.

It will be apparent that the overprotection does not remain consistent throughout childhood. In the example cited, the complete shift in overprotection to the newcomer is evidence of the inconsistency of the maternal response to her first-born. The mother discards number one for number two with the ease of a primitive parent. There are a number of cases in which a mother, ignorant and emotionally immature, overindulges her infant, creates an excessive dependency on her, and when, as a result, the child becomes difficult, discards him. Such easy release does not occur in the so-called pure cases of overprotection. Numerous attempts by mothers to become emotionally free of the infant who grows up to overburden the family with tyrannical demands ordinarily end in failure. Maternal release from the infant becomes difficult after overprotection during the first 2 years. When a struggle for release by either mother or child from the bonds of the

391

powerful overprotective relationship becomes apparent, the overprotective features may be concealed.

The Characteristics of Maternal Overprotection

Maternal overprotection is synonymous with excessive maternal care of children. Its manifestations in the mother-child relationship have been grouped, according to the manner in which they occur, under four headings. Three of these concern maternal activity primarily and paraphrase the common observations "The mother is always there," "She still treats him like a baby," and "She will not let him grow up" or "She will not take any risk." These observations are classified as expressions of *excessive contact, infantilization,* and *prevention of independent behavior*. All the manifestations of overprotection as revealed by maternal activity are classifiable under these three headings, excepting activities that denote anxious behavior.

The fourth heeding of overprotection is *lack or excess of maternal control*. The former indicates a breakdown in the mother's ability to modify her child's behavior. In extreme form, the mother is subservient to the demands of her nursery despot who has retained full possession of the mother's attention and services, as in the first year of life. The latter indicates excessive maternal domination of the child.

When overprotection is revealed by all four criteria, the picture presented is well-portrayed by a mother who holds her child tightly with one hand and makes the gesture of pushing away the rest of the world with the other. Her energies are directed to preserving her infant as an infant for all times, preserving her baby from all harm and from contact with the rest of humanity. For her child she will fight hard, make every sacrifice, and aggressively prevent interference with her social monopoly. Her aggression, directed so strongly against the intruder, yields, however, before the child. Toward him she is submissive; her discipline falters when he becomes assertive in the latter half of infancy, and is gradually destroyed.

In one group of overprotection, the general picture is that of inadequately modified behavior in respect to infantile power over the mother. The infantile aggression is manifested in having one's way, in dominating every situation, in manipulating the scene in order to be the central figure, and in displaying temper when crossed. The overprotection may be described as a process in which infantile power, unmodified, expands into a monstrous growth that tends to subjugate the parents.

In the second group, the dependency phase of the infant's relationship with the mother is fostered through lack of development or overmodification of the dominating phase. In regard to infantile aggression, the overprotection in the second group is a process of constriction rather than expansion—a constriction in the growth of aggressive tendencies.

In their clinical manifestations of overprotection, mothers show a distinct difference in the two groups. Mothers of the dominating children are indulgent; mothers of the submissive children are dominating. The statement as it stands is merely a description implied by the meaning of the terms employed. For if a child is submissive to his mother, it is implied that he readily yields to her demands, that he keeps away from the company she forbids, that he goes to bed on time, and the like. She appears to be dominating the child, and the child is submissive to her. On the other hand, if a child goes to bed when he pleases or eats only what happens to suit his fancy, the implication is that his mother has been consistently indulgent.

The question remains: Is the type of maternal overprotection determined primarily by maternal attitude or by the type of response in her offspring? Before we can attempt an answer, we must study the significant phases of overprotection in detail as well as the backgrounds of the mother and child and their response to family life.

MATERNAL AND PATERNAL FACTORS

In studying the maternal factors, we must explore the influences exerted in every phase of the mother's life on the overprotective relationship. This leads to an inquiry of experiences related to the period immediately preceding the birth of her offspring, to her marital and social life, and to her childhood.

Factor 1: Prolonged Anticipation

Assuming a normal desire for children, all types of experience that thwart or threaten the possibility of pregnancy or its successful outcome are potent sources of increased maternal longing. Mothers

393

who suffer the trials of prolonged anticipation of the first-born, of long periods of relative sterility, or of spontaneous miscarriages or still-births are rendered obviously more apprehensive and protective in their attitude toward the offspring than if childbirth occurred without these circumstances.

A preliminary period of barren years is a different type of experience from a series of pregnancies that end in disaster. The feeling of hopelessness and impotence is greater in the former. A pregnancy that aborts raises a hope at least that another pregnancy will ensue and that it will go to term. The difference in maternal attitude resulting from a period of anticipation featured chiefly by waiting, contrasted with a period featured chiefly by disappointment, cannot be determined from our data. It would seem that the mothers who suffered a long period of sterility are especially concerned with that phase of overprotection that concerns risks to the life of the child.

So far we have assumed that a child was wanted and that a normal maternal need was magnified by a period of tantalizing waiting and disappointment. But suppose our reliance on the mother's statements as to frustration is false; or that, at least, an unconscious wish to be unencumbered by pregnancies or children was a motivating influence. There is supporting evidence for this viewpoint in our records. Two mothers postponed for a long time an operation recommended as a cure for their sterility. Another rode horseback, thereby endangering the pregnancy by a possible accident—which actually occurred.

Studies of maternal attitude by the method of psychoanalysis indicate that hostile feelings toward pregnancy and children are universal in our culture. Such feelings vary in a quantitative sense, like physical energy. A similar variation is found in the counteracting force of repression, enabling the individual to check the dangerous activity impelled by hostile feelings and also to conceal any recognition of them. It is possible that a mother, consciously yearning for a child but unconsciously hostile to her destiny as the impregnated female, might accept a period of sterility all too readily. In that sense, the reason given for postponing an operation designed to cure the sterility—fear of death, inconvenience, and the like—would be regarded as a rationalization and a concealment of the hostility to pregnancy. Indeed, as Groddeck asserts, the sterility itself would be explained on the same basis as a state psychically determined.

394

Reasoning along the same line, we can say that all maternal overprotection could be regarded as compensatory to unconscious hostility, and its quantitative variation simply an index of the strength of the compensatory device. So-called pure overprotection would be pure only in the sense that its manifestations are consistent in every phase of maternal care, whereas in compensatory or guilt overprotection inconsistencies or special emphasis on one phase of the mother-child relationship become apparent.

Differences in maternal feelings related to constitutional factors would be regarded then simply as increasing or diminishing the compensatory device. This consideration would be necessary since it is known that the same condition—for example, infidelity on the part of the husband—is followed by increased maternal protection in some women and by rejection of the child in others. The difference in reaction is then attributed to differences in makeup, the overprotective reaction being the reaction of maternal types.

The psychopathology of maternal overprotection resembles obsessional neurosis more than any other form of neurosis—in the compulsory quality of the behavior, the stubborn resistance to therapeutic modification, and the high degree of responsibility that characterizes the overprotecting mother. The similarity to "compulsion neurosis" is enhanced by the superego value of maternal attitudes. Being a "good mother" is an ego ideal of the woman and being, in any sense, a "not-so-good mother" is a loss of self-esteem. Thus motherliness is a demand on the superego. This resemblance also would lend support to the theory that maternal overprotection represents a type of neurosis in which, especially, processes of guilt result in exaggerated maternal care.

Before considering other possible neurotic elements in mother-child relationships, it is important to weigh the possibility of pure overprotection, pure not only in the consistency of the clinical symptoms, but also in the sense of an excess in maternal response not primarily determined by psychic conflict. Granting a normal maternal response to the helpless infant, one readily grants an increased response to an increased helplessness. That the sickly infant evokes more care and concern than the healthy one or that a previously healthy infant elicits through a sudden convulsive seizure increased maternal behavior requires no explanation in terms of neuroses. Numerous conditions act primarily as an aggregate of powerful stimuli

395

that evoke a correspondingly powerful maternal response. So also with various frustrations of pregnancy. They would especially increase the longing for a child in maternal women. When feelings of guilt are to be found in pure overprotection, as they are likely to be in any mother-child relationship, they may therefore be secondary factors, and not primary determinants, as in the impure cases. Otherwise we would be in the precarious position of maintaining that when a response in a human relationship is increased above normal, the increase is effected only through a neurotic mechanism.

Factor 2: Sexual Maladjustment

When husband and wife are sexually compatible and have social interests in common, they thereby set up a number of conditions that operate against a mother-child monopoly. The parents' own life as husband and wife withdraws certain time and energy from the parent-child relationship. A wife devoted to her husband cannot be exclusively a mother. In a more fundamental sense, the release of libido through satisfactory sexual relationship shunts off energy that must otherwise flow in other directions—for example, in the direction of maternity. The child must bear the brunt of the unsatisfied love life of the mother. One might theoretically infer that a woman sexually well-adjusted could not become overprotective to an extreme degree. Certainly she would not make the relationship to the child her exclusive social life.

There is certainly definite evidence that the sex difficulties of these mothers have, at least, reinforced the overprotective relationship. In one case it was clear to the mother that her overprotective attitude became intensified after learning of her husband's infidelity. From her own point of view she had more love to give and also, having lost her husband, wanted to make sure she would never lose the children. Such instances are common enough, but not sufficient to explain the original overprotective attitude, for it appears clear from our studies that the difficulty in the sexual adjustments acts chiefly as a strengthening factor rather than a causal one. As will be seen later, a large number of mothers in this group also curtailed their general social activity after the coming of the child. Most have difficulties in sexual life, varying from passive adaptation without pleasure to various methods of preventing sexual activity.

Lewenberg compared forty-five overprotecting mothers with forty-five nonoverprotecting mothers, the cases taken at random from the files [7]. Her contrast group showed 46 percent sexual maladjustment as compared with 87 percent of the overprotecting group. In a study of 35 rejecting mothers Figge found sexual incompatibility in 66 percent [3].

Where difficulties prevent outlets of energy in one direction, a compensatory flow in another is readily understood. This time-honored idea has been utilized to explain the exaggerated mother love of widows, of mothers of only children, of mothers who, for whatever reason, have only their children to look after. It does not explain why, under the circumstances given, some mothers reject their children, or continue, even intensify, a previous rejection. The explanation of simple compensatory increase in mother love, through blocking other channels of expression, is used typically in cases where maternal love was previously in evidence.

Why sexual maladjustment occurs so frequently in this group of overprotecting mothers is a problem difficult to solve without psychoanalytic data. *At this point it may be said that the overprotecting mothers were found to be aggressive women, as was consistent with their strong maternal behavior.*

Factor 3: Curtailment of Social Activity

Consistent with our findings on sexual incompatibility, there is little social life in common among the parents of the overprotected children. The rate of social disharmony or of curtailment of mutual social activity seems high. This finding is not to be explained by a generally impoverished social life due to economic or cultural factors, since the majority of mothers were socially active before marriage. Nor is it to be explained by infidelities or extramarital social activity of the fathers, since they represent on the whole a faithful and stable group of men. The explanation is not to be found entirely in the sexual incompatibility, for it is a common observation that many husbands and wives have an active social life together in spite of sexual disharmony.

There is clearly a difference in the dynamics of protecting the child against extramaternal experiences when this activity represents an outgrowth of the original absorption in the infant, and when it represents an extension of a generally suspicious attitude manifested long before marriage. Overprotection of the latter type shows, especially, evidence of "excessive contact" and "prevention of independent behavior," since these data are consistent with social isolation. Theoretically, in contrast with mothers who are truly excessively maternal (pure overprotection), there should be a paucity of data on infantilization because of basic mistrustfulness. Cases of pure overprotection do also involve more than the usual amount of "guarding against the stranger," but such an attitude is a derived and not a primary phenomenon.

Factor 4: Affect Hunger

The childhood experience of these mothers reveals a number of glaring accounts of privation of parental affection and of childhood play. Lack of maternal love featured the lives of most of these mothers. Foley studied this problem by applying the factors "no affection" and "early responsibility" to three groups of mothers—overprotecting, rejecting, and neither [4]. After this process a much larger contrast was discernible between the overprotecting and the neutral group, the former showing 68 percent, the latter 15 percent, of the criteria "no affection" and "responsibility."

The impoverishment in the child of all the positive feelings implicit in parental love—recognition, security, affection, sympathy, and the like—has been called *affect hunger*. The term was derived from clinical studies in which various symptoms demonstrating exaggerated need of love were traceable to early love privations. The assumption that love is a basic need of the child, a need unfulfilled by care and protection alone, can be readily utilized as an aid in explaining an overprotective relationship. For, assuming an insatiable hunger for love, based on early privations, its gratification through maternity would engender a relationship of the closest degree.

The insolubility of affect hunger in marriage could be explained in two ways. In one, the husband may be regarded as unable, through a mature love, to satisfy a requirement made possible only in maternity, namely, the establishment through the child of a new childhood for the mother, free from all early privation.

The second explanation is in the high degree of sexual and social incompatibility in the marriages of the overprotecting mothers. As a solution of affect hunger, the marital relationship failed in the large majority of these cases, and hence offered no offsetting influence to the exaggerated maternal behavior.

We are left with the problem of these difficult marriages. It is easy to understand how, when a maternal overprotective relationship is established, a bad marriage will help to reinforce it. But it still remains obscure why there is such a high degree of incompatibility in the marriages of this group.

Factor 5: Household Cares and Responsibilities Early in Mother's Childhood

These mothers represent predominantly responsible, stable, aggressive women. To a number of them, other members of the family, as well as friends, come for help and advice.

The term *responsible* in this connection is attested by helping, beyond ordinary chores, with the housework and care of siblings in childhood; by helping to support the family through steady employment before marriage; by self-maintenance through steady employment, saving money for education, and other evidence of stable, competent, reliable care or support. There is little difficulty in determining the responsibility of the group in the manner indicated, since it occurs in high degree. "Household cares early in childhood" amounts to a serious curtailment of childhood play.

A feature of the responsibility described, of special interest in terms of the overprotecting behavior to follow in motherhood, is its aggressive or active quality. For the responsible attitude determined by the measure of stability in work is not merely the stability of acquiescence, of obedience. It appears to be an active helping-out, a responsible attitude in a truly maternal sense.

The active or aggressive feature of responsible behavior may be regarded as distinctly maternal, representing the active helping-out on the mother's part in the mother-child relationship. The majority of these mothers play a maternal role in the sense of an aggressive, responsible role from childhood. Although there is no direct evidence linking maternal behavior with spontaneous mothering of children during childhood, the conclusion seems warranted that the overprotecting mothers show, in the main, strongly maternal behavior from an early age.

Factor 6: Thwarted Ambitions in the Mother

One of the effects of educational privation in the parent is seen in strong ambitions for the education of the child. Fulfillment through the child of the parent's thwarted ambition is easily comprehended and directly stated by the parents themselves—to "make up" to the child what they themselves were denied. One readily comprehends the possibilities in this regard of an increased valuation of the child, through increased identification with it. Other features of the overprotective relationship are in themselves sufficient to explain strong ambitions for the child, as the esteemed love object and as a protective measure in the struggle for existence. The thwarted ambitions of the parents represent an additional factor.

The attempt to experience through the child the satisfactions of demands necessitated by an experience of love hunger would theoretically be enhanced by any other privation; hence the significance of a thwarted career would, under such circumstances, be of much greater import than if love hunger were absent.

Affect hunger and strong maternal tendencies are basic findings in the life histories of the overprotecting mothers. Of the two findings, the latter occurs in the group with greater frequency, and in the absence of the former. Hence it is not necessarily its derivative. Certain cases of affect hunger reveal a marked overvaluation and attachment to a love object. The love object may be understood in terms of the original hunger for maternal love, protection, and support. The excessive demands, so typical of affect hunger cases, are seen in the light of the child's need of contact and care. Variations in the patterns of demands can be understood in terms of varying stresses in the familiar criteria of maternal care; in one case for constant proximity and caresses (contact), in another for money and indulgence (care and overindulgence), in another for constant reassurance (protection against loss of love), and so forth.

Presumably the concept of affect hunger could be employed to explain both the excessive need of love and the aggression of the overprotecting mothers, since the experience of affect hunger has been found in relation with a high degree of aggressive behavior. Affect hunger occurs also in rejecting mothers, however, explained in such instances as an attempt on the part of the mother to play toward the husband the role of demanding child, in competition with her own children. Since the overprotecting mothers in one group we studied showed maternal tendencies in childhood, an assumption was made that the influence of affect hunger in the direction of overprotection was effective only in definitely maternal women.

400

Factor 7: Maternal Aggressiveness

Aggressive behavior is part and parcel of maternal behavior. The aggression in relation to the infant is involved in various dominating, protecting, and training activities.

The various forms of maternal behavior may be described in terms of protecting and giving. Apparently the giving function has often been used as synonymous with the word *maternal,* including activities in which aggressive behavior appears indirectly as in nursing, body care, and the like. Stress on the giving function of maternal behavior involves also the idea of sacrificing one's interests on behalf of the child, of submitting to its needs. It has given rise to theories of feminine passivity and masochism. There has been a tendency to regard maternity in the light of femininity, and hence to dwell on those aspects of maternity consistent with that psychology. The aggressive phase has thus come to be regarded as evidence of masculinity. Theories of femininity, emphasizing especially passive, receptive behavior in a woman, in keeping with her role in overt sex activity, have embraced all her functions, and hence have confused feminine and maternal behavior.

Aggressive behavior, manifested in its protecting phase, is an integral part of the maternal pattern. It is distinctly maternal.

In the cases of pure overprotection there is consistent exaggeration of both the giving and the protecting function. DeGroot's observation that highly maternal women are often sexually maladjusted[2] is consistent with our findings [2]. She attributes the difference, however, to their high degree of masculinity. She states that the woman achieves active love, and satisfies her masculinity in relation to her child, in nourishing it and caring for it, later educating it. This statement is tantamount to making maternal behavior synonymous with masculinity.

There is evidently a relationship between aggressive and maternal behavior. DeGroot's observation that very feminine women are usually poor mothers appears logical in view of the fact that hardly one of the overprotecting mothers can be so described. Further, it

[2] *Editors' note:* "Seeking refuge from their loveless marriages, these [frigid] women find it vicariously in an ecstatic devotion to their children whom they idolize. Hence the consequence of frigidity may be exaggerated devotion or hatred . . . very severe at one time, they change . . . and spoil their children by pathological tenderness" [8].

appears consistent with the observation that there may be a clash between maternal and sexual drives; a high degree of maternity developing at the expense of femininity [2].

Although the sharp cleavage between sexual and maternal behavior is not observed in human beings, there is evidence in women of sexual and maternal cycles, as of menstrual cycles, according to the investigations of Benedek [1].

The overprotective mothers manifested from childhood aggressive and helping tendencies, both characteristic of maternal behavior; the question now arises as to its biologic nature. There are a number of animal studies of pseudopregnancy and prolactin-induced behavior in which maternal activity is revealed without an external stimulus. This would seem to indicate a drive impelled exclusively by internal stimuli and would suggest that maternal behavior has a powerfully endogenous nature that can function without the presence of the object which normally stimulates it into activity. The integral components are therefore biologic and not psychogenic. Its aggressive features may be regarded as a protective framework for the insurance of suckling and rearing during infancy, just as the aggressive features in the sexual behavior of males may be regarded as an insurance of the insemination of the female.

There are also natural variations in the strength of the component maternal drives both in animal and human mothers. Variations in maternal behavior of girls, in which some become "neighborhood mothers," preferring the care of a baby to any other pursuit, are consistent with the finding of such constitutional variations in animals. In other words, some women may be more naturally maternal than others and manifest such differences at an early age.

The attempt to show that aggressive behavior is part and parcel of maternal behavior, and that variations in this regard may indicate natural differences in maternal makeup, does not preclude the influence of social and psychic factors. There is a varying degree of plasticity in the different components of maternal behavior.

The expression of aggression in maternal behavior, in which the giving function, its very core, is diminished or even absent, is seen in various forms. Of these the following may be differentiated: (1) the dominating mother who gives no love but whose dominating tendencies embrace every social relationship; (2) the dominating mother

402

who utilizes only her children, or a particular child, as an object of domination, though without love—disguised often as conscientious motherhood: (3) the thwarting or denying mother, whose aggression appears in the form of oppositional tactics, as a projected asceticism; (4) the spiteful mother, jealous of her children for having more opportunities or pleasure than she had in childhood, jealous of a daughter because of looks, or charm, or intelligence, jealous of a son because of his sex; (5) the brutal or sadistic mother who utilizes every opportunity to punish, deride, or embarrass her offspring.

These are various types of rejecting mothers who must utilize the children as outlets for inner emotional difficulties. The dynamic mechanisms consist of numerous restorations of the mother's unsolved childhood experiences or of old hostilities to cruel or denying parents; intense jealousies of brother or sister; the experience of being thrust aside or belittled in social life by more attractive or intelligent children, inside or outside the family; various masculine drives and sexual complexes.

The same type of unconscious hostilities may, however, be expressed in exaggerated love and protection. One may conjecture that the direction is determined by the relative intensity of the maternal drive. Given the same quantum of unconscious hostility, the direction toward hostility or love will be determined by the weakness or strength of the maternal tendency. Thus, instances of maternal oversolicitude based on unconscious hostility to the child may represent an intensification of a true mother love, rather than its entire structure.

Factor 8: Breast-feeding

In 1905, Giard proposed the interesting theory that among mammals lactation is the source of maternal love, a source of symbiosis that unites mother and child [6]. He regarded the sucking child as a source of pleasure to the mother, through releasing tension in her breasts. The feeling for the child would thus be based on a series of positive conditioning experiences through pleasurable release of tension.

Although observations and experiments disproved lactation as a source of maternal love, they do not diminish the value of Giard's theory when utilized as a powerful reinforcement of the mother-child "symbiosis." In the studies of long and short breast-feeding periods, the proportion of overprotecting attitudes was found significantly correlated with the former. It was not possible, however, to factor out the stimulus value of the lactation experience in itself.[3]

*Factor 9: Unresolved Masculine Drives
in the Mother*

Psychoanalysis regards maternity primarily as a derivative of the sexual instinct, and the child, as love object, a substitute for a longed-for penis. The girl's infantile sexuality, at first, like the boy's, directed to the mother, is thrown into a state of turmoil when first awareness of the penis occurs. In the usual case the girl develops penis envy, considers herself castrated and, in a state of hostility to the mother, for which the usual denials of love and gratification have prepared her, turns to the father, hoping to derive a penis from him. This transformation also occurs in her play with dolls. At first they represent children, merely objects upon which she releases activities exercised on her by the mother. Later, when the desire for a penis begins, the doll represents a child by the father. "The feminine situation is only established when the wish for a penis is replaced by the wish for a child." Through a son alone the mother attains "undiluted satisfaction" and "the most complete relationship between human beings," since through him she is able to transfer all her suppressed ambitions and derive "the satisfaction of all that has remained of her masculinity complex" [5].

The maternal drives, according to Freud, thereby have a dual basis: one purely biologic, its source in sexual hormones; the other purely psychologic, its source in the ideas of the child [5]. These are derived by observing and contrasting differences in genitalia and concluding that they have been brought about by castration. The girl's previously formed hostilities to the mother are then intensified, since the mother is regarded as the responsible agent of the castration, and, in pursuit of the illusory penis, she turns her love to the father.

Freud's theory of maternal behavior is in marked contrast with his theory of sexual behavior. For the latter his orientation as to its origin is simply biologic and rests on the discovery of sexuality in the infant on the proof that sex life does not arise full-blown in pu-

---

[3] *Editors' note:* Human motherliness is more complex than the "prolactin" effect alone. Many motherly women never lactate.

berty but starts practically with life itself. He sees no evidence, however, of maternal behavior in the little girl as an early expression of the mature maternal instinct. Though he uses observations of marked activity in the sex life of certain female animals to question the naive use of the word *passivity* as a synonym for femininity, he employs none of the observations of maternal behavior of animals on behalf of his theory of maternal function in human beings. Otherwise he would not propose a theory that by inference would limit so basic a drive as the maternal to human society alone, since its complex psychic origin could not be ascribed to animals.

Though unnecessary in explaining the origin of maternal love, the theory of penis envy is useful in explaining its intensification and, also, the maternal preference for males. Favoring the boy, especially the first-born son, is a common observation in our culture. A high degree of aggression in the female, however consistent with a high degree of maternal behavior, is blocked in numerous other ways; hence the utilization of the son as a means, through identification, of satisfying unfulfilled ambitions and aggressions, is very comprehensible. The universality, in our culture, of penis envy in females is a generalization not yet established. However, it must be a very frequent phenomenon—and in normal children.

The gratification of a strong maternal drive may be enhanced through a male child by various psychic experiences. The theory of penis envy helps to explain reinforcing factors in maternal overprotection in regard to the marked predominance of male children and of aggressive mothers in that group. That a high degree of aggression in females is in itself prognostic of overprotection is not to be inferred. Rejecting mothers, whether of sons or daughters, are also more likely to be aggressive than other mothers. It may be that aggressive women are more likely than others to be either overprotecting or rejecting of children. The direction would then be determined by the strength of the maternal drive. The point is not proved, but it is consistent with the observation recorded that overprotecting mothers show constant maternal behavior from childhood.

Factor 10: The Peripheral Father

The fathers of the overprotected children may be generally characterized as submissive, stable husbands and providers who play little or no authoritative role in the life of the child. They offer little counteracting influence to the overprotection after their several attempts to discipline the child have been firmly resented by the mother. The discipline of the child is left entirely to the mother. In a few instances, fathers aid the overprotection by indulging or infantilizing, or interfere with the mother's attempt to discipline. There was not one instance of a dominating father in the group studied.

The fathers of overprotected children have to deal with mothers who monopolize the child. Their rather ready adjustment to that situation is not difficult to understand, in view of our typical cultural patterns of family life. These fathers appear, however, readily adaptable to such complete surrender of the paternal role by virtue of their generally submissive traits.

The important influence of the father, in his authoritative role and as a counteracting agent to maternal infantilization, indulgence, and overprotection, in its strict sense, is thus either nullified or used merely to strengthen the overprotection.

To these facts must be added the derogatory attitude of the child toward the father, which is in some instances fostered by the mother, thereby reducing the paternal influence to its lowest degree.

An analysis of the background of the fathers yields the information that they are in general the favorite children and obedient sons of dominating mothers, and sometimes the obedient sons of dominating fathers as well. There is rarely any instance of aggressive behavior.

In view of the main trends revealed in their personalities, their selection of dominating women and of maternal women appears a logical and determined choice. With few exceptions, the fathers are also stable and responsible workers. In contrast with their responsible, aggressive wives they may be described as responsible and submissive. That they were selected as husbands appears, therefore, equally consistent, especially when we add the factor of affect hunger, so frequent in the history of the overprotecting mothers—a factor that would determine selectivity in favor of kindness, sympathy, and devotion. If a strong maternal drive is assumed in the mothers of the group and certain freedom in range of choice, the selection of men of a dependent type of personality becomes the more likely. Certainly the factors that favor the development of aggressive, maternal, love-hungry women, and of submissive, responsible men would, at the same time, favor their selection of each other.

Factor 11: Interfering Grandparents

The usual patterns of interfering grandparents are found also in the families of the overprotecting mothers: the indulgent grandparent, relieved of the responsibilities of parenthood, who enjoys the process of spoiling a grandchild; the grandmother, jealous of her daughter-in-law, who regards her son's child as her own; the grandmother who still maintains a maternal hold on her married daughter and grandchild. To the overprotecting factors there are added the interferences of grandparents, especially the maternal grandparent, who contact the child frequently, shower him with gifts, augment the maternal indulgence by resenting any corrective measures, and sabotage the discipline of the parents.

A THEORY OF MATERNAL OVERPROTECTION

The theory that emerges in this chapter is simply that "pure" maternal overprotection occurs in naturally maternal women whose behavior as mothers has been intensified by the operation of certain psychic and cultural forces. By true overprotection is meant exaggerated maternal love, that is, overprotection which is not determined primarily by neurosis. By "naturally maternal" is meant a strong maternal drive. Evidence for this feature lies in manifestations of behavior consistent, throughout the lives of most of these women, with both the giving and protecting phases of maternal function. Evidence of specific maternal behavior in childhood and proof of a constitutionally maternal type are lacking.

The psychic forces in operation are represented by such powerful agents as affect hunger, experience of relative sterility, or their equivalents in the "period of anticipation"; life-threatening illnesses in the life of the child; or marital sexual incompatibility. The sociocultural forces are represented chiefly by the experience of meeting harsh realities too early in life, through deaths of parents, or poverty, or both, necessitating the substitution of work for childhood play, and of premature responsibility. The attitude toward such experiences is based, however, by assumption, on a strong maternal tendency. Other factors in our culture that play into the hands of the potentially overprotecting mother are represented by the high degree of freedom given to mothers in influencing the life of the child and in the superior role

407

given to the male. In regard to preference for the male child, the psychic influence of penis envy was assumed to be a primary determining factor.

Since our theory represents in the main the utilization of psychic forces by a constitutionally maternal personality, its general application to the field of psychosomatics should be noted. It may be true that the maternal drive, a drive so basic to survival, has a higher degree of resemblance in man and animals than does the sex drive. Certainly there is a remarkably close resemblance of the criteria of maternal care used in our study in all mammalian behavior. The sexual life of man may be determined by psychic and cultural influence to a much higher degree than the maternal life. If experiments on human beings show decisive effect of prolactin on maternal attitude—that is, go beyond a physiologic effect, as the induction of lactation, into a psychologic effect, as in animals—the primary hormonal determination of maternal behavior will be proved. Even if this occurs, it will not follow necessarily that the same rule applies to all other human drives.

CASE 1.   Dominating-type mother
Excessive contact: Mother of this 10-year-old boy slept with him until he was 6 years old. During the entire 5 years, mother and patient lived alone with practically no other contacts after the father deserted during his wife's pregnancy.

Prolongation of infantile care: Patient was breast-fed to age 3, with mother's excuse, "You know he was all I had."

Prevention of independent behavior: Mother changed patient to another school because the walk there was a little shorter. Until age 8 he was never allowed to play with other children because they were rough. Now allowed to play with boys in front of the father's store. Mother hired an older boy to accompany patient to school because he complained that the boys molested him.

Maternal control: Anxious, obedient child. Accepts mother's domination. Accepts mother's infantile methods of discipline without protest. Mother's "slightest disapproval" is very effective in making him mind. Wants to do exactly what mother does, helping her with the housework. Overresponsive to her approval or disapproval.

CASE 2.   Indulgent-type mother
Excessive contact: Mother frequently kissed and fondled this 12-year-old boy. Practically never let him alone during infancy. Kept him away from all but a few adults because she was afraid of infection. Patient still sleeps with mother when father is out of town (continued to age 13).

408

Prolongation of infantile care: Patient was breast-fed 12 months. Mother still waits on him, gets water for him, butters his bread, etc.

Prevention of independent behavior: Mother has prevented patient from bicycling, making his own friends, and has generally prevented the development of responsibility.

Maternal control: Patient is disrespectful and impudent to parents. Constantly demands mother's service. Had a temper tantrum at age 12 because she did not butter his bread for him. Resents giving up his chair for mother. Leaves the table and refuses to eat when he does not get the biggest serving.

Bibliography

1. Benedek, T., and Rubenstein, B. B. Ovarian activity and psychodynamic processes: Ovulative phase. *Psychosom. Med.* 1:245–270, 1939.
2. DeGroot, J. L. Problems of femininity. *Psychoanal. Quart.* 2:489–518, 1933.
3. Figge, M. A. Quoted in D. M. Levy, *Maternal Overprotection.* New York: Columbia University Press, 1943.
4. Foley, P. Quoted in D. M. Levy, *Maternal Overprotection.* New York: Norton, 1966.
5. Freud, S. *New Introductory Lectures on Psychoanalysis.* New York: Norton, 1933. Pp. 175, 182.
6. Giard, A. Les origines de l'amour maternel. *Bull. Inst. Gén. Psychol.* 5:3–32, 1905.
7. Lewenberg, M. P. *A Study of the Marital Relationships of Overprotecting and Non-overprotecting Mothers* (1932). Cited by D. M. Levy. In D. M. Levy, *Maternal Overprotection.* New York: Norton, 1966.
8. Stekel, W. Frigidity in Mothers. In V. Calverton and S. D. Schmalhausen (Eds.), *The New Generation.* New York: Macaulay, 1930.

20

The Concept of
Maternal Perplexity

William Goldfarb
Lillian Sibulkin
Marjorie L. Behrens
Hedwig Jahoda

Parental perplexity is a mental attitude of exaggerated and thus "deviant" bewilderment in the parent-child relationship. In this chapter we will consider the phenomenon from the point of view of the mother mainly. She acts out and feels doubtful, indecisive, and caught in a quandary. She vacillates or, in a state of inner confusion, totally suspends her responses to the child. Of course, perplexity occurs to some degree in any parent. Thus, there is the average uncertainty of any individual learning a new task. This is seen commonly in the young mother with her first-born, or with new counselors at the residential center. Hilde Bruch and others have pointed to a culturally determined uncertainty among middle-class parents today [1]. Presumably these parents have been robbed of their spontaneity because they have been intimidated by the flood of professional warnings and enjoinders given them. The parent who is anything but totally permissive is made to suffer pangs of guilt. Finally, there is the universal uncertainty of a parent faced with any kind of illness or disability in his child.

We have applied the term *parental perplexity* to a special type of parental response. We have observed that parental perplexity is especially characteristic of parents of schizophrenic children under our observation. With these parents, the response to ordinary child-rearing experiences is far beyond normal expectations. Further, the parents possess an underlying psychodynamic core which predisposes them to this extreme behavior. When observed, parental perplexity in the parents of our schizophrenic children combines several elements:

1. Outwardly, a striking lack of organized parental activity. The parents are outstandingly passive and uncertain. They do not stand out from the environment and are hollowly bland.

2. A lack of parental spontaneity, and a lack of immediate natural awareness of the child's needs. The parent performs mechanically the parental tasks without ability to empathize with the child.

3. When pressed by the bizarreness or destructive nature of the child's symptoms, the parent gives overt signs of bewilderment. Often these are verbalized as "I don't know what to do," or "Tell me what to do."

4. The child reacts as though there were no controls, either outer or inner. One sees perseverative, uncontrolled aimlessness, confusion, and uncontained and enduring emergency responses of fear and rage.

CLINICAL ILLUSTRATIONS

The nature of parental perplexity in its maternal expression is illustrated in the following observations made of Tommy T., age 6.

Case 1. On a visiting day at the Henry Ittleson Center, the psychologist's attention was arrested by this scene: Tommy was under his mother's skirts. He had dropped his trousers and was masturbating. In addition, he was poking at Mrs. T.'s genitals. She stood frozen and unmoving, with tears in her eyes. Pleading, she asked the psychologist: "What shall I do?"

The following observations of Tommy were made during an actual home visit.

It was planned that the observer would dine with the family. Tommy ran down the stairs, walked in and out of the living room several times, and then went to the kitchen. The observer accompanied Tommy to the kitchen where he saw the boy take a handful of Jello out of a bowl as he passed by, pushing some of it into his mouth and dropping the rest on the floor as he left the room. There was no intervention by the parents. The boy then opened the back door, and Mrs. T. said to the observer that Tommy wanted to go out. It had snowed the night before, and Mrs. T. explained to Tommy that he had to put his coat and boots on. Mr. T. brought Tommy's clothes and urged him to put his coat on, but Tommy ignored him, going directly to the car outside, with the father running after him. When Tommy came back with his father, he walked into the kitchen, picked up a slice of fish from a plate, stuffed it in his mouth, and dropped the rest on the floor. Mrs. T. immediately picked up the fish from the floor. Mr. T. took Tommy's outer clothes off, but as soon as they had been removed, Tommy made for the front door and went out. Both parents chased after him again with his clothes. A few minutes later Tommy ran back into the house with his father following. Mr. T. wanted to take Tommy's jacket off, but the boy would not let him. Instead, he walked around the kitchen and dining room, taking food from the plates and dropping it on the floor. Mrs. T. said in a reasonable fashion that he was hungry and prepared a plate of food for him. Tommy was out of the house again with Mr. T. after him. When Tommy came back, Mrs. T. said to him she understood he was hungry, and she urged him to sit at the table. He sat there for a few minutes, ate from a plate, dropped food on the floor, got up, walked around the table, took food from the other plates on the table, pushed the food into his mouth, and dropped the rest on the table or on the floor. This occurred repeatedly during the next hour. Mrs. T. scolded Tommy in a calm, sweet voice and explained each time that his plate was at the table, that the food was for everyone, not just for him, but he just ignored her. When he put his hand on the wine decanter, his father offered him some, but he ignored him. Then he ran out of the house and Mrs. T. said "Go after him, he is not properly dressed." Her husband quickly did what she asked.

We have supplied two discrete events that typify every moment of interaction between Tommy and his parents. In his random explorations, Tommy is faced with an environment that is totally amorphous and unorganized. His experience is ambiguous and unstructured. At no point do the parents offer direction or control in a spontaneous and assertive way. They "run after" the child, so to speak, as he moves about aimlessly. They do not intervene to break up, or to control, the boundless fluidity of his behavior. The mother is dominant in the situation and requires that the father and the other children submissively meet her unorganized pattern of behavior with the child. Mr. T. merely perpetuates the ambiguity of Tommy's human environment. The family tone, therefore, is set primarily by the mother. Similarly, the aberrant family setting for Tommy reflects a deviation in the execution of maternal function. The parents show a persistent, exhausting concentration on, and for, Tommy. Mrs. T. even has the magical belief that she has a special capacity to communicate with him and to understand his needs. In actual fact, she seems inadequate in achieving genuine empathy with the child. She does not seem to know what he needs at the moment he needs it. For example, she offers him an abundance of food with the remark, "I can tell he is hungry." The food she encourages him to eat immediately slips to the floor from his loose mouth. Mrs. T.'s behavior is like that of a mother who mechanically plays with her baby in accord with a rule for maternal behavior at a time when he needs to be relieved of his wet, chafing diaper. The unusual nature of Mrs. T.'s relationship to her son is most dramatically seen when he is destructive, or aggressive, or involved in acts that challenge the average individual's characteristic reaction formations such as indiscriminate soiling, masturbation, fingering his anus, or smearing his food. The usual response of his mother is a persistent, hollow, sweet smile or total bewilderment.

In brief here are some salient facts in Tommy's history, and the psychodynamic conclusions drawn from our total contact with the family. Tommy was referred to the Center at age 6 by a child guidance clinic to which Mrs. T. had originally gone. Mrs. T. sought help because she found it difficult to comprehend or relate to Tommy. The onset of the illness was put at 3½ years. Up to then he was presumably bright and well-developed, although continued contact with the family revealed that for some time before this Tommy had also been withdrawn and disturbing. Precipitating circumstances included a very tense household in which Mrs. T. felt criticized by her mother-in-law. In a state of desperation and temper, Mrs. T. gave up Tommy entirely to the care of his paternal grandmother.

The grandmother was constantly correcting, disciplining, and disapproving of Tommy. After three days, the boy became extremely hyperactive and cried incessantly. He seemed frightened of airplane noises. He wanted only to be in his mother's lap. He stopped speaking and felt her eyes and ears with his hands. At the time of referral, he had no speech at all, was hyperactive, demanded his mother's attention, and had temper tantrums if she gave any attention to a younger baby. He was quick and agile. In a few moments he would upset everything in the house, pulling out drawers, throwing things around the rooms. He needed constant supervision. There was an extreme preoccupation with cars and a persistent effort to get into unlocked cars. He could not be permitted outdoors alone. He frequently covered his ears with his hands. He never had a full meal at any time, but would eat frequently during the day. He spilled food over himself and the house.

Tommy was unwanted and unplanned for, but the mother insists she was pleased with him after his birth. He weighed 7 pounds at birth. Mrs. T. describes him as a helpless baby who lay in the crib with his eyes closed. She contrasted him with her youngest baby who "opened her eyes to see the world." Mr. T. was himself hospitalized at this time for an arthritic condition and was invalided for a year. For the week following their return from the hospital, Mrs. T. cared for her husband while Tommy was cared for by a nurse. Mrs. T. recalls her irritation because she was not strong enough to care for both. According to Mrs. T., her husband "did not open his heart up to Tommy." He would not respond to the baby when he was put in his lap. When Tommy came home he could not urinate easily, cried, and was tense. Mrs. T. recalls also that he had colic as a baby. Tommy was given a bottle every hour or two because it was felt that he could drink only a little at a time. He frequently vomited the milk. Mrs. T. said she was always patient and spent much of her time feeding him. Tommy was able to take normal amounts of food at about 6 months of age. At 3 years he fed himself and "ate like a little gentleman." He was bowel-trained at 9 months and stopped wetting early, although the exact age was unknown. He lost control of his sphincters with the onset of his acute illness at the age of 3½. He walked at 1 year and talked before he walked. At 3 years of age he spoke in full sentences and was completely comprehensible. As noted, there was a rapid loss of speech function at 3½ years. Mrs. T. recalls that Tommy was always "weakish" and easily frightened, inclined to be withdrawn, but was also loving and affectionate. With the onset of schizophrenia at age 3½, he masturbated openly. Tommy had always been shy with children but at 3½ was openly fearful in their presence.

Mrs. T. was born in Europe and was the oldest of ten children. She describes her father as a successful, gregarious businessman who liked to have company around and who was inclined to pay more attention to company than to his children. Mrs. T.'s mother was distant and unaffectionate. As a child, Mrs. T. was compliant and "so

415

sensitive and gentle that I always fainted." Although Jewish, she was sent to a convent to learn handwork and how to become a lady. In her words, she learned a "genial acceptance of responsibilities." She was given and accepted maternal responsibilities at a young age. When 12 years old, she recalls intervening, in adult fashion, in a physical struggle between her father and one of his employees.

She is an intelligent, articulate individual who smiles in a tense, rigid, persistent fashion. She feels herself to be a very strong person. She expresses great expectations and high ideals. She feels people should accept things stoically. She sometimes feels "impotent and helpless," but is annoyed that she is not stronger. "I steel myself when there is trouble; then I have no feelings at all. I stiffen and straighten out." She must always be serving others, and sees herself as the all-giving mother. She is deeply religious. There is a dissociated quality in her magical omnipotent feelings of closeness to God. She has great difficulty in admitting weakness. She talks of Tommy as a psychologist would, and has given very thorough written descriptions of his behavior. Her attitude is one of resigned willingness to perform her special function with Tommy in a belief that she alone can bring him out of his illness.

Mr. T. is less well-known to us. He has always been the passive parent. He acknowledges all his wife's values and meets her demands at home. He is a very intelligent person and successful in his teaching job. He seems depressed, cries when he speaks of his father's death, and is very anxious about the possibility of his mother dying.

We now have had fairly intensive contact with the family for over a year. We have been interested particularly in the psychodynamics of Mrs. T.'s performance as a mother. She seemed to have had very little in the way of direct emotional response from her mother. She was required to grow up precociously and act as a parent both to her own parents and to her other siblings. From the beginning, however, she complied, repressed her own frustrated wishes and her rage at nongratification of her own childhood needs. Instead she was always sweet and gentle, stoical, ever ready to take care of everyone else. All through her life, she has denied her own spontaneous wishes and her rage at frustration of these wishes. Instead, there has been a compensatory need to believe in her own overpowering gift to mother and to care for others. Nevertheless, she possesses an unusual amount of rage and an unconscious belief in her omnipotence and her potentially destructive powers. There is a consequent denial of her rage, with resultant inability to be spontaneous, and an outer facade of smiling detached tolerance, combined with the air of frozen bewilderment.

DISCUSSION

There is a quality of specificity to the perplexity reaction, in that the parents show varying degrees of perplexity response to the different siblings. Parental perplexity is most extreme with the schizophrenic child.

In its immediate impact on the schizophrenic child, the atmosphere of the families studied appears to be mother-dominated. Often, as in the T. family, the father and siblings become extensions of the mother and elaborate her reaction pattern with the disturbed child. In other families, the father's relationship to the mother acts to exaggerate her perplexity with the child. In others, the father is unable to counteract the impact of the mother.

We have been able to study the psychodynamic structure of the mothers best of all. The overt picture of the mother is that of stiff, wooden passivity, an absence of decisive, organized response, a lack of spontaneity, and an awkwardness in anticipating the child's needs. The mother is aware of vague confusion and bewilderment. She feels entangled and paralyzed. Underlying the bewilderment there appears to be an immense reservoir of repressed rage toward the schizophrenic child. Sometimes this rage emerges explosively for brief intervals. More usually it is diverted retroflexly into a state of clinical depression. Equally important is the mother's unconscious wishful image of her omnipotent magical power. Murderous rage is thus combined with an unconscious belief in her catastrophically destructive powers. Any move toward the child is potentially capable of destroying him. Incidentally, persistent fear of the child's death is extremely common in this group. The mother inhibits her rage and becomes blocked in the execution of her mothering role. We have sought to explore clinically the basis for the mother's unconscious rage toward her schizophrenic child and her continued fantasy of personal omnipotence. Uniformly, the mothers themselves seemed to have had an early infantile experience of affective deprivation at the hands of their own mothers. Frustration occurred at the oral-nutritional level, at which stage normal infants usually achieve magical gratification by the mother. This deprivation is the probable basis for what has been called the narcissism of the mothers of schizophrenic children. The mothers themselves are helplessly caught in their own dependency needs and are preoccupied with fantasies of omnipotence and effortless gratification. This is true of those mothers who present a patent and outward picture of total helplessness and dependency. It is equally true of the mothers who hide their deep sucking needs under a disguise of exaggerated overcompensated concentration on their maternal functions.[1] When the child, who later becomes schizophrenic, is born, the mother experiences him as a monstrous challenge to her own needs for infantile gratification. She cannot bring herself to empathize spontaneously with the child's minimal needs for protection and care.[2] The demands of the new child for quick gratification assail the frustrated mother's own omnipotence, and she feels overpowering rage. As noted earlier, the overcompensated inhibition of the rage results in parental perplexity. We need to test further our impression that in most of our histories the unconscious rage seems to have preceded the mother's awareness of the child's illness as such. Fear of the child's death was common in the maternal histories, even at the moment of delivery of the child.

Because of our special interest in the interrelationship between repressed omnipotent strivings and outer parental perplexity, we looked for similar reactions in our counselors. For example, the following incident came to our attention.

CASE 2.　Before beginning a case conference, it was casually noted that one of the counselors had a painful finger. Somewhat reluctantly she permitted the clinical director to look at the finger. It was swollen and blue, and there was an obvious fracture. On inquiry, the counselor admitted that the injury had occurred about 4 hours previously, in the arts and crafts shop. One of the aggressive children had been very disruptive to the group. At one point, when the counselor tried to restrain the child

[1] We have had occasion to psychoanalyze a perplexed mother of this kind. She literally nursed her baby all day long, and told of having nursed her baby for as long as 4 to 5 hours at a time. Her own major and dominating fantasy was that of consuming the maternal breast.

[2] Mrs. T. did not stop Tommy and watched helplessly as he climbed to the garage attic and finally hung down dangerously from the window ledge high in the air.

418

from throwing an object the object hit her finger. The next day, about 30 hours later, we held another conference. This time the counselor said she wanted to raise a question in the handling of the boy. Should she let him know that he had injured her? We were taken aback at the remarkable control and passivity of the counselor, and asked her if there had been any pain. She denied this entirely. On inquiry, she affirmed her fear of letting the boy know he had hit her, because she did not want to increase his anxiety. She denied steadfastly any resentment toward the boy. It seems that the counselor, out of misinterpretation of her task and from devotion to it, behaved like a perplexed masochistic mother.

It is hypothesized that the complex pattern of parental perplexity is the manifestation of a conflict between the repressed omnipotent strivings and actual experience of helplessness. This leads to the disorganization of the child's psychologic surroundings, which has serious consequences for the child. It is believed that these parents contribute to the confused mental state of the schizophrenic child. This is especially true of his problem in orienting himself to his own body and in differentiating himself from his outer reality. Time and space orientation are also affected. The child has no definitive guides for action, no way of learning bounds, no basis for control of motility. He cannot know what to expect. The parental passivity and detachment destroy the foundation for internalization of a defined parental image. There is no clear-cut prototype or design for achieving control and a system of either painful or pleasurable anticipations. The emergency emotions of rage and fear can become overwhelming and unmanageable to the child himself. Also what is normally accepted as a reward is not received as such by these children.

Regardless of the etiology of childhood schizophrenia, the schizophrenic child deserves and requires an organized and directed environment as much as, perhaps more than, the normal. In treatment we have become impressed with the slow, albeit partial, definite reversibility of the child's confusional pattern. This seems to occur in an atmosphere of benevolent certainty, where there is a consistent 24-hour adult interaction and intervention with and for the child. We have had example, too, of a child in partial recovery becoming disorganized and psychotic in the specific presence of a counselor whose behavior and underlying psychodynamics were similar to those attributed to the mothers of schizophrenic children.

With parents of schizophrenic children, the following simple principles are helpful. An active, authoritative role with the parents is assumed and the parents' fear of their own aggression is cut through directly. The objective is to diminish their ambivalence and frozen indecisiveness so as to get them to react with normal assertiveness to the child's behavior. In one way or another, the formula is communicated: "Put bounds on the child's behavior. Introduce normal expectations. Do not worry so about hurting the child. No single act of yours will be permanently and catastrophically dangerous to the child." This may be illustrated in the following brief incidents.

CASE 3. An 8-year-old schizophrenic boy, Robert, and his mother were waiting for the doctor. As the doctor came into the waiting room, he saw Robert punching his mother viciously in the face with the full weight of his body. She was sitting with unflinching passivity, indeed, without any expression at all. The therapist asked in a firm loud voice that both the mother and child could hear: "Why do you permit Robert to beat you up so?" The mother and child both looked up startled, but the beating had stopped. The mother asked: "What should I do?" The therapist answered unhesitatingly "Stop him, of course." Later Robert's mother admitted she became aware at that moment of how angry she had been for years over the beatings the boy had administered to her. Another mother came for office consultation with her 9-year-old son, Harry. Harry was found in her lap, pressing roughly against her. Repeatedly and without immediate provocation, he jabbbed both elbows with all his strength into his mother's breasts. The mother sat unmoving. The doctor asked why she permitted Harry to hurt her, and she in turn asked the usual question: "What should I do?" Our direction, of course, was not to permit him to hurt her. Subsequently the direct physical attacks on this mother stopped.

The symptomatic relief in both parent and child has sometimes been dramatic. The rationale essentially is to buttress and protect the parent. Thereby her wishes for infantile gratification and dependency are met. Her own sense of omnipotent complacency is enhanced. Further, she lends her omnipotence to the therapist. She no longer experiences her assertiveness with the child as her own. Rather, she borrows it from the therapist, who at the same time assures her nothing will happen to damage the child and assuages her guilt. More organized management of the child becomes possible.

Bibliography

1. Bruch, H. *Don't Be Afraid of Your Child.* New York: Farrar, Straus & Young, 1952.

Parental Aggression
in Fantasy, Actuality,
and Obsession

Parental behavior is motivated by the psychologic derivatives of the parents' own experiences in infancy and by their immediate and often affect-laden responses to their child's needs. A part at least of this motivation is accessible to the conscious experience of the parent and also to the observer. It can be analyzed from the developmental and psychoeconomic point of view, although the latter may remain incomplete unless the personality integration of the parents at the time of observation can be fully considered.

The aim in this multiauthored book is to show the many viewpoints, general and specific, from which parenthood, both normal and pathologic, can be investigated. The investigator, however, must always be aware in describing any particular phenomenon of parenthood that the steadily changing vector of the interacting processes between parent and child may bring about unpredictable results, since it is never possible to take all the relevant factors into account. Within this multitude of factors that motivate parental behavior, there exists an hierarchy of biologic, economic, and cultural entities in various combinations with the psychologic derivatives. These include the child's fantasy of the child being beaten and the mother's repressed fantasy of the same theme. This has been investigated by Dr. Brody as a crucial determinant of mothering behavior. She puts forward the challenging hypothesis that this unconscious derivative of the oedipus complex eventually becomes, as a universal occurrence, the central organizing factor of motherhood. It at once raises the significant question of whether a fantasy (unless one adheres to the concept of archetypes in a collective unconscious) can become a universally motivating factor. Up to the present, it has generally been held that however frequently the fantasy appears, it is still an outcome of individual ex-

421

periences activated by social and cultural events. It is clearly not universal in the biologic sense, and it is open to question whether it is even widely disseminated culturally. There are, for example, many primitive, and many highly civilized cultures as well, in which child-beating is by no means as usual as it is in the Judeo-Christian tradition. In such societies, parents also become frustrated and angry, and their children also experience insecurity, but it would appear that sadomasochistic transactions between parents and children are a much less frequent and consistent part of the educational ideology than the Western world has become accustomed to accept as normal. It would constitute an important anthropologic study to determine the frequency and rootedness of fantasies motivating sadomasochistic transactions between parents and children beyond the degree of frustration necessary for the child to grow up within the limits and customs of the culture.

There is no doubt that the need to implant in the child the necessity to control his impulses is more urgent in Western civilization than in any other of the studied cultures. The relationship between early established impulse controls and the proclivity on the part of parents to regress and lose control toward the child deserves careful research. The emphasis in the next three chapters is on the use of investigated material to indicate the motivating force of fantasies originating in derivatives of developmental conflicts. In Dr. Brody's study, one can observe "the hopeful attitude of the expectant mother" changing to a growing defensiveness toward the 6-week-old infant, and eventually to an impatience toward her 6-month-old child. None of these women was analyzed, so there is no direct analytic evidence of the "beating fantasy" in individual mothers, but the evidence is carefully built up by implication and inference from the beautiful observations of the mother and infant in transaction. This would be, of course, within the child-rearing system of a patriarchal organization. It would not necessarily follow in other types of family structure.

The subjects of the investigation are "good enough mothers," to use Winnicott's expression. They came to the clinic because they wished to raise their children properly. Once there, they carried out their maternal functions under the scrutiny of the investigators. Under such "laboratory" conditions, they would be more likely, one might imagine, to show effects due to "the stresses of motherhood" sooner than in everyday circumstances. Nevertheless, one can assume that they represent the normal mothers of our urban population who will be able to satisfy the complex demands of their growing children without danger to the emotional development of the family as a whole.

As the child gets older and his behavior is increasingly motivated by his need for activity, his parents are faced with the immediate educational task of controlling his impulsive behavior. This in itself increases the stress on the mother. As the child's spontaneous behavior becomes more and more unpredictable, his parents may find it necessary to punish him, not only to release their own emotional tensions but because they may be convinced that physical punishment is the best way to achieve the aims of child-rearing. Whether the parents actively repeat what they themselves have suffered passively as children or whether their punitive behavior has other origins, it should be clear that the so-called battering parent is not simply the punishing parent, but something different, as will be seen from Dr. Steele's chapter.

The difference lies mainly in the ego integration, the battering individuals, because of various constitutional and environmental factors, having remained extremely labile in their responses. Because of their low frustration tolerance, any tension in the psychic apparatus tends to throw their tenuous emotional stability off balance. This is followed by ego regression and release of hostile, aggressive impulses. When the frustrating agent is their own child, parental love and empathy become disregarded and savage impulses take over until satiated. When the parent is not actually psychotic, he may very well behave normally in between episodes, and he may even try to make amends for his attacks.

In other instances, especially when no consequences, legal or otherwise, follow the battering, an aggravation of such behavior may go undetected, since the cruelties that are perpetrated are generally not overt or easily identifiable as such. They go on behind closed doors, in dark rooms, and in circumstances of great fear. All through history, children have been tortured, beaten, and grossly neglected, but much of this is hidden under acts of apparent discipline, and the parental "right to chastise" is often upheld in courts even in the face of blatant sadism.

There are many indications that violence in general and toward children in particular is on the increase in these troubled times. The arithmetic of cruelty has assumed horrendous proportions. In the year 1966, for example, convictions for cruelty to children (mainly by parents) were reported as follows: U.S.A. (population 197,000,000), 5,778 cases; U.K. (population 55,000,000), 398 cases; France (population 49,500,000), 815 cases; West Germany (population 59,500,-000), 250 cases; and Austria (population 7,250,000), 913 cases. In these five countries therefore, in one year alone, 8,154 acts of extreme violence toward children were investigated and proved. Humane societies everywhere are certain that for every convicted case there are many more that never reach the stage of official investigation.

Not all brutality of parents toward children can be explained on the basis of impulsive behavior. Although many parents involved are immature and ineffectual, and a great number have distorted personalities of various types, a large group falls within the category of "normality," although overloaded at times with moral fanaticism. Among these are the parents whose "justified" punitive attitude combined with a perverse need is acted out not impulsively, but rather under the control of a compulsively rigid and even self-righteous ego. An American newspaper inquiry revealed a startling number of parents, all staunch citizens and churchgoers, who professed to believe in preventive chastisement for their children. One righteous pair told how every Sunday morning after breakfast they made their two daughters, aged 11 and 13, lie bare-bottomed across a bed and gave each a "good licking." Walking behind the little girls to church, "It makes us," they said, "feel good to know that their bottoms under their pretty Sunday dresses are well-reddened as a warning." Such instances do not enter the caseloads of social agencies, which deal largely with inadequate parents, men with habitual criminal records, alcoholics, deeply primitive or mentally subnormal people, or young, incapable, unmarried mothers and, consequently, this type of parent does not come under welfare supervision. It is well to remember their existence, however, when considering the theoretical implications of parental aggression.

The clinical condition described in the chapter on murderous obsessions is a derivative of postpartum depression, although the latter may not have been recognized as such at the time of birth. It is common knowledge that women often become depressed after childbirth. Transitory tearfulness in the early puerperium has been found in 60 to 80 percent of deliveries, and in 25 percent of these symptoms continue for longer than a few weeks. The commonest complaints are those of fatigue, irritability, tension, and anxiety. A "vomiting baby" is not infrequently the presenting symptom of the mother's puerperal depression. Psychiatrists are also familiar with women patients who report having been unwell since the birth of the last child. The condition has been ascribed to a marked ambivalence toward the infant and to a "narcissistic loss before rediscovery of the child." It has also been attributed to the onset of lactation, perineal soreness, and hormonal changes. In the severe postpartum depression, there is always the risk of suicide and sometimes infanticide, the rate being about one in five hundred births. The "natural history," therefore, of the murderous obsession begins at the time of parturition, with an overt or covert depression which gradually subsides and is replaced somewhat later by hypochondriac and phobic developments involving the child.

The condition constitutes a pathologic condition of motherhood which differs in some important respects from the states described by

424

Brody and Steele in the following chapters. Clinically, one can envisage a spectrum of maternal aggressiveness ranging from psychotic filicide and psychopathic cruelty on the one side to normal aggressiveness and beating fantasies on the other with neurotic murderous obsessions somewhere intermediate. The differences are based on the ego strength of the obsessional character who, when relieved of the pressing fear of the murderous impulse, can concentrate on the task of repression. For this reason, although relatively accessible to psychotherapy, these women tend, with the passage of time, to become more rigid and constricted. They live for long periods with their ambivalence and hostility under repression, at which times their outward behavior is "good," and they may even gain the reputation of being devoted mothers. Eventually, some critical event disrupts their vulnerable defensive system and triggers off a dissociation of affects so that hostility returns to consciousness and threatens the parent's superego by the presence of the murderous idea. The vulnerability of the defenses is due to their becoming exhausted in the course of their repressive work by the insufficient supply of integrating energy.

There is some support for the view that this type of illness tends to occur in women who find particular difficulty in their biologic role but function adequately otherwise. A significant association with dysmenorrhea has also been found.

E. J. A.
T. B.

21

A Mother Is Being Beaten: An Instinctual Derivative and Infant Care

Sylvia Brody

This chapter resumes a discussion of propositions originally set forth some years ago in an inquiry into some unconscious determinants of mothering behavior and attitudes [5]. That inquiry grew out of a study of 32 mother-infant pairs, each of whom were observed at one of four intervals during the first 6 months of life. The propositions dealt with the ways in which the unconscious wish to be beaten by the father might be reflected in maternal behavior in general, and they were applied to the mothers of the infants only indirectly [8]. Clinical examples that were used to illustrate the proposed connection between the unconscious fantasy and the observable behavior were drawn from cases of disturbed mother-child relationships and were very brief.

The same relationship between the unconscious fantasy and forms of maternal behavior has been explored further in data gathered in the Infant Development Research Project,[1] a longitudinal investigation of maternal behavior with infants in the first year of life. A primary goal of the research was to replicate the classification of maternal behavior resulting from the earlier study [5]. The new classification elaborates upon the earlier one and will be described in a separate publication.

Portions of this chapter are included in S. Brody and S. Axelrad (Eds.), *Anxiety and Ego Formation in Infancy*, International Universities Press, 1970.
[1] Conducted at a large metropolitan hospital in New York City, 1963–1967. This work was supported by N.I.M.H. Grant 1429.

427

For this presentation, the original propositions have been reexamined in data gathered for 122 mother-infant pairs, consisting of interviews with the mother prenatally and during confinement; neonatal examinations; and at the infant ages of 6 weeks, 6 months, and 1 year, interviews with the mother, observation of her behavior and attitudes, psychologic tests of the infants, and 16-mm films of entire feedings of the infant by the mother. Because of the longitudinal nature of the Infant Development Research Project, the large number of cases, and the abundant clinical and behavioral material, causal statements could be formulated concerning relationships among the typology of maternal behavior, the role of the unconscious fantasy, and the defenses against it. Considerations of space make it impossible to include in this context the highly detailed clinical material needed to illustrate the defensive operations. For the same reason it is assumed, but no attempt is made here to prove, that the beating fantasy is universal, and that although it can hardly furnish a full psychoanalytic explanation of a mother's behavior toward her child, it contains a central organizing factor.

THE BEATING FANTASY AND ITS VICISSITUDES DURING DEVELOPMENT

The beating fantasy derives from an unconscious wish of the phallic phase and is represented by three successive statements: first, "My father is beating the child," second, "I am being beaten by my father," and third, "A child is being beaten." The second statement, or stage, is most subject to repression, and usually comes to light only as a reconstruction in analysis. Freud interpreted it as a wish to be sexually gratified by the father, disguised in a regressive wish to be beaten by him. "This being beaten is now a convergence of the sense of guilt and sexual love" [8].

The patently aggressive content of the first statement may find a common expression in judicial or religious themes. The further displaced aggression in the third statement may find a common outlet in preoccupations with subject matter ranging from murder mysteries to reports of criminal behavior and acts of war. But the second statement is most clearly passive in aim, is less ego-syntonic than the other two, and finds fewer overt forms of discharge. In view of its greatest vulnerability to repression, we should expect that its unconscious influence also will be greatest and will most undergo defensive distortions.

Freud stated that the central fantasy of being beaten may persist and be satisfied perversely, may be subjected to repression, may be replaced by reaction-formation, and may be transformed by sublimation. Bonaparte proposed a fifth outcome of the masochistic wish, the facilitation of the biologic functions of the female necessary for pregnancy, childbirth, and breast-feeding [4]. Consequently, I suggested:

Psychologically normal maternal behavior will depend upon the mother's ability to imbue the child with phallic attributes, and to sublimate a part of her masochism to the passive aim of symbolically receiving its blows . . . The sublimation can occur . . . if the mother can accept a more passive role than she has previously had and can award a more and more active role to the child. . . . She has to adopt the passive aim of receiving the clamorings of the child. Concretely, this means that she inwardly agrees to tolerate his demands and to cushion his "blows"; that she identifies unambivalently with his gratification, supplied by her; *but that her passivity does not go so far that she derives masochistic gratification from it* [5].

In retrospect I should say that Bonaparte's "fifth fate" of the beating fantasy provided a transitional link for my application of the fantasy to maternal behavior. Thus the defenses against the fantasy that were discussed earlier, and those following here are actually only special cases of the processes originally outlined by Freud.

The main proposition here is that major aspects of maternal behavior and attitudes are significantly determined by unconscious resolutions of the unconscious wish to be beaten by the father. The proposition is based upon two assumptions: The first is that the second phase of the beating fantasy, "I am being beaten by my father," is an expression of the oedipal conflict, is unconscious, and is universal. The matrix for this assumption is found in Freud's paper [8]. The bridge between the beating fantasy and the oedipus complex is the childhood fantasy of violence in the primal scene.[2]

While there are many salient unconscious determinants of ma-

[2] Discussions of the beating fantasy most relevant to the present theme are to be found in Bonaparte [4]; in an especially clear clinical illustration by Lester [12]; in a consideration of auditory hallucinations emanating from primal scene experiences during infancy by Niederland [14]; and in connection with primal scene fantasies by the Kris Study Group [11].

ternal behavior—the influences of preoedipal conflicts upon a mother's body-image, the history of active and passive aims toward her parents and the extent of her aim-displacements upon siblings, the degree of narcissistic injury with which her instinctual aims have been tempered since childhood, the rigidity of defenses erected against instinctual demands and narcissistic injuries—in this context the defenses against the unconscious wish to be beaten and sexually gratified by the baby as an unconscious representative of the father's penis will be the focus of discussion. The infant, by virtue of his conception and birth passage, acquires the unconscious significance of the male genital. If upon delivery the mother sees the infant as a penis lost (again), he may bear the brunt of her envy and aggression; if she sees him as a penis regained, his narcissistic value is liable to augment her ambivalence toward him. By and large, our human histories and our culture place massive limits on the opportunities for a stable sublimation of the anal, sadomasochistic wish; and only when prephallic conflicts have been appreciably resolved can we expect derivatives of the beating fantasy to be available for sublimation.

Whatever the quality of a woman's psychosexual development, the experience of childbirth draws her objectively into the problems of the genital phase. Her psychologic readiness to relate to a child may be assumed to vary with her capacity to integrate that relationship with others previously established, in fact or fantasy. Ideally, there will be few regressive pulls toward responding to the infant on a phallic or prephallic level. Among women whose genital drives do find appropriate genital discharge, one might expect optimal capacity for maternal behavior, with least admixture of pregenital demands. Realistically, it may be presumed that most mothers will bring to their mothering position many components of pregenital drive derivatives.

The second assumption is that data of interviews and direct observations can provide inferences about the mother's defensive measures in the same way that such inferences can be made in series of diagnostic interviews and observations. Although the mothers who participated in the research did not come for diagnosis of their maternal behavior or of their personality structure, the information that they gave or withheld, and their manner of doing so, provided considerable material regarding the dynamics of their conscious conflicts, ideas, and affects. Study of these dynamics throws light on defenses especially when objective data about mother and infant stand in sharp contradiction to the mother's reports. Statements about defenses so inferred remain general, of course. They do not allow for any conclusions about how and why specific defenses were adopted.

To recapitulate the foregoing propositions:

1. The fantasy of being beaten contains a mixture of progressive and regressive aims, reflecting ego strengths and weaknesses that refer to the mental representation of the female body-image of childhood.

2. The greater the psychosexual maturity of the mother, the more stable her genital relationships and the greater the possibility of sublimation of the beating fantasy in her mothering.

3. The regressive aims may be discerned in behavior and attitudes that are objectively inappropriate or defensive, and mask subjective needs in the mother that are irrelevant to the immediate condition or maturity of the infant.

4. The greater the fixation or arrest of pregenital impulses, defenses, and affects in the mother, the more regressive or perverse their influence will be upon her unconscious wish to be beaten by the child who, by displacement, takes on the attributes of the beating father.

The passive quality of the infantile wish to be beaten, being itself a defense against active incestuous wishes, makes it particularly elusive. One must look for active means (sublimations, defensive and adaptive activities, perversions) by which the mother gratifies an originally active aim which since childhood has been disguised as a passive aim. The problem is further compounded by the evocation of clusters of defenses against associated ideas and affects. As in the case of any unconscious wish, the influence of defense in the determination of behavior and personality depends upon the genetic chronology with which the defenses—or sublimations or perversions—have been called up, under what dynamic conditions they were retained, the duration and stability of their functioning, the fixedness with which they were established, the success with which they have protected repressions, the degree to which they have interchanged and combined, and the secondary gains they have netted. Study of the case material can thus yield only glimpses into segments of the composite structure of a

431

mother's adult response to the beating fantasy at a given point in her life as a mother. It can make no attempt to provide a picture of her general personality, much less the genesis of her particular beating fantasy.

Mothers with overtly different behavior and different defenses may show comparable conflicts, and mothers with many different kinds and degrees of conflict may show similarities of expressive behavior and comparable defenses. It is to be expected that with so potent a conflict as that represented by the unconscious beating fantasy, the full range of defenses would be employed. The defenses apparent in the clinical material range from sublimation to such regression that frank perversion is evident.

The Beating Fantasy in Relation to Types of Maternal Behavior with Infants

Seven types of maternal behavior with infants were found through the analysis of the maternal feeding behavior in the Infant Development Research Project. The seven types were differentiated behaviorally at 6 weeks, according to a series of ratios between feeding acts and duration of feeding episodes, and clinically at 6, 26, and 52 weeks, according to the quality and consistency of the mother's empathy, control, and efficiency during feedings. After these types were isolated and discovered to be statistically significant, it was possible to order the data in each type in terms of the vicissitudes of the beating fantasy.

Very brief descriptions of the maternal behavior characteristic of each of the seven types, and of the chief defenses typically employed by mothers in each type, follow:

TYPE I (27 Mothers). Type I mothers take pleasure in observing and reporting about their infants, and give information agreeably and with appropriate affect. Many are able smoothly and confidently to divide their attention between infant and interviewer. They place little explicit emphasis upon standards of behavior for themselves or for their infants, or upon their competence as mothers, and they are open to influence regarding child-rearing.

They are genuinely interested in the infants' moods and activities, and their physical care is considerate and economical. Most are

432

consistently free to initiate social or motor activities with the infants; to communicate by glance, voice, or touch; and to respond to the infants' wishes for activity and sociability. They show much affection to the infants, and encourage, and praise them. Usually their enjoyment of mothering extends well beyond providing routine care.

The type I mother appears to be more likely to sublimate the wish to be beaten than the mother of any other type. By reaction-formation the wish to be beaten is changed to a wish to be needed and loved; and by identification with the father of childhood, the passive position is changed to an active one in which the mother, by regarding the needs of her child as greater than her own needs, and by providing proper care and control, enables him to develop initiative and frustration tolerance. It is also evident that the mother's willingness to accept the baby's demands may be interfered with by anxiety at times, lest she surrender too passively and fail to be adequately demanding or consistent.

A sublimation is the result of an identification and a reaction-formation.[3] Neither of these defenses used singly would produce sublimation of the unconscious wish to be beaten. For while the wish must be altered to a wish to receive demands, that receiving borders on masochistic surrender unless the passive role of the beaten child is also altered, by the mother's taking active charge of her infant in ways approvable by the superego.

TYPE II (19 Mothers). Type II mothers observe their infants casually and give limited information about them. Although they are attentive mothers, they show little or no curiosity about matters of child-rearing. All but one are agreeable and cooperative toward the interviewer, but in all cases their manner is bland and unaffected.

---

[3] In the original discussion of this subject the defense of reaction-formation was explained as an alteration of the wish to be beaten into a wish to beat, to command [5]. That explanation was incorrect. It resulted from confusions between instinctual aim and overt behavior, and between some of the *effects* of reaction-formation and of identification with the aggressor. As now formulated, the reaction-formation consists of the reversal of *aim,* i.e., the aim is no longer to be the object of aggression, and instead is to be the object of libidinal strivings. The appropriate unconscious statement of the mother would be, "I do not wish to be beaten, I wish to be needed and loved." Identification with the aggressor consists of a change of *subject:* in the place of the beating father of childhood or of the primal scene, we see the mother in the present. The appropriate unconscious statement of the mother would be: *He* does not beat, *I* do the beating."

433

Often they profess an assurance about mothering which is not convincing. Their emotional investment in the maternal role is subdued.

Their handling of the infants is dispassionate, restrictive, and impersonal. Occasionally it is both sensitive and careful; it is rarely grossly incompetent. These mothers seldom initiate social activity with the infants, and playfulness is markedly absent in the relationship. The mothers seem to take for granted their infants' development and capacity to conform to the mothers' attitudes or standards. They express little or no pleasure about the infants' behavior, but often stress early promotion of skills.

The chief defense against the wish to be beaten employed by the type II mother is repression, as described previously:

> In the case of repression the masochistic impulses have been kept out of consciousness with the result that the energy attaching to them as well as countercathectic energy is no longer available to the conscious ego. Maternal activities that require empathy and attitudes of giving are derogated if not avoided altogether; the maternal role is regarded as involving extra responsibilities but as otherwise not unlike other interpersonal roles . . . [the mother] feels little conflict about leaving [the baby] alone or in the care of others . . . She may care for him quite well materially but does not extend herself emotionally. It does not occur to her to make demands of the child other than that he not lean upon her for emotional support and that he conform to conventionally accepted standards of behavior. Such a mother often deplores her child's dependence in a way that betrays an unconscious longing to be the mothered one rather than the mother [5].

The repression requires mild support of other defensive measures, usually denial and, less often, turning against the self and projection. Nevertheless, the mother is vulnerable to occasional breakthrough of anxiety stirred up by the unconscious wish to beat or to be beaten.

TYPE III (21 Mothers). Type III mothers, with few exceptions, are unwilling observers and poor reporters. They barely show interest in their infants' development and have almost no curiosity about child-rearing methods. Their overt cooperation varies: Many are grimly restricted, many are emotionally shallow and do not take the interview seriously, and a few show artificial elation. Gentle emotions seem to embarrass them. Only one expresses any lack of confidence as a mother; most declare an overweening confidence.

Most of these mothers show a capacity to handle their infants adequately or adeptly, but mainly their actions are mechanical, rough, or abrupt. They are peremptory and impatient, often condescending and critical. Tenderness is manifested only briefly or sporadically. Attitudes that at first appear to be permissive shortly are seen to reflect the mothers' disposition to ignore or to neglect the infants' passing needs or states; and a contradictory sharpness, visible in scolding, teasing, threatening, and dominating behavior, is common. These mothers seldom encourage their infants to experience age-appropriate curiosities or activities. A few show pride in isolated aspects of their infants' performance. Pleasure in contact with the infants is rare or very short-lived.

In the type III mother identification with the aggressor is the conspicuous defense against the unconscious beating fantasy. She assigns a passive position to the baby and arrogates to herself a high level of activity. Her repression of passive aims is much less successful than it is in the type II mother, and her equilibrium is apt to be disturbed by breakthroughs of aggression more than by breakthroughs of anxiety. Frequently she is assailed by ambivalent impulses; she shows strong inner approval of the baby's physical activity and, on the other hand, sullen refusal to recognize his active demands upon her. The conflict between these opposing tendencies is masked by an overt disinterest in or carelessness of affectionate mothering. It seems crucial for the type III mother to maintain a defensive position which states that she has no wish to be beaten, and thus no cause to sublimate the wish, that is, to alter it to a wish to be loved. Her infant must cope with a great deal of tension unaided.

TYPE IV (10 Mothers). Type IV mothers are exceedingly poor and unwilling observers. Their reports are vague, evasive, and self-centered. Cooperation with the interviewer is superficial and often marred by irritability and negativism. These mothers are either tense, dissatisfied, and angry, or they are flippant and make a show of being nonchalant in the maternal role. All assert disinterest in learning more about infant care, and all refer to their infants' behavior critically, sarcastically, or with open hostility. Eight of the ten mothers in this group appear to be overconcerned with their appearance; five show a distinctly masculine manner; three are overdressed and put on feminine airs. Although a few mothers in other groups, mainly in type III, also exaggerate feminine or masculine qualities of behavior, the con-

435

spicuous masculinity appears only in type IV mothers. No mother in this group shows any interest in increasing her maternal competence or confidence.

These mothers respond to their infants very mechanically and as little as possible. They carry out bare routines with remarkable absence of sensitivity to the infants' feelings. The interaction they do provide is almost always impatient, delayed, begrudging, or condescending. They ignore the infants' visible distress, and speak to them abusively, complain about them, neglect them, or punish them. While they all show exaggerated affection at times, some especially in the form of kissing, all seem devoid of any kindly feelings toward the infants. With one exception, all express maternal pleasure only in regard to the infants' being undemanding. Their positive or their negative involvement with the infant is exaggerated, and their general maternal behavior is neutral and joyless. No natural intimacies between mother and infant are seen.

The type IV mother shows an identification with the aggressor so intense that any passivity required of her in the course of fulfilling her maternal obligations quickly invokes counteraction. She seems compelled to demand that the infant behave in ways that will satisfy her own oral-passive and anal-passive needs. She projects onto the infant her own feelings of badness and dirtiness, and she denies needs and affects in the infant as well as in herself. All of these measures may not suffice. The mother's oral and anal sadism break through; she invites counteraggression, feels beaten, and thus finally justifies her own harshness, which she believes has been provoked by the child. A sadomasochistic entente becomes visible as the mother acts out the wish to beat along with the wish to be beaten.

TYPE V (21 Mothers).   Type V mothers are, with one exception, poor or superficial observers, and are uneasy when questioned. Their reports contain many clichés and generalizations. Insight into the needs of their infants is meager, and methods of infant care do not interest them. Some show apathy or petulance, most are emotionally remote, and rapport is difficult to achieve. On the whole these mothers lack spirit and confidence, and show neither strong positive nor strong negative involvement in the maternal role.

With the infants they are cautious and apprehensive. They are slow to respond, may do so impersonally, or may be unmoved by

436

obvious needs of the infants. They are passive and aloof, and offer little stimulation of any kind. Several explicitly say that they expected to be bored by their babies. They take pleasure in telling how the infants are easy to care for, but hardly comment upon the infants' behavior or personalities. The relationship is encompassed by routine care. The overall attitude is one of detachment, and the mother-infant relationship is impoverished.

In the type V mother repression of the wish to be beaten is fortified by severe inhibition, weak reaction-formation, and turning against the self. The defensive structure resembles that of the type II mother, but is much less effective. As a result, the type V mother is more disposed to maintain a pattern of avoidance of maternal activity. She appears to be arrested by severe conflict between her wish to give adequate care to her infant and her intense fear of feeling forced to do things for him. While active and passive aims remain opposed, superego pressure leads the mother to feel burdened and beaten by the internalized image of the beating father. She appears to be either chronically depressed or chronically anxious.

TYPE VI (15 Mothers).   Type VI mothers vary in their capacities to observe and report and in their interest in methods of child-rearing, but all see their maternal position as important. They relate thoughtfully to the interviewer. Most express or imply high confidence in their mothering abilities. They handle their infants carefully, properly, with ease, but they lack sensitivity to the infants' changing states. They are steadily in charge, with variable degrees of animation, communication, and pleasure. In almost all cases the mother appears to be the dominant partner in the interaction. In other ways, these mothers fall into three groups: (1) Five, who are the least adequate observers, show more concern with the proper conduct of the interview than with accommodation to the infants' needs. Unless they have specific duties to perform they leave the infants alone and communicate with them minimally or not at all. They do not show pleasure in mothering, are imperturbable, rarely stimulate their infants, and in general lack spontaneity. (2) Three, who observe and report well, are also well-organized and often didactic to the interviewer. Their efficiency is rote or rigid or subtly restrictive. Communication with the infants is almost entirely of a corrective nature. They do not seem to enjoy mothering, but they do express pride in the infants' accomplish-

437

ments. (3) Three are talkative and so exuberant that their observing and reporting suffer. Their enthusiasm leads them to be excessively playful and dominating. They are sincere and voluble in expressing pride and pleasure in their infants.

The type VI mother shows as her chief defenses identification with the *active* aim of the internalized father rather than identification with the aggressor, relatively successful repression of the passive aim, and isolation. She is self-reliant and expects her infant to suppress inner needs with equanimity. Her attentiveness to the infant is often rote and affectless. She is often identified with parent figures in whom strictness, efficiency, and independence were prominent attributes. She rationalizes the correctness of her maternal procedures and shows an unquestioning confidence in her own judgment, but often acts insensitively. Projection of aggressive demands upon the infant is frequent. In the type VI mother, who is often skillful, reaction-formation by way of acknowledgement of a need to be loved either is starkly absent, or is dramatized.

TYPE VII (5 Mothers). Type VII mothers believe themselves to be, and are, inadequate observers and reporters. They are highly amenable, friendly, responsive to the interests of the interviewer, and eager to learn about infant care. Being fearful of taking action, they sometimes wait for the interviewer to direct their maternal activities.

All try to be competent in handling the infants, but are generally awkward. They are self-conscious and insecure both in recognizing and in responding to the infants' needs. They blossom when the infants respond to them, they can be very attentive and affectionate, yet are not often free to initiate communication or play, or to make demands upon the infants. Despite their obvious difficulties, they show strong positive involvement with the infants and enjoy their mothering.

The defenses shown by the type VII mothers are in sharp contrast to those shown in type VI. A striving toward reaction-formation against the passive wish to be beaten is seen in the mother's eagerness to accommodate and to please her infant, and to receive his reciprocal love. Sometimes her devotedness has the quality of masochistic subservience. And as her identification with an active object is weak, her potential for sublimation is limited. When her mothering efforts are ineffective she becomes inhibited. It is as though the assumption of a normally active leadership in the maternal position might interfere with the capacity to maintain kindliness. The type VII mother is more ready than most to recognize insecurity and anxiety in herself, and she does not intellectualize. In these ways her attitudes have a resemblance to the attitudes of some type I mothers.

UNCLASSIFIED GROUP (4 Mothers). The clinical and behavioral ratings of four mothers place them neither in any of the seven types that were statistically significant nor in a type by themselves. Each mother shows maternal behavior that is unusual in its childishness, ineptitude, or stereotypy.

A prominent defense among the mothers in the latter group is regression. In different ways, each of these mothers is monotonously playful with her infant on primitive erotic levels, and treats him like an amusing doll. Childish devotion to the momentary needs of the infant is alternated with childish domination of his activity.

THE ROLE OF INTROJECTION AND PERVERSION IN THE VICISSITUDES OF THE BEATING FANTASY

Two vicissitudes of the beating fantasy found almost exclusively in types III, IV, and V have been reserved for discussion outside the context of the specific typology of mothers because of their special pathologic nature: These are the defenses of introjection and perversion, which express the passive and active aims of the beating fantasy in most crude form.

Introjection

At the 6-week visit, nine mothers reported mild postpartum depressions. They complained of extreme fatigue, feelings of incompetence, inability to enjoy their babies, and bad moods. At the 6-month visit all but two had recovered, and they recovered shortly afterward. During the remainder of the infants' first year, however, the mothers' maternal behavior was very inadequate, except in one case. In the latter case, once the depression lifted, the mother treated her baby very tenderly and conscientiously, and although she was often anxious and overactive, she was not inadequate. In a second case, the mother never felt able to care for the baby, and as her husband was able and willing to do so when he was not busy studying, she found outside employment after a few months. She was scarcely acquainted with her baby.

The other seven mothers, after overcoming their partial depres-

439

sion and withdrawal, were openly negative, harsh, or angry toward their infants, hypercritical of them, and negligent as well. In terms of the beating fantasy, it could be said that during their depressions these mothers introjected the hated, beating father, devaluating themselves as in the classic picture of the melancholic. After the depression passed they devaluated the infants. Again in terms of the beating fantasy, it could be said that they tried to rid themselves of the hated introject by projecting the beating impulses to their "bad" babies.

The first medical publication about postpartum psychosis and depression appeared in this country in 1894, the next not until 1911. These and a few more were first reviewed as a group in 1926 [16]. While this relatively late interest in the illness may be accounted for by the late growth of dynamic psychiatry itself, its actual incidence was probably increased by the reduced maternal and infant mortality after the turn of the century, and by the change in the social position of women. That is to say, the greater real number of mother-infant pairs naturally would have made for more awareness of conflicts inherent in the maternal role, and the social pressure for women's work outside the home presumably would have led to an increased internalization, among women, of conflicts inherent in a psychologic position to which connotations of "feminine-passive" have been attached. In addition, defensive aspects of maternal conflict may have been hidden or entirely snuffed out, even a century ago, by practices of infanticide and abandonment. In present times the same conflict may appear in various forms of withdrawal from the infant, as well as in frank depression, and may become conspicuous only later on, in the projection of badness to the child. Such a projection becomes dramatically visible in the battered child syndrome (see Chap. 6).

It is of special interest that Asch considers that many "crib deaths" may be a form of infanticide during postpartum depression [1]. His clinical evidence supports the probability that some crib deaths result from a displacement of the mother's suicidal impulses during the postpartum period, when the self and the object representations are confused [2]. This writer knows of one case in which an infant of a few weeks was barely rescued from suffocation as a result of maternal carelessness, in a period of emotional stress, by the timely appearance of a nurse; and one case in which an infant of a few months was almost smothered intentionally by a depressed mother who could not bear to hear the baby's crying. The latter mother maintained a pathologically anxious and angry behavior toward the child well into his adult years.

The separation of the mother from the infant in childbirth, because it produces psychologic, physiologic and endocrinologic changes in the mother, generally has been considered the major precipitant of postpartum depression. The hypothesis offered here takes account only of psychic determinants, and is more specific. It is that the postpartum depression is a manifestation of an earlier introjection of the father's activity in the beating fantasy; and that, depending upon the severity of illness, the introjection gradually gives way to projection or to other pathologic defense measures which can end in battery or infanticide. The reasoning is that the primary dynamic factor in the onset of the depression is not the actual separation from the infant and the attendant change in the narcissistic balance of the mother, but that the birth of the baby provides the setting for the actualization of the unconscious beating fantasy. After delivery, a real object exists which at first arouses guilt attaching to the introjection, and which subsequently arouses the wish to beat and the fear of being beaten, and the converse fear and wish. This hypothesis is in harmony with the one proposed by Asch, who also has noted the probable relationship between infanticide and the battered child syndrome. Similarly relevant are the descriptions by Wasserman of characteristic oscillations between lifelong depression and explosive behavior, and of anal preoccupations, among "battering parents" [17].

Perversion

A perverse acting out of the wish to beat is not common among mothers of young infants. Nevertheless, 8 of the 122 infants studied were by age 1 habitually involved in physical fights with their mothers. These mothers, and numerous others, justified spanking the infant, sometimes as early as at 6 months of age, to teach him obedience. A relationship between the rationale for spanking and the unconscious beating fantasy would seem to be obvious. Certain refinements of this rationale may have broad significance for maternal behavior.[4]

The first of these refinements is moral masochism, in which the

[4] Although all the propositions regarding the role of the beating fantasy are expected to apply to fathers as well as to mothers, the discussion has throughout made reference only to mothers because only they were regularly studied.

beating activity is unconsciously displaced from the internalized father to the child, the form of the beating is changed from physical to mental, and the aim of the mother remains passive. An ideal form of moral masochism may be seen in the traditional picture of the self-sacrificing mother. She appears figuratively in religious themes, and actually in social groups in which few nondomestic sublimations are available to married women. The "selfless" mother was more familiar in a prefeminist era.[5]

If the wish to be beaten may be enacted in moral masochism, so it may be proposed that the converse wish may be enacted in moral sadism, that is, in instinctual excitements achieved through the inflicting of mental pain upon another, for *moral* purposes. The dynamics of this moral sadism may finally put in proper focus the relationship between the beating fantasy and maternal behavior.[6]

An archetype of moral sadism might be the hell-fire sermon against sin, in which the culpable listener must be threatened with the pain that is likely to result from waywardness. Parents with any psychologic enlightenment are likely to disavow such moralizing as much as they would speak out against cruel beatings, or out-of-fashion thrashings and canings. Parental opinions about hitting, slapping, or spanking are different, however. Rarely do parents agree in principle that there are *no* instances when a child should be hit, slapped, or spanked. These disciplinary measures are commonly assumed to be necessary and inevitable in the education of nearly every child, at least in certain emergencies, or at least if the hitting is spontaneous and well-meant.[7]

[5] Another form of masochism in motherhood is to be found among women whose unconscious wish is to bear a child for their mothers or fathers, either as a form of expiation or to propitiate parental love. "Having a child for the grandparents" expresses this motive half-humorously. Bearing an out-of-wedlock child often has the selfsame basis, but is motivated by a far greater quantity of ambivalence [18].

[6] This is not the place to expatiate upon the general dynamics and varied manifestations of the phenomenon which I am calling *moral sadism*. "Mental cruelty" is one example. Wit and sarcasm provide other examples of moral sadism, with different origins and different outcomes. Wit usually has as one aim the infliction of mental pain upon an equal; sarcasm, upon an inferior (cf. Humour [7]).

[7] At the 6-week visit, the "burping" activity of the mothers (helping the baby to bring up the bubble of air) was remarkable in several ways. Most infants need a little help to expel swallowed air, and usually burping is facilitated by the infant's being held erect or placed prone. A few pats may also help. (See Nelson [13] and Hood [9].) For the purpose of burping, infants were placed in almost thirty different positions. The number of pats, strokes,

Because in matters of discipline parents often delegate responsibility to each other, the splitting of punitive measures between mother and father may represent a cooperative working out of the beating fantasy.

The original discussion of the beating fantasy as a determinant of maternal behavior called attention to *spanking* as the preferable term by which to describe the typical punishment meted to the child [5]. The merit of the homelier and more equivocal word is that it stirs up an indisputably seductive connotation, recalls more familiar childhood affect and, most important, takes into serious account the more common forms of physical assault. Morality demands of the parent that he exert certain controls upon the child's unsuitable or harmful acts. At first he may try to do so with quiet words, then with firm or angry words. By and by, as words fail, he finds himself resorting to the quick slap, push, or hit. The mild appeals have been directed to reason, the more serious commands and rebukes are intended to arouse the child's conscience and remorse, and then there is a sharper shift to condemnation and anger. The latter may carry very considerable force. It may be regarded as a form of moral sadism, intended to arouse guilt and mental pain, both of which may still be assimilated by the ego of the child. Impelled by psychic pain, he may be enabled to correct his actions in harmony with the normal demands of his superego. But when a further shift occurs—and such shifts may be exceedingly swift—and the parent strikes the child, the narcissistic wounds to the parent's self-esteem and to the child's body feeling and self-esteem may be overwhelming. The wound to the child occurs

---

circular rubs, etc., applied to each infant ranged from 14 to over 5,000, with a median of 408.2. The number of episodes of burping during single feedings ranged from 1 to 15, with a median of 5.7. (Feeding duration averaged about 35 minutes.) On inquiry all the mothers said that the observed burping activity was customary; and while talking to the baby, smiling at him, cleaning his face, changing his diaper, caressing, comforting, or kissing him were not common activities among all of the mothers during feeding, every one of the mothers burped her baby. Unconscious determinants might be a wish to overcome feelings of passivity normally experienced during the feeding of a very young infant, and a wish to discharge emotional tension through a licit contact with the baby's body. Nevertheless, very often the vigor and rapidity of the burping activity gave it a definite appearance of a hitting procedure, as noted by observers of the films [6]. Viewing of the raw film data showed, additionally, that often the mother's patting hand strayed downward from the baby's back to his buttocks, which then also received the impact of her rhythmic hand movements. A reasonable hypothesis may be that in part the burping represents a displacement of the wish to beat.

443

even if no physical pain results, because the physical assault violates the boundaries of control and of personal separateness. The fleeting loss of ego organization felt by the parent who suddenly strikes out has the quality of a momentary tantrum: an exquisite, exciting surrender to inner forces that become spent in an attack upon the child. This excitement is contagious. Identification of the child with the regressive, anal-sadistic elements of the parental superego is likely to be grossly facilitated.

According to the distinctions between feelings of guilt and the need for punishment made by Nunberg, guilt has as its aim an undoing of the crime, a reconciliation with the loved object; and it is a mark of ungratified libido [15]. The need for punishment represents the turn of aggression against the ego and is a mark of ungratified aggression. The one always implies existence of the other. Which of the two predominates in any given instance depends upon degrees of instinct fusion and defusion. Or, as one might now say, upon the patterns of discharge of and defense against instinctual drive derivatives. Both guilt and the need for punishment emanate from the demands of the superego. Guilt may induce self-punishment; but as its aim is to undo through intrapsychic struggle and adaptive measures, its effects can be limited to influencing actions and attitudes. But the need for punishment is regressive, demands suffering, and can be satisfied only by a real wound or loss, entailing lowered self-esteem, heightened narcissism, and threats to the development of or stability of identifications on a genital level. The question may be raised whether the verbal rebuke, however harsh, may be more likely to arouse guilt, shame, or anxiety; and whether the physical assault, however slight, may be more likely to stir the need for punishment.

Isakower's classic paper postulated that the auditory structure and hearing function of human beings are fundamental for the regulation of relationship with the environment—for the development of judgment, language, and thinking—and thus are nuclear to superego formation [10]. It then may follow that the word, the moral exhortation, however severe, still belongs to the sphere of judgment and mentation, still leaves the child a way open to act with a degree of autonomy. The sternest command that he control his impulses does not violate the integrity of his physical person. It enters into his consciousness through a receptive organ and through a natural hearing and thinking process. Certainly the borderline between mental and physical pain may be blurred if the command is screamed, or conversely, if the physical attack consists of a mild touch. But it remains true that aggressive speech, reason, argument, and even restraint are directed to the arousal of affects, including guilt and mental pain, whereas aggressive blows instantly alienate mental processes, offend narcissism in the profoundest sense, provoke counteraggression in sadomasochistic form, and so in due course provoke the need for punishment as well.[8]

In sum, it is submitted that the predilection to hit or to spank the child is rooted in a defense against the fantasy of being beaten. Regardless of whether the act is approved or disapproved as an educational measure, it signifies a loss of ego organization and a simultaneous and often frantic assertion of control. The impulse to hit breaks through when moral sadism—threats and condemnations—are felt to be ineffectual. It comes in a wild effort to direct the child's aggression back upon the child. The psychic aims are to quell the anxiety (in the parent) stemming from a return of the repressed passive wish to be overcome or beaten, to give way to the active impulse to beat, and to relieve affective tension that has been reinforced by guilt for either the parent's or the child's insufficiencies. In pursuit of these aims the parent is inwardly pushed to regression in the form of an actual assault.[9]

Two psychologic considerations follow: that moral sadism, though ominous in its sound, is safer than the physical blow in which the sadism is cruder, and regressive; and that in child-rearing gener-

[8] Of course it is not assumed that the unconscious need for punishment stems only from the beating fantasy. The need may have many other sources, particularly identification with an overaggressive parent, in fact or fantasy. One example lies in the relationship between the need for punishment and gang activities [3]. Similarly, recidivism may be accounted for by the lack of reformative influences in correctional institutions, and by the failure of any given period of incarceration to quench the drive-like character of the need for punishment.

[9] A tempering of the universal lust to beat may be illustrated by the following excerpt from the New York Times: "Prisons in Britain Ordered to Destroy Tools for Flogging." London, Sept. 24, 1967. The Home Office has ordered the burning of birches and cat-o'-nine-tails and the destruction of all related equipment by Oct. 1. A new criminal justice act, barring any form of corporal punishment, goes into effect then. . . . The spokesman said that before the [metal] triangles [to which prisoners were tethered] were thrown away they were to be beaten out of shape under the supervision of a senior officer in each prison. The cloth and leather parts used as bindings were to be burned and the wooden parts cut up, he said.

445

ally so little use is made of the intermediate measures of moral *or* physical restraint *without* counteraggression that the need for punishment almost automatically becomes a constant in our culture. Inherent in the need for punishment is the need to project, and projection carries along a chain of defenses: The child is accused of hurting the parent, the child accuses the parent of taking unfair advantage, and the sadomasochistic affair is entrenched. In our times, the upraised arm and the menacing hand did become a charismatic sign of strength and leadership in Fascism and Communism.

It is no wonder that the dramatic struggle for power in the adolescent period may have an unconscious determinant discernible in the beating fantasy, for in a more real way than ever before in his life the adolescent has the physical potential to be the active beater of the parent. The connection between reawakened fantasies of sexual brutality and reawakened fears of passive "childlike" surrender in the adolescent is obvious enough. The sadomasochistic complementations of parent and child need to undergo radical revisions, and both feel themselves to be stepping on dangerous thresholds. The threat to both may be reduced eventually only by flight or by further displacements of active and passive positions to nonfamilial objects and to the next generation. In passing, it may be noted that it is very rare for an adolescent to be pictured in the beatific representations of mother and child so common throughout history and in many cultures. Perhaps a mutual tenderness between mother and child may be expectable only so long as the physical capacity to beat lies with only one of the partners.

Bibliography

1. Asch, S. S. Psychiatric Complications. A: Mental and Emotional Problems. In J. J. Rovinsky and A. F. Guttmacher (Eds.), *Medical, Surgical and Gynecological Complications of Pregnancy* (2d ed.). Baltimore: Williams & Wilkins, 1965.
2. Asch, S. S. Crib deaths: Their possible relationship to postpartum depression and infanticide. *J. Mount Sinai Hosp. N.Y.* 35:214–220, 1968.
3. Axelrod, S. Juvenile delinquency: A study of the relationship between psychoanalysis and sociology. *Smith Coll. Stud. Social Work* 35:2, 1965.

4. Bonaparte, M. *Female Sexuality*. New York: International Universities Press, 1953.

5. Brody, S. *Patterns of Mothering*. New York: International Universities Press, 1956. Pp. 384–386.

6. Brody, S., and Axelrad, S. Mother-Infant Interaction: Forms of Feeding at Six Weeks (Film), 1967. Available from New York University Film Library.

7. Fowler, H. W. *A Dictionary of Modern English Usage*. London: Oxford University Press, 1937.

8. Freud, S. A Child Is Being Beaten. In J. Strachey (Ed.), *The Standard Edition of the Complete Psychological Works of Sigmund Freud,* Vol. 17. London: Hogarth, 1955.

9. Hood, J. H. Effect of posture on the amount and distribution of gas in the intestinal tract of infants and young children. *Lancet* 2:107–110, 1964.

10. Isakower, O. On the exceptional position of the auditory sphere. *Int. J. Psychoanal.* 20:340–348, 1939.

11. Joseph, E. D. (Ed.). *Beating Fantasies*. Monograph I, Kris Study Group of the New York Psychoanalytic Institute. New York: International Universities Press, 1965.

12. Lester, M. The analysis of an unconscious beating fantasy in a woman. *Int. J. Psychoanal.* 38:22–31, 1957.

13. Nelson, W. E. (Ed.). *Textbook of Pediatrics*. Philadelphia: Saunders, 1956.

14. Niederland, W. Early auditory experiences, beating fantasies, and primal scene. *Psychoanal. Stud. Child* 13:471–504, 1958.

15. Nunberg, H. *Practice and Theory of Psychoanalysis: A Collection of Essays*. New York: Nervous and Mental Disease Monographs, 1948. Pp. 89–101.

16. Strecker, E. A., and Ebaugh, F. G. Psychoses occurring during the puerperium. *Arch. Neurol. Psychiat.* (Chicago) 15:239–252, 1926.

17. Wasserman, S. The abused parent of the abused child. *Children* 14:5, 1967.

18. Young, L. *Out of Wedlock*. New York: McGraw-Hill, 1954.

22

Parental Abuse of Infants and Small Children

Brandt F. Steele

T he actual incidence of child abuse is difficult to determine, but it seems likely that each year in the United States at least 40,000 children are seriously injured by their parents or other caretakers.[1] Such abuse of infants and small children may in some cases be continued until later years, but it is a different phenomenon from abuse which begins only when the child is older. The latter is more directly related to problems of sexuality and aggressive competition. Direct murder of children is also a different form of behavior.

Original reports of child abuse came largely from welfare agencies and charity hospitals, leading to the assumption that there might be direct correlation between socioeconomic factors and abusive parental behavior toward children. Other studies, however, show child abuse existing in all strata of society, regardless of educational or socioeconomic levels. Financial crises, social distress, unemployment, poor housing, broken families, and alcoholism are obvious stresses that disturb psychic equilibrium and activate latent potentials for child abuse. But these factors are neither necessary nor sufficient.

This study was supported by the Children's Bureau of the Department of Health, Education, and Welfare, Project No. 12:HS, Project 218.

[1] Accurate statistics are not available, and it is well known that a high percentage of cases of abuse are not recognized or reported. Personal experience leads us to make the estimate given above. Approximately one-third of the children are age 3 or under. We do not believe that published surveys, such as that of Gil [12], have produced accurate or useful data.

Abuse occurs in families in which none of these stresses is present. More basic and constant in the instigation of abuse is the psychologic set of the parent which creates a recognizable style or pattern of parent-child interaction in which abuse is likely to happen. This chapter presents the findings from our previously published study of 60 families in which child abuse occurred [23], plus subsequent observations on a nearly equal number of less intensively studied cases. In our sample of abusing parents approximately four-fifths were mothers, one-fifth fathers. This preponderance of mothers should not be considered a valid statistic, but merely an accidental result of skewed sampling. The essentials of the psychologic patterns involved in abuse are the same in men as in women; they are not gender-linked. With few exceptions, such as references to pregnancy, the descriptions of abusing parents given below apply equally to both sexes.

There is no common psychiatric diagnostic category into which even a majority of abusing parents can be placed. True sociopathy is rare. Moderately active psychotic states, either schizophrenic or depressive, are occasionally seen. Much more common are the various types of psychoneuroses and character disorders. Psychosomatic illnesses are frequent. There is the almost universal presence among abusing parents of some degree of depression, either overt or latent. It is predominantly a rather chronic, low-grade, anaclitic type of depression. Child abuse cannot be considered an integral part of any of our usual psychiatric entities, but is best understood as a particular type of parent-child interaction which can exist in combination with any other psychologic state.

PATTERN OF CHILD-REARING

Basic in the abuser's attitude toward infants is the conviction, largely unconscious, that children exist in order to satisfy parental needs. Infants who do not satisfy these needs should be physically punished in order to make them behave properly. Further, this demand for satisfying behavioral response from the infant to parental need is highly premature and expressed very early in the infant's life. As an inevitable corollary there is parental disregard of the infant's own needs, wishes, and age-appropriate abilities or inabilities to respond properly. It is as though the infant were looked to as a need-satisfying parental object to fill the residual, unsatisfied, infantile needs of the parent.[2]

The following somewhat ironic description of parental ideals for child behavior appeared in *The New York Times* in E. LeShan's article, "The 'Perfect' Child"[17]:

> Grandma had brought 4-year-old Lauri a walking-talking doll for her birthday. Lauri, her parents and grandparents watched in wonder as the doll walked across the floor in jerky steps, a mechanical voice from within saying, "Hello, I love you, hello, I love you, hello, I love you."
> "Now *that's* what I call a perfect child!" exclaimed Lauri's mother.

The counterpart of this was poignantly expressed by our patient Mrs. C. who told us, "I have never felt really loved all my life. When the baby was born, I thought he would love me, but when he cried all the time, it meant he didn't love me so I hit him." Kenny had been hospitalized at age 3 weeks with bilateral subdural hematomas.

This particular style of child-rearing, which is first evidenced soon after the infant is born, continues through the subsequent years of the child's life.

CASE 1. Mr. J., in speaking of his 16-month-old son, Johnny, said: "He knows what I mean and understands it when I say, 'Come here.' If he doesn't come immediately, I give him a gentle tug on the ear to remind him of what he is supposed to do." On hospitalization, Johnny showed multiple contusions, abrasions, lacerations, skin infections, malnutrition, and anemia. His ear was lacerated and partially torn away from his head. A younger brother, Dennis, age 3 months, was hospitalized at the same time with multiple bruises, fractures of the clavicle and femur, and bilateral subdural hematomas.

Mr. J. was unemployed and doing much of the baby care while his wife was out working. He felt he had been doing the best job he could in the face of great difficulty and that the children were not properly responsive and apppreciative. Mr. J. had been raised by a rigid, authoritative father who beat him and his siblings to make them behave correctly. He felt his mother had been cool and distant; she had not only failed to protect him from his father but had also beaten him occasionally.

In early life the infant is most likely to be attacked during the normal care-taking, mothering functions of feedings, diapering, bath-

---

[2] This is the "role reversal" phenomenon described by Morris and Gould as "a reversal of the dependency role, in which parents turn to their infants and small children for nurturing and protection" [18]. Olden also noted "Again and again we find adults whose children represent their own parents" [19].

ing, dressing, and comforting, and in later months during training and "obedience" situations. If the infant responds with cooperation and pleasure, the parent feels approved of and loved, and all goes well. Should the infant be uncooperative, however, continuing to cry, or persisting in wriggling and thwarting the parental care-taking efforts, the parent may feel disappointed, disapproved of, unloved, and criticized, and will respond with attack in the form of yanking, slapping, hitting, and throwing about in an effort to make the baby behave. This leads to the bruises, lacerations, visceral injuries, and fractures which we call the "battered child syndrome" [7, 15].

Although children may die of repeated severe injuries inflicted by their parents in this pattern of child-rearing, it is important to bear in mind that this is very different from the direct murder of children. The latter is done mostly by psychotic parents or relatives who involve the child in their psychotic systems [1]. There is a great deal of difference between disciplinary attack of a child in order to get it to shape up and behave better and a direct attempt to destroy a child out of psychotic hatred. The abusing parent has a great investment in a live child who will *perform* satisfactorily.

Probably all parents have a need for the infant to respond in rewarding fashion. Benedek has clearly described the mutually rewarding interaction between mother and child in which each of the partners adequately satisfies the needs and expectations of the other [4]. The abusing parent differs from the "normal" in the excessive intensity of expectations that are expressed too early in the infant's life. Further, such parents are deficient in true empathy and disregard the infant's lack of ability to understand commands and its limited repertoire of responses. Difficulty inevitably arises because of the discrepancy between the premature, excessive demand of the parent and the inability of the infant to respond properly. The parent feels that the infant is failing to do what he should, and solves the problem by scolding and criticizing the child and punishing him physically in order to get him to behave better.

CULTURAL FACTORS

Child abuse is widespread in our culture. Reports of abuse appear in the medical literature and daily press in most countries of our

Western world. Abusing parents voice common clichés such as "Children need to be taught respect for parents and obedience to authority," "You have to use discipline on children or they'll grow up to be delinquent," "If you give in to babies and pick them up when they cry, they will be spoiled rotten," and "Children have to be taught they can't have their own way in this world." One father expressed it: "I'd rather see my kids disciplined and afraid of me than loved, pampered, and spoiled." The warning "Spare the rod and spoil the child" is still a basic tenet in our culture, even though now less openly expressed than in the past. One need only go to the supermarket or playground, or observe one's neighbors, to see how much yelling, criticism, slapping, and yanking is vented on small children. Our society seems to condone such behavior despite some dismay. All of us are aware that children need to be "civilized" during their early developmental years. It is a necessary part of psychic maturation that we develop the mechanisms that control the unbridled expression of basic instinctual drives. Abusing parents are characterized by their implementation of this culturally accepted goal, with exaggerated punitive attack and less empathic consideration for the infant early in the child's life. This particular style of parental behavior toward children can be considered "culture-bound" in the sense that it is widespread and is passed from one generation to the next as a socially useful pattern.

The Clinical Picture

Like all parents of very young children, the great majority of abusing parents are in their late teens, twenties, or early thirties. In addition to their chronologic youth, they usually show several of the characteristics lumped under the vague terms *immature* and *dependent*. A few talk openly of how they have mistreated their infants and hesitantly, embarrassedly ask for some sort of help. Most often they are evasive, either denying any knowledge of how the baby could have been hurt or giving glib, inadequate, inappropriate, inconsistent explanations of how the injuries occurred. They tend to avoid or actively rebuff the medical, psychiatric, and social service personnel, either insisting there is nothing to talk about or failing to keep appointments. If insensitively accused of abusing their child, they often respond by denial, feeling insulted, being angry, or even making threats. On the

453

other hand, some respond by superficial submissive cooperation and talk freely, but give only information which seems peripheral, useless, or camouflaging. This puzzling variety of reactions becomes understandable upon further investigation of the parents' lives.

Abusing parents are lonely people, yearning for love and understanding, yet plagued by a deep sense of inferiority and an inability to have any confidence in being lovable or in finding real understanding and help. Such feelings may be overt but often are covered by a superficial, defensive facade of social competence and protestations of "everything is all right." The deep convictions of helplessness and ineffectuality are frequently hidden beneath attitudes of righteous certainty about their ideas and actions and strong expressions of their right to run their own lives without interference. Related to this righteous attitude of doing only what is appropriate and necessary to make a child grow up and behave well is the rather striking absence of a sense of guilt over their actions, often noted in abusing parents. Some reveal a pseudoparanoid attitude of suspiciousness and ideas that others in the world will make trouble for them. At different times they present distinctly different pictures of themselves and their style of living, suggesting a problem in the area of identity.[3] This is not an amorphous lack of identity, but rather a lack of integration of disparate, strong identifications that will be discussed more fully later in this chapter.

All the abusing parents we have seen were brought up in much the same manner as that employed in raising their own children. They may or may not have been subjected to severe physical abuse in early life but, even if not physically punished for their failure to behave well, they felt deeply crushed by disapproval. Invariably they tell of insistent demands from their parents for proper response and behavior. From their earliest years on, they felt the necessity to be alert and sensitive to parental needs, no matter how excessive, and to attempt to meet them. At the same time, they felt that their own desires, feel-

[3] At this time there is no concensus among the psychoanalysts on either the definitions or the metapsychology of introjection, internalization, identification, identity, self, self-representation, etc. Various conceptual frameworks have been presented by Freud, Hartmann, Kris, Lowenstein, Jacobson, Erikson, Rapaport, Loewald, Schafer, and others. The author is describing clinical observations in terms that have some general understandability without trying to fit them into any specific conceptual system. The reader is encouraged to interpret the observations in any frame of reference he prefers.

454

ings, and thoughts were largely disregarded or belittled. (Mrs. P., who had fractured the skull and pelvis of her infant son because he was "lazy and stubborn," told us: "Mother never paid any attention to what I thought or felt. I was just her servant.") Such persons had been subjected to recurrent criticism and felt they had never been able to do well enough to gain real parental approval for their efforts or performance. Nothing they had done was ever good enough. This sense of ineptness, unworthiness, and unimportance felt by abusing parents is primarily in relation to their mothers. They had looked to their mothers, as do all children, for the deepest understanding, sympathy, and comfort but had failed to find it. Throughout life they have pathetically yearned for good mothering, returning again and again to their mothers, seeking for it but not finding it, and ending up with disappointment, disillusionment, lowered self-esteem, and anger. A similar, but usually less intense situation, existed in their relationships to fathers. Some abusive parents had overidealized their fathers and turned to them to find the mothering they had never had. To a degree, their fathers seemed more rewarding, more able to satisfy some dependency needs. But inevitably the fathers too were disappointing and failed to meet emotional needs adequately and the child again felt helpless and defeated.

Among those abusing parents who had been physically abused in childhood, attacks by mothers were more disturbing than attacks by fathers. Even when the father was the attacker, the child felt more devastated by the mother's failure to protect him against attack than by the actual paternal attack itself. This is not surprising in view of the universal human conviction that mother should be the original, basic, and most reliable source of protection and comfort. It was, however, an extremely distressing experience when a temporarily successful pattern of "child being good to parent" broke down with father. The child was thrown back on the mother with no method of seeking self-esteem. Sometimes there was a superficial sense of self-esteem arising from a belief of having pleased a parent, but it was readily shattered by recurrent criticism.

Abusing parents felt that their siblings, either older or younger, were favored over themselves. This was not a problem of masculinity or femininity, but simply an obvious fact of life that the parents were more accepting and approving of the siblings. They could rarely understand or verbalize why or ever hope to solve the problem; compensation was not possible. (In some girls, superimposed upon this more basic sense of inferiority, there developed the additional mechanism of penis envy.) Even though all children in the family were exposed to the same general demand and criticism, disregard, and punishment, the patient felt subjected to the greatest degree of it; but we have seen a few instances in which an abusing parent had a sibling also involved in child abuse.

The few only children we have seen have given no evidence of having been "spoiled or coddled"; on the contrary, they gave the same history of experiencing intense early parental demand, disregard, and punitive attitudes. A very few abusing parents have told us they felt that they had been their mother's favorite. On investigation, this proved to be a reference to a few instances in which the mother had been kind and giving in a useful way, but this was a material gift of money, or a car, or clothes; not evidence of a deep, personal, loving, understanding regard. The belief of being mother's favorite was really a clinging to a few good memories in a desperate attempt to maintain a sense of being loved and to deny the painful awareness of having been repeatedly criticized and disregarded.

Parents in our study had rarely been able to disagree openly with their parents or rebel against them, and had developed the pattern of submitting to parental criticism and punishment without open complaint. Intense feelings of anger and resentment toward the parents were common, but these could not be directly expressed toward them without making our patients feel unbearably endangered.

Most of the information about the early lives of abusing parents is derived from their own retrospective histories. This could be challenged on the basis of the inevitable instances of amnesia and distortion that occur during history-giving. We had the good fortune, however, on several occasions to interview the abusing parents' own parents and sometimes to see direct interaction among them. From such observations we were able to corroborate, often in great detail, the elements outlined above. We obtained some data from the abused infants' grandparents about their own childhood. They, too, had been brought up in much the same way. We believe that we have seen the basic ingredients of this pattern of child-rearing and style of parent-child interaction that leads to abuse in three successive generations.

A mechanism for the transmission of such patterns from generation to generation has been described by Benedek, who tells how an adult, on becoming a parent, experiences an upsurge of two sets of early intense memories, largely unconscious. One of these is a group of memories of what it was like to be a child, as far back as one can recall. The other is a cluster of memories of how one was parented, of what one's parents did to one, and the way in which they did it. The integration of these two sets of memories or identifications constitutes the basis for the parents' relationships to the newborn child and the style of interaction with him. If one's own infancy was good, with a rewarding experience of being parented, the integration of these two memories enables one to be empathically sensitive to an infant's needs and to have a useful repertoire of care-taking responses. Abusing parents do not enjoy this happy state. Their concept of the self as an infant is that of being incapable and unrewarding and not understood. Their memory of parental behavior is that of disregard, demand, criticism, and often physical punishment. These two concepts cannot, of course, be integrated into a comfortable pattern of parent-child interaction, and trouble will develop. It seems likely that the basic elements in all styles of parental behavior have their origin in this mechanism and that undesirable patterns are transmitted in the same way as healthy ones [5]. Just as "good" parents can draw on the good experience of their early lives, abusing parents reenact a less useful experience of the first early years.

MISPERCEPTIONS OF THE INFANT

Commonly noted are misperceptions of the baby as being "bad." Abusing parents in various ways describe their infants as too dependent, too fussy, uncooperative, stubborn, disobedient, inconsiderate, unloving, worthless, and bothersome. To an outside observer the baby looks helpless, little, sometimes content, sometimes fussy, crying, and hard to comfort. He is not a bad baby; he is just a normal baby, busy being a baby. A clue to the meaning of such misperceptions are statements made by abusing parents, such as "the baby gets his stubbornness from me," "she's as bad as me when I was a kid," "I was always doing the wrong things when I was little, too, and had to be punished." In short, the abusing parent sees the offspring as another edition of his own bad childhood self.

Such misperceptions of the infant, which are intimately involved with the act of abuse, have been noted by many observers and have often been considered evidence of a serious psychopathologic state. Kaufman, for instance, has described them as probably indicative of a psychotic process of schizophrenic nature involving great use of the mechanisms of denial and projection [14]. It may be that Kaufman was working with more seriously disturbed parents. We, too, have seen abusers who were schizophrenic, but by far the great majority of our patients have not shown evidence, either from clinical data or from thorough psychologic testing, of a thinking disorder of psychotic nature. Hence, it seems more likely that the misperceptions of the infant are expressions of potent, unconscious residuals of the parents' early childhood experience. He has a strong image of himself as an unrewarding, worthless child, and an equally strong identification with the critical parent who considers children unsatisfactory. The identification of the infant as bad is not a psychotic identification accomplished by denial and projection, but rather what Fenichel described as reverse identification[4] [10].

A further determinant of these feelings about the child is the abusing parent's firm conviction that those to whom one looks for need satisfaction will fail to respond appropriately, which is a direct result of the childhood experience with his own parents. In this context, "misperception" of the child as a need-satisfying object which will be unrewarding is a transference phenomenon. The poor reality-testing is not of a psychotic nature but only that which is inherent in all illogical transference reactions. This same transference pervades all other relationships in the abusing parent's life. Other adults are seen as unsatisfying objects, and it is useless to look to them for help. When in need of comfort, the parent falls back on his identification with his own parents and looks to an infant to take care of his needs. This transference problem is obviously a source of great difficulty in therapy.

Some of the clearest statements of the psychologic set which plagues the abusing parents' relationship to infants are the thoughts expressed by mothers during pregnancy. Both the identification with the punitive parent and the misperception of the child as a new edi-

---

[4] We consider normal identification as "I am like him." Reverse identification is "He is like me." Psychotic projective identification would be "It is not I; it is he."

tion of the bad childhood self are pictured. Examples are the following: One mother said, "If my baby is a girl, I am likely to treat her as mother treated me. I will hate her the way my mother hated me. She will be as angry at me as I am at my mother. It will be a mess." Another mother, Mrs. H., had often been told how she had damaged her mother's pelvic organs, ruined her marriage, and had been berated for having too close a relationship with her father. Her mother had repeatedly beaten her from infancy to the teens. During pregnancy she felt she did not want her unborn child because it would ruin her figure, deny her freedom, and shatter her chances for a good marriage. She often spoke to her husband about her fear that he would spoil the baby when it came, and asked him many times how soon she could start disciplining it. The baby, a girl, had a fractured femur at age 1 month and a fractured skull with subdural hematomas at 3 months. The problem is not always gender-linked, as it is in the two above examples. Both mothers and fathers can express these attitudes toward both boys and girls.

Fantasies about what an unborn child will be like, and how one will parent it, are ubiquitous among mothers- and fathers-to-be. Normally there are high expectations of success and satisfaction, and the fears of difficulty are ameliorated by the confidence that useful help can be found in the environment. The abusing parent has expectations of trouble and dissatisfaction, and is convinced that no understanding help can be available, no matter how desperately it is needed. Problems are inevitable and will have to be solved by aggressive discipline, with the infant bearing the brunt of it.

The Lack of Motherliness

It is possible to describe the essence of abusive behavior in simplified terms as a deficit in motherliness. Usually the more mechanical aspects of mothering, such as feeding, diapering, bathing, and clothing, are carried out adequately well. Significant breakdown occurs in the maternal affectional system in the area of sensitive, emotional interaction with the infant and the warm, empathic awareness of its needs, feelings, and abilities, which we call "motherliness." Caretaking actions of the abusing parent are carried out with an unconscious hope of satisfying unmet parental needs, and a corresponding

459

disregard of the infant, a significant lack of motherliness. This deficit in an abusing parent can be explained by the lack of motherliness in the parent's own early infantile experience. Benedek [2–4] has written of the importance of the early, primary, symbiotic relationship of mother and child and its profound influence on later psychologic development. Adequate experience in infancy with an empathic mother lays the foundation for being an empathic adult and vice versa. Kohut and Olden have also described this origin of adult empathy [16, 20].

It must be borne in mind that motherliness is not limited to biologic mothers. It can be fully present in adoptive mothers, foster mothers, maiden aunts, nurses, and matrons in foundling homes. Children, both boys and girls, can demonstrate it with each other and with babies. Men, too, can show it if they are not too fearful of being "unmasculine." Josselyn wrote that the ability to show tenderness, gentleness, and empathy "is not a prerogative of women alone; it is a human characteristic" [13]. During the routines of baby care, it is a deficit in motherliness which sets the stage for abuse to occur. This is true of fathers and mothers and of baby-sitters and other care-takers.

Deficiency in empathic mothering experience during infancy leads to a lack of confidence or basic trust in the adult [2, 9]. Abusing parents show this lack of confidence to a high degree. They have no deep sense that they could be cared for or cared about, or that the world could be good to them. They are not easily able to ask for help or to stimulate a helpful attitude in the environment. The very idea of help is foreign to them because they feel that the ones to whom they look for help are the ones who will attack them.

CASE 2.   Mrs. S., a bright, well-educated, attractive young woman came to us voluntarily, hesitantly asking for help with her feelings of mild, pervasive depression and concern over abusive behavior toward her infant son. In the first three sessions she told us of feelings throughout her life that her mother had never really listened to her or understood her. She described how disapproving and angry her mother had been when she did not behave properly and did not suit the mother's expectations. No matter how hard she tried, she had rarely been able to find out how to please her mother. She told of her anger and punitive behavior toward her 5-month-old son when he did not do as she wished. She felt great anguish and distress that she was just as bad as her mother was. In her fourth session, she reported a dream: "I was with mother. There was the usual feeling of tension. We were in a motel and had gone to bed in twin beds. I woke up. Something in white was standing over me, very threatening. It was terrifying. I called to my mother for help and she answered, 'I am your mother' and it turned out that she was the creature in white who was threatening me. I woke up screaming." Mrs. S.'s associations to this dream were variations on the themes of lack of closeness to her mother, fear of her mother's recurrent critical attacks upon her, feelings of helplessness and hopelessness, coupled with resentment of her mother.

In this brief vignette we see the interweaving of many ideas, "I have a bad mother," "My mother hates me," "I want my mother but I am afraid of her," "I am like my mother and I am mean to my child," "I do not believe that I can ever get help or understanding." This material, appearing in the early stage of her looking to us for therapeutic help, carries significant transference implications. Other patients have given us similar material, although rarely with such concentrated clarity.

The abusing parents' ideas of people being unhelpful and attacking can in some instances become so pervasive and intense that they have a paranoid-like quality. The mechanism of projection, however, is not involved. Rather, there is a widespread expression of feelings that originated toward parents in early childhood. Whenever there is a need for love and understanding, the object becomes dangerous, a direct transference reaction. This lack of confidence is a most important element in the pattern of abuse. When spouse, family, friends, and neighbors cannot be looked to for aid in time of difficulty, the abusing parent has nowhere to turn except to his own infant for this comfort. This desperate "last-chance" turning to the infant for comfort is another determinant in the misperception of the child as a need-satisfying object. In view of the lack of confidence, it is not surprising that many persons, particularly female social workers, interested in doing something for abusing parents, have felt they either do not want help or are unavailable to therapeutic intervention. The intense, fear-ridden ambivalence which such patients feel toward mother-figures makes seeking or believing in help a frightening or impossible task for them.

Ego and Superego Development

As already implied, study of parents who abuse children has led us to the belief that the essence of the abusive behavior had its origin in the early pregenital phases of the parents' lives, predominantly in relation to lack of empathic mothering combined with early excessive demand and control. The oedipal phase and later developments may have significant effect on the choice of which child is abused when, and for what reason, but during the stress and turmoil that lead to the act of abuse, there is regression to pregenital conflicts and fixations. The belief in this origin comes from several sources. First, the gross observation that the parents are repeating with their infants the manner in which they were raised as children. Second, the reconstructions we can make of the parents' early mother-child relationships from their factual histories and associations, plus data from their own parents. Third, the direct observations of the responses of abused infants to the treatment they receive. We believe we see in the abused infant's development a reenactment of what went on in the parent's own infancy.

It seems likely that the major difficulty begins at the time there is a change from the state of primary narcissism into the beginning of object relationships, when the I and the non-I begin to be separated. This is probably around age 3 months, when the smiling response becomes established. It is at this time that the earliest rudiments and precursors of the ego and superego begin to be recognizable. The perceptions the infant has of the primary object, the mother, begin to be introjected and become the earliest primitive identifications, some of the first elements of later psychic structures. The empathic pleasure-giving mother forms the basis of the ego ideal, and the pain-giving, frustrating, controlling mother forms the anlage of the superego. The abusing parent had an insufficiently empathic and pleasure-giving mother. The result is an impoverished ego ideal, which leads eventually in the adult to unempathic behavior with children. On the other hand, the controlling, frustrating, punitive mother was a much stronger image, leading to a strong, controlling, punitive superego primordium.

Spitz describes the precursors that antedate the final formation of the superego at the time of the resolution of the oedipal conflict. He considers physical restraint to be the earliest rudiment and says:

. . . among the primordia which will form up the superego there are some to which we have paid little attention up to the present. They belong to the perceptual sector of tactile and visual impressions, such as restraining the child physically on the one hand, the facial expression, as well as the tone of voice which accompanies such prohibiting interference on the other. Similarly, imposing physical actions on the infant, whether he likes it or not, in dressing, diapering, bathing, feeding, burping him, etc., will inevitably leave memory traces in the nature of commands. These physical primordia of prohibitions and commands are not easily recognizable in the ultimate organization which is the superego [22].

We agree with Spitz entirely in this concept of the earliest beginning of superego structure and would add that in the abusing parent we can clearly recognize the results of this early state in the ultimate superego organization.

We have observed parents during their routine care-taking behavior with infants express great amounts of physical restraint and physical attack, accompanied by angry vocal command and facial expression. If the infant persists in crying, despite all efforts to comfort him, or keeps wriggling too much during diaper-changing or bathing, or interferes with feeding, or refuses to eat rapidly enough, the parent is likely to attack. These events occur early in the infant's life, before, during, and after his crucial phase of transition from narcissism to early object relationships. We have seen infants respond very quickly and accurately to such parental control. They often show restrictions of spontaneous behavior and a rechanneling of action into forms that suit parental demand. A simple example is that of a mother who told us in a righteous, angry tone: "When I fed Timmy his first solid food, at age 3 weeks, he got hold of the spoon and messed the food around. I slapped his hands. He never reached for that spoon again." Much later we saw her with her 7-month-old daughter, who sat in her high-chair with her arms held rigidly up in the air, quickly eating from the spoon her mother offered her.

Such response by the infant indicates to us that some kind of intrapsychic change has taken place. We interpret it as early superego formation because, functionally, it demonstrates control and suppression of certain instinctual drive discharges. It is also apparent that the development of elements in the conflict-free sphere of the ego has been hampered. Not only has spontaneous exploratory motor discharge been interrupted, but sensory experiences of touching and feeling have been inhibited.[5] More subtly, possibly more importantly, an early imitative identification has been negated. These babies cannot

[5] In Piaget's terms, these infants have suffered a distortion of their very earliest sensorimotor schemata, with inevitable developmental consequences.

463

interact with the mother, by putting food to her mouth as she feeds them, a happy experience which infants can have and which helps them make identification with a loving, feeding object. It seems likely, too, that such early control and limitations of free, independent motor and sensory experience will diminish or distort to some degree the development of the integrative function of the ego. Under the pressure of parental demand there is forced adherence to parental ideas and expectations, and the infant is limited in obtaining and using data from his own exploration and experience. Further, he is not allowed to integrate in the ego his own feelings and desires; these must be kept isolated, and to a large extent denied. This is an early determinant of what we see in the adult as lack of integration of the concepts of the self as a helpless, needy child and the concepts of self as adult parent.

A second superego precursor is the mechanism of defense, described by Anna Freud as "identification with the aggressor" [11]. This could probably not occur before the second year of life, when object relationships and ego functions have become more sophisticated. Spitz associates it with the child's acquisition of the semantic "No" [21]. It is our impression, however, that previous to clear identification with the aggressor, something else has already happened, which we might call a primitive "imitative identification with aggression." Although some infants may become more cooperative and docile under the influence of repeated parental attack, others begin to show increasing amounts of insistent clamoring, more resistant behavior, and angry, glaring facial expression. This seems to be different from the activity of the congenitally more assertive infant and from the usual aggressive response to frustration. It seems more likely that the infant's copious exposure to aggressive parental behavior has led the primitive ego to take over the use of aggression as a customary "way of life." In this sense, it is in resonance with, or an imitation of, the parental behavior, and is somewhat analogous to the well-recognized pattern of infants being happy or depressed or irritable as responses to the mother's moods. We do not know, either from historical data or longitudinal studies, whether this leads to greater aggressive behavior in adults or not. In our patients, the classic mechanism of identification with the aggressor has a very special flavor of an identification with a parent-aggressor against child object. The adult parent shows a residue of this, not only in the intrapsychic denigrating

attacks on the self as an inept child, but also in the tendency to criticize spouse, other adults, and children for what is considered unacceptable child-like behavior (or what was considered bad behavior in
himself as a child). Most obviously, abusing parents overtly repeat
toward their children the aggressive attitudes of their own parents toward themselves.

NARCISSISM AND MASOCHISM

Relics of the early, primitive, narcissistic state persist into the
abusing parent's adult life. Although often unable to express it, these
parents have a strong, demanding need for care, love, and approval in
a very infantile way, and this is accompanied by a "selfish" disregard
of the objects from whom they want this attention. Closely related is a
residue of the early sense of omnipotence; a feeling of "I can and I
will make the world around behave to suit me." This has been merged
with, and enhanced by, the superego identifications with the authoritative, punitive parent. Also, persistent relics of injured narcissism
plague abusing parents, evidenced in the recurrent tendency toward
an anaclitic type of depression. They are exquisitely sensitive to any
hint of lack of love or approval and to rejection and desertion in any
form. They react to such environmental stimuli with hopeless feelings
of depression, inferiority, and anger. The arousal of this constellation
of feelings is often a most important factor in setting the stage for
individual abusive acts.

Moral masochism, often of high degree, is commonly found as
a significant element in the abusing parent's personality. There is the
instigation of many self-defeating actions in general living, and the
prolonged toleration and unconscious creation of extremely unpleasant interpersonal relationships. Our understanding of the origin of this
process in these patients essentially agrees with that of Berliner [6],
whose position is that moral masochism is not a person's own sadism
directed against the self but, as in our patients, a persistent search for
love from the primitive object who is sadistic rather than loving. The
sadistic love object is, of course, incorporated into the superego. Our
patients have persistently returned again and again to their mothers or
mother substitutes seeking love and understanding but getting only
criticism, inconsideration, and demand. In a similar way, although

465

some abused infants show fear and withdrawal, most often we see the small child turn with open arms to the parent who has injured him or has been his constant, unloving critic.

LATER DEVELOPMENT

The same style of child-rearing continues through the subsequent phases of the infant's development. Toilet training may be instituted as early as the fourth to sixth month of age, and is often accomplished by incessant demand, much criticism, belittlement, and excessive physical abuse. At the same time, the infant's increasing activities of crawling, walking, talking, and playing are met by high parental expectations, prohibitions, and specific, directive channelings.

CASE 3. Mrs. P., who had seriously injured her baby and bitterly complained of having been nothing but a servant of her own mother, had an older son, Sammy, not quite 2½ years old. She spoke with pride and pleasure of how he always washed the breakfast dishes, vacuumed the living room, and efficiently baked cakes from ready-mix materials. Often he was with her during office visits, and when I gave him things to play with, she would say angrily: "Be careful. Don't break that or Dr. Steele will spank you. He'll get a needle and give you a shot." Spontaneously, he would empty my ash tray in the wastebasket, and if he spilled any ashes on the floor, would quietly find a Kleenex and wipe them up. His mother beamed and said he always did this at home, too, rarely letting more than one stub accumulate in a tray. Sammy was remarkably adept at tying his shoes and putting on and buttoning his coat, but if he made mistakes, his mother would call him "stupid" and whack him. Occasionally, he would imitate his mother's angry glare and voice, then grin. At times, this seemed to amuse her, but at other times she slapped him for being "sassy." Sammy is doubtless a very handy servant to have around the house, but he is far from being an average 2½-year-old boy. Mrs. P. told us that she always picked the boys up and held them twice a day, but that it was a mistake to do so because it spoiled them. She told how her mother frequently criticized her for the way she raised the boys, telling her that the babies were too demanding, that they had to be taught to take care of themselves, and that Sammy "ought to have his butt blistered every time he turns around."

It is not surprising that the recurrent frustrations and frequent exposure to aggressive behavior during the infant's first two years lead to the expression in the adult of behavior categorized as "oral" and "anal" aggression.

The child growing up under these circumstances can hardly have a normal oedipal phase. Genital strivings are markedly colored and hampered by the already existing pregenital conflicts and fixations. The little boy cannot look toward his mother with full, warm, sexual yearning and fantasies. He is still too involved with desires for unmet oral satisfaction, and is too fearful of her rejection or attack. His conflict with the father has as much the flavor of a genderless sibling rivalry for mother love as it has of masculine competition. Likewise, the girl turns to her father with her genital strivings much diminished or overshadowed by her need for him to supply the basic mothering she has lacked. She is also excessively concerned lest she lose the meager love she has had from her mother or be attacked by her. The resolution of such an orally oriented oedipal conflict is characterized by inadequate identification with a sexual adult and by a superego which remains predominantly concerned with the suppression of pregenital drives.

Later development through adolescence follows the same pattern. Parental demand and criticism continue. The growing child's efforts to explore, observe, and think for himself are restricted. Attempts to find new models with whom to identify are considered erroneous or are clearly prohibited. Parents express to the child a potent, personal version of the biblical commandment, "Thou shalt have no other gods before me." There is constant repetition of two mutually reinforcing pressures: to respond to parental authority and to disregard inner feelings and thoughts. As a consequence, there is diminished internalization and development of integrated self-directed standards of behavior. Correspondingly, there is a greater than normal dependence upon fear of criticism and punishment from external sources as guides and controls of behavior. The balance between internalization and external orientation varies from patient to patient, but the relative diminution of internalization is one determinant of the lack of a conventional sense of guilt, often observed in abusing parents.

THE INFLUENCE OF OTHER PARENTAL PSYCHOPATHOLOGY

Up to now we have discussed only the basic pattern of parent-child interaction considered to be the essential minimum in abusive behavior. Abusing parents also have a wide spectrum of other conflicts and character structures, depending upon the individual variations of their developmental experience. Some of these other character traits are significant in determining which child is more likely to be attacked when and for what, and they interact intimately with the developmental phases of the infant.

Obsessive-compulsive characters with rigid attitudes toward dirtiness, messiness, disorder, and disobedience are much more likely to attack when their infants show these qualities. According to the parent's specific concerns, the attack may occur early in situations of food-messing, slobbering, or vomiting, or it may occur later in relation to excretory messiness, or still later when clothes are dirtied during play and toys are strewed around. We assume that the infant's behavior threatens the parent's stability by stimulating unacceptable, unconscious impulses to be messy. The parent must forcefully maintain his own repression and aggressively attack the stimulating infant. Such attacks appear on the surface to be very simple and direct, but they occur in the already existing setting of excessive premature parental demand and intolerance for infantile errors and inabilities.

Unresolved, intense sibling rivalry is another frequent contributing factor. Both men and women have a great tendency to abuse an infant toward whom they transfer and relive the resentment felt toward either brothers or sisters who were preferred over themselves. In some abusive mothers, there is the additional impetus of anger and envy toward males. An example of the latter is as follows.

CASE 4. Naomi was a fourth child, raised largely by baby-sitters until age 6, and then by a grandmother, who, she felt, did not love her. She did not think either her mother or her father really cared for her, especially her mother. An older sister was the only person she loved or felt loved by. A brother 3 years older was the family favorite, and she felt that her life was ruined by being neglected while he got everything. She hated and envied her father, brother, husband, and all men. A belligerent sense of rightness in her behavior thinly covered deep feelings of being inadequate and worthless as a mother. Her first child, a girl, was raised strictly and became very submissive, obedient, and cooperative. However, Naomi said: "I'd beat her, too, if she rebelled or got angry at me."

An unwanted pregnancy produced a boy 2 years later. Naomi said, "He came too soon after the girl and cheated her out of her childhood. I weaned him at 2½ months because nursing him upset her. I hate him; the mere sight of his genitals upsets me. I don't have time for him; I wish he'd never been born or that I could give him away to someone who'd love him. I want to hit him, hurt him, shake him, get him out of the way." She also said she saw all her own undesirable qualities in him. Naomi slapped, bruised, and roughed up this baby boy, and by age 2 he had had three head wounds requiring stitches.

Abuse of the infant son is obviously related to sibling rivalry and envious anger toward males. Yet Naomi shows the basic pattern of demand and criticism with her daughter, too. Only the fortunate accidents of sex, time of birth, and ability to respond correctly prevented abuse of her first child. A more common variation is exemplified by another mother who had some episodes of abusing her baby boy triggered by emotional turmoil arising when her own mother came to help her care for him. She would become angry because he seemed to be getting the good mothering which she had not had, but which had been bestowed on her only sibling, a younger sister. Not only did she feel that her baby was taking her own mother away from her, but also that any success her mother had with the baby was a critical belittlement of her own mothering ability.

The effects of unresolved oedipal conflict and excessive oedipal guilt are more difficult to assess. Although, as noted before, our patients tended to have inadequate or distorted development, there was great variation and a few had a more nearly "normal" oedipal phase. Mrs. H. (page 459) probably revealed the clearest evidence of oedipal difficulty as an instigator of abuse. She recalled having a warm, close relationship with her father when she was a little girl, and that her mother had berated her and beaten her for this. After delivery of her first baby, a girl, she had recurrent dreams of her husband being seduced away from her by a sexy brunette whom she described as looking as Cindy would look when older. By the time Cindy was 3 months old, Mrs. H. had fractured the child's femur and skull. This type of material was not frequently seen in our patients. What appeared superficially to be oedipal rivalry was found not to be so when deeper, unconscious motivation was explored. The fathers who became abusive toward a baby boy for having too much close warmth with the mother, or a mother who attacked a baby girl who was happily "being spoiled" by the father, actually were angry because the baby seemed to be getting the motherly love they had missed and still yearned for. It resembled sibling rivalry more than an oedipal problem.

Zilboorg has described parental antagonism and attack of older children and its close relationship to oedipal conflict [24]. We would agree that abuse of children over 3 or 4, especially if it begins at that time, is profoundly influenced by parental concern over sexuality and competitiveness. Zilboorg also clearly noted two factors that have impressed us: the parental tendency to see the child as the reincarnation of the bad self, and the strength of the punitive superego. He wrote:

. . . the stronger the parents' "conscience," that is, the stronger their inhibitions, the greater will be their hostility against the child's freedom. To put it in technical terms: to the unconscious of the parents the child plays the role of the Id; the parents follow it vicariously for a time and then hurl upon it with all the force of their Super Ego; they project onto the child their own Id and then punish it to gratify the demands of their uncompromising Super Ego.

In the situation of abuse of infants, however, the parental behavior is much more the result of pregenital determinants than of oedipal residues.

THE ATTACK

Varying degrees of physical attack are superimposed on the basic parental attitude of unempathic premature demand and scolding of the infant. Some parents frequently slap and spank during all routine care-taking acts: they whack, poke, or severely pinch the infant each time they pass the crib, and they may burn the infant with a cigarette or hit him with handy household objects. Although no serious injuries or fractures occur, the infant shows bruises, minor lacerations, and burns. Such children have been called "tormented" children. Other infants have periods of relatively good care interspersed with isolated attacks of yanking and hitting of great severity, causing fractures, massive bruising, lacerations, or visceral injury. These are the typical battered children. Frequently seen are welts and bruises produced by belts and electric cords, burns from hot electric appliances or dipping in hot water, bruises and fractures caused by choking, shaking, or throwing the baby against the wall or side of the crib. There are many variations and combinations of these patterns. It would seem impractical and of little value to place tormented and battered infants in separate diagnostic categories except from the standpoint of gross pathologic description of injuries. Parents may torment one of their children and batter another, or one child who has been tormented may later be battered. Some children in a family may be physically abused while others are not. In short, the type of abuse is not an accurate guide to the pathologic state of the parent.

Despite minor variations, the psychologic state of the parent seems basically the same in all the different forms of abuse. It is, however, in the more violent, explosive attacks leading to serious injury that we can see most clearly the full operation of the psychopathologic condition of the parent. Usually the mother approaches the care-taking tasks with the good intention of doing well for the baby, both because she wants to and because she thinks it is her duty. She is handicapped, however, by her own lifelong, unsatisfied need to be loved and cared for and her conviction that she is basically unable to do well enough at anything expected of her. If, previous to her care-taking activity, she has been criticized, misunderstood, or deserted by spouse, family, or any other important figure, she feels especially inferior and lonely, her needs for loving approval are increased, so she turns as an unloved child herself to the only available object, her baby, to get this desperate need satisfied. If the baby happens to respond well, cooperates, and seems happily satisfied by her efforts, all goes well. If the baby continues to cry in spite of what she does, however, or if the baby in any way interferes with what she is trying to do, she becomes increasingly frustrated and feels criticized and unloved. Some patients tell us, "When the baby keeps crying, it sounds just like my mother yelling at me and criticizing me." This situation of generation reversal, in which the parent feels like an unloved, criticized child and sees the infant as a critical, unloving parent, involves considerable regression. Regression opens the way for resurgence of infantile anger toward the parents of childhood, anger which has always been prohibited and inhibited. The regression also makes possible the full use of an equally early ego defense, the mechanism of identification with the aggressor. A shift takes place. The mother identifies with her own punitive parent and sees the child as equivalent to her own bad childhood self and, therefore, deserving punishment. This makes possible the release of aggressive attack on the infant, with full superego approval and a sense of righteousness. Having inadequate empathy and an overstrict, punitive superego, there is nothing else for the mother to do. Fathers exhibit the same psychologic processes[6] [19].

---

[6] After developing the above understanding of the attack we found that Olden [19] had previously described a similar phenomenon: ". . . the child,

Many persons are distressed by not finding a sense of guilt in the abusing parent. It is obvious from the above description that the parent might not have a sense of guilt. Obedience to the demands and dictates of the superego automatically makes guilt unlikely. The attack on the child is a superego syntonic function. There are, of course, variations in this phenomenon. In some patients, there is a degree of empathy for the child and sympathy with his hurts, related to the identification of the child with the parent's own hurt-child self. As one mother told us: "After I hit Johnny, I sat down by the crib and cried and cried. I felt as if I had hit myself." Some parents have told us that in the midst of the turmoil of feeling like an unloved child, unloved by their own baby, they are aware of a deep sense of sadness. They say: "When the baby is crying, I feel like crying myself." Interestingly, if they can break down and cry themselves, they do not go ahead and hit the baby. It is as if the breakthrough of previously repressed true feelings of sadness prevents the shift into identification with the aggressor. Another variation described by a very few patients is a curious sense of relief, almost pleasure, which follows hitting the child. This does not seem to be a fusion of erotic and aggressive drives as would occur in true sadism. Rather, it resembles the process of recovery from depression in which aggression which has been directed against the bad self is redirected and discharged onto an external bad object.

THE ROLE OF THE INFANT

There is no doubt that some babies, by their very nature, are more likely than others to stimulate parental attack. A baby conceived premaritally, or coming too soon after a previous child, may well start life as an embarrassing, interfering, and unrewarding object in his parents' lives. Premature and sickly infants, and those with congenital defects, require much more care and are less able to respond to parental needs. Either boys or girls can be thought of as unsatisfactory

---

representing the parent's own parent, and especially the mother, causes in the parent a fear and a feeling of helplessness and an aggressiveness similar to what the parent felt for his own parent. Aggressiveness toward the children may at the same time derive from a reversal of this situation; that is, in addition to the aggressiveness of which he was the subject, the parent takes over the aggressiveness of which he was the object. By the defense mechanism of identification with the aggressor he acts out with his children the aggressiveness his parents aimed at him."

because the other sex was desired. Parental displeasure can be aroused if the baby is temperamentally either very active or too passive when the opposite type was hoped for. Yet none of these situations, which create obvious burdens and disappointments for parents, can be used as an adequate cause or excuse for acts of abuse. The possibility of a baby's being different from a hoped-for ideal is a normal hazard faced by all those who have children. The common denominator in the situations where abuse occurs is the innocent infant's failure to meet exaggerated, unyielding parental need.

More subtle are the cases of abuse of older infants and young children whose behavior is described by their parents as extremely disobedient, rebellious, basically bad, provocative, or uncontrollable. Observers can corroborate the described behavior and may even agree with the need for strong discipline. Aggressive hyperactivity due to obscure neural abnormality may be suspected. Investigation, however, often reveals that the child was relatively normal for a variable period of months before the bad behavior started. Further, such children may show great shifts toward normal behavior soon after placement in a more protective home. Thus, it seems possible in these cases that the child has responded to earlier aggressive parental action by becoming more aggressive himself, rather than the parents responding appropriately to a stubbornly recalcitrant child. The situation is reminiscent of a remark made by comedian Sam Levenson who, when asked if he believed mental illness was inherited, replied: "Yes, you get it from your children."

THE NONABUSING SPOUSE

With few exceptions only one parent attacks the child. The husband or wife of the abusing parent may show indifference or approval, but, even if openly disapproving of the abuse, is almost invariably covertly condoning or abetting it. The nonabusing spouse usually has a background and personality structure similar to the abuser. Attitudes toward children are the same, although less intense. The care-taker can be directly encouraged to attack a child if the spouse says such things as, "That kid is getting spoiled; you've got to discipline him more." Criticism of the care-taking parent's behavior, disregard of pleas for help, attitudes of emotional withdrawal or deserting be-

473

havior can be potent stimulators of abuse. Such actions toward the potential abuser not only arouse anger but also intensify the need for love, so the abuser turns to the baby with an increased demand for satisfaction which cannot be met. The unconscious collusion of the nonabusing spouse may become apparent only during therapy of the abuser. As the latter becomes gentler, the previously nonabusing parent begins to attack the infant. Therefore, it is often necessary to involve both parents in treatment or counseling of some sort to alleviate the problem.

TREATMENT

In a previous publication we have described the treatment of abusing parents in some detail, with additional case material [8, 23]. The following discussion will be confined to basic principles. In general, treatment can follow recognized principles of dynamic psychotherapy, but some special problems require attention. Often the first task a therapist faces is dealing with his own feelings. No matter how accustomed a psychiatrist may be to the foibles and misbehaviors of human beings, the knowledge or sight of a baby seriously hurt by his care-taker can be a potent stimulus to emotional reaction. There is a strong tendency to deny parental abuse and blame the injuries on accidents and obscure diseases, or on the other hand, to feel angry and punitive toward the abuser. A more useful neutral position may be reached if the therapist can realize that the patient is really a frightened, hurt child himself, although angry or unlikable at the moment.

The patient's disbelief in the very idea of help and his hypersensitivity to disappointment makes establishment of a working alliance slower and more difficult. Nonjudging, sympathetic listening is of paramount importance, but must be balanced by noncritical verbal observations. Too much silence will be felt as lack of interest, but persistent questioning is likely to be understood as criticism. Because of their obligation to please authorities, some patients present a picture of cooperation which can be very misleading, and the therapist suddenly finds what he thought was real involvement in therapy is only superficial compliance. Other patients may for some time, based on fear, maintain an attitude of antagonism and disinterest while their deep yearning for help remains hidden. If this first phase can be

474

weathered tolerantly, the patient develops a sense of trust and confidence in the therapist and treatment begins to be meaningful. At this time, feelings of dependency appear and may become intense. It is important to accept such neediness for some time; to shatter it or attempt to reduce it too soon is likely to bring an end to treatment and return the patient to his previous hopeless disbelief in help. The extreme sensitivity of these patients to lack of interest or desertion necessitates unusual openness and care in dealing with changes of appointments and vacations. Effort must be made to maintain a positive therapeutic alliance and minimize the persistent tendency toward negative transference reactions. In long-term deeper therapy, however, skillful management of limited regression and negative transference can be effective in leading to significant resolution of conflicts.

The psychiatrist may be involved in evaluating a parent suspected or known to be abusing soon after injuries are discovered. His opinion may be needed to determine whether a child may be returned home or placed in protective custody. He should avoid, if possible, taking an active part in reporting injuries or petitioning the court for a dependency hearing. His therapeutic role is protected if the procedures are handled by other physicians, hospital administrators, or social agencies. Although protection of the child from further injury is a main concern, the parent's therapist should not focus interest on the child, but pay primary attention to the parent's problems. The more that concern is expressed about the child, the more the parent feels left out, unimportant, and angry. Rarely is it useful to probe into "who did what to the infant" in order to determine guilt. Such data will emerge naturally in the course of treatment. Probing tends to arouse more anger and defensive denial.

The aid of a sensitive, skilled social worker is enormously valuable [8]. She can provide crucial information, obtained from home visits, about family interactions and parental behavior with children. She provides another welcome outlet for the intense dependency needs of the patient, thereby making the psychiatrist's task of resolving the patient's conflicts easier and more effective. A main goal of treatment is enabling the parent to look to other adults for help in time of trouble rather than turning to the infant for gratification. The social worker, by her presence, example, and gentle encouragement, provides the bridge for the parent to become involved with a wider group

475

of adults to find satisfaction and help. For women she provides a new and different, more empathic, less aggressive surrogate mother with whom to identify and from whom to learn new patterns of mothering.

Treatment is primarily oriented toward modification of parental attitudes involved in abuse. Other aspects of the total personality may be worked with, either because they are significant accessories in the abusing behavior or because the patient desires to change other patterns of living. Despite difficulties and disappointments, therapy can be rewarding, not only in relieving current problems, but also in minimizing the chance of the transmission of damaging patterns of child-rearing to another generation.

Bibliography

1. Adelson, L. Slaughter of the innocents. *New Eng. J. Med.* 264:1345–1349, 1961.
2. Benedek, T. Adaptation to reality in early infancy. *Psychoanal. Quart.* 7:200–215, 1938.
3. Benedek, T. The psychosomatic implications of the primary unit: Mother-child. *Amer.·J. Orthopsychiat.* 19:642–654, 1949.
4. Benedek, T. Psychobiological aspects of mothering. *Amer. J. Orthopsychiat.* 26:272–278, 1956.
5. Benedek, T. Parenthood as a developmental phase: A contribution to the libido theory. *J. Amer. Psychoanal. Ass.* 7:389–417, 1959.
6. Berliner, B. On some psychodynamics of masochism. *Psychoanal. Quart.* 16:459–471, 1947.
7. Children's Bureau, U.S. Dept. of Health, Education, and Welfare. *Bibliography on the Battered Child.* Washington, D.C.: U.S. Government Printing Office, 1965.
8. Davoren, E. The Role of the Social Worker. In R. E. Helfer and C. H. Kempe (Eds.), *The Battered Child.* Chicago: University of Chicago Press, 1968.
9. Erikson, E. *Childhood and Society.* New York: Norton, 1950.
10. Fenichel, O. *The Psychoanalytic Theory of Neurosis.* New York: Norton, 1945.
11. Freud, A. *The Ego and the Mechanisms of Defense.* London: Hogarth, 1942.
12. Gil, D. G. Incidence of Child Abuse and Demographic Characteristics of Persons Involved. In R. E. Heffer and C. H. Kempe (Eds.), *The Battered Child.* Chicago: University of Chicago Press, 1968.

13. Josselyn, I. Cultural forces, motherliness and fatherliness. *Amer. J. Orthopsychiat.* 26:264–271, 1956.
14. Kaufman, I. Psychiatric Implications of Physical Abuse of Children. In *Protecting the Battered Child*. Denver: Children's Division, American Humane Association, 1962. Pp. 17–22.
15. Kempe, C. H., Silverman, F. N., Steele, B. F., Droegemueller, W., and Silver, H. K. The battered-child syndrome. *J.A.M.A.* 181: 17–24, 1962.
16. Kohut, H. Forms and transformations of narcissism. *J. Amer. Psychoanal. Ass.* 14:243–272, 1966.
17. LeShan, E. The 'perfect' child. *New York Times Magazine,* August 27, 1967.
18. Morris, M. G., and Gould, R. W. Role Reversal: A Concept in Dealing with the Neglected/Battered Child Syndrome. In *The Neglected/Battered Child Syndrome*. New York: Child Welfare League of America, 1963. Pp. 29–49.
19. Olden, C. On adult empathy with children. *Psychoanal. Stud. Child* 8:111–126, 1953.
20. Olden, C. Notes on the development of empathy. *Psychoanal. Stud. Child* 13:505–518, 1958.
21. Spitz, R. *No and Yes.* New York: International Universities Press, 1957.
22. Spitz, R. On the genesis of super-ego components. *Psychoanal. Stud. Child* 13:375–403, 1958.
23. Steele, B. F., and Pollock, C. B. A Psychiatric Study of Parents Who Abuse Infants and Small Children. In R. E. Helfer and C. H. Kempe (Eds.), *The Battered Child*. Chicago: University of Chicago Press, 1968.
24. Zilboorg, G. Sidelights on parent-child antagonism. *Amer. J. Orthopsychiat.* 2:35–43, 1932.

23

Murderous Obsessions in Mothers Toward Their Children

E. James Anthony
Norman Kreitman

T he extract that follows is from a letter written by a woman who had completed an analytically oriented treatment 8 years previously. She is doing well, but she complains about her 16-year-old son.

Dear Doctor:
Things haven't been too good with Bill since he left school. In fact, as time goes on, it gets worse. Wherever he works, there is always someone who is apparently out to harm him. He seems to want to hide himself in the four walls. He cannot go out or make friends, and he dreads being left at home alone. He is like a frightened child. He is ever so lonely and all he says is that he wishes he was dead. Imagine a boy of sixteen talking like that! All the time, he feels he is being punished for some reason unknown to him and that he deserves it otherwise he would not be so unhappy. Can you help him?

The writer of this letter had sought treatment 12 years previously because she felt dominated by the conscious desire to kill her child by strangling him at night while he was asleep. The problem was acute at the time because she had separated from her husband and lived alone with the little boy. When she put him to bed at night, she would lock his bedroom door and place the key between the pages of a book on the bookshelf and would then "forget" which book it was until she searched for it again the next morning.

She fell into a special group of mothers who suffered from more than the transient irritation that women normally endure when in

479

close and continuous contact with their children. They were severely disturbed individuals, in considerable distress over these "unnatural" feelings and desperate to receive help for a very painful symptom. Their concern was largely centered on the possible harm they might do their children, for whom they otherwise expressed various degrees of positive affection. Many of them were what would conventionally be described as "good mothers." As a rule, they emphasized one critical aspect of their mental state that differentiated them from hostile and cruel women who killed, maimed, or battered their children: In their case, the aggressive idea was well encapsulated within the setting of very benign feelings so that it seemed absurd, incongruous, and "cold." It was different from the "hot," angry feelings that led normal women to scold or chastise their children. It was also different from the affects or lack of affects usually associated with psychotic infanticide or psychopathic battering by virtue of the overwhelming experience of remorse, shame, and tenderness. *It was this profound ambivalence that especially characterized these women.*

Diagnostic Types

In the 40 women studied therapeutically, a diagnosis of compulsive-phobic reaction was made in 18, depressive reaction in 14, and mixed neurotic reaction in 8. In the first category, the murderous wish was expressed in the form of a classic obsessional-phobic symptom, ranging in severity from a distressing but "absurd" idea to an impulse the actuality of which came perilously close to reality. Four of the less severe cases had no additional symptoms and claimed to have no personal problems. They gave an impression of being in tight control of themselves, were socially poised and polite, but perhaps a little aloof, and prided themselves on the care with which they ministered to the child's material wants. The majority, however, had a varied collection of additional symptoms, chiefly obsessions not directly related to the child, rituals and counterphobias, and a shifting amount of secondary depression.

In the second category, the women were primarily depressed, but about half of them had secondary phobic-ruminative symptoms. They lacked the cool and detached attitude of the obsessional group and they were much more frightened that the impulses might easily

480

erupt into action. The gap between thought and action seemed altogether narrower. Three of these patients reported suicidal ideas, and it seemed of great theoretic interest that the suicidal impulses in two of these patients varied inversely with the hostility feelings toward the children. Another patient in this group reported an alternation between aggression directed toward her child and toward her own mother, while two reported nightmares of attacking their mothers during suicidal phases or phases of increased hostility toward their children.

The reactions of patients in the third category were characterized chiefly by attacks of anxiety and panic. We were particularly struck with two patients whose chief symptoms, apart from the hostile impulses, were exclusively hypochondriacal. They described their troublesome viscera in exactly the same terms as their children, and spoke of clawing at themselves when in distress. One other patient had, in addition to the anxiety and hostile feelings, a number of minor hysterical symptoms; she was also one of the few in the series who had made any kind of aggressive attack on their children.

THE SYMPTOMS

In the great majority of cases, the patient expressed concern about attacking the child in one or, sometimes, two specific modes. Of these different forms of attack, the most frequent was strangling. Among the obsessional group there was a marked predilection for sudden and direct violence rather than the slower, oblique forms. This tendency was not shown by the depressive characters.

The murderous wish remained a fantasy in nearly all instances. Even though some patients reproached themselves with having made one or more "attacks," inquiry usually revealed that these so-called attacks consisted of leaving potentially dangerous objects near the child or encouraging him to play in dangerous surroundings. Though the significance of such behavior was clearly evident to these patients, in no case was any child actually harmed.

Parenthetically it might be mentioned that although a few of the mothers reported episodes of cruelty, such as harsh punishment of the children over trifles, the majority expressed a fear of touching their children at all and would never chastise them physically. A few were apprehensive about even verbal rebukes, and attempted to ignore their children. On the whole, however, it was striking how often these mothers expressed reactive overconcern at their children's health and material satisfactions.

Half the patients of menstrual age reported a premenstrual intensification of their aggressive tendencies (see Fig. 23–1).

Seven women undertook to keep a record of their impulses (filicidal and suicidal) over a period of 6 months. These diaries were subsequently correlated with their menstrual cycles, the impulses being averaged out for the group. The mean duration of the menstrual period was 5.3 days. A high frequency of premenstrual tension was also reported.

In addition to impulses centered on the child, there were other phobic reactions that involved outgoing aggression (fears of attacking strangers, husbands, or mothers); ingoing aggression (fears of going mad, of committing suicide, of being attacked, of being raped, of developing cancer or tuberculosis, and of dropping dead); sexual impulses (of shouting obscenities, of exhibiting or masturbating in public, especially when menstruating, of attacking men's penises, and of

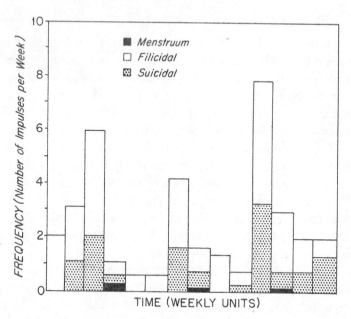

Fig. 23-1.   Suicidal and filicidal impulses in relation to menstruation (N = 7).

being seen undressed); and common or garden fears (of being alone, of being in the dark, of crowds, of traveling, of being in open spaces, of trains, of being closed in).

Almost all the patients reported an avoidance of horror films and dramatic television features, newspapers, and books. Many of them also said that they would leave the room or the house if the impulse to kill was particularly strong. Some would be forced to wake the child from its sleep to make certain he was still alive; others would have to take the child into their own beds to counteract the impulse to walk into his room and attack him; and still others had elaborate routines for systematically hiding all sharp objects and for locking all the doors.

Many patients mentioned the reassurance they derived from having another person present, especially the husband, though even the presence of another child, no matter how young, was often appreciated.

Most of our patients had been depressed at some stage of their illness. The interesting pattern of alternation of suicidal and child- or mother-directed hostility has already been mentioned. In other cases, anxiety was the cardinal feature, sometimes with the occurrence of almost continuous panic states.

Hypochondriacal symptoms, displayed by two patients, appeared to be of considerable theoretic interest.

One of these patients reported having been sexually attacked by her father at the age of 15. Since then she had experienced a variety of painful symptoms, centered over her lower abdomen, which often caused her to scratch furiously at her thighs and abdominal wall. She also became very conscious of some tiny marks on her legs, and expressed much concern that men would stare at them. During therapy she reported that the tension she experienced when in pain had a sexual component: she also reported that her antagonism to her first child had made her want to scratch at her in exactly the same way as at her own body.

The second patient was unusual in that she reported a fairly clear-cut progression of symptoms. From her teens she had been preoccupied with masochistic masturbatory fantasies. These were replaced later by a fear of having damaged herself irrevocably. Subsequently she developed fears of damaging other people. These fears were largely resolved after the birth of her first child, when she became afraid of attacking him.

Loosely organized paranoid feelings were present in many of these patients.

The Mother and Her Family of Origin

The majority of the women expressed very marked positive or negative feelings or painful ambivalence toward their parents, while a small number professed indifference to one or both parents. Positive and ambivalent attitudes toward the mother were commoner than toward the father, but the converse was true of indifference or active dislike.

The reaction of the parents to the mother during her childhood, as recalled by her, was equally unhappy. The mothers complained of undemonstrativeness and rejection, and of gross physical cruelty. Only a very few reported an absence of striking cruelty.

In spite of this, there was a strong tendency to cling to the ideal of a good mother and, in contrast to the father, her behavior was often exonerated or else the good and bad images were set together incompatibly, as if this was in the nature of things.

The pattern of interaction between the parents was described as one of frequent and severe quarrels, with separation by choice or divorce in more than half the cases. Altogether, about two-thirds of the group came from severely disturbed homes, and in a fifth of the cases a parent had received psychiatric treatment.

With regard to their attitudes toward brothers and sisters, half of the women expressed a marked dislike of at least one sibling, usually with reference to their childhood feelings, but often these were still persisting.

Relationships with Husbands

About half the women claimed that they had achieved a satisfying orgasm at some stage of their lives, but only a few were still orgastic during intercourse. There was a history of overt homosexual activity in one patient, and another was judged to have very strong lesbian interests. Two patients said that they had had incestuous relations with either a father or a brother.

We were impressed by the number of women who expressed a strong dislike for sexual intercourse: This was true of almost every patient. At the same time, many said they felt sexually very frustrated but hated to be touched by their husbands, or that if they did reach a climax they still felt unfulfilled. Over a third of the patients stated that men had the better of it sexually, and were frankly envious of the masculine sexual role.

When questioned about any change in relationship with their husbands following the onset of symptoms, more than half declared that they had become more aggressive toward them. One obsessional patient said that her murderous impulses alternated between her son and husband, but never involved both simultaneously. (She felt no hostility toward her other child, a girl.) The antagonism to the husband was most marked in the depressive subgroup. The development of a more hostile attitude toward the husband did not seem to be associated with the sex of the initially "disliked" child, or with the patient's declared parental preference or her reported attitude to her father. There did appear to be a clear association between the aggression suffered at the hands of the father and the change in attitude toward the husband.

The Disliked Child

In 19 out of 21 cases, where the family contained at least two children, the hostile feelings of the mother had been directed initially at one particular child. In the remaining 17 cases, it was an only child that was disliked. Thus in 36 patients, the symptoms had initially been centered on one child: subsequently, however, the impulse had spread to involve other children, and at the time of review there was a total of 45 "disliked children."

The age of the child at the onset of the mother's hostile feelings occurred in 40 percent of the cases in connection with pregnancy (or in anticipation of it) or within 6 months of parturition: in the remaining 60 percent the symptoms began after the child had reached 1 year (eleven under 5 years and eleven over 5 years).

These two groups also differed in some other respects. Some external precipitating factor was evident in only a quarter of the early-onset cases, as compared with about half the late-onset group: Presumably this discrepancy was met by childbirth itself acting as a relatively stronger "precipitant" in the younger group. The patients' relationship to their own mothers also differed in that, of those patients expressing a parental preference, only half the early group chose their mother as against three-quarters of the older group.

The inference here is that a relative dislike of the patient's mother is coupled with a stressful pregnancy and parturition, and an early onset of aggressive feelings. Conversely, subjects with relatively close attachment to their mothers found pregnancy and childbirth less stressful, and their aggressive impulses tended rather to be triggered by some "extraneous" event which was unrelated to the age of the child.

Three-quarters of the disliked children were firstborn, i.e., only and eldest children, boys and girls being equally represented. An *only* "disliked" child, however, is much more likely to be a son than a daughter.

Before commencing this study we had formed the impression that maternal antagonism was often highly selective, and that the disliked child evidently held some special significance for the mother. From our findings, it would seem that there is a clear tendency for the patients to dislike their sons if they have disliked their fathers, and a less marked tendency for patients who disliked their sisters to dislike their daughters.

A number of the patients were certain that their attitude toward the disliked child would be difficult if the child were of the opposite sex. All these patients had distinct preferences for one or other parent, and in almost all cases the disliked child was of the same sex as the least-favored parent; in the remaining, there were disliked siblings of the same sex as the child.[1]

THE PSYCHODYNAMICS OF THE
MURDEROUS RELATIONSHIP

It was evident that certain dynamic factors were common to many of the patients, some of which would doubtless be encountered in other groups of mothers who had disturbed relationships with their children. Among the factors encountered in therapy with these women were the following:

1. *A general sense of being unloved in childhood* by one or both parents. This led, among numerous other sequelae, to a sense of emotional poverty: patients would make observations such as "how can I love my child? I've never known what love is."

[1] In the final analysis, there is no doubt that the "disliked child" is basically the "hated self-hated child."

486

The continuing influence of this factor in the patient's current life-situation could often be discerned. This is well illustrated by one patient, the middle sibling of three, who felt that both her own parents had been emotionally aloof, unpredictable, and disinterested in her, though she always maintained a warm attachment to her father. She married a man who repeatedly deserted her. As soon as he would go, she would be terrified by a flood of murderous rage against her three children, which would cease as soon as her husband returned.

2. *The absence of maternal models* for identification sometimes led to an inability to understand the maternal role, let alone fulfill it. Many women had practically no concept of how to meet the most elementary needs of their children, with the consequence that they felt inadequate, frustrated, and tense. "I still feel like a child; how can I possibly be a mother?" One result of this was that often their relationship with their child took on the character of a struggle, in which the mother viewed any unhappiness in the child as an insufferable reproach and the child himself as a persecutor to be fought. This seemed particularly true in the mixed neurotic subgroup, in whom anxious feelings of inadequacy and immaturity were prominent. This was also true of some of the depressed patients, but applied much less to the obsessional group. It is of interest that one of the most powerful "triggers" for the hostile impulse was the sound of the child crying, which was interpreted both as an accusation and a demand on the mother's limited maternal capacities.[2]

3. *Profound ambivalence to the parents* invariably underlay both the feelings of emotional insecurity and the defective maternal functioning already mentioned. It also led to numerous other conflicts, as will shortly be discussed. It is true that many patients, notably from the obsessional group, often described their mothers as "perfect angels," but that their experience was in fact as unsatisfactory as that of any other subgroup was evident from the violence of their fantasies toward their children, and often toward the mothers themselves. Typically such fantasies were well "encapsulated," their aggression being

[2] In the development of healthy maternal attitudes, the importance of the patient's relationship to her own father should not be overlooked. In many —though by no means all—of our cases, it could be seen that inadequate maternal feelings were closely linked with an immaturity of sexual development, due in great part to disturbed relationships with the father. The consequent lack of sexual "polarity" in turn led to the numerous marital problems characteristic of many of our patients.

countered by denial and oversolicitude for the child (and sometimes for their mothers also) at a conscious level.

4. *Exposure to interparental aggression,* such as was frequently encountered during childhood, seems to have resulted in the heightened awareness of the patients of aggressive components in all their relationships. This led not only to a painful state of instability, but in some instances to a true sadomasochistic orientation. Such patients were especially difficult to treat. Those functioning primarily in the sadistic mode felt helpless in the face of apparently endless ambivalence toward their children (and husbands), though in some cases they became aware that their hostility formed the basis of a desired and valued relationship. Those at the masochistic pole, who comprised some of the most deeply depressed patients, posed the classic psychotherapeutic problem of the "self-defeating" patient in its most extreme form. We had occasion to note how, in the therapeutic groups, these depressed patients would often compete strenuously with each other in terms of self-abasement, as though no other way of claiming the therapist's interest was available to them.

5. *An inadequate system of ego defenses* was of course evident in all cases, but it is of interest to note that in addition to the various general factors already mentioned as contributing to the maternal antagonism, the child was often sensed as a specific threat to the primary defense mechanisms of the patient's personality structure. Thus the obsessional group was frequently unable to tolerate any dirtiness or untidiness in the child, or even a display of emotion of any kind. One such patient first became ill at the time one of her children developed diarrhea during a gastrointestinal illness. We have already referred to the vulnerability of the mixed neurosis group to any stressful situation involving the child. With the depressive group it was less easy to distinguish any one main pattern of "threat," except perhaps in instances when the child demonstrated some similarity of temperament with the patient or was obviously unhappy.

On a general level, it would seem that a common factor between our patients and "normal" mothers who display occasional irritability might be the vulnerability of the mother's defense mechanisms; in this respect the differences would be quantitative rather than qualitative. Moreover, since unconscious hostility to a child is frequently found in a variety of disorders, it may be that it is this specific threat to the defense mechanism, or their defeat, which resulted in the hostility in our patients being fully conscious.

SPECIFIC FACTORS

In addition to these general influences, we were particularly interested in the genetic analysis of the hostile feelings in the mother, and in what determined which one of a number of children was signaled out as a target. In considering patterns of identification, for example, it rapidly emerged that the identification of the child with a parent or sibling played a significant role in the selection of the disliked child.

The extent to which such identifications took place and the complexity of the patterns involved, often with multiple splitting and oscillation, were remarkable. One patient complained that she was powerless and ineffective before the "will" of her son, aged 3. Another had dressed her boy in girls clothes till the age of 5, and admired "what a pretty girl" he made. In some instances, the children refused to act out their expected roles in the unconscious fantasy of the mother, and the anxiety this occasioned was sometimes a secondary source of hostility. Some of the commoner patterns of identification are as follows:

The simplest is probably that in which a particular child is directly identified with a disliked parent or sibling. All the fear, hostility, and guilt experienced in relation to the original family member is then worked out on the person of the child. This process seems more especially marked in women with disliked fathers and sons (when the sexual component is often easily recognized), and in those with disliked sisters and daughters.

Another common pattern may be described as a more complex variant of the one just mentioned. Here the identification is less complete, in that certain aspects of the parent are projected onto the child while the patient herself identifies with other parental aspects. Sometimes it is the hostile features of the mother that are seen in the child, and the patient then sees herself as basically "good" but under constant attack from the "wicked" child. Frequently, however, the pattern is reversed; the children have all the virtues of the parents, includ-

489

ing the right to criticize and condemn, while the patient is totally without merit. Often the pattern oscillates, and occasionally both forms exist side by side as a result of multiple divisions of the parental image. This emerges clearly with depressed patients who feel (either alternately or simultaneously) both suicidal and filicidal. The precise significance of the aggressive impulse may thus range from paranoid counterattack to compulsive "identification with the aggressor," i.e., the parent.

This last point should be noted. Identification with an aggressive parent was a relatively common mechanism and has been noted by other workers, but it sometimes led to a particular pattern which we would like to call the "transposition of the generation." Here a new element appears, namely, the identification of the patient herself with her child. In this pattern, the birth of the child leads first to an assumption of the maternal role based on close identification with the patient's own mother. Secondly, the child is identified with the patient herself. In consequence, all the hostility attributed to the patient's mother is now incorporated and directed at the child.[3] Sometimes it is a disliked sister rather than the patient's mother who provides the initial traumatic figure, though conceivably such sibling rivalry is also to be traced in many cases to aggressive tendencies originally experienced toward the mother.

The sexual infantile significance of the impulse against the child has already been mentioned. Sometimes it is the dominant feature. It is our impression that ambivalent attitudes toward a hostile father lead to more complicated (and more distressing) relationships, especially toward sons, than does "clean" hostility. The parallel situation of fixation on the mother who has been rejected also leads to psychosexual retardation and to disturbances of a homosexual type, but this is often difficult to distinguish clearly in the attitude toward the children. In such patients, it is the maternal role in general that is rejected (witness those women whose hostility *preceded* pregnancy) with consequent rejection of all children, irrespective of sex.

Given any particular combination of identifications, the manner in which such processes are synthesized with other personality func-

[3] As the reader will readily appreciate, the mechanism of "transposition" is considerably more complex than has been outlined here, and it involves further processes of incorporation and projection. The depressed patient described in Case 1 later in this chapter beautifully illustrates the process.

tions can vary. In the obsessional patients, for example, the parental image often remains relatively encapsulated and the patient fights a continuous battle to prevent herself from becoming engulfed by it. In the aggressive patients, the identification is often conscious and is accepted in a mood of despair and hopelessness.

A further consequence of the patient's double orientation toward her family, both past and present, is the kind of concept she forms of herself. We were interested to note how some patients used this self-concept extensively in endeavoring to meet some further need. For example, one patient had been fostered out by her mother, a prostitute, when she was 5. Three years later her mother died, having visited her regularly in the interim. Her foster mother, who later developed paranoid schizophrenia, treated her harshly. This patient had a profound need to see her real mother as ideal, if only as a compensatory fantasy for the hardships she had to endure, yet she felt that she had been abandoned and vividly recalled the shock of being handed to her unkind foster mother. She met this dilemma by believing that it was she herself who was wicked, so that her mother could still be seen as good. Her destructive attitude toward the members of her own family both derived from and further encouraged this belief. Other patients, not necessarily depressive subjects, similarly displayed a deep need to preserve a self-image of destructiveness to perpetuate the only relationships they could maintain with their parents, living or dead.

ILLUSTRATIVE CASES

We have already described some of the characteristics of the hypochondriacal-neurotic group. The two following accounts (which do not aim to be complete) illustrate some features of the depressive and obsessional types, and indicate how the different patterns of identification may oscillate or coexist.

CASE 1. The patient recalled that her childhood was made wretched by a cruel, depressed mother who was also a heavy drinker, and toward whom she early developed predominantly hostile, if ambivalent, feelings. Her father never humiliated or maltreated her, as did her mother, but was a rather aloof, remote figure. There were one older and two younger sisters, all of whom she disliked intensely, especially the oldest, but she was very fond of her brother, one year her senior, with whom she had some form of sexual relationship in her early teens. When she was 15 and her mother 41, the latter committed suicide by hanging; it was the patient who discovered the body. At this point she seems to have regressed severely, spending many weeks in bed in a state of apathy, though she denied being depressed. This phase was followed by one of social activity and sexual promiscuity.

In her early twenties she married, and at 31 she had her only child, a daughter. She had not wanted a child and had difficulty in realizing that the child was her own, disliking her from the outset. Though there is some question of her having been unduly strict with the girl, the patient remained free from major symptoms until she reached her late thirties. She then became frightened that she too would commit suicide by cutting her throat at the age of 41, not from choice but "by fate" (anniversary reaction). She grew increasingly depressed, and when she did in fact reach that age she requested hospital admission.

While in the hospital (during which period her father died) she was given a Methedrine abreaction interview, in the course of which she declared she would either commit suicide or kill her daughter by cutting her throat, to preserve her from some terrible fate. What this might be she would not specify, but believed it had something to do with the child's growing up to resemble herself. The critical date in the year having passed, she improved sufficiently to leave hospital, but was now preoccupied with murderous feelings toward the child, whom she accordingly tried to avoid as much as possible. These feelings fluctuated markedly in intensity, but when the child entered her teens, the patient again became depressed, with intense fear that when the girl reached 15, she would kill her; vague suicidal ideas were also present, though to a less extent than formerly, and were visualized chiefly as an alternative to attacking the child. She again sought hospital treatment and reported additional symptoms of intense jealousy of her husband, sexual frustration, coitus reversus, and envy of the male sexual function. In the psychotherapeutic group she professed antipathy to all the other members, whom she despised for being women, and was at great pains to stress her "wickedness" in a competitive manner. She related to the therapist in an aggressive-seductive manner throughout.

CASE 2. According to this patient, her mother, who had suffered from asthma most of her life, was meticulously tidy and constantly restricted her children's activities in a typical overprotective manner. The mother died of asthma when the patient was only 6, but was recollected by the patient as "an angel." Her father, who died of tuberculosis when the patient was 7, was remembered as a moody, irritable, and intolerant individual who drank heavily. There were frequent quarrels between the parents, though neither was physically cruel to the patient. Despite these descriptions of her parents, the patient was often uncertain of her "real" feelings for her mother, while for her father she professed only affection despite his aggressiveness. She was the thirteenth child of a sibship of sixteen, and had apparently got on reasonably well with all her siblings.

With the death of her parents she was sent to an orphanage, where she grew up in the care of a kind but rather strict and undemonstrative housemother; there was no father figure of note. At 14 she left to live more happily with a married sister. Having completed her schooling, with average success, at 17 she went to work and continued to work throughout her life, usually at a factory bench.

At 23 she married an equable, industrious man and considered her marriage a very good one. Sexual relations were marred, however, by constant fears of pregnancy: contraception was apparently unknown to them. At 23 she had a daughter, and at 25 a son, though she had not wanted a second child. Much later she reported that she had always resented the boy for being in some unspecified way so "different" from herself.

Her first symptoms began at 36, with excessive concern about the children's welfare. She grew anxious, irritable, and tense and developed indigestion and vomiting. After 2 years of medical treatment she recovered.

At 40 menopause occurred, and at about this time she had a brief, unenthusiastic extramarital affair, which her husband discovered but forgave. Also at about this time her pet dog developed diarrhea, and the patient was very worried about catching a similar illness. Her precautions were extravagant, and included rubbing carbolic acid over the furniture. Her anxiety mounted, and the nervous indigestion recurred. While still being treated for this she read a newspaper account of a man with "nerve trouble" who had killed his children and then himself. She at once grew very agitated, fearing that she too would attack her children, and especially her son, by squeezing them to death.

These murderous phobic ruminations, which she strenuously attempted to dismiss, had continued with fluctuating intensity (but never entirely abating) for the next twenty years: She was 60 when we saw her. During that time she had frequently consulted various hospitals but had never persevered with therapy. She had managed to continue her work, her social activities, and an ostensibly harmonious relationship with her husband. Currently she still had fears of squeezing her son to death, although he is now 37 years of age, is 6 feet tall, and has for some years been living some 6,000 miles away in South Africa!

DISCUSSION

The universality of the theme of child destruction in literature, religion, mythology, folklore, and even nursery rhymes has frequently been noted. Stern has collected many such instances, including anthropologic data [15]. In the latter context, it seems especially interesting in view of our findings how commonly the sacrificed children are firstborn males, while among European legends it is noteworthy that prominent among the many victims of parental hostility was Oedipus himself!

There are two other categories whose relationship to our patients pose many unresolved and important problems.

First, there is the group of postpartum psychoses. The question

493

of child-directed hostility in relation to puerperal reactions deserves closer study. Aggressive attitudes have been frequently noted among such patients, and conversely, it will be recalled that about half of our patients developed their symptoms within a year of childbirth[4] [4, 8, 18, 19]. There is further evidence that puerperal reactions of all varieties are particularly associated with firstborn children (72 percent firstborn "disliked" children in our series) and even that postpartum illness, especially of the depressive variety, may be further related to the sex of the child [14]. The age of the patients in the two groups is also very similar, tending to be in the late twenties. Moreover, among postpuerperal neurosis, Vislie states that "neurotic-phobic" and "neurotic-obsessional" reactions account for about a quarter of all postpuerperal neuroses, which is presumably higher than would be found in a random sample of hospital-treated neurotic patients [17]. Lastly, there appear to be many similarities in the psychodynamic processes involved in both groups, although it would be desirable to have further details of the mechanisms involved in postpartum neuroses before drawing any firm conclusions. Thus there is evidence of similarities between our series and postpartum illness on the counts of time of onset in relation to parturition; age; attitude toward the child; and possibly with respect to the sex of the child and psychodynamic factors. This is enough to warrant a more detailed study of postpartum illness, with care to distinguish the different subgroups. If antagonism to the child is in fact an important feature of puerperal illness, then such data should reveal close similarities between the two groups.

Secondly, our cases invite comparison with those of infanticide, filicide, and female homicide in general. Such comparison is difficult, as most of the detailed reports on infanticide and filicide relate to overtly psychotic mothers [3, 9, 10, 16]. There appear to be further differences. Infanticide is said by some authors to be particularly associated with social stress [3, 11], though this is denied by others [10]. Clearly case selection plays a large part in such differences of opinion; we simply wish to point out that social pressures were certainly not a feature in our series. Further, we found a high proportion

[4] The authors quoted believe such attitudes to be nuclear to all puerperal depression, and widespread in other forms of postpartum illness, while Anderson reports an incidence of about a third in a mixed group of puerperal psychoses [1]. Smalldon reports hostile attitudes toward the child in 75 percent of both depressive and schizophrenic illness [14].

494

of obsessional disorders, which has not been reported in the filicide or homicide cases, although conceivably the "impulse disorders with tension states" of Tuteur and Glotzer [16] and the obsessional depression of Podolsky [12] might overlap.[5] On the other hand, certain similarities also emerge. Noteworthy in both groups are the absence of hostility and revenge motives directed primarily against the child, the fundamental importance of identification processes, and highly disturbed parental relationships. Hypochondriacal mechanisms have also been noted [12], though the two patients reported by us appear to be the first in whom somatic hypochondriasis has coexisted with a view of the child as a malignant component of the mother's self.

It would appear from reports on female homicides in general that such subjects also have certain affinities with our patients, especially as regards the psychologic relationship between the killer and her victim [5, 11]. We may also note in passing that while poisoning is said to be the commonest mode of attack for female homicides in general and in filicide [12], suffocation, strangulation, and wounds to the head are more common in infanticides [7, 13]. It will be recalled that none of our patients mentioned poisoning, whereas suffocation, strangulation, and head wounds accounted for the contemplated mode of attack in the majority of cases. Thus, if these quoted statements are true, our series more closely resemble infanticide than filicide despite some of the children approaching middle age. Their ages in their mothers' fantasies is another matter.

A few points might next be made about our therapeutic groups, which were conducted along group-analytic lines [6]. (One group has already been described elsewhere [2]). On comparing the two groups after they had both been terminated, certain common factors emerged which differed from most therapeutic groups in the following respects.

The initial "honeymoon phase" was particularly well marked. Without exception all the patients expressed their great relief at discovering they were not unique in having such socially unacceptable symptoms. The support so afforded was invaluable to them even when no further progress occurred. As a corollary, it emerged that only in the group situation were the patients prepared to face the full extent

[5] Podolsky describes this group as characterized by the absence of precipitating factors. In our series, such factors occurred with equal frequency among all subgroups.

495

of their hostile tendencies, with all the fear these engendered: Patients often reported that their impulses were more frightening when discussed in the group than they appeared to be at home. Silences were very tense, and competition for attention was often ruthless.

In the intermediate period, we noted a particularly marked tendency to subgroup formations. The major polarity was between the obsessional patients and the depressive patients. The former group was often much envied by the latter for their apparent ability to control their lives and emotional expressions, despite their manifest concern with the "absurdity" of their feelings and their phobic sense of horror. The depressed patients felt frustrated in conveying their sense of urgency; they believed their impulses as only too real. Both groups, in fact, developed a special terminology for this phenomenologic differentiation in the immediacy of their aggression. One group referred to "hot" and "cold" hostility, the other to impulses "right in front" and "not in front." Other subgroupings, usually transient, were based on complementary sadomasochistic needs, and on the "prolific-devouring" principle (feeding versus oral aggression).

To a striking extent, the groups both tended to institutionalize their proceedings. A recognized practice in one, for example, was for any patient in particular distress to leave and stand just outside the door, whereupon another member, after brief discussion, would go and bring her back with an almost ceremonial introduction to the others. Concern about absent or late members was always marked; seating arrangements were rigidly preserved throughout. These attempts to render the group as concrete as possible, plus the theme of who was "inside" and who "outside" probably symbolized the patients' relationship of the mother's body to the child. Children who were "part" of the body outside were vulnerable to catastrophe (viz, the mother's aggression), those inside were safe.[6]

The vissicitudes of the aggressive drives during the course of treatment were too complex to detail. Essentially we noted that complaints about the "wickedness" of the disliked children, which incidentally were confined to a minority of patients, gradually became less. Once the honeymoon period was over, a great deal of aggression was released into the group situation, often along the lines of the pa-

[6] Two patients in our series became pregnant while under treatment. Their hostile impulses against their existing children at once ceased.

496

tients' early familial patterns. As may well be imagined, the atmosphere was often electric, and one patient made a suicidal gesture during a therapeutic session. Progress tended to be slow despite ostensible high motivation, since underlying anxieties and aggression were invariably deeply embedded and painful.

In both groups a female observer was present who soon became idealized by the groups and subsequently the target for paranoid attack.

In the general management of these patients, we did not in any instance recommend the removal of the child from the mother, though in a few instances this had been effected already by those having psychiatric care of the child. No attacks were made on the children by the mothers in treatment, which may be attributed not only to the improvement derived from psychotherapy but also to the confidence engendered in these mothers through having the children left in their care.

Finally, we would like to stress one cardinal consideration in the treatment of these patients. They possessed considerable, if unexpressed, positive feelings toward their children. It was the demonstration and elaboration of this which created the necessary security for the control and further exploration of the murderous impulse.

Bibliography

1. Anderson, E. W.   A study of the sexual life in psychoses associated with childbirth. *J. Ment. Sci.* (London) 79:137–149, 1933.
2. Anthony, E. J.   A group of murderous mothers. *Acta Psychother.* (Basel) 7 (Suppl.): 1–6, 1959. Proceedings of the Second International Congress on Group Psychotherapy, Zurich, 1957.
3. Bender, L.   Psychiatric mechanisms in child murderers. *J. Nerv. Ment. Dis.* 80:32–47, 1934.
4. Brew, M. F., and Seidenberg, R.   Psychotic reactions associated with pregnancy and childbirth. *J. Nerv. Ment. Dis.* 111:408–423, 1950.
5. Bromberg, W.   Psychological Study of Murder. In E. Podolsky (Ed.), *Encyclopedia of Aberrations.* London: Arco, 1953.
6. Foulkes, S. H., and Anthony, E. J.   *Group Psychotherapy.* Middlesex, Eng.: Penguin, 1957.

497

7. Hopwood, J. S.   Child murder and insanity. *J. Ment. Sci.* 73: 95–108, 1927.
8. Linn, L., and Polatin, P.   Psychiatric problems of the puerperium from the standpoint of prophylaxis. *Psychiat. Quart.* 24: 375–384, 1950.
9. McDermaid, G., and Winkler, E.   Psychiatric study of homicide cases. *J. Clin. Exper. Psychopath.* 11:93–146, 1950.
10. McDermaid, G., and Winkler, E.   Psychopathology of infanticide. *J. Clin. Exper. Psychopath.* 16:22–41, 1955.
11. Morton, J. H.   Female homicides. *J. Ment. Sci.* 80:64–74, 1934.
12. Podolsky, E.   The psychodynamics of filicide and matricide. *Dis. Nerv. Syst.* 19:475–477, 1958.
13. Pollak, O.   *The Criminality of Women.* Philadelphia: University of Pennsylvania Press, 1950.
14. Smalldon, J.   A survey of mental illness associated with pregnancy and childbirth. *Amer. J. Psychiat.* 97:80–101, 1940.
15. Stern, E. S.   The medea complex: Mother's homicidal wishes to her child. *J. Ment. Sci.* 94:321–331, 1948.
16. Tuteur, W., and Glotzer, J.   Murdering mothers. *Amer. J. Psychiat.* 116:447–452, 1959.
17. Vislie, H.   Puerperal mental disorders. *Acta Psychiat. Neurol. Scand.* Suppl. 3:3–42, 1956.
18. Zilboorg, G.   Depressive reactions related to parenthood. *Amer. J. Psychiat.* 10:927–962, 1931.
19. Zilboorg, G.   Sidelights on parent-child antagonism. *Amer. J. Orthopsychiat.* 2:35–43, 1932.

Part V

Some Clinical Correlations Between Parents and Children

24

The Effect of Personality
Disturbances in the Mother
on the Well-Being
of Her Infant

René A. Spitz

EDITORS' INTRODUCTION

It is revealing to introduce the following chapter with a biblio-graphic note. Dr. Spitz published two papers in the same year which demonstrated his deep involvement with the interrelatedness of physio-logic and psychologic processes in early development (actually before one could speak of psyche as distinguished from soma). The first of those papers was the often-cited "Hospitalism," a clinical investiga-tion of the effects of emotional deprivation during infancy [1]. The next one was entitled "Diacritic and Coenesthetic Organization" [2]. This is a study of the earliest maturational processes of the neonate that can be considered the rudiment of psychophysiology.

The term *coenesthetic organization* refers to that period of the newborn infant's existence when his sensorium is not yet developed to differentiate "inside" and "outside"; all stimuli are perceived as expe-rienced within the body. Thus the sensations of the coenesthetic or-ganization are mainly visceral; they take place on a deep level of sen-sibility involving mostly the smooth musculature. Soon, however, the infant's sensorium shifts from the receptive mode of functioning that characterizes the coenesthetic system to perception, which is the mode of functioning of the diacritic organization. The sensations of the dia-critic system are intensive, involving the sensory organs and the striate musculature. One may assume that the coenesthetic organization is the source of self-directed (receptive) functions while the diacritic organization is the source of the object-directed, psychic functions.

Farfetched and difficult as this condensation must appear, it is necessary because it outlines the two spheres of the mental apparatus and its psychodynamic functioning. In a later paper, Spitz described the steps of early maturation by which the purely physiologic recep-tive processing of stimuli becomes integrated and forms the precursors of gradually evolving object-relatedness [3].

501

In the impenetrable depth of rudimentary psychic organizations are hidden the memory traces of sensations from which the smiling baby emerges and into which he submerges again; when crying, he regresses and "forgets" his pain. Since the newborn infant does not relate the sensations to his surroundings, he does not reward and does not punish the mother. Yet the mother may feel rewarded by the sleeping of her satiated baby just as she may feel blamed and punished by his crying. This well-known experience of mothers indicates that the state of emotional symbiosis begins with the affective attitude of the mother toward the infant at a time when the infant has only global discharge reactions and reacts with somatic responses of thriving or with somatic responses of discomfort and symptoms which might lead to a pathologic state.

The following chapter is the result of extensive clinical observations conceptualized in terms of psychoanalytic theory. The constitutional factors of the child are implied, but the material has been selected with the focus on the maternal attitude that activates the particular somatic disposition in the infant.

E. J. A.
T. B.

Bibliography

1. Spitz, R. A.   Hospitalism: An inquiry into the genesis of psychiatric conditions in early childhood. *Psychoanal. Stud. Child* 1:53–74, 1945.
2. Spitz, R. A.   Diacritic and coenesthetic organization. *Psychoanal. Rev.* 32:146–162, 1945.
3. Spitz, R. A.   The primal cavity: A contribution to the genesis of perception and its role for psychoanalytic theory. *Psychoanal. Stud. Child* 10:215–240, 1955.

In the mother-child relationship, the mother is the dominant, active partner. The child, at least in the beginning, is the passive recipient. This leads us to our first proposition: Disturbances of the maternal personality will be reflected in the disorders of the child. If we limit the psychologic influences which become effective during infancy to the mother-child relationship, we obtain our second hypothesis: In infancy damaging psychologic influences are the consequence of an unsatisfactory relationship between mother and child. Such unsatisfactory relationships are pathogenic and can be divided into two categories: (1) improper mother-child relationship and (2) insufficient mother-child relationship. Stated differently, in the first case the disturbance of the object relationship is due to a qualitative factor, while in the second case it is due to a quantitative factor. The second case, that of insufficient mother-child relationship, has been discussed extensively elsewhere [16]. In this chapter our attention will be restricted to the impaired mother-child relationship arising out of a personality disturbance in the mother.

IMPROPER MOTHER-CHILD RELATIONSHIP

This can lead to a variety of disturbances in the child. I have been able to distinguish several clinical pictures of such disturbances; each seemed to be linked to a specific inappropriate mother-child relationship. Indeed, the clinical picture appeared to be the consequence of a given maternal behavior pattern. Some of the clinical pictures have been described in the pediatric literature. I do not claim that the psychogenic etiology of these diseases has been adequately demonstrated through the fact that I succeeded in uncovering a linkage between specific disturbances of object relations and given clinical pictures. Indeed, in certain of these diseases one can demonstrate specific congenital elements which also seemed to play an etiologic role. However, neither the psychologic factor alone nor the congenital element alone would lead to the onset of the disease in question—only the conjunction of the two.

By the nature of things, the mother's personality is dominant in the dyad. We may then assume that where an improper mother-child relationship prevails, the mother's personality makes her unable to offer her child a normal relationship, or that, for reasons of her personality, she is compelled to disturb the normal relationship which a mother would ordinarily have with her baby. In either case we can say that the mother's personality acts as the disease-provoking agent, as a psychologic toxin. For this reason, I have called this group of disturbances in object relationships, or rather their consequences, *psychotoxic diseases of infancy*. I was able to distinguish a series of damaging maternal behavior patterns, each of which appeared to be linked to a specific psychotoxic disturbance of the infant. These maternal behavior patterns are enumerated below:

1. Primary overt rejection
2. Primary anxious overpermissiveness
3. Hostility in the guise of manifest anxiety
4. Oscillation between pampering and hostility
5. Cyclical mood swings of the mother
6. Maternal hostility consciously compensated

PRIMARY OVERT REJECTION

Primary Active Rejection

In this syndrome the maternal attitude consists of a global rejection of motherhood; this rejection includes both pregnancy and the child, and probably also many aspects of genital sexuality. I have a motion picture of such a case; however, the follow-up is lacking. These cases are difficult to follow, for the child frequently dies ("accidentally" or through infanticide), is abandoned, or, at best, is given for adoption.

Primary Passive Rejection

The reaction of the newborn to the mother who will not accept him was first described by Margaret Ribble [14]. In extreme cases the newborn becomes comatose, with Cheyne-Stokes type dyspnea, extreme pallor, and reduced sensitivity. These patients appear to be in a state of shock; treatment consists of saline enema, intravenous glucose, or blood transfusion. After recovery, these babies have to be taught to suck by repeated and patient stimulation of their oral zone. The condition endangers the life of the newborn.

CASE 1. The mother of the child was a 16-year-old, unusually good-looking girl; she was unmarried. She had been employed as a servant and seduced by the son of her employer. Allegedly only one intercourse took place, resulting in impregnation. The child was undesired and the pregnancy was accompanied by very severe feelings of guilt, as the girl was a devout, practicing Catholic. The delivery took place in a maternity hospital and was uneventful. The first attempt to nurse, after 24 hours, was unsuccessful and so were the following ones. The mother, allegedly, had no milk. We had no difficulty, however, in obtaining milk from her by manual pressure. Neither was there any difficulty in feeding this milk to the infant from a bottle. During nursing the mother behaved as if her infant were completely alien to her and not a living being at all. Her behavior consisted of withdrawal from the baby, her body, hands, and face rigid and tense. The nipples, though not inverted, were not protruding and nursing did not appear to provoke turgor.

This went on for 5 days, while the baby was kept alive with the milk expressed from the mother's breast. In one of the final attempts, the baby was seen to sink back into the stuporous, semicomatose condition described by Ribble. Energetic methods had to be applied, including tube-feeding and saline clysis, to bring the baby out of this condition.

Concurrently, an attempt at indoctrination of the mother was made, and she was shown how to treat her nipples to produce turgor, making nursing possible. From the fifth day on, after this indoctrination, nursing went on relatively successfully; the child recovered, at least for the subsequent 6 days during which I could observe him.

One may well ask how a child will develop when he is confronted from the beginning with as massive a rejection as this. I assume that it is highly likely in these archaic reactions that even when the danger to life has been overcome, other, perhaps less critical, psychosomatic sequelae will appear.

The following case of infantile vomiting is one of these sequelae, though in this case the mother's passive rejection of motherhood probably was admixed with active rejection of her child.

CASE 2. This child was first breast-fed by his mother. Subsequently she refused to continue nursing and formula was introduced. Both during breast-feeding and formula-feeding, the mother was full of complaints and recrimination. Breast-feeding, she said, was unsatisfactory, because the child vomited; but the formula was not right either, because the child vomited with that also. After 3 weeks the mother contracted influenza, was hospitalized, and separated from her child. The child's vomiting

505

ceased immediately. Six weeks later the mother returned. The child started vomiting again within forty-eight hours.

To date, cases like these have not been sufficiently investigated. In my opinion passive maternal rejection is not directed against the child as an individual but against the fact of having a child. That is to say, it is a rejection of motherhood; it is objectless. This attitude can exist only during the first few weeks after delivery, and at most during the first couple of months. Later, when the child begins to develop, his specific individuality, his personality, will begin to make itself felt, and maternal hostility will also become more specific, more directed to what her child is, namely, an individual different from all others.

The attitudes of these mothers and their generalized hostility to motherhood originate in their individual histories, in their relationship with the child's father, in the manner in which they succeeded or failed to solve their own oedipal conflict and their castration anxiety.

The preceding considerations took into account primarily the hostile mother's response to her child; as for such an infant's response to a hostile mother, it must be realized that at the outset, at the very beginning of life, the neonate has not even begun to develop the rudiments of adaptation, let alone of defense. The child, as Freud stated, is born helpless; he is in the primary narcissistic stage, the most archaic way of existence known to man. This archaic mode of existing slowly evolves into the earliest modes of oral behavior, which later gradually become integrated into behavior patterns associated with what is known in psychoanalysis as the oral stage. In this archaic period, the infant's relations with his surroundings have only just been transferred from the umbilical cord to the mouth and have changed from being passively transfused to incorporating actively. It is logical that the manifest symptoms of the child's disturbance in the cases just described will be expressed through oral symptoms as a paralysis of incorporation during the first days of life—and as vomiting at a somewhat more advanced stage.

PRIMARY ANXIOUS OVERPERMISSIVENESS

Primary anxious overpermissiveness is a maternal attitude which can be considered a subdivision, that is, a special form, of what Levy has called maternal overprotection [9]. Unfortunately, maternal overprotection has become an omnibus concept, used indiscriminately by authors in different disciplines, to describe a wide scale of behavior patterns and attitudes without regard for the diversity of the underlying motives. In the following chapter I shall attempt to distinguish a number of different forms of this maternal overprotection. I shall try to elucidate the motivation which leads to these different forms, and to relate these forms to the specific clinical picture presented by the child.

Connected with anxious overpermissiveness is, I believe, the disturbance which Spock has called the "three-month colic." In pediatric circles the three-month colic is a familiar clinical picture: after the third week of life, and continuing to the end of the third month, the infant begins to scream in the afternoon. Feeding may calm him, but only temporarily. Within a relatively short time, the baby again shows the symptoms of colicky pains. Whether one shifts the baby from the breast to the bottle, or from the bottle to the breast; whether one changes the formula or leaves it alone—nothing seems to help. Drugs have been tried, among them atropine, mostly without result. The stools of these infants show no pathologic condition, though in certain cases one may see some diarrhea. The pains of the infant last several hours, then stop, and begin again the next afternoon. Toward the end of the third month, the disturbance has the tendency to disappear as inexplicably as it appeared—to the great relief of mother and pediatrician.

Theoretic Considerations

From the findings of the various observers, two factors emerge which appear to me to be significant in the etiology of three-month colic: these are maternal overconcern on the one hand, and hypertonicity of the infant from birth on the other. I therefore advanced the hypothesis of a *two-factor* etiology: *If newborn infants with congenital hypertonicity are raised by mothers who are anxiously overconcerned, they may develop three-month colic.*

This hypothesis is in good agreement with Freud's postulate of a complemental series in the etiology of neurosis. The hereditary constitutional factor which predisposes these cases to the three-month colic is a somatic compliance, namely, hypertonicity [5, 6].

Unlike in the adult, conditions are rather simple in the infant;

there is no conflict between ego and superego, since in the neonate neither the one nor the other is present. Instead, a vicious circle is established between the infant's hypertonicity and the mother's anxious overpermissiveness, and particularly so when the self-demand schedule is practiced. One surely may assume that an oversolicitous mother tends to react to any unpleasure manifestation of her infant by feeding him or nursing him. One may even surmise that the unconscious hostility to the child of some of these mothers produces guilt for which they overcompensate. Due to this tendency to overcompensate they readily accept and even insist on the self-demand schedule. Clinically this looks as if they wanted to atone for their unwillingness to give anything to their child—and least of all the breast.

It is relatively easy to uncover the psychologic factor of the complemental series and its dynamic aspects in the behavior of these mothers. It is rather more difficult to detect these factors in the undifferentiated personality of the 3-week-old infant. Here, however, physiology helps us. Tension has to be discharged; a hypertonic infant will have to discharge much larger quantities of tension at more frequent intervals than a calm and placid child.

We may assume that an overconcerned mother is less capable than a mother with fewer guilt feelings of distinguishing whether her child is really hungry or whether he screams for other reasons. Consequently she responds to his cries by feeding him.

At this point the constitutional hypertonicity, the somatic compliance of the infant, meshes with the mother's psychologic overconcern. The digestive system of these infants is more active, peristalsis faster—possibly more violent—and excess food will produce excess intestinal activity. A vicious circle results: The hypertonic child is unable to get rid of his tension normally in the course of the nursing process. Instead he discharges it through the postprandial screaming and motor agitation typical of these children. The oversolicitous mother immediately feeds the child again, in an exaggerated compliance with the tenets of self-demand. During this unscheduled feeding, some tension will be discharged through oral (sucking and nursing) activity and deglutition; for a brief period the child becomes quiet. However, the food which the infant has ingested again overloads the digestive system, increases tension, and causes a recrudescence of the state of unpleasure, leading to renewed colic and screaming. The anx-

508

ious mother is able to interpret the cries of the child only within the framework of self-demand, and will again feed the infant, and thus the vicious circle goes on.

How can we explain that around the age of 3 months of life the syndrome disappears? In the first place, we may assume that, after 3 months, even mothers with guilt feelings or inexperienced mothers will tire of the constant sacrifice required by exaggerated self-demand. Or perhaps they will learn to interpret a little bit better the screams and vocalizations of their infants and will give up the all too single-minded interpretation of the child's demands.

But, more important, in the course of the third month of life the infant will develop his first directed and intentional responses, namely, volitional behavior directed toward his surroundings. This is the age when the first social responses emerge, the first precursor of the object appears, the first cathectic displacement on memory traces take place, and mental activity begins. Body activities multiply; we witness "experimental" movements, the inception of the first attempts at locomotion, the active striving of the child toward the things in his reach, enabling him to discharge actively the tension to which up to this stage of development he had to submit passively.

HOSTILITY IN THE GUISE OF MANIFEST
ANXIETY (INFANTILE ECZEMA)

The maternal attitude which we observed in the great majority of mothers whose infants suffered from infantile eczema[1] was that of manifest anxiety, mainly about their child. It soon became clear that this manifest anxiety corresponded to the presence of unusually large amounts of unconscious repressed hostility.

At birth the skin of these children may seem more than usually vulnerable because of cutaneous excitability. If that were true, how-

---

[1] Throughout this presentation I shall speak of infantile eczema. Consultation with different dermatologic authorities did not show consensus in regard to such terms as eczema and atopic dermatitis. I have therefore elected to use the old-fashioned term, *infantile eczema*. The picture in question is that of a skin infection, beginning in the second half of the first year of life, localized predominantly on the flexor side, favoring skin folds (inguinal, axillary, popliteal, cubital, the crease behind the ear, etc.) with a tendency to weeping exfoliation in the most severe cases. In the subjects studied it seemed to be self-limiting and to disappear in the first half of the second year.

509

ever, eczema should appear already in the first few weeks of life, or at the latest a month or two after birth. But such is not the case; it actually begins in the second half of the first year. Therefore we may rule out the vulnerability of the skin, and say that the eczema of these children is due rather to an increased readiness for response; or, in analytic terms, an increased cathexis of cutaneous reception. That actually is another way of saying that at birth the group of future eczematous children had an increased reflex excitability. And one may wonder whether the phenomena described by Greenacre in her article "The Predisposition to Anxiety" as the consequence of a "dry birth" cannot be explained equally well by a higher excitability of the newborn's skin [8].

As to the second factor, influence of the environment (that is, the influence of the object relations) on these children, we found the following: In a subtle way their object relations were different from the average. In one area of the child's functioning with the persons of the surroundings, namely, in the manifestations of the 8-month anxiety, there was a statistically significant difference between the two groups. Of the children suffering from eczema, 15 percent showed 8-month anxiety; in children without eczema 8-month anxiety was present in 85 percent of the cases.

The psychiatric exploration of the mothers of the eczematous children yielded significant information. The majority of these mothers showed an attitude of manifest anxiety about their children. It soon became clear that unusually large amounts of unconscious repressed hostility were concealed behind this manifest anxiety.

It was striking that among the mothers we investigated the great majority of manifestly infantile personalities was concentrated in the group of the mothers of eczematous children.

These mothers also had other notable peculiarities: They did not like to touch their child; they always succeeded in talking one or the other of their friends into diapering him, bathing him, giving him the bottle, etc. At the same time they were concerned about the fragility, the vulnerability of their child; one of them used to say, and this is characteristic: "A baby is such a delicate thing, the least false movement might harm him." This exaggerated concern is an overcompensation for unconscious hostility. The actions of these mothers contradict their words. Our interpretation is supported by the numerous instances in which the same mothers exposed their babies to unneces-

510

sary risk, to real danger. They often barely avoid inflicting serious damage on the baby, such as feeding it an open safety pin in the cereal; some of these mothers consistently and intolerably overheated the baby's cubicle on the plea that he might catch cold; one of them knotted the baby's bib so tightly that the baby became blue in the face and only my timely intervention saved him from strangulation. In this group one was not surprised to learn that this baby or that had fallen out of bed on his head more than once.

Our study of the infants who develop eczema has thus revealed two anomalies of the mother-child relationship: (1) The mothers had infantile personalities, betraying hostility disguised as anxiety toward their child; they do not like to touch their child or care for him, and deprive him systematically of cutaneous contact. (2) The child patient has a congenital predisposition for increased cutaneous responses, leading to increased cathexis of the psychic representation of cutaneous perception—in loose analytic terms, to a libidinization of the skin surface. This is the very need which his mother refuses to gratify. Accordingly these babies' needs and their mothers' attitudes stood in an asymptotic relation to each other.

Primary identification consists in the infant's experiencing everything in his environment which pertains to need gratification (drive gratification) as part of his own person and body, outside of which nothing exists. Glover appears to be thinking on similar lines: "For the primitive mind, all states having the same pleasure tone tend to bring about identification with the objects connected with these states" [7].

Primary identification is accordingly made difficult by those anxious mothers who withhold from their children the need gratification inherent in being touched. They extensively restrict the occasions for primary identification through withholding tactile experiences. Yet, if the infant is to differentiate himself from his mother, these primary identifications—tactile and other—have to be dealt with, severed, and overcome. Perceptual development plus action-directed motility first, and locomotion later, are the child's devices for dealing with primary identification and achieving differentiation. When differentiation from the mother has been accomplished, the infant can form those secondary identifications which pave the way to autonomy and independence.

Elaborating on Mahler's concept of "the process of individua-

tion-separation" [11, 12], we would then say that the road to individuation leads through secondary identifications. For the child must acquire the mother's techniques of taking care of him, of watching over
him (and he can do so only through identification), before he becomes able to separate himself from her and to become an independent individual. I believe that the process of individuation-separation,
which Mahler places after the eighteenth month of life, has two precursor stages. The first of these stages I would call the process of
primary individuation, in which the child deals with primary identifications, severs, and overcomes them. Stage two is that of secondary
identification, which begins in the second half of the first year of life.
In the course of this stage the child acquires techniques and devices by
means of which he achieves independence from his mother [15].

The inadequately integrated ego of the eczematous children's
mothers made it particularly difficult for them to develop devices for
controlling and compensating their unconscious anxiety in a consistent manner. This difficulty obviously is at the root of the chaotic affective signals which they present to their offsprings.

That such anxieties do indeed affect the child most vitally has
been observed by Anna Freud and Dorothy Burlingham in their
studies of displaced children in wartime [4]. Their observations demonstrated that infants up to 3 years did not become anxious during the
terror of the London blitz unless their mothers began to feel anxious.
The infants remained unaffected by external stimuli until the meaning
of these stimuli was transmitted to them via their mother's affective
attitude.

The operation of these processes is well-illustrated in the case
of the depressed mother whom we watched one day feeding her infant
with an expression of deep concern on her face. Manifestly she was
pouring far too much at a time into his mouth. At the same time,
swallowing movements of her throat showed that she was identifying
with her child, so to say, encouraging him to swallow by performing
the act herself. But it immediately became clear that her swallowing
represented a desperate effort to overcome an overpowering nausea,
which soon began to express itself in her face. The child of course was
not experiencing nausea; it was only the mother who was nauseated,
for neurotic reasons of her own, at the idea of swallowing milk. Consequently she was overdoing the pouring-in, to get it over with

512

quickly, and she succeeded in making the child regurgitate, to her own increased revulsion.

This is a drastic example, taken from the feeding situation, in which a mother can most easily be observed and her conflicts detected. However, it should be realized that conflicts will interfere in all the relationships of such a mother with her baby. For example, a particular mother who was diapering her child suggested a slow-motion film because of the hesitancy, the extraordinary retardation of her movements. She placed the baby on the scale as if she were lifting a heavy weight, which she might drop at any moment. And while fixing the diaper with a safety pin which she had been handling as if it were a loaded gun, she succeeded in the end in drawing blood. Throughout this procedure changing expressions alternated in her face. The benign look with which she approached the child quickly gave way to rigid effort when she was lifting him onto the scale, then changed to gloom, replaced by a forced smile while she was fumbling with the safety pin.

These isolated examples are in effect characteristic of the totality of the emotional climate in which the eczematous child is raised. He is constantly faced with affective signals coming from his mother that ostensibly correspond to the given situation. But in the next moment her unconscious conflict reasserts itself, anxiety wells up, she suppresses all signals, only to shift into an overcompensation of the cause of her anxiety and to transmit signals contrary to her feelings; though on the next occasion she may just as well exaggerate the signals which are appropriate to her feelings.

In a word, what she transmits will be neither consistent with her inner attitude nor will it correspond to her actions in regard to the child. What she does cannot be taken as a signal in the usual sense of the term, for it is not related to the partner. What she expresses depends not on her conscious or even on her unconscious relationship with her child but rather on the variable climate of her unconscious guilt feelings, ghosts from her past, provoking anxiety which does not permit her truly to identify with her child. And so she particularly avoids the most elementary form of identification, that of immediate, of affective physical contact.

In other words, her messages are not signals but only signs or symptoms. To the adult, to the psychoanalyst, they might be meaningful. As road signs on the path of normal development they are meaningless and confusing for the child.

Accordingly, forming object relations in response to ambiguous and inconsistent signals becomes an uphill task for the child. A selective lesion has been inflicted on both primary and secondary identification. This lesion is the direct result of interference with, and impairment of, the forming of the first object relations. This lesion is particularly striking in the area of human relations; it is less striking in regard to the child's relationships with inanimate objects. Hence the lesion is noticeable in the nonappearance of the 8-month anxiety. As these infants have not formed normal object relations, they are unable to distinguish affectively the mother from the stranger and therefore show no anxiety when approached by a stranger.

It is interesting to note that infantile eczema, just like the three-month colic, is limited to a certain developmental phase; a spontaneous cure occurs, usually after the end of the first year. Again, we may ask ourselves: Why is this disturbance self-limiting? I believe that these limits are contingent upon the progress of maturation, just as in the three-month colic. After the end of the first year, the child acquires locomotion; that makes him increasingly independent of the signals originating from the mother. He now becomes capable of substituting normal object relations—of which the eczema-afflicted child has been deprived—by stimuli which he can obtain himself. He now can get on without so many contacts with his mother; he can replace maternal stimuli by contacts with things, with other persons whom he can seek out; for he has left passivity behind and progressed to directed activity. It is to be expected that the interlude of eczema during the first year of life will leave permanent traces, fixation points, on the psychic development of the child; what they are we can only surmise.

OSCILLATION BETWEEN PAMPERING AND
HOSTILITY (ROCKING IN INFANTS)

A very common motility disturbance known as rocking behavior is particularly frequent in infants in the institutional setting. In itself the behavior can hardly be called pathologic, for practically every child engages in it at one time or another. Before the age of 6 months, rocking is rare, however, and when it occurs it is carried out in the supine position. In general, children perform their rocking activity after the first 6 months of life in the knee-elbow position. After the tenth month, rocking—or its equivalent—may be performed in the standing position also.

When rocking in infancy takes a pathologic turn, it becomes the principal activity of the children affected by this condition and substitutes for most of the usual activities common at the same age level. Furthermore, we were struck by the violence with which rocking is carried out, involving motor behavior and expenditure of energy far in excess of that generally seen in children of the same age.

The relationship between the rocking children and their mothers is a peculiar one. It certainly is not absent; but it is far from being a well-balanced, close relationship. In general, the mothers of these children are extrovert personalities with a readiness to intensive, positive contact, and definitely alloplastic tendencies. They are mostly infantile personalities, with a lack of control over their aggressions, expressed in frequent outbursts of negative emotions and violent manifest hostility.

These mothers are victims of their own emotions, and, due to their infantile personality, they are unable to realize the consequences of their behavior and are unusually inconsistent in dealing with their environment. Their babies are the main outlet for their labile emotions, so that these babies are exposed alternately to intense outbursts of fondling, of "love," and to equally intense outbursts of hostility and rage. In one word, there are rapid oscillations between pampering and hostility.

The two sectors in which rocking children are retarded are the sector of social adaptation and that of manipulative ability. The manipulative sector reflects the way in which the child handles and masters toys, tools, inanimate things in general. It measures the child's relation to "things." The sector of social relationships, on the other hand, reflects the child's progress in human relations. Combined, the retardation in both sectors adds up to the incapacity of the rocking children to relate either to their living or to their inanimate surroundings, to their inability and lack of initiative in dealing with their environment.

How does the mother's behavior contribute to this developmental deficiency? The late Katherine Wolf advanced the proposition that only after relationships with the libidinal object had been established, only after object constancy had been achieved, will the infant be able to relate to inanimate things.

Our assumption, then, is that the mother of a rocking child has stunted the establishment of the primal, of the libidinal object, and thereby made all later object relations difficult or impossible for him. In other words, the mother's behavior, self-contradictory and inconsistent, leads her baby to store in his memory conflicting object presentations. This fund of memory traces does not lend itself to being amalgamated into a unified libidinal object through the fusion of the drives directed to the mother. Such experience impairs the formation of an object which can remain identical with itself in space and time. The object presentation genetically is not identical with itself, because of the vagaries, because of the ups and downs, of the mother's emotional temperature. The original experience with the libidinal object-to-be creates, above all, an expectancy pattern. Where that is lacking, each single object presentation will have to be approached on a trial-and-error basis, as an experiment, as an adventure, as a peril.

This can be observed in children beginning to recover from the damage done by hospitalism: They move toward any object, animate or inanimate, with utmost caution, which expresses itself in their behavior. They slowly approach the object with one outstretched finger, without touching it, withdrawing, advancing again, and repeating this several times until they finally touch it. This behavior is pathognomonic.

The less severely damaged (deprived) rocking baby who still has surplus aggression at his disposal cathects his own body as an object. And he uses it as something to be actively manipulated for the discharge of aggression through volitional involvement of the totality of his body musculature. Why this relatively harmless avenue of discharge is chosen in preference to the much more severely pathologic somatization of internal organ systems, or the elaboration of pathologic adaptive-defensive mechanisms, we do not know yet.

This choice may be determined by the phase in which the etiologic factor has become effective in the given child. The observations of Myrtle McGraw [13] on the inception, proliferation, and subsidence of behavior patterns support such a proposition as much as our own infant observations. The latter situate the proliferation of muscular activity of every description and subsequently the development of locomotion just in the period when pathologic rocking becomes most conspicuous. It might be worthwhile to investigate whether pathologic rocking is not a substitute for erect locomotion, or rather a deviant development of erect locomotional maturation. Or we might surmise that pathologic rocking is the manifestation of a specific psychologic process—for instance an early precursor of the ambivalence so characteristic for the second year of life. On the other hand we could assume a congenital predisposition for rocking movements, anchored in phylogeny. And finally, a concurrence of all three factors cannot be excluded.

In summary, inconsistent, contradictory behavior of the mother makes the establishment of adequate object relations impossible and arrests the child at the level of primary narcissism, so that he is limited to the discharge of his libidinal drive in the form of rocking.

CYCLICAL MOOD SWINGS OF THE MOTHER (FECAL PLAY AND COPROPHAGY)

Fecal play was recorded in our nursery population as early as 8 months and 3 days of age. Most of our cases fall between the tenth and the fourteenth months of life. In 67 percent of the cases, the fecal play culminated in coprophagy. We will, therefore, speak of coprophagy and fecal play interchangeably. Though the play with feces as such went on for long periods at a time and showed many variations, the mouth movements accompanying it, the facial expressions, and the sequence of gestures indicated that all this playing was but a preliminary to the final act of putting the feces in the mouth and, in several cases, to swallowing them. We therefore came to the conclusion that fecal play during the first year of life is intimately connected with oral ingestion.

Highlights of the Mother's Personality

We again begin with an account of the mother's personality. It came as a surprise to find that the near totality of psychoses present in the population under observation was concentrated in the group of the mothers whose children manifested fecal play. Among these

517

mothers, 69 percent showed the clinical symptoms of depression; 2 of them were paranoiac; of the remaining 3, 1 was homicidal.

Mother-Child Relationship

A closer study of the relationship between the depressive mothers and their children reveals further meaningful details. In the first place we found that these mothers showed marked intermittent mood changes toward their children. The duration of a given mood ranged from 2 to 6 months. In some of the cases we recorded mood reversals up to four times in the course of 1 year. These moods varied from extreme hostility with rejection to extreme compensation of this hostility in the form of "oversolicitousness."

I have put the term *oversolicitousness* in quotes for a good reason. The protocols of many of the coprophagic cases contain remarks to the effect that the mother is tender or loving to her baby; but the remarks are qualified by the statement that this love has some exaggerated traits. We noted, for instance, a hungry, fascinated incapacity of the mother to tear herself away from her child. Or we found a mother saying, "I cannot look at other children, only at my own." Or such a mother may dislike her other children to the point where she not only neglects them but does them actual harm.

The rejecting or hostile behavior is, in its way, equally peculiar. Overt rejection in the mothers of noncoprophagic children usually takes the form of a mother's declaring that she does not want her child, and offering him for adoption. However, such overt rejections are rare in our coprophagic cases. Equally infrequent are overt hostile statements of these mothers about their children. One such mother said, "I hate my child to be called 'darling.'" Whatever the overt manifestation of feeling, we found unconscious hostile behavior to their children in all 16 of the mothers.

A surprisingly large number of the coprophagic children suffer injury at the hands of their own mothers. In the group we studied they suffered burns; they were scalded; one was dropped on his head; one was nearly drowned during bathing. We had the impression that without the alert supervision of the staff few of these children would have survived. In passing, it is worth mentioning that the only two cases of actual genital seduction of children by their own mothers were found among the group of depressive mothers.

The coprophagic children show the affective state of depression. Besides those who look depressed, for instance, others at times show a facial expression resembling that of paranoid suspicion; a third group look as if they are in a catatonic daze. Therefore I consider this a clinical picture sui generis, which at an early level of infantile development appears to combine the characteristics of orality (hence the depressive looks of some of these children) with anality.

The mothers of our coprophagic child patients have a personality characterized by deep-seated ambivalence. Periodically when their superego has the upper hand, the hostile components are repressed; the picture is that of a self-sacrificing, self-debasing mother who envelops her child with love. During this period such mothers may, for instance, constantly pester the observer with worries about their child, particularly during the first month, when they often believe that the child is deaf or blind. Or, as another example, one mother said: "My baby is so little [at the time he was one year old], I am afraid of hurting him." Or again in another case, an unsophisticated observer, a nurse, remarked about a mother: "She is defiant, like a lioness with her cub." These "love" periods lasted for an appreciable time, never less than 2 months, and would then be replaced by a swing to hostility. The hostile periods again lasted for an appreciable time.

The child is in effect confronted with a potential libidinal object which maintains a consistent attitude long enough to permit the forming of object relations. However, this period comes to an end; the second phase of the cycle begins, in which the potential object becomes its own opposite. Now this "new" object remains constant long enough so that the child can form a set of new object relations; but it also compels the child to establish a compensatory reaction to the loss of the first, the "original" object.

How does the inconsistency, the oscillation, of the mothers of the rocking children differ from the mood swings of the mothers with coprophagic children? Rocking children were exposed by their mothers alternately to intense but brief outbursts of love and equally intense and brief outbursts of rage. The mothers of these rocking children had infantile personalities which were incapable of consistent attitudes lasting for days, let alone months. Their tantrums alternated with kissing jags within the hour, and at no time could their behavior be anticipated by the child. His potential libidinal object alternates between opposite poles and passes so rapidly through every point of the compass of emotions that all attempts at forming an object relation must fail. But it would be an error to equate this picture with the long-wave periodicity observed in the mothers of the coprophagic children.

I have commented on the peculiar nature of love in the depressive mothers; on their hungry fascination with their child, which can go to the point of cunnilingus. In the original study I advanced the proposition that coprophagic children identify with the unconscious tendencies manifested in their mothers, and that this identification leads the child to oral incorporation.

Anna Freud discussed certain aspects of the child's relationship to the depressed mother [3]. She remarked that the child's behavior does not reflect a process of simple identification. The mother's depressive mood generates in the child an inclination toward depressive tendencies. The depressed mother retreats from the child, and the child, in Anna Freud's words, "follows her into the depressive mood."

Anna Freud made it clear that she considers this phenomenon to be in the nature of "infection" and that it is not an imitation of the mother's gestures which produces this mood in the child. The child simply responds to the affective climate, not to the cause of the affect; he is thus infected by the affective climate.

It seems to me that in the symptoms of coprophagic children we have a working example of Anna Freud's proposition. Perhaps I should no longer speak, as I did in the past, of an identification of the coprophagic child with the unconscious tendencies of the mother, but of an "infection" of the child with the mother's devouring tendencies. Or, as I would say now: The child follows the mother's attitude, but he follows it in global terms, which are the only ones he is as yet able to assimilate. These are the terms of "taking in" and "spitting out." This would lead the coprophagic child to the oral incorporation of his object.

Given the fact that the coprophagic syndrome arises in the wake of a radical change of the mother's attitude, which, for the child at this age, is tantamount to losing her, we can now discern three components in the clinical picture of coprophagy:

1. Depression leads to oral incorporation of the lost object.
2. The child follows the mother into depression.

3. The coprophagic child has suffered what amounts to the loss of the "good" object (eventually destined to fuse with the "bad" object into the libidinal object proper).

The "loss" of the mother going into depression is not a physical loss, as when the mother dies or disappears for some reason. It is an emotional loss; for the mother, in changing her emotional attitude, also radically changes the signals which identified her as a good object for the child. Physically, she remains the same mother she was. Emotionally, the good mother, the libidinally invested object, is lost. This is a loss which can be experienced in this form only in the first year of life, at this developmental stage; in other words, it is stage-specific.

The depressive mother blocks this normal development when she withdraws from the child into her depression; the radical change of her emotional attitude transforms her into a bad object. While the good object invites the opportunities for action exchanges with the child, the mother who has withdrawn into her depression avoids and withholds them. The child is thus deprived of the opportunity to complete the fusion. In his need for action exchanges, he follows the mother into the depressive attitude and so acquires her global incorporative tendency, attempting to maintain what he had already achieved in the way of object relations.

The infant's actions either originate in the actions of the mother and then extend them, or the situation may be reversed: The infant's actions trigger the mother's actions, which will then continue and complete the infant's action. Within the first year, those of the infant's actions and attitudes which proceed independently from those of the mother are limited. Therefore, one has to conceive of the infant's actions within the dyad as forming, together with those of the mother, a continuity of which they are a part. This interlocking, which corresponds in part to Benedek's [1] and Mahler's [10] concept of symbiotic relations, begins as identity of infant and mother, that is, as primary identification. But even by the end of the first year, differentiation between child and mother is far from complete.

To summarize: in the first year of life, coprophagy is covariant with depression in the mother. Two elements in the mother's depressive picture provoke the child's pathologic state:

1. The periodic nature of her mood swings.
2. The unconscious oral-incorporative tendencies characteristic of depression.

In the child we found three factors relevant to coprophagy which all serve and facilitate the child's striving to get back to the mother:

1. The facilitation provided by "following the mother's mood." This is a precursor of identification; identification proper is not available at this stage because of the ego's incompleteness.
2. A dynamic facilitation arising out of the child's reaction to the loss of the "good" object.
3. A phase facilitation through the child's having arrived at the transition from the oral to the anal phase.

MATERNAL HOSTILITY CONSCIOUSLY COMPENSATED (THE HYPERTHYMIC CHILD)

Maternal behavior in these cases is the result of a conscious conflict. For such mothers the child serves as an outlet for narcissistic and exhibitionistic satisfaction—and not as a love object. However, such a mother is aware that her attitude toward her child is improper, she feels guilty, and therefore she overcompensates consciously by a subacid, syrupy sweetness. This maternal attitude is primarily found in intellectual and professional circles.

The fathers in these cases are aggressive and successful in their jobs. This may be due to their capacity for overt expression of hostility. In their relationships with the children, they are hearty, loud, and somewhat exhibitionistic, not knowing where to stop, and as often as not frightening the children through rough and ready handling, over the concerned mothers' protests.

The children themselves impress the observer by their manipulative proficiency. That is not particularly surprising; I recall a few cases where as a rule the children were practically crowded out of their playpens by the mass of toys accumulated there by the overcompensating parents who were trying to buy off their guilt feelings. Naturally, the children were exceedingly familiar with inanimate objects and clever in manipulating them. But in the social sector of their

522

personality their developmental profile shows a conspicuous retardation, in line with the kind of human relations offered them by the parents. By the time they are in their second year, they are apt to be hyperactive, not very sociable, and destructive with toys. On the other hand, they are uninterested in contact with human beings and become hostile when approached. The catamnesis of the cases followed by us leads me to believe that their personality tends to develop in the direction of children described by John Bowlby under the name "aggressive hyperthymic" [2].

CONCLUSION

I have discussed deviations in the establishment of object relations and the disturbance of the infant's psychic development frequently associated with such deviations. Some of these disturbances of early infancy, be they psychogenic affections or psychosomatic conditions, bear a striking resemblance to disturbances with which we are familiar also in the adult. I have stated that these resemblances do not make the two, the disturbance in the infant and the psychiatric disease in the adult, either homologous or even analogous. On the contrary, I have stressed that the pathologic conditions seen in infancy are independent clinical pictures sui generis, because they affect an organism having a psychic structure very different from that of the adult. However, when disturbances as serious as some I have described occur during the formative period of the psyche, they are bound to leave scars on the psychic structure and function. Such scars are likely to constitute a locus minoris resistentiae on which disturbances occurring at a later age can find a foothold. The disease appearing later may belong to a completely different nosologic category or it may not; these are questions which await investigation. However, I believe that it is highly probable that early infantile psychogenic disturbance creates a predisposition for the subsequent development of a pathologic state.

Bibliography

1. Benedek, T. Adaptation to reality in early infancy. *Psychoanal. Quart.* 7:200–215, 1938.
2. Bowlby, J. *Forty-four Juvenile Thieves.* London: Baillière,

Tindall & Cox, 1946.

3. Freud, A.   Quoted from four lectures on child analysis, New York, September 1960.

4. Freud, A., and Burlingham, D.   *War and Children.* New York: International Universities Press, 1943.

5. Freud, S.   Fragment of an Analysis of a Case of Hysteria (1905). In J. Strachey (Ed.), *The Standard Edition of the Complete Psychological Works of Sigmund Freud,* Vol. VII. London: Hogarth, 1953.

6. Freud, S.   Introductory Lectures on Psycho-Analysis (1915–1917). In J. Strachey (Ed.), *The Standard Edition of the Complete Psychological Works of Sigmund Freud,* Vols. XV & XVI. London: Hogarth, 1963.

7. Glover, E.   *On the Early Development of Mind.* New York: International Universities Press, 1956.

8. Greenacre, P.   The predisposition to anxiety. *Psychoanal. Quart.* 10:66–94, 1941.

9. Levy, D. M.   *Maternal Overprotection.* New York: Columbia University Press, 1943.

10. Mahler, M. S.   On child psychosis and schizophrenia: Autistic and symbiotic infantile psychoses. *Psychoanal. Stud. Child* 7: 286–305, 1952.

11. Mahler, M. S.   On two crucial phases of integration concerning problems of identity: Separation-individuation and bisexual identity. Abstracted in panel, Problems of Identity, reported by D. Rubinfine. *J. Amer. Psychoanal. Ass.* 6:131–140, 1958.

12. Mahler, M. S.   Symposium on psychotic object relationships. III: Perceptual de-differentiation and psychotic "object relationships." *Int. J. Psychoanal.* 41:548–553, 1960.

13. McGraw, M. B.   The Neuro-muscular Maturation of the Human Infant. New York: Columbia University Press, 1942.

14. Ribble, M. A.   Clinical studies of instinctive reactions in newborn babies. *Amer. J. Psychiat.* 95:149–160, 1938.

15. Spitz, R. A.   *No and Yes: On the Genesis of Human Communication.* New York: International Universities Press, 1957.

16. Spitz, R. A.   *The First Year of Life.* New York: International Universities Press, 1965.

25

Effects of Adaptive and Disruptive Aspects of Early Object Relationships upon Later Parental Functioning

Peter L. Giovacchini

EDITORS' INTRODUCTION

The pathogenic effects of delayed and deficient separation-individuation of the infant from his mother has been well studied from the point of view of the child.[1] The author of this chapter presents clinical material to illustrate derivatives of such unpropitious infancy in the serious psychopathologic conditions of adults. As the unconscious motivations of these pathologic states become experienced in the transference, they seem to prove the fundamental significance of the primal mother-child relationship. The psychopathology of adults discussed in this chapter, however, serves mainly as a link between the generations. The infant who shared such "symbiotic fixation" suffers the consequences of that predicament throughout his life. Even if the developmental adaptations relieve and compensate for many of its symptoms and even if he succeeds in various aspects of his life, such an individual can rarely escape reliving the derivatives of his infantile experiences through his parental attitudes.

The observations reported in this chapter based on manifestations of transference phenomena in the psychoanalytic process might be viewed as a continuation of the experience described in Chapter 10; it goes, however, beyond the mutuality of the analyst-patient experience in a single instance. It rather attempts to illustrate the biopsychologic significance of the experiences of the symbiotic phase of development as it is transmitted by the mother to her child.

E. J. A.
T. B.

[1] See the Bibliography to Chapter 11 in this volume.

Early childhood experiences determine the adult's character structure. In this chapter, the impact of early object relationships upon the course of emotional development and how they determine parental functioning in particular will be examined.

Recently, considerable attention has been directed to a phase of development referred to as the symbiotic phase. Benedek, focusing upon the mothering process [1--3], and Mahler, directing herself primarily to childhood psychosis [8, 9], have discussed symbiosis extensively and present convincing arguments why it is useful to postulate such a developmental phase. Benedek especially has shown its relevance to development in general as the child is mothered and as the mother develops further by being a parent [4].

Benedek has also stressed that emotional development can be viewed as a continuum in the development from preobject and symbiotic phases at one end to maturity. The role of the external world in facilitating this development, of course, varies, but in very early stages the mother is responsible for preparing a setting in which maturational processes are unimpeded and object relations can develop.

Structuralizing processes initiated by innate maturational forces are characterized by responses that are, at first, massive and general, and later become coherent, discrete reactions. Postulating the existence of a symbiotic phase as a beginning state in the development of the psyche is a logical extension of what has been observed in the structural elaboration of the soma. Consequently, the formation of psychic structure must proceed from a global symbiotic phase to complex object relations (such as parenthood) that are used in the service of adaptation.

The reconstruction made from the study of the transference neurosis also points to the plausibility of postulating such a phase. Psychopathology, although distorting, also emphasizes psychic features that may have been otherwise unnoticed. Fixation upon the symbiotic phase by highlighting what impedes emotional development broadens our understanding of structuralizing processes and the formation of character structure. These are all-important elements that determine how the adult functions later as a parent.

Patients in psychoanalysis can teach us about the difficulties

526

encountered in the resolution of the symbiotic phase. The transference regression may reenact some early developmental vicissitudes that later lead to difficulties in the consolidation of the parental role. In addition, direct observation of the mother-infant relationship can also lead to insights. The latter is a more accurate replication of what actually occurs, whereas the former enables us to make "microscopic" formulations about defective adaptation.

Clinical Illustrations of Symbiotic Fixation

To illustrate the effects of fixation upon the symbiotic phase, I will present the following vignettes.

Case 1. A middle-aged patient found that he was unable to work. He felt totally paralyzed and not capable of coping with the external world, which he experienced as having become inordinately complex. He did not consider himself a person with a separate identity and had no interest whatsoever in relating to anyone. His only concern was about his relationship to me.

Recently, he had changed jobs, moving from a position of financial comfort and status, but in which he was stabilized without hope of further advancement, to one where his horizons were unlimited.

His associations were prominently oral, being preoccupied with swallowing and eating me or being eaten by me. He was also obsessed with the fear that I would kill him or that he would commit suicide.

He believed that a job with upward mobility would cause him to become separated from me. Upward mobility was equated with independence. His old job, insofar as no forward movement was possible, meant a fixated state without the threat of change.

His fears had many facets. His moving away from me (the symbiotic fusion) caused him to be afraid of my anger. He believed that I wanted to maintain the status quo and would kill him if he showed any evidence of "growing away" from me. He was also afraid that he would kill me if we separated. His fantasies were that as he literally pulled away he would be tearing some vital part out of me and then I would die.

In addition, he wanted to kill me in order to be rid of the hated part of himself which had to some extent become projected into me through the symbiotic fusion. On the other hand, because of the fusion, he believed this would also constitute suicide.

In summary, all the symptoms and transference reactions could be understood as results of the threatened dissolution of the mother-child symbiosis which was being reenacted in the transference regression. He was ambivalent. He wanted to feel autonomous and separated from me. Still, such independence was frightening and in many fantasies he questioned whether he could handle the responsibility inherent in autonomy and whether he could survive without my "omnipotent support." Symbiotic fusion also meant annihilation of his psychic existence as an individual entity. This was experienced as terror. Consequently, he was faced with the unbearable conflict of wanting an independent identity in the context of magical fusion.

There are many direct observations of the mother-child relationship that seem to have similar meaning as the one described above.

CASE 2.   A toddler who could barely walk was very actively playing. His mother was sitting in the same room, one that had an ample supply of toys. The child's attention span was limited but he was able to play vigorously with several toys. He broke several and could not manage others, but he doggedly continued playing even though obviously feeling frustrated. The mother simply sat there; the child never turned to her for either help or comfort. The mother could have been on another planet, the child displaying a remarkable independence which, in spite of the many frustrating toys, was characterized by determined calm. The mother finally left the room. The child's reaction was surprising in view of the above. Even though he seemed to be ostensibly nonchalant about her presence, he broke down completely when she left. His expression changed to one of terror and he had a temper tantrum. He looked miserable, and his previous aplomb was replaced by chaotic and purposeless screaming and kicking. Others entered the room trying to supply comfort but caused only an intensification of the tantrum. Nothing could stabilize this child until the mother returned. She walked back into the room and he gave no sign that he even saw her; not once did he directly look at her, but his anguish vanished and he returned to his "autonomous" play.

In normal development ego boundaries become consolidated during the subsequent structuralization following the symbiotic phase. Consequently, a fixation upon this stage also leads to a blurring of ego–non-ego boundaries which has many manifestations. The middle-aged adult patient often did not know what was not part of himself. He demonstrated this frequently during the transference regression but he also spoke of other situations that could be explained by his inability to distinguish "me from not-me." For example, during his first week of analysis he often pounded the wall with his fist. By so doing, he would establish where his "body ended" (fist) and the outside world (wall) began. This patient had the not too unusual symptom of difficulty in paying his bills. Paying money meant surrendering part of himself to me. Since his ego boundaries were so tenuous, he was sensitive to many situations that he believed threatened his integrity.

In other cases, the patient's "blurring" of ego boundaries is manifested by lack of perceptual discrimination. What is, in fact, outside the self is perceived as belonging to the self. Consequently, the external object is only dimly perceived and its distinct qualities are not recognized. The lack of distinction between me and not-me affects the perception of the external object insofar as the difference between object and nonobject is also not recognized. As a parent, this lack of discrimination will involve the relationship with the child.

Obese and alcoholic patients often show marked identity disturbances and perceptual difficulties. The markedly overweight person often does not really enjoy food. Bruch has described such phenomena [6]. Some patients hardly ever feel hungry and seldom have any appetite. This is a manifestation of nondifferentiation of drives, but there is an added factor in that these patients do not distinguish between food and nonfood.

CASE 3. One such patient, a 32-year-old mother, actually did not know what she was eating. Eating had become a mechanical, automaton-like procedure which she did not cathect sufficiently to be aware of what she was doing. Her basic pathologic condition included a fluid ego boundary which encompassed the *universe*. If, by chance, something managed to be perceived outside of herself, this was only momentary because she was continually incorporating and maintaining a state similar to symbiotic fusion and infantile megalomania. This patient never had an organized meal where one sat down at the table at a prescribed time eating a particular type of food appropriate to what is conventionally served at that time of day. Her eating habits were a reflection of her general lack of structure, her ego being unable to relate to structured, distinct situations because her diffuse boundaries contained an amorphous, unorganized ego.

This blurring had marked effects on her ability to function as a mother. She reacted to her two daughters, 6 and 8 years old, as if they were part of herself (see next section). They were not recognized as separate and distinct persons.

As could be anticipated, her associations and fantasies were constantly concerned with oral incorporation and with what could be conceptualized as fusion with external objects leading to their obliteration. She saw herself as self-sufficient, not requiring or acknowledging any reality outside of herself. Still, the fact that she desperately sought treatment emphasized her helplessness and vulnerability.

One finds similar constellations in many alcoholic patients. They do not enjoy liquor and are often unaware of what or whether they are drinking.

CASE 4. A 49-year-old married woman described alcohol as being another of her body secretions [7]. She could not buy anyone a drink because this was equivalent to giving away part of herself and thereby establishing a distinction between herself and the surrounding world. When drunk, she was very generous and wanted a partner to drink with her, but she clearly indicated these were moments where she was totally fused with her companion and emotionally speaking she was giving nothing away. Through a vicarious identification she would be merely giving drinks to herself, thereby not being forced to distinguish between herself and the outer world, i.e., to disrupt her symbiotic fixation.

Here, too, the distinction between drink and nondrink simply was not made. She was never aware of drinking (when she naively stated she never drank, she believed it) because she was drinking all the time. Alcohol had become so much a part of her that it was not perceived as a separate, distinct entity, nor was drinking perceived as a specific activity.

When a person is unable to distinguish an external object as separate from himself, there is the further problem of being unable to perceive the self. All the patients described above had difficulties in knowing who and what they were and questioned the purpose of their existence. The obese patient sometimes found everything to be in a haze, including her body, which seemed to "blend" with her surroundings. She then "forgot" her name and other facts about herself which would identify her as a person. Similarly, other patients, especially when the transference regression recapitulated the symbiotic fusion, lost their precarious sense of personal identity. Loss of identity and fixation upon the symbiotic phase are related.

Children, usually of parents such as the above, often demonstrate similar phenomena. Dramatic malfunctioning of the identity sense is often found in autistic children. Autoerotic activities such as head-banging, body-rocking, and trichotillomania are frequently found in conjunction with developmental arrests that are associated with symbiotic fixations [5, 10]. These children highlight the need to "define themselves" by withdrawing from the intrusive outside world upon which they feel hopelessly and helplessly dependent.

Furthermore, parents suffering from relative fixations upon the symbiotic phase often reveal histories of the above autoerotic activities. To summarize briefly, both the observation of children and the retrospective reconstructions made from the treatment of adults emphasize that when there are difficulties in the symbiotic phase: (1) drive differentiation is impaired, (2) ego–non-ego boundaries are blurred, leading to a defective identity sense, and (3) there is a defensive need for omnipotent control resulting in the interesting paradox of autonomy within the framework of symbiotic fusion.

EFFECTS OF VICISSITUDES OF SYMBIOTIC FIXATION UPON LATER PARENTAL FUNCTIONING

The middle-aged patient described above who reacted adversely to a promotion and a 32-year-old woman whose transference reactions indicated similar developmental problems are particularly germane to our topic, since they are both parents. They spent considerable time in their treatments discussing their children.

The mother has one child, a daughter, with whom she has an extremely disturbed relationship. She had been ambivalent about becoming pregnant, concerned whether she would be adequate to the task of child-rearing. Her pregnancy, however, was relatively calm except for the occasional recollection of a "monster" dream (giving birth to a deformed fetus).

After delivery she suffered from a postpartum depression, but was still capable of taking care of her child. As she improved she felt more and more that the child was still part of herself, whereas immediately after delivery she was upset because she had "lost a part" of herself. These reconstructions were made 5 years later after she had been in treatment for 3 years.

Although she seemed able to relate to her child during the first 6 months, the situation became increasingly difficult later. It was apparent that as long as her daughter represented an amorphous extension of herself, she was able to relate to her. The monster dreams, which were repeated during analysis, clearly indicated her need to rid herself of the hated part of herself. Still, she had to maintain a symbiotic union because complete separation would lead to both her destruction and her daughter's. By remaining fused, she could strive for magical reparation; however, the daughter's maturation made it difficult to maintain such an undifferentiated relationship. She suffered intensively the latter half of the first year up to the time she sought treatment two and a half years later. Taking care of her daughter became an agonizing ritual. Whereas previously she was relatively efficient in feeding, diapering, and bathing her child, she now found these routine activities inordinately complex.

She could not relate to her child as a separate being, and this was recapitulated in the transference relationship. She relived with me feelings identical to those she had toward her mother. She believed that her behavior toward her daughter represented a repetition of what she had experienced with her mother during early childhood, in reverse. The transference relationship indicated that this was a plausible reconstruction.

During a regressed phase she did not differentiate herself from me or her child. Her dreams and associations indicated that we were a unit, indistinguishable from each other. Surprisingly, at this time, she began acting out sexually with several men and running the risk of becoming pregnant.

This behavior was especially interesting because she was reacting to the tensions created by primitive pregenital impulses rather than truly sexual ones. At first she referred to her inner emptiness and the need to have it "filled" by a child or by my "maternal self." She reported fantasies where the core of her personality was "occupied" by a boundless but vague and amorphous parent. She had considerable anxiety at this time because she did not know whether this state of "fusion" was going to be blissful or destructive.

She described my presence inside of her as "global" but her reactions to her daughter as well as her mother were similar. During this period of treatment she could not retain a distinct detailed image of me. She could not describe my appearance and, as was true with her child particularly, she was not able to discern individual qualities that would distinguish us from other persons. Her lack of discrimination of her own identity sense and of myself seemed to indicate that the transference was recapitulating an early symbiotic phase which now included her daughter as well as her mother.

Finally this patient was able to feel my "inner presence" as benign rather than destructive, as apparently had been the prototypic relationship with her mother and as she had perceived me during the beginning of the symbiotic regression, which was characterized by promiscuity. She felt that I was gradually shrinking within her but, in so doing, I was becoming more distinct (structured), losing my previous amorphous vagueness as well as my all-pervasive and encompassing attributes. She could now see me more clearly, and simultaneously began "discovering" her daughter as a person in her own right.

She was emphasizing a progression from the global to the discrete. Insofar as she was able to experience aspects of our relationship as nondestructive, she could differentiate beyond the symbiotic stage. Each step was reflected in her ability to mother her daughter and how she perceived her.

This progression emphasized the transitional aspects of the symbiotic phase which were demonstrated in the parent-child relationship. For several months she treated her daughter and later me as if we were transitional objects [11]. She felt we were fused inside of her but under her "control." At the same time she was able to acknowledge our external presence without being particularly concerned.

Her indifference gradually subsided and she became aware of feelings toward me, both affectionate and hostile, that were not necessarily directed toward herself at the same time. Metaphorically it seemed that this differentiation was accompanied by an ego "shrinkage" from its previous vast, amorphous, diffuse, amoeba-like qualities. Both her daughter and I underwent a similar shrinkage so that now external objects were perceived in a more sophisticated fashion and registered within the ego system as more discrete entities. They were not only more sharply delineated but there was more "space" between the object representation and the ego boundaries, signifying from a functional and structural viewpoint a developmental advance.

Behaviorally, she developed confidence in her ability to relate to and care for her daughter. She gradually achieved a relaxed attitude about mothering, feeling that being a parent was "natural" to her. It seemed that she had been able to construct a mothering introject that was no longer a discrete entity but one which had become amalgamated into various ego systems. She considered mothering a modality rather than a separate and distinct function isolated from the general ego organization as she had previously. Of course, there were many factors involved in the lengthy therapeutic relationship besides those descibed above.

I will now briefly describe how the middle-aged male patient related to his children. This next case will be abbreviated considerably in view of the more detailed exposition above.

The male patient had 8 children, and this in itself was interesting, especially since he had no religious scruples against birth control. He did not particularly want any children but he stated that he was fond of them.

Although his relationship to his children seemed phenomenologically different from that described above, there were fundamental similarities. His preoccupation was with eating and being eaten, as stated, and his associations before he was able to confine his projections to me often referred to eating his children. However, here again was an undifferentiated situation. He did not distinguish between one child and another. The large number of children enabled him to keep them anonymous. He did not accept them as well-delineated individuals but thought of his family as a "formless mass."

THE SIGNIFICANCE OF A TRAUMATIC SYMBIOTIC PHASE ON IMMEDIATE AND LATER FUNCTIONING

Parenthood has been considered from a more "microscopic" viewpoint than phenomenology. The mother's role also has to be distinguished from the father's. Still, whether looking at overt behavior or the symbiotic transference, there are some common denominators. *Both mothers and fathers who suffered these types of developmental vicissitudes are unable to relate to a child who has achieved a measure of autonomy and differentiation.*

The histories of parents who have difficulties in resolving the symbiotic phase with their children repeatedly suggest that they have had similar difficulties with their own parents. Behaviorally, as parents, they find themselves to have intense feelings of inadequacy when they try to minister to their children's more individualistic needs. Their relationships with their parents is reported as being similar to that observed between the child in the playroom and the mother.

Similar to the obese and alcoholic patients' attitudes about the amorphous qualities of the external world, these parents encompass their children as narcissistic extensions that are part of their amorphous selves. To see their children as individuals in their own right is a massive threat because they lack the differentiated ego mechanisms required to adapt to a complex and sensitive person. Even though the overt technique involved in taking care of a neonate and a somewhat older child may not be radically different, the interpersonal qualities of the latter relationship require considerable flexibility and maturity. Parenthood is traumatic because these patients lack the synthesis and differentiation to relate to a distinct external object.

534

The woman just described resorted to many obsessional rituals when caring for her daughter, not only to protect herself and her child from her murderous rage, but also because she lacked the adaptive techniques that would have made mothering an intrinsic part of her self-representation. She referred to mothering as something she might have read about in a mechanic's manual. Insofar as the mothering introject was imperfectly and tenuously formed, she dealt with her child clumsily, relying upon what she had memorized, since she was incapable of warmth and spontaneity.

The child, as a narcissistic extension of the self, becomes the recipient of the parent's projections. The mother, especially, can project the hateful parts of the self-representation upon the relatively undifferentiated neonate (note the frequent occurrence of "monster" dreams). This establishes psychic equilibrium as she has "rid" herself of disruptive rage.

A traumatic symbiotic phase leads to the formation of threatening introjects in subsequent developmental stages and there will be difficulties in the "absorption" of the maternal introject into the general ego structure. The self-representation will eventually incorporate the mother's hatred [1] and self-hatred, feelings of worthlessness, and inadequacy.

The ego, therefore, has two monumental tasks: First, it has to protect itself against the maternal introject. This means it must be powerful enough so that it will no longer feel threatened. It must be capable of handling the disruption the maternal introject creates. This is achieved by a rent in the ego's unity, a partial fragmentation where one part maintains control over the other which contains the disruptive introject. The second task is one where the ego has to master problems "autonomously." Since the maternal introject is split off, the child or patient has to deny that the mother has any influence whatsoever, either negative or positive, as the clinical examples illustrate. He cannot turn to her for the satisfaction of inner needs and he cannot rely on his own resources because he has acquired only a minimum of adaptive techniques from her.

As an adult and a parent, this need to be rescued from a de-

[1] Granted, the horrendous monstrous qualities of the archaic maternal image described in the transference regression are the outcome of projection of primitive hatred. Still, hateful self-feeling must have been to some extent the residual of the partial resolution of the symbiotic phase.

535

structive self will crucially affect relationships with children. Since the parental introject is a threatening one, these patients feel both threatened and ineffective when functioning as parents. Insofar as they recapitulate their traumatic symbiosis in the parent-child relationships, they impede their child's development and do not foster his autonomy.

Thus, parenthood recapitulates early phases of the relationship with one's own parents [3]. When a child has undergone the type of disturbances of the symbiotic relationships described here, his parental functioning will reflect these early disturbances. As they had difficulties in "emerging" from the symbiotic phase, they will present similar difficulties to their children. They will have problems when their children "threaten" to become persons rather than amorphous extensions; consequently, anything that leads to separation is also traumatic *for the parent*. How this trauma is mastered varies and may result in obsessive ritualism or a defensive maintenance of anonymity as seen in these patients.

SUMMARY

The impact of early object relationships upon the developmental sequence is emphasized. The adult character structure is discussed primarily in terms of its capacity to function in the parental role.

As parents, these patients recapitulate with their children the difficulties they had in resolving their symbiotic phase during childhood. Primarily they require the presence of the child upon whom they can project the unacceptable portions of their destructive self-image, to a large extent determined by a nonfunctional, devouring, maternal introject. Still, they cannot allow the child to structuralize to a stage of relative separateness as (1) they cannot relate at a higher structural level because of their lack of psychic differentiation, and (2) once a child ceases to reflect their amorphous self-image he is no longer available for their projections.

536

Bibliography

1. Benedek, T. Adaptation to reality in early infancy. *Psychoanal. Quart.* 7:200–215, 1938.
2. Benedek, T. The psychosomatic implications of the primary unit: Mother-child. *Amer. J. Orthopsychiat.* 19:642–654, 1949.
3. Benedek, T. Psychobiological aspects of mothering. *Amer. J. Orthopsychiat.* 26:272–278, 1956.
4. Benedek, T. Parenthood as a developmental phase. *J. Amer. Psychoanal. Ass.* 7:389–417, 1959.
5. Bettelheim, B. *The Empty Fortress; Infantile Autism and the Birth of the Self.* New York: Free Press, 1966.
6. Bruch, H. Falsification of bodily needs and body concept in schizophrenia. *Arch. Gen. Psychiat.* (Chicago) 6:18–24, 1962.
7. DeLevita, D. J. *The Concept of Identity.* New York: Basic Books, 1965.
8. Mahler, M. On child psychosis and schizophrenia: Autistic and symbiotic infantile psychoses. *Psychoanal. Stud. Child* 7:286–305, 1952.
9. Mahler, M., and Elkisch, P. Some observations on disturbances of the ego in a case of infantile psychosis. *Psychoanal. Stud. Child* 8:252–261, 1953.
10. Spitz, R. A. Life and the Dialogue. In H. Gaskill (Ed.), *Counterpoint.* New York: International Universities Press, 1963.
11. Winnicott, D. W. Transitional objects and transitional phenomena. *Int. J. Psychoanal.* 34:89–97, 1953.

26

The Clinical Effects
of Parental Neurosis
on the Child

Melitta Sperling

EDITORS' INTRODUCTION

This chapter represents a further elaboration of Spitz's thesis regarding the significance of the coenesthetic and diacritic organizations in the early biopsychologic integration of the maturational processes of the infant and their influence upon dispositions for psychosomatic pathology. Dr. Sperling's method of investigation was psychoanalysis of the child and the mother, sometimes conducted simultaneously or successively by the same analyst, and at other times carried out by different psychoanalysts. It proved fruitful in revealing the symbiotic nature of the unconscious and nonverbal communication between mother and child. Since her subjects were children of different ages and much older than the infants directly observed by Spitz, she was able to collect data on their active and passive participation in transactions with their mothers. Even when they were not the primary influences in the children's pathologic conditions, the illness sooner or later affected the mothers, thus setting up the spiral of transactional processes and the consequent aggravation of symptoms in both participants.

The variety of cases studied by Sperling enabled her to classify the symptoms according to the customary developmental phases. On this basis she found that the "oral" symptoms, such as anorexia or vomiting, originated in predispositions established earlier than the "anal" ones, such as spastic and mucous colitis and the more serious manifestations of ulcerative colitis.

Whatever the importance of this, the conditions investigated in this chapter would seem to corroborate the significance of the "primal cavity" in producing "early acquired dispositions" even though the pathologic condition becomes manifest later as a result of evolving conflicts and their persisting stress effects [1]. Since these subsequent developments might well influence psychosomatic dispositions, it would seem useful to differentiate the symbiotic phase of development from the transactional processes occurring later between the child and his mother or with other "significant objects"—transactions that might activate an earlier established disposition through the pressure of the latent conflict.

This elaboration of the following chapter points to its significance for the general theory of psychosomatic medicine.

E. J. A.
T. B.

Bibliography

1. Spitz, R. A. *No and Yes: On the Genesis of Human Communication.* New York: International Universities Press, 1957.

F or the past 27 years, a considerable part of my time has been devoted to the psychoanalytic treatment of children and adolescents suffering from psychosomatic diseases such as ulcerative colitis, mucous colitis, asthma and allergies, cyclic vomiting and anorexia, migraine, petit mal, epilepsy, and skin disorders.

In the treatment of these children, I found that at certain phases during their analysis a seemingly unmotivated exacerbation of their condition took place or treatment was suddenly terminated with or without a rationalization. Invariably, these occurrences turned out to be the result of unconscious resistances on the part of the mothers to the treatment of their children. In adults, resistances to therapy are manifested as such in the patients themselves and can be handled directly, but in children the resistances of the parents may show themselves in various forms that gain expression through children and often cannot be dealt with directly, that is, through the children alone.

I discovered that this crucial phase in the treatment of the psychosomatically ill child was the time when the child was attempting, with the help of analysis, to dissolve the symbiotic relationship with the mother, and the mother, because of her own unconscious needs, was unable to accept this [16, 32]. Unless she could be helped through psychoanalytic intervention to understand and to overcome her resistance, she could not or would not permit this basic change in the relationship to occur. However cooperative her conscious attitude appeared, the treatment of the child was doomed to failure. In children like these, in whom resistance manifested itself in somatic symptoms that developed with surprising speed, it was essential to recognize this tendency in the mother and analyze it at once. This was best done by the analyst who was treating the child, particularly in the case of younger children, where mother and child seemed to function as an inseparable unit.

THE METHOD OF SIMULTANEOUS ANALYSIS

The great merit of the method of simultaneous analysis of mother and child lies not only in the fact that it represents an essential technical aid in the treatment of certain psychosomatic diseases in

541

children, important as this may be, but also that it has proved to be a new and rewarding approach to the study and understanding of a crucial area of child development, namely, the psychology and psychopathology of the mother-child relationship. It permitted the immediate observation of interactions between the *unconscious* of the mother and her child, of the ways in which the unconscious wishes of the mother were transmitted, received, and reacted to by the child, and of the changes brought about in their responses to each other by the analytic process. Resulting from this, a new understanding of the etiologic factors and deeper dynamic mechanisms operating in certain psychosomatic diseases of children was gained. The method was applied successfully to the treatment of ulcerative colitis in children and provided a means of conceptualizing the illness in a more satisfactory way [13, 16, 25, 27, 29, 42]. It also made it possible to study and to compare the conditions under which, given a symbiotic mother-child relationship, either a psychosomatic disorder or a psychotic development occurred.

My application of this method to the study and treatment of severely disturbed children, whose bizarre, explosive, and unpredictable behavior could not be fully understood or influenced by individual treatment alone, proved equally fruitful. In the cases so studied, behavior which might have been ascribed to inherited factors was shown to be reactive to the mother's unconscious wishes [18, 21, 32]. Similarly, behavior that might have been explicable only in terms of some speculated mechanism, such as extrasensory perception, became more understandable in the context of acceptable theory. Because the manifest behavior of the parents in these cases appeared appropriate, it was difficult for either the parents or observers to relate the disturbed behavior of the child to parental attitudes. The child, it seemed, reacted to the latent feelings and needs of the parents and not to their overt behavior. This is well-illustrated in the following two examples.

An 8-year-old boy was referred to me by the school where his abusive language and behavior presented a serious problem. The mother had no complaints; he was very devoted and attentive to her, and he presented no problems at home. The father was alternately seductive and sadistic with him. The son was afraid of his father and sadistic with others, especially with younger children. On the surface and to the casual observer, the behavior of these parents appeared to be beyond reproach. It soon became obvious that the child's mother had agreed to treatment under the pressure of school, but actually resented and opposed any interference in her relationship with her son.

During the treatment of the mother, I found that she had been using her son as her mouthpiece. She had been a shy and fearful child, who could never speak up in school or elsewhere. She was still afraid of people and had difficulty in expressing herself or voicing an opinion. Her son was saying and doing some of the things which she herself wanted to say and do but had never dared.

The perceptiveness of a child to the intonation of his mother's voice is revealed by the following little episode.

A teacher asked her pupils to talk freely about their feelings concerning their parents. She was astonished when one complained that her mother yelled at her all the time. The teacher, who knew this mother to be a very gentle, soft-spoken woman, expressed her disbelief. The little girl responded, "But she yells at me from the inside."

The reactions of infants to the neurotic problems of parents also pose problems similar to those described for the psychosomatic child. They are difficult to diagnose as such, because infantile reactions to tension (from whatever source) are also expressed somatically and because parents and pediatricians are inclined to look for somatic rather than emotional causes for such reactions.

The severity of a child's reaction to parental neurosis and the consequences for later development depend to a large measure upon the age of the child at which this pathologic interaction begins, and upon the nature and severity of the parental neurosis. Because the disposition to react in a specific pathologic way to experiences and situations in later life is acquired very early, the question of early acquired constitution versus inherited constitution is of the utmost importance for prophylaxis.

A maternal neurosis can affect every area of the child's developments from birth onward. The child may even have been assigned a specific unconscious role by the mother prenatally based on a specific sex identification, identification with a member of the mother's family from childhood, or with a rejected part of herself, etc.

Disturbances in the Mother-Child Relationship

The earliest indication of a disturbed mother-child relationship usually manifests itself in a disturbance of the vital functions of the child, such as food intake, sleep, excretion, and respiration. There are sometimes severe disturbances of these functions for which no apparent reason or remedy can be found, and which are of more serious significance than the mild and transitory disturbances encountered during the developmental phases. In these cases, superficial psychotherapy, reassurance, advice, or manipulations are ineffectual. It would seem that only interpretations exposing the unconscious motivations and conflicts of the mother are helpful. This can often be accomplished even in brief contacts with the mother. With young children, treatment of the mother alone is often sufficient to dissolve the pathologic relationship. Such indirect treatment is the only method by which infants or preverbal children can be treated successfully. In the very young, even severe psychosomatic disorders are still reversible if something is done to alter the disturbing relationship between mother and child.

Feeding and eating disturbances in children are the earliest and most frequent psychosomatic disorders in childen. They are the first indications of something amiss in the mother-child relationship, and seldom reach the child analyst or child psychiatrist. The following is an example.

CASE 1.   The mother of a 5-month-old infant was referred to me by a pediatrician who had recognized that the mother's psychologic problems were the cause of the child's symptoms. The situation was as follows: The woman had given birth to a healthy, well-developed 8-pound boy whom she breast-fed in the hospital. She experienced much anxiety and worried that she might not have enough milk and urged the doctor to prescribe a formula to have on hand at home in case breast-feeding should prove insufficient. At home she began to add the formula after each feeding. She would wake the child when he fell asleep after breast-feeding and force the bottle upon him. When he began to vomit after each feeding, she consulted a pediatrician who advised her to stop the additional feedings. She did not accept this advice. As time went on, the child refused to take the breast, continued to vomit, and developed colic. She consulted another pediatrician who advised her to starve the child for some time until he could take food again. At this the mother became panicky, abandoned any schedule, and was obsessed by only one desire, i.e., to get food into the child. The child was losing weight rapidly, and she again consulted the pediatrician who referred her to me.

I learned from the mother that she had not wanted this child, and particularly not a boy. She had wanted to end the pregnancy, which was not planned for, but her husband would not agree. She feared that something would happen during birth or that the child would be born dead. She had a 12-year-old daughter who had never presented any difficulties to her. Psychoanalytic investigation revealed that she had unconsciously identified her son with her younger brother who had died in infancy when my patient was 5 years old. She had always felt guilty over the death of this brother, without having been conscious of her death wishes against him. She had, by the force of repetition-compulsion, reenacted with her own child this unresolved conflict with her brother. Awareness of this helped her to accept the baby as her son and restored her ability to feed and care for him properly [27].

The progressive development of a severe feeding disturbance arising from a distorted mother-child relationship and the therapeutic approach which takes into consideration both partners of this relationship are illustrated by the following case, in which mother and child were treated by me in concomitant analysis.

CASE 2. When Ann started psychoanalytic treatment, she was 4 years of age. She had been referred to me (but not brought in) when she was 3 because of severe and persistent vomiting, anorexia, and abdominal cramps with periodic episodes of diarrhea for which no organic cause could be found. A year later, when the child developed an intense phobic attachment to her mother, refusing to allow her out of her sight, the mother acted upon the referral.

In the treatment of the mother I learned that prior to Ann's birth she had had an obsessional concern regarding her husband, who suffered from mild diabetes. Her attitude toward him had changed markedly upon the discovery of this condition, as had her entire behavior. She could not work, developed a sleep disturbance, and found it impossible to concentrate on anything except her husband's condition. As soon as Ann was born she completely lost her anxious preoccupation with her husband's ailment and devoted herself exclusively to her baby. Soon after the child's birth, she thought that Ann was not taking enough food; she changed the formula and increased the number of feedings, with the result that at 7 weeks of age, Ann developed anorexia, vomiting, and diarrhea, for which she had to be hospitalized. After a short stay in the hospital, she was discharged and put on a diet and new formula. Her symptoms continued and she was hospitalized again at 11 months of age. Her condition, however, remained unchanged up to the time she began treatment with me. At the age of 4, she had not been given any solid foods but was still on a formula elaborately prepared and fed to her with a spoon by her mother. The mother maintained that only she knew how to prepare the child's food and how to feed her. Up to the time treatment began, Ann had vomited with every feeding.

Analysis of the mother revealed that Ann's intense need to hold on to her mother was a reflection of the mother's inability to let her out of her sight even for a moment. She was in constant dread over the child. She did not permit her to taste candy or solid food for fear that she would

545

choke on it instantly. Even when Ann had been in need of glucose because of the acidosis caused by her continuous vomiting, the mother could not carry out the doctor's suggestion to allow her to suck on a lollipop.

Ann's mother was the youngest of five children and had been a particularly demanding and possessive child. She had to have her way and would threaten suicide if her own mother did not comply immediately with her wishes. To her mother's illness and death when she was an adolescent she had reacted in a way which she could not understand before her analysis. During the illness, she had been so concerned about her mother that when the doctor came, he had to attend to her first. Throughout this period, she had a rapid pulse and could neither eat nor sleep. On the day of her mother's death, she heaved a sigh of relief, ate a complete meal, and had her first sound sleep. She had never realized how dependent she had been nor aware of the way in which this dependency had expressed itself in her possessive and controlling behavior. In retrospect, she could understand her intolerance of the suspense created by her mother's illness, a situation over which she had no control. She accepted the death as something that she had wanted to happen in order to put an end to the agonizing uncertainty. Her reaction could also be understood as a defense against an impending depression and as an attempt to maintain her fantasy of omnipotence.

She had carried over her dependency to her husband whom she controlled similarly to the way she had her mother. When he developed a mild diabetic condition she became extremely disturbed, reacting to his illness as she had to her mother's. As soon as Ann was born, she transferred this relationship from her husband to the child, keeping the baby in a state of complete dependency.

After she had gained some understanding of her need to control her child completely, she began to relinquish her hold on Ann to some extent. The latter reacted to this not only by giving up her phobic clinging, but also, to her mother's surprise (and frustration), by demonstrating a strong desire for independence. When the child first began her play analysis, she insisted on having her mother with her in the playroom and continually asked her permission for everything we did. She apparently understood and accepted my interpretations regarding her insecurity in relation to her mother—casually injected—because, on her fourth visit, she decided to come into the playroom by herself. Leaving my office that day, she said to her mother: "I don't want you to come in with me into the playroom anymore. I have a much better time without you." This was a big step forward in Ann's life, as well as in her mother's. Throughout the past year, Ann had refused to remain with anyone but her mother, not even accepting her father or the nursemaid who had been with her since infancy.

About 6 months after the beginning of treatment, an episode occurred which illustrated the interplay between the unconscious of the mother and her child and the way in which an immediate phobic reaction of the child could be induced by the mother's unconscious needs. At the time when this occurred, Ann's condition had improved to the extent that she had given up clinging to her mother and was playing outdoors with other children. She had also been asking for some solid foods—bread, fish, meat—which she would eat when her father or grandmother were in the house but not at her regular mealtimes when her mother fed her. She had also completely stopped vomiting. All of a sudden, there was a relapse into the phobic clinging and refusal of any solid food. In the session with the mother, it was revealed that this had set in on the day after the mother's visit to her gynecologist for a checkup. During her pregnancy with Ann, the mother had undergone a gynecologic operation and there was some question as to whether she should or could have another child. She had seen this doctor once before, more than a year ago, and the day after that, as she distinctly remembered, Ann's phobic behavior had started. On her way to the doctor this time, she had thought about this and wondered whether the same would happen again. At the doctor's she found out that she could not have another child. After discussing this, the mother was able to recognize clearly that she had been unwilling to let go of Ann and that the fleeting thought she had had about a recurrence of Ann's symptoms had expressed her unconscious wish for her daughter to remain attached to her.

The morning after this session the mother said to Ann in a casual way: "I am going shopping now and Mary [the maid] will take you out this morning." Instead of clinging, crying bitterly, vomiting, and complaining of abdominal pain as she previously had whenever her mother attempted to leave her, Ann accepted this suggestion very readily. Her mother was now able to realize that it was actually she who clung to her daughter and experienced difficulty in leaving her, and now that she was determined to let go of her, Ann was accepting it without disturbance.

It was difficult for the mother to surrender her food control, even though she permitted the child more freedom now in other areas. When Ann began to bombard her mother with questions as to when she would have "regular food," the mother felt guilty but could not accede with ease to the child's request. She understood that this meant setting Ann free, allowing her normal independence. Ann, in turn, was testing her mother constantly during this period. Often she would come and tell her that she had cramps, and would carefully watch for her reaction. On one occasion, she was sucking hard candy at home, something which she did in every one of our play sessions, but which she had not yet done at home. She suddenly made a noise, as if she was choking, and watched her mother's face very closely. When the mother remained calm ("It does take a lot out of me," the mother would tell me), Ann said: "Don't you hear? I am choking!" The mother replied: "You're a big girl now and you know how to suck a candy." Ann continued to test her mother for some time before she was convinced that this change in the mother's attitude was a real one [27].

Eating disturbances in young children can be severe and, in some cases, can be regarded as somatic equivalents of depression [31]. Anorexia nervosa and pernicious vomiting in older children and adolescents are always serious conditions, and a pathologic mother-child relationship is an important factor in these cases [38].

I have described this relationship, which originates early in life, as the "psychosomatic type." In it a premium is set by the mother on her child's illness and consequent dependence upon her, but the child is rejected by the mother when he is healthy and manifests strivings for independence [29]. This relationship can be transferred later by the child to another person, who then unconsciously becomes a mother (substitute). Such a mother substitute does not necessarily have to be an older female or a female at all. Particularly in the case of girls it can be, and very often is, a boyfriend or, later, a husband. The girl then becomes as dependent on this substitute as she once was on her mother, and shows an exaggerated need to control this person. For example, in the case of Helen, a 15-year-old girl whose history will be given a little later, the mother substitute had been first a girl friend and later a boyfriend. This is rather typical for girls in this relationship, namely, to attach themselves in this way to another girl in preadolescence or early adolescence and later transfer the connection to a boy.

The Father's Role in a Disturbed Mother-Child Relationship

The father in these cases is usually a follower, like the child, who goes along with the mother as the leader. The father is often in competition with the child for the mother's attention and can, as exemplified in the case of Ann, be suddenly dropped in favor of the child. It then frequently happens that the father too, in his own ways, will try to use the child for instinctual gratifications denied him by the spouse, thus contributing to the seduction and overstimulation of the child. In the case of Ann, the mother, by inducing the phobic clinging, tried to frustrate her husband also in this area and to make sure that she alone controlled the child. In the case of a 4-year-old boy (suffering from ulcerative colitis) the father, whenever he felt frustrated by his wife, would take the little boy to bed with him as a substitute for the wife [25].

Even with older children the seduction and overstimulation by the father is often blatant. Nevertheless, it does not seem, in these cases in which the peoedipal symbiotic relationship with the mother is the determining factor, that the neurosis of the father constitutes a major hazard in the child's development. The father rarely opposes

548

the treatment recommendation for the child and may become positively supportive when he begins to reap the benefits gained by it, such
as the regaining of the lost relationship with his wife. In some cases
where the marital relationship was so unsatisfactory that the "sick
child" was the only tie keeping the marriage together, successful treatment of the child was often followed by a breakup of the marriage.
Experience has shown that the treatment of the mother preceding the
treatment of the child not only helped to modify her relationship with
her child but at the same time helped to restore the relationship between the marital partners by reinstating the husband in the role to
which he was entitled. Even in cases in which the neurosis in the father was severe enough to handicap its familial situation, the treatment of the mother alone may be sufficient to permit the child to
extricate himself from his pathologic involvements if one is able to
motivate the mother genuinely into helping the child. For example, a
9-year-old boy with severe ulcerative colitis had a father who was a
latent psychotic type who had not been seen or spoken to by the
child's therapist in the 3½ years of treatment. The father had displaced some of his hypochondriacal and paranoid fears onto his son,
whom he prohibited from playing with other children or from being
outdoors. Because of his illness this boy had missed school for nearly
2 years, and was unable to ride a bicycle or play ball. Nevertheless,
the mother could overcome her husband's objections and carry out
the therapist's suggestion (made at a phase of the treatment when the
child's destructive impulses, previously bound up in the somatic symptoms, were being released and required adequate outlet), that they
hire a male companion to teach the boy how to ride a bicycle, play
games, swim, etc., so that he could join his contemporaries without
being ridiculed and called a "queer."

Surprisingly, these marriages did not break up in the course of
or following the wife's treatment, although in many cases the women
had anticipated such an outcome and had made use of it as a resistance during analysis. In one instance the marriage had been broken
off by the mother of a 7-year-old girl suffering from ulcerative colitis
before she began her own treatment and before the child's treatment
was started. In another, the parents separated when their daughter,
who had been treated for ulcerative colitis when she was a child, and
for residual psychologic problems in adolescence, got married. In this

549

case the wife left her husband, who was very dependent on her, but returned to him after a short time to resume the sadomasochistic relationship they had had from the start of their marriage.

In the previous case, the husband, too, was very dependent upon his wife who, after the divorce, married a much younger man in order to make herself into a real woman and thus help her to sever her tie with her sick child. The husband did not remarry but remained close to his former wife, who needed the dependence and devotion which she could not get from her second husband, although she had made him financially dependent upon her.

It would appear that the personality of the fathers of psychosomatically sick children is characterized by their own need for a parent-child relationship with their wives, in which they may alternately play the father, the mother, or the child with the spouse, instead of the husband. This manifests itself also in their sexual relationship, which may appear adequate on the surface but which is never satisfactory. In many cases there are manifest sexual disturbances such as periods of impotence, premature ejaculation, lack of sexual desire, or a preference for sex play other than sexual intercourse. In other instances there was sexual hyperactivity rather than hypoactivity, but this was seen as an overcompensatory activity employed in the service of pregenital sexual fantasies and needs. In such marriages it is the wife (although she may simulate the role of child with her husband) who is the real leader in the sexual relationship as well. Because of her own infantile sexual needs, she may not only accept but may actually seduce the husband into this type of sexual relationship, thus promoting his sexual impotence.

The treatment of the mother that aims at helping her to accept herself as a women, a wife, and a parent is often sufficient to bring about a more mature relationship in which the roles of the parents and that of the child are more clearly defined. These facts should explain why the role of the father appears somewhat neglected in my concepts and treatment of psychosomatic diseases in children, because the central issue is, in my opinion, related to the uniqueness of the psychosomatic relationship, which originates and ends with the mother or her substitute. It is only rarely in our society, or elsewhere, that a male takes the place of a mother with a young infant and, when this happens, he will be regarded and responded to as a mother by the child.

The Psychosomatic Relationship

In this situation the mother tries to maintain, in several disguised ways, the kind of control over her child which she had prenatally. The unconscious meaning of this control is to preserve the fantasy of omnipotence involving life and death. In most instances, the death of the pregnant woman actually means the death of her unborn child. The preoccupation with life, death and birth, and separation and reunion is a basic dynamic feature in these mothers and also in the child with whom they establish this relationship, but it is not exclusive to them. The same dynamics, in fact, have been found operating in phobic children and their mothers [41]. There is a dynamic interrelationship between phobic and psychosomatic symptoms that may coexist or alternate in the same patient [20, 24, 35, 40]. These are two different aspects of the same problem, namely, the unresolved symbiotic relationship between the mother and her child. This phenomenon could be observed in the case of Ann, whose mother accepted the fact that she needed treatment only after the girl had developed a phobia in addition to her somatic symptoms. This was because the mother then resented the control which the child exerted over her through the phobia. It was only after the mother, in her own therapy, discovered that she had been responsible for inducing the phobia in her daughter, and realized the reasons for this, that she was able to allow Ann to separate from her.

In many psychosomatic diseases of children the somatic symptoms may actually cover up a severe phobia, which has to be brought to the fore and resolved in order to insure a permanent relief from the somatic tendency. This is particularly true for asthma and colitis [20, 24, 35]. In some cases the psychosomatic condition not only camouflages a phobia of the child but also a severe phobia of the mother. In these cases both the phobia of the child and that of the mother have to be uncovered and resolved to allow for sufficient independence and growth of the child [40].

From these considerations it follows that the psychosomatic relationship between mother and child has to be taken into account if treatment of the child is to be successful. This presents a particular problem in cases of older children and adolescents, when it is not advisable for the analyst to work with the youngster and the mother or parents concomitantly. There are situations, however, in which the

adolescent refuses to accept treatment, or in which it can be anticipated that treatment will be broken off by the patient or that the patient will be withdrawn by the mother as soon as there is any interference in their pathologic relationship [19, 32]. In such cases, it may
be necessary to start with the treatment of the mother in order to
enable her to accept a change in the relationship. This type of situation can be illustrated from the treatment of an adolescent girl with
anorexia and vomiting, and from that of her mother. Both partners of
this psychosomatic relationship were treated intermittently and, for a
brief period, simultaneously. As a result it was possible to study the
vicissitudes of such a relationship during adolescence and the special
problems that it presented to the mother and to her daughter.

CASE 3.   Helen was referred to me when she was 15 years old,
following a 9-month period of illness during which she had been hospitalized three times in different hospitals because of severe anorexia, vomiting,
and a low-grade fever for which no organic basis was found. In the hospital her condition would improve, but the cycle repeated itself as soon as
she returned home. I saw her three times and I realized that she would not
accept treatment at present because of the relationship with her mother.
The latter's overeagerness for Helen to start therapy concealed opposing
unconscious wishes, and it was to these that Helen was reacting. I did not
exert pressure upon the girl when she indicated her unwillingness for therapy. We agreed that she should return to school in spite of her mother's
apprehension and that she would contact me should she experience any
difficulty.
Without Helen's knowledge I arranged with the mother for psychoanalytic therapy for herself, because this seemed the best way in which to
help Helen at that time and also, perhaps, to render her more amenable to
psychoanalytic treatment in the future. The mother revealed very strong
guilt feelings regarding her daughter's illness. She had felt intuitively that
her child's condition was in some way related to her, although she did not
know how. She had expressed this feeling to the attending physicians, and
it was actually through the mother's prompting that the case was finally
referred to me. She had been very much aware of the fact that Helen had
been able to eat and that her condition improved whenever she was away
from home and that she stopped eating and vomited when she returned
home. Helen was her only child and she had always given her much attention and care. Until the girl was about 13, they had been very close to one
another. At that time, Helen had begun to detach herself from her mother
and became very close to a girl friend. Upon her mother's instigations, she
broke off this friendship shortly before her fourteenth birthday. The
mother now blamed herself for having destroyed this relationship and connected this event with the onset of Helen's illness. She tried to rationalize
that the friend was not a good influence on her, but came to realize that

she had actually resented the friend for taking her daughter away from her.

As could be seen, Helen, in her attempts to separate herself from her mother in early adolescence, had transfered her pathologic relationship from mother to friend upon whom she became as dependent as she had been upon her mother. For some time preceding the onset of the acute anorexia and vomiting the mother, who previously had been overindulgent with Helen (reward for dependence), had become very critical and disapproving of her (rejection for strivings for independence). During her treatment the mother was able to understand that she had not been able to differentiate herself from the child and to accept her as a separate being with an individuality of her own. The relationship with Helen made up for an unsatisfactory marriage, and she could not bear to lose her to the girl friend but even less to a boyfriend. When Helen began to show interest in boys, the mother blamed the influence of the girl friend for what she considered a premature interest. She managed to bring about the social isolation of her daughter who, instead of having a birthday party (to which she had no one to invite), got sick on her fourteenth birthday. I am focusing here on only one aspect of Helen's illness, namely, her relationship with her mother. Helen's fear of growing up, accepting her femininity and heterosexuality (which also derived from her dependence upon her mother), were dealt with later when she started her treatment in her sixteenth year.

It is of some interest that even at adolescence indirect treatment (that is, the understanding by the mother of her role in her child's illness and its modification of the relationship) can be so effective. Helen improved remarkably during the first few months of her mother's treatment. She lost her symptoms and gained almost 20 pounds. I had arranged with the mother that Helen was not to be coaxed by her but should be permitted to take her food herself and to eat her lunches in school. Helen also had made up with her girl friend and had a number of other friends at school. She spent very little time at home.

Helen came for psychoanalytic treatment at the age of 16½ when the mother, who by this time felt that she had gained sufficient understanding of her relationship with her daughter, discontinued her analysis. The precipitating event was a disappointment in her boyfriend, to which Helen had reacted with somatic symptoms, developing a sore throat and persistent fever which resisted medication. She accepted readily her doctor's suggestion (he knew of her past history) to see me. She told me that she had been seeing a young man before she became ill and that she had expected him to call her. Two days before she became sick, she had stayed home to guard the telephone, constantly expecting his call. Because they had had an argument she was not certain that he wanted to see her again, and it was on the second day of her anxious waiting that she fell ill. It was brought out that although she had many friends, both boys and girls, she felt insecure in her relationships with people.

Helen was able to understand and work out these feelings of dependence and helplessness. The effect of this understanding upon her behavior was significant indeed; she gradually relinquished her innumerable and rather superficial friendships, which had served only to gratify her

553

neurotic needs and as a protest to her mother who did not want her to have any friends, and became interested in one particular boy. It was during the period of treatment, when she had assimilated interpretations, that she was able to give up this boy, of whom her mother disapproved, without recourse to illness.

Helen had what could be diagnosed as a cyclothymic personality, with a tendency to depressive and to mild hypomanic states. In her psychosomatic pattern of response, the depressive aspects were in her anorexia and the hypomanic behavior in the vomiting and hyperactive behavior [30]. The change in her relationship with her mother brought about by the treatment of the mother and by her own therapy, and the change in her personality structure enabled her to become aware of and to tolerate her feelings consciously without recourse to somatic symptoms or overt depression. A certain amount of adolescent rebellion has to be regarded and accepted as a normal feature in an adolescent girl's struggle to find and to establish her identity independent of her mother. The deeper dynamics underlying her anorexia and vomiting, such as oral pregnancy wishes and defenses against it, and the role of the positive and negative oedipal conflict, which was particularly severe because of the seductive attitude on the part of both parents, were additional features of her psychopathologic state.

Helen's mother had suffered from severe insomnia from adolescence all through her married life until Helen's birth. She remained free of it until the girl was 6 years old and had started school, and also during Helen's illness. There was a strong latent homosexual attachment of mother to daughter. When Helen was 19 and became engaged to be married, her mother had a recurrence of the insomnia with depressive feelings. She returned for more treatment, this time with the knowledge of her daughter who had by then finished her therapy.

Her sleep was particularly disturbed on weekends when her daughter had dates. She would wait up until the girl came home and could not fall asleep afterward. She could not sleep on nights when a certain boy came to see Helen because he was "a nice fellow and in too much of a rush." Her dreams and associations made it clear that she could not tolerate losing Helen, whom she wanted to keep either dependent as a helpless child or to possess as a homosexual love object. Some of her dreams were self-explanatory. She dreamed, for example, that she had lost Helen when she was a teen-ager but did not realize it until later. She offered her half a grapefruit but it was refused. (To "grapefruit," she associated "breast.") In another part of the dream, she bought figs (associated with testicles, sperm, babies), expressing her wish for another baby and her regret that she could not replace Helen. She had frequent nightmares during this phase of the analysis: A woman was pursuing a young girl on a big empty lot—the girl was escaping. She saw a young girl in a wedding gown, but the wedding changed into a funeral and the girl was dead. She knew even in the dream that the girl was Helen. The day before she had offered to have a ring made for the girl, with a diamond which Helen had inherited from her grandmother. Helen had said to her: "I don't want a ring from you." The mother, who had found out that Helen had been looking at engagement rings, was hurt and resentful. In the dream, therefore, she had Helen dead rather than married. When, in the course of the analysis, the mother had worked out these feelings, she once remarked: "Now I realize why I found fault with every young man that Helen went out with as soon as I felt that she was definitely interested in him, and why I always praised those for whom she did not care" [17].

The choice of defenses against instinctual impulses and the choice of illness which grows out of a conflict situation depend to a large measure upon the quality of the relationship with mother. In the psychosomatic type of relationship, the child reacts with the psychosomatic pattern to conflicts such as separation, loss, and other traumatic situations to which others might respond with manifest disturbed behavior.

The mothers in these cases do not tolerate frank neurotic or openly rebellious behavior of the child. When Ann became overtly phobic and in this was attempting to exert control over her mother, the mother resented it and it was then that she acted upon the referral to me. She had an intense fear of losing control—that is, losing her mind—which she tried to counteract by her exaggerated need for control over others, especially Ann. This was true also for Helen's mother, and was brought out very clearly when she returned for more therapy at the time Helen contemplated her engagement.

THE SIGNIFICANCE OF THE PREGENITAL PHASES IN PSYCHOSOMATIC CONDITIONS

The importance of the oral phases and the role of a disturbed mother-child relationship during these phases upon personality development and in the genesis of severe emotional disorders in children has been stressed by many investigators such as Benedek, Fries, Ribble, and Spitz, to name only a few of the outstanding pioneers [3, 9, 12, 44]. The earlier part of this chapter was concerned primarily with some of the somatic consequences of such a disturbed mother-child relationship, as manifested in eating disturbances in childhood and anorexia nervosa in adolescence. To the infant, mother and food are equated, and the relationship with the mother is a determining factor in the child's attitude to food and eating. This primary symbolic equation can be revived in the *unconscious,* especially in conflict situations which involve giving up or separating from the mother. This oral fixation or regression causes the child or adolescent to employ oral fantasies and oral mechanisms in the struggle with unresolved conflicts during subsequent (anal, phallic, and oedipal) stages of development. In the severe eating disturbances of children and in anorexia nervosa of adolescents, the predominant fixations are at the oral phases due to oral problems and to preoccupations of the mother with food and eating.

While the development during the oral phases has been the focus of psychoanalytic interest and research for some time, and the contributions in this area are too numerous to be listed here, development during the anal phases has remained a comparatively neglected area of psychoanalytic research, which is surprising considering that the management of the anal phases plays a significant part in determining character and symptom formation [1, 8]. Many psychopathologic manifestations indicating maldevelopment actually make their appearance at this time. To name only some: sleep disturbances; phobic behavior; obstinacy; defiance; temper tantrums; ritualistic, fetishistic, and transvestite tendencies; speech difficulties (especially stammering); tics (multiple, single, and vocal); and head-banging. Many so-called habits also make their appearance around this period, such as: sniffing, nose-picking, pica, hair-pulling and hair-eating, nail-biting, and encopresis and enuresis [2, 4, 6, 7, 15, 20, 23, 24, 27, 28, 30, 32, 34–38, 40–42, 45, 46].

My work with children suffering from various psychosomatic disorders—particularly ulcerative colitis, mucous colitis, psychogenic diarrhea and constipation, allergy and asthma—directed my attention to the significance of the anal phases in the genesis of these conditions and to the role which anal preoccupations and unresolved anal conflicts of the parents play in the etiology of the child's psychosomatic illness. The observations and findings made in the simultaneous treatment of mothers and of children suffering from these conditions were confirmed subsequently by the psychoanalysis of adolescents and adults also suffering from such psychosomatic disorders. With these patients, analysis needed to go back to the pregenital phases, and the anal fixations and conflicts had to be systematically exposed and resolved [13, 14, 16, 17, 20, 22, 24, 25, 27–29, 32–35, 39, 40, 42]. It is now necessary to discuss some of the somatic consequences resulting from the experiences of the child during the anal phases, with the

556

focus on the role which parental attitudes play in the etiology. The main concern here is with neurotic attitudes and feelings of parents who are well-informed, of above-average intelligence, and consciously well-meaning. The following brief illustration will suffice to make these points.

A mother whose 5-year-old son was severely disturbed and inclined to withhold his feces for a week or longer at a time told me of an incident that happened when he was 2 years old. This boy had had a nursemaid until he was 20 months of age and had been successfully bowel-trained. After the dismissal of the nursemaid he relapsed into soiling. On one occasion when he soiled himself the mother, "to teach him," stuck his face into his feces. The cleaning woman, who was a simple, uneducated person in contrast with the mother, who held two college degrees, said to her: "Don't do this, you don't teach a child that way."

It would seem that certain attitudes of the parents, and particularly of the mother, may interfere with a satisfactory development of the child during the anal phases and provide not only the basis for a bowel disturbance, but also for a disturbance of the child's ability to handle and to express aggression and sexuality later in life. During the anal phase, from about 1½ to 3 years of age, the child is required to give up soiling and the pleasure in his excretions and to acquire sphincter control. During this period the child also undergoes an important psychologic transformation. From being a passively dependent infant of the oral phase, the child develops into the aggressive and even destructive toddler of the anal phase, who now has the necessary physical equipment to execute at least some of his strivings for self-assertion and independence from mother [2, 8].

During the preceding oral phases of development, separating is a passive experience for the child and is initiated by the mother. While separation-anxiety is operative from the beginning of life, separation conflicts become manifest during the anal phases, when the child can actively initiate separation and, most significantly, when he can utilize bowel functions for the symbolic representation and attempted solution of this conflict. The pregenital roots for the development of character disorders go back to these phases, and as pointed out before, the first manifestations may appear at this age. These symptoms are indications of the child's struggle with anal impulses and of his developing defense mechanisms, especially reaction formations.

In some cases the anal needs of the mother, sometimes concealed by reaction formation, may lead to a relationship with the child which I have referred to as "toilet symbiosis" [40, 42]. This can be seen especially clearly in childhood cases of ulcerative or mucous colitis, when mother and child often spend much time together in the toilet during the day as well as during the night. Such behavior can be well rationalized with the illness of the child, and certain ministrations which involve handling of fecal matter can be carried out by the mother for the sake of her child.

Nonbloody psychogenic diarrhea and constipation often develop during this phase [28]. They are an outcome of an unsatisfactory resolution of anal conflicts, especially of the conflict over holding on to or letting go of feces. The diarrhea may alternate with constipation, and this condition, termed *mucous colitis,* is frequently associated with phobic behavior [20, 24, 27, 28]. Fears of the toilet and refusal to use the toilet for defecation are more commonly recognized by parents and pediatricians as psychologic problems and as related to traumas during the period of toilet-training.

The ambivalence characteristic of the anal instincts and the anal phases may become the basic conflict affecting every area of development, including the child's relation to his love objects. The conflict over clinging to or letting go of the parents, taken over from the anal conflict proper (retention or expulsion of feces), appears now as the separation conflict. The intensity of this also depends on the degree of resolution of the symbiotic relationship with the mother during the oral phases and reflects the outcome of the weaning process. *This unresolved symbiotic relationship turns into a psychosomatic relationship in those cases in which the mothers do not permit overt expression of aggression or self-assertion, and eventually into certain psychosomatic disorders when anal fixations are added and predominate,* such as ulcerative colitis, mucous colitis, and bronchial asthma, to name a few.

Within the framework of this chapter only a few brief illustrations can be given to highlight this interplay of anality between child and mother.

CASE 4.   An 8-year-old girl who suffered from ulcerative colitis developed abdominal cramps and diarrhea usually during mealtimes, interrupting her eating to run to the toilet. The mother frequently took food to her and continued to feed her there. In analysis, this woman proved to be an anally fixated person who spent many hours every day with her own excretory procedures in the toilet. However, she was afraid to be there when there was no one at home, and she would always leave the toilet door open. When her child improved and was ready to attend school, this became a problem for the mother, who needed someone in the house in the morning when she had to spend time in the toilet. This phobia was only one manifestation of the generalized chronic and crippling phobic state from which this mother suffered and which she had been able to cover up by rationalizations and manipulations and with the help of her sick child [40].

CASE 5.   The mother of a young boy who suffered from ulcerative colitis expressed her feelings by saying: "I am such a clean woman and he has such a messy disease!" In this case, the forbidden and deeply repressed anal pleasures could be indulged in only under the guise of illness. This boy showed very early reaction formations and signs of a compulsion neurosis. Already, at less than age 2, he was anxious and concerned when a drop of food dirtied his bib. At age 4½, when he entered treatment, he was afraid to touch clay in the playroom and had a hand-washing compulsion. But due to his "illness" he soiled himself often fifteen times daily [16, 25].

In such cases, in spite of the sometimes manifest signs of disgust by the mother and child shown in handling fecal matter, both derived significant instinctual gratifications from it.

In the psychoanalytic treatment of children suffering from persistent or recurring attacks of nonbloody psychogenic diarrhea and abdominal cramps, certain common features in the personality structure and also certain common experiences in the period of toilet training were found consistently. The personality of the mothers of these children also showed certain features in common: Especially marked were compulsive traits, ambivalent attitudes, a need for control over the child, and overemphasis upon anal functions. Toilet training was usually conducted early and rigidly and led to abrupt repression of anal impulses. It did not allow overt expression of aggression and self-assertion. In some cases in which the child had colic in infancy there was a marked exacerbation of the symptom around age 2. In cases where toilet training had been accomplished early, before age 1½, short-lived soiling occurred around age 2 before the condition of chronic or intermittent diarrhea had established itself fully.

Prugh, investigating the role of emotional factors in idiopathic celiac disease, found no single etiologic factor operative [11]. His observations regarding the personality of the mothers and the time of onset of symptoms in the children suggest some similarity between factors prevailing in celiac disease and psychogenic diarrhea. Finch, in discussing a case of constipation in a 4½-year-old child, portrayed the situation as follows: "There was a battle for the stools raging between the child and his family." He also drew attention to the fact that the routine giving of enemas (for which the child in this case had to be restrained forcibly) had been instituted upon medical advice, and he cautioned pediatricians about this practice [5].

With encopretic children the anality of the parents and of the child is much more overt, and coprophilic impulses are gratified in a less-disguised way. Persistent encopresis, like persistent enuresis, especially in older children, has to be considered a form of impulse disorder. This explains the tenacity of the symptoms and the difficulty in treating of such children. The anality of the parents of encopretic children is very marked, and unless the senior partner in this encopretic relationship is dealt with, it will be very difficult to get the child to give up his soiling.

Anal incontinence is much more frequent than is commonly believed and as might appear from the scarcity of published case reports in the literature [2]. The reason for this is that this condition is treated with more secrecy by both the parents and the child than psychogenic diarrhea or mucous colitis, which are "legitimate" forms of anal incontinence. This close-mouthed attitude on the part of the parents is found also in deviate sexual behavior of children.

CASE 6.   In the analysis of a mother whose two children, aged 4½ and 3, were both soiling, it was found that the mother's anality was instrumental in producing the incontinence. Both children soiled themselves daily during their afternoon nap. The mother cleaned the children and their beds without any reprimand, but she would punish them severely for slight transgressions in other areas, especially for not obeying her. She was aware that the children were soiling when they were up and awake, because she would hear them giggling and talking. She would stand at the closed door listening but not interfering. They also soiled while she was bathing them together in the tub, but they would not defecate when put on the toilet. Again, she refrained from interfering and cleaned the children and the tub with much pleasure. She had been aware of this, but had tried to deny it by rationalizing that she was not "rushing" their toilet training.

In her analysis, which she had sought for reasons unrelated to the soiling, it was found that she had intense coprophilic and coprophagic impulses. She consciously enjoyed handling feces and had encouraged this behavior in her children. The following incident is illustrative. One evening her younger child was walking through the playroom and pieces of

560

feces were dropping out from her panties. The dog, who was following the little girl, was licking up the feces from the floor and eating them. That night the mother awoke from a dream, which she could not remember, with an olfactory hallucination: She smelled feces. She suddenly realized that she had envied the dog and would have liked to have been in his place.

CASE 7.   In the analysis of another patient with very marked coprophilic and coprophagic impulses I made the following observation. She mentioned in her analysis that her 3-year-old son suffered from an anal prolapse and that she had to push back his prolapse after each defecation. After she had gained some understanding of her needs and stopped handling his anus, the prolapse disappeared without any further therapy. There was apparently no motive for the little boy to push out his rectum if his mother no longer wanted to play with it. She had also maintained that the little boy refused to have the toilet door closed and that she had to take him with her into the toilet. She realized in her analysis that she could not be alone in the toilet. She had many fears—particularly of fainting or choking in the toilet—which were related to her coprophagic impulses. She was surprised to find that after she had worked out in treatment some of her problems her little son developed a strong sense about toilet privacy.

The struggle for sphincter control and impulse control becomes a problem with the interfering, alternately permissive and prohibiting —that is, confusing—parents, and may result in failure to achieve sphincter control. The two following examples illustrate, in the first case, the failure of achieving bladder control in such a situation and, in the second case, a failure to achieve bowel control.

CASE 8.   A 4-year-old girl who wet herself during the night and also during the day was in the habit of hitting her mother whenever this occurred. She correctly felt that her mother was responsible for the control or lack of control of her bladder. Up to age 3, her mother had picked up the child whenever she thought she should urinate. She had done this upon the advice of her husband, who had had some medical training. The husband had a sister, a chronic schizophrenic patient, who also wet herself during both the day and the night. From the time his daughter was born, the father had a fear that she would turn out to be like his sister and therefore insisted on a very rigid system for bladder training. The mother had to pick up the child several times during the night and carry her to the toilet, and she had to see to it that the child urinated almost hourly during the day.

CASE 9.   In the history of an encopretic boy of 8 years of age, I found that his mother had not allowed him to develop control of his anal sphincter. From infancy on she would give him an enema whenever she felt he should have a bowel movement so that she would not need to take diapers and clothing with her when they were out or have to clean him in inconvenient situations. She continued this practice through the anal phases, thus preventing him from becoming aware of the signal for defecation and responding to it. She had "appersonated" him anally, so to speak, and was treating his anal urges and his feces as if they were her own, with the result that at the time when he should have been toilet trained he was a severe soiler [43]. The degree of narcissism, omnipotence, and bisexuality in this boy was remarkable. It reflected the character disorder of the persistently encropretic child as well as of his mother.

Too much interference with motility and aggressive drives during this phase of motor and muscle development is another parental action which can have general and far-reaching consequences through encouraging passivity rather than activity. It may also have more specific consequences concerning locomotion, such as poor coordination. In some cases, too much physical restraint is a contributing factor in head-banging and various tic disorders. In one case of severe head-banging in a 1½-year-old boy the mother maintained that she had to swaddle him or restrain him physically by holding his head, because the banging was so severe that it disturbed the neighbors. Helping the mother to relax these restraints by enabling her to recognize her need for the severe physical restriction of her son was followed by immediate lessening of the head-banging. This was only one aspect of this condition but important from the standpoint of a practical therapeutic approach by manipulating the environment.

In tic disorders of children, the removal of restrictions in motility and the provision of adequate motor outlets such as sports, dancing, singing, etc., can be very helpful. Impatience with the child's developing speech and restrictions in the use of anal words and noises play a part in stammering and other speech difficulties. For example, a 4-year-old boy with multiple body tics developed a vocal tic (made up of strange sounds and startling noises) following the birth of his sister. His mother had imposed severe restrictions of motility and had forbidden shouting, especially when the baby was sleeping. The dynamics of stammering are based on a displacement upward from the rectum and anus to the pharynx and mouth and, of course, on many other factors as well.

The Dynamics of Allergic States

Food can assume an anal significance during the anal phases. This meaning may be retained and appear as a food idiosyncrasy or food phobia in later life. The anal meaning of food comes from the child's identification of food with feces and is related to the child's coprophilic and copophagic impulses. This identification may be based on the similarity in consistency, color, smell, or other qualities, and is often taken over from an "idiosyncrasy" toward such food from the mother, that is, from her own unresolved anal problems. In some cases mothers have told me that they had an aversion to certain foods but that they did not show this to their child "because, if I make a face, he won't eat it."

There is a connection between such food phobias or food avoidances and food allergies. Taboos concerning forbidden anal impulses may attach themselves to certain food, which then becomes taboo. The transgression of such a food taboo may then be followed by certain physiologic reactions which are the anticipated consequences and punishment for the anal (sexual) transgression. These reactions can affect various organ systems and their functions, for instance, the gastrointestinal and respiratory systems or the skin. It is usually a reaction which is specific for the individual child in that a certain food item will produce a certain reaction in a certain organ system or organ. The specific unconscious meaning of such a food offender (allergen) can be established only by psychoanalytic investigation where also the separation of the unconscious meaning of the food from the food itself can be accomplished.

In children, this "psychologic desensitization" can be achieved in a rather simple way by the indirect approach through and with the mother. She can, by lifting these taboos and gradually introducing the previously forbidden foods with a positive attitude, help to "desensitize" her child.

It has been demonstrated that asthmatic children develop a resistance to allergens in psychoanalytic treatment or psychotherapy although they remain sensitive to them in skin tests. In other words, these children no longer produce asthmatic attacks when exposed to these allergens [10, 35]. This would indicate that the constitutional factor, even when present, is not the decisive factor but that various factors (extrinsic and intrinsic) are operative in producing the complex syndrome of asthma.

The method of "psychologic desensitization" has been found to be effective in various types of allergic conditions, including food allergy. In 1949 a report from the indirect treatment of an asthmatic child threw light on the understanding of the phenomenon of self-desensitization.

CASE 10. As soon as the mother of this asthmatic boy gained insight and could understand how through her behavior she had transmitted to her son the expectation for allergic reactions that culminated in severe asthmatic attacks, previously forbidden foods and inhalants were gradually introduced with excellent results. There were no allergic reactions or asthmatic attacks that previously had required emergency treatment with prolonged bed rest and absence from school. All these changes occurred within less than half a year and concomitant with the cessation of all medical treatment. The boy, who had been demonstrably sensitive to animal hair, could later own first a hamster and then a dog, and was able to go horseback riding. Prior to his mother's and his own treatment, he had severe wheezing culminating in asthmatic attacks when he only came close to a horsetrack or stable [17].

The phenomenon of interest here is that an innate somatic property, such as allergy, can be stimulated or inhibited by certain behavior of the mother, father, or both parents. This would appear to be similar to what we know about the vicissitudes of innate mental endowment. Specific mental development can be encouraged or discouraged by environmental attitudes, especially those involving parent-child relationships. The same is also true of intellectual development and its inhibition.

It would appear, then, that certain innate somatic endowments, such as allergy, respond in a similar way. Of further interest is the fact that the same stimulus, e.g., a specific food allergen such as chocolate, can trigger off different allergic reactions in different children; in one a respiratory, in another an intestinal, and in a third perhaps a skin reaction. One method of medical treatment and prophylaxis in allergies, frequently used by allergists, is desensitization aimed at decreasing the child's sensitivity to the offending allergen. This treatment needs to be repeated frequently, and the results are in many cases lacking or short-lived. Psychologic self-desensitization seems to operate similarly in that it decreases immunologic sensitivity. In psychologic desensitization this is achieved, in psychoanalytic treatment, by separating psychic content and affect from the physiologic vehicle and by rendering them harmless. The results are impressive and last for a lifetime. With children, this procedure can be simplified by treating the mother and by getting the physician who issued the specific prohibitions to withdraw them.

It appears then that somatic patterns of behavior, such as allergies, are established in childhood. Further, the emotional attitudes of the parents, such as their unconscious needs and anxieties relating to instinctual activities of the child, can "trigger" off the allergic reactions by promoting or intensifying the child's own conflicts.

The undoing of food taboos is also an important aspect in the treatment of children suffering from psychogenic diarrhea and mucous and ulcerative colitis. These children are often kept on very limited and strict diets for long periods of time.

CASE 11.   A 9-year-old girl, being treated for ulcerative colitis, had been on a very limited diet for the past 2 years. She could not have most of the things which children like—ice cream, chocolate, cake, sodas, candy, nuts, mayonnaise, pickles, catsup, franks, hamburgers, no red meats, salads, fruit, rye bread, fresh bread or rolls; in fact, anything that was tasty was forbidden. The mother of this child had severe oral and anal problems and a very disturbed relationship with her own mother. Therapeutic work focused at first on some of her marital problems and on the relation of these to her child. It was then necessary to help the child, who by now had completely accepted these taboos and who, in her attitude to the "forbidden" goods, reflected not only her own but also her mother's anxieties.

The pediatrician, who had been delighted with the cooperation of the mother and the child in the matter of diet, had to be convinced. He was organically oriented and very skeptical. He could not be replaced because he represented a father figure both for the mother and for the child, whom he had attended since her birth. It took diplomacy and patience, but it worked. The release from the food restrictions also meant a release from the mother's control over the child. She could now eat her lunch at school, at her friends' homes, at restaurants, at parties, and be away from her mother. The mother was now able to use her talents to make a part-time career for herself instead of devoting herself "completely" to her sick child.

Parental Guilt Feelings

It is commonly supposed that a therapeutic focus on the interaction between parental unconscious feelings and wishes and the child's reactions to these arouses excessive guilt in the parents because it puts the blame for the child's neurotic behavior onto them. It is the author's experience that this approach tends rather to relieve than to generate such feelings. These neurotic parents bring their child for treatment, sometimes against the advice of the treating physician, because they are unhappy and guilty with regard to their unconscious ambivalence toward the child. Many mothers of children suffering from psychosomatic diseases are aware that their children have psychologic problems, but they are aided and abetted in their denial by attending physicians who misdirect their attention to organic causes and treatment. In fact most mothers are relieved when the child gets into psychotherapy or psychoanalysis and can be helped to disentangle himself from the pathologic relationship, especially if the mother has been given some understanding of the situation and of her role in it. There are cases in which the neurosis of the mother is very severe and this pathologic relationship with the child is the only important relationship that the mother has. In these cases the mothers require help to enable them to establish new and more meaningful relationships.

The orientation and approach of the child therapist or child analyst are important factors in allaying rather than rousing guilt feelings in the parents. The parents are not blamed for their neuroses. Instead, they are helped to understand themselves and the part they have played in promoting and maintaining undesirable behavior in their child. The guilt feelings of the parents in many cases stem from their own unconscious unresolved conflicts, which are carried over to their child.

The situation is different with parents of children with deviate sexual behavior and other severe characterologic problems manifested in delinquent or psychopathic acting-out behavior. These parents usually will bring their children for treatment only under external pressure from school or other authorities. While the characterologic difficulties manifested by the child may not be readily detected in his parents, closer investigation always reveals that the child has taken the clues for his behavior from one parent or both. In these cases, it is often necessary to stimulate guilt feelings in the parents so they will accept and permit treatment of their child and perhaps be activated to do something about their own problems.

SUMMARY

In this chapter an attempt has been made to delineate some of the somatic disturbances in children that are consequent to parental neurosis. The material has been arranged according to the developmental stages in order to make the interwoven clinical material more comprehensible. The pregenital phases (the oral and anal) have been covered, demonstrating that traumatic experiences can bring about fixations and later regressions to the fixation points. These pregenital fixations are felt to be important factors in the etiology of psychosomatic and severely neurotic disorders in children, adolescents, and adults.

Attention has also been drawn to the influence of parental attitudes during the anal phases in the genesis of some psychosomatic disorders and of many character, neurotic, and behavior disorders. A better understanding of the role of parental attitudes and a proper assessment of the early indications of the effects of parental neurosis upon the child would be of considerable help in efforts toward the prevention and treatment of mental illness.

Bibliography

1. Abraham, K. A Short Study of the Development of the Libido, Viewed in the Light of Mental Disorders. In E. Jones (Ed.), *Selected Papers on Psycho-Analysis.* (Translated by D. Bryan and A. Strachey.) London: Hogarth, 1927. Pp. 418–501.
2. Anthony, E. J. An experimental approach to the psychopathology of childhood: Encopresis. *Brit. J. Med. Psychol.* 30:146–175, 1957.
3. Benedek, T. Adaptation to reality in early infancy. *Psychoanal. Quart.* 7:200–215, 1938.
4. Bornstein, B. Phobia in a two-and-a-half-year-old child. *Psychoanal. Quart.* 4:93–119, 1935.
5. Finch, S. M. Psychosomatic problems in children. *Nerv. Child.* 9:261–269, 1952.
6. Fraiberg, S. On the sleep disturbances of early childhood. *Psychoanal. Stud. Child* 5:285–309, 1950.
7. Freud, S. The Predisposition to Obsessional Neurosis. In E. Jones (Ed.), *Collected Papers,* Vol. 2. London: Hogarth, 1913. Pp. 122–132.
8. Freud, S. Three Contributions to the Theory of Sex. In A. A. Brill (Ed.), *Basic Writings of Sigmund Freud.* New York: Modern Library, 1938.
9. Fries, M. E. Psychosomatic relationships between mother and infant. *Psychosom. Med.* 6:159–162, 1944.
10. Gerard, M. W. "Bronchial" asthma in children. *Nerv. Child.* 5:327–331, 1946.
11. Prugh, D. G. Preliminary report on role of emotional factors in

idiopathic celiac disease. *Psychosom. Med.* 13:220–241, 1951.

12. Ribble, M.   *The Rights of Infants.* New York: Columbia University Press, 1944.
13. Sperling, M.   Psychoanalytic study of ulcerative colitis in children. *Psychoanal. Quart.* 15:302–329, 1946.
14. Sperling, M.   Analysis of a case of recurrent ulcer of the leg. *Psychoanal. Stud. Child* 3–4:391–408, 1949.
15. Sperling, M.   Neurotic sleep disturbances in children. *Nerv. Child.* 8:28–46, 1949.
16. Sperling, M.   Problems in analysis of children with psychosomatic disorders. *Quart. J. Child Behavior* 1:12–17, 1949.
17. Sperling, M.   The role of the mother in psychosomatic disorders in children. *Psychosom. Med.* 11:377, 1949.
18. Sperling, M.   Children's interpretation and reaction to the unconscious of their mothers. *Int. J. Psychoanal.* 31:1–6, 1950.
19. Sperling, M.   Indirect treatment of psychoneurotic and psychosomatic disorders in children. *Quart. J. Child Behavior* 2:250–266, 1950.
20. Sperling, M.   Mucous colitis associated with phobias. *Psychoanal. Quart.* 19:318–326, 1950.
21. Sperling, M.   The neurotic child and his mother. *Amer. J. Orthopsychiat.* 21:351–364, 1951.
22. Sperling, M.   A psychoanalytic study of migraine and psychogenic headache. *Psychoanal. Rev.* 39:152–163, 1952.
23. Sperling, M.   Animal phobias in a two-year-old child. *Psychoanal. Stud. Child* 7:115–125, 1952.
24. Sperling, M.   Psychogenic diarrhea and phobia in a six-and-a-half-year-old girl. *Amer. J. Orthopsychiat.* 22:838–848, 1952.
25. Sperling, M.   Psychotherapeutic Techniques in Psychosomatic Medicine. In G. Bychowski and J. Despert (Eds.), *Specialized Techniques in Psychotherapy.* New York: Basic Books, 1952.
26. Sperling, M.   Food allergies and conversion hysteria. *Psychoanal. Quart.* 22:525–538, 1953.
27. Sperling, M.   Psychosomatic Medicine and Pediatrics. In R. Cleghorn and E. Wittkower (Eds.), *Recent Developments in Psychosomatic Medicine.* London: Pitman, 1954.
28. Sperling, M.   Observations from the treatment of children suffering from non-bloody diarrhea or mucous colitis. *J. Hillside Hosp.* 4:25–31, 1955.
29. Sperling, M.   Psychosis and psychosomatic illness. *Int. J. Psychoanal.* 36:1–8, 1955.
30. Sperling, M.   Pavor nocturnus. *J. Amer. Psychoanal. Ass.* 6:79–94, 1958.
31. Sperling, M.   Equivalents of depression in children. *J. Hillside Hosp.* 8:138–148, 1959.

32. Sperling, M.   A Study of Deviate Sexual Behavior in Children by the Method of Simultaneous Analysis of Mother and Child. In L. Jessner and E. Pavenstedt (Eds.), *Dynamic Psychopathology in Childhood*. New York: Grune & Stratton, 1959.
33. Sperling, M.   Psychosomatic Disorders. In S. Lorand and H. Schneer (Eds.), *Adolescents: Psychoanalytic Approach to Problems and Therapy*. New York: Hoeber, 1961. Pp. 202–216.
34. Sperling, M.   Fetishism in children. *Psychoanal. Quart.* 32:374–392, 1963.
35. Sperling, M.   A Psychoanalytic Study of Bronchial Asthma in Children. In H. Schneer (Ed.), *The Asthmatic Child; Psychosomatic Approach to Problems and Treatment*. New York: Hoeber Med. Div., Harper & Row, 1963. Pp. 138–165.
36. Sperling, M.   The analysis of a boy with transvestite tendencies. *Psychoanal. Stud. Child* 19:470–493, 1964.
37. Sperling, M.   Dynamic considerations and treatment of enuresis. *J. Amer. Acad. Child Psychiat.* 4:19–31, 1964.
38. Sperling, M.   Trichotillomania, Trichophagy and Cyclic Vomiting: A Contribution to the Psychopathology of Female Sexuality. *Int. J. Psychoanal.* 49:682–690, 1968.
39. Sperling, M.   Acting-Out Behavior and Psychosomatic Symptoms: Clinical and Theoretical Aspects. *Int. J. Psychoanal.* 49:250–253, 1968.
40. Sperling, M.   The Role of Pregenital Conflicts and of Somatic Symptomatology in Phobia. Read at the fall meeting of the American Psychoanalytic Association in New York, December, 1967.
41. Sperling, M.   School phobias: Classification, dynamics and treatment. *Psychoanal. Stud. Child* 22:375–401, 1967.
42. Sperling, M.   Ulcerative colitis in children: Current views and therapies. *J. Amer. Acad. Child Psychiat.* 8:336–352, 1969.
43. Sperling, O.   On appersonation. *Int. J. Psychoanal.* 25:128–132, 1944.
44. Spitz, R. A.   The psychogenic diseases in infancy: An attempt at their etiologic classification. *Psychoanal. Stud. Child* 6:255–275, 1951.
45. Sterba, E.   Analysis of a psychogenic constipation in a two-year-old. *Psychoanal. Stud. Child* 3:227–252, 1949.
46. Wulff, M.   Phobie bei einem Anderthalbjahrigen Kinde. *Int. Z. Psychoanal.* 13:290–293, 1927.

27

The Influence
of Maternal Psychosis
on Children — Folie à Deux

E. James Anthony

EDITORS' INTRODUCTION

The earlier chapters in this section illustrate the disturbances originating in the early, preobject phase of development that normally does not extend beyond the first 3 to 6 months of the infant's life. In the mother, this coincides with that phase of her motherhood during which she enjoys her infant and her mothering functions without being aware of her active influence upon the child's psychic development. The pathologic conditions discussed in this chapter, although they indicate an intense symbiotic relationship between mother and child, differ in that they seem to have developed later; they show the symbiotic process in a more differentiated level of the ego-object relationship.

The children seem to have avoided fixation to the phase dominated by the "primal cavity," and the integration of their coenesthetic and diacritic functions have apparently outgrown the oral and anal phases of development. The pathologic conditions in these cases stem from what seems to be an inborn sense of weakness of the ego; the infantile sensorium shows from the very beginning such an oversensitivity to external stimuli that when they are "hatched" from the symbiotic phase and able to differentiate "inside" from "outside," they are unable, and later even unwilling, to accept that which is not I. Such children become autistic or schizophrenic if the mothers cannot maintain the degree of emotional symbiosis necessary for the developing egos to carry through the processes of differentiation and individuation.

The mothers who initiate and maintain the pathologic states discussed in the following chapter represent the opposite pole. They are always there for the children who feel their presence as the mothers seem to feel secure in their delusional assumption that they, and only they, can protect their children from any harm or anxiety. Since separation anxiety is the basis of the maternal pathologic state, these mothers consciously induce and deliberately maintain the emotional symbiosis far beyond the psychophysiologic needs of the children. They create a tendency in the children to identify solely with the mothers. Fostering a strong dependency on themselves, they isolate their children from other children and from adults. The unconscious communication is maintained through the transactional processes of the manifest and often goal-conscious behavior of the mothers whose reactions sharpen the children's anticipation so that they gradually become automatons, surrendering their volition to the mothers who remain, despite all their pathologic conditions, surrogate egos.

Yet there are different degrees and levels of folie à deux. The pathologic states of the mothers, serious though they may be, do not point to early levels of symbiotic fixation since they often occur in individuals with highly differentiated perceptual systems, elaborate fantasy lives, and often genuine artistic talent. Perceiving what is true and important for the mothers, the children go beyond imitation and even beyond the mothers' expectations of them. In this way, the pathologic transactions of the symbiotic process develop a reversed phase. The mothers repeat the process by identifying with their grown and successful children, demanding with great intensity that they cling to them and become their protectors in old age.

E. J. A.
T. B.

The generating of research ideas is an inscrutable process. Much of it is carried on, supposedly, in some penumbral region of the mind, such as Binet's "Intellectual Unconscious," wherein observations, experiences, questionings, readings, and ruminations swirl about disconnectedly until some powerful catalyst activates a chain of associations that struggles eventually into consciousness in a coherent, communicative form. From then onward it cuts itself off from its intuitive origins and is gradually molded by scientific canons into a testable and refutable hypothesis. The successive stages in this cognitive counterpart of "working through" have been vividly described by Poincaré, Wallas, and other insightful thinkers, all of whom have emphasized the fact that a large part of this process never reaches awareness. It is possible that "free association," having proved so effective a technique in uncovering buried emotional conflicts, could prove equally operative in helping scientific workers to recapture the hidden steps in their research ideation.

In this chapter, an attempt will be made, albeit on a modest scale, to follow one such stream of association to the point when it crystalized around an organizing set of constructs. My concern focuses on the curious phenomenon of *folie à deux* as it occurs in the relationship of mother and child during a certain phase of development to which the epithet *critical* might justifiably be applied, and the clinical impact of a number of such cases in which the ego boundaries are apparently nonexistent and the maturational process of individuation fails to take place. These weakly integrated mothers leave the child so defenseless that he unconsciously absorbs the mother's fears and fantasies rather than setting up neurotic or psychopathic systems of resistance or resorting to psychosomatic modes of reaction.

The associations evoked by the clinical encounters will be presented as they emerged successively into my working consciousness.

Supported by U.S.P.H.S. Research Grants MH12043-01 and MH-14052-01.

This chapter is also included in a festschrift in honor of Dr. Margaret Mahler entitled *Folie à Deux—A Developmental Failure in the Process of Separation-Individuation* which is being published by International Universities Press.

FIRST ASSOCIATION

Clinical research begins by definition at the bedside, that is, with the patient. It begins with a question or a series of questions which may refer to the patient as a whole or in part; to the patient in isolation or in relationship to his environment; and to the patient as he is, or to the way he has become what he is.

The clinical cases about to be described belong to a research population of children and their psychotic mothers or fathers. The primary aim of this investigation is to explore the immediate and remote consequences that might result from children being brought up for a while in close association with a psychotically disturbed parent. At the present stage of the study it looks as if the effect of the psychosis is dependent on the age of the child, on the duration of his exposure to the disturbing influence, and on the type of psychosis manifested by the parent.

In a certain number of the cases, a most unusual state of affairs was detected within the mother-child dyad and clearly demanded closer scrutiny. The relationship had all the characteristics of a symbiosis, the child seeming to exist almost completely within the maternal ambience with little or no intervention of any "placental barrier" to impede the free flow of noxious thoughts and feelings between the encapsulated pair. The child's condition in many respects simulated that of the mother, but it could as easily be said that the mother's condition resembled that of the child. It was only a small number of deluded women who provoked such an outcome, and, in these instances, the delusional ideas implicated the safety of the children or, more often, of a particular child, and thereby provoked a primitively protective response, almost as if the mothers were in danger themselves. The children participating in these situations were characteristically psychologically undifferentiated, of less than average intelligence, dependent, submissive, suggestible, and deeply involved in the ill parent and in her illness.

CASE 1. A little girl aged 5, living alone with her widowed mother, one day saw a scarecrow in a field adjacent to her home. It waved to her and whistled. She heard it say that it would come and get her. She told her mother, who was perturbed by what she heard and said that when she was small scarecrows sometimes got free and came into the house, and that

574

when they did you could usually expect a death to take place. The mother warned the child to be careful and to keep away from that side of the field. The next day the child came running into the house screaming that the scarecrow had been coming after her and that it was going to kill her mother. The mother immediately rushed out with a broom and the neighbors heard her shouting that she was not going to let any devil get into her house. That night the child had a severe night terror and screamed that the scarecrow was in the room and sitting on her chest. The mother put on the light, barricaded the door with a heavy chair, and took close hold of the child who continued screaming. The next morning the mother told her neighbor that "they" were not going to get her or her child and that she knew what they were up to. She and the child now slept in the basement, both in a state of great apprehension, and the mother began to have nightmares. She explained to the child that the "scarecrow people" were now devising all sorts of tricks such as dreams to get into the house and kill the occupants. According to the mother, it was the child that they were after and according to the child, it was the mother. Four days later, the police broke in and found the pair virtually starving and panic-stricken. The mother was hospitalized with the diagnosis of schizophrenia and the child placed in a residential home. For about 4 weeks the child continued to interpret events in her environment in terms of the "scarecrow people," but this then gradually subsided and eventually disappeared.

CASE 2. A 5-year-old boy, much addicted to television cartoons, began to worry that the world was going to be taken over by a superguy who could change himself into anyone or anything and would thus be able to spy on people without their being aware of it. He could become a clock or a lamp and could send out messages by means of the ticking of the clock or the light waves of the lamp. There was no way of hiding from superguy since he could get in anywhere. The reason why he focused on this boy's home in particular was that he knew it was the center of the whole world.

The child's mother had once worked for a crime commission as a secretary, and within the last year she had begun to imagine that some of the crooks and gangsters at large, about whom she had typed reports, were now out to pay her back for the part she had played in getting them punished. There was a "Mister M." who had been a much-wanted man and "devilishly clever." The authorities had been unable to catch him because he disguised himself so well. Every car that drew up on the street and every passerby was associated with "Mister M.," and at the sight of a strange face, the mother would immediately dial for the police. Her husband tried to obtain evidence from all quarters indicating that she had nothing to fear and that "Mister M." was largely a figment of her imagination. The character became increasingly bizarre. She began to refer to him as the gangster king and claimed that he had magical powers that allowed him to outwit the police and F.B.I. He also used electronic listening devices, and she became suspicious of any article in the house that could be tampered with for this purpose. She stopped all the clocks in the house as a special precaution. She sat by one of the windows all day with the blinds drawn, and her son kept watch near her. Her husband called in neighbors, and eventually doctors, but to no avail. He became increasingly alarmed at the growing agitation of his wife and son.

They now appeared to have a common persecutor whom they both referred to as "super" because he had such superior powers. They would not be separated from each other and paid little or no attention to the father. At last, much against his will, he called the hospital and had the mother hospitalized. The boy became acutely panic-stricken with the departure of his mother, but with the loving care of his kindly paternal grandmother, he soon settled down and gradually ceased to talk about "super." The mother's diagnosis in the hospital was paranoid schizophrenia.

In both of these transactions, and in several others of similar nature, it was difficult to tell where fantasy ended and delusion began or who was influencing whom. The interplay of fantasy and delusion would lead to the transformation of fantasy into a delusional fantasy which was never systematized because of the cognitive ineptness of the child.

There was sometimes a marked variability of response within the same family, one child accepting the maternal delusions completely and with conviction, another rejecting them out of hand, while a third learned to adapt to a double standard of reality, conforming to realistic expectations outside the home while maintaining an irrational orientation within the family circle. The ego's reality-testing often clashed with the needs of object relations, the mother frequently making the acceptance of her delusion a test of loyalty.

There was clearly some degree of folie à deux in each of the cases presented, set against the background of an unresolved symbiotic relationship and a lack of individuation in the child. It raised the immediate question as to whether there was any evidence that folie à deux could exist at such an early age, which leads to the second association.

SECOND ASSOCIATION

There are more than 150 reports of folie à deux in the literature as collected by Michaud [19], but very few of these have to do with children, which is, in a way, surprising, since the vulnerability has been especially emphasized in this context.

The possibility of a "mental contagion" that could mysteriously leap over the gap between individual minds has preoccupied and perplexed psychopathologists for a very long time. In 1658, an eminent Jacobean physician, Sir Kenneth Digby, had this to say about it:

Now let us consider how the strong imagination of one man doth marvelously act upon another man who hath it more feeble and passive . . . Women and children, being very moist and passive, are most susceptible of this *unpleasing contagion of the imagination* . . . All the effects of a strong and vehement imagination working upon another more feeble, passive and tender, ought to be more efficacious in the mother acting upon her son than when the imaginations of other persons act upon those who are nothing to them [italics added] [8].

Sir Kenneth then proceeded to offer in the way of explanation a musical metaphor with the implication that a mechanism analogous to sympathetic resonance was probably at work.

I pray you to remember, when two lutes or two harps, near one another, both set to the same tune, if you touch the strings of the one, the other consonant harp will sound at the same time, *though nobody touch it* [italics added].

He was not alone in his mystification. Another early commentator, Dr. Whytt, writing in 1746, remarked on the "wonderful sympathy between the nervous systems of different persons whence various emotions and morbid symptoms are often transferred from one to another *without any corporeal contact or infection"* [italics added].

In the century that followed, interest in the phenomenon appeared to be intensified, and a spate of explanations was offered without too much supporting evidence. In 1819, Berlyn, for example, described a mother and son who shared identical hypochondriacal delusions which were quickly healed "by psychic means," and Ideler, in 1838, presented a series of case histories purporting to demonstrate "madness through the imitative instinct." Twenty-three years later Finkelnburg also invoked "the influence of the imitative instinct on the spread of sporadic insanity" as an explanation in 12 cases. On the other hand, Feuchtersleven, in 1845, had felt that the contagion of delusional ideas was more understandable on the basis of "pathologic sympathy."

Other authors of the same period were more concerned with finding the right label for the newly recognized condition, and a host of synonyms were introduced, such as "communicated," "simultaneous," "collective," "contagious," "reciprocal," "double," "induced," "influenced," "imposed," "associated," "mystic," etc. In 1877, Lasègue and Falret coined the name of *folie à deux* that has since stuck to the condition and is now in fairly general use [13].

In their perceptive and authoritative account these authors made the first clinical references to folie à deux in impressionable children as young as 8 years of age, the preconditions, in their view, being low intelligence, a passive docility, a close and constant relationship with the deluded person, and some form, however obscure, of secondary gain. This is what they had to say:

Naturally apprehensive children, confined in a limited environment, are most disposed to become *the echoes of a delusion* with which they are associated. Their indecisive reason cannot defend itself and if only the insane person has made them a participating partner, they hope or fear on their own account with the limitations of the self-interest characteristic of their age. *Their faith, in some cases, goes so far that the lunatic himself hesitates to follow, and at first glance, one would believe that the children had created the delusions they reflect.* In general, with rare exceptions, the ideas transmitted are more terrifying than agreeable. We know how accessible to fear are children predisposed to cerebral troubles. The spontaneous manifestations consist of bedtime terrors, fears of darkness, nightmares, frights of imaginary dangers or threatening individuals; *the artificially provoked manifestations assume the same forms* [italics added] [13, pp. 4, 5].

They also refer to the bind in which the child finds himself and to the means he employs to resolve his dilemma of the double standards of reality:

The child finds himself between two currents; one, that of the insane parent who has provoked the conceptions; the other, that of the bystanders who minimize the unlikely aspects and modify the acceptable sides to fit their own wishes. *Misled by the one, corrected by the others, the child finally believes and convinces others of his second-hand inventions. This double development is very striking.* . . . [italics added] [13, p. 5].

Lasègue and Falret had originally observed that the delusional relationship included a dominant partner who created the delusion and a submissive partner who colluded in its production, and that when the two were separated, the delusional ideas tended to persist in the first and to weaken and eventually disappear in the second. This would be in keeping with our experience.

578

In 1939 Coleman and Last also outlined certain preconditions to the establishment of folie à deux: the inductor, they postulated, would need to be strongly motivated to have his ideas accepted and even to modify them to some extent in order to achieve this; his delusion would have to be not too idiosyncratic so as to allow personal involvement by another; the partner would have to be a somewhat hysterical, suggestible person whose wishes would gain equal fulfillment by the delusion; and, finally, the two needed to have lived together in close association for some time [2].

Most authors have stressed the immaturity, dependence, suggestibility, passivity, and poor contact with reality that is characteristic of the submissive partner, and the way in which the deluded pair band together for the most part against a common enemy, the majority of the delusions in cases of folie à deux being persecutory in nature. The paranoid anxiety, present in both, would act as solvent to the weak ego barriers of the symbiosis and conduce to a further dedifferentiation of the personality structure. Such conditions are highly reminiscent of the child's state even under normal circumstances.

The concepts of contagion and resonance, stemming from a physical model, were replaced in the following more psychologically minded century by those of empathy and identification, but neither one nor the other point of view has proved wholly adequate in explaining the condition. That the puzzlement continues to persist into the present day is evident from the following quotations:

The interesting phenomenon of one person inducing mental illness in another is not uncommon but little understood, and still presents a challenge to all theories of mental illness [8].

Folie à deux . . . is a puzzle to those who adhere to the idea that mental illness is biological and hereditary, theoretical proof to those who regard mental illness as contagious, and fertile ground for speculation by those interested in the dynamics of family interaction [23].

In the model of folie à deux lies the clue to mental illness [6].

The geneticists were equally perplexed by the phenomenon and complained that the label was overinclusive. Kallmann suggested limiting the term to the transference of circumscribed delusions between closely associated but unrelated persons [11]. By so doing he felt that it might be possible to separate the interacting effects of genetic and nongenetic elements in the etiology of the condition. He chided those whose subscription to the psychology of influence and to the inheritance of acquired characteristics had led them to perpetuate the notion of a magic phenomenon inducing mental disease through personal contact. He obviously felt that the geneticist stood behind the psychologist and would ultimately provide the answer to the problem.

What seemed to be lacking in all these considerations was a developmental point of view. Folie à deux in its partial and incomplete forms was not well-recognized in childhood, and therefore very little investigation and therapeutic work have been done on it. That it should not have been better recognized was surprising, since the mechanisms of imitation and identification in the child were freely used to account for both normal and abnormal childhood behavior. In addition, social learning theory in recent years has also placed special emphasis on the factors of "shaping" and "modeling" on the conditioning of the child's responses. Nevertheless, the sharing of a common psychopathologic condition between parent and child has not been accorded a crucial role in psychopathogenesis by clinicians, perhaps because it seemed to imply the existence of a special nosogenesis which was not in keeping with the classic psychoanalytic theory of a gradual evolution of neurosis or psychosis out of certain psychosexual vicissitudes during early development. Such phenomena as symbiosis and individuation were not too well explained in terms of classic theory. Parental psychopathology was admitted to have precipitating, facilitating, or exacerbating functions impinging on the more or less autochthonous growth of disturbance in the developing child, whereas folie à deux seemed to demand a psychologic transplant or grafting in the manner of the earlier conception of the trauma theory. In recent years the lines of development have been regarded in more complex fashion and attempts have been made to separate out the varying effects of development, conflict, and trauma, some theorists even including large-scale introjections of pathologic elements in the parent. This would be akin to the formation of the superego, but, apart from the mechanism of identification, it would be difficult at the present time to delineate this alleged process more fully and clearly.

It may well be that the preconditions to the genesis of folie à deux unfold developmentally like an infantile neurosis or psychosis, but this would still be begging the question, since there are no indications in classic theory of how this might take place.

580

THIRD ASSOCIATION

The influence of a disturbed and disturbing mother on the individuation of her child is in sharp contrast to that of the ordinary "good enough" mother working under average expectable conditions. Over a century ago Kierkegaard recognized the differences involved and wrote of them vividly. In the one case:

The loving mother teaches her child to walk alone. She is far enough from him so that she cannot actually support him, but she holds out her arms to him. She imitates his movements, and if he totters, she swiftly bends as if to seize him, so that the child might believe that he is not walking alone. The truly loving mother can do no more if she really intends for her child to walk alone. And yet, she does more. Her face beckons like a reward, an encouragement. Thus, the child walks alone with his eyes fixed on his mother's face *not* on the difficulties in his way. He supports himself by the arms that do not hold him and constantly strives towards the refuge in his mother's embrace, little suspecting *that in the very same moment that he is emphasizing his need of her, he is proving that he can do without her,* because he is walking alone [italics added] [12, p. 85].

And in the other, it is very different:

There is no beckoning encouragement, no blessing at the end of the walk. There is the same wish to teach the child to walk alone, but not as a loving mother does it. For now there is fear that envelops the child. It weighs him down so that he cannot move forward. There is the same wish to lead him to the goal, *but the goal becomes suddenly terrifying* [italics added] [12, p. 85].

The fearfulness, the ambivalence, the unconscious hostility, the need to encapsulate hinders the child from stepping off on his own. With his delicate insight, Kierkegaard crystallizes the moments of development when the toddler feels the pull of separation from his mother and at the same time asserts his individuation. It is a mixed experience of enormous developmental significance, the child demonstrating that he can and cannot do without his mother, and his mother demonstrating that she can and cannot let him walk alone. The psychotic mother fills these moments with apprehension so that not only has the child got nowhere to go, but also he is afraid to get anywhere.

581

FOURTH ASSOCIATION

In the very next phase of development, when the child is becoming aware of his environment, the psychotic mother may help to perpetuate his naive, distorted representation of the world, so that it remains unrealistic.

Spiegel offered an analysis of a common nursery situation in which the child bumps himself on the chair and his mother says: "Naughty chair!" perhaps giving it a playful smack. Why, asks Spiegel, does she do this? The pain, he says, produces anger, and in order to avoid a possible angry interchange in which the child displaces his rage onto her, she involves the child in a make-believe conflict with the chair, with herself as some sort of referee. In doing so, she also avoids any possible negative evaluation of herself as an incompetent protector, the carelessness now being attributed to the chair. This allows her to preserve stability in the relationship between herself and her child [22].

This may be good, continues Spiegel, for the relationship, but it may carry some disadvantages for the child's ability to test reality.

She conceals the important information that pain and accidents can occur without motive and need to be endured in the inevitable process of maturation and acquisition of autonomy by the child. Thus her masking ties the child to her in a dependent relationship in which she plays the role of protector. *She conceals both from herself and her child information about her resentment at the growing independence of the child, which, if it were available as a message, would read, "If you are going to act so independently, you ought to be punished.* But I don't want you to know that I think this, so I'll pretend that it's not your behavior I resent but the chair's. You will understand that the world is full of hostile chairs, and you need me to protect you from them." If the child does not see through this masking, he will take the complementary dependent role which his mother desires for him [italics added] [22, p. 376].*

If the ordinary mother experiences difficulty in accepting the anger of her child or recognizing her own resentment at the process of individuation, how much more will the child's capacity to test reality be affected in the case of a psychotic mother, which brings us to the next association.

* From N. W. Bell and E. F. Vogel, *The Family*. Copyright © 1960 by The Free Press, A Corporation.

582

FIFTH ASSOCIATION

Sandor Ferenczi described three stages in the development of the sense of reality [5]. First, there is an introjective phase, in which all experience is still incorporated into the ego, and the feeling of omnipotence is rampant so that the world obeyed and followed every nod. Next there is the animistic phase, during which the growing objectification of the outer world still leaves intact some part of the tie between the ego and the nonego. The child learns to be satisfied with having only a part of the world—the ego part—at his disposal, with the outer world often opposing his wishes; nevertheless, he still invests a lot of his ego qualities in this outer world, so that objects appear endowed with life, feeling, thought, and motivation. Finally comes the projective phase which introduces "a painful discordance" into the child's experiences. This is the stage of brute reality when clear distinction is made between the perfidious things "out there" which do not bend to his will and are experienced as sensations, and what is inside him and experienced as feelings. Prior to the development of this third stage, the child feels himself to be in possession of magic capacities.

Ferenczi pointed out what a hard fight the achievement of reality is for the young child and how influential the adult in the child's environment can be in helping or hindering this crucial development. Even in the most average environment, transient setbacks could be brought about in imaginative children by the fairy tales told to them by grown-ups in search of their own lost omnipotence of childhood.

In fairy tales, man is immortal, he is in a hundred places at the same time, sees into the future, and knows the past . . . In the fairy tale, man has wings, his eyes pierce the walls, his magic wand opens all doors . . . He may live in perpetual fear of attack from dangerous beasts and fierce foes but a magic cap makes him inaccessible [5, p. 238].

These represent the normal, cultural fantasies to which children are exposed as they grapple for reality in the outside world. How overwhelming it must be for a child to be constantly confronted by the delusional fantasies of a highly significant person whose love he would wish to preserve beyond the calls of reality!

SIXTH ASSOCIATION

Approaching the matter from a different theoretic framework, Piaget outlined three stages similar to those of Ferenczi in the child's construction of reality. First, there is an autistic phase, which is dominated by an adualistic confusion involving self and nonself, internal and external, and thought and things. Next comes an animistic phase, which is similar to the one described by Ferenczi but more fully and richly depicted. During this phase the child's egocentrism gives him an intense subjective perspective so that he is unable to empathize with another's point of view. Thirdly there is a logical, social development in which the child sees himself as an object among other objects and is able to look at the world objectively [21].

Piaget had written to Freud in 1923 about his notion of an intermediate, prelogical animistic phase which lay between primary and secondary process thinking and received no reply. Perhaps Freud was too tactful to point out that Ferenczi had developed the same conception 10 years earlier. Piaget pursued this study of the partial egocentric stage of individuation and made it one of his major contributions to early development.

Its significance is such that it can be described as a critical stage of development from which the child needs to shift if he is to undergo further individuation. These shifts involve ways of thinking, ways of conceiving the world, and ways of communicating to others. The phase, as a whole, is characterized by a deficiency in operational thinking with its logical coherence and flexible, reversible reasoning. Instead, it is dominated by intuitive and magical modes of thought which helps to inculcate a naively primitive and dynamic conception of the universe loaded with inconsistencies, incompatibilities, inconsequences, and muddle, referred to more elegantly by Piaget as *syncretism*. It is a world in which inanimate things come to life, the sun and moon follow you around, dreams arrive through your bedroom window, and magical causality rules the world. In an older child manifesting the same phenomena, the clinician would be alert to a borderline or full psychosis. The stage is summarized into its component parts in Figures 27-1, 27-2, and 27-3.

It was very understandable that when this sort of magic-phenomenistic system came into close contact with the psychotic sys-

584

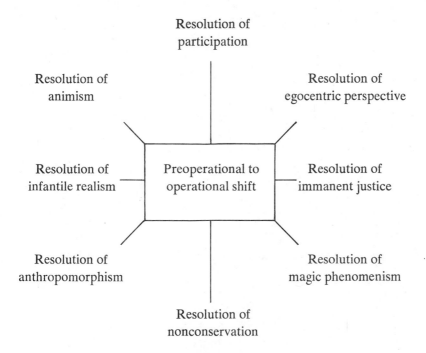

Fig. 27-1. The critical period (ages 4 to 7) seen in terms of Piaget's developmental theory—phenomenal shift.

tem of the mother, the two would powerfully reinforce each other.

Piaget was fully aware of the similarities between the child's preoperational system and the delusional system of the psychotic subject. His picture of the latter system is summed up in Figure 27-4, which he derived from Dromard [3].

Speaking of the small child's astonishing capacity for answering any question and disposing of any difficulty with the most farfetched and unexpected reason or hypothesis, Piaget compared this with the verbalism of delusional psychotic patients, especially in the early stages of the illness.

He quoted Dromard in his description of the peculiarities characteristic of the "interpretational" psychoses [3]. These included reasoning based on fantasy, in which every possibility may become a probability or a certainty; diffusion of interpretation, in which there is a linking up of ideas on the basis of juxtaposition; radiation, in which

585

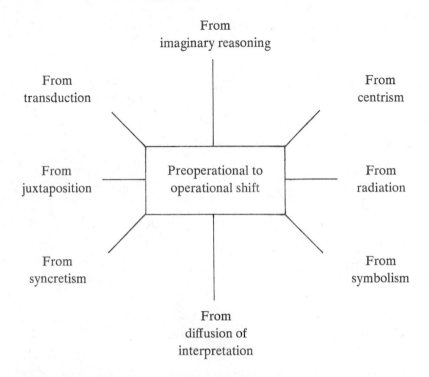

From
imaginary reasoning

From
transduction

From
centrism

From
juxtaposition

Preoperational to
operational shift

From
radiation

From
syncretism

From
symbolism

From
diffusion of
interpretation

Fig. 27-2. The critical period (ages 4 to 7) seen in terms of Piaget's developmental theory—cognitive shift.

there is a spread of fortuitous interpretations stemming from some central idea; and symbolism, in which there is a tendency to find in every event and every statement a hidden meaning of greater depth.

From his own studies Piaget concluded that Dromard was perfectly justified in believing that "in their manner of thinking, of perceiving and of reasoning, delusional psychotics recall some of the essential traits of child thought."

There is likewise, he added, a similar propensity for imaginative interpretation of imperfectly understood words, for arbitrary justification of their ideas at any price, and for syncretism in their reasoning and perceiving. This latter phenomenon is closer to autistic or dream thought than to logical thought, in that associations of all varieties float about in the mind until two or more are brought together by chance and juxtaposition. As in the dream, syncretism condenses dis-

586

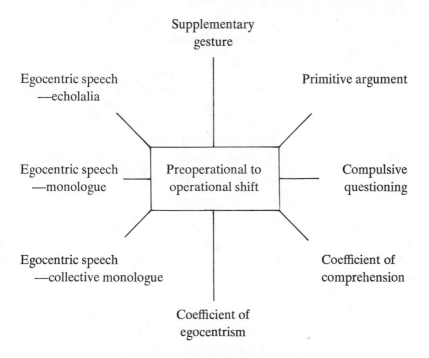

FIG. 27-3. The critical period (ages 4 to 7) seen in terms of Piaget's developmental theory—communicational shift.

parate elements into a whole, and, as in the dream, it transfers from one idea to another on the basis of purely external resemblance. In many ways, therefore, this preoperational thinking is actually not too far removed from the thinking disorders found in psychosis [20].

It was perfectly reasonable to suppose that when these two unusual systems, belonging to the deluded mother and to her preschool child, came into contact, they would tend to create a common pool of paralogical ideas fed by unrealistic and irrational sources, and leading in time to the efflorescence of bizarre ideas and associations.

SEVENTH ASSOCIATION

Lidz and his co-workers, in discussing the familial milieu in which there is a psychotic member, argued that the child is exposed to the parental interpretations of reality and that these could be regarded

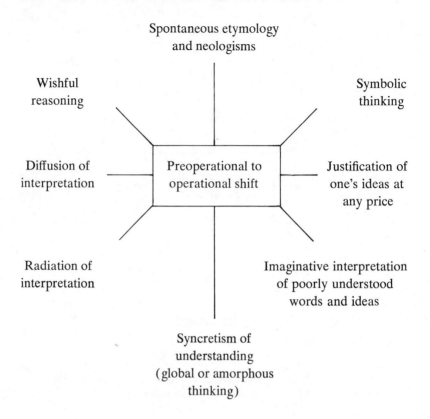

FIG. 27-4.   The cognitive process in delusional psychosis [21].

as having limited value where they serve primarily to maintain the parents' own precarious mental equilibrium. The wishful perception of events could result in:

. . . a strange family atmosphere into which the children must fit them-selves and suit this dominant need or feel unwanted. Often children must obliterate their own needs to support the defenses of the parent whom they need. They live in a Procrustean environment, in which events are dis-torted to fit the mold. The world as the child should come to perceive or feel it is denied. Their conceptualizations of the environment are neither instrumental in affording consistent understanding and mastery of events, feelings, or persons, nor in line with what persons in other families experi-ence. Facts are constantly being altered to suit emotionally determined needs. The acceptance of mutually contradictory experiences requires par-alogical thinking. *The environment affords training in irrationality* [italics added] [14, p. 180].

Our own findings would lend support to these views. The children living within this "subculture of psychosis" do indeed find themselves in a "Procrustean environment" and struggle to accommodate themselves to the opposing attractions of reality and object relationship. They are often confronted with the challenge "love me, love my delusion" and, in place of making an agonizing choice, they may develop distressing, conflicting symptoms. Conflict, however, implies some measure of individuation and, in its absence, one can expect the insidious development of folie à deux.

EIGHTH ASSOCIATION

Karl Jaspers has had some pertinent remarks to make about the sense of reality in the deluded individual, and, although he does not adopt the developmental standpoint, it is possible to infer certain things about this important mediating function between the self and the nonself [10]. The sense of reality, for him, grows in the individual from infancy onward and is closely related to personal experience. One's reality is constantly tested against the judgment of others and modified by familial, group, and cultural experiences. From this point of view, reality-learning begins with the mother and acquires her permanent imprint. To put it in yet another way, individual reality is always embedded in the general reality and, more particularly, in the mother's reality. *The reality of the child is therefore a function of the maternal reality and an index of its validity.* The function of reality is also a matter of individuation, since the awareness of the existence of an objective world is linked to the primary awareness of one's own existence, and the awareness of one's own existence is separate existence from that of the mother, that is, some resolution of the symbiosis.

The delusion, according to Jaspers, is a transformation of the total awareness of reality. Since the sense of reality in the child is closely bound up with the total awareness of reality in the mother, a transformation in the latter inevitably induces some degree of transformation in the child's reality-testing.

Jaspers makes the important statement that "reality is not a single experience in itself," but an ongoing experience, relative, variable, flexible, and sensitive to the context of the experience. It is, therefore, highly modifiable in the child when delusional pressures emanating from highly significant persons are exerted upon it.

NINTH ASSOCIATION

This association brings us into the psychodevelopmental framework to which we look for our major understanding. Jacobson and Benedek have described the relationship between mother and infant as "truly symbiotic" in nature since not only does the infant need and feed upon the mother, but the mother also needs and feeds upon her baby [1, 9]. At any developmental stage, says Benedek, the parents identify with their child's need by reviving their own experiences of this phase, and this mutual identification between parent and child is especially significant for the development of the sense of identity [7]. This tendency toward identification with the child on the part of the parents stems from reactivated memories of their own infantile past, and it helps enormously in the empathic understanding of their child. It is important for them, however, not to overdo such identifications, as this may serve to undermine their parental position.

Even in the earliest phase of symbiosis the mother needs to prepare herself for the individuation of her child and does this by showing a loving awareness of the differences between her own and the child's needs as she attempts to gratify both. (As quoted earlier, Kierkegaard showed a sensitive realization of this crucial piece of maternal functioning.)

When the mother attempts to sustain the symbiosis by ignoring the existence of developing barriers or indulging herself in undue penetration and merging, a pathologic prolongation and intensification of symbiosis may result. This has been described brilliantly by Mahler and her colleagues in a series of papers [4, 15–17].

The maternal fantasies of merging with the child are strengthened by the child's reciprocal wish to fuse with the mother. The symptomatic developments in symbiosis—the overprotection, the oversolicitude, the dominance, the wish to keep the child passive and dependent, and the tendency to treat him as an extension of herself—all help to blur the demarcation between the maternal and self-images within the child. His fear of separation and his desire to maintain or regain the original mother-child closed unit may grow so strong that

590

he abandons any attempt to build up an enduring and consistent self-concept. His psychic organization remains undifferentiated, unstructured, and unorganized.

CLARIFICATION AND INTERPRETATION

After the period of active association, according to Poincaré, comes the stage of incubation, and then the moment of illumination as things begin to fall into place. The clinical cases triggered off a number of associations, each of which attempted to deal with the circumstances within a mother and child symbiosis that led to a failure in the separation-individuation process and eventually to the establishment of folie à deux.

Sir Kenneth Digby introduced us to moist, passive, feeble, and tender children who were "most susceptible" to an "unpleasing contagion of the imagination," and Lasègue and Falret extended the clinical picture by emphasizing the "passive docility." Kierkegaard then described the fearfulness that enveloped the child in his first attempts "to walk alone," and Spiegel carried the matter further by pointing to the resentment experienced by the mother at the growing independence of the child and her unconscious wish to punish him for it. We then followed the vicissitudes in the development of a sense of reality. Ferenczi hinted at the holdups that might ensue should a parent apply omnipotent, wishful, unrealistic solutions to everyday difficulties, and Piaget prepared us for a breakthrough in our understanding by bringing together the prelogical system of the child and the paralogical system of the psychotic. When the two systems came together in the same "Procrustean environment," as depicted by Lidz, the child's sense of reality was distorted to fit the mold and the environment afforded him training in irrationality. This line of associations culminated in the work of Jaspers, who related the sense of reality in the child to the reality in which he was brought up and to the extent to which he was able to become aware of himself and his own existence as distinct from the existence of the rest of the world. This brought us to the work of the developmental psychoanalysts—Benedek, Jacobson, Greenacre, and Mahler—who began to introduce us to new developmental concepts that heralded the revolutionary understanding provided by Mahler and her associates. It was Mahler's description and

591

microanalysis of normal separation-individuation during development and the clarification it provided for the formation of the autistic and symbiotic psychoses of early childhood that made us hopeful that it would be of equal help in explaining the occurrence of childhood folie à deux.

One of the confusing problems that Mahler has clarified in her characteristically luminous manner has been the differentiation between *physical separation* of mother from child and *intrapsychic separation* of self from nonself representations "within the physical and emotional availability of the mother" [18]. The former is a pathogenic action which can have deleterious effects on personality growth; the latter is a normal developmental process that leads to healthy individuation.

Our cases of childhood folie à deux were in no instance caused by physical separation although often mitigated by it. On the other hand, in every instance there appeared to be a failure in intrapsychic separation against a background of persistent symbiosis as well as a regression from a low level of individuation to a stage of poor differentiation of self and object representations. The extent of the symbiosis and the pathologic regression were never as extreme as in the symbiotic psychoses. Nevertheless, there was a parasitic exchange of magical thinking and omnipotent wishes. There was also less internal conflict between the desire and fear of "reengulfment by the object," and the degree of individuation that remained allowed for an "identification with the crazy one" and impeded the further development of a symbiotic or autistic psychosis. In place of the delusion of oneness with the "mothering principle," there was a shared delusion of togetherness against a common persecutor; both mechanisms, however, served the function of survival.

In the symbiotic psychosis the child clung to a representation of the part maternal object which functioned as a transitional or fetish substitute for the actual maternal object. In the folie à deux case the delusional idea was hypercathected and clung to as part of the mother although no more than a deanimated symbol.

The stress generated by the maternal psychosis sometimes leads to the appearance of symbiotic-like behavior in one or more of the children in the family, and this may be a prelude to the eventual development of folie à deux. In one particular family in our sample a

mother offered convincing evidence in support of her delusional belief, but this was rejected out of hand by most of the children, who
appeared to have established stable identities. One girl, however, remained uncertain, confused, submissive, frightened, and very much
involved in her mother. She not only shared the delusional belief with
equal conviction but was even able to bring further supporting evidence in favor of the mother's position.

Our research hypothesis as it has now evolved could be stated
as follows: In childhood folie à deux there appears to be a biologically predetermined deficiency in the maturation of the ego which
manifests itself in a general incompetence of ego functioning
(self-assertiveness, self-confidence, self-awareness, self-control, self-
esteem, self-knowledge, self-determination, self-mastery, self-
possession, self-reliance, self-satisfaction, and self-sufficiency). Associated with this there is a factor abetting the development toward
separation-individuation. Under conditions of stress, a symbiotic state
is established in this predisposed child and, in the absence of a psychologic "placental barrier," pathologic thought and fantasies circu-
late freely within the symbiosis.

The child in question has generally shown some degree of independent functioning although lacking in ego competence and prone to
anxiety in each new step of separate functioning. During development
he has been less actively experimental with separation and return to
the mother, less exploratory, less curious, less daring, and more inclined to operate within a large margin of safety. He has also shown a
consistently deficient sense of reality with constant resorting to fantasied solutions and comforts. The world outside the maternal orbit has
been perceived as malevolent and threatening, and this perspective
has been strongly reinforced by the mother. The child has also shown
less awareness of his body and body boundaries and is more inclined
to experience stranger anxiety.

When interviewing these children it was difficult to regard them
as separate individuals, since only a part of them appeared to be in
contact with the interviewer. They seemed lacking in attention and
concentration, inept at establishing social rapport, confused by direct
questions, and puzzled by any reference to their feelings and functions. It almost looked as if a part of them was absent and lay somewhere outside the interviewing room. They would look toward the

door or out of the window as if their thoughts were elsewhere. We felt that they did not expect to be understood or have their wants anticipated, and there was little or no interest in the person of the interviewer or in the interviewing environment. The delusional ideas of the mother were often repeated in parrot-like fashion, as if they were reciting a lesson that had been overlearned, and there would be a blank stare at any question that seemed to challenge the veracity of the delusional ideas.

We were most impressed by the absence of a sense of humor. In one family the folie à deux child reiterated her convictions in a solemn and even pompous manner, whereas her cheerful young brother, when asked how he came to eat dinner at home when his mother believed that the food was being poisoned, responded with a humorous shrug of his shoulders: "Well, I'm not dead yet." It would seem that the acquisition of a sense of humor, like the sense of reality and the sense of identity, was part of the separation-individuation process that led to a diminution of egocentrism, to use Piaget's term, a greater objectivity, and altogether a better perspective on life.

With our research hypothesis now in hand, we can continue, in a more orthodox scientific manner, to investigate this most unusual clinical syndrome.

Bibliography

1. Benedek, T. Parenthood as a developmental phase. *J. Amer. Psychoanal. Ass.* 7:389–417, 1959.
2. Coleman, S., and Last, S. A study of folie à deux. *J. Ment. Sci.* 85:1212–1223, 1939.
3. Dromard, G. Le délire d'interprétation; essai de psychologie. *J. Norm. Path. Psychol.* (Paris) 8:189, 406, 1911.
4. Elkisch, P., and Mahler, M. S. On infantile precursors of the "influencing machine" (Tausk). *Psychoanal. Stud. Child* 14: 219–235, 1959.
5. Ferenczi, S. *Sex in Psychoanalysis.* Boston: Gorham, 1916. Pp. 213–239.
6. Gralnick, A. Folie à deux: The psychosis of association. *Psychiat. Quart.* 16:230–263, 1942.
7. Greenacre, P. Early physical determinants in the development of the sense of identity. *J. Amer. Psychoanal. Ass.* 6:612–627, 1958.

594

8. Greenberg, H.   Sir Kenneth Digby on "folie à deux": An historical note. *Brit. J. Med. Psychol.* 29:294–297, 1956.
9. Jacobson, E.   *The Self and the Object World.* New York: International Universities Press, 1964.
10. Jaspers, K.   *General Psychopathology.* Chicago: University of Chicago Press, 1963. Pp. 93–107.
11. Kallmann, F. J.   Discussion of two papers. *Amer. J. Psychiat.* 117:804–805, 1961.
12. Kierkegaard, S.   *Purity of Heart.* New York: Harper & Row, 1938.
13. Lasègue, C., and Falret, J.   La folie à deux. (Translated by R. Michaud. *Amer. J. Psychiat.* 121 (Suppl.):1–23, 1964.
14. Lidz, T., Fleck, S., and Cornelison, A.   The Transmission of Irrationality. In *Schizophrenia and the Family.* New York: International Universities Press, 1965.
15. Mahler, M. S.   Problems of identity. From panel report by D. L. Rubinfine. *J. Amer. Psychoanal. Ass.* 6:131–142, 1958.
16. Mahler, M. S., and Elkisch, P.   Some observations on disturbances of the ego in a case of infantile psychosis. *Psychoanal. Stud. Child* 8:111–126, 1953.
17. Mahler, M. S., and Furer, M.   Certain aspects of the separation-individuation phase. *Psychoanal. Quart.* 32:1–14, 1963.
18. Mahler, M. S., and Furer, M.   Development of symbiosis, symbiotic psychosis and the nature of separation anxiety. *Int. J. Psychoanal.* 47:559–561, 1966.
19. Michaud, R.   Bibliography to La folie à deux. *Amer. J. Psychiat.* 4 (Suppl. 121):18–23, 1964.
20. Piaget, J.   La psychanalyse dans ses rapports avec la psychologie de l'enfant. *Bull. Soc. Alfred Binet* 56:131–133, 1923.
21. Piaget, J.   *The Language and Thought of the Child.* London: Routledge & Kegan Paul, 1926.
22. Spiegel, J.   The Resolution of Role Conflict Within the Family. In N. W. Bell and E. F. Vogel (Eds.), *The Family.* Glencoe, Ill.: The Free Press of Glencoe, 1960. Pp. 361–381.
23. Sturges, S. G.   Folie à deux in a husband and wife. *Bull. Menninger Clin.* 31:343–351, 1967.

Part VI

Summing Up

Summing Up

E. James Anthony
Therese Benedek

T here is a period, at the end of some hard intellectual work, when one sits back, somewhat exhausted by the energy and time expended, and quietly ruminates and speculates on the meaningfulness and worthwhileness of it all. No matter what the conclusion to this work there is always a little sadness connected with the process, as there is always a little sadness at the finishing of any protracted task. There is also a certain amount of relief, as well as a certain amount of anxiety as to how it will all be received. The mood of this period is nowhere better captured than by William James when he had completed his monumental *Principles of Psychology* and had this to say:

I came home very weary, and lit a fire, and had a delicious two hours all by myself, thinking of the big étape of my life which now lay behind me . . . and the possibilities that the future yielded of reading and living and loving out from the shadow of this interminable black cloud.

Although not by any means a "black cloud," parenthood has haunted us over the past 2 years so that much of our reading and writing and thinking has referred to it in some way. The time has now come to turn this preoccupation over to a larger audience so that others, too, can experience the lively interest occasioned by many distinguished minds elaborating variations on the same basic theme.

In editing the book, our main concern was to provide the text with as much continuity as possible, and, in order to accomplish this, we assumed the role of intermediary between authors and readership, attempting to relate the one more intimately to the other and both to ourselves. Very much in keeping with the general nature of the book, we regarded our function as still another aspect of transaction in the triadic setting of editor, author, and reader. To bring this about, we set ourselves to write an introduction, a series of interlinking commentaries, and a summing up, and, in this form, we hoped to weld the different parts together into a continuous and comprehensive whole, adding consistency and coherence where these were needed.

In order to understand the several contributions to this volume, it needs to be viewed as a whole, since each of the parts helps to complete the others by calling attention to theoretical or practical issues discussed or implied in other chapters. Psychoanalytic theory has, for the most part, been presented obliquely by the confirmation or disaffirmation of analytic propositions or by a concentration on some particular aspect of psychoanalytic psychology as it proved useful in theory or practice.

The building up of a significant spectrum of meaning is well illustrated in Part III where the term *development* is given a new twist in referring to the development of the parents rather than of their children. In striking fashion, this sequence of chapters, taken together, provides corroboration of the underlying postulate, so often and so necessarily reiterated in the book, that parenthood is a developmental process. The section begins, for example, with the biopsychologic processes that occur during pregnancy and continues with the mutual interaction of parents and children at each subsequent stage of the life cycle. Although a true metapsychology of interpersonal communication within the family has yet to be formulated, the necessity for one is becoming increasingly obvious as investigators become more and more aware of the shifts in the psychic economy of the mother brought about by her child's needs and behavior.

There are many repetitions during early development of the transient disequilibrium occurring in the psychoeconomic balance between mother and infant and reflected typically in a rise in tension in each. For example, the increased tension in the mother hearing her infant cry is relieved by the diminution in its tension as the child falls asleep, and, less obviously, the infant's first tendency toward sacrific-

600

ing its immediate gratification may represent an archaic effort to procure for itself the comfort of a tension-free mother. In the more usual presentations, the problems of psychic economy are viewed unilaterally, whereas the successive chapters herein on development have attempted to consider an interlocking, interacting system.

Normal development, of either parent or child, is psychologically silent unless the transaction is disturbed and a disequilibrium results. This is especially likely to happen in the parent as an "anniversary reaction" that takes place when the child reaches the developmental age at which the parent, as a child, suffered from some intrapsychic conflict. At this point, parental anticipation and the behavior of the child enter a spiral of transactions that may cause the parent to become highly stressed. The subsequent conflicting reactions to the child are then internalized and influence the parent's development as a parent.

The mutuality of interpersonal communication and contact helps to explain the effects of the fluctuating psychic economy. In responding to their child's behavior, parents experience not only mood changes that motivate their surface behavior but also shifts in their intrapsychic systems that arouse latent conflicts and thereby are conducive to various kinds of pathologic states. The different investigations in this section of the book offer many examples, behavioral as well as situational, of internal processes in the parents that, on analysis, reveal that the psychoeconomic balance depends on the outcome of tensions arising from conflicts between the parent's internalized developmental experiences and his current response to the needs and behavior of the child. This double origin of the psychology of parental behavior is universal and holds true for all the adaptations that parents have to make concomitant with the growing autonomy of their developing children.

The propositions illustrated by the chapters dealing with normal parental psychology are also highlighted in the following parts, although we feel justified in assuming that the authors did not consciously pursue any such aims of theoretic generalization. Chapters 18, 19, and 20 depict the mother's defenses against anxieties aroused by the characterlogic conflicts stemming from the biologic assumption of motherhood. These character trends, with their deeply ingrained psychologic motivations, place an undue burden on the psychic economy of the mother, sometimes for short periods when defenses are mobilized in response to external problems concerning the child, but even more so when they are required to function all the time to guard the mother against insights into the shortcomings of her motherliness. Whatever the behavioral manifestations of this fluctuating but permanent stress, they might lead, sooner or later, to a depletion of the psychic energy that sustains adequate motherly attitudes and behavior, as shown in Chapters 21, 22, and 23. Chapter 21 illustrates the transient frustration of the mother by the child and the resulting activation of anger in normal mothers. On the other hand, Chapter 22 demonstrates a pathologic breakdown of the regulatory system with ensuing diffusion of instinctual energies so that brutal aggression becomes unleashed against the child. Chapter 23 depicts still another type of psychopathology in mothers, in which their internal regulatory system is well established but controlled by a powerful superego that makes them continue to use up their psychic energy to protect themselves from guilt and their children from harm.

In general, one could say that the psychic economy is regulated by the mother alone during the symbiotic phase, and that only with the beginning individuation of the child is it possible to speak of a new phase when regulation becomes interpersonal. This is true only in cases where the mother is completely happy with a satisfactory, healthy infant. In instances in which the mother has a neurotic conflict toward her motherhood or is unhappy for other reasons, she might implant her ambivalence into the infant. On the other hand, an infant who is colicky, crying, and unhealthy can activate ambivalence in the mother. The symbiotic phase in which the mother and infant have, so to speak, a common regulation for their "psychic economy" is not without its pitfalls. In Part V, Chapters 24 to 27 illustrate the possible pathologic effects of the mother's influence upon the infant and upon the later development of the child if she cannot give up her oneness with the child and attempts to maintain a closely transactional regulation of their mutual psychic economy.

This is where our book must end, and, as we glance backward through its pages, we are made aware that whatever cohesion it possesses comes from its rootage in psychoanalytic principles and practice and in its primary concern for *man as a parent* striving, at all times and in all places, to fulfill his generative needs, reconciling the basic constancy of his inner dynamic forces with the changing circumstances to which he is constantly exposed. This is especially apparent when the text focuses on the mutual influence of developing parents on developing children. It is our hope that this approach, with its emphasis on the interaction of current experience and biologic process, will not only stimulate new interest in the psychology and psychopathology of parenthood, but also help others to take a new look at the family and its present state of turmoil in a similar way.

Index

Index

Abortion and rage, 144
Abuse, parental, 449–477
  attacks and, 470–472
  child-rearing pattern and, 450–452
  clinical picture, 453–457
  cultural factors in, 452–453
  dependency and, 453
  ego development and, 461–465
  immaturity and, 453
  lack of motherliness and, 459–461
  later development of child and, 466–467
  masochism and, 465–466
  misperceptions of infant, 457–459
  narcissism and, 465–466
  nonabusing spouse and, 473–474
  obsessive-compulsive personality and, 468
  role of infant in, 472–473
  superego development and, 461–465
  treatment of parents in, 474–476
Acceptance, parental, alternation with rejection, 384–385
Adaptation, biologic, and social structure, 6–9
Adaptive aspects of slow growth and development, 19–25
Adaptive behavior of mother, infant's experiences of, 249
Adolescence. *See also* Adolescent
  alienation and, 134
  "good" reaction to, 323

sexuality and, 194
stereotypes and, 309–311
stereotypic reactions to, 311–323
Adolescent. *See also* Adolescence
  as lost object, stereotypic reaction to, 319–320
  as maladjusted individual, stereotypic response to, 320–323
  as object of envy, stereotypic response to, 317–319
  as sexual object, stereotypic response to, 314–317
Adoption, 353–371
  infertility and, 360–362
  maladaptive responses in, 362–367
  stress in psychology of adopters, 356–360
  telling the child about, 367–370
Adulthood phases, 293
Affect hunger and maternal overprotection, 398–399
Aged, narcissism of, 204
Aggression
  dominance hierarchy and, 8
  expression of, and psychosomatic conditions, 558
  interparental, and murderous obsessions in mothers, 488
  maternal overprotection and, 397, 401–403
  parental, in fantasy, actuality, and obsession, 421–425
Alienation and adolescence, 134

Allergic states, dynamics of, 562–565
Ambitions, thwarted, in mother, and
　　maternal overprotection, 399–
　　400
Ambivalence, 118
　in monkey, 31
　profound, and murderous obsessions
　　of mothers toward children,
　　480, 487–488
Amok, 70
Anaclitic love, 110
Analysis. *See* Psychoanalysis
Anorexia and pregnancy, 144
Anthropology
　definitions of, 58
　personality development and, 61
　psychoanalysis and, 59–60
Anxiety
　castration, 213–214
　hostility in guise of manifest anx-
　　iety, 509–514
　overpermissiveness and, 506–509
　separation, of mother, 160
Appetite and pregnancy, 142–143
Attachment, in monkey, 31
Attacks and abuse, 470–472

Baby. *See* Infant
Beating fantasy
　introjection and, 439–441
　perversion and, 441–446
　types of maternal behavior and,
　　432–439
　vicissitudes during development,
　　428–432
Behavior
　adaptive, of mother, infant's experi-
　　ences of, 249
　"instinctual," 119
　maternal
　　beating fantasy and, 432–439
　　phylogenetic considerations,
　　　9–12
　need-related, as individual subcul-
　　ture, 62
　paternal, phylogenetic considera-
　　tions, 12–16
　sexual, phylogenetic considerations,
　　16–17
Behavioral dimorphism, 23
Behavioral program of mammals, 5
Biologic adaptation and social struc-
　　ture, 6–9

Biologic aspects of bond formation,
　25–35
"Biologic symbiosis" and conception,
　141
Biosocial bond, 26
Biotaxic relationship, 27
Biotaxis and psychotaxis, 26
Bond
　biosocial, 26
　formation
　　biologic aspects of, 25–35
　　parent-young, and territory, 34–
　　　35
　group, 26
　"pair-bonds" in care of offspring,
　　169
　psychosocial, 27
　social, formation of, 25
Breast-feeding. *See* Nursing

Castration anxieties, 213–214
Character, national, studies of, 63
Child. *See also* Infant
　abuse of. *See* Abuse
　anticipation of parental reactions,
　　126
　failure of, parental anticipation of,
　　130
　folie à deux and. *See* Folie à deux
　hyperthymic, 522–523
　idealization of parent, 129
　identification with, 172
　image of, changing, 292–295
　married, parents separating from,
　　197
　-mother monopoly, 388
　-mother relationship. *See* Mother-
　　child relationship
　murderous obsessions of mothers
　　toward. *See* Murderous obses-
　　sions
　oedipal. *See* Oedipal child
　reality of, and maternal reality, 589
　sexuality of, parental reactions to,
　　193–195
　simultaneous analysis with mother,
　　541–555
Childbearing
　delay after nubility, 23
　fantasies about, 146
Child-rearing
　lower-class goals in, 97
　middle-class goals in, 97
　pattern, and abuse, 450–452

Pampering, oscillation between pampering and hostility, 514–517
Parent. *See also* Father, Mother
abuse by. *See* Abuse
adoptive. *See* Adoption
aggression in fantasy, actuality, and obsession, 421–425
anticipating child's failure, 130
-child relationship, social class differences in, 97
child's idealization of, 129
guilt feelings of, 565–566
narcissism of, 174
perplexity of, 374–375, 411–412
reactions
child's anticipation of, 126
to oedipal child. *See* Oedipal child
to sexuality of children, 193–195
readjustments during child's latency, 302
separating from married child, 197
superego of, 129–130
in transition, 291–292
-young bond formation and territory, 34–35
-young relationship and social structure, 7
Parental care in mammals, 5
Parental functioning
role of empathy in, 119–121
symbiotic fixation and, 531–536
Parenthood
commitment to, 211–212
critical periods of, 186
decision for multiple pregnancies, 215
as developmental process, 124–131
drive organization of, 169
early phase of, 188–193
estrangement between marital partners arousing wish for, 214–215
expectant, 239–242
grandparenthood, 199–205
indulgence and, 201
insecurity at approach of, 240
marriage of child and, 196
middle phase of, 195–199
part-time, and latency, 189
phylogenetic considerations, 4–25
problems during latency, 192–193
prolonged anticipation, and maternal overprotection, 393–396

structured strain in, 101–104
total, 188
Passionate love, 112
Passivity and female psyche, 139
Paternal. *See* Father
Patriarchal family, 132
Perfectionistic mother, 162
Perplexity
maternal, 411–420
clinical illustrations, 412–417
parental, 374–375, 411–412
Personality
development
family as psychologic field and, 115
socialization and, 61
obsessive-compulsive, and abuse, 468
Perversion and beating fantasy, 441–446
Phallic phase, 292–293
Phenomenal shift and folie à deux, 585
Phobias, food, 563
Phylogenetic considerations of parenthood, 4–25
Physical separation and intrapsychic separation, 592
Pituitary, 138
Placenta, 4
Play, fecal, 517–522
Poverty, 99
Practice and learning, 21–22
Preadult phase, 293
Pregenital phases, 292
psychosomatic conditions and, 555–566
Pregnancy
anorexia and, 144
appetite and, 142–143
depression and, 144
illicit, 91
licit, 91
loneliness and, 217
morning sickness of, 143
motivations for, 211–216
multiple, decision for, 215
nausea and, 143
as proof of womanhood, 217
psychopathology of, 142–145
quickening, 218
redefining femininity during, 219
regression and, 144
unwanted, 91